CW00669981

PUBLICATIONS OF

THE NAVY

RECORDS SOCIETY

Vol. 167

NELSON'S LETTERS TO LADY HAMILTON

AND RELATED DOCUMENTS

THE NAVY RECORDS SOCIETY was established in 1893 for the purpose of printing unpublished manuscripts and rare works of naval interest. The Society is open to all who are interested in naval history, and any person wishing to become a member should either complete the online application form on the Society's website, www.navyrecords.org.uk, or apply to the Hon. Secretary, email address honsec@navyrecords.org.uk. The annual subscription is £40, which entitles the member to receive one free copy of each work issued by the Society in that year, and to buy earlier issues at much reduced prices.

SUBSCRIPTIONS should be sent to the Membership Secretary, 19 Montrose Close, Whitehill, Bordon, Hants, GU35 9RG.

Members are advised that the Annual General Meeting of THE NAVY RECORDS SOCIETY takes place in London on a Wednesday in July. Members should consult the Society's website, www.navyrecords.org.uk, for more details

---

Pastels of Nelson and Lady Hamilton by Johann Heinrich Schmidt (done in Dresden in 1800). [NMM]

NELSON'S LETTERS TO LADY HAMILTON AND RELATED DOCUMENTS

Edited by

MARIANNE CZISNIK, M.Sc., Ph.D., F.R.Hist.S.
Regierungsdirektorin

PUBLISHED BY ROUTLEDGE
FOR THE NAVY RECORDS SOCIETY
2020

LONDON AND NEW YORK

First published 2020
by Routledge
2 Park Square, Milton Park, Abingdon, Oxon OX14 4RN

and by Routledge
52 Vanderbilt Avenue, New York, NY 10017

Routledge is an imprint of the Taylor & Francis Group, an informa business

British Library Cataloguing-in-Publication Data
A catalogue record for this book is available from the British Library

Library of Congress Cataloging-in-Publication Data
Names: Nelson, Horatio Nelson, Viscount, 1758–1805. | Czisnik, Marianne, editor.
Title: Nelson's letters to Lady Hamilton and related documents / edited by Marianne Czisnik.
Description: London, UK ; New York, NY : Routledge/Taylor & Francis Group, 2020. | Series: Navy Records Society Publications | Includes bibliographical references and index.
Identifiers: LCCN 2020006046 (print) | LCCN 2020006047 (ebook) | ISBN 9780367495138 (hardback) | ISBN 9781003047070 (ebook)
Subjects: LCSH: Nelson, Horatio Nelson, Viscount, 1758–1805—Correspondence. | Hamilton, Emma, Lady, 1765–1815—Correspondence. | Admirals—Great Britain—Correspondence.
Classification: LCC DA87.1.N4 A4 2020 (print) | LCC DA87.1.N4 (ebook) | DDC 359.0092—dc23
LC record available at https://lccn.loc.gov/2020006046
LC ebook record available at https://lccn.loc.gov/2020006047

ISBN: 978-0-367-49513-8 (hbk)
ISBN: 978-1-003-04707-0 (ebk)

Typeset in Times LT Std
by Apex CoVantage, LLC

Printed and bound in Great Britain by
TJ International Ltd, Padstow, Cornwall

CONTENTS

ILLUSTRATIONS

ACKNOWLEDGEMENTS

This edition has had many supporters in the course of the more than ten years that I have been working on it. It would not have been completed without the help of a great number of people in archives and libraries. Friends and family gave advice and a Caird Fellowship of the National Maritime Museum supplied financial aid. Among the many supporters Professor H. T. Dickinson, and Professor Roger and Jane Knight stand out. Harry Dickinson has read the introductory texts, corrected mistakes and made important suggestions as to how to clarify the contents. Roger and Jane Knight have provided me with a wealth of support, ranging from historical advice to accommodation in London. I am grateful to have experienced their friendship in the long journey leading to this edition.

PREFACE

Sadly, this volume cannot be called *Correspondence of Horatio Nelson and Emma Hamilton*. In order to justify such a title, more of her letters to him would need to have come down to us. Nevertheless, it is worth publishing what is left of this correspondence.

It is fortunate that nearly all of Nelson's letters to Lady Hamilton can be traced and read. The business of tracing them, however, is so difficult that this alone would have justified publishing them in one volume. The original manuscripts are spread over public and private collections across Britain and America. Those that have been published are distributed over several printed sources and have not always been transcribed reliably. Apart from changes in spelling, punctuation and the like, whole paragraphs have sometimes been omitted. The aim of this edition is therefore to render a complete and easily accessible collection of as much as there remains of this correspondence.

Nelson's part of the correspondence alone is worth publishing as a whole, because – even more than in his other letters – Nelson is outspoken in expressing his views and feelings. The story of his last and historically most interesting years is here told by himself. The value of this collection is enhanced by the authenticity of Nelson's compositions. He appears never to have composed a standard letter, but rather wrote in a stream-of-consciousness style and often in haste. As a result his rather curt style, trained by years of writing logbooks, often conveys the impression of listening to him talking. This immediacy of style is also reflected in the subjects covered. Nelson's letters deal with the great variety of matters that were on his mind at the time of writing, from political and strategic issues, through practical worries of the day-to-day running of a fleet at sea, to private and intimate matters. The lack of inhibition that some of the letters betray may be explained by strength of feeling towards the addressee or by the confidence (at least in 1801) that she would burn his letters. As a consequence the lack of much pondering is a value of Nelson's letters to Lady Hamilton rather than a weakness.

Lady Hamilton's letters are marked, if possible, by an even greater immediacy. Nelson repeatedly described their effect on him: 'all your letters my dear letters are so entertaining and which paint so clearly what you are after that they give me either the greatest pleasure or pain, it is the next best thing to being with you' [283]; 'You write so naturally that I fancy myself almost, not *quite*, in your dear company' [347].

Missing letters and meetings of the correspondents necessarily create gaps in the correspondence. In order to bridge these gaps an introduction is placed before the letters in each of the chronologically arranged chapters. Details and references mentioned in the letters are explained in footnotes.

Past hesitations about publishing this very particular and in part very intimate correspondence stemmed from the wish to keep Nelson's image unsullied by what later generations saw as embarrassment or even immorality. During Lady Hamilton's lifetime the publication, in 1814, of even a small portion of Nelson's letters appears to have hurried her to an early death on 15 January 1815. Now, more than two hundred years after her death, we can allow Nelson to have the last word [in 321]: 'Dearest beloved Emma (Read that whoever opens this letter and for what I care publish it to the world)'.

GENERAL INTRODUCTION

A. *Choice of Documents*

As pointed out in the Preface the collection of letters published here is sadly incomplete, since most of Lady Hamilton's letters to Nelson have disappeared. As mostly early letters of her to him and one of September 1805 that reached the fleet only after the Battle of Trafalgar have been traced so far [2, 4, 5, 10, 13, 15, 17, 19, 21, 22, 23, 37, 279 and 397], it appears that Nelson burnt them, although he only mentions burning her letters in the first three months of 1801, just before and after the birth of their daughter, a difficult and decisive period in their relationship [59, 96, 112, 123 and 139]. As the relationship could not be socially sanctioned, the couple was forced to observe a degree of secrecy. Nevertheless, the two lovers acted very much within a wider framework of friends and family. In the early stages of their correspondence and again during Nelson's time ashore after the preliminary articles of peace with France had been signed (1801–3) they sometimes wrote letters together or maintained a correspondence that included a third person, namely Sir William Hamilton or Captain Ball or even both [see 7, 36 and 39; and the introduction to Chapter IV]. Before their relationship had become a love affair they often appear to have assumed that their letters were read out or shown to others – at least to Sir William Hamilton [11 and 14]. Later their correspondence bears ample evidence of the importance that friends and acquaintances played in their lives. This network of contacts is explained and put into context in the introductions to the chronologically arranged chapters of this edition and in the many footnotes elucidating the contents of the individual letters.

Offering the correspondence of Nelson and Lady Hamilton to an interested public requires, first of all, the presentation of their letters to each other. This volume adds to these letters further documents that are closely linked to the relationship, but do not form part of another correspondence, such as: Nelson's wills with their codicils [34, 118, 120, 132, 259, 260, 285, 303, 311, 355, 382 and 402], a draft of a speech delivered at Palermo [with Lady Hamilton at his side, 28], Nelson's letters to their daughter [who was too young to answer, see 294, 301, 314 and 400], his and her poems, which focused on their relationship [his: 89 and 141; hers: 18, 109 and 359]. These documents can been seen as indirect messages to the correspondent, be it Nelson or Lady Hamilton, since, for example, it needs to be assumed that Lady Hamilton read the letters Nelson wrote to their daughter and her verse can help to take the place of those of her letters to him that have not come down to us. To these manuscripts have been added Nelson's last letters to Lady Nelson that he wrote at the end of 1800 and beginning of 1801, after returning from the Mediterranean with Lady Hamilton, when his marriage was breaking up [53, 55, 57, 58, 71, 107 and 117].[1] These letters are an essential key to an understanding of how Nelson's emotional commitment finally shifted from his wife to his lover. For the last six weeks of Nelson's life an exception has been made to include his journal entries that refer to Lady Hamilton's importance in his life – most famously his last entry before the Battle of Trafalgar, which is also the last codicil to his will [383 and 402].

B. *Editorial Procedures*

In order to give as complete a picture of the correspondence of Nelson and Lady Hamilton as possible, this edition has relied not only on manuscript sources, but also on printed primary sources, ranging from facsimiles to printed extracts from their letters. In some cases letters had to be pasted together from different sources, such as one page from a facsimile and the rest of the letter from a printed primary source [52, 62, 63, 74, 86, 91, 185, 230, 300 and 392]. In one case, the text of an incomplete manuscript could be completed from a printed primary source [275]. Consequently, it needs to be made clear, first, how the edition deals with the existing variety of sources, including a description of how a range of sources was combined to produce one single letter. Second, the editorial technique applied in transferring manuscript sources into the printed text of this edition will be explained.

[1]George Naish (ed.) was not able to copy the first six of these letters from a direct sight of them in his *Nelson's Letters to His Wife and other Documents. 1785–1831* (London, 1958) [hereafter: Naish] and was thus forced to add them as addenda (pp. 618–20), copied 'from an article in *The Huntington Library Quarterly*, Vol. XI, no. 1, pp. 81–6 (Nov 1947), by Hardin Craig, Junior'. The very last of these letters, which is located in the British Library, is reproduced in Naish, p. 580.

1. *Documents That Can Be Found in a Variety of Sources*

It was assumed for this edition that the reader would like the texts rendered as close as possible to the way in which they were written. If several sources existed, a hierarchy was deployed that had manuscripts as its top priority, followed by facsimiles and photocopies. If none of these was available, a printed primary source was used. The printed primary sources, then, had to be prioritised again. The reliability of the three major printed primary sources of Nelson's letters to Lady Hamilton and hers to him can be tested, where the manuscripts of the printed documents exist. This led to a preference for the '1814-letters' and Morrison (there are no documents that appear in both works) over Pettigrew for the following reasons.

What are referred to as the '1814-letters' are *The Letters of Lord Nelson to Lady Hamilton with a Supplement of Interesting Letters by Distinguished Characters*, edited anonymously in two volumes (London: Thomas Lovewell & Co.) in the year 1814. Some refer to this publication as 'Harrison', since it has been assumed that James Harrison, commissioned by Lady Hamilton to write a biography of Nelson (published in 1806),[1] had tricked her out of the possession of these letters. This assumption appears to be based on the mere idea that he was an unscrupulous hack writer with the advantage of being in contact with her and thus with the letters in her collection.[2] This assumption, however, cannot convince and carries the danger of creating confusion. First of all, none of the letters published in 1814 was used in the biography of 1806 and, second, Harrison's biography contains a unique letter, not found anywhere else [7]. 'Harrison' should thus remain responsible only for the biography of 1806. Harrison's biography was not taken very seriously and appears not to have had any noticeable influence on later publications.[3] The 1814-letters, by contrast, attracted widespread attention. Lady Hamilton herself, having heard of their publication, vehemently, but ineffectually protested that she knew 'nothing of these letters'.[4] Apart from Nelson's posthumous reputation, the publication of the letters also damaged Lady Hamilton's

[1]James Harrison, *The Life of the Right Honourable Horatio Lord Viscount Nelson ...* (2 vols, [London], 1806).

[2]See for example, Flora Fraser, *Beloved Emma* (London, 1986) [hereafter: Fraser], p. 364, possibly influenced by earlier attributions.

[3]Marianne Czisnik, *Horatio Nelson. A Controversial Hero* (London, 2005), pp. 62–3 about Harrison and pp. 63–6 about further literature from the first half of the 19th century dealing with Nelson's relationship with Lady Hamilton.

[4]Fraser, p. 364

own reputation and it was even assumed that she herself had sold them for profit.[1] When they came up for sale in 1817, two years after her death in penury, John Wilson Croker, then first secretary at the Admiralty, was commissioned to buy the collection, using government money, in order to keep these manuscripts out of the public domain.[2] The collection was later bought by the Victorian collector, Sir Thomas Phillipps, thus gaining the name Phillipps-Croker, and only found its way into a public archive (that of the National Maritime Museum) in the twentieth century. Somewhere on the way eight letters became separated from the main body of the collection; three to end up in different collections at the British Library [11, 127 and 392], one to resurface in the Nelson Museum Monmouth [65], another to be found in Clive Richards' Collection [77], while three were lost [252, 314 and 361]. From the great majority of the 1814-letters that can be traced as manuscripts it is possible to claim that the anonymous publication is true to the originals – excepting for minor weaknesses such as 'improving' Nelson's spelling and punctuation as well as structuring the text by dividing it up into paragraphs. Only in one of the letters that can be checked against the manuscript source have a few words actually been omitted, perhaps accidentally [394].[3]

Of similar quality are the documents in *The Collection of Autograph Letters and Historical Documents formed by Alfred Morrison (Second Series, 1882–1893) – The Hamilton & Nelson Papers*, produced in two volumes in 1893. The private collector got this collection (and several others) printed for private circulation only. Not under any pressure to make money from a publication, Morrison was not interested in appealing to a scandalised readership. Consequently, the volumes were soberly produced, arranged in strictly chronological order and complemented by footnotes. Apart from applying the contemporary editing standards of changing (modernising, standardising and sometimes correcting) spelling and adding punctuation, Morrison's anonymous editor adopted the technique of omitting to copy the opening of the letter or the closing signature, except if incorporated into the main body of the letter.[4] This

[1]Fraser, p. 365.

[2]Roger Knight, *The Pursuit of Victory. The Life and Achievement of Horatio Nelson* (London, 2005) [hereafter: Knight], pp. xxv–xxvi.

[3]Between 'affectionate heart' and 'blessing on you' the words 'you ' fly up to my mind and my last breath happen when it will, will be offered up in a prayer for a' are not given in the 1814-letters; nor are they, by the way, in Pettigrew's biography of Nelson.

[4]See for example, 'my dear friend' (Doc. No. 83), 'my own Dear Wife' (on 1 Mar 1801, Doc. No. 112), 'My Dearest amiable friend' (Doc. No. 152), 'my Dearest best friend' (Doc. No. 154) and 'My Dearest best amiable friend' (Doc. No. 173).

means a significant loss, since it is of consequence to see the evolution of how Nelson addressed Lady Hamilton as well as how he signed his own name. Just using Morrison, the reader misses greetings such as 'your truly faithful and affectionate' [44],[1] as well as the development of how 'Horatio Nelson' [6], 'Nelson' [24], 'Bronté Nelson' [44], 'Nelson + Bronte' [62] addressed Lady Hamilton as: 'My dear Madam' [first in 6], 'My dear Lady' [first in 24], 'My dear Lady Hamilton' [first in 35], 'My dear M^{rs}: Thomson' [first in 70, at the beginning of February 1801, just after the birth of their daughter], 'My dearest friend' [first on 16 February 1801, 91] until 'My Dearest Emma' [first on 18 February 1801, 96], which was thereafter to become his standard address to his lover. Nelson merely reverted to 'My dearest friend' in October 1801 [first in 237] and sometimes refrained from using an address altogether [as in 76], both probably for reasons of secrecy.[2] Otherwise, he stuck to 'my dearest Emma', which he developed in his last letter to her, that of 19 October 1805, into: 'My Dearest beloved Emma the dear friend of my bosom' [401].

These omissions in Morrison could be easily rectified, whenever the original manuscripts were at hand, but of the 108 documents that have been used in this edition from Morrison's volumes, only two-thirds could be traced. Of these 72 documents, 49 were examined in manuscript collections, while the remaining 23 could only be traced to auction catalogues (though often in facsimile). Of the 49 manuscripts only three were acquired by government institutions [11, 160 and 401 at the British Library]. The others were either later handed over to public collections (two to the National Maritime Museum and eight to the Nelson Museum Monmouth) or are accessible in private collections, mostly in America (20 at the Huntington, six at the Houghton Library in Harvard, three in the Hubert S. Smith Naval collection in Ann Arbor, two in the Kislak collection in Florida). In Britain, Clive Richards has four manuscripts from the Morrison collection that were used for this edition and Christie's holds one letter from Morrison. There still remain 36 documents from the Morrison edition that have not been traced.

Between the 1814-letters and Morrison's collection of the late nineteenth century, Thomas Joseph Pettigrew's two-volume work, published in 1849, stands out as the major printed primary source for Nelson's

[1]Abbreviated by Morrison into '&c'.

[2]This standard was merely interrupted by variations, such as: 'My Dearest only friend' (Doc. No. 128) and 'My dear Emma' (Doc. No. 215).

letters to Lady Hamilton. It contains most of the letters that are to be found in the 1814-letters and Morrison as well as a great many more. The publication contains a major flaw, however. It does not even aspire to be an edition. Pettigrew's *Memoirs of the Life of Vice-Admiral Lord Viscount Nelson, K.B. Duke of Bronté etc. etc. etc.*[1] is a biography that largely consists of copies of manuscripts. The fact that Pettigrew was indeed looking at original manuscripts is borne out by the variations in his transcriptions; one major example being numerals, such as: '2 or 3 days' [62], which Pettigrew converted into 'two or three days', while Morrison later rendered them true to the original. While Pettigrew was in the enviable position of having had the most complete collection of the correspondence between Nelson and Lady Hamilton at his disposal, he did not seek to adopt a consistent editorial standard. While the manuscript text which he copied was rendered reasonably faithfully, he did not always indicate where he had decided to omit passages in the letters. Some of the (unmarked) omissions from the letters were later reproduced in supplementary chapters about 'Lady Hamilton' and 'Horatia Nelson' at the end of Volume II, in which he aimed to prove that Horatia was Nelson and Lady Hamilton's daughter. But sometimes the texts given there are incomplete [112] and most of the omissions that plague nearly all of Pettigrew's transcriptions can only be reconstructed by consulting the original manuscripts. Unmarked omissions, by the way, were not a weakness of Pettigrew's alone and they lead to the seemingly contradictory versions of Document 218 given by Pettigrew and by Sichel. Both failed to mark their different omissions, thus providing the letter with different endings.[2] These omissions marring most of Pettigrew's transcriptions must be borne in mind when reading each of the 65 letters from his two volumes, whose manuscript source I was unable to find.

Other printed primary sources in addition to these three works rarely contain letters from Nelson to Lady Hamilton or vice versa that can be found nowhere else. One exception is Nicholas Harris Nicolas', *The Dispatches and Letters of Vice Admiral Lord Viscount Nelson*[3] [31, 33 and 288]. The only other case in which I was not able to trace a manuscript

[1](2 vols, London, 1849) [hereafter: Pettigrew].

[2]Compare Pettigrew, ii, pp. 186–7, to Walter Sichel, *Emma Lady Hamilton. From New and Original Sources and Documents. Together with an Appendix of Notes and New Letters* (3rd edn, revised, Edinburgh, 1907), p. 515. The original manuscript is kept at the NelMusMon E 107.

[3]7 vols (London, 1997; first edition: 1844–46) [hereafter: Nicolas].

from a printed primary source is from Jack Russell, *Nelson and the Hamiltons* [50].[1]

The hierarchy of sources according to their reliability as described above (manuscript – facsimile – photograph – printed primary source, with a preference of 1814-letters and Morrison above Pettigrew) was observed in the choice of source for a document to be printed in this edition. Above each document in this collection the source is given, so that the reader can see from how reliable a source the text is taken. If more than one source is given, the document had to be pasted together from different sources. In this case as much as possible was taken from the source that was regarded as more reliable and the gaps were filled from the other, less reliable, source. In these cases the sources are given lower case letters in Italics (*a), b), c)* and so on) above the text of the document. Within the text these lower-case letters were added in square brackets at the beginning of the passage copied from the respective source.

2. *Transcription from Manuscripts*

Fortunately most of the documents presented in this edition could be taken in their full length from original manuscripts, kept in public and private collections in Britain and the United States of America. This made it possible to convey the letters' contents as closely to the authors' handwriting as possible in print. In order to achieve this aim, the following editorial practices have been adopted.

The overall structure of the letters, marked by a nearly complete lack of paragraphs or indentations, has been maintained. This superficial first impression of the manuscripts already indicates a continuous flow of thoughts. Structuring the texts in print by breaking them up into paragraphs would mislead the reader into believing that they were composed in order to cover different subjects rather than written down in a brainstorming fashion. Nelson did not even feel a need to start a new line, when he continued the letter at a later time. In such cases he merely put a date or time of day wherever he had stopped and continued the letter; the relatively short text of document 268, for example, contains six new starts, marked within the text: 'May 26th: … May 30th: … June 2nd: … June 3rd: … 2 oclock … June 4th:'. In order to gain a chronological

[1](first published 1969; Harmondsworth, Middlesex, 1972).

overview of the documents written, Appendix 2 lists them with all their new starts.

Another indication of the lack of the writers' editorial work on the letters is the scarce number of insertions and crossings out. If Nelson inserted anything at all, it was rarely more than a word that he had forgotten to write or wanted to exchange for a crossed-out word. As the insertions were always of minor size, they could easily be accommodated above the line into which they were meant to belong, with a Λ-shaped insertion mark from below the line indicating the exact gap into which the word/s was or were meant to be inserted. If Nelson, in the process of writing, changed his mind about how to word a text, he crossed out a word and continued with the expression that he had found to be more appropriate [see, for example, 59].[1] Whenever words or letters were crossed out, this is indicated in this edition by a single line crossing through the respective ~~word~~ or le~~tter~~/s. In the rare cases when the crossing out made some letters illegible, the assumed number of letters are represented by ~~xxxx~~. As a whole, Nelson's as well as Lady Hamilton's letters apparently did not undergo much revision and they therefore convey an immediacy of thought and feeling that would be lost, if minor mistakes were corrected. In very few cases, the texts were later tampered with (most probably by Lady Hamilton). In one of these cases cold light, ultraviolet light and a microscope at the Paper Conservation Department of the National Maritime Museum allowed me to see that somebody had tried to scratch away the ink with a blade, before crossing out a name with ink of the early nineteenth century that contained iron and thus made the letters underneath illegible even with ultraviolet light [340]. In such cases, the respective words are crossed out with ~~double lines~~. When the word was thus made illegible, the rough number of letters is given: ~~xxxxx~~ [see, for example, 16 and 139].

In Nelson's as well as in Lady Hamilton's letters the flow of writing was structured by little punctuation. Nelson sometimes underlined the last letter of a word or name. This finishing underlining is transcribed as a full stop. Much more often than such full stops, Nelson used commas. Even when a full stop appeared more appropriate, commas have never been transcribed into full stops, because this again would have implied a structure that the flow of the writing did not have. Nelson and Lady Hamilton never used question marks or exclamation marks. This did not stop earlier editors adding such marks generously to their

[1] 'I delivered to Mr. ~~Thompson Mrs.~~ ---- M[rs]: Thomsons message + note'.

transcriptions [for example exclamation marks in 92 by Morrison, and in 361 in the 1814-letters]. Adding punctuation could give the text a meaning that might not have been intended by the writer, as in the following phrase: 'we could burn Copenhagen would thet win an affection towards England,' [144]. While this phrase could be interpreted as a neutral statement of possible consequences, Pettigrew transcribed, if not dramatised, it into: 'We could burn Copenhagen. Would that win an affection towards England?' In rare cases, Nelson used brackets [for example in 96, 192 and 307] that often rather looked like slash marks. Similarly rare were quotation marks. If used at all, they only denoted the beginning of a quotation [see 236]. For the continuation of the quotation over the following lines Nelson used an equals sign at the beginning of each line (this edition indicates in the footnotes that accompany the text, when this is the case). He also used the equals sign, both at the end of a line and at the beginning of the following line, as a hyphen, when splitting a word (this use is also indicated in footnotes in this edition).

In their near-spoken style of writing, neither Nelson nor Lady Hamilton used many punctuation marks when writing words. For example, unlike the earlier editors of these letters, Nelson himself never hyphenated words, so that what Pettigrew transcribed as 'Commander-in-chief'[1] reads in the original manuscript 'Commander In Chief' [133]. His writing is sometimes not even clear as to whether words should be written together or separate. The words 'I have', for example, are nearly always written together, and the indefinite article 'a' is often added to the following noun. In this edition these words have been separated, because it appears that they were merely combined out of convenience in writing. On the other hand, some words were often split into different parts and written leaving wide gaps between these parts, as in the words 'vis it' and 'Med iter rane an' in document 144. In transcribing such words, the gaps have been closed. Nelson also usually saved himself the trouble of using an apostrophe. As a consequence he gave the time as 'O Clock', 'OClock', 'oclock' or even 'of clock' [29, 40, 41 and 68] and attached the genitive ''s' to the end of the word like a plural, as in 'for heavens sake' [145], 'Sir James Saumarezs' [190], 'Midshipmans' [297]. Similarly, Nelson contracted 'don't' to 'dont' [see, for example, 103] and 'can't' to 'cant' [for example, in 209]. All these time-saving measures have been maintained in the texts of the letters as printed in this edition.

[1]Pettigrew, i, p. 445.

Capitalisation of words does not help in giving the text a structure, either. In most words a capital first letter can merely be gauged by size, which is difficult to assess, since it is merely a relative measure in comparison to the other letters of the word. In the case of the letters s and c this is further complicated by the fact that they always tend to look like capital letters at the beginning of a word. In these cases I have adopted the common rules of capitalisation. Only in the case of the letter Y at the beginning of You, Your and Yours, where Nelson's capitalisation varies, have I tried to follow his preference in any specific case. Only the letters B, D, F, H, I, J, L, P, R and T (and sometimes N and M) are written distinctly differently from their lower-case equivalents. As a consequence I have not glossed over inconsistencies in capitalisation, but rather rendered the letters as written in the manuscript source: for example, 'french' (among the many examples see 274 for inconsistent capitalisation of French/french, and 321 for repeated use of 'french').

Similarly inconsistent was Nelson's use of abbreviations. The only rule one can make out is that Nelson sometimes abbreviated words when he reached the end of a line and had not left space enough to write out the full word. Otherwise, abbreviated words appear to merely reflect on the spontaneity of Nelson's writing. In order to convey the original impression of reading Nelson's letters, they have all been maintained. As they follow a simple pattern, they tend to be self-explanatory. Traditional abbreviations of words at the time consisted in the beginning of the word with the last letter(s) superscribed (sometimes with a colon underneath), as in: 'mom^{t}' and 'mom^{t}:' for moment [86 and 221]. If the significance of the abbreviated word or name is not self-evident, it is explained in a footnote. Numbers (if not used in date and time) were sometimes, but not always, rendered as figures, as in: 'next two or 3 days' [229]. Apart from numbers, only the word 'and' was abbreviated into a symbol: '+', particularly in 'Nelson + Bronte', also '+^{c}:' or '+c' for etc. [for first uses see 24 and 46 respectively], not '&' or '&^{c}' as earlier editors rendered it.

Nelson's spelling tended to be fairly consistent. Spellings that were common in his day have been maintained without marking them with '[*sic*]' in this edition. Examples are: cabbin, chuse, cloaths, compleat, doat, encrease, gulph, inclosed, œconomy, shew and shewn as well as endings in expence(s) / (non)sence / suspence / dispence / advice (as verb), cotts / sett / fitt, surprize (as noun), honor / honorable / dishonor, favorable / favor / favorite, vigor, color[1] and diplomatick / domestick /

[1]But also: rumours, Valour, humour, harbour.

politicks / republick / rhumatick (but: public). The same, of course, needs to apply for Lady Hamilton's spelling, including 'frantick' [10]. Beyond these spellings, common at the time, Lady Hamilton's spelling is of a very individualistic kind. In most cases I have refrained from the use of '[*sic*]', as this would have overburdened the letters and there is no great risk of her imaginative orthography being taken as an editor's typing errors. I should generally state, however, that the vowels a and u as written by Lady Hamilton often look like o. Assuming that Lady Hamilton meant to write a or u when these vowels should be used, I have rendered for example what looked like whot into what, couse into cause and hosband into husband [10].

The '[*sic*]' has also been omitted to indicate those idiosyncrasies of Nelson's spelling that he used consistently or at least repeatedly. Apart from specific words that will be listed below, he was weak in spelling vowels, particularly in distinguishing between a and e. It appears intriguing that this weakness can be observed in such a common word as 'that', which he frequently spelt 'thet'. As 'a' and 'e' are often difficult to distinguish in handwriting, I was at first reluctant to actually copy 'thet', but several cases were so obvious that I eventually decided to transcribe them true to the manuscript source. The difficulty in distinguishing between a and e was also reflected in other common words that Nelson sometimes spelt with an 'e' instead of an 'a', such as 'hes' [for example, 159], 'then' [where 'than' is meant, as in 173], 'whet' [for example, 112], 'seperate' [for example, 42], 'shell' [where 'shall' is meant, as in 131, but corrected by Nelson himself in 141], 'teke' [for example, 144], 'petent' [for example, 184], 'pendents' [for example, 178], 'neture' [238] and even 'Gibralter' [for example, 275]. On the other hand, Nelson sometimes over-compensated his tendency towards 'e' by writing 'existance' [113], 'independant' and 'independance' [for example, 267 and 272 respectively], 'avarage' [325], 'correspondant' and 'correspondance' [297 and 321 respectively] and 'prudance' [323]. Nelson also misspelt 'codocil' [for example, 118], 'Docter' [267] and 'compliment', where complement is meant [for example, 62 and 66]. Whether this particular weakness in the use of vowels may be attributed to Nelson's pronunciation, coloured by his Norfolk accent, or to some more profane reason, is left to the reader to judge.

Other idiosyncrasies of Nelson's spelling that appear fairly frequently and have therefore not been marked '[*sic*]' in this edition are:

1. arrainge / arraingement [for example, 161]; even: arreinge [182]; similarly: 'Champaigne' [191],
2. attatched / attatch'd' / attatchd / attatchment [for example, 62]; similarly: detatched [for example, 91],

3. carraige [for example, 24]; similarly: miscarraige [306], marraige [262],
4. rout [where 'route' is meant; first in 322],
5. Streights of Gib^{r}: [first in 268],
6. 'weither' instead of whether' [first in 16],
7. spelling the ending of the participle of a verb (–ed) without the 'e', as in 'join'd' and 'joind' [164 and 367 respectively] and in many more cases; in a few cases the ending was changed into –t, as in 'vext' [first in 362] and 'stopt' [first in 393],
8. words ending in –ll, instead of –l, such as: untill [first in 14], Channell [first in 232], fullfill [first in 16], 'bowells' [244].
9. Nelson usually did not change the 'y' at the end of a word into 'ie' when he formed the plural of it, as in 'Sicilys' and 'Majestys' [14] and in many other cases, or when he used the third person singular in the present tense of a verb, as in 'carrys' [114],
10. Nelson put the '£' after, instead of in front of the number [first in 57].[1]

Nelson's as well as Lady Hamilton's writing were also marked by a number of grammatical idiosyncrasies that – in order to maintain readability – have not been marked '[*sic*]' in this edition. Whether these characteristics can be explained as old forms, remnants of dialect or otherwise is again left for the reader to judge.

Nelson often used the verb 'to be' in a striking fashion. As in German, he used it as an auxiliary verb, as in: 'Defiance is just joined' [396][2] and 'I expected Sir John Orde was come out to relieve me' [362].[3] Nelson also often used 'was' instead of 'were', as in 'if you was' [first in 66], 'you was recovering' [310] and 'there was three pictures taken' [321]. Sometimes it appears that Nelson used the verb 'to be', because he did not mean to combine it with a participle as verb form, but rather with an adjective. This, for example, appears to be the case of the participle of the verb 'to arrive', as in: 'the box you mention is not arrived' [333 and many more examples] in comparison to 'your letters … I found just arrived' [302]. A similar use of 'to be' can be observed in Lady Hamilton's letters, as in: 'some of the ships are this moment come to anchor' and 'the Army is marched' [21].

[1]An exception is Doc. No. 323, in which Nelson put £, s and d above the respective numbers.

[2]The 'is' was changed by Pettigrew, ii, p. 511, into 'has'.

[3]Colin White (ed.), *Nelson. The New Letters* (Woodbridge, Suffolk, 2005), no. 57, p. 48, has 'has come'.

Other grammatical idiosyncrasies of Nelson's writing that appear so frequently that the use of '[*sic*]' would have disturbed the reading are:

1. When Nelson meant to write a verb in the past participle, he often used the auxiliary verb with the verb in the simple past, as in: 'I have wrote' [first used in 16 and frequently thereafter] or even 'is wrote' [340]. Such combinations of the auxiliary verb with the verb in the simple past, occur with a great number of verbs, such as 'have forgot' [first in 106] and 'have drove' [310].
2. Nelson sometimes (as Germans do) omitted the verb 'to do' with a negation, as in: they or I 'care not' [first used in 41].
3. Nelson also often used an adjective, where an adverb belonged, as in: 'a real kind letter' [240].
4. Nelson often wrote 'who' instead of 'whom' [for example, 112],
5. Nelson inconsistently used 'fleet' as plural or singular, as in: 'the fleet is gone' [300][1] and 'the French fleet have again escaped me' [375].

C. *Conditions under Which the Letters Were Written*

The style and contents of the letters in this edition may sometimes have been influenced by external factors, such as the pressure of professional demands and the insecurity of means of conveyance. Nelson himself sometimes mentions these factors. Whether at all or in how far they affected what he was writing is difficult to say and remains for the reader of this edition to assess. This introduction can merely help to give some guidance.

Professional demands sometimes meant that Nelson simply did not have much time or privacy to compose a letter to his mistress. On his way to the Baltic he wrote in a short note: 'I am writing in a room full of interruption' [80]. Even in the Mediterranean in 1804, when one might assume Nelson to have been in calmer circumstances, he wrote in one letter: 'I have not a moment I am writing + signing orders whilst I am writing to my own Emma' [348]. Pressure could also derive from external turmoil, be it caused by weather conditions or human interference. While in the Channel in the autumn of 1801 the wind forced him to adapt within a few lines of one letter from 'I intend to go on shore' to 'The wind is now freshing, and I do not think I shall be able to land' [220].

[1]Again changed by Pettigrew, ii, p. 346, into 'has'.

Being close to land could also require his constant attention and this could result in stress. On 7 August 1801 Nelson, then on board *Medusa* in 'Margate Roads', wrote:

> I have given directions to cap^{n}: Gore (or rather requested) not to let any body[1] come into the ship but who had business with me for the Medusa would be full from morning 'till [night] 50 boats are rowing I am told about her this mom^{t}: to have a look at the one armed man

This unwanted attention distracted him enough to forget what he had just written, so that he mentioned twice that he was about to go to 'to Hosely bay or Harwich' [192]. Such stress contrasts markedly with expectant excitement, when Nelson himself could shape events. On 30 March, two days before the Battle of Copenhagen, he wrote: 'I must have done for breakfast is waiting. and I never give up a meal for a little fighting' [139]. Sometimes signs of hurry are more subtle, as in the letter of 10 August 1801, in which one of the last words is imprinted on the opposite page, so that one can assume that Nelson folded the letter before the ink was dry [195].

The technical difficulties in sending letters could also influence the contents of a letter. On a superficial level this is the case, when a letter deals with these technicalities. On a less obvious level, the difficulties in sending letters could affect a letter's safe conveyance and thus the author's trust in the means of conveyance and what he or she might dare to write.

On a practical level, a considerable part of the documents here reproduced (particularly Nelson's) deal with how and where to send letters. At the beginning of the year 1801 as well as during the Channel campaign later that year, Nelson was in English waters and thus able to use the service of the Post Office. The Royal Mail had originally been created as a courier service of the crown that could be used for 'letters to and from members of both Houses of Parliament and certain Officials … free of charge'.[2] By the time Nelson was created a peer and became a member of the House of Lords, 'restrictions [had been] placed on Free letters' in order to stop abuses.[3] In '1795 the limit of weight was reduced to one ounce, and each Member was allowed to send only ten letters and receive fifteen each day'. Apart from the reduction in the numbers of letters sent free of postage per day, 'the Member [of Parliament] must

[1]Both words are underlined twice.
[2] R. M. Willcocks, *The Postal History of Great Britain and Ireland* (Perth, 1972), p. 4.
[3]Ibid.

be within twenty miles of the place at which letters bearing his frank were posted, on that day or the day before.'[1] As a consequence, Nelson had to write the exact date as well as place from whence he sent his letters on the outside of the letter. When too far away from the next post office, Nelson's ability to use the postal service was restricted: 'I will send you … tomorrow, as my frank will not send free of postage the Exeter occurrence and Plymouth' [60]. If he wanted to use the mail service free of postage, he also had to consider the weight of each letter: 'I would send you the letter to which it is an answer but it would be over weight' [250]. Convenient as the postal service was for Nelson, he was subject to its timetable of deliveries and had to accept if his letter was 'too late for the post' [119]. This was a fact of which he needed to remind his lover: 'You must be aware, my dear friend, that the letters cannot be answered by the same day's post, for the letters are delivered at 3 o'clock, and the post goes out for London at 2 o'clock, it arrives at one.' [121]. Particularly when Nelson was moving about the Channel, he had also to think ahead and plan where Lady Hamilton should send letters for him, sometimes making rather complicated arrangements:

> do not write here after you receive this I shall be gone, You can in Sir W^{ms}: name write a note to Sir H. Parker, asking if the S^{t}: George is ordered to Spithead, if so write to Portsmouth desiring my letters to be left at the Post Office 'till the ships arrival.' [97]

Particular arrangements were necessary, when parcels were to be sent. Nelson even advised Lady Hamilton on how to wrap them: 'I shall therefore give the print to Hardy, I think they might come by the mail coach as a parcel wrapt up round a stick any print shop will give you one, and direct it as my letters the coach stops for parcels at the White Bear, I believe, Piccadilly' [77].

Sending letters became more difficult the further Nelson was from home. In order to spread the risk of letters getting lost or read, Nelson liked to use different means of conveyance. From the Baltic he wrote: 'God knows how this letter goes, or one which is aboard the London, under cover to Troubridge, wrote 3 days ago. I daresay they are all read' [152]. In May and June 1801 Nelson sent his letters to Lady Hamilton by a variety of means: 'with all my public letters, by way of Rostock and Hamburgh … more letters by the Danish post' [163], 'by Troubridge,

[1] R. M. Willcocks, *England's Postal History With notes on Scotland, Wales and Ireland* (Perth, 1975), p. 56.

and ... by Davison' [177]. Similarly, in the Mediterranean, Nelson had to make use of various different means of conveyance: 'I hope that Captain Murray will be the bearer of a letter from me to you' [292], 'a boat which is going to Torbay having brought out a cargoe [*sic*] of potatoes ... the Lisbon packet' [346] and many more (see Appendix 6).

While a greater variety of means of conveyance may have increased the likelihood of the majority of letters actually getting to their destination, it also carried the constant risk of letters being seized and read by others. Nelson worried not only about letters being taken by an enemy, but also about the British government 'smoking' (that is: opening by applying heat) and reading his letters [357, 365 and 380]. From the Baltic, in May 1801, Nelson suspected even: 'this letter will be read ten times at least before you get it' [163]. Without specifying who may be the unintended reader, Nelson often hinted that he did not feel free to write what he thought or felt: 'I cannot write Politicks' [146, 147 and 150] and 'I cannot write all I wish' [269]. In some cases he expressed his worries more explicitly: 'I cant say more by such a conveyance' [346] and 'by this rout I do not chuse to say more on this subject' [326].

Beyond the simple fear that others would read his letters, Nelson was also worried that these letters would be published. Such a publication could, in Nelson's view, be an act of revenge against the publication of *Copies of Original Letters from the Army of General Bonaparte in Egypt, Intercepted by the Fleet under the Command of Admiral Lord Nelson. With an English translation* (London: J. Wright, 1798): 'we ~~xxx~~ may read them [intercepted letters] in a book as we printed their correspondance from Egypt'. Such a danger of publication repeatedly preoccupied Nelson, on his way into the Baltic in 1801 [134] as much as in the Mediterranean in 1804 [315 and 321]. While it was a mere theoretical possibility in the Baltic, it appeared to be a real danger in the Mediterranean, when documents sent out to Nelson's fleet were in fact intercepted by the French and passed on to Paris. Nelson, however, overestimated the importance of public discourse in a country with a controlled press (see Appendix 5).

In order to counteract the use of his letters by any interceptor, Nelson used different measures that would probably all have been equally insufficient, if brought to the test. One means was simply not to sign his name 'after we get Into the Baltic', an intention that he announced in his letter to Lady Hamilton of 19 March 1801 [134], but appears to have been put into action only once, less than two weeks later, in his last letter before the Battle of Copenhagen [140]. At the beginning of his command in the Mediterranean in 1803 Nelson attempted to keep his authorship secret by referring to himself in the third person singular, as 'the Admiral' [267, 269 and 272] and – over a longer period of time – as 'Lord Nelson' [271, 302, 304, 305, 320 and 358]. His most famous alias, however, was the one he started using in January 1801 when he described himself as Mrs Thomson's friend [first in 61]. This young man (read: Nelson) was not allowed to marry Mrs Thomson (read: Lady Hamilton), because his aunt (read: Lady Nelson) and her uncle (read: Sir William Hamilton) were against the match. Nelson himself, however, got quickly confused by these aliases. At first he wrote as Nelson to Lady Hamilton about the lovers [62, 63, 65, 66, 68 and 69], then he wrote to Mrs Thomson herself about her 'good and dear friend' as well as 'Lord N.' [70]. Then he reverted to writing a letter as himself to Lady Hamilton about the lovers [73], immediately followed by a letter signed by himself to Mrs Thomson, but also about 'Lord Nelson' [74]. Although he every now and then wrote to Mrs Thomson [75 and later], he from now on mostly wrote as himself to LH about the lovers [76 and later]. In mid-March 1801 Nelson already appears to have become impatient about the illegitimate affair between Mrs Thomson and her friend, and referred to him as her 'husband' [129 and 130]. By the end of May Mrs Thomson's friend had become Mr Thomson [170]. Although Nelson had stressed the spelling of Thomson, without a 'p', at the end of April 1801 [152], he later came to spell the name 'Thompson' [255 and 353] and referred to his daughter as Horatia Nelson Thompson. After the summer of 1801 Nelson rarely referred to Mrs or Mr Thom[p]son. An attempt to hide the true addressee of one of his letters of mid-September of 1801 by putting 'M^{rs}: Thomson care / of Lady Hamilton' on the address panel was particularly clumsy, since the letter started: 'I came on board but no Emma, no no my heart will break I am in silent distraction' [213]. On his way to the Mediterranean Nelson finally amalgamated Lady Hamilton and Mrs Thomson as he wrote to the former: 'be assured that my attatchment + affectionate regard is unalterable nothing can shake it, and pray say so to my Dear M^{rs}: T. when you see her, tell her that my love is unbounded to her + her dear sweet child and if she should have more it will extend to all of them' [266; similarly: 269 and 284].

D. *Outer Appearance of Letters*

To appreciate the original appearance of the documents reproduced in this collection it is necessary to understand the paper on which they were written, the ink that was used, the method that was employed to fold them and the seals with which they were closed. All these factors influenced the extent of the paper that could be written upon.

The paper on which the letters in this collection were written is naturally of the standard of the time. The watermarks show that nearly all of the documents were written on paper produced in Britain. This paper was usually produced in sheets of about 37 × 23 cm that were folded to form two leaves or four pages of about 18.5 × 23 cm each. As the sizes of the sheets tended to vary, however, so did the size of the pages, ranging normally, in different proportions, between 18.3 and 19 cm in width and 22.2 and 24 cm in height (in auction catalogues imprecisely described as '4to' or quarto format). Deviations from the standard of laid paper with its characteristic ribbed texture, usually watermarked and in a light beige colour existed in respect to quality [wove paper without ribbed structure, 3 and 144], colour and size. As to colour, Lady Hamilton used in Naples thin bluish paper that was slightly smaller [4, 18 and 22; the half-sheet measuring 17 × 22 cm] and, judging from the watermark 'Honig' (honey in German) came from north of the Alps. As a rule, however, Lady Hamilton used British paper, even in Naples [clearly to be seen, for example, in 10, 19 and 23]. Even British paper did not always keep within the range of sizes described above (a page measuring 18.3–19 cm × 22.2–24 cm). Pages (that is half of a sheet) were often bigger and could sometimes measure 20.5 × 25 cm or more [69, 73, 76, 77, 94, 95, 97, 127, 131, 132, 136, 151] or be produced in awkward proportions, such as 19.6 × 31.6 cm [161] or even 19.2 × 32 cm [183]. In some exceptional cases Nelson was content using half-sheets [65, 80, 81 93, 100, 106 and 173].

Sheets of impressive size were sometimes used for official or legal documents such as wills and codicils [34 was folded into two leaves or four pages of about 32 × 20 cm] and in one rare case for a letter [143]. If such huge sheets were not at hand, sheets of normal size were sometimes not folded and thus used as one leaf with two pages for deeds such as a last will and codicils [118, 120]. In any case, big formats were preferred, as with Nelson's last will of 10 May 1803 and the first codicil to it, which were written on pages in the format of 32.5 × 40.5 cm [259 and 260]. Even at sea Nelson used bigger sheets than normal for the second and third codicils to his will [285 and 303], but reverted to ordinary sheets for the fourth, fifth and sixth codicils [311, 355 and 382]. The seventh and last codicil to his will was written in a small leather-bound journal of 17 × 10.7 cm that he used as a weather logbook [402; see also 383].

One document shows marks of having undergone treatment, either at the time or later [16]. When The Victory Museum (now The National Museum of the Royal Navy) purchased this early letter from Nelson to Lady Hamilton in 1964, it had it examined by A. W. H. Pearsall, Custodian of Manuscripts at the National Maritime Museum. Pearsall assumed it to be authentic, partly because of 'the extraordinary way in which the second sheet is upside-down, and partly because the outline of the white patch suggested that the letter had been deliberately heated'. Pearsall made these observations: 'Munday[1] pointed out that letters from overseas were often so disinfected and the white outline represented the Tongs'.[2] Although I, too, take the paper and writing to be authentic, I rather suspect that the strange marks (mostly darkened paper) are not of the time. The 'extraordinary way in which the second sheet [rather: leaf of the sheet] is upside-down' may be explained by the letter having been repaired that way. This appears likely, because the fold is clearly glued together after having been torn. The marks of the tong show that the treatment was performed after the letter was put together with the second leaf upside down. Though it needs to be pointed out that 24 days before Nelson wrote this letter at the end of October 1798, on 3 October 1798 he wrote another letter to Lady Hamilton with the second leaf written on upside down [11]. Pearsall's comment that 'letters from overseas were often so disinfected' may be true for a letter sent to Britain. This document, however, was sent from Malta to Naples. The strange treatment it appears to have undergone may rather have been a botched attempt to preserve it. An indication that the darkening of the letter occurred only in the twentieth century is an article in *The Times* of 29 May 1913, in which the letter is described, but no mention is made that it is strangely coloured and that the second leaf is upside-down in relation to the first.[3]

The ink Nelson and Lady Hamilton used is without exception black and contains iron as was common at the time. In one letter one may assume that Nelson had problems with the quill [189], but the ink stains in a letter of 1 March 1801 [112] can be explained perhaps by emotional agitation rather than by technical problems. In general, the writing is clear and the paper so far unaffected by slow fire that can be caused by the acid in historical ink.

Once the letters were finished they were only rarely folded in order to be put into an envelope [272 and 274 apparently were, and envelopes have survived for 17, 126 and 384]. Usually the half-sheet was first folded from the top and from the bottom of the first page and then

[1]John Munday, formerly curator at the National Maritime Museum and, among other publications, contributor of an essay about 'The Nelson Relics' to *The Nelson Companion*, ed. Colin White (Portsmouth, 1995), pp. 59–79.

[2]Pearsall's letter is kept with the manuscript at the NMRN 49/64.

[3]It said there on page 6: 'We have received from Miss Anne Miles, of 97, Priory-road, West Hampstead, copies for publication of two letters from Nelson to Lady Hamilton, the originals of which are now in Miss Miles's possession.'

from both sides so as to leave the centre of the fourth page for the address and the other side to be sealed.[1] Sometimes both Lady Hamilton and Nelson closed their letters with a kind of (often reddish) glue between the layers of paper, used like a wafer, so that no image could be impressed [23, 32, 153, 159, 160, 165, 166, 179, 304, 317, 320, 321, 325, 326, 333, 337, 340 and 343]. If wax was used it was usually of red colour. Nelson used black wax after the deaths of Edward Parker at the end of September 1801 [226, 227, 229, 230, 232, 234, 236, 237, 240, 245, 248–251, 254–257, 262] and Sir William Hamilton in April 1803 [267], but also in May 1801 [158, 169 and 171].[2] Lady Hamilton and Nelson used different seals over the years, not all of which can still be made out. In some cases the wax was damaged when still warm (probably by piling the letters), in other cases the wax was simply torn away on opening the letter. Lady Hamilton used a seal with the inscription 'Nelson / 1 August / 1798' [21]. Those of the seals used by Nelson to close the letters in this collection that can still be discerned have the following motifs:

- bearded man with a helmet looking to the right [29, 30, 115 and 128],
- palm-tree [34, 46, 144, 187 and 302],[3]
- female profile looking to the right [38, 40, 59, 66, 89, 94, 114, 116, 127, 139, 146, 171, 175, 180, 182, 186, 190, 192, 218, 221, 223, 226, 232, 236, 247, 251, 253–257, 262, 267, 275 and 313],
- profile of a woman whose curls are held by ribbons, looking to the right [41, 69, 73, 95, 97, 101, 104, 113, 134, 141, 147, 158, 169, 176, 178, 195, 234, 240, 244, 245 and 248],[4]
- Nelson's coat of arms [71, 82 and 202],[5]
- 'N' written in Italics in a circle crowned by a little crown [183]

On opening the letter the paper around the wax or wafer had to be torn. This affected the sides of the third page. In order to avoid parts of the text thus becoming unreadable, Nelson either left the central third of the page (from left to right) empty or merely wrote in a kind of narrow column,

[1]See illustration on p. 323.

[2]The first written in early May from Køge Bay (stretching southwest of Copenhagen), the other two written on 24 and 27 May from off Rostock; none of them with a clear reference to a reason for mourning.

[3]The image can be seen in Martyn Downer, *Sotheby's. Nelson: The Alexander Davison Collection* (London, 21 Oct 2002) [hereafter: Downer], pp. 55, 123.

[4]Downer, p. 60.

[5]Downer, pp. 70–71, 124.

when writing on this central part of the third page. The latter technique was also applied by Lady Hamilton in the last letter from her to Nelson that we know of [397]. Nelson sometimes even marked the parts to be left empty with curved lines [165, 169 and 309]. Considering how much space he lost through not writing in this gap, it is interesting to see how rarely such gaps were necessary to ensure readability. Only in a few cases was the paper actually torn on opening [66, 127, 144, 236, 238, 240, 243, 244, 249, 253, 254, 271 and 309] and never across the whole page. When he needed more space for writing than the first three pages allowed, he continued writing on the parts of the fourth page, above and below the address field, that would be folded into the back of the letter. Such cases are denoted in the accompanying footnotes in order to allow a better understanding of possible disruptions of the flow of writing.

ABBREVIATIONS AND SHORT TITLES USED IN CITATIONS

1814-letters	[Anon.] (ed.), *The Letters of Lord Nelson to Lady Hamilton with a Supplement of Interesting Letters by Distinguished Characters*, 2 vols (London: Thomas Lovewell & Co., 1814).
BL	British Library
Add	Additional Manuscripts
Egerton	Egerton Manuscripts
Bonhams	sale of 14 November 2012
Christie's	sales of: – 21 June 1989 (*Medieval and Illuminated Manuscripts*), – 20 July 1990 (Edwin Wolff), – 9 December 1998 (Christie's New York, Printed Books and Manuscripts) – 3 December 2003 (Spiro Family Collection), – November 2014 – 19 October 2005
	Corporate Art Collection
CRC	Clive Richards Collection
Harrison	James Harrison, *The Life of the Right Honourable Horatio Lord Viscount Nelson* ... 2 vols ([London]: C. Chapple, 1806).
Houghton Library	Harvard University, Houghton Library pf MS Eng 196.5 John Husband Collection MS Hyde 77, 7.111.7 individually acquired piece MS Lowell 10 collection of 'Lord Nelson / Love letters to Lady Hamilton', bequest of Amy Lowell of Brookline, 1925
Huntington Library	HM
Morrison	[Alfred Morrison], *The Collection of Autograph Letters and Historical Documents formed by Alfred Morrison (Second Series, 1882–1893) – The Hamilton & Nelson Papers*, 2 vols) ([n. pl.]: printed for private circulation, 1893).

Monmouth	Nelson Museum and Local History Centre, Monmouth
Nicolas	Nicholas Harris Nicolas (ed.), *The Dispatches and Letters of Vice Admiral Lord Viscount Nelson*, 7 vols (London: Chatham Publishing, 1997; first edited 1844–46).
NMM	National Maritime Museum; now part of Royal Museums Greenwich Various individually acquired pieces (AGC [41, 54, 117, 221]; PBE2591 [243]; JOD/14:1–2 [383]; PST/83 [179])
CRK	Croker Collection
MAM	Matcham Collection ('xerox copies of Matcham Collection of Nelson Letters. Originals returned to owner, Mr. Jeffreys, June 1977')
MON	Nicholas Monsarrat Collection
RUSI	miscellaneous papers formerly owned by the Royal United Services Institute
SUT	Sutcliffe-Smith Collection
TRA	Trafalgar House collection of Nelson manuscripts, purchased from Earl Nelson in 1947
WAL	Walter Collection
Pettigrew	Pettigrew, Thomas Joseph, *Memoirs of the Life of Vice-Admiral Lord Viscount Nelson, K.B. Duke of Bronté etc. etc. etc.*, 2 vols (London: T. and W. Boone, 1849).
Pierpont Morgan Library	Pierpont Morgan Library, New York
MA321	Autograph letters of Horatio Lord Nelson
RNM	Royal Naval Museum, Portsmouth
Russell	Jack Russell, *Nelson and the Hamiltons* (first published by Anthony Blond, 1969; Harmondsworth, Middlesex: Penguin Books, 1972).
Sichel	Walter Sichel, *Emma Lady Hamilton. From New and Original Sources and Documents. Together with an Appendix of Notes and New Letters*, 3rd edn, revised (Edinburgh: Archibald Constable, 1907).
Sotheby's	sale of 2010 (consulted on 19 May 2010)
TNA	The National Archives
Prob. 1/22	Wills and probates before 1858
William Clements	Library, University of Michigan, Ann Arbor, Hubert S. Smith Naval Collection, volume 1 'Naval Affairs'

CHAPTER I

THE BEGINNING OF AN ENDURING RELATIONSHIP, JUNE 1798–DECEMBER 1800

The outbreak of the French Revolutionary War in 1792 would bring changes to all the countries of Europe – directly or indirectly. It would also change individual lives. Among the many lives it changed were those of Horatio Nelson and Emma Hamilton.

The French declaration of war on Britain on 1 February 1793 had an immediate effect on Nelson's life: he was being employed again after five years on half-pay. Since December 1787 he had been on half-pay ashore. Most of that time he had spent with his wife Fanny in his father's[1] parsonage at Burnham Thorpe, his birthplace. He looked after the education of Josiah,[2] Mrs Nelson's son from her first marriage, but did not succeed in getting him an apprenticeship. On being re-employed he therefore decided to take Josiah with him to sea. On 30 January 1793 he received his commission as captain of His Majesty's ship *Agamemnon*, a third-rate ship of the line of 64 guns.

His orders were to join the fleet in the Mediterranean under the command of Lord Hood.[3] As revolutionary upheaval was still going on in France itself, the British Mediterranean fleet was expected to play an active role in supporting royalist forces in France. These forces had assembled in the naval port of Toulon. The British Mediterranean fleet under Admiral Hood's command was supporting these French royalist forces from the sea. Hood, however, realised that he would need support – both in goods and men. In order to ask this support from the king of Naples, he sent Nelson to Naples. Ferdinand IV of the kingdom of Naples and III of Sicily[4] resided in his capital, at the time the third largest city in Europe. There Nelson would have to report to Sir William Hamilton, KB, who had been living in Naples with few interruptions since 1764, and, since 1789, as Envoy Extraordinary and Minister Plenipotentiary.

Nelson arrived in Naples on 11 September 1793 and stayed for the following four days. While he was arranging to be presented at court, he had an opportunity to meet the ambassador's wife, Emma Lady Hamilton. On 14 September he wrote to his wife: 'Lady Hamilton has been

[1]Edmund Nelson (1723–1802).

[2]Josiah Nisbet (1780–1830).

[3]Samuel Hood, 1st Viscount Hood (1724–1816), in command of the British Mediterranean fleet since 1793.

[4]Ferdinand of Bourbon (1751–1825), younger brother of Charles IV of Spain (1748–1819), married to Maria Carolina of Austria (1752–1814, daughter of empress Maria Theresa); the oldest of their many children, Maria Teresa (1772–1807) was married to her first cousin, the Emperor Francis II (1768–1835).

wonderfully kind and good to Josiah. She is a young woman of amiable manners and who does honour to the station to which she is raised.'[1] The focus of Nelson's attention shifted, however, after he was presented to the king of Naples. He proudly wrote to his brother, William, that he met him three times. The king had even planned to visit Nelson on board his ship, when Nelson had to leave in a hurry. Nelson then merely mentioned Lady Hamilton as one of many whom he had to get off his ship in order to receive the king:

> [The king] was to have visited my Ship the day we sailed, when she was full of ladies and gentlemen. – Sir William and Lady Hamilton, the Bishop of Winchester,[2] Mrs. North[3] and family, Lord and Lady Plymouth,[4] Earl Grandison[5] and daughter, besides other Baronets, &c. I gave them breakfast, manned Ship, &c., and was to have sent them off at one o'clock, when the King was to come on board. I had everything ready to have entertained him . . .[6]

After these first encounters Lady Hamilton merely appears in the few letters Nelson had occasion to write to the British ambassador. Nelson then courteously presented his 'most respectful compliments'[7] and in one letter of 1794 he also requested Sir William 'to present' his letter to Lady Hamilton.[8]

Although Nelson stayed in contact with Sir William Hamilton,[9] his further activities as a captain serving in the Mediterranean offered no

[1] *Nelson's Letters to His Wife and other Documents. 1785–1831*, ed. George Naish (London, 1958) [hereafter: Naish], p. 91.

[2] Brownlow North (1741–1820).

[3] Henrietta Maria, née Bannister (d.1796).

[4] Other Hickman Windsor, 5th Earl of Plymouth (1751–99) and his wife Sarah, née Archer (1762–1838).

[5] George Bussy Villiers, 4th Earl of Jersey, Viscount Grandison (1735–1805).

[6] *The Dispatches and Letters of Vice-Admiral Lord Viscount Nelson*, ed. Nicholas Harris Nicolas, 7 vols (London, 1997; reprint of first edition 1844–46) [hereafter: Nicolas], i, p. 328.

[7] Nicolas, i, p. 379 (letter of 27 Mar 1794); similarly: Nicolas, ii, p. 135 'With my best respects to' (letter of 11 Mar 1796) and *The Collection of Autograph Letters and Historical Documents formed by Alfred Morrison (Second Series, 1882–1893) – The Hamilton & Nelson Papers*, 2 vols ([n. pl.], 1893) [hereafter: Morrison] i, p. 181 (no. 226) 'I beg my Respectful Compliments to Lady Hamilton' (letter of 27 Sept 1793).

[8] *The Letters of Lord Nelson to Lady Hamilton with a Supplement of Interesting Letters by Distinguished Characters*, ed. [Anon.], 2 vols (London, 1814) [hereafter: 1814-letters], ii, p. 225; quoted in Nicolas, i, p. 401.

[9] Nelson's letters to Sir William Hamilton are published in Nicolas and Morrison, but also partly unpublished; for an example of an unpublished letter, see Roger Knight, *The Pursuit of Victory. The Life and Achievement of Horatio Nelson* (London, 2005) [hereafter: Knight], p. 154 [quoted from the collection at the Nelson Museum in Monmouth].

reason to return to Naples and visit the Hamiltons. Apart from a cruise along the coast of Northern Africa, to Tunis and to the west of it, in November 1793, his sphere of action was mostly between Leghorn Roads and Corsica with occasional service off Genoa, Sardinia and Toulon, which he helped to evacuate at the end of 1793. On Corsica Nelson had an opportunity to show whether he was able to be entrusted with independent command. Admiral Hood wished to cooperate with the Corsican patriots under Pasquale Paoli, but was not supported in this plan by the British general, David Dundas, so he decided to attempt a conquest with his marines. After Nelson had taken command the towns of Bastia and Calvi surrendered. The conquest of the latter cost Nelson the sight of his right eye, but his personal engagement in the campaign confirmed his valour and ambition. His spirited actions gained him the colonelcy of the marines, a sinecure for senior captains.

After Admiral Hood was recalled home, Nelson was not given as much opportunity to prove himself as he would have wished. He was sailing with the British fleet, when it met with the French fleet on 13 March 1795. The French were aiming to retake Corsica. Admiral Hotham,[1] who was at that time acting commander-in-chief of the British fleet, only captured two French ships, letting the greater part of the French fleet escape unopposed. Nelson complained to his wife:

> My disposition can't bear tame and slow measures. Sure I am, had I commanded our fleet on the 14th, that either the whole French Fleet would have graced my triumph, or I should have been in a confounded scrape. I went on board Hotham so soon as our firing grew slack in the van, and the *Ca Ira* and *Censeur* struck, to propose to him leaving our two crippled ships, the two prizes, and four frigates, to themselves, and to pursue the enemy, but he is much cooler than myself and said "We must be contented. We have done very well", but had we taken 10 sail and allowed the 11th to have escaped if possible to have been got at, I could never call it well *done*. Goodall backed me. I got him to write to the Admiral, but it would not do. We should have had such a day as I believe the annals of England never produced but it can't be helped.[2]

After Nelson went with the fleet to Minorca in May and June of 1795, he was given a small squadron to co-operate with the Austrian army on the Ligurian and Tuscan coasts. On the Ligurian coast, the city of

[1]William Lord Hotham (1736–1813).
[2]Naish, p. 204.

Genoa, though nominally neutral, pursued a policy that was very much influenced by French interests. In contrast, Leghorn, on the Tuscan coast and thus further removed from French influence came to be an important base for Nelson. There Nelson shared in the social network around the English factory (an association of British merchants) and the British consul, John Udney.[1] This social circle included women, which some officers readily passed from one to another. Nelson, however, in the course of two years appears to have stuck to one, Adelaide Correglia.[2] Different references to her in contemporary documents show that Nelson even took her to sea with him. Only one note of Nelson's to her, however, survives.[3]

The new commander-in-chief, Sir John Jervis,[4] arrived in January 1796. From the start, Nelson got on very well with him and his career continued as promisingly as it had done under Admiral Hood. Nelson took command of the 74-gun ship *Captain* and was soon created commodore. The position of the British in the Mediterranean, however, did not develop as promisingly. Neither Nelson's cooperation with the Austrians nor other attempts of the British to maintain a strong position in the Mediterranean were very successful. The British government therefore decided to retreat from the Mediterranean and from the end of 1796 until the beginning of 1797 Nelson was busy helping to achieve this. He was aware that leaving the Mediterranean also meant a separation from the friends he had made there, even though he had not been able to maintain personal contact with the Hamiltons. He wrote to Sir William Hamilton on 1 December 1796 that he was 'grieved and distressed . . . till now [England] never was known to desert her friends while she had the power of supporting them . . . I wish any mode could be adopted that individually as an officer . . . I could serve the King of Naples.'[5]

Nelson had just left the Mediterranean and joined Jervis's fleet, when, on 14 February 1797, the fleet encountered a Spanish convoy,

[1]John Udney (1727–1800), consul at Leghorn from 1776 until 1796, when he fled from the French invasion.

[2]Knight, pp. 185, 197–9, 211, 630.

[3]Kept in the Huntington Library, San Marino, California, HM 34180 (A facsimile of this letter of Nov 1796 can be found in Knight, p. 197). It reads: 'Ma Chere Adelaide, / Je suis partant en cette moment pour la mere, une vaisseau neapolitan partir avec moi pour Livorne, Croire moi toujours / Votre chere amie / Horatio Nelson. / Avez vous bien successe.'

[4]Sir John Jervis (1735–1823); to be made Earl St Vincent after the Battle of Cape St Vincent.

[5]Morrison, i, p. 226 (no. 290).

accompanied by a fleet of twenty-two Spanish men-of-war. Jervis led his line of battle through a gap in the Spanish fleet, thus cutting off the Spanish rear and focusing on the centre. When the Spanish rear managed to interrupt his movement and the Spanish vanguard attempted to support its centre, Jervis ordered the rear to interrupt this movement. The British admiral in command of the rear did not react, however, but Nelson took the *Captain* out of the rear of the British fleet and manoeuvered it towards the centre of the Spanish fleet.[1] Helped by some confusion in the Spanish centre and his old friend Collingwood's[2] ship, Nelson daringly attacked two Spanish ships that were much superior in size to his own and managed personally to board and take them both.

Nelson was disappointed not to have been mentioned in Jervis's official dispatch, but he was created Knight of the Order of the Bath, thus becoming Sir Horatio. Soon after he was promoted Rear Admiral and Jervis, now Earl St Vincent, kept giving him independent tasks to perform. Nelson was sent to maintain a tight blockade on the southern Spanish port of Cadiz. As a result of the mutinies at Spithead and the Nore, in 1797, he was given a new ship, the *Theseus*, the crew of which had taken part in the mutiny. With the captain exchanged and Nelson as admiral on board, it was dispatched with a squadron to take the island of Tenerife, where a Spanish treasure ship had moored. The attack began badly as the Spanish noticed the British advance in time to prepare their defence and the attack itself went disastrously wrong, costing many lives and Nelson personally lost his right arm.

After months of painful convalescence Nelson again was able to join the fleet of Earl of St Vincent, the recently ennobled Sir John Jervis, in April 1798. At this time the British government had decided to send a small force into the Mediterranean and St Vincent entrusted Nelson with the task of leading it. The choice of Nelson was St Vincent's own and he was heavily criticised by Sir John Orde,[3] who was senior in rank to Nelson, had spent all the winter in the fleet under St Vincent's command, and had thus regarded himself the natural candidate for this attractive post. As Nelson was returning into the Mediterranean, the chances increased that he might meet Lady Hamilton again.

[1]How this independent action was interpreted in the course of time is shown in my book *Horatio Nelson. A Controversial Hero* (London, 2005), p. 21.

[2]Cuthbert Collingwood (1748–1810), whom Nelson had befriended in the West Indies in the 1770s, would be his second-in-command at Trafalgar and then succeed him in the command after the battle.

[3]Sir John Orde (1751–1824), described by Knight, p. 660, as a 'universally unpopular officer'.

After Nelson left Naples in September 1793, the life of the Hamiltons had continued much as before. Apart from the news of the evacuation of Toulon at the end of 1793 and the suffering of the refugees, the British ambassador and his wife mostly dealt with social refugees, who had escaped the restraints of British society. Earlier in the year the Dowager Countess Spencer[1] had arrived with her two daughters, Georgiana Duchess of Devonshire[2] and Elizabeth Lady Bessborough,[3] as well as Lady Elizabeth Foster (friend of the Duchess of Devonshire and her successor as wife of the 5th duke).[4] The three younger women of the company were all taking a break from their troubled marriages. The Duchess and her friend had returned to Britain, but the Countess, who had avoided meeting the newly wed Lady Hamilton in England in the summer of 1791,[5] and Lady Bessborough, were still around. Lady Hamilton entertained them at Caserta, north of Naples, where the Neapolitan court spent the summer of 1794, while Nelson was fighting in Corsica. Another refugee from British morality was Prince Augustus, sixth son of George III,[6] who in March 1794 had secretly married Augusta Murray in Rome and now did not dare to return to Britain. In November 1794 Lady Foster's father, the Bishop of Derry, Earl of Bristol, and an old friend of the Hamiltons, arrived to stay for a while. The wealthy William Beckford,[7] an old friend of Sir William Hamilton and outcast of elegant society because of a homosexual affair, who had welcomed the Hamiltons on their honeymoon, kept promising to visit, but never made it.

Lady Hamilton was beginning to involve herself in political matters, too. This was mostly due to her intensifying relationship with the queen of Naples,[8] an isolated foreigner within Neapolitan society herself, whose confidence she had gained. In September 1796 the queen lent

[1]Margaret Georgiana Spencer, née Poyntz (1737–1814), wife of John Spencer, 1st Earl Spencer (1734–83).

[2]Georgiana Cavendish, née Spencer, Duchess of Devonshire, (1757–1806), wife of William Cavendish, 5th Duke of Devonshire (1748–1811).

[3]Henrietta Frances Lady Bessborough, née Spencer (1761–1821), wife of Frederick Ponsonby, 3rd Earl of Bessborough (1758–1844).

[4]Elizabeth Christiana Foster, née Hervey (1758–1824), daughter of the Earl-Bishop of Bristol (1730–1803), later to become the second wife of William Cavendish, 5th Duke of Devonshire.

[5]Flora Fraser, *Beloved Emma. The Life of Emma Lady Hamilton* (London, 1986) [hereafter: Fraser], p. 162.

[6]George III of Great Britain (1738–1820).

[7]William Thomas Beckford (1760–1840), heir to a vast fortune, poet, traveller, collector, art-lover, friend of Sir William Hamilton's.

[8]Maria Carolina of Austria (1752–1814), thirteenth child of Empress Maria Teresa (1717–80), by marrying Ferdinand IV (1751–1825) became queen of Naples and Sicily.

Lady Hamilton a letter from the King of Spain[1] in which he informed his brother, Ferdinand of Naples, of his plan to join France in her war against Britain. Lady Hamilton quickly copied the letter, returned the original to the queen and sent the copy on to the British Foreign Secretary, Lord Grenville.[2] Important as the information was, it can hardly have arrived in Britain in time to influence policy.[3] Following the treaty of alliance between Spain and France, signed at San Ildefonso on 19 August 1796, Spain declared war on Britain in October 1796. When the Neapolitans celebrated peace with France in December 1796, the British fleet was already leaving the Mediterranean.

With the political situation turning ever more difficult for Britons in the Mediterranean, a new type of refugee turned up at the ambassador's residence. One of them was Sir Gilbert Elliot,[4] till lately Viceroy of Corsica. Other British refugees, in this case from Leghorn, were the wealthy Wynnes. One of the two daughters of the family, Elizabeth (Betsey) married Thomas Freemantle at the British embassy (Palazzo Sessa) on 12 January 1797 and went on to accompany her husband on board ship, even to the attack on Tenerife on 24 July 1797, where Nelson lost his right arm. After the French occupation of Rome on 10 February 1798 and the declaration of the Republic there five days later even more Britons arrived at Naples, among them Lady Knight,[5] widow of admiral Sir Joseph Knight, and her daughter Cornelia Knight.[6] While the British in Naples felt the increasing uncertainty of the political situation, Nelson was under intense pressure to deal with the very specific uncertainty as to the aims of the French fleet.

Nelson had avoided staying with his squadron in sight of Toulon. On 22 May 1798 his ships encountered a heavy storm off the western coast of Sardinia and the ships-of-the-line lost contact with the frigates in the squadron. As soon as the ships were patched up, Nelson sailed northwards again and on 5 June met the *Mutine*, Captain Hardy,[7] with

[1]Charles IV.

[2]Fraser, p. 205; William Wyndham Grenville, 1st Baron Grenville (1759–1834), Foreign Secretary 1791–1801.

[3]For a detailed discussion of this matter, see: John Knox Laughton, 'Nelson's Last Codicil' [first part] in *Colburn's United Services Magazine* 1889, 647–62, esp. 652–5.

[4]Sir Gilbert Elliot (1751–1814) had been viceroy of Corsica 1794–96 and became Lord Minto in 1797.

[5]Philippina Knight (d. 1799), widow of Sir Joseph Knight and mother of Cornelia Knight.

[6]Cornelia Knight (1757–1837), writer who had settled with her mother in Italy, living in Naples at the time Nelson arrived; she had become friend of the Hamiltons and Nelson, and returned with them to England.

[7]Thomas Masterman Hardy (1769–1839) had served with Nelson in the Mediterranean 1793–97, at Tenerife 1797 and at the Nile 1798; 'Thereafter, Nelson always asked for Hardy to serve with him' (Knight, p. 643).

St Vincent's orders to rendezvous with Captain Troubridge[1] and ten 74-gun ships-of-the-line and the *Leander* with 50 guns off Toulon, take command of the whole fleet and destroy the French fleet, wherever it was to be found in the Mediterranean. This task was urgent, as the French fleet had left Toulon on 20 May. Consequently, Nelson's actions were not only the focus of attention for his fellow officers, but also for the British government. While the French fleet sailed southwards, Nelson – still without frigates – searched for it along the coast of Italy, sending a letter to Lady Hamilton, as he assumed he would not go ashore at Naples [1]. On 17 June he reached Naples for the first time since 1793. Instead of going ashore himself, he merely sent Captain Troubridge into the city of Naples in order to enquire of news of the French fleet. Lady Hamilton used the opportunity to send a letter by the queen of Naples for Nelson to read and return. He accompanied the returned letter with a few lines [3]. Just before Troubridge left Naples again, Lady Hamilton penned down some emotional lines, wishing Nelson well [see 2 and 4]. The following day, at sea again, Nelson wrote a 'private' letter to Sir William Hamilton, and concluded it with a personal note: 'Pray, present my best respects to Lady Hamilton. Tell her, I hope to be presented to her crowned with laurel or cypress. But God is good, and to Him do I commit myself and our Cause.'[2] Only after crossing the straits of Messina did Nelson learn that the French had taken Malta just a few days before and sailed on. He conjectured that they were heading for Alexandria and after consulting with captains Troubridge, Saumarez,[3] Darby[4] and Ball[5] made directly for that place. He arrived in Alexandria with his fleet on 29 June, finding the harbour without a French ship. In order to continue his chase he left again on 30 June, a day before the French arrived. In desperate search of the French fleet Nelson went northwards towards Turkey , then westwards along the coast of Crete, back to Sicily.

On 19 July 1798 Nelson arrived with his fleet at Syracuse. Although he had not yet received Lady Hamilton's letter of 30 June,[6] he himself

[1]Thomas Troubridge (1758–1807), whom Nelson first met when they were both midshipmen, in 1773.

[2]Nicolas, iii, p. 34.

[3]Sir James Saumarez (1757–1836).

[4]Henry D'Esterre Darby (d. 1823).

[5]Alexander John Ball (1757–1809), captain of the *Alexander* at the Battle of the Nile, later to become first Governor of Malta.

[6]In her letter of 30 June 1798, Lady Hamilton writes that she takes 'the opportunity of Captain Hope to write a few lines'. Captain Hope was in command of the *Alcmene* which joined Nelson's fleet only twelve days after the battle, on 13 Aug 1798, when Nelson immediately answered it (see Doc. No. 9).

wrote to her two letters on 22 July [5 to 7]. In one of these letters Nelson complains about 'the treatment we receive from the power we came to assist + fight for'. In the other, written to both Sir William and Lady Hamilton he writes happily: 'Thanks to your exertions, we have victualled and watered: and surely watering at the Fountain of Arethusa, we must have victory'. It is impossible to assess, what exactly made Nelson think at the time that he was indebted to Sir William and Lady Hamilton for the victualling and watering.[1] In any case, he stuck to this idea, reduced over time to Lady Hamilton alone as the helpful influence. On the last day of his life he wrote in the codicil to his will:

> the British fleet, under my command, could never have returned the second time to Egypt, had not lady Hamilton's influence with the Queen of Naples, caused letters to be wrote to the Governor of Syracuse, that he was to encourage the fleet being supplied with everything, should they put into any port in Sicily. We put into Syracuse, and received every supply, went to Egypt, and destroyed the French fleet.[2]

Lady Hamilton attempted to confirm this claim after Nelson's death. She assumed that her support was contained in the queen of Naples' letter which she had passed on to Nelson on 17 June 1798, when he stopped at Naples in order to get information about the whereabouts of the French fleet.[3]

Still without frigates, but 'amply supplied' Nelson left Syracuse on 23 July 1798.[4] After a second fast crossing he reached Alexandria and on 1 August 1798 found the French fleet in Aboukir Bay to the east of the city. In this bay at the mouth of the Nile the French fleet had anchored in a supposedly secure position, while a French army under Bonaparte had started to conquer Egypt. Nelson attacked immediately with thirteen of his fourteen ships-of-the-line; the *Culloden*, commanded by Troubridge, ran aground before entering the battle. Nelson's fleet took or sank nearly all of the thirteen French ships-of-the-line, allowing only two to escape.

[1]John Knox Laughton, 'Nelson's Last Codicil' [second part] in *Colburn's United Services Magazine* 1890, 10–23, esp. 22–3; Jack Russell, *Nelson and the Hamiltons* (Harmondsworth, 1969) [hereafter: Russell], p. 48.

[2]See Doc. No. 400.

[3]See her note on Doc. No. 3.

[4]Letter to Sir William Hamilton of that day in Nicolas, iii, pp. 47–8; the original is at the Huntington Library, HM 34019.

The French flagship *L'Orient* of 120 guns (the biggest British ships in the battle had only 74 guns) blew up at the height of the battle.

Although Nelson himself had been wounded in the head during the battle, he now had to make sure the news of the event arrived in Britain as soon as possible. On 8 August, only a week after the battle, he wrote a letter to the British ambassador at Naples, beginning: 'Almighty God has made me the happy instrument in destroying the Enemy's fleet, which I hope will be a blessing to Europe'.[1] He wrote that he would be 'sorry to have any accounts get home before my dispatches', but in the end it was through the second set of dispatches that he had sent to Naples that the news would reach Britain, as the first set was lost, when the *Leander* with Captain Berry[2] and the documents on board was taken by *Le Généreux*. Having decided to refit in Naples, Nelson wrote his first letter after the battle to Lady Hamilton, three days after that to her husband, announcing his arrival [see 8]. Two days later, still in the bay of Aboukir, Nelson received her letter of 30 June, which he answered immediately [5 and 9]. Still without an account about whether and how the news of the Battle of the Nile had been received in different parts of Europe, Nelson set sail on 19 August, slowly moving northwards with a small squadron of three ships-of-the-line. While Nelson was cruising from Crete towards the Straits of Messina, the news of the Battle of the Nile reached Naples, on 3 September. When Lady Hamilton, five days later, recorded the reaction of the inhabitants of Naples to the news in a letter to Nelson she described herself as 'delerious with joy' and 'impatient to see +embrace you' [10]. Nelson, meanwhile, having passed the straits of Messina, merely signed a list of the 'Force of the English and French Fleets at the Battle of the Nile' for Lady Hamilton.[3] When he received Lady Hamilton's enthusiastic letter still at sea, he copied in a letter to his wife what the queen of Naples had exclaiming according to Lady Hamilton: 'Oh, brave Nelson; Oh God bless and protect our brave deliverer. Oh Nelson, Nelson, what do we not owe you. Oh victor, saviour of Italy. Oh that my swollen heart could now tell him personally what we

[1]Nicolas, iii, p. 93; the original was sold be Christie's on 3 Dec 2003; a facsimile of the letter can be found in the catalogue of the sale as lot 219.

[2]Edward Berry (1768–1831), captain of Nelson's flagship, the *Vanguard*, at the Battle of the Nile.

[3]NMM: SUT/1; including, for the British: names of ships, numbers of guns, men, killed and wounded; for the French: names of ships, numbers of guns and men, 'how disposed of' (burnt, taken or sunk) or 'escaped'; with a list of what became of the French (sent on shore, escaped, prisoners on board the fleet – 3,705 – or 'Kill'd, drownd, burnt, and missing' – 5,225).

owe to him.' On this outburst of enthusiasm he dryly commented: 'I only hope I shall not have to be witness to a renewal'.[1] Four days later, on 20 September, he began a letter to his commander-in-chief, Earl St Vincent: 'I detest this voyage to Naples'. How Nelson reacted to the emotional reception he received, when he arrived at Naples, can be guessed at from the continuation of his letter to his wife three days later:

> The poor wretched Vanguard[2] arrived here on the 22nd. I must endeavour to convey to you something of what passed, but if it was so affecting to those only who are united in bonds of friendship what must it be to my dearest wife. My friends say everything which is most dear to me in this world. Sir William and Lady Hamilton came out to sea attended by numerous boats with emblems etc. My most respectable friends had really been laid up and seriously ill, first from anxiety and them from joy. It was imprudently told Lady Hamilton in a moment. The effect was a shot. She fell apparently dead and is not yet perfectly recovered from severe bruises. Alongside my honoured friends came, the scene in the boat appeared terribly affecting. Up flew her ladyship exclaiming: 'Oh God is it possible' fell into my arms [*sic*] more dead than alive. Tears however soon set matters to rights, when alongside came the King. The scene was in its way affecting. He took me by the hand, calling me his deliverer and preserver, with every other expression of kindness. In short all Naples calls me 'Nostro[3] Liberatore' for the scene with the lower classes was truly affecting. I hope one day to have the pleasure of introducing you to Lady Hamilton. She is one of the very best women in this world. How few could have made the turn she has. She is an honour to her sex and a proof that even reputation may be regained, but I own it requires a great soul. Her kindness with Sir William to me is more than I can express. I am in their house, and I may now tell you it required all the kindness of my friends to set me up. Her ladyship if Josiah was to stay would make something of him and with all his bluntness I am sure he likes Lady Hamilton more than any female. She would fashion him in 6 months in spite of himself. I believe Lady Hamilton intends writing you. . . .[4]

[1]Naish, p. 399 (letter of 16 Sept 1798).

[2]Nelson's flagship at the Battle of the Nile.

[3]Naish has here 'Nostra', which I assume is an error in transcription.

[4]Naish, pp. 400–401; in her letter to Lady Nelson of 2 Dec 1798 Lady Hamilton refers to a 'former letter with an account of Lord Nelson's arrival and his reception from their Sicilian Majesties . . .' (Naish, p. 461).

In his next letters to his wife on 28 September and 1 October, Nelson continued to describe how he was celebrated in Naples. It appears that the experience of 'what is called pleasure' was so overwhelming ('I am not my own master for 5 minutes') that it drew him closer to the Hamiltons: 'The continued kind attention of Sir William and Lady Hamilton must ever make you and I love them and they are deserving of the love and admiration of all the world'.[1]

The adulation he received did not distract him from analysing the political situation. He judged rightly of the importance of his victory at the Nile in breaking a long chain of uninterrupted conquests by Napoleon Bonaparte. It remained difficult, however, to decide how best to build upon this success. With impatience he observed a culture of political 'procrastination'. Ignoring the possibility that the same procrastination could be found in the military forces of Britain's ally in southern Italy, he urged the King of Naples to fight the French on land. On 3 October 1798, less than ten days after his arrival at Naples, he drafted a letter to Lady Hamilton that was meant to be shown to the government of Naples [11]. This draft shows many changes and differs slightly from the letter actually sent. In this letter he regarded the expected arrival of the Austrian general, Mack,[2] as an opportunity to encourage 'the government not to lose any more of the favourable time which Providence has put in their hands'. The Neapolitan government, in Nelson's view, should not 'wait for an attack in this country, instead of carrying the war out of it'. Nelson declared that if the government did not act, it would have to prepare for the evacuation of the court.

Rather than staying at Naples in order to influence policies, Nelson had to fulfil his naval duties. One of these duties was to support the Maltese who had risen against their French occupiers. Nelson thus sailed for Malta on 15 October 1798, where he arrived nine days later. This first absence from Naples after the Battle of the Nile triggered the first flow of correspondence between him and Lady Hamilton. Luckily letters from both sides of this correspondence have come down to us, so that we can get an idea of the kind of relationship that had built up between Nelson and Lady Hamilton in the course of less than a month in Naples (22 September to 15 October). His first letter was merely a note signed

[1]Naish, p. 403.

[2]Karl Mack von Leiberich (1752–1828) did indeed arrive and take command of the Neapolitan troops, with which – after initial successes, particularly the conquest of Rome – he was devastatingly defeated and forced to flee to the French, who unsurprisingly took him prisoner.

'Nelson' and thus signifying that he had received the news of being elevated to the peerage [12]. Lady Hamilton in the meantime had followed the Neapolitan court to Caserta, its residence north of Naples. From there she reported not only gossip about the wife of the crown prince being in labour, but also about the political worries of the influential queen, how Nelson was 'wanted at Court', and how she herself tried to 'inspire' the court 'with some of our spirit + energy' [13].

On arrival off Malta, on 24 October 1798, Nelson wrote to Lady Hamilton about the difficult situation he encountered there, but also about his worries concerning French 'shipping in Egypt' and 'how to best meet [the queen of Naples'] approbation'. He trusted Lady Hamilton with an enclosed letter which has not come down to us, commenting: 'I believe scarecly any thing I hear' [14]. Three days later, still off Malta, Nelson received some 'interesting' letters from Lady Hamilton. He told her that he was 'totally displeased' with the results of Neapolitan policy and was struggling with different scenes of action in the eastern Mediterranean as well as Italy [16].

In her next letter Lady Hamilton enthused about the honours that the Ottoman Sultan had conferred on Nelson and what kind of titles she herself would give him, if she were King of England: 'I wou'd make you the most noble puisant Duke Nelson Marquis Nile Earl Alexander vicount pyramid Baron crocadile + prince victory That posterity might have you in all forms' [15]. On 27 October she continues to describe presents for Nelson from Turkey, enthuses how he is appreciated by the queen of Naples and encloses her version of 'See the conquering Hero comes', dedicated to Nelson [17, 18]. She also deals with political issues, reporting more gossip from Caserta, about the uncertain position of Austria and her own role in encouraging the queen to send Mack to fight [17]. With an urgent note of 2 November Lady Hamilton sent Nelson 'the latest papers' and announced that 'the King marches the 8th thank god' [19].

In the meantime, Nelson was on his way back to Naples. He had left Malta on 30 October and arrived at Naples on 5 November. The Neapolitan troops appeared to be successful at first. When they moved northwards, Nelson again went to sea, this time transporting troops to Leghorn in the hope that military success could be carried further north. On leaving, Nelson sent Lady Hamilton a personal note, assuring her of his friendship [20]. Lady Hamilton kept writing to Nelson during his absence, mentioning her worries about the bad weather, congratulating him on the present of a sword, informing him about the movements of the Neapolitan troops, and repeatedly imploring him not to go on shore in Leghorn, perhaps knowing of his earlier amorous affair there, years before [21, 22, 23]. Awaiting Nelson's return, Lady Hamilton wrote to Lady Nelson in a similar vein to the style of her letters to Nelson himself. She described how 'Lord Nelson is adored here + looked on as the deliverer of this country' and that the king of Naples begged 'my Lord Nelson . . . to advise + consult with her Majesty, who is Regent' during his absence.' Lady Hamilton also mentioned – rather worryingly for the addressee – how she nursed Nelson with 'asses milk' and of her judgement that 'Josiah is so much improved'.[1]

On Tuesday, 4 December 1799, Nelson announced his immediate return to Lady Hamilton in a quickly written note. He trusts her with a 'private memorand^m' and information about the position of different ships [24]. Political decisions were now urgently needed as the Neapolitan troops had been unable to hold Rome. With French troops advancing towards Naples, it was decided that the royal family must leave the city. Supposedly in mistrust of their own navy, they embarked on 21 December 1798 on Nelson's flagship. In a letter of 7 January 1799 to her former lover, Sir William Hamilton's nephew and heir, Charles Greville,[2] Lady Hamilton described the events:

> for 6 nights before the embarkation I sat up at my own house receiving all the jewels, money; & effects of the Royal family, and from thence conveying them on board the *Vanguard*, living in fear of being torn to pieces by the tumultuous mob who suspected our departure, but Sir W^m & I being beloved in the country saved us. On the 21st, at ten at night, Lord Nelson, Sir W^m, mother, & self went out to pay a visit, sent all our servants away, & orderd them in 2 hours to come with the coach, & ordered supper at home. When they were gone we sett off, walked to our boat, & after 2 hours got to the *Vanguard*. Lord N. then went with armed boats to a secret passage adjoining to the palace, got up the dark staircase that goes into the Queen's room, & with a dark lantern, cutlasses, pistols, &c., brought off every soul, ten in number, to the *Vanguard* at twelve o'clock. If we had remained to the next day we shou'd have all been imprisoned. But we remained 2 days in the bay to treat with the Neapolitans – but, alas, with such vile traitors what can you do?

[1]Letter of 2 Dec 1798; BL Add 34,989 ff. 8–11; printed in Naish, pp. 461–2. Nelson wrote to his wife on 11 Dec 1798: 'The improvement made in Josiah by Lady Hamilton is wonderful' (Naish, p. 479).

[2]Charles Francis Greville (1749–1809).

Nelson's squadron sailed on 23 December 1798 and suffered a heavy crossing to Palermo, the capital of the Sicilian kingdom. Lady Hamilton described the dramatic crossing to Palermo as follows:

> the *Vanguard*, Lord Nelson, brought us off with all the Royal family, & we arrived here on Christmas Day at night, after having been near lost, a tempest that Lord Nelson had never seen for thirty years he has been at sea the like; all our sails torn to pieces, & all the men ready with their axes to cut away the masts, & poor I to attend & keep up the spirits of the Queen, the Princess Royall, 3 young princesses, a baby six weeks old & 2 young princess, Leopold & Albert, the last six years old, my favourite, taken with convulsion in the midst of the storm, & at 7 in the evening of Christmas Day expired in my arms, not a soul to help me, as the few women her majesty brought on board were incapable of helping her or the poor Royal children

While Lady Hamilton was supporting the queen and her children, her mother, Mrs Cadogan,[1] was with Sir William, the king, several politicians and their helpless 'attendants'.[2] After their arrival at Palermo, Nelson invited Lady Hamilton, her mother and husband for a small Christmas party [25]. About two weeks later, in her letter to Charles Greville, Lady Hamilton summarised their new situation:

> We have left every thing at Naples but the vases & best pictures, 3 houses elegantly furnished, all our horses, & 6 or 7 carriages I think is enough for the vile French, for we cou'd not get our things off not to betray the Royal Family, & as we were in councel we were sworn to secrecy, . . . We cannot at present profit of our leave of absence, for we cannot leave the Royal family in their distress. Sir William, however, says in the spring we shall leave this, as Lord St Vincent as order'd a ship to carry us down to Gibraltar, God only knows what yet is to become of us, we are worn out: I am, with anxiety and fatigue; Sir W^{m} as had 3 days a bilious attack, but is now well; my dear, adorable queen, whom I love better *than any person in the world* is allso very unwell, *we weep together*, & now that is our onely comfort. Sir William & the King are philosophers; nothing affects them, thank God, . . .[3]

[1]Mary Cadogan (d. 1810).
[2]Morrison, ii, pp. 35–6, no. 370.
[3]Morrison, ii, pp. 35–6, no. 370; Sir William described himself as a 'philosopher' in his letter of 8 April 1799 to the same addressee (Morrison, ii, pp. 40–41, no. 381).

The party now settled in Palermo, where they spent the next five months together. As a consequence their correspondence diminished. What has come down to us relating to their joint activities consists of a few short notes: Nelson's assurance of his loyalty to the queen of Naples [26]; a letter of Nelson's to Ball, who was maintaining the blockade of Malta, with a postscript by Lady Hamilton [27]; and Nelson's notes for a speech made on the occasion of being created a citizen of Palermo [28]. By April Sir William had learned that his vases, which Lady Hamilton had described as saved from the upheavals at Naples, had been lost on their way to Britain in the *Colossus* off the Scilly Islands. Sir William could not find much more joy in their situation in Palermo:

> From being driven from my comfortable house at Naples to a house here without chimneys & calculated only for summer, we have all suffer'd in our health, . . . I am still most desirous of profiting of the King's leave and of returning home by the first ship that Lord Nelson sends down to Gibraltar, as I am worn out and want repose; but as I realy now see a very good prospect of Ld Nelson's carrying back their Sicilian Majesties to Naples in the *Vanguard* & placing them again on that throne, and that hitherto Lord Nelson, not knowing the language, could not have done without our assistance, and I see that his Lordship is very desirous of my staying with him a little longer, as is the Court, I will have patience. . . . You cannot conceive their gratitude, and also of this whole island, towards the English, for you see Genl Stuart has secured Messina for them. You may judge, my dear Charles, what it is to keep a table for all the poor British emigrants from Naples, who have none, & for the officers of the fleet, as Lord Nelson lives in the house with us, & all the business, which is immense, is transacted in our house. . . . Emma makes a great figure in our political line, for she carries on the business with the Queen, whose abilities you know are very great. . . . I love Ld Nelson more & more – his activity is wonderfull, and he loves us sincerely.[1]

In letters to his wife, Nelson, too, described the heavy workload under which he was labouring: 'With more writing than two hands could get through you must take a line for a page and a page for a sheet of paper'.[2]

[1]Letter to Charles Greville of 8 April 1799, Morrison, ii, pp. 40–41 (no. 381); in another letter to Charles Greville of 28 April 1799 Sir William again described how much all three of them had to work (Morrison, ii, p. 45, no. 384).

[2]Letter of 2 Feb 1799 (Naish, p. 481); similarly in letters of 10 April, 5 May, 10 May and 5 June 1799 (Naish, pp. 482, 483 and 485).

As he was now merely writing short letters and rarely more than one letter a month, his concern about Lady Nelson's son weighed the more heavily: 'I wish I could say much to your and my satisfaction about Josiah but I am sorry to say and with real grief, that he has nothing good about him, he must sooner or later be broke.'[1]

Nelson only left Palermo and the Hamiltons to go to sea, when he learned that the French admiral Bruix[2] had left Toulon with the French fleet. He went on board the *Vanguard* on 19 May 1799 in a depressed mood [29]. While sailing he constantly kept Lady Hamilton informed about his movements and considerations [30–33 and 35]. In between naval and broader political subjects these letters are interspersed with assurances of friendship. So are Sir William's letters of the period. It appears that, instead of an exchange of letters between two persons a network of correspondence was developing. Nelson sent Lady Hamilton letters he received from the queen of Naples as well as from the Portuguese admiral Niza[3] [33] and he referred Sir William to a letter he had written to 'Lady Hamilton this morning'.[4] He also sent Sir William and Lady Hamilton 'Hallowell's[5] letter to Troubridge'.[6] Similarly, Sir William Hamilton kept Nelson informed: 'Whilst Emma was writing to your Lordship, I have been with Acton[7] to get a felucca, to send Ball's dispatch to you.' With the same letter Sir William supplied Nelson with 'an interesting letter I have just received from our Consul at Trieste: and Acton's answer to my yesterday's letter' as well as 'a strange rhapsody from Lord Bristol'. This mixture of naval and political information was combined with strong assurances of friendship: 'We miss you heavily: but, a short time must clear up the business; and, we hope, bring you back to those who love and esteem you to the very bottom of their souls'.[8] The feeling was mutual. On 25 May 1799, still at sea, Nelson composed on a huge sheet of paper[9] the first codicil to his will in which he bequeathed something to Lady Hamilton – as well as to Sir

[1]Letter of 17 Jan 1799, Naish, p. 481; Josiah himself sensed the strain on the relationship to his stepfather and tried to assuage Nelson's anger (Morrison, ii, p. 45, no. 385).

[2]Étienne Eustache Bruix (1759–1805).

[3]Domingos Xavier de Lima, 7th Marquis consort of Nisa [also spelt Niza] (1765–1802).

[4]Morrison, ii, p. 46, no. 388 (letter of 21 May 1799).

[5]Benjamin Hallowell (1760–1834), had been with Nelson in the Mediterranean 1794–96 and had been captain of the *Swiftsure* at the Battle of the Nile.

[6]1814-letters, ii, p. 192 (Sir William acknowledging receipt on 19 May 1799, 'Sunday night late, near winding-up-watch hour').

[7]General Sir John Francis Edward Acton (1736–1811; 'prime minister' of Naples under Ferdinand IV).

[8]1814-letters, ii, pp. 194–6 (letter of 26 May 1799).

[9]33 × 20.8 cm; the sheets Nelson normally used were about 23 × 18.5 cm.

William Hamilton [34]. Both were meant to receive some memento of their friend.

Geographical separations, reunions and journeys together were to dominate the lives of Nelson, Sir William and Lady Hamilton until they set off for their journey home together in the summer of 1800. When Nelson returned to Palermo on 29 May 1799, the three were again busy maintaining their naval network [36, joint letter to Captain Ball]. On 8 June Nelson went on board the *Foudroyant* which remained anchored at Palermo. Lady Hamilton kept him informed about the queen's worries and what she expected from him [37]. Nelson sailed for Naples on 13 June with the king on board, but had to return to Palermo two days later, because he had received news about the movements of the French fleet. After disembarking the king, Nelson sailed to Maritimo, an island at the western tip of Sicily. During the five days of his absence he wrote four letters to Lady Hamilton [38–41], to one of which Captain Ball added a postscript. The last letter he wrote on 20 June, the day before his return to Palermo, was written rather in the style of a logbook, in three instalments (at 'noon . . . 3 oclock . . . 4 oclock'), showing his tense mood ('my anxiety is great'). On 21 June, Nelson merely stopped at Palermo in order to embark Sir William and Lady Hamilton in order to take them with his Squadron to Naples.

The events of the following weeks, until the beginning of August, particularly at the end of June, have been controversially described and interpreted.[1] Nelson and Lady Hamilton, however, saw themselves as instruments of the rightful restoration of the Neapolitan monarchy. In a letter to Mrs Cadogan, Lady Hamilton's mother, Nelson commented on the verbose petitions to Lady Hamilton that tried to explain involvement in the Neapolitan republic as involuntary:[2] 'Our dear Lady is also, I can assure you, perfectly well; but has her time so much taken up with excuses from rebels, Jacobins, and fools, that she is every day most heartily tired.'[3] Lady Hamilton herself explained matters to Charles Greville: 'The Queen . . . sent me as her Deputy; for I am very popular, speak the Neapolitan language, and [am] consider'd, with Sir William, the friend of the people.' She unflinchingly described how the 'Calabreas',[4] in support of the restoration of the Neapolitan monarchy, 'were committing

[1]For a summary, see: Marianne Czisnik, 'Nelson at Naples. A Review of Events and Arguments', *Trafalgar Chronicle* 2002, 84–121, and particularly 'Nelson at Naples. The Development of a Story', *Trafalgar Chronicle* 2003, 35–55.

[2]See Morrison, ii, p. 52, no. 401 and 403; ii, 56, no. 409; ii, 58, no. 412.

[3]Morrison, ii, p. 55, no. 408, letter of 17 July 1799.

[4]Calabrians; 'Calabreas' is an Anglicised version of the Italian 'Calabrese'.

murders', so that 'the citty [was] in confusion'. This encouraged her to get involved:

> I sent for this Pali, the head of the Lazeroni,[1] and told him, in great confidence, that the King wou'd be soon at Naples, and that all we required of him was to keep the citty quiet for ten days, from that moment. We give im onely one hundred of our marine troops. He with these brave men kept all the town in order, and he brought the heads of all his 90 thousand round the ship on the King's arrival; and he is to *have promotion*. I have thro' him made 'the Queen's party', and the people at large have pray'd for her to come back, and she is now very popular. . . . I have given audiences to those of her party, and settled matters between the nobility and Her majesty. She is not to see on her arrival any of her former evil counsellers, not the women of fashion, alltho Ladys of the Bedchamber, – formerly her friend and companions, who did her dishonour by their desolute life.

As a result Lady Hamilton was confident that the queen of Naples 'has sense enough to profit of her *past unhappiness*, and will make for the future *amende honourable* for *the past*. In short, if I can judge, it may turn out fortunate that the Neapolitans have had a dose of Republicanism.'[2]

While Lady Hamilton's optimism proved tragically unjustified, she and Nelson watched events in the bay of Naples and on 5 August 1799 sailed with the king of Naples back to Palermo. The rest of the year they spent together at Palermo with only the exception of Nelson's employment at Minorca, which kept him away from Palermo for sixteen days in October 1799. Although shorter periods of separation had previously and would later produce many letters to Lady Hamilton, none has survived for this period. From other correspondence, however, it is clear that they were indeed separated. On 5 October, the day he left Palermo, Nelson wrote to Captain Ball: 'I am not well, and left our dear friends Sir William and Lady Hamilton very unwell.'[3] From Port Mahon he wrote to Troubridge: 'All my letters from the Marquis de Niza and Ball you will open, but not those from Sir William Hamilton or Palermo, as there may be many things in them which I do not wish any one to be acquainted with.'[4]

Nelson and Lady Hamilton were next separated from 16 January until 3 February 1800, when Nelson was ordered to join his new

[1]The Lazzaroni were from the lowest classes of Naples.
[2]Morrison, ii, pp. 56–8, no. 411, letter of 19 July 1799.
[3]Nicolas, iv, p. 45.
[4]Nicolas, iv, p. 58, letter of 17 Oct 1799.

commander-in-chief, Lord Keith,[1] at Leghorn. Only two letters from Nelson to Lady Hamilton survive from that period [42 and 43], but they contain a continuous flow of writing from 29 January until 3 February (with the exception of 1 February) and the first unrestrained outbursts of passion. Over the course of a few days he appears to have worked himself into a state of intense sexual longing and outward despondency. At the beginning of this series of messages, on 29 January, he remarked, rather soberly: 'my love and affection for you . . . is founded on the truest principles of honor'. Next day he described himself as 'your own faithful Nelson who lives only for his Emma'. The following night he wrote that he 'did nothing but dream of you', in a passage which culminated: 'we enjoy'd the height of love'. On 2 February he concluded, somewhat exhausted, but determined: 'no love is like mine towards you'. In this state of passion, Nelson pitied himself, because he was '20 Leagues farther from you than yesterday noon [because] my Commander In Chief knows not what I feel by absence' [42]. He complained of not being able to command, but 'only obey' [43].

On his return to Palermo, Nelson was with Keith and he remained moored in the bay from 4 until 11 February 1800. On 12 February they left for Malta and he kept Lady Hamilton informed in cautiously worded letters. He appears to have taken up the multi-party correspondence as, on 13 February, he refers to a letter written to her and Sir William, which appears to have been lost. He remarks: 'I do not send you any news or opinions as this letter goes by post and may be opened' [44]. His next letter, on 18 February [45], reflects his anxiety to get at *Le Généreux*, one of the two French ships that had escaped from the Battle of the Nile. Having taken *Le Généreux* the following day Nelson resigns himself to self-pity: 'My head ache, dreadfully and I have none near to give me a moments comfort' [46, letter of 20 February], 'I really want rest and a great deal of your kind care' [47, letter of 25 February; similarly, 48, letter of 4 March]. On 16 March Nelson returned to Palermo, where he stayed until 24 March, moored in the bay.

With Sir William having received his recall and Nelson longing for rest, they managed to spend their last months together in the Mediterranean rather pleasantly, ignorant of or ignoring the gossip which was spreading about them.[2] From 25 March until 23 April Nelson stayed with the Hamiltons in Palermo. In the meantime, Ball managed to take the *Guillaume Tell*, the last French ship of the Battle of the Nile not yet taken by the British. Nelson could therefore decide to undertake a cruise with

[1]George Keith Elphinstone, Lord (later: Viscount) Keith (1746–1823), since 1798 second-in-command of the British Mediterranean fleet and since 1800 commander-in-chief.

[2]Russell, p. 167–8, 170–71.

the Hamiltons. After some sightseeing in Syracuse they proceeded to Malta. Some details of this cruise were recorded decades later by Lieutenant (then: Midshipman) Parsons:[1]

> I must return to a more serious subject (at least, in Lord Nelson's opinion), the illness of Lady Hamilton, who was very feverish; and to give her rest, the Foudroyant was run off before the wind, with her yard braced by, for the whole night, which had the desired effect; for to his great joy – and, indeed, it gave pleasure to all on board – she was pronounced convalescent. . . . The expectation of an early surrender, formed upon this known state of destitution, I imagined influenced Lord Nelson, the ambassador and his lady . . . to hope they might be present at the surrender. . . . A breeze unexpectedly came in from the sea, and the ship dragged her anchor. . . . Hunger, I suppose, kept the Frenchmen waking, and at peep of day he made us a target for all his sea-batteries to practise on. "All hands up," – "Anchor a-hoy!" resounded fore and aft; and we hove short to the music of the shot, some of them going far over us.
>
> Lord Nelson was in a towering passion, and Lady Hamilton's refusal to quit the quarterdeck did not tend to tranquilize him. When short a-peak, the breeze failed, leaving only its disagreeable concomitant – a swell.
>
> [Nelson prepared to get the *Foudroyant* towed out of the range of French artillery fire.] Just at this moment a shot . . . struck the unfortunate fore-topmast, inflicting a deadly wound. His lordship then insisted upon Lady Hamilton's retiring, who did not evince the same partiality for the place of "de safety" as our illustrious friend the Prince of *****,[2] and leaving them in high altercation, I proceeded to his Majesty's frigate Success. . . . Hamilton, finding that the French governor would not surrender, until he had made a meal of his shoes, influenced Lord Nelson to turn her head for Palermo, a much more agreeable place, and where the balls were not all of iron. On our passage we fell in with . . . Lord Keith, come to supersede our hero. This caused many long faces on our quarter-deck . . .[3]

Parsons forgot to mention in his account the more relaxing parts of the cruise: a week in St Paul's Bay and another week in Marsa Scirocco Bay.[4] At one of these stops it is most likely that Lady Hamilton conceived their daughter, as she gave birth nine months later and Nelson referred back to this period in his letter of 23 April 1801: 'My Dearest amiable friend this

[1] G. S. Parsons, *Nelsonian Reminiscences. Leaves from Memory's Log* (London, 1843) [hereafter: Parsons].

[2] Parsons, pp. 27, 35–6.

[3] Parsons, pp. 59–60, 62–5.

[4] Knight, p. 339; St Paul's is north of La Valetta and Marsa Scirocco (or Marsaxlokk) south of it.

day twelve months we sail'd from Palermo on our tour to Malta, ah those were happy times, days of ease and nights of pleasure'.[1] On his return to Palermo, he stayed moored in the bay from 1 to 9 June, before he sailed with the Hamiltons to Leghorn (10 until 14 June).

Nelson stayed moored off Leghorn, first on the *Foudroyant* and then on the *Alexander*, for about a month (until 13 July), when he struck his flag and went ashore. As to his plans how to get back to England, Nelson explained in his letter to Keith of 24 June: 'If Sir William and Lady Hamilton go home by land, it is my intention to go with them; if by water, we shall be happy in taking the best Ship we can get.'[2] He was apparently hoping to be allowed to sail home in the *Foudroyant*. Probably Keith did not even have time enough to take the hint and would most probably not have been prepared to part with a major ship, anyway. On 2 July Cornelia Knight, who was accompanying the party, wrote to Berry: 'Lady Hamilton cannot bear the thought of going by sea; and, therefore, nothing but impracticability will prevent our going to Viena'. She added on 16 July: 'It is, at length, decided that we go by land'.[3]

The resulting journey across central Europe was hazardous, expensive and scandalous. Hazardous, because Nelson and the Hamiltons travelled close to French outposts in the north of Italy and had to take a Russian frigate from Ancona to Trieste in order to avoid the French. Expensive, because the whole four-month trip cost them a small fortune.[4] And scandalous, as remarks in the British press about the odd menage à trois increased and culminated in open ridicule when they arrived in London in November.[5] Quite a few private comments as well as local reports about how the three were seen and Lady Hamilton's attitudes were admired, have come down to us.[6] It remains a matter of speculation, however, how they themselves felt about the sumptuous receptions and shows of public admiration they – particularly Nelson – received.

[1]Russell, p. 175; Ernle Bradford, *Nelson. The Essential Hero* (London, 1977), pp. 249–50; Doc. No. 151.

[2]Nicolas, iv, p. 260.

[3]Nicolas, iv, p. 263.

[4]Russell, p. 216, reports that Nelson had to sell about £ 8,000 of his holdings in stocks in order to pay off the debts he had incurred in Palermo and on the journey back home. An undated list of what Nelson had 'laid out for Sir William' amounts to £ 3,588 (BL Egerton f. 13; see also: Pettigrew, i, pp. 403–4); another list, included in Morrison, ii, p. 405, gives the amount 'drawn for & paid out by Ld N. between July 13th & Nov, 18th' as '£3431 16 0'.

[5]Russell, pp. 198–9 and 206–12.

[6]See for example Knight, 341–4; Deutsch, Gitta and Klein Rudolf (eds.), *Otto Erich Deutsch, Admiral Nelson und Joseph Haydn. Ein britisch-österreichisches Gipfeltreffen* (Vienna, [1982]); Marianne Czisnik, 'A Unique Account of Lady Hamilton's Attitudes in Hamburg', in *Trafalgar Chronicle*, 2010, 108–20.

Nelson resumed writing to Lady Hamilton in November 1800 in London [49–51], when expectations of propriety forced them to part. These letters are mere notes about when or where they might meet next. With the pressure of public attention on them, it is not surprising that they accepted William Beckford's invitation to his folly, Fonthill:[1]

> you have many worse things to get over but our November fogs. The intellectual fog we labour under in this phlegmatic country is the very devil. If any rays can dissipate this gloom, your's will; but you must shine steadily, rise early, set late, and keep above the horizon, almost without relaxation, till we have animated the dull clod. . . . Pray tell Lord Nelson, that though dead to the world in general, and to almost all its great and small characters,[2] I am perfectly alive to his transcendent merit, and feel towards him those sentiments of grateful admiration which glow in the heart of every *genuine* Briton. I exist in the hopes of seeing Fonthill honoured by his victorious presence, and if his engagements permit, his accompanying you here; we shall enjoy a few comfortable days of repose, uncontaminated by the sight and prattle of drawing-room parasites. . . .[3]

On their arrival on 23 December, Beckford arranged a spectacular, torch-lit celebration for his special guests.[4] After returning from his joint Christmas holiday with the Hamiltons at Beckford's gothic folly, Nelson received the news of the death of William Locker,[5] his old mentor from West Indian days, when Nelson had been a young captain. He attended Locker's funeral in a depressed mood: 'believe me when I say that I regret that I am not the person to be attended *upon* at this funeral, for although I have had my days of glory, yet I find this world so full of jealousies and envy that I see but a very faint gleam of future comfort' [52]. At the end of the year 1800 Nelson could not know, what life would bring him in future – professionally as well as privately – with his wife still expecting him to resume their married life and his lover eight months pregnant.

[1]Sir William and Lady Hamilton had been there before in the summer of 1791 after their wedding in London (see Fraser, p. 162). They had planned to return; see letter of Lady Hamilton to William Beckford, 23 Feb 1798 (Morrison, ii, p. 39, no. 378).

[2]William Beckford had been ostracised by polite society after he had been caught in a suspected sexual affair with Lord Courtenay.

[3]Pettigrew, i, pp. 403–5, letter of 24 Nov 1800.

[4]Knight, p. 349.

[5]William Locker (1731–1800) had been Nelson's patron in the West Indies.

1. *To Lady Hamilton*

[Jean Kislak: 1993.002.00.0001]

My Dear Madam,

as soon as I have fought the French fleet, I shall do myself the honor of paying my respects to Your Ladyship at Naples and I hope to be congratulated on a Victory, Lord S^{t}: Vincent hav^{g}:[1] wrote me that you and Sir Willm:[2] are desirous of getting down the Med^{ean}: on your way to England I beg leave to assure[3] You of my sincere desire to do whatever your Lady^{p}:[4] wishes me, the Duke of York has promised Your Protegée [*sic*] M^{r}: Pearson a Cap^{tn}: Commission but the Young Man is a little in too much hurry, the truth is (I believe) that he intends to marry so soon as he gets his Commission, therefore he is in some measure excuseable [*sic*], with my sincerest good wishes for Sir William and your Ladyship

Believe me ever your
Most faithful servant

Horatio Nelson

Vanguard
June 13th: 1798,[5]

If Capt: Troubridge has the honor of delivering this note I beg leave to introduce him to the honor of your Ladyships acquaintance[6]

[1]The word is abbreviated, because it stands at the end of the line.
[2]The name is abbreviated, because it stands at the end of the line.
[3]Inserted.
[4]The word is abbreviated, because it stands at the end of the line.
[5]Written off Civitavecchia (port north-west of Rome).
[6]There are blots of ink on the letters a and q at the beginning of the word.

2. *Lady Hamilton to Nelson*

[BL: Add. MS 34,989 f. 3] [17 June 1798][1]

Dear Sir

I send you a letter I have recevd this moment from the Queen[2] Kiss it + send it me Back by Bowen[3] as I am bound not to give any of her Letters ever yours

Emma

3. *To Lady Hamilton*

[BL: Egerton 1614 ff. 1–2, no. 1]

My Dear Lady Hamilton,

I have kissed the Queens letter pray say I hope for the honor of kissing her hand when no fears will intervene, assure her Majesty that no person has ~~hers~~ her[4] felicity more at heart than myself,[5] and that the sufferings of her family will be a Tower of strength on the day of Battle, fear not the

[1]For the dating of the letter see the introduction to this chapter and Russell, p. 48, who provides a letter from Sir William Hamilton of 17 June 1798 that most probably refers to this letter by his wife: 'Emma writes to you herself and sends a charming letter she has just received from the Queen of Naples – such an Original letter will give you pleasure, and I desired her to send it you as it will prove to you what they are at heart here and how sensible they are that you have saved them from ruin.'

[2]Russell, p. 49, suggests that the queen's letter referred to here is this one of 17 June 1798: 'My dear Miledi, I am affected even to tears by the true delicacy of the just English – our circumstances, or rather those of the other great powers, prevent our opening our ports and our arms entirely to our brave defenders, but our gratitude is none the less. I hope events will so occur that we shall see the squadron again, with its brave officers crowned with new victories, and that I and all my dear family may go on board to drink to the health of a nation that possesses all my esteem and gratitude. I should have much wished to see the brave Trowbridge, and they said it would not be prudent . . .'.

[3]Thomas Bowen (d. 1809); Russell comments 'Captain Bowen took these letters out in the Transfer and returned with Nelson's answer'; see also letter of LH of 30 June 1798.

[4]Nelson has inserted 'her' above a crossed-out 'hers'.

[5]'than myself' is written above 'at heart,'. Both are at the end of the line.

event, God is with us, God Bless You and Sir William pray say I cannot stay to answer his letter Ever

Yours faithfully,

Horatio Nelson

17th May 6 PM[1]

this letter I[2] receved after I had sent the Queens letter for Receving our ships into Their ports – ~~xxx~~ for[3] the Queen had decided to act in opposition to the King who wou'd not then break with France + our fleet most have gone down to Giberalter to have watered + the battle of the Nile wou'd not have been fought for the French fleet wou'd have got back to Toulon

4. *Lady Hamilton to Nelson*

[BL: Add. MS 34,989 f. 1, 2] [17 June 1798]

my dear admiral

I write in a hurry as Capn T.[4] cannot stay a moment. God Bless you + send you victorious oh what glory see you bring back buona parte with you pray send Capn Hardy out to us for I shall have a fever with anxiety the Quen [*sic*] desires me to say every thing thats kind + bids me say with her whole heart + soul she wishes you victory god bless you my dear dear sir I will not say how glad I shall be to see indeed I cannot describe to you my feelings in your being so us ever ever dear Sir

Your oblidged + gratefull Emma Hamilton

[1]It is most likely that Nelson wrote this letter on 17 June 1798, in the Bay of Naples. The letter was clearly written in answer to a letter by Lady Hamilton, so that by the time Nelson wrote the letter he was aware that his arrival in the Mediterranean was known in Naples. A few days before his arrival at Naples, however, Nelson was still not sure, whether news of his arrival had reached Naples. He wrote to Sir William Hamilton in a letter of 12 June 1798: 'If the Transfer Sloop of War has arrived at Naples, you will know that the British Fleet is in the Mediterranean, and that I have the honour of commanding it' (see Nicolas, iii, p. 28). Also, the fact that Nelson gives a time of day on which the letter was written indicates close proximity to the addressee.

[2]This note (f. 2), written on the outside of this folded, but unsealed piece of paper, is in Lady Hamilton's handwriting.

[3]There is a word crossed out after the dash. Nelson has inserted 'for'.

[4]Troubridge.

5. *Lady Hamilton to Nelson*

[NMM: CRK 20/55] Naples,
June 30th, 1798

Dear Sir,

I take the opportunity of Capn Hope[1] to write a few lines to you + thank you for your Kind letter by Capn Bowen[2] the Queen was much pleased as I translated it for her + charges me to thank you + say she pray's [*sic*] for your Honner [*sic*] and safety victory she is sure you will have[3] we have stil [*sic*] the Regicide minister here Garat[4] the most impudent insolent dog making the most infamous demands every day + I see plainly the Court of naples [*sic*] must declare war if they mean to save their Country her Majesty sees + feils [*sic*] all you said in your letter to Sir Wm dated of [*sic*] the Faro di Misina [*sic*][5] in its true light so does General Acton but alas Their first minister Gallo[6] is a frivolos [*sic*] ignorant self conceited Coxcomb that thinks of nothing but his fine embroidered Coat ring + snuff Box + half naples thinks him half a Frenchman + God knows if one may judge of what he did in making the peace for the emperor[7] he must either be very ignorant or not attached to his masters or the Couse Commune[8] the Queen + Acton Cannot bear him + Consequently [he][9] Cannot have much power but still [*sic*] a first minister all tho he may be a minister of smoke yet he [h]as allways [*sic*] something enough at least to do mischief The jacobins have all been lately declared innocent after suffering 4 years imprisonment + I know they all deserved to be hanged long ago + since Garrat[10] [h]as been here + through his insolent Letters

[1]George Johnstone Hope (1767–1818), at that time commanding the *Alcmene*.

[2]Commanding the *Transfer*.

[3]The words 'victory she is sure you will have' are in one line.

[4]Dominique-Joseph Garat (1749–1833) had, as minister of justice, signed the death warrant for Louis XVI and was now French ambassador to Naples (from 1797 until July 1798).

[5]Letter of 20 June 1798, printed in Nicolas, iii, pp. 34–6.

[6]Marzio Mastrilli marchese (in 1813, under the Napoleonic rule of Joachim Murat: duca) di Gallo (1753–1833)

[7]Gallo negotiated and signed the treaty of Campo Formio between France and Austria in 1797 for Austria; the Emperor referred to was Francis II.

[8]Here Lady Hamilton mixes French (chose commune) and Italian (causa commune) for 'common cause'.

[9]Added by 1814-letters.

[10]Misspelling of Garat.

to Gallo these pretty Gentlemen that had planed [*sic*] the death of their Majesties are to be let out on society again[1]

in short I am afraid all is lost here + I am grieved to the Heart for our dear charming Queen who deserves a Better fate I write to you my dear Sir in Confidence + in a hurry I hope you will not quit the medeterenian [*sic*] without taking us we have our leave + every thing ready at a day'[s] notice to go but yet I trust in God + you that we shall destroy those monsters before we go from hence surely their reign cannot last long if you have any opportunity write to us pray do you do not know how your letters comfort us God bless you my dear dear Sir + believe me ever your most sincerly [*sic*] obliged + attached friend Emma Hamilton

Naples June 30th 1798

6. *To Lady Hamilton*

[Huntington: HM 34077]

Vanguard Syracuse
July 22nd: 1798

My Dear Madam,

I am so much distressed at not having had any account of the french fleet and so much hurt at the treatment we receive from the power we came to assist + fight for, that I am hardly in a situation to write a letter to an Elegant Lady, therefore You must on this occasion forgive my want of those attentions which I am ever ambitious to show You, I wish to know Your and Sir Wms: plans for going down the Medn: for if we are to be[2] kicked in every port of the Sicilian dominions, the sooner we are gone the better Good God how sensibly I feel our treatment, I have only to pray I may find the french and throw all my Vengeance on them

With my affectionate Regards to Sir William
Believe me with the greatest Respect
Your Ladyships
Most faithful Servant
Horatio Nelson

[1]After the word 'again' there is a gap until the end of the line that strongly suggests that a paragraph was intended.
[2]Inserted.

7. *To Sir William and Lady Hamilton*

[Harrison, i, p. 256] 22nd July, 1798.

My dear Friends,

Thanks to your exertions, we have victualled and watered: and surely watering at the Fountain of Arethusa, we must have victory. We shall sail with the first breeze, and be assured I will return either crowned with laurel, or covered with cypress.[1]

8. *To Lady Hamilton*

[NMM: CRC/18] August 11th, 1798

My Dear Madam,

I may now be able to show your Ladyship the remains of Horatio Nelson and I trust my mutilations will not cause me to be less welcome, they are the marks of honor, I beg leave to introduce Capt: Capel[2] who is going home with my dispatches to your notice, He is a son of Lord Essex[3] and a very good young man, And I also beg your notice of Capt: Hoste[4] who to the gentlest manners joins the most undaunted courage, he was brought up by me and I love him dearly I am afraid you will think me very impertinent[5] in introducing all these young men, but You and Sir William have spoiled [me], Believe me,

Ever my Dear Madam
Your Ladyships
most obedient servant
Horatio Nelson

[1]For a discussion of this letter, see the introduction to this chapter.
[2]Thomas Bladen Capel (1776–1853).
[3]William Anne Capell, 4th Earl of Essex (1732–99).
[4]William Hoste (1780–1828).
[5]At the end of the line it reads 'imper=' and above these letters 'tinent'.

9. *To Lady Hamilton*

[RNM: 48/64]

My Dear Lady Hamilton,

I have this moment your favor of June 30th: I am penetrated with the Queens condescension to think of such an animal as I am, God Almighty has made me the happy Instrument of destruction this Army will be ruined, why will not Naples act with Vigor, these Scoundrels only need to be faced like men, and what are they thanks to Sir W^{m}: for his letters, God Bless You and Believe me Ever your obliged

Horatio Nelson.

Nile
Aug^{t}: 13th: 1798.

[*added on the outside in Lady Hamilton's handwriting:*] in consequence of this note we made naples act with vigour

10. *Lady Hamilton to Nelson*

[BL: Add. MS 34,989 ff. 4–7]

Naples
Sep^{br} 8th 1798

My dear dear Sir

How shall I begin what shall I say to you. tis improbable I can write for since Last Monday[1] I am delerious with joy + assure you I have a fevour caused by agitation + pleasure Good God what a victory never never has their been any thing half so glorious so compleat I fainted when I heard the joyfull news + fell on my side + am hurt but what of that I shou'd feil it a glory to die in such a cause no I wou'd not Like to die tell I see + embrace the victor of the Nile[2] how shall I describe to you the transports of Maria Carolina tis not possible she fainted cried Kiss'd her Husband her children walked frantick with pleasure about the room cried kiss'd + embraced every person near her exclaiming oh brave nelson oh God Bless + protect our Brave deliverer oh nelson nelson what do we not owe to you oh victor savour of itali oh that my swoln hert cou'd now

[1] 3 Sept 1798.
[2] The word 'Nile' is underlined twice.

tell him personally what we owe to him,[1] you may judge my dear Sir of the rest but my head will not permit me to tell you half of the rejoicing the Neapolitans are mad + if you was here now you wou'd be Kill'd with kindness Sonets on Sonets illuminations rejoicing not a french dog dare show his face how I glory in the Honer of my Country + my Country-man I walk + tread in air with pride feiling I was born on the same Land with the victor nelson + his gallant band but no more I cannot dare not trust my self for I am not well Little dear Cap^{n} Hoste will tell you the rest he lives with us in the day for he will not sleep out of his ship + we love him dearly he is a fine good Lad Sir William is delighted with him + says he will be a second Nelson if he is onely half a nelson he will be superiour [to] all others I send you 2 Letters from my adorable Queen one was written to me the day we receved the glorious news the other yesterday keep them as the one her own hand writing I have kept Copies onely but I feil that you ought to have them if you had seen our meeting after the Battle but I will keep it all for your arrival I cou'd not do justice to her feiling nor to my own with writing it we are preparing your apartment against you come I hope it will not be Long for Sir William + I am so impatient to see + embrace you I wish you cou'd have seen our house the 3 nights of illumination tis was coverd with your glorious name their were 3 thousand Lamps + Their shou'd have been 3 millions if we had had time all the english vied with each other in celebrating this most gallant + ever memerable victory Sir William is ten years yonger since the happy news + he now onely wishes to see his friend to be compleatly happy how he glories in you when your name is mentiond he cannot contain his joy for god sake come to naples soon we receve so many sonnets + letters of congratulation I send you some of them to show you how your success is felt here how I felt for poor Troubridge he must have been so angry on the Sand Bank so brave an officer in short I pitty all those who were not in the Battle I wou'd have been rather an english powder monkey or a swab in that great victory than an Emperor out of it but you will be tired of all this write or come soon to ~~our Gxxx~~ rejoice your ever sincere + oblidged friend Emma Hamilton turn over[2]

[1]Nelson quoted this passage from Lady Hamilton's letter (with corrected spelling) in a letter to his wife of 16 Sept 1798, commenting: 'You may judge of the rest, but my head will not allow to tell you half. So much for that.' (Naish, 399). The queen of Naples herself wrote in a similar vein to Lady Hamilton: 'Ma chere Miledy quel Bonheur quelle Gloire quelle Consolation pour cet unique Grande et illustre Nation que Je vous suis obligé reconoissante. J'ai pleuré rié embrasse mes enfans mon mary' (Russell, p. 61).

[2]The text continues on the second page of the second sheet.

the Queen as this moment sent a dymond Ring to Cap^{n} Hoste, six Buts of wine 2 Casks for the officers + every man on board a Guinea each her letter is in english + comes as from an unknown person but a well wisher to our Country + us admirers of the gallant admiral as war is not yet declared with France she cou'd not show herself so openly as she wish'd but she as done so much + rejoiced so very publickly that all the world sees it she bids me say that she longs more to see you than any woman with child can long for any thing she may take a fancy too + she shall be for ever unhappy if you do not come God bless you my dear Dear friend my dress from head to foot is alla nelson ask Hoste even my shawl is in Blue with gold anchors all over my ear rings are nelsons anchors in short we are be Nelson'd all over I send you some sonnets but I must have taken a ship on purpose to send you all whats written on you once more god Bless you my mother desires her Love to you I am so busy + haste in such a hurry I am affraid you will not be able to reed this scrawl.

11. *To Lady Hamilton*

[BL: Add. MS 34,989 ff. 12–13]

Naples
Oct^{r}: 3rd: 1798

My dear Madam,

The anxiety which you + Sir Willm: Hamilton have always had for the happiness and welfare of their Sicilian Majes^{tys}: was also planted in me five years past and I can truly say[1] that on every occasion which have [*sic*] offered (which have been[2] numerous) I have never faild to manifest my sincere regard for the felicity of these kingdoms, under this attachment[3] I cannot be an indifferent spectator to what has and is passing in the ~~Kings~~ two Sicily, nor to the misery which (without being a Politician) I cannot but see plainly is ready to fall on those very king$^{dms:}$ now so loyal, by the worst of all policy, that of procrastination, since my arrival in these seas in June last I have seen in the Sicilians the most loyal people to their Sovereign with the utmost detestation of the French and their principles, since my arrival at Naples I have found all Ranks from

[1]Inserted.
[2]Inserted.
[3]*Sic*; unlike his usual spelling, Nelson did indeed not write a 't' before the 'ch'.

the very highest to the lowest[1] eager for War with the French who all know,[2] are preparing an army of Robbers to plunder these kingdoms and to[3] destroy the monarchy, I have seen the minister of the insolent French[4] pass over in silence [the] manifest breach of the 3rd Article of the treaty between His S. M.[5] + the French Republic, ought not[6] this extraordinary conduct to be[7] seriously noticed have [*sic*] not the uniform conduct of the French ~~been~~ been[8] to lull ~~countrys~~ Governments[9] into a fatal security and then to destroy them, ~~what has this Governmt: done that they should~~ as I have before stated is it not known[10] to every person that Naples is the next marked object for plunder – with this knowledge (~~which done we contradict what am I to th~~, ~~none will deny~~[11] and that H. S. M. has an army ready (I am told) to march into a Country ~~ready~~ anxious[12] to receive them with the advantage of[13] carrying on the war from[14] ~~into the Enemies County~~[15] instead of waiting for it at Home ~~the evils of which are well known and in the present situation of this country~~[16] I ~~pronounce that if His M. troops wait~~ am all astonishment[17] that the Army has not march'd a month ago, I trust that the Arrival of Genl: Mack will ~~not~~

[1]Nicolas, vii, p. clxiii, produces a transcript of the letter actually sent, the original of which he claimed to have in his possession. In this version the words 'from the very highest to the lowest' are omitted.

[2]Nicolas, vii, p. clxiii, renders the final version of the letter with the words 'every one knows', instead of 'all know'.

[3]Inserted.

[4]This refers most probably to Jean-Pierre Lacombe-Saint-Michel (1751–1812), who followed Garat as ambassador of France, after he left Naples in July 1798; Lacombe-Saint-Michel went home to France in December 1798 (see Nelson's passport for him in Nicolas, iii, 189, where he is referred to as 'La Combe de St Michel'. Garat, is mentioned by Lady Hamilton in her letter of 30 June 1798 (Doc. No. 5).

[5]Sicilian Majesty.

[6]Inserted.

[7]Inserted.

[8]The word 'been' was first inserted, then crossed out and then again inserted (this time under rather than above the line).

[9]The word 'Governments' is added above the crossed-out word 'countrys' and the letters 'in' of 'into'.

[10]Inserted.

[11]Above '~~done we contr~~' Nelson has crossed out '~~none will deny)~~'.

[12]The word 'anxious' is written above the crossed-out 'ready'.

[13]The words 'with the advantage of' are inserted.

[14]Inserted.

[15]The word 'Country' was inserted.

[16]The passage starts at the bottom of the second page and continues at the same end of the third page, upside down.

[17]The words 'am all astonishment' are written above the crossed-out words 'pronounce that if His M.'.

[18]Inserted.

induce the Governmt: not[18] to lose any more of the favorable time which Providence has put in their hands for if they do, and wait for an attack in this country instead of carrying the war out of it, it requires no gift of prophecy to pronounce that these[1] ~~country~~ kingdoms[2] will be ruin'd + the monarchy destroy'd, ~~and if any long=~~ but shou'd unfortunately[3] this miserable Ruinous system of procrastination be persisted in, I wou'd recommend that all your property and persons are ready to embark at a very short notice, It will be my duty to look and provide for your safety and with it (I am sorry to think it will be necessary),[4] that of the amiable Queen of these Kingdoms and her family,[5] I have read with admiration her[6] Dignified + incomparable letter of Sepr: 1796, ~~the same reason and~~ may the[7] councils of these kingdoms[8] ever be guided by such sentiments of dignity honor + justice, ~~You~~ and may the ~~words advice~~ words[9] of the great Mr. Pitt Earl of Chatham[10] be instill'd into the ministry[11] of this country, <u>The Boldest measures are the safest</u>[12] is the sincere wish of Your L. [Nelson][13]

PS. Your Ladyship will I beg, receive this letter as a preparative [*sic*] for Sir Wm: H. to whom I am writing, with all respect the firm + unalterable opinion of a British Admiral, anxious to approve himself a faithful sert:[14] to His Sovereign by doing everything in his power for the Happiness ~~of this~~ + Security[15] of their Sicilian majesties + their Kingdoms.

[1]Here Nelson originally wrote 'this', but changed the word into 'these'.

[2]The word 'kingdoms' is written above the crossed-out word 'country'.

[3]The words 'but shou'd unfortunately' are written above the crossed-out words 'and if any long='.

[4]The words 'it will be necessary)' are inserted.

[5]Nicolas, vii, p. clxiv, renders the final version of the letter with the words 'their *Sic*ilian Majesties and Family', instead of 'the amiable Queen of their Kingdoms'.

[6]Nicolas, vii, p. clxiv, renders the final version of the letter with the words 'the Queen's', instead of 'her'.

[7]Above the crossed-out words 'the same reason' stand the words '~~and~~ may the'.

[8]Inserted.

[9]Nelson had originally written 'words', then crossed out this and wrote 'advice' above it, but crossed out that again and wrote again 'words' under the first, crossed-out 'words'.

[10]William Pitt, 1st Earl of Chatham (1708–78), father of the then Prime Minister, William Pitt the Younger (1759–1806).

[11]Nicolas, vii, p. clxiv, renders the final version of the letter with the words 'engraved on the heart of every Minister', instead of 'instill'd into the ministry'.

[12]A popular expression of Nelson's; see also his letter to Sir Hyde Parker of 24 Mar 1801 (Nicolas, iv, p. 297–8); on different websites of the internet this quotation is now attributed to Nelson himself.

[13]After 'L.' follow a few illegible scribbles. The 'L.' has been interpreted as 'Ladyship's' and the scribbles as 'Nelson'. Both are doubtful, but I have no better suggestion to offer.

[14]Servant.

[15]The words '+ Security' are written above the crossed-out 'of this'.

12. *To Lady Hamilton*

[BL: Egerton 1614 ff. 3–4, no. 2]

My dear Madam,

I honor and respect You and my Dear friend Sir Willm Hamilton and Believe me ever

Your faithful + affectionate

Nelson.

Naples
Oct^{r}: 16th: 1798.

[*Lady Hamilton added below:*]

the first letter written by our gallant + immortel Nelson after his dignity to the peerage may God bless + preserve him + long may he live to enjoy the Honners he so deservedly won prays his true friend Emma Hamilton

13. *Lady Hamilton to Nelson*

[BL: Add. MS 34,989 ff. 14–15] Caserta October 20th 1798

My dear respectable friend

We have this moment had a letter from Troubridge to say the flora cutter is going to join you + I feil so happy to have an opertunity to write allto but a line to our dear dear Admiral ah how we feil our Loss cou'd you but know how miserable we were for some days but now hopes of your return revives us we are oblidged to be here now tell her Royal Highness[1] squaling is over + thank God her Belly is fell so all the Ladies in the pallace say I know nothing about it[2] yesterday we heard

[1]Maria Clementine of Austria, the wife of Francesco (1777–1830), heir to the thrones of Naples and Sicily. She was to give birth to a daughter, Maria Carolina, on 5 Nov 1798.

[2]Thus, in passing, Lady Hamilton suggests that she has never given birth. Nelson took that to be so; see Doc. No. 112 of 1 Mar 1801, in which Nelson wrote: 'I never had a dear pledge of love 'till You gave me one and you thank my God never gave one to any body else.'

talk of nothing but the pancia caduta[1] which is a sign she will son Bring forth then we go to naples for it is impossible to [stay] here to be happy when our ships are there + my anxiety for news is such I have no rest however here we go on with vigor + I flatter myself we spur them for I am allways with the Queen + I hold out your energick Language to her Mack is writing he does not go to visit the frontiers but is now working night + day + then goes for good + I tell her Majesty for god sake for the countrys sake + for your[2] own[3] sake, send him of as soon as possable no time to be lost + I belive he goes after tomorrow the rebellion in Ireland being finish'd + the French Troops taken as given them fresh courage I translate from our papers for her to inspire her or them I shou'd say with some of our spirit + energy, how delighted we Booth were to sit + speak of you she loves respects + admires you for myself I will leave you to guess my feelings poor dear Troubridge staid that night with us to comfort us what a good dear soul he is I have not time to say more + not being at naples I have nothing to send you how provoking the Queen desires her kindest compliments + thanks you for leaving Troubridge he is to come I own soon + I am to present him she says she shou'd not feil happy if she had not an English ship here to send of her poor children give my compliments to good dear Tyson[4] I love him for his real attachment to you remember me to Hardy + Mr Commins he is a worthy good man I am sure + his profesion must gain him respect allways + shake little Fady[5] + Noodin[6] by the hand for me I hope your doctor is satisfied with your health how do you do for your cook the dog I will have him taken as a deserter but all is for the Best perhaps your stomach is better with John Bulls roast + Boil then the Italian spoil stomach sauce of a dirty Neapolitan God bless you how we abused Gallo yesterday how she hates him he wont reign long so much the Better write to me + come soon for you are wanted at Court all their nodles are not worth yours, ever ever yours

Emma

[1]Literally translated: 'fallen belly'.

[2]The word 'your' is additionally underlined by three further lines.

[3]The word 'own' is underlined three times.

[4]John Tyson (d. 1816); had served under Nelson as purser of the *Badger* in the late 1770s; he was Nelson's secretary from after the Battle of the Nile until July 1800.

[5]Son of Captain of Marines William Faddy, of the *Vanguard*, who was killed at the Battle of the Nile (Nicolas, iii, p. 7, fn 2; v, p. 439, fn 6).

[6]Probably Dr Nudi.

14. *To Lady Hamilton*

[NMM: CRK/19/1]

Vang[d]: off Malta
Oct[r]: 24th: 1798,

My Dear Madam,

After a long passage we are arrived, and it is as I suspected, the ministers at Naples know nothing of the situation of the Island, not a house or Bastion of the town is in possession of the Islanders, and the Marquis de Nz[a][1] tells me they want arms, Vict[s]:[2] + support, he does not know that any Neapolitan officers are in the Island, perhaps although I have the names none are arrived and it is very certain by the Marq[s]: account that no supplies have been sent by the gov[rs]: of Syracuse or Messina, however I shall and will know every thing, as soon as the Marquis is gone which will be to morrow morn[g]: he says he is very anxious to serve under my command and by his changing his Ship it appears as if he was so, however ~~it appe~~ I understand the trim of our English Ships better[3] Ball will have the management of the Blockade after my departure, as it seems the Court of Naples think my presence may be necessary and useful in the beginning of Nov[r]: I hope it will prove so, but I feel my duty lays at present in the East for untill I know the shipping in Egypt are destroy'd I shall never consider that French Army[4] as compleatly sure of never returning to Europe, however all my Views are to serve + save the two Sicilys and to do that which their Majestys may wish me, even against my own opinion, when I come to Naples + that Country is at War, I shall wish to have a meeting with Gen[l]: Acton on this Subject, You will I am sure do me Justice with the Queen for I declare to God my whole study is how to best meet her approbation May God Bless You + Sir William and ever believe me with the most affectionate Regard Your obliged + faithful friend

Horatio Nelson.

I may possibly but that is not certain send in the enclosed letter shew it to Sir William, this must depend on what I hear + see for I believe scarcely [*sic*] any thing I hear once more God Bless You.

[1]The words 'de Nz[a]' (Niza) are inserted.
[2]Victuals.
[3]Last word on this page.
[4]Inserted.

15. *Lady Hamilton to Nelson*

[BL: Add. MS 34,989 ff. 16–17] october 26 – 1798

my dear friend

I must say one word more to you we have just now another letter the Grand Signor[1] has written to the King of England to beg his permission that you may wear the order or feather that he took out of his own Turban to decorate you + which is the sign of sovranity I do not exactly know how many thousand piastres its worth but unprecedented[2] is the present viva il Turco Say[s] Emma if I was King of England I wou'd make you the most noble puisant Duke Nelson Marquis Nile Earl Alexander vicount pyramid Baron crocadile + prince victory That posterity might have you in all forms pray is the Turkish frigate comes to you ~~xxx~~ I beg you to[3] bring it here then I may have the pleasure of entertaining the Good Turband soul + sending him home satisfied + convinced that an english woman has a soul for I fancy they don't belive we have one + shewing him our gratitude for the justice his master has done to the friend of our hearts for so Sir William + I call you once more god bless you + belive me ever your gratefull Emma Hamilton

If you see our Captain Ball pray remember me most kindly to him + to all the Brothers[4] Gold[5] Foley[6] + Louis[7] –

16. *To Lady Hamilton*

[RNM: 49/64] Vanguard off Malta
Oct[r]: 27th 1798

My Dear Madam,

Your letters are so interesting that I am gratified beyond belief at receiving them, and your whole conduct has ever been to me so very

[1]Selim III, Ottoman Sultan (1761–1808, reigned 1789–1807).

[2]This refers to the aigrette or chelengk that Nelson received; for the further history of the item see Appendix 3.

[3]The words 'I beg you to' are above a crossed-out word that cannot be deciphered.

[4]This refers to the 'band of brothers', a term with which Nelson liked to refer to the captains under his command at the Battle of the Nile.

[5]Probably Captain Davidge Gould (1758–1847).

[6]Thomas Foley (1757–1833).

[7]Thomas Louis (1758–1807).

much above my deserts that I am absolutely at a loss how to express myself, but believe me, my heart is as alive to kindness as it is to anything like an insult, my letter by the Marquis de Niza (who is totally ignorant of the forms of our Service and led wrong by his Major) would not convey I believe much satisfaction at the appearance of affairs in this Island the more I enquire the more reason I have to be totally displeased with the Grand Vizir of Naples[1] I do say that he must have neglected full-filling the beneficent wishes of his honor'd Master towards the Maltese I have wrote Sir W^{m}: so fully on this Subject[2] that I refer you to his letter, something must be done directly either protect or at once give them up, I have very much to say to the Queen on this Subject as well as on many others, my letters from Egypt which I hope Troubridge has read, makes [*sic*] me think seriously of that quarter, I wish to state my Ideas fully to Her Majesty for I have not a thought that I wish to keep from her, and weither I think it right to send or go with my ships East, West, North, or South, it is all from my belief that the plan I may have will best serve their Majestys in whose service I feel myself placed by our Good and gracious King, but as none of us are Infallible I should wish to consult with that person her Majesty may point out, I do not understand the Marquis de Gallo therefore I only beg it may not be him, I should be much reliev'd had I the use of two Neapolitan[3] frigates and a corvette, the Sword is drawn and why hide it for a day, none can know that the ships of their Majesty[4] are under my orders 'till after the War is begun, (indeed I hope it will be begun before my arrival) I want to have force enough to keep this Blockade compleat, that of Alexandria, to have a very respectable Squadron off Corfou, and those Islands to have another, (equal to the French force at Toulon) to the North of Civita Vecchia, to prevent the 7000 French at Massa[5] from getting alongshore to Civita V^{a}: a thing very easy to be accomplish'd, before the War begins some ships should be in Telamon[6] bay and on that coast, I have ships enough if

[1]*The Times*, 29 May 1913, comments: 'The "Grand Vizier of Naples" appears to be the Marquis de Gallo, subsequently mentioned in the same letter as a Neapolitan Minister whom Nelson did not understand'.

[2]Nelson wrote on the same day to Sir William Hamilton: 'When I come to Naples I can have nothing pleasant to say of the conduct of his Sicilian Majesty's Ministers towards the inhabitants of Malta, who whish to be under the dominion of their legitimate Sovereign. The total neglect and indifference with which they have been treated, appears to me *cruel* in the extreme. . . .' (Nicolas, iii, pp. 161–3, 161).

[3]Inserted.

[4]The letter is continued upside down on the next page.

[5]North of Leghorn.

[6]Nowadays Talamone, part of Orbetello (then in Tuscany), north of Civitavecchia (then port of the Papal States).

they were English, but the Portugeze [*sic*] are all with the Rank of Rear Admirals therefore will not serve under any of my[1] brave Captains, and I doubt if they will serve well, sure I am I would not trust my word for their accomplishing any particular service, my recommendation at this moment is succour Malta directly, and have all the ships in Commission ready to weigh anchor at a minutes notice victualled stored and manned, From these scenes of War let me turn to that of your + Sir Williams goodness, my heart wa[r]ms[2] when I think of you, If you are at Caserta when I arrive I will come to you directly then all my business will be done w[i]th (the (Court) say Queen to thom I beg you will present my humble duty had you [t]he goodness to write a line ~~to xxxdy xxxon~~[3] may God Almighty Bless you and Sir William are my prayers each day and may I be worthy of your friend^{p}: is the si[n]cere wish of your affectionate

Horatio Nelson.

17. *Lady Hamilton to Nelson*

[BL: Add. MS 34,989 ff. 18–24]

Caserta
October 27th 1798

My dear Sir

We have had our good Trowbridge here a day + half he is gone to Naples to send a frigate to you I cannot let the least opertunety pass without writing to our dear respectable admiral + we have been so happy with Troubridge[4] in having such an occasion to speak of you as you deserve I presented him + Captain Waller[5] to the Queen we staid with her 2 hours poor dear Troubridge was affected in seeing her with her children he thought of his own we lived with General Acton how you are beloved for not onely with her Majesty but at the Generals you was our theme

[1]Inserted.

[2]The paper is broken at the folding line, which is why the 'r' here and the 'i' in 'with', 't' in 'the' and 'n' in 'sincere' in the following lines needed to be added.

[3]Here at least one word is crossed out at the end of the line and at least one more at the beginning of the next. The passage at the end of the line appears to begin with 'to' and to end with 'dy' and the crossed-out passage at the beginning of the next line appears to end with 'on', so that it appears possible that Nelson had written here 'to Lady Acton'.

[4]*Sic*, not 'Trowbridge' as before.

[5]Captain Thomas Moutray Waller (d. 1818), who had just arrived in the Mediterranean from Lisbon with the Emerald (36 guns).

and my full heart is fit to Burst with pleasure when I hear you honoured name but enugh now for the joy I receved yesterday in a letter from Spencer Smith[1] your present is a pelicia[2] of Gibelini[3] with a feather for your hat of dymonds large + most magnificent[4] + 2 Thousand sechins[5] for the wounded men + a Letter to you from the Grand Signor God bless him There is a frigate sent of on purpose we expect it here I must see the present how I shall Look at it smel it taste it + tuch it put the pelice over my own shoulders Look in the glas + say viva il Turk + by expres desire of his Imperial Majesty you are to wear these Badges of Honner so we think it is an order he gives you for you are particularly desired to wear them + his Thanks to be given to all the officers god bless or Mahomet bless the old Turk I say no longer Turk but good Christian the Queen says that after the English she loves the Turks + she as reson for as to viena the ministers deserve to be hanged + if Naples is saved no Thanks to the Emperor for he is kindly leaving his father[6] in the lurch we have seen 2 days desperate on account of the weak + cool acting of the Cabinet of viena Tugood[7] must be gained but the Emperor oh but he is a poor sop a machine in the hands of his corrupted ministers the Queen is in a rage Belmonte[8] expected back not having been permited to go on their arrived here Sunday last 2 couriers one from London one from viena The first with the comforting news of a fleet to remain in the medit[n] a treaty made of the most flattering kind for Naples in short everything amicable friendly and most truly Honerable t'other from their dear son and daughter[9] cold unfriendly mistrustfull frenchified + saying plainly help yourselves how the dear Maria Carolina cried for joy at the one and rage at the other but Mack is gone to the army to prepare to march emediatly

[1]John Spencer Smith (1769–1845), then at the British Embassy in Turkey.

[2]Pelisse, see Appendix 3.

[3]This probably means 'Gobelin', that is tapestry.

[4]This describes the aigrette; see Appendix 3 for more details.

[5]Seçin, a Turkish coin.

[6]In 1790 Francis II (1768–1835) had married Maria Theresa (1772–1807), a daughter of the king and queen of Naples.

[7]Johann Amadeus Franz von Thugut (1736–1818); Austrian 'prime-minister' who was one of the decisive promoters in Austria of what was to become the second coalition against France (1799–1801).

[8]There are several persons belonging to various branches of the Belmonte family; Ventimiglia, to whom Lady Hamilton refers further down in this same letter, was also a prince of Belmonte; the 'Belmonte' referred to here may have either been Gennaro Pignatelli, 9th prince of Belmonte (1777–1829), or Antonio Maria Pignatelli Pinelli Ravaschieri Fieschi (d. 1828), prince of Belmonte (since 1794).

[9]Franz II and his wife Maria Theresa.

+ I flatter myself I did much for whilst the passions of the Queen were up + agitated I got up put out my left arm like you spoke the language of truth to her painted the drooping situation of this fine Country her friends sacrificed her husband children + herself led to the Block + eternal dishoner to her memory after for not having been active in doing her duty in fighting bravely to the last to save her Country her Religion from the Hands of the rapacious murderers of her sister[1] + the Royal family of france that she was sure of being last if they were inactive + their was a chance of having saved if they made use of the day + struck now while all minds are imprest with the Horrers their neighbours are suffering from these Robbers in short their was a councel + it was determined to march + help themselves + sure then their poor fool of a son[2] will not cannot but come out he must a hundred + fifty thousand men in the venetian state the french cou'd be had in between the 2 army[s] italy cleared + peace restored I saw a person from millan yesterday who say that a small army wou'd do for the milanese have had enough of Liberty whilst the nobility are starving at home + Ladies of the first fashion without a gown to their Backs their are 2 hundred French common w—s the priest cloaths coaches sadle horses + attendant dancing a way every evening + putting virtue out of Countenance by their infamous publick prostitution + Libertinage so you see a little wou'd do now is the moment + endeed here every thing is going on as we cou'd wish the King is to go in a few days not to return the Regency is to be in the name of the prince Royal but the Queen will direct all her head is worth a thousand I have a pain in my head + much so Take an airing 3 o'clock allegramente[3] Sir Wm has been with Acton the Emperor as thought better and will asist them the war to be declared Religious but he will tell you more for I am to go to the pallace + this must go off tonight we are tied by the feet here the princess is got well after being in pain all one night + us all dress'd in galla 24 hours so we must wait with patience the King say[s] it will not be these ten day[s] (how shou'd he know) prince ventimiglia[4] desires his kind compliments the King + Queen beg'd to be most kindly remember'd to you + prince Leopold[5] was yesterday contriving to escape to get a board

[1]Marie Antoinette (1755–93, beheaded in the French Revolution), had married the Dauphin of France, who was to become Louis XVI, making her queen of France.

[2]Probably Francesco, heir to the throne.

[3]Italian for 'cheerfully' or 'merrily'.

[4]Giuseppe Emanuele Ventimiglia Cottone, prince of Belmonte (1766–1814).

[5]The then 8-year-old son of the king and queen of Naples. Leopold (Leopoldo Giovanni, prince of Salerno, 1790–1851) was the 16th child and 6th son, and by 1799 only the second of two surviving sons, of Maria Carolina and Ferdinand of Naples.

a ship to come to you + cried himself sick becose they wou'd not let him but how every body loves + esteems you tis universal from the high to the low oh do you know I sing now nothing but the conquering hero[1] I send it to your altered by myself + sang it to Troubridge + Waller yesterday God bless you prosper + assist you in all you undertake + may you live long long long for the sake of your Country your King your family all Europe Asia Affrica + America + for the scorge of france but particularly for the happiness of Sir William + self who love you admire you + glory in your friendship, compliments to Hardy Tyson Mr Commins[2] my dear little fatherless Fady tell him to keep his head clean + when he comes back I will be his mother as much as I can comb work + cut his nails[3] for with pleasure I cou'd do it all for him, in London you are not abuse alltho tis known you are return'd to Syracuse you are call'd their gallant admiral but there is not an Idea that you will meet with them + yet you are praised what a joy must it be to England when the glorious news arrives glad shou'd I be to be there for one moment your statue ought to be made of pure gold + placed in the middle of London never never was there such a Battle + if you are not requited as you ought I wish I will renounce my country + become either a mamluck or Turk the Queen yesterday said to me the more I think on it the greater I find it + I feil such gratitude to the worrior the glorious nelson that my respect is such I cou'd fall at his Honer'd feet + Kiss them you that know us boath + how alike we are in many things that is I as Emma Hamilton + she as Queen of naples imagine us boath speaking of you we touch ourselves in to tears of rapture wonder respect + admiration + conclude this is not such another in the world I told her Majesty we onely wanted Lady Nelson to be the female tria juncta in uno[4] for we all love you + yet all three differently + yet all equally if you can make that out Sir William laughs at us but he owns women have Great souls at least his has I would not be a luke warm friend for the world I am no ones enimy + unfortunately am difficult + cannot make friendship with all but the few friends I have I would die for them + I assure you now if things take an unfortunate turn here and the Queen dies at her post I will remain with her if she goes I follow her I feil

[1]'See, the conquering hero comes'; see Appendix 4.

[2]Perhaps Rev. Steven Comyn (fl. 1798–1805), chaplain who had served with Nelson on board *Vanguard* at the Battle of the Nile.

[3]Nelson appears to have reacted to this way of Lady Hamilton's expressing motherly care; see his letter of 13 June 1801 (Doc. No. 178), in which he expresses a wish for her to cut his fingernails.

[4]Allusion to the motto of Order of the Bath, which both Nelson and Sir William Hamilton had been awarded.

I owe it to her friendship uncommon for me[1] thank god the first week in november is near I write in such a hurry I am affraid you will be [need] ing[2] patience but take the will for the deed if I fail Love Sir William + myself for we love you dearly he is the best Husband friend I wish I cou'd say father also but I shou'd be too happy if I had the blessing of having children so must be content god bless you prayes most since[re] ly your ever

Emma Hamilton

18. *Verses to 'Heart of Oak' by Lady Hamilton*[3]

[BL: Add. MS 34,989, f. 25]

See the conquering Hero comes
Sound the Trumpet beat the drums
Sports prepare the Laurel Bring
Song[s] of Triumph to him sing.

See our gallant Nelson comes
Sound the Trumpet beat the Drums
Sports prepare the Laurel Bring
Song[s] of Triumph Emma sings
Myrtle wreath[s] and roses Twine
To deck the Hero[s] brow divine
————Nelsons arrival from Egypt as conqueror.

19. *Lady Hamilton to Nelson*

[BL: Add. MS 34,989 ff. 26–27]

Caserta Friday
nov[br] 2[d] 1798

God knows wether this will reach you my dear admiral however I will risk + send you the latest papers the King marches the 8th thank god – I

[1]The following passage is written lengthwise on the inside of another sheet of paper, which was used as an envelope.
[2]This word is indeed hard to decipher. My reading can merely be a suggestion; 'aving' and 'onely' are possible, too.
[3]A comparison to the original text by Thomas Morell (to which Handel composed the music) can be found in Appendix 4.

hope you will be here soon now theirfore will not say more onely love + compliments to all + belive me ever my dear dear admiral your ever oblidged + sincere

E. Hamilton

the Pincess[1] not brought to bed oh dear what can the matter be god bless you

20. *To Lady Hamilton*

[Monmouth: E 425][2]

My dear Madam,

Not being able to get our anchor out of the ground, allows me to say on paper that I am your and Sir Williams affectionate friend May God Almighty Bless and protect you both is the fervent prayer of your Nelson.

Thursday noon,
Pray grant me the favor of getting well.

21. *Lady Hamilton to Nelson*

[BL: Add. MS 34,989 ff. 28–29]

Saturday evening
Novr 24 1798

My dearest Lord

how unhappy we are at the bad weather how are you toss'd about why did you not come back we have not slept these 2 nights thinking on all your sufferings God protect you I find some of the ships are this moment come to anchor but what are these to us if you was to come back we are afraid you will be sick pray keep your self well for our sakes + do not go on shore at Leghorn there is no comfort their for you[3] – the Army is marched the Queen is in Town praying for their success I have not

[1]Maria Clementine (1777–1801).
[2]On the 'outside' of the letter somebody noted: 'Lord Nelson Nov^{er} 22^{d} 1798'.
[3]This may be proof of Lady Hamilton knowing about Adelaide Correglia (Russell, p. 79).

seen her for I have not been out since you went nor can I for 2 or 3 days yet as I have been ill but now getting better as Sir William sends you a manifest of the King[s] I will not[1] your dear venerable father is to be made a Bishop at how happy I am at every ma[r]k of honner shown you why did Troubridge go out in such weather he knew it was not Good how is Tyson Compliments to all friends may God Bless you my dear Lord ever yours sincer[e]ly + affectionat[e]ly Emma

22. *Lady Hamilton to Nelson*

[BL: Add. MS 34,989 f. 30–31] Sunday evening[2]

My dear Lord

I write you 2 Lines more to say I am better but how are you oh this weather if we cou'd know how you are + were [*sic*] you are we shou'd be happy the King is to sleep at Frescati[3] to night + tomorrow enters Home we have had 2 or 3 skirmishes Malilerni the prince with one eye as cut To pieces 4 hundred poles That clever Saxe[4] as taken Teracina[5] to day is to be the French Battle of veletria[6] God prosper them you have shewn them the example the French may date their downfall from the glorious first of August every body here pray[s] for you even the Neapolitans say mass for you but Sir William + I are so anxious that we neither eat drink or sleep + till you are safely landed + come back we shall feel much we have been beset to tell the secret but I wou'd have my flesh torn off by red hot pinchers sooner then betray my trust we send you one of your midshipmen left here by accident [so Abrams][7] pray don't punish him oh I had forgot I wou'd never ask favours but you are so good I cannot help it I write in such a hurry I am afraid you will not be able to read we have got Josiah[8] how glad I was to see him. Lady K Miss K.[9]

[1]A line ends here. 'I will not' apparently refers to who sends the 'manifest of the Kings'. The new line opens a new subject.

[2]Probably 25 Nov 1798.

[3]Frascati is a town south-east of Rome.

[4]Possibly Karl Mack von Leiberich (1752–1828), who, though strictly speaking not from Saxony, was in command of the Neapolitan troops, conquering Rome.

[5]Terracina, town on the coast between Rome and Naples. The Rada di Terracina is at the southern end of the Pontine Marshes.

[6]Velletri is a town south-east of Rome (a bit further from the city than Frascati).

[7]These words cannot be clearly deciphered.

[8]Josiah Nisbet (1780–1830), Nelson's stepson.

[9]Lady Knight and Miss Cornelia Knight.

Cam[p]bell[1] + Josiah dined to day with us but alas your place at table was occupied by Lady K I cou'd have cried I felt so low spirited for God sake turn back soon pray do you have no occasion to go on shore at Leghorn[2]

God bless protect + keep you from all danger + restore you my dear Lord to your ever sincere + affect[io]nate

Emma Hamilton
Sir Williams Love to you

23. *Lady Hamilton to Nelson*

[BL: Add. MS 34,989 ff. 32–33]

God bless you I congratulate you on the sword I belive wealth is taken for sure how are the Generals I have taken a Bath am a little better God protect you my dear Lord ever your since[re]ly

E. Hamilton

make haste back Emma + Sir W^{m} entreats you

24. *To Lady Hamilton*

[Monmouth: E 424]

My Dear Lady,

If you have not rec^{d}: my letter from Leghorn Roads you will like to know that we took possession last Wednesday,[3] I send a paper for you and Sir Willm: to read it is my private memorand^{m}: and not to be communicated If you will have the goodness to have the carraige at the mole,

[1]Probably Donald Campbell (d. 1819), Commodore in the Portuguese navy.

[2]This may be another indication of Lady Hamilton knowing about Adelaide Correglia; see above note to her letter of 24 Nov 1798 (Doc. No. 21).

[3]Nelson arrived in Leghorn on Wednesday, 28 Nov 1798; as he returned to Naples on Wednesday, 5 Dec 1798, and as Nelson refers to writing on 'Tuesday', this letter can be dated 4 Dec 1798.

I shall have great pleasure in coming to you as soon as possible, Ever your faithf^{l}:

Nelson

Tuesday night.[1] Turn over

God bless you for comforting me with your letters, I have had nothing else like comfort, I saw the Marq^{s}:[2] at a distance in Porto ferraio also had Com^{dr}: Cambell[3] on board to breakfast saw Josiah +^{c}: under Monte Christe, I hope for good news from the army, several vessels with runaways from Civita Vecchia arrived on Wednes^{y}: at Leghorn.

25. *To Lady Hamilton*

[NMM: MON/1/11]

My Dear Lady Hamilton,

I shall most certainly expect the happiness of seeing you Sir W^{m}: + M^{rs}: Cadogan at dinner, come and let us have as merry a X^{t}:mas as circumstances will admit,[4] + Believe me Ever yours most truly

Nelson.

26. *To Lady Hamilton*

[NMM: CRC/19]

My Dear Lady Hamilton,

I grieve on reading the Queens letter to you, only say for me, Nelson never changes, Nelson never abandons his friends in distress, on the

[1]4 Dec 1798 (see previous fn.).
[2]De Niza.
[3]Donald Campbell.
[4]See Lady Hamilton's account of the crossing, dealt with in the introduction to this chapter.

contrary those are the moments that knits him closer to them, Nelson you know his heart

Vouch for the uprightness of your
old Friend

Nelson.

Nelson never quits Palermo but by the desire of the Queen.

Palermo
January 25th: 1799

27. *To Ball, with a postscript by Lady Hamilton*

[Morrison, ii, p. 38 (No. 376)]

Palermo,
February 9th, 1799.

I send you the *Benjamin*, Captn Thompson,[1] but I beg you will endeavour to keep him out of the way of the Tunisan cruisers, for I should be sorry if any action took place which might loosen our friendship with the Bey.[2] We have nothing new here as yet, all is quiet at Naples and its environs. The French flag is flying, and they have fitted out the frigate and brigg, and I have my fears they will drive off the *Mutine*. When I get the *Minerva* she shall cruise off Naples, God bless you! Sir Wm & Lady Hamilton desire their regards. You are loved by the fair and esteem'd by the brave; so say yours, [&c]

[*in Lady Hamilton's handwriting:*] I have only time to say, my dear friend, that Sir William & I shall be most happy to see you *make haist*. Do, or else *entre nous* Fate will carry me down. I cannot enter now into the false politicks of this country. *A ora*, ever yours.[3]

[1]Thomas Boulden Thompson (1766–1828).

[2]Hamuda Pasha, Abu Mohamed (French: Hammouda Pacha; 1759–1814), Bey of Tunis 1782–1814.

[3]Nelson's and Lady Hamilton's joint letter-writing appears to reflect a mutual sentiment; Captain Ball at about the same time (on 5 Feb 1799) wrote thus to Lady Hamilton: 'I will not attempt to describe how much I feel flattered by the attention with which I have been honoured by your Ladyship and Sir William Hamilton, for which I am in a great measure indebted to Lord Nelson's friendship. You both feel such a regard for him, that you never lose an occasion of proving it. I may be quoted as a strong instance. . . .' (Morrison, ii, pp. 39, no. 378: 'Dated *Alexander*, off Malta, February 5th, 1799').

28. *Draft for speech in Palermo*

[Christie's, 3 Dec 2003, lot 224][1]

Few events could give me greater happiness than finding myself in the midst of my fellow citizens, and I can assure them that I wear every true Sicilian in my heart, and that it shall be my pride to imitate my new countrymen in love for our Gracious King . . . and in hatred and detestation of the French

29. *To Lady Hamilton*

[NMM: CRK/19/3]

Vanguard
May 19th: 8 O Clock,

Calm,[2]

My Dear Lady Hamilton,

Lieu^{t}: Swiney coming on board enables me to send some Blank passports for Vessels going to Procida with Corn +^{c}: and also one for the Courier boat, to tell You, how dreary and uncomfortable the Vang^{d}: appears is only telling You what it is to go from the pleasantest Society, to a Solitary Cell, or from the dearest friends to no friends, and not I am now perfectly the gr<u>eat</u> <u>man</u> not a creature near me, from my heart I wish myself the little man again, You and Good Sir William have spoilt me for any place but with You, I love M^{rs}: Cadogan You cannot conceive what I feel when I call You all to my remembrance, even to Mira[3] do not forget Your faithful + affectionate[4]

[1]The catalogue comments: 'Autograph manuscript notes for a speech made on the occasion of his being created a citizen of Palermo, with several autograph corrections and alterations, one page, . . . endorsed on verso in Lady Hamilton's hand, "Lord Nelson's address to the Senate of Palermo after having been made a Citizen", n. p., n.d.'; dated 4 March 1799.

[2]The word 'Calm' was added by Nelson in much lighter ink than the rest of the beginning of this letter.

[3]This appears to have been a pet, perhaps a dog.

[4]Greek cross drawn by Nelson in his letter to Lady Hamilton of 19 May 1799 (Doc. No. 29) [NMM CRK 19 3, detail]. © National Maritime Museum, Greenwich, London.

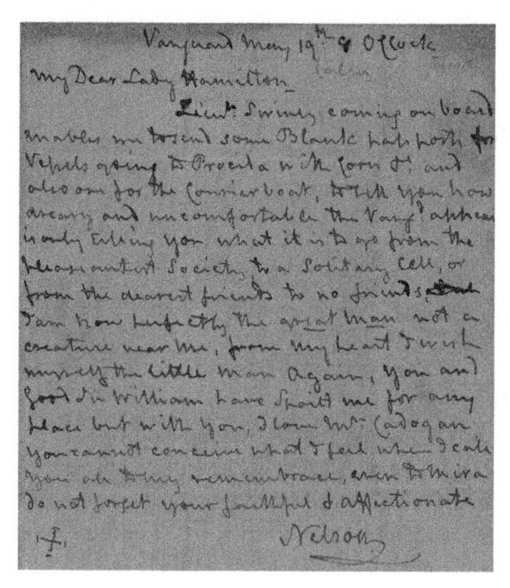

Vanguard May 19th 9 OClock

My Dear Lady Hamilton

Lieut: Swiney coming on board enables me to send some Blank passports for Vessels going to Procida with Corn &c: and also one for the Courier boat, to tell you how dreary and uncomfortable the Vang: appears is only telling you what it is to go from the pleasantest Society to a Solitary Cell, or from the dearest friends to no friends, I am now perfectly the great man not a creature near me, from my heart I wish myself the little man again, you and good Sir William have spoilt me for any place but with you, I love Mrs: Cadogan you cannot conceive what I feel when I call you all to my remembrance, even to Mira do not forget your faithful & affectionate

Nelson

Nelson.[1]

30. *To Lady Hamilton*

[NMM: CRK/19/4] May 20th: 1799

My dear Lady Hamilton,

Many thanks to you and Sir William for your kind notes, You will believe I did not sleep much with all my letters to read +^{c}: +^{c}: My letters from L^{d}: S^{t}: V^{n}: are May 6th: he says 'We saw the Brest Squadron pass us yesterday under an easy Sail, I am making every effort to get information to L^{d}: Keith[2] who[m] I have ordered here, to compleat their water + provisions I conjecture the French Squadron is bound for Malta + Alexandria, and the Spanish fleet for the attack of Minorca,['] I must leave you to judge weither the Earl will come to us I think he will, but entre nous M^{r}: Duckworth[3] means to leave me to my fate I send you

[1]Later the same day Nelson wrote to Sir William Hamilton about his letter to Lady Hamilton: 'I send you Ca^{tn}: Hallowell's note to Capt: Troubridge. If Duckworth joins I shall have a respectable force; you may depend I will do my best. I have wrote good Lady Hamilton a line this evening, but sent it to Lieu^{t} Lamb, it being of no very particular consequence weither the passports got to her at night or in the morning. The moment I get my dispatches I shall write to her, although this will come to you very late, yet it is of too much consequence to keep from you one moment.' (Morrison, ii, p. 46, no. 386); the following day, Nelson even wrote Sir William Hamilton, referring to Lady Hamilton as 'my good Lady' (Morrison, ii, p. 46, no. 387).

[2]At that time second-in-command to St Vincent.

[3]Sir John Thomas Duckworth (1748–1817), commodore of the squadron that secured Minorca in 1798.

(under all circumstances) his letter,[1] never mind if I can get my 11 sail together they shall not hurt me God Bless you Sir William and all our joint friends in your house Noble[2] Gibbs[3] +c: and Believe me Ever for Ever your affectionate Friend

Nelson.

31. *To Lady Hamilton*

[Nicolas, vii, p. clxxxii] May 21st [1799], near Ustica; foul wind.

My dear Lady Hamilton,

The Sparanaro's[4] leaving me last night prevents my sending you Hood's[5] information from Naples. He is sure, if this event had not happened (of the French Fleet's arrival) that we should at this moment have been in Naples. How unlucky this foul wind, and half calm. I am very anxious about the Ships off Malta; for should my friend Ball have stopped to settle any arrangement for the island, he may be too late to effect his escape. I am not well pleased at the Minorca Squadron not joining me. With them I could and would have fought the French Fleet. They should not have relieved Malta, but I must submit – *not patiently*; for that is not in my disposition. I have sent Cockburn[6] off Maritimo: others to Pantelaria, to get me information. Oh, God! how I regret Duckworth's decision.[7] The Earl cannot, I am sure, leave Gibraltar before the 12th, and then, if the Spanish Fleet comes out of Cadiz, he cannot come to me:

[1]This probably refers to John Duckworth's letter of 11 May 1799 (kept at the NMM, CRK/4/156), in which he writes: 'Your Lordship may be sufficiently apprized of the Enemies approach to avoid the risqué [*sic*] with which you may be possibly surrounded. My little squadron by a combination of fortunate events are all collected (except Eurora which I have apprehensions about) and I wait with anxiety the approach of Lord St Vincent [John Jervis, Earl St Vincent, 1735–1823]. I don't detain the Portuguese Frigate a moment, but I have the honor to be under all circumstances with real Respect, and Regard'.

[2]Edmund Noble; Knight, p. 659, writes: 'fl. 1799–1805; Merchant who accompanied the Hamiltons to Palermo in 1799 . . . Took care of Hamilton's effects that had been left behind at Palermo and Naples'.

[3]Abraham Gibbs; Knight, p. 639, writes: 'fl. 1799–1804; Merchant from Naples who moved to Palermo in 1799 and lived with the Hamiltons in the Palazzo Palagonia; later looked after Nelson's business affairs, including the administration of his estate at Bronte'.

[4]The word 'sparanaro' is a variant of 'speronara', a small, three-masted, lateen-rigged Mediterranean sailing boat, used especially for transport between Sicily and Malta. The name 'speronara' derives from the distinctive spur or ram (Italian: speróne) at the bow of the boat (Wiktionary).

[5]Samuel Hood (1762–1814), not to be confused with his cousin Samuel Viscount Hood (1724–1816).

[6]George Cockburn (1772–1853).

[7]Duckworth's decision to leave Nelson; see Doc. No. 30.

therefore why D. should have not made haste to join I cannot conceive. If he shelters himself under *nice punctilios* of orders, I do not approve of an Officer's care of himself. O: conscious of my upright intentions, I would risk my life, much less my commission, to serve my Country.

I have just been to visit Niza. He is very much better, and of course, made many kind inquiries after you. What shall I say, for what you tell me of the missing me out of your charming house? Indeed, I will endeavour to deserve all your good opinions. With kindest regards to Sir William, Mrs. Cadogan, the Greffers,[1] little Mary,[2] Noble, Gibbs, Nudi,[3] &c., and believe me ever, with the sincerest esteem, your faithful and affectionate friend, Nelson

Hardy and the whole Squadron desire to be remembered.

I have been fighting, with the Marquis,[4] Troubridge, Louis, and Hood, my new plan of attack. They all agree it must succeed.[5] Say everything proper for me to the King or Queen for the butter.

Two Sparanaroes returned.

32. *To Lady Hamilton*

[NMM: CRK/19/2]

My dear Lady Hamilton,[6] Accept my sincere thanks for Your kind letter, nobody writes so well therefore pray say not You write ill for if You[7] do I will say what Your goodness sometimes told me You L-e [*sic*] I can read

[1]John Graefer (d. 1803) and his wife, who managed Nelson's estate at Brontë.

[2]See Docs Nos 32 and 46.

[3]Dr Nudi.

[4]de Niza.

[5]This choice of words is similar to that in the letter of 1 Oct 1805 (Doc. No. 394), where Nelson wrote about the reaction to his plan for the Battle of Trafalgar: 'it was like an electric shock, some shed tears all approved, it was new, it was singular, it was simple and from Admirals downwards it was repeated it must succeed'.

[6]This letter has been dated in the 1814-letters as of 12 May 1799, but Nelson only left Palermo on 20 May; also Troubridge (who is referred to in this letter) joined Nelson only on 18 May, so that Nicolas (iii, p. 363) suggested the letter being of 21 May 1799. A further reason for this date can be deduced from the fact that Nelson starts this letter by referring to receiving a letter from Lady Hamilton. In his letters of 19 and 20 May 1799 (Docs Nos 29 and 30) he had also mentioned receiving letters, so that it appears that yet another letter had been delivered to him. This further letter could have been delivered by one of the sparanaroes mentioned in the letter given as Doc. No. 31 or by the ships that reached his squadron in the morning of 21 May (letter of Nelson to St Vincent; Nicolas, iii, p. 365).

[7]Here Nelson had first written 'I', but then wrote 'You' over the 'I'.

and perfectly understand every word you[1] write, We drank Your + Sir Will^{ms}: health, Troubridge, Louis, Hallowell and the new Portugeze [*sic*] Capt: dined here I shall soon be at Palermo for this business must very soon be settled, No one believe me is more sensible of Your Regard than Your obliged + grateful Nelson. Turn over[2]

I am pleased with little Mary, kiss her for me, I thank all the house for their regard, God Bless You all,

I shall send on shore if fine to morrow for the felluccas[3] are going to leave us and I am sea sick I have got the piece of wood for the Tea Chest it shall soon be sent,

Pray present my humble duty + gratitude to the Queen for all her marks of Regard and assure her it is not thrown away on an ungrateful soil.

33. *To Lady Hamilton*

[Nicolas, vii, pp. clxxxiii] May 22nd, 1799

My dear Lady Hamilton,

The wind is as bad as bad can be. I am not nearer Maritimo than if I had been all this time at Palermo. How unlucky, in every sense of the word! Ball has not joined: I am under the greatest apprehension that he has not quitted Malta on the first report of the French, and has either been surprised, or taken the route by way of Messina. Although the first would be unpleasant for England, yet the last is equally distressing to me. Altogether I am not pleasantly situated. If Malta, Toulon, or Minorca is the object of the French, I can do nothing. I almost hope it is the first, when no Battle will yet have taken place. It is difficult to know what to wish. I am sea-sick, and uncomfortable. I send you some of the Queen's letters. How anxious I am to hear of these French! Should Sicily be their object, if I have not force enough to fight them, you may depend I shall return to Palermo, and take care of all my friends, amongst the first of which, I need scarcely say, stand you and good Sir William. I shall dispatch this

[1]Inserted.
[2]The text continues on the next page of the original manuscript.
[3]*Sic*. A felucca is a small sailing or rowing vessel of the Mediterranean, used for coastal transport or trading (Peter Kemp (ed.), *The Oxford Companion to Ships and the Sea* (Oxford, 1988)).

Sparanaro the moment one of the others join, or that I get off Maritimo, which I still hope will be tomorrow morning.[1]

May 24th, 8 o'clock. – Neither of the two Sparanaroes sent to Palermo having joined, I cannot send this for Palermo, till her return from Maritimo, which I am now five miles from. No sight of Ball's Squadron. There is but two guesses to be made about him – viz., that he is either gone round by Messina, or he is taken. Whichever is the case, Nelson is abandoned to his fate; for Mr. Duckworth will not come near me. But on this you may depend, that if my little Squadron obeys my signal, not a Ship shall fall into the hands of the Enemy; and I will so cut them up, that they will not be fit for even a summer's cruise; and one of them at least shall have the Fire-ship laid on board. In short, I am, my dear Lady, so cursedly out of humour with our friends below us[2] (not even a Brig with information), that a Frenchman had better be at the devil than come near. I have five English Ships which are not to be matched in this world. God bless you. I shall write a line to Sir William, when the Boat returns from Maritimo. With kind regards to all in the house, believe me ever your faithful and affectionate friend, Nelson

I send you some letters from Niza. Pray forward them.[3]

[1]On 23 May Nelson wrote to Sir William Hamilton: 'My Dear Sir William, No sight of Balls Squadron I do not like it, I have sent off the Swallow Protugueze corvette to Minorca, the Cutter to Pantaleria, and the sparanarro to Maritimo the latter shall go to You the moment she returns so shall something else when I get any news, or no news, this moment I have had an account that the French fleet were seen off Cagliari stand[g]: to the NE, however this news on closer examination proved to be false, but if true it made me form my plan for the defence of Palermo from a Capture by a Sea attack, and You may assure their Majestys and Gen[l]: Acton that If the whole fleet pursue me I will not pass to the Eastward of Palermo but will there make my stand, and I believe should prevent the whole F. Fleet from Destroying us, I will stand or fall with their Majestys and You + Lady H[n]: Noth[g]: shall swerve me from this determination, 1/2 p[t]: 11 the sparanaro is just return'd from Maritimo where they have heard nothing of the French fleet, God Bless You + Believe me Ever Your affectionate Nelson.' (Huntington Library: HM 34032; Morrison, ii, pp. 46–7, no. 389).

[2]The Portuguese?

[3]On 25 May 1799 Nelson wrote to Sir William Hamilton, referring to Lady Hamilton again as 'my lady': 'My Dear Sir William, Your two letters of the 21st: + 22nd: arrived at 3 oClock with 2 from G[l]: Acton and one from Col[l]: Graham, for the perusal of which I thank You, the cutter gone to Pantelleria goes to Minorca the moment of her return and If she has heard nothing of the French fleet I shall return and anchor with the whole squadron in the Bay of Palermo, as many of our Naples ships want to compleat their Water + provisions which they will do in 24 hours, the Protugeze want every thing, for as Duckworth means not to Join me I can only hold myself in readiness at moments notice for any service either in a whole body or detatchment as the Earl may direct, If the Enemy are gone to Toulon and the news from Paris and Italy is true they will not come out at present, The Line of Battle ships with me must not be again separated therefore Malta must trust to the Russians, I will direct the Lion to remain at Procida for the protection of the Islands but nothing more is in my power at present, You will my Dear Sir William communicate this in confidence to Gen[l]: Acton, the mass may believe the ships are going to their former destination, I shall write my Lady she may tell the Queen for she is a great woman, and is satisfied I act as I really think best for the common cause with sincere + cordial thanks for all Your kindness when present + good wishes when absent Believe me Ever Your obliged and affectionate Nelson. . . . Troubridge who was with me + Hardy desire their kindest regards.' (Huntington HM 34033; Morrison, ii, p. 47, no. 390).

34. *Codicil to Nelson's will*

[CRC]

Whereas I Horatio Lord Nelson K. Bth: Rear Admiral in His Majestys fleet have belonging to me two Gold Boxes set with Diamonds one bearing the Picture of His Imperial Majesty the Emperor of all the Russias,[1] The other a nearly Round Box set with Diamonds said to have been sent me by the Mother of the Grand Signor,[2] I do hereby give and Bequeath the last mentioned nearly Round Box +^{c}: +^{c}: +^{c}: to my Dear Friend Emma Hamilton Wife of the Right Honb^{bl}: Sir William Hamilton which I request she will accept (and never part from) as token of Regard and Respect for her every [*sic*] eminent Virtues (for She the said Emma Hamilton possesses them all to such a degree that it would [mean] doing her Injustice was any particular one to be mentioned) from Her Faithful and affectionate Friend

Nelson.

I also request that my friend the R^{t}: Honb^{le}: Sir Willm: Hamilton K. Bth: will accept of ~~50~~ fifty[3] Guineas to purchase a Ring which I beg he will wear for the sake of His Sincere Friend Nelson.

I declare this as a Codicil to my last Will and Testament on Board His Majestys Ship vanguard this 25th: May 1799 off Maritimo Island of Sicily

Nelson

Delivered in the presence of us.
T. Troubridge
T.M.Hardy

35. *To Lady Hamilton*

[Monmouth: E 444] May 26th: 1799

My Dear Lady Hamilton

Many many thanks for your letters, but as neither of ours can go by post, we must trust to the mercy of a boatman who cares not for our

[1]Tsar Paul I of Russia (1754–1801).
[2] See Appendix 3 for a possible confusion about the donors of these boxes.
[3]The word 'fifty' is written above a crossed-out '~~50~~'.

anxietys, I send you the passports for the vessels, only tell me how I can be most useful and that is enough, the thing is done, there is not a vessel in sight theref[re]: I can send you nothing new, pray do not trouble yourself to send me fruit for to say the truth I have no stomach for eating, May God Almighty Bless you and all my friends about you and Believe me amongst the most faithful and affectionate of your friends Nelson.

I have no boat with me, therefore I cannot send again[1] till one comes.

36. *Nelson, Lady Hamilton and Sir William to Ball*

[*c)* Christie's, 3 Dec 2003, lot 227; *d)* Nicolas, iii, p. 371]

[*c)*] June 1st: 1799

My Dear Ball,

I will give You a frigate as soon as I can get one liberated from other very important services which the present moment call for, I will not lose sight of the maltese + I sincerely pray that you may soon[2] be able to see the inside of la Villette + the ships, no one man in this world deserves success so much as Yourself, and Believe me no one is more truly sensible of Your great merits than your affectionate Friend

Nelson.

Cap[t]: Ball[3]

If you cou'd but have come to us for five minutes my dear Sir how happy shou'd I have been to see you how I pitied you when you were call[ed] from Malta knowing your energy + attachment to these unfortunate people but I hope all will yet go [*d)*] well, and that you will have the pleasure of soon driving the monsters out. I have not been well: can anybody, with a little sensibility, be well in these moments of anxiety? But at all times, and in all circumstances, I shall ever be, my dear Sir, your attached, and obliged, and grateful – Emma Hamilton

June 1st, 1799.[4] My dear Sir, I received your letter from off Marsala this day at noon, from a handsome man, with a monstrous deal of hair

[1]Inserted.

[2]Inserted.

[3]Up to here in Nelson's handwriting; from here in Lady Hamilton's.

[4]Nicolas adds: 'The other addition was by Sir William Hamilton'. Christie's catalogue remarks: 'Sir William Hamilton's signature excised'.

under his chin and on his throat, and communicated it directly to Lord Nelson. I rejoice in your going back to Malta, for my heart already bled for the consequences that might arise from your being obliged to quit that station. God bless, and give you the success your assiduity so well deserved. General Acton has assured me that Cordoni shall have the rank he wishes for, as it is Captain Ball that intercedes for him.

37. *Lady Hamilton to Nelson*

[NMM: CRK/20/56] Thursday Evening, June 12th [1799]

I have been with the Queen this evening she is very miserable + says that altho the people of naples are for them in general yet Things will not be brought to that state of quietness + subordination till the fleet of Lord Nelson appears off Naples she therefore begs intreats + conjures you my dear Lord if it is possible to arrange matters so as to be able to go to naples Sir William is writing for general Actons answer for god sake consider it + do we will go with you if you will come + fetch us Sir W is ill I am ill it will do us good God bless you

ever ever yours sincerely
E Hamilton

38. *To Lady Hamilton*

[NMM: CRK/19/7] June 16th: 7 O Clock

My Dear Lady Hamilton.

What a difference but it was to be from your house to a boat, Fresh breeze of Wind the Ship 4 or 5 leagues from the mole getting on board into truly a hogstye of a Cabbin, leaking like a Sieve consequently floating with water, what a change, Not a Fellucca[1] near us I saw them come out this morning but they think there is too much Wind and Swell, pray do not keep the Cutter as I have not a thing if any thing important should

[1] *Sic*, it should be 'felucca', which is a small sailing or rowing vessel of the Mediterranean, used for coastal transport or trading.

arr^{ve}: to send to you, Only think of Tysons[1] being left, May God Bless you my Dear Lady and Believe me Ever your truly affectionate + Sincere friend

Nelson.

Lady Hamilton. put the candlestick on my writing-table.

39. *To Lady Hamilton, with postscript by Ball*

[BL: Egerton 1614 ff. 5–6, no. 3] June 18th: 1799

My Dear Lady Hamilton,

Since I sent off the vessel yesterday forenoon and dispatched the Telegraph Brig to Lord S^{t}: V^{n}: I have received not the smallest information, this morning brought us in sight of the Alexander + Goliath and by noon they will have joined me, As to my feel^{ngs}: My Dear Lady I know not[2] how to express them, but I know how to feel them for they have made me very unwell Jefferson[3] wants to give me castor oil but that will not smooth my anxious mind, I long to be at the French fleet as much as ever a Miss longed for a husband, but prudence stops me Ought I[4] to risk giving the cursed French a chance of being mistress of the Med^{n}: for one hour, I must have reinforcements very soon, Ah Lord Keith you have placed me in a situation to lower me in the Eyes of Europe, they will say this cried up Nelson is afraid with 18 Ships to attack 22 The thought kills me I know what I am equal to and what ships + men can do and I declare to God if no more ships could join me that I would instantly search out the French fleet and fight them, for believe me I have no fear but that of being lowered in the opinion of those I love + esteem. The Ad^{l}:[5] Troubridge and Campbell dined here yesterday they all love you and Sir William + charge me to say so, Martin[6] came after dinner and amongst them they told such things of

[1]For letters from Nelson's secretary Tyson to Lady Hamilton see: Pettigrew, i, pp. 335–337.

[2]Inserted.

[3]Surgeon Michael Jefferson, who had treated Nelson on Corsica (after he had lost the sight of his right eye) and in London after the loss of his arm.

[4]Inserted.

[5]Probably the Marquis de Niza.

[6]George Martin (1764–1847), whom Nelson had first met in the West Indies.

Palermo ladies that I was all astonishment, that one who may is a Lady we saw oddly lifted up on the quarter deck of the Principe Reale gives herself up for Money Price named a great deal[1] more I am sure than She is worth, in short we of Your house know nothing of the Infamy of C – n, P – t – r – and a Lady who is with child was not shared, where have I been not to have known as much as these Gentlemen, living in a house of Virtue + goodness, there anecdotes I only catched as they flew for I was thinking of other things much more interesting to me. I shall keep this letter open till Ball joins, Troubridge's pilot + wife wished to be considered as Prisoners, She is a Jacobin + t[h] reatened her husband to have him hanged as a Royalist when I can get a good cargoe they shall be off, Allen[2] has left my New plain hat in the hat box pray send it, and I take the liberty of sending a cover to be washed for I am in the midst of dirt + filth, poor Hardy is very unwell + Tyson they are taking Physic, pray say everything kind for me to M[rs]: Cadogan M[r]: G[r]:[3] the child[n]: Gibbs Noble +: +: Emma is very well and growing fat and saucy, she goes to all parts of the ship at the different meal times She seems to prefer Roast Goose to all other things, To the Queen you will I am sure say everything which is proper, Answer for my Attachment and that I will fight in defence of her crown and dominions whenever the proper time arrives, and that the damn'd French shall not get Sicily with their fleet but thro' my hearts blood May the God of heaven Bless you and be assured I am your faithful + affectionate Friend

Nelson.

No boats remaining – Ball and Foley on board.[4]

My Lord Nelsons kindness allows me to assure Sir William and Lady Hamilton of my inalterable esteem and regard. I am this moment come on board of the Foudroyant and I feel happy in having joined in time to fight under his Lordships Banners – Lord Keith has given us a hard task but I feel sanguine that our dear Friend will be followed by fortune

[1]Inserted.
[2]Tom Allen (1764–1838), Nelson's manservant from Norfolk.
[3]Graeffer.
[4]The following text is written on the last of the four pages, upside down against Nelson's text.

which will crown him with additional laurels. Foley sends his best regard

God Bless you
Your ever obeyed and devoted
Alex Jn Ball
Foudroyant
18 June 1799

40. *To Lady Hamilton*

[Monmouth: E71] June 19th: 1799.

My Dear Lady Hamilton.

Sir Williams packet came last night at 10 Oclock and although the Public news was good it gave me great pain to hear both Sir Wm: + yourself were so very unwell, I wrote Sir William yesterday that if you both thought the Sea air would do you good I have plenty of Room I can make you private apartments and I give you my honor the Sea is so smooth that no glass ever was smoother, I am anxious to hear of the F. Ft: return to Toulon for then they will return for we have no fleet to stop them, I should instantly send one half the fleet under Duckworth off Malta which would secure its surrender and with the other go to Naples that their Majestys may settle matters then and take off (if necessay: the head of) the Cardinal, nothing in sight a Fresh West wind quite cool, may God bless you get well + Believe me Ever your most affectionate Friend Nelson.

Kind regards to Mrs: Cadogan, Greffer + the children. Wind fresh at Wt: + cool.

41. *To Lady Hamilton*

[NMM: AGC/N/3] June 20th: noon, off Trapani.

5 oclock most secret,
no one knows my determination but
Duckworth[1]
My Dear Lady Hamilton,

[1]Nelson appears to have added the words from '5 oclock' until 'Duckworth' later. They are written in a lighter shade of black ink and squeezed in the empty space to the right of 'My Dear Lady Hamilton'.

Many thanks for your flying letter I will call it by the Pallas, Cap^{n}: Edmonds had the goodness to make the signal to the Incendiary he had a letter for me and I received it last night, it is very natural that we should like them that like us therefore Cap^{n}: E. must in future be a favorite of mine, I wish you and Sir William where here this moment, my anxiety is great at the frigate in sight and she does not near us more than 1 mile an hour + I want her to fly to me with news, and then you would have it at the same moment, curse the felluccas [*sic*]they care not for news I send a letter Niza to the Princess and he desires I will make his best Comp^{ts}: which I tell him I always do, this must be a Portugeze [*sic*] corvette she manages so ill + can not fly to give us news. 3 oclock three feluccas are in sight about 8 miles to leeward, the Portugeze [*sic*] corvette will be with me in half an hour no appetite but for news. I have been in chace [*sic*] of this ship all day, some of the fleet 4 Leagues distant. 4 oclock The Swallow arrived I send you Lord S^{t}: Vincent [*sic*] letter I have made the signal for Ad^{l}: Duck^{h}: my determination is taken for my sake[1] by all the regard you and good Sir William have for me[2] oppose not my resolution,[3] nor suffer the Queen to prevent me,[4] my honor is at stake for Gods sake prevent not my gaining a little more, we will annihilate these rascals + give peace to the world, I shall be with you I hope before this letter, may God Bless you + Sir William + Believe me your most faithful + affectionate Friend.

Nelson.

I will not be absent 8 days. If I should be in Sight have a Carraige at the Beach near the Colin, the command of the fleet I leave with Duckworth.

42. *To Lady Hamilton*

[CRC/24] Wednesday 29th: Jan^{ry}: [1800]

Seperated from all I hold dear in this World what is the use of living if indeed such an existance can be called so, nothing could alleviate such

[1]A new page begins here.

[2]Inserted and written in a much lighter shade of ink than the rest of the text.

[3]The words 'my resolution' are inserted and written in a much lighter shade of ink than the rest of the text.

[4]Inserted and written in a much lighter shade of ink than the rest of the text.

a seperation but the call of our Country but loitering time away with nonsence is too much,[1] no seperation no time my only beloved Emma can alter my love and affection for you, it is founded on the truest principles of honor, and it only remains for us to regret which I do with the bitterest anguish that there are any obstacles to our being united in the closest ties of this worlds rigid rules, as we are in those of real love, Continue only to love Your faithful Nelson as he loves his Emma, Your [*sic*] are my guide I submit to You, let me find all my fond heart hopes and wishes with the risk of my life I have been faithful to my word never to partake of any amusem^t: or to sleep on shore, Thursday Jan^ry: 30th: we have been six days from Leghorn and no prospect of our making a passage to Palermo, to me it is worse than death, I can neither eat or sleep for thinking of you my dearest love, I never touch even pudding[2] you know the reason, no I would starve sooner, my only hope is to find you have equally[3] kept your promises to me, for I never made you a promise that I did not as strictly keep as if made in the presence of heaven, but I rest perfectly confident of the reallity [*sic*] of your love and thet[4] you would die sooner than be false in the smallest thing to your own faithful Nelson who lives only for his Emma, friday[5] I shall run mad we have had a gale of wind that is nothing but I am 20 Leagues farther from you than yesterday noon, was I master notwithstanding the weather I would have been 20 Leagues nearer but my Commander In Chief[6] knows not what I feel by absence, last night I did nothing but dream of you altho' I woke 20 times in the night, In one of my dreams I thought I was at a large table you was not present, sitting between a Princess who I detest and another, they both tried to seduce me and the first wanted to take those liberties with me which no woman in this world but yourself ever did, the consequence was I knocked her down and in the moment of bustle you came in and taking me in your embrace whispered I love nothing but you my Nelson, I kissed you fervently and we enjoy'd the height of love, Ah Emma I pour out my soul to you. If you love any thing but me you love those who feel not like your N.

[1]The words 'is too much' are inserted.

[2]Coarse slang for 'penis'; probably derived in sailors' language from the nautical meaning of any rope padding or binding which prevents chafing or impact damage.

[3]Written 'equ' and above 'ally'.

[4]Quite clearly an 'e'.

[5]31 Jan 1800.

[6]Lord Keith: George Elphinstone, Viscount Keith (1746–1823).

Sunday[1] noon fair wind which makes me a little better in hopes of seeing you my love my Emma to morrow, just 138 miles distant, and I trust to find you like myself, for no love is like mine towards you,[2]

43. *To Lady Hamilton*

[NMM: CRK/19/5] feb^{ry}: 3rd: 1800.

My dear Lady Hamilton.

Having a Commander in Chief[3] I cannot come on Shore 'till I have made my manners to him, times are changed, but If he does not come on Shore directly I will not wait, in the mean time I send Allen to enquire how You are, send me word for I am anxious to hear of You, it has been no fault of mine that I have been so long absent, I can not comm^{d}: and now only obey, M^{r}: Tyson + the Consul[4] have not been able to find out the bettrosed[5] wife of the Priore altho' they were 3 days in their Enquiries and desired the Neapolitan Consul to send to Pisa, I also desired the Russian Ad^{l}:[6] as he was going to Pisa, to enquire If the Countess Poushkin had any letters to send to Palermo, but as I received none I take for granted she had none to send, May God Bless You my Dear Lady and be assured I ever am and shall be Your obliged and affectionate Bronte Nelson.

44. *To Lady Hamilton*

[Jean Kislak: 1988.013.00.0003] Feb^{ry}: 13th: 1800,

My Dear Lady Hamilton

I do not send You any news or opinions as this letter goes by post + may be opened and as I wrote to You and Sir William yesterday nothing particular has occurred, we are now off Messina with a fresh breeze and

[1]2 Feb 1800.

[2]The letter ends thus unfinished in the upper half of its third page.

[3]Lord Keith.

[4]Probably Charles Lock (1770–1804), at that time Consul-General at Naples. Nelson had a row with him over his allegation of irregularities in the victualling of the fleet. The row lasted from July 1799 at least until the end of the year and was never properly resolved.

[5]*Sic*. Betrothed.

[6]Fedor Fedorovich Ushakov (1745–1817).

fair, Mr: Roach[e][1] has had the goodness to come on board, to say how I miss Your house and company would be saying little, but in truth You and Sir Wm: has [*sic*] so spoil'd[2] me that I am not happy any where else but with You, nor have I an Idea thet [I][3] ever can be, all my newspapers are purloingd [*sic*] at Gibr: and I suspect a Gentleman [t]here[4] has sent them to Ld: Keith, for they are all stars, I see in Lord Grenvilles note to Paris he concludes with say[ing][5] thet the best mode he can recomm[end][6] for France to have a Solid Peace is to replace its ancient Princes on the Throne, May the heavens bless You and make You ever be satisfied thet I am Your truly faithful and affectionate Bronte Nelson[7]

You will make my kindest regards to Sir Willm: and to all the house[8] also duty to the Queen.

45. *To Lady Hamilton*

[Morrison, ii, p. 86 (No. 456)] [18 February 1800]

I feel anxious to get up with these ships & shall be unhappy not to take them myself, for first my greatest happiness is to serve my gracious King and Country, & I am envious only of glory; for if it be a sin to covet glory I am the most offending soul alive. *But there I am* in a heavy sea & thick fog – Oh, God! The wind subsided – but I trust to Providence I shall have them.[9]

[1]The 'h' is at the end of the line with no space left for an 'e'; Morrison has added an 'e' here.

[2]Nelson used this phrase before in his letters to Lady Hamilton of 11 Aug 1798 (Doc. No. 8: 'You and Sir William have spoiled [me]') and 19 May 1799 (Doc. No. 29: 'You and Good Sir William have spoilt me for any place but with you').

[3]Added in pencil by somebody else.

[4]The 't' is torn from the bottom left corner of the first page.

[5]Glued in at the end of the line.

[6]Glued in at the end of the line.

[7]Underlined twice.

[8]After 'house' the writing continues in a new line.

[9]Morrison comments on this first part of the 'letter': 'in Emma's handwriting, endorsed by Sir William: "I desired Lady H. to make me a little extract from Ld Nelson's letter to her, which was a sort of journal. I fear your Lp will scarcely be able to make out her hasty scrawl; but Lord Nelson's sentiments, expressed in his own words, doe [*sic*] him so much honor [*sic*] that I trust your Lp will excuse the liberty I take in having sent this paper for your lordship's private perusal. W. H."' It is not clear for whom this copy of Nelson's letter, originally addressed to Lady Hamilton, was intended.

18th in the evening, I have got her – *Le Généreux* – thank God! 12 out of 13, onely [*sic*] the *Guillaume Telle* [*sic*] remaining; I am after the others. I have not suffered the French Admiral to contaminate the *Foudroyant* by setting his foot in her.[1]

46. *To Lady Hamilton*

[NMM: CRK/19/6]

Off La Villette
febry: 20th: 1800

My Dear Lady Hamilton,

had you seen the Peer[2] receive me I know not what you would have done, but I can guess, but never mind I told him, thet I had made a Vow if I took the Genereaux[3] by myself it was my intention to strike my flag, to which he made no answer, If I am well enough I intend to write a letter to Prince Leopold and to send him the French Admirals flag which I hope you will approve of, as it was taken on the Coast of his Fathers Kingdom, and by as faithful a Subject as any in his Dominions, I have had no communication with the Shore therefore have seen neither Ball, Troubridge or Graham,[4] nor with the Lion, when I have, I shall not forget all your messages and little Jack I only want to know your wishes that I may at least appear grateful, by attending to them. My head ache, dreadfully and I have none near to give me a moments comfort, I send the packet to Genl: Acton as I think [it] may go quicker, and he will be flattered by presenting the flag + letter to the Prince Malta I think will fall very soon if these other corvettes do not get in, pray make my best regards acceptable to Mrs: Cadogan, Miss Knight, little Mary Re Geovanni [*sic*],[5] Gibbs, +c +c, and ever believe me your truly faithful and affectionate

Bronte Nelson.

[1]Rear-Admiral Jean-Baptiste Emmanuel Perrée (1761–1800) was struck by a shot from the *Success* and died a day later; so he could hardly have been in a state to set foot into the *Foudroyant*.

[2]Lord Keith.

[3]*Le Genereux* was the only French ship present at the Battle of the Nile that had not yet been taken by the Royal Navy.

[4]Thomas Graham (1748–1843), later to become Lord Lynedoch.

[5]Most probably a misspelling for Giovanni.

47. *To Lady Hamilton*

[CRC/25] Feb^{ry}: 25th: 1800.

My Dear Lady Hamilton,

Your letters by Girgenti[1] are not yet come here. The weather has been bad sent [*sic*] them in charge to the Consul I fancy under cover to our friend Ball and they will be safe, Macauly[2] was to go over that way to Palermo and it is the only way I can send to you, for by L^{d}: Keiths order to me Palermo is no longer to be the rendez vous of our Ships,[3] You will I am sure thank Miss Knight kindly for her high and unmerited compliment – it is a little of a prophecy, but I wish not to trust dame fortune too long she is a fickle dame and I am no courtier, I long to give it all up 19 Sail of the Line + 4 Ad^{ls}: is enough for one man at the taking of 16 I have bore my flag. My health has been so bad that yesterday I wrote a letter to L^{d}: Keith for 2 or 3 weeks leave of absence to go to Palermo + rest quiet, but I found if I went at this moment perhaps we might lose Malta therefore for a very short time I have given way as I have often done to the Public Service but I really want rest and a great deal of your kind care, for ever believe me my Dear Lady Hamilton Your Obliged affectionate and Sincere Friend

Bronte Nelson.

There is another letter sent herewith,

[1]Until 1927 the official name of Agrigento; the letter from Palermo, where Lady Hamilton was staying, went probably via the nearby port of Porto Empedocle (Southern Sicily) from where it would be sent by sea to Malta, as Nelson was at this time cruising with *Foudroyant* off Malta. Nelson expected letters from Lady Hamilton via Girgenti, because Sir William had informed Nelson: ‘Emma has just let me into the secret that she sends her dispatches to your Lp. tonight to Girgenti’ (quoted in Russell, p. 162).

[2]*Sic*. Alexander Macaulay was at that time Treasurer of Malta.

[3]Nelson complained more openly about his situation in a letter to Sir William Hamilton of the same day: ‘my situation is to me very irksome but now at this momt: to get rid of it is a great difficulty, The French ships are here preparing for Sea, the Brest fleet L^{d}: Keith says may be daily expected and with all this I am very unwell, I was in hopes I could have come and staid 2 or 3 weeks quiet in your house with^{t}: a care or a thought of the service, but for a short time that prospect is vanish’d something must come forth in 2 or 3 weeks credit to myself I shall assuredly give you my company, Lord Keith will tell you that he is going first to Syracuse and then to the Gulph of Genoa but every moment may change his plans if he has any, I am made truly happy by the event of the Grand Masters favor to our Dear and highly meritorious Lady + to Ball the Cross never before was so well bestowed, . . . L^{d}: K. is Commander In Chief when I can rest a little quietly I hope I shall be well enough to get thro’ this compaign, when you see me it may be unexpected perhaps crossing the country from Girgenti for a visit of rest I am determined to take, . . .’ (NMM: MON/1/15; Morrison, ii, p. 88, no. 460).

I intended to have wrote more by[1] Capt: C. is arrived + I cannot detain him.

48. *To Lady Hamilton*

[BL: Egerton 1614 ff. 7–8, no. 5] March 4th: 1800.

My dear Lady Hamilton,

My health is in such a state and to say the truth an uneasy mind at being taught my lesson like a School Boy, that my determination[2] is made to leave Malta on the 15th: morning of this month on the first moment after the wind comes favourable, unless[3] I am sure[4] that I shall get hold of the French ships then my friends would have me attend to the last sprig of laurel which will ever be plucked by my Dear Lady your faithful and affectionate

Bronte Nelson.

I beg my best regards to Sir William.

49. *To Lady Hamilton*

[BL: Egerton 1614 ff. 9–10, no. 6] [November 1800]

My Dear Lady Hamilton,

Lady Nelson[5] + myself will as it is so much desired come for a few minutes to Lady Elcho's after the play I am tired it will be midnight, Ever Your truly affectionate

Bronte Nelson of the Nile.[6]

Sunday I dine with M^{r}: Nepean[7] from my heart I wish you could have join'd here, may God Bless you, best regards to Sir William.

[1] *Sic*. Nelson left a gap here. There seems to be the name of a ship missing in the text.

[2] Underlined thrice.

[3] Underlined twice.

[4] Underlined four times.

[5] Frances Nelson, née Herbert (1758–1831), whom Nelson had married in 1787 on Nevis in the West Indies.

[6] Signature used by Nelson until 6 Nov 1800 (see Nicolas, iv, p. 267), when on his return to Britain he stopped using his Sicilian title; Nelson started signing 'Nelson + Bronte' on 21 Jan 1801, after having been permitted to use his title in Britain (Doc. No. 59).

[7] Sir Evan Nepean (1751–1822), since 1794 Secretary of the Admiralty.

50. *To Lady Hamilton*

[Russell, p. 212]

My dear Lady Hamilton, I have had but a very indifferent night, but from Sir William Beechey's will come to you to know weither it is fixed for me to dine with the Duke of Queensberry, to say the truth I am not fond of meeting strangers.

51. *To Lady Hamilton*

[Bonhams,
14 Nov 2012][1]

My Dear Lady,

I shall not come to Your house after what passed last night 'till You send for me when I shall fly, I never will retract one syllable I utter'd, or one thought I felt, never will I sit tamely and see You my Dear friend neglected or Insulted, for Believe me, as Ever Your most sincere and affectionate

Nelson
Sunday morn[g]:

52. *To Lady Hamilton*

[*a)* Pettigrew, i, p. 392; *c)* Christie's, 21 June 1989, lot 234][2]

[*a)*] My dear Lady Hamilton,

It is now six o'clock, and I dread the fatigue of the day, being not of the best spirits, and believe me when I say that I regret that I am not the

[1]Nov or Dec 1800; for the dating of this letter, see Marianne Czisnik, 'Nelson's Letter to Lady Hamilton Sold by Bonhams on 14 Nov 2012: A Suggestion on How to Date It', in *The Nelson Dispatch*, vol. 11, part 6 (April 2013), 360–64.

[2]The first part of the letter is taken from Pettigrew, i, p. 392; from 'that I see . . .' the text is a transcript from the facsimile given in Christie's Catalogue of 1989, *Medieval and Illuminated Manuscripts including a Portolan Chart Early printed Books autograph letters historical document, . . . which will be sold at Christie's Great Rooms on Wednesday 21 June 1989 at 10.30 precisely*, lot 234; when the letter went again on sale at Christie's London, *the Spiro Family Collection, part I: English Historical Documents and Letters* Wednesday 3 Dec 2003 at 2.30 p.m., lot 132, the letter was dated (doubtfully, see next fn.) 3 Jan 1801, 'Provenance: Edwin Wolf 2nd Collection (Christie's sale, 21 June 1989, lot 234)'.

person to be attended *upon* at this funeral,[1] for although I have had my days of glory, yet I find this world so full of jealousies and envy [*c)*] that I see but a very faint gleam of future comfort, I shall come to Grosvenor Square[2] on my return from this melancholy procession + hope to find in the smiles of my friends some alleviation for the cold looks and cruel words of my Enemies. May God Bless you My Dear Lady and Believe me Ever Your unalterable Nelson.

Saturday Morning

[1]This refers to the funeral of Nelson's old friend Captain Locker, who died on 26 Dec 1800 (Nelson sent a letter of condolence to Locker's son John on 27 Dec and agreed to attend his funeral on 29 Dec 1800; see: Nicolas, iv, pp. 270–71).

[2]The home of William Beckford in London, where Sir William and Lady Hamilton were staying at the time.

CHAPTER II

THE BALTIC CAMPAIGN, JANUARY–JUNE 1801

Professionally, the year 1801 started promisingly for Nelson. On 1 January he was promoted to the ship he himself had captured from the Spanish at the Battle of Cape St Vincent in 1797. In his new position Nelson was again to be subordinate to Admiral St Vincent, then commander-in-chief of the Channel fleet. This answered his wishes, as he had already asked the Admiralty in November 1800 to be sent on 'active service' again and he had shown a preference to serve under St Vincent.[1] The new posting also allowed him to evade his current situation in England: he had just been coldly received at a royal levee on 7 January and his private situation at the time was awkward, to say the least. While Lady Hamilton was now in her ninth month of pregnancy, Nelson was apparently not yet able to separate from his wife. Part of the problem may have been the difficulty at this time of securing a formal separation; a divorce was even more difficult. On 9 January, the day on which he received his orders to join the Channel fleet, he and his wife signed the document which sold the house at Roundwood that she had chosen for them. Nelson settled a generous pension on his wife, the first instalment of which was paid on the day on which Nelson left London, 13 January 1801.[2] While these technicalities about the state of the marriage are documented, the state of their emotional relations remains elusive.

Authors of the mid- and late-nineteenth century have tried to prove that it was really Lady Nelson who decided to end the marriage. For their arguments they use biased or untraceable sources. The biased source is a letter from Nelson's solicitor, William Haslewood, written 45 years after the event to the editor of *The Dispatches and Letters of Lord Nelson*, Nicholas H. Nicolas:

> Dear Sir, – I was no less surprised than grieved when you told me of a prevailing opinion, that Lord Nelson of his own motion withdrew from the society of his wife, and took up his residence altogether with Sir William and Lady Hamilton, and that you have never received from any member of his family an intimation to the contrary. . . In the winter of 1800, 1801, I was breakfasting with Lord and Lady Nelson, at their lodgings in Arlington-street, and a cheerful conversation was passing on indifferent subjects, when Lord Nelson spoke of something which had been done or said, by 'dear Lady Hamilton;' upon which Lady Nelson rose from her chair, and exclaimed, with much vehemence, 'I am sick of hearing of dear lady Hamilton, and am resolved that you

[1]Roger Knight, *The Pursuit of Victory. The Life and Achievement of Horatio Nelson* (London, 2005) [hereafter: Knight], p. 350.

[2]Terry Coleman, *Nelson. The Man and the Legend* (London, 2001), p. 244.

> shall give up either her or me.' Lord Nelson, with perfect calmness, said – 'Take care, Fanny, what you say. I love you sincerely; but I cannot forget my obligations to Lady Hamilton, or speak of her otherwise than with affection and admiration.' Without one soothing word or gesture, but muttering something about her mind being made up, Lady Nelson left the room, and shortly after drove from the house. They never lived together afterwards. . . . to the day of her husband's glorious death, she never made any apology for her abrupt and ungentle conduct above related, or any overture towards a reconciliation.[1]

The untraceable source is the note that Nelson is said to have written to his wife on the first evening of his journey to Plymouth to take up his post. According to John Cordy Jeaffreson, Nelson, having just left London, wrote more than the short note, reproduced in Nicolas [53]. He supposedly also wrote: 'Dear Fanny, Forgive the husband, who loves you, what he repents.'[2] The letter to which this is supposedly added, is preserved in the Huntington Library and does not contain the quoted addition. It is short and there remains much empty space on the sheet on which Nelson wrote it, so that is appears very unlikely that Nelson added an expression of repentance on a separate sheet of paper. Moreover, both sources appear doubtful as to their contents. Neither appears to be in keeping with the partners' characters. As to Lady Nelson, no similar shows of determination are known to have come from her and several, supposedly missing 'overture[s] towards a reconciliation' from her are documented in drafts of letters, of which, however, we can merely assume that and in which form they were actually sent.[3] As to Nelson, no other signs of repentance are documented.

Whatever Nelson's emotions or thoughts were, he was clearly torn between his wife and his lover. The letters he wrote to his wife and his lover on different days of his journey to Plymouth and at his arrival

[1]Nicolas, vii, pp. 391–2; doubts about this source have been brought forward by Edgar Vincent, *Nelson. Love & Fame* (New Haven and London, 2003), p. 388. James Stanier Clarke and John M'Arthur, *The Life of Admiral Lord Nelson, K.B. from His Lordship's Manuscripts* (in 2 vols, London, 1809) [hereafter: Clarke & M'Arthur], ii, p. 256, make Nelson's words on the occasion of his supposed separation from his wife on 13 Jan 1801 even more dramatic: 'In taking his final leave of Lady Nelson on the 13th of Jan, 1801, he acted, however wrong, with that greatness and liberality of mind which nothing could subdue: "I call God to witness", exclaimed he, "there is nothing in you or your conduct I wish otherwise."'

[2]John Cordy Jeaffreson, *Lady Hamilton and Lord Nelson. An Historical Biography Based on Letters and Other Documents in the Possession of Alfred Morrison Esq. of Fonthill, Wiltshire*, 2 vols (London, 1888), ii, p. 218.

[3]Naish, pp. 585 (draft of April 1801), 588 (draft of July 1801, unfinished); in a last letter of 18 Dec 1801 Lady Nelson refers to 'my letter of July' (Naish, p. 596).

there attest to this [53–56].[1] Interestingly he started the series with a letter, or rather note, to his wife on his first evening away from London [53, without the supposed expression of repentance]. A day later Lady Hamilton received some lamentations that 'various workings of my imagination gave me one of those severe pains of the heart that all the windows were obliged to be put down the carraige stop'd and the perspiration was so strong that I never was wetter, + yet dead with cold'. These reactions had disappeared, when Nelson encountered 'the same crowds + applauses thet you for ever join in' [54]. On the day of his arrival at Torre Abbey,[2] St Vincent's residence, Nelson, probably distracted by naval business, wrote to neither of the two women. Having received a letter from his wife, he sent her a note the following day [55]. The messages to his wife included wishes to his sister-in-law and to his father. The next letter to Lady Hamilton, after Nelson's arrival in Plymouth again told her about the reception he had received ('the parade was exactly like Salisbury') and it contained some reports about his encounters with the mother of the captain who had been killed at the Battle of the Nile and with St Vincent. He added his regards to Sir William [56].

Lady Hamilton, in the meantime, appears to have been equally confused about how to continue her relationship with Nelson. She, too, appears to have assumed that Lady Nelson would have as much a part to play in their future as Sir William. Naish quotes a letter from her to Lady Nelson that must have been written during the days after Nelson's departure to Plymouth. It conveys slightly confused messages of friendship:

> I would have done myself the honour of calling on you and Lord Nelson this day, but I am not well nor in spirits. Sir William and self feel the loss of our good friend, the good Lord Nelson. Permit me in the morning to have the pleasure of seeing you and hoping, my dear, Lady Nelson, the continuance of your friendship, which will be in Sir William and myself for everlasting to you and your family. Sir William begs to say, as an old and true friend of Lord Nelson, if he can be of any use to you in his Lordship's absence, he shall be very happy and will call to pay his respects to you and Mr. Nelson, to whom I beg my compliments and to Capt. Nesbit.[3]

[1]The letters to Lady Nelson have already been published by Naish (pp. 618–20). They are inserted here again, not only because Naish did not have the originals at his disposal, but mostly because reproducing them together with those to Lady Hamilton, allows the tracing of Nelson's emotional state at the time.

[2]Now part of Torquay.

[3]Naish, p. 562, where no manuscript source is given.

No messages from Lady Nelson to Lady Hamilton from this period have come down to us.

Nelson was now apparently busy taking up his post in Plymouth. For some days he did not write any letter to either of the two women. The silence was broken by two letters on consecutive days to his wife. They contain nothing but complaints, if not reproaches, about the bad state in which his luggage had been packed and sent [57 and 58, of 20 and 21 January]. The second letter was followed by one to Lady Hamilton, commenting: 'I have not got I assure you scarcely a comfort about me excapt the two chairs, which you ordered of Mr: Foxhall[1] I have wrote her a letter of truths about my outfit' [59]. In this letter Nelson first mentions 'Mrs Thomson'. This fictitious lady was in love with an equally fictitious junior officer on board Nelson's ship. Although her uncle (read: Sir William Hamilton) and his aunt (read: Lady Nelson) stood in the way of them marrying, Nelson sometimes referred to Mrs Thomson's lover as 'Mr Thomson' [first in a deletion in 59]. Mrs and 'Mr' Thomson's relationship was to increase in intensity after the birth of their daughter (read: Lady Hamilton and Nelson's daughter).[2] Otherwise Nelson's letter to Lady Hamilton contains gossip and overall it is written in a slightly incoherent manner.

After another two days of not writing to either of the two women, a flow of letters to Lady Hamilton followed. The numbers alone are telling: eleven letters to Lady Hamilton in as many days [60–70], then, on 3 February, one rather cold letter to his wife [71], followed by thirty-five letters to Lady Hamilton written within twenty-one days [72–106], at the end of which, on 24 February, Nelson sent a harsh message to his wife (probably after an earlier similar message)[3] and spent three days

[1]Foxhall was a merchant or producer of furniture; in an undated list of what Nelson had 'laid out for Sir William' (BL Eg 1614 f. 13), the amount of £350 is mentioned as having been given to 'Mr: Foxall for furniture'.

[2]Horatia Nelson Thomson (1801–81).

[3]Nelson referred to this letter: 'I had a letter from thet person at Brighton saying she heard from my Brother thet I was ill + offering to come and nurse me but I have sent such an answer thet will convince her she would not be received I am almost afraid you will think I have gone too far for she must see there is some strong reason, but my intentions are in every thing to give you satisfaction, therefore do not be angry for the strength of my letter' (Doc. No. 95 and again Doc. No. 105). Lady Nelson copied it out in a letter to Alexander Davison (1750–1829) of 24 Feb 1801: 'I have received Your letter of the 12th: I only wish People would never mention My Name to You, for wether I am blind, or not, it is nothing to any person, I want neither nursing, or attention, And had You come here, I should not have gone on shore nor would You have come afloat. I fixed as I thought a proper allowance to enable You to remain quiet, and not to be posting, from one end of the Kingdom to the other, Wither I live, or die, am sick or well I want from no one, the sensation of pain or pleasure, And I expect no comfort till I am removed from this wold']

in London with his lover and their child. The eleven letters written between 24 January and 3 February to Lady Hamilton at first appear to continue in the same vein as the preceding letters to her after he had left London. Nelson reported professional matters, conveyed gossip and gave accounts of how he was fêted. An emotional bond was at first most strongly expressed in worries about postal matters, which – technical as they may appear – convey an urgency to stay in touch [60]. A closing line to his 'dearest friend' and a note about how 'uneasy' Mrs Thomson's friend was 'about her' [60 and 61] merely indicated deeper feelings. Nelson's letter of 25 January then showed an emotional reaction to the 'truly kind and friendly letters' from Lady Hamilton. He described his 'friendship' to her being 'as fixed as Mount Etna, and as warm in the inside as that mountain'. After some naval news and a disparaging remark about his wife ('she is a great fool and, thank god! you are not the least bit like her') Nelson continued to write about the anxieties of Mrs Thomson's friend [62]. On the following day, in anticipation of their child's birth, he remembered her birthday 'this day nine months'. He started to worry about her meeting the Prince of Wales[1] and assured her of not socialising himself [63]. The following letters continued to deal with worries about how to arrange for post to be sent, complaints about health problems with his eye, assurances of lack of contact with other females and of the importance of Lady Hamilton to him [64–67]. After having learned of the birth of his daughter, Nelson burst out emotionally in his letter of 1 February 1801: 'I believe poor dear M^rs^. Thomson's friend will go mad with joy. He cries, prays, and performs all tricks, yet dare not shew all or any of his feelings'. Nelson by now had sailed in the *St Josef* to Torbay, where he received orders to move his flag to the *St George* and 'go forth as the Champion of England in the North' [68]. While Nelson waited for the *St George* to arrive, postal arrangements and assurances of affection dominated the next few letters [68–70].

. . . Lady Nelson wrote on Tuesday, 24 Feb 1801, to Alexander Davison about this letter: 'I beg you will candidly give me your opinion of the following extract. "I have received Your letter of the 12th: I only wish People would never mention My Name to You, for weither I am blind, or not, it is nothing to any person, I want neither nursing, or attention, And had You come here, I should not have gone on shore nor would You have come afloat. I fixed as I thought a proper allowance to enable You to remain quiet, and not to be posting, from one end of the Kingdom to the other, Weither I live, or die, am sick or Well I want from no one, the sensation of pain or pleasure, And I expect no comfort till I am removed from this World" 17th of Feby I received this on Saturday [21 Feb 1801] You may suppose the consternation it threw me into . . .' (NMM, DAV/2/30)

[1] George Augustus Frederick (1762–1830), to become Regent in 1811 and King George IV in 1820.

On 2 February, one day after having learned of the birth of his daughter by Lady Hamilton, Nelson received a letter from his wife, to which he answered a day later, hypocritically assuring her: 'it never was my intention to find [fault]', continuing: 'but the fact is I have nothing'; he went on to give an extensive list of practical worries supposedly caused by his wife's inefficiency [71]. On the following day Nelson again took up his correspondence with Lady Hamilton, though with much increased frequency. The thirty-five letters Nelson wrote to Lady Hamilton until their meeting in London on 24 February reflect the strain he felt because of the insecurity of their common future, both emotionally and socially. Nelson commented on relatively few political or naval events [72, 83 and 85] and professional matters usually circle around the question of when he might get leave to go to London [75, 91, 95, 97, 101 and 104–106].[1] Close to the English coast, but still separated from Lady Hamilton, much of his thoughts were taken up with how to send letters to his lover, how to make sure her letters would reach him, and to explain when weather conditions would not allow for the sending of any messages [72, 73, 76, 77, 79, 84, 86–88, 91, 94, 95, 97 and 101–104]. The fact that these rather technical issues were recurrent themes indicates the main concern of Nelson's letters, which was to keep in close connection with Lady Hamilton and to confirm as well as stabilise their relationship. At first, in direct reaction to the news of the birth of his daughter, Nelson's thoughts circled around the provisions of a will that would provide for his child as well as her mother [72 and 73]. In the draft he intended for Lady Hamilton, 'a pattern for all wives + mothers', 'to have the full power of naming any child she may have In or out of wedlock' [73]. This appears to have been, in the opinion of Lady Hamilton, too outspoken, so that Nelson assured her, twelve days later, that he had 'burnt the memorandums of my will', but went on to suggest new plans for his will [95]. Nelson also pondered the christening his daughter [74 and 75] or rather not yet [76], but assured Lady Hamilton that 'Mrs Thomson's friend' 'submits himself to your prudence' [76]. He felt sorry about Lady Hamilton's troubles 'about the nurse' [75] and frequently expressed his love or sent his blessings for his 'godchild' [90, 91, 94, 95, 100, 102 and 103], 'a love begotten child' [102].

Nelson had to remain in Torbay, so that no major naval tasks prevented him from worrying about his personal future. He pondered the conflicting interests of love and duty, which he tried to reconcile in a letter to

[1]An exception to this rule are Nelson's worries about his case against St Vincent in Docs Nos 56, 65, 77 and 95.

Lady Hamilton: 'You are so true and loyal an Englishwoman thet you would hate those who would not stand forth in defence of our King Laws Religion and all which is dear to us' [77]. More than by his own absence, Nelson was worried by the presence of other men in Lady Hamilton's company. Thoughts that other men might be interested in Lady Hamilton and concerns that she might not be as interested in him as he in her plunged him into doubts and led to outbursts of jealousy [72, 78, 93, 97, 98 and 102–105; particularly 92, 96]. Nelson regarded Sir William Hamilton as responsible for exposing his wife to ruthless admirers, particularly the Prince of Wales [72, 78 and 103]. Such fears appear to have been – at least partly[1] – nourished by Lady Hamilton herself. From his reply to one of her letters we can assume that Lady Hamilton had informed Nelson about being pursued by different admirers. He responded: 'you try to irritate me', an attempt to which he reacted with some jealousy, but also with the appeasing comment: 'Let us be happy, that is in our power' [86]. In two other letters Nelson expressed dismay at Lady Hamilton's having written a 'truly unkind' letter [82 and 83]. It would be interesting to know what made Lady Hamilton's letter so 'truly unkind'.

In order to understand what might have made her a difficult correspondent at this time, just remember her situation. She had given birth to her lover's child, while still living with her husband in rented accommodation without a clear prospect of settling down anywhere, let alone with her lover. As can be seen from the 'Thomson letters' there was an agreement between her and Nelson that the true character of their relationship was to be kept secret. It may even be assumed that this secrecy was more important to her than to him, as her social standing was much more precarious. Her apparent reaction to Nelson's draft of a will [commented on in 95] indicates that Nelson's outspoken wording – even though meant to be to her advantage – rather worried her. Nelson himself appears to have been aware of her wariness when he wrote about a letter to his wife: 'I am almost afraid you will think I have gone too far for she must see there

[1]Sir William Hamilton appears to have had his own part in the matter, too. The day before Nelson wrote Doc. No. 103, Sir William wrote to him: '... we have been drawn in to be under the absolute necessity of giving a dinner to ***** on Sunday next. He asked himself; having expressed his strong desire of hearing Banti's and Emma's voices together. I am well aware of the danger that would attend ****** frequenting our house. Not that I fear, that Emma could ever be induced to act contrary to the prudent conduct she has hitherto pursued; but the world is so ill-natured, that the worst construction is put upon the most innocent actions. As this dinner must be, or ****** would be offended, I shall keep it strictly to the musical part; . . . In short, we will get rid of it as well as we can, and guard against its producing more meetings of the same sort. Emma would really have gone any lengths, to have avoided Sunday's dinner. But I thought it would not be prudent . . .' (1814-letters, ii, pp. 200–201).

is some strong reason' [95]. Nelson apparently assumed that separating openly from his wife would not benefit Lady Hamilton, as it would cause a scandal that would have repercussions on her reputation. It appears that Lady Hamilton, not seeing a possibility of living with Nelson, demanded that Nelson would not socialise with other women, to which he repeatedly assured her: 'I shall religiously stay on board, as you like me to do so, and I have no other pleasure' [86; similarly, 83, 91 and 101]. On a more practical level news from Nelson were not always comforting. He frequently complained about conditions on board his ship and described himself as a 'miserable fellow shut up in wood' [85; similarly, 79, 80 and 86].

The strain on their relationship was intermittently relieved, so that expressions of bliss were expressed on both sides. Two undated letters at the beginning of February focus on expressing love ['thou art present ever to my eyes', 80] and promising a joint future ['instantly . . . come and marry you', 81].[1] Nelson's two letters to Lady Hamilton of 12 February [84 and 85],[2] when he had just transferred from the *San Josef* to the *St George*, were calm and full of declarations of affection. Moreover, when he was cut off from receiving letters for two days in mid-February, Nelson wrote in a relaxed and rather matter-of-fact vein [88, written on 15 and 16 February]. When he finally received letters from Lady Hamilton again, he was made 'happy' by them and, though he had many other letters to answer to, he elaborated on some postal issues, disparaged certain women whom he might come across, and even composed a poem [89], including a note to Mrs Thomson [90].

Such indications of an apparent calming of their relationship are misleading, however. In between his rather relaxed correspondence Nelson had to deal again with an unsettling letter from Lady Hamilton, to which he sent a lengthy reply [86]. After learning that he was to be 'destined for the north' [91 of 16 February 1801], while still off Torbay, Nelson suffered a severe bout of jealousy that took five days to dissipate [92, 93, 96–98 and 102–105 of 17 to 22 February 1801]. Even these expressions of emotional upheaval were interspersed with moments of apparent relief: 'Forgive every cross word. I now live.' [97 of 19 February] and many assurances of affection [99–103 and 105]. Lady Hamilton, in the meantime, appeared keen to keep up her correspondence, since she even 'commissioned' her husband to send a note to Nelson, 'to tell you that she is much better – having vomited naturally'.[3] On the same day,

[1]See also Docs Nos 73, 76 (remembering time spent in Naples: 'ah those were happy times') and 78.

[2]Doc. No. 85 cannot be dated with certainty.

[3]1814-letters, ii, p. 205 (letter of 20 Feb).

20 February 1801, Lady Hamilton, still in bed, found enough energy to write a lengthy letter to Sarah Nelson, the wife of Nelson's brother, the Reverend William.[1] Strengthening her links to Nelson's family to the disadvantage of her lover's wife, she protested that 'from the moment we met our souls were congenial not so with Tom tit [read: Lady Nelson] for their was an antipathy not to be described'; and concluded: 'tom tit might go to the devil for what I care'.[2] Nelson's suffering was to be cured by knowing that he was about to see Lady Hamilton again and his 'godchild' for the first time. Leaving for London, he wrote to 'Mrs Thomson': 'Poor Thompson seems to have forgot all his ill health and all his mortifications and sorrows in the thoughts that he will soon bury them all in your dear dear bosom he seems almost beside himself' [106].

Nelson flew to Lady Hamilton, at whose place he arrived on 24 February in the 'morning by seven o clock'. He appears to have been so 'beside himself' as to forget that a few days ago his wife had offered to 'nurse him and . . . to do everything . . . to please him'.[3] According to Lady Hamilton, writing rather triumphantly to Sarah Nelson: 'tom tit does not come to town she offer'd to go down but was refused'.[4] Nelson's refusal was contained in a rather harshly worded letter [107], written the same day. It is not clear, whether Nelson had seen his daughter by then, but all his other movements were meticulously recorded in letters that Lady Hamilton wrote to Sarah Nelson. He used the second day of his stay, 25 February 1801, to go to the Admiralty, 'coming Back to Dinner with Morice his Brother, whom he brings with him + Trowbridge also'.[5] Next day Sarah Nelson was informed that they had 'had a pleasant evening', that they 'supped + talked politicks', finishing in real time:

> oh my dearest friend our dear Lord is just come in he goes off tonight + sails emediatly my heart is fit to Burst quite oh whot pain god only knows I can only say may the alllmighty god bless prosper + protect him I shall go mad with grief oh god only knows whot it is to part with such a friend such a one we were truly call'd the tria juncta in uno for Sir W. he + I have but one heart in 3 bodies my beloved friend I can only

[1] William Nelson (1757–1835).

[2] BL, Add. MS 34,989, ff. 36–37 (also: Naish: p. 577).

[3] She wrote to Davison on 20 Feb: 'My affection My anxiety My fondness for him all rushed forth and I wrote to him on last Wednesday Week and offered to nurse him and that he should find me the same I had ever been to him faithful, affect. and desirous to do everything I could to please him, to this letter which was directed at Torr Bay, I have had no answer' (NMM DAV/2/29).

[4] BL, Add. MS 34,989, ff. 38–39 (also: Naish, p. 578).

[5] BL, Add. MS 34,989, ff. 40–41.

say god bless you he our great nelson sends his love to you give mine to Mr Nelson my grief will not let me say more heavens bless you amen

Your aflicted Emma Hamilton[1]

Nelson felt much the same, writing on his arrival at Portsmouth: 'Parting from such a friend is literally tearing one's own flesh' [108]. The encounter, emotional as it was, appears to have been reassuring on the whole, as Nelson put it: 'my very short trip to London has, if possible, given me an additional confidence' [110]. Separation appears to have been no less painful to Lady Hamilton, of whom a farewell poem survives [109]. Nelson continued for a while to write at least one letter a day, but – though emotional – elements of jealousy and disparaging of other women diminished [see minor passages in 110–113, 116, 119 and 121]. Instead Nelson wrote of their 'dear child' or rather his 'godchild' [108 and 110–113, but then only again in 119] and gave constant assurances of his affection for Lady Hamilton. These appear to have been reassuringly mutual: 'I must naturally be happy thet Your affection is such as You describe and so exactly a counterpart of my own feelings' [110]. The friend of Mrs Thomson felt 'sorry that she was a little unwell when he was in London as it deprived him of much pleasure but he is determined to have full scope when he next sees her' [110] and Nelson himself admitted more openly in another letter: 'Would to God I had dined alone with you. *What a desert we would have had*' [111]. When he felt free to write a letter to his 'own Dear Wife' (read: Lady Hamilton), he planned to go with their 'dear little child' to Bronte, where he assumed their marital status would not matter, because he still thought that 'it would bring 100 of tongues and slanderous reports if I seperated from her [read: Lady Nelson]' [112].

In addition to the repeated assurances of affection to Lady Hamilton [also in 113–116] other people were mentioned in Nelson's letters to Lady Hamilton. Although he warned that she would find his brother William 'a great bore at times', he appears to have been pleased that Lady Hamilton got on well with his brother's wife, Sarah, and that his lover thus established contact with his family [110, 114 and 116].[2] He also started to write about naval matters and to report on officers under his command [108, 111 and 114]. While his relationship to Lady Hamilton was still socially fragile, it did begin to stabilise as Nelson became more active in his profession again. On 3 and 4 March 1801 he sailed to the

[1]BL, Add. MS 34,989, ff. 42–44 (extract in: Naish, p. 579).

[2]The new connection between the two women is borne out by Lady Hamilton's letters to Mrs. Nelson (BL Add. MS 34,989, ff. 47–48 and 49–50).

Downs, when he appears to have come to a decision about his private affairs. On 4 March he sent his wife what she called 'my Lord Nelson's letter of dismissal'. He coolly stated what arrangements he had recently made for her son, Josiah, then went on that 'whether I return or am left in the Baltic' it was his 'only wish . . . to be left to myself' [117]. Having thus dismissed his wife from his life, he went on to settle matters, by setting up his will on 5 March [118], adding a first codicil a day later [120]. In both cases he dutifully provided for his wife, while bequeathing specific, valuable items to Lady Hamilton. In doing so, he probably still assumed that Lady Hamilton would be provided for by Sir William Hamilton or by a state pension as his widow.

Before leaving the Downs for Yarmouth (now: Great Yarmouth), Nelson suggested a meeting there with Sir William and Lady Hamilton [119]. Sir William, however, declined the invitation as he was 'now totally occupied in preparing for the sale of my pictures, and what I have saved of my vases', and Lady Hamilton, still 'not quite free from bile',[1] could not respectably do the trip on her own. Nelson's passage to (Great) Yarmouth extended by calm weather, with snow and rain, 'from what is often done in fourteen hours to three days' [119]. At least he was consoled on the way by receiving letters from Lady Hamilton, which were 'the comfort of my life' [121 and 122]. Off Yarmouth, Nelson joined his commander-in-chief, Sir Hyde Parker[2] [121 to 123], but it appears that the two men did not meet in person, though Nelson at least made sure Lady Hamilton knew that Sir Hyde's young wife, whom he 'saw for a moment' was 'skinny and may be called ugly'. Nelson stubbornly stayed aboard the *St George* in order not to alarm Lady Hamilton: 'Sir Hyde wanted me to dine with him to day or to morrow my answer was My ship was my home' [122]. Nelson had just repeated his plan to go with Lady Hamilton to Bronte 'to part no more' [122], when he received another attempt from her to make him jealous: 'Your letters to-day have made me miserable; there is a turn in them that I have noticed, it almost appeared that you liked to dwell on the theme that that fellow wished, and what he would give, to enjoy your person' [124]. This setback did not prevent him from dreaming: 'we will take our fill of love. No, we never can be satiated till death divides us' [125]. A day later he was rewarded with a letter that gave him 'infinite satisfaction': 'and believe me, my feelings and affections keep pace with yours', although this did not quench his jealousy: 'My blood boils' [126]. This emotional rollercoaster would

[1] 1814-letters, ii, pp. 207 and 209 (letter of 7 Mar 1801).
[2] Sir Hyde Parker (1739–1807).

reach calmer waters after Nelson sailed eastward with Sir Hyde Parker's fleet, into the rough wintery North Sea.

Nelson himself had contributed to Sir Hyde being ordered to sail by informing Troubridge at the Admiralty about the delay in leaving.[1] Not surprisingly the cooperation with his commander-in-chief did not begin promisingly and, four days after having sailed from Yarmouth, Nelson complained to Troubridge that he was 'yet in the dark, and . . . not sure we are bound to the Baltic'.[2] In any case, Nelson's mind was increasingly busy with naval matters which was reflected in his correspondence with Lady Hamilton. He had already mentioned his movements, when sailing to the Downs and to Yarmouth [114 and 121] as well as mentioning to her when he was expecting to sail from Yarmouth [123]. The day before actually sailing thoughts of his child and traces of jealousy were intermingled with plans for the campaign to come, questions of patronage and other naval matters [127 and 128]. Two undated letters, that appear to have been written about the same time, focus on their child and their future as a family, with Lady Hamilton as his 'heaven-given wife' [129 and 130]. The day after sailing Nelson offered solace to his lover by stating that it was 'duty to our country' that made them both suffer: 'In the cause of our country You have sent your dearest friend and I have left mine'; promising: 'but never mind Nelson will be first if he lives, and you shall partake of all his glory' [131]. During three of the following four nights he dreamed of Lady Hamilton, plagued by jealousy [131, parts of 14 and 16 March, and 133]. He was keen to get his will, that he had already made on 5 March, signed and sent to Davison[3] [131], which he managed on 16 March, together with the first codicil of 6 March and a second codicil of 16 March [118, 120 and 132]. Having settled his bequests he elaborated on the naval and political situation relating to Denmark in an unprecedentedly lengthy passage [131], so that it appears that Lady Hamilton's description of them talking 'politicks' in London for the first time finds a reflection in one of Nelson's letters. Nelson continued such reports [133, 135, 136, 139 and 140, up to the Battle of Copenhagen] and declared explicitly how he appreciated Lady Hamilton's interest and analytical ability in such matters:

> these Ideas my sensible friend the vicinity of Denmark naturally gives rise to, and I let them out to you as one of the most sensible women of the age and if I was to add of men to[o] I should be more correct, your beauty which I own is beyond thet of all other women is still below

[1]Knight, pp. 360–61.
[2]Knight, pp. 364–5.
[3]Alexander Davison (1750–1829), Nelson's prize agent after the Battle of the Nile (Knight, p. 631–2).

thet of your understanding, for I believe that either Johnson[1] or Burke[2] would be struck with your excellent writings, and both these rare and most extraordinary qualifications are almost eclipsed by your goodness and gentleness of heart, there you shine with unequalled lustre the first make you the Envy of all the women ~~+ age~~ in this world (your wisdom they do not envy your for they know not the worth of it [...])' [136]

The increasing frequency and length of political news in Nelson's letters to Lady Hamilton coincided with a constant awareness of death, which he used to express in the final lines of his letters, such as 'your friend till death' [134 and 136–140]. The possible finality of anything he was writing and doing also appears to have induced him to burn Lady Hamilton's letters, 'although it goes to my heart' [139]. Tenseness of style gave way to elation after Nelson had had his conversation with Sir Hyde Parker on 23 March 1801 and as the battle was approaching.[3] Nelson now even joked that a poet friend of Lady Hamilton's should not get into 'too great a hurry with his songs, I beg we may deserve them first'; and two days later: 'I must have done for breakfast is waiting. and I never give up a meal for a little fighting' [both in 139].

The prospect of action appears to have released an enormous amount of energy in Nelson. On 30 March he had confessed himself 'tired' [140] and after the Battle of Copenhagen, on 2 April 1801, he noted in the evening: 'I have scarcely slept one moment from the 24th: of last month' [141]. The stress caused by preparing and leading through the battle, however, kept Nelson going long enough to enable him to write an account of it on the evening after the battle. In its immediacy this account conveys an authentic picture of Nelson's view of the battle, including the concession that the 'cessation of hostilities' was 'not very inconvenient to me as the Elephant had run on shore alongside a 74 and two or three floating batteries' [141]. Nelson's amazing outburst of energy culminated in the composition of a poem that summarised in eighteen lines how his 'guardian angel' (read: Lady Hamilton) supported him on his path to fame. Two corrections in one line appear to prove that the piece was indeed composed on the spot [141]. The extreme strain on Nelson had taken its toll, however, as he only wrote the next surviving letter to Lady Hamilton

[1] Samuel Johnson (1709–1784).

[2] Edmund Burke (1729–1797).

[3] For Nelson's accounts of this report see his reference to it in a letter to Sir Hyde Parker (1739–1814) himself (Nicolas, iv, pp. 295–8) and his letter to Davison (BL Egerton 1614, ff. 30–31).

three days later. In reporting on the negotiations he had conducted after the battle with the Danes ashore, he mentioned a Danish captain who had been 'at Naples [and] enquired kindly after you and Sir Willm: he had often been at your house' [142]. In expressing his impatience at the slow advance of his negotiations he took Lady Hamilton to be his kindred spirit: 'we Mediterranean people are not used to it' [143]. After another three days of silence, Nelson resumed his fairly detailed reports to Lady Hamilton of his negotiations, interspersed with declarations of love for her and their child together with hopes of retiring to Bronte [144–151].

The period from 15 April until the beginning of June was overshadowed by ill health. In his letter of 8 June 1801 Nelson summarised: 'I may now tell you that I have been since April 15th: rapidly in a decline'; acknowledging, however, that her letters helped him to recover [175]. Mentions of this 'decline' of his health can be found in several letters to Lady Hamilton during this period. Ill health is a recurrent theme in his letters, particularly from the end of April onwards [155, 156, 159, 163 'it is downright murder to keep me here', 164 'I did not [...] come to the Baltic with a design of dying a natural death', 166 'after 17 days not out of my cabbin', 167, 168 and 169], culminating in asking why no admiral was sent to supersede him: 'unless it is wished to kill me; for a pistol put to my head would be charity to keeping me here dying a lingering death' [172]. As Nelson had learned of the death of Paul I of Russia, who had been the driving force behind the 'Armed Neutrality of the North' that Nelson had been sent to break, there was no reason for further action and the conclusion of peace appeared imminent [146, 151, 161]. Accordingly, Nelson's impatience to get home or to Bronte increased [152–155, 157, 159, 163–167, 170, 172, 173 and 176] and his accounts of the current naval and political situation became less frequent and less detailed [151, 162, 165, 169–171, 174 and 176]. Instead, Nelson had time to contribute to his public image.

He had learned that the armistice he had concluded had been criticised at home as a ruse de guerre. This induced him to write a letter on 8 May 1801 to 'My dearest friend' (the way of address he used at the time for Lady Hamilton) in which he explained that 'humanity' had been his driving force. At the end of this letter Nelson asked her to 'get M^{r}: East or some other able man to put these truths before the Public' [160, manuscript kept at the British Library]. On the same day, he wrote another note on the same subject, this time without addressing it explicitly to Lady Hamilton, but sending 'best regards to Sir William + all our friends, to my Brother M^{rs}: Nelson +^{c}: Hardy Colonel + Stewart[1] desire their remembrances' [161], so that it can be assumed that this note, too, was meant

[1]William Stewart (1774–1827), had cooperated with Nelson at the siege of Calvi.

for Lady Hamilton.[1] Together with this second document the Huntington Library keeps a secretary's copy of both documents, which added the headline 'on the armistice' to the second document and omitted the greetings at the end of both documents. To this secretary's copy Nelson added the date, the expression 'rue [*sic*] de guerre' and a personal note to Lady Hamilton at the end [also 161]. Both documents, the letter in the British Library [160] and the note in the Huntington Library [161] in Nelson's handwriting, or a secretarial copy of the two, were then, together with an introductory letter, also sent to Addington, the then Prime Minister, omitting the closing remarks, but maintaining the address to 'My dearest friend'.[2] It is intriguing to think that Nelson originally wrote a declaration of such political importance to his lover as his moral judge at home [see also 158], rather than to the politician to whom he had to explain his actions. Just to make absolutely certain that his motivation for the flag of truce would be understood, Nelson added a remark to the same effect to another letter to Lady Hamilton, also written on 8 May 1801 [163].

He was trying to ensure that her importance to him was being noticed by the people around him. On her birthday he 'invited the Admirals, and all the Captains who had the happiness of knowing' her 'to assist at the fete of Santa Emma' [153]. Those who did not know Lady Hamilton were made to admire her portrait [170 and 171], while he himself preferred to remain unseen [166]. Particularly in May, during his illness, he does not appear to have felt very self-assured. He thanked Lady Hamilton for not having scolded him in her letters and pleaded: 'for God [*sic*] sake do not scold me' [158 and 159], as he was 'a for~~xx~~lorn outcast except in your generous soul' [169]. With hardly any traces of jealousy left after mid-April [only 154 and 157], declarations of love, nostalgia for 'happy times' together and hopes for a joint future with his mistress were recurrent themes in the letters written during his period of ill health [152–154, 157, 159, 164, 166, 169, 175]. At least in one letter he also worried about her [164].

The few letters he wrote to Lady Hamilton between his recovery (8 June 1801) and his return to England were dominated by frustration at the lack of information [176], hopes of returning to England [176], pleasure at the news of being superseded [177 and 178] and the announcement of his arrival in Yarmouth [179].

[1]An indication that Nelson may have had (also) the prime minister in mind is the use of the word 'you' in the following context: 'all political subjects were left for the discussion of the ministers of the two powers – Peace Denmark could not in the moment make with you, as the moment she made it with you, she would lose . . .'.

[2]Nicolas, iv, pp. 359–61.

53. *To Lady Nelson*

[Huntington: HM 34039]

Southampton
Jan^{ry}: 13th: 1801

My Dear Fanny

We[1] are arrived and heartily[2] tired, so tell M^{rs}: Nelson, + with kindest regards to my father and all the family Believe me Your aff^{te}:

Nelson.

54. *To Lady Hamilton*

[NMM: AGC/18/26]

Axminster
Jan^{ry}: 14th: 1801.
8 o'clock

My Dear Lady Hamilton,

We sett off from Southampton at 8 oclock this morning and got to Mr. Roses[3] at ½ p^{t}: 9, but found him gone to London therefore I had my trouble for nothing but the pleasure of trying to serve my brother,[4] Anxiety for friends left and various workings of my imagination gave me one of those severe pains of the heart that all the windows were obliged to be put down the carraige stop'd and the perspiration was so strong that I never was wetter, + yet dead with cold however it is gone off + here I am and while I live your affectionate

Nelson.

I find the same crowds + applauses thet you for ever join in. Make my best regards to S^{r}: W^{m}: the Duke[5] Mr. Beckford, + tell Lord W.

[1]Who else?

[2]Separated 'hear=/=tily'.

[3]George Rose (1744–1818), secretary of the Treasury 1783–March 1801; privy councillor from January 1802 and member of the Board of Trade from February 1802; from June 1804 joint paymaster-general and vice-president of the Board of Trade.

[4]In a letter of 29 May 1806 to Haslewood Lady Hamilton wrote about Nelson's brother William: 'He owes all to me for I kept Him + His glorious Brother friends and I had match to do it' (NMM SUT/2).

[5]of Queensberry (William Douglas, 4th Duke of Queensberry, 1725–1810).

Gordon[1] his last verses are perfectly true.[2] My brother desires his regards.

55. *To Lady Nelson*

[Huntington: HM 34040]

My Dear Fanny,

this moment of the posts departure we arrived, Your letters I rec^{d}: this morn^{g}: at Torr Abbey[3] for which I thenk You, I have only time to say God Bless You + my Dear Father + Believe me

Your affectionate

Nelson.

5 oClock, Jan^{ry}: 16th: 1801.

56. *To Lady Hamilton*

[Pettigrew, i, p. 410] January 17th, 1801, Five o'clock.

I write through Mr. Nepean

that this letter may get to you on Sunday.[4]

My dear Lady Hamilton,

I am this moment arrived, and truly melancholy. I feel as if no friend was near me. *How different!* We left Axminster yesterday morning at eight. At Honiton, I visited Captain Westcott's[5] mother – poor thing, except from the bounty of Government and Lloyd's, in very low circumstances. The brother is a tailor, but had they been chimney-sweepers it was my duty to shew them respect. Being dragged out of the town we broke down half-way between that place and Exeter, at five miles from which we were met by the Devon Cavalry Volunteers, and escorted into

[1]Lord William Gordon (1744–1823).

[2]In the postscript to his letter of 21 Jan 1801 (Doc. No. 59), Nelson probably again refers to this poem: 'pray send me the last lines wrote by Lord W^{m}: Gordon + 'Henrys anchors fixed in . . . heart'.

[3]Home of St Vincent; Torre Abbey is now part of Torquay.

[4]18 Jan 1801.

[5]George Blagden Westcott (1753–1798); fell at the Battle of the Nile where he was in command of the *Majestic*.

the town, through which we were dragged to the hotel, where the Foot Volunteers met us. The rest of the parade was exactly like Salisbury.[1] At half-past four arrived at Torr Abbey. The Earl[2] received me with much apparent cordiality, and we parted this morning good friends; but not a word of prize-money, which I certainly will not give up.[3] I will write you fully to-morrow, but the post is almost gone. May God bless my dear friend, and believe me ever your

Nelson

Best regards to Sir William.

57. *To Lady Nelson*

[Huntington: HM 34041] Jan^{ry}: 20th: 1801.

My Dear Fanny,

All my things are now breaking open for only one key can be found, my steward says I have no one thing for comfort come, but a load of useless articles from Burgess's and a large chest of Green Tea, I have been buying a few things just to make me <u>un</u>comfortable for in fact I have nothing useful but two chairs, 100 £ I have paid for carraige 20 £ would have bought more then I could want from M^{r}: Burgess. I know not where I shall be in a week, with my kindest regards to my father + M^{rs}: Nelson I am Your affectionate

Nelson.

[1] *The Times*, 24 Dec 1800, had reported about the event: 'Lord Nelson accompanied Sir W. and Lady Hamilton on their visit to M. Beckford at Fonthill. On arriving on Saturday [20 Dec] at Salisbury, they were met at the verge of the county near Winterflow Hut, by some Gentlemen of the Corporation and escorted in from thence by the Salisbury troop of Yeomanry Cavalry. The party alighted at Mr. Alderman James Goddard's, in the Market–place, from whence Lord Nelson walked to the Council Chamber and, being introduced to the Mayor, his Worship presented his Lordship the copy of his Freedom, emblazoned on vellum, decorated with the Arms of the City and those of the Hero . . . enclosed in a box of English Heart of Oak, carved with naval trophies . . . The noble Admiral made a short reply to the Mayor, expressing the great happiness he felt, in hearing that his efforts against the common enemy met the approbation of his countrymen, and particularly in that testimony or it, by which he was enrolled among the freemen of Salisbury. From Salisbury Lord Nelson and his party proceeded to Fonthill. The cavalry escorted them out; but when a short distance on the road, his Lordship addressed the officers, thanked them for the honour the corps had done him, requested they would take no further trouble, and politely bade them adieu. . . .'. Similar reports were published in *The Morning Chronicle*, 24 Dec 1800, and *Gentleman's Magazine*, 71 (1801), 206–8.

[2] of St Vincent.

[3] This refers to the court case Nelson had with St Vincent; for details, see fn. to Doc. No. 65.

58. *To Lady Nelson*

[Huntington: HM 34042] Jan^y: 21 1801

My dear Fanny, Cap^n: B. tells me You have changed your house[1]

Half my wardrobe is left behind and thet Butler a French rascal ought to be hanged and I hope you will never lay out a farthing with M^r: Burgess, had the Waste of Monny [*sic*] been laid out in Wedgewoods ware knives forks for servants or cooking utensils it would have been well, but I am forced to buy every thing even a little Tea for who would open[2] a large chest, In short I find myself with^t: any thing comfortable or convenient, In glasses of some kind the steward tells me he finds a useless quantity[,] of decanters as yet not one can be found, and if He cannot find them today I must buy, In short I only regret thet I desired any person to order things for me, I could have done all in Ten minutes and for a 10 part of the expense, but never mind I can eat of [*sic*] a yellow ware plate, It is now too late to send my half ward robe, as I know not what is to become of me nor do I care. My Brother is very well + desires his regards [as] I to M^rs: Nelson. Yours truly Nelson.

59. *To Lady Hamilton*

[BL: Egerton 1614 ff. 14–15, no. 8] January 21st: 1801.

My Dear Lady Hamilton,

It is a dreadful rainy day, and the ship cannot be got out of the harbour, therefore letters will certainly find me here till Monday[3] that is you may safely write till Saturday,[4] I have not got I assure you scarecly [*sic*] a comfort about me[5] excapt [*sic*] the two chairs, which you ordered of M^r: Foxhall I have wrote her a letter of truths about my outfit,[6] You ought to have receiv'd a letter on Sunday[7] it was put under cover to M^r: Nepean and was with him on Sunday morn^g: with one for

[1]This remark appears to have been inserted later, as it is written on top of the page into a small space.

[2]Inserted.

[3]26 Jan 1801.

[4]24 Jan 1801.

[5]Inserted.

[6]See above.

[7]18 Jan 1801.

her, I well knew your friendly anxiety ab^{t}: my arrival + I had no other way of your getting a letter on Sunday, You are my Dear friend always like yourself, and your goodness to poor dear M^{rs}: Thomson is a proof of it no person feels like you, poor Nile was bought at a large Dog shop in Holborn, M^{r}: Davison was with me, Those active dogs will not do for the house if he is not found and you buy another do get a more domestick animal, I sincerely hope thet your very serious cold will soon be better,[1] I am so much interested in your health + happiness that pray tell me all, I delivered to Mr. ~~Thompson Mrs.~~[2] — M^{rs}: Thomsons message + note he desires me poor fellow to say he is more scrupulous than if M^{rs}: T. was present he says he does not write letters at this moment as the object of his affections may be unwell and others may open them not that he cares only for her sake, I have refused to dine with Lady Louisa Lennox[3] although she is 65 and very much the looks of a Gentleman but fame says our Ad^{l}:[4] is attentive he is about the same age [+]one[5] Leg, – the persons desires me to tell you for M^{rs}: T^{s}: information thet every letter is burnt, and to beg her to be assured of his sincere regard + true affection.

You have had a large party does [*sic*] Ladies J. Halliday + Rodney take after their amiable mamma,[6] but I am sure you will not ape their Manners, for yours are compleat perfection, Yesterday there being no port I thought one of the longest days I ever past, with my best regards to Sir W^{m}: the Duke M^{rs}: Dennis[7] +c +c[8] Believe me as Ever my dear Lady your fast + unalterable friend

Nelson + Bronte.[9]

[1]Reference to Lady Hamilton's confinement.

[2]'Thompson M^{rs}:' appears to be washed away with water. The letter is continued in the next line.

[3]Louisa Conolly, née Lady Louisa Lennox (1743–1821).

[4]Nelson was at this time under the orders of Earl St Vincent, who at that time was 65 years of age, but had no reputation as a womaniser.

[5]At the beginning of this word Nelson appears to have changed a letter; it is not clear what this phrase is supposed to mean.

[6]Elizabeth and Louisa-Martha (1748–1814), the eldest two of the three daughters of John Stratford, 3rd Earl of Aldborough (d. 1823) and his wife Elizabeth Hamilton, had married John Halliday, later Tollemache, and John Rodney (son of George Bridges Rodney, 1st Baron Rodney) respectively.

[7]Mrs. Denis was a singer (Flora Fraser, *Beloved Emma. The Life of Emma Lady Hamilton* (London, 1986, p. 288).

[8]Not '+^{c}:'.

[9]This appears to have been the first time Nelson signed a letter 'Nelson + Bronte'. Naish, p. 573, fn. 3, explains: 'Nelson did not use his foreign title of Bronte in England until he had received royal licence to do so'.

pray send me the last lines wrote by Lord W^{m}: Gordon + 'Henrys anchors fixed in Σ[1] heart[2]

60. *To Lady Hamilton*

[Pettigrew, i, p. 414] Jan. 24th, 1801

My dear Lady Hamilton,

No orders to man my San Josef; therefore, instead of being paid this day as I wished, it will be Monday.[3] They are not so active at the Admiralty as I am. Your letters of Thursday[4] are this moment arrived, for which I sincerely thank you. I will, if possible, write to Admiral Man,[5] who has the regulation of appointing Lieutenants, requesting him to give Mr. Champion a good frigate. If I could take him I would on your recommendation. This day has made me a freeman of Plymouth. I will send you the address tomorrow, as my frank will not send free of postage the Exeter occurrence and Plymouth.[6] Miss Troubridge is our friend's sister, about fifty-five, pitted with the small-pox, and deafer by far than Sir Thos. T. Respect to him, and his having prepared his house for me made it proper. Mrs. K. I met in her walk, but should have called, as she is a near relation of hers, and known to me for eighteen years. Write to Brixham, as I directed, to the care of Troubridge, and if any alteration should take place respecting myself, I will write him what to do with my letters. May the heavens bless and preserve my dearest friend, and give her every comfort this world can afford, is the sincere prayer of your faithful and affectionate,

Nelson and Bronté.

Send the letter to Admiral Man, and give it to Mr. Champion.

[1]Here Nelson made a horizontal zig-zag movement in the shape of a mirror-image Sigma or laying M (with its top turned to the right), which is continued downwards with what can be interpreted as 'ton'.

[2]This poem is also referred to in letter of 14 Jan 1801 (Doc. No. 54).

[3]26 Jan 1801.

[4]22 Jan 1801.

[5]Robert Mann (c. 1748–1813).

[6]See p. 15.

61. *To Lady Hamilton*

[Pettigrew, ii, p. 645] [1]

Pray tell Mrs. Thomson her kind friend is very uneasy about her, and prays most fervently for her safety.

62. *To Lady Hamilton*

[Jean Kislak: 1993.151.00.0004] January 25th: 1801,

My dear Lady Hamilton,

If You'll believe me, nothing can give me so much pleasure as Your truly kind and friendly letters, and where friendship is of so strong a cast as ours, it is no easy matter to shake it, mine[2] is as fixed as mount Etna and as warm in the inside as thet mountain, the Audacious Gould will be paid off tomorrow, and he bears the talking of Miss Knight with good humour he has enquired where she lives, he is not grown much wiser since we left him or he never would have wished to leave such a Ship + Ships Company, I am quite vexed ~~xx~~[3] not to have[4] orders for compleating the San Josefs complim^ent[5] of men, or to proceed to Sea, therefore I shall certainly not be at Torbay on Wednesday,[6] I shall write to Troubridge this day to send me Your letter which I look for as constantly and with more anxiety than my dinner, let her[7] go to Briton[8] or where She pleases I care not She is a great fool and thank God You are not the least like her, I deliver'd poor M^rs: Thomsons note her friend is truly thankful + grateful for her kindness and Your Goodness,[9] who does not admire Your benevolent heart, poor man he is very anxious and begs you will if she is not able, write a line just to comfort him[10] he appears to me to feel very

[1] According to Pettigrew (ii, p. 645) this was written 'on the 24th'.

[2] Here Nelson had apparently first written 'my is' and then changed the 'y' into 'ine', which ends below the 'is'.

[3] Here a short insertion is crossed out.

[4] The 'e' at the end of 'have' has disappeared under an ink blot.

[5] The letters 'ent' are written above the 'm' in order to fit into the line at the right-hand margin of the page.

[6] 28 Jan 1801.

[7] Most probably a reference to Lady Nelson, who was then heading for Brighton.

[8] *Sic*, see also Doc. No. 71.

[9] There is another ink blot above the letter 'n'.

[10] Inserted.

much her situation, he is so agitated and will be so for 2 or 3 days thet he says he cannot write and that I must send his kind love and affectionate regard.

What dreadful weather we have got a deep snow I wish I was just setting off for Bronte I should then be happy, as I cannot now sail before Thursday[1] You may direct Your letter on Tuesday[2] to me at Plymouth and if ever so ready will not sail 'till the post is arrived, on Wednesday[3] direct to Brixham as I mentioned before, and Believe me as Ever Your obliged attatched + most affectionate[4] Friend

Nelson + Bronte

My Brother is as vexed as I am and fears he shall lose his trip to Torbay, I should have lived on board before but as the ship[5] will be paid tomorrow I hope to get on board on Tuesday,[6] I hate Plymouth I shall write every day

63. *To Lady Hamilton*

[*a)* Pettigrew, i, pp. 416–17, and ii, 645;
b) Morrison, ii, p. 109 (No. 503); *c)* Christie's,
3 Dec 2003, lot 134] [*c)*] January 26th: 1801.

My Dear Lady Hamilton when I consider that this day nine months was Your birth day and thet although we had a Gale of Wind, Yet I was happy, and Sung come cheer up fair Emma, +c +c'.[7] even the thoughts compared with this day makes me melancholy, my heart some how is sunk within me I long to hear you are well keep up Your Spirits all will end well the dearest friends must part and we only part I trust to meet again, I own I wonder thet Sir Wm: should have a wish for the Prince of

[1] 29 Jan 1801.
[2] 27 Jan 1801; the letters 'ay' are written onto the empty page 3.
[3] 28 Jan 1801.
[4] The letters 'nate' are written onto the empty page 3.
[5] Nelson had hoisted his flag on board the *San Joseph* on 17 Jan 1801, but was to shift it to the *Saint George* in Torbay on 12 Feb1801, before leaving for the Baltic.
[6] 27 Jan 1801.
[7] This song to the tune of 'Heart of Oak' was 'addressed to Lady Hamilton on her Birthday, April 26th 1800, on board the Foudroyant, in a gale of wind, by Miss Ellis Cornelia Knight'; for the text, see Appendix 4.

Wales to come under Your Roof, no good can come from it, but every harm, You are too beautiful not to have enemies and even one visit,[1] will stamp you as his chère amie and we know he is dootingly [*sic*] fond of such women as Yourself, and is without one [*b)*] spark of honour in those respects, and would leave you to bewail your folly. But, my dear friend, I know you too well not to be convinced you *cannot be seduced* by any prince in Europe. You are, in my opinion, the pattern of perfection. I have no orders, and can have none before Wednesday, therefore sooner than Thursday or Friday[2] the ship cannot move. I have told my brother of your intentions of giving him a paste.[3] He would have had a hard matter to get one of mine. He proposes, if no orders arrive very soon, to leave me, when I shall instantly return on board. I feel no loss in not going to these balls and assemblies. My thoughts are very differently engaged. I know nothing of my destination more than I did when in London, but the papers and reports of my being to be put in a bad ship which, although I can hardly credit, fills me with sorrow, which joined to my private feelings, makes me this day ready to burst every moment into tears. I will try and write to the Duke to-morrow; this day I could not if millions lay in my way. Mrs. Thomson's friend is this moment come into my room; he desires me to thank you for your goodness to his dear friend. He appears almost as miserable as myself. He says you have always been kind to his dear Mrs. T. ; and he hopes you will continue your goodness to her on this trying occasion. I have assured him of your innate worth and affectionate disposition: and believe,[4] as ever and for ever, your [*a)*] attached and truly affectionate friend, NELSON AND BRONTE.

[*b)*] My best respects to Sir William, M[rs] Denis, &c. &c.

[1] *Sic*, a comma here.

[2] 29 or 30 Jan 1801.

[3] Portrait medallion (probably of Lady Hamilton). Such jasperware medallions were modern variants of antique cameos (such as the Portland vase that had belonged to Sir William Hamilton), made fashionable by James Tassie in the late eighteenth century.

[4] Pettigrew, ii, p. 645, has here 'he lives'.

64. *To Lady Hamilton*

[Pettigrew, i, p. 417] January, 27th 1801.

My dear Lady Hamilton,

I have got so dreadful a cold in my good eye, that it is all I can do to see a word I write, and I am anxious and uneasy till you can tell me some news of our dear Queen. Her situation at this distressing time fills me with apprehension. I pray God she may get well through it. Troubridge will send me your letter to morrow. Hardy was with me this morning, and I delivered him your regards. * * *[1] I cannot, my dear friend, see a word, therefore must finish, and only beg you to believe me to be, &c. &c.

Nelson and Bronté

I dine quiet at home with an old purser, seventy years of age. I refuse all invites except the Commissioner[2] and Admiral[3] – these I cannot get off.

65. *To Lady Hamilton*

[Monmouth: E 91] Jan^{ry}: 28th:

What a fool I was my Dear Lady Hamilton to direct thet your cheering letters should be directed for Brixham I feel this day[4] truly miserable in not having them and I fear they will not come till tomorrows post, what a Blockhead to believe thet any person is so active as myself I have this day got my orders to put myself under Lord S^{t}: Vincents command, but as no order is arrived to man the ship it must be friday night or Saturday morning[5] before she can sail for Torbay, direct my letters now to Brixham, my Eye is very bad I have had the Physician of the Fleet[6] to examine it[7] he has directed me not to write, (and yet I am forced this

[1]Marked thus by Pettigrew; in vol. ii, p. 646 he writes, referring to Doc. No. 63: 'On the 27th, he writes in a similar strain, and requests her "to do everything which was right."'

[2]Charles Saxton (1732–1808); commissioner of the navy at Portsmouth from 1789 until 1806; DNB: 'a low-profile commissioner who disliked administrative innovations'.

[3]Earl St Vincent.

[4]Inserted.

[5]30 or 31 Jan 1801.

[6]Dr. Thomas Trotter (1760–1832).

[7]Inserted.

day to write Lord Spencer[1] S^{t}: Vincent, Davison about my lawsuit,[2] Troubridge, M^{r}: Locker[3] +^{c}: but you are the only female I write to), not to eat any thing but the most simple food, not to touch wine or porter to sitt in a[4] dark room to have green shades for my Eyes, will you[5] my Dear friend make me one or two nobody else shall, and to bathe them in cold water every hour I fear it is the writing has brought this complaint my Eye is like blood and the film so extended thet I only see from the corner farthest from my nose, what a fuss about my complaints but being so far from my sincere friend I have leisure to brood over them,

I have this moment seen M^{rs}: Thomsons friend poor fellow he seems very uneasy + melancholy he begs you to be kind to her, and I have assured him of your readiness to relieve the dear good woman, and Believe me for Ever my Dear Lady your faithful attatched + affectionate

Nelson + Bronte.

I will try + write the Duke a Line, my Brother intended to have gone off tomorrow afternoon but this half order may stop him

66. *To Lady Hamilton*

[BL: Egerton 1614 ff. 16–17, no. 9] Jan^{ry}: 29th: 1801.

I have this moment my Dear Lady receiv'd your truly kind letter sent to Brixham on Monday and also yours of Tuesday, which I shall reply to in rotation, You may tell Lord Abercorn[6] that His Eleve M^{r}: Sotherby [*sic*] if he comes in my way may be sure of my assistance the lad really without a compliment to parental feelings deserves it, but you can answer there is not the smallest probability of my going to the Mediterranean.

[1]George John Spencer, 2nd Earl Spencer, (1758–1834); brother of Georgiana, Duchess of Devonshire, and Lady Bessborough ; 1st Lord of the Admiralty 17 Dec 1794 until Feb 1801.

[2]Nelson had a dispute about prize money with St Vincent concerning ships taken in Oct 1799, when Nelson was temporarily commander-in-chief in the Mediterranean and St Vincent was in England. The legal proceedings are analysed in: Grahame Aldous QC, 'Lord Nelson and Earl St Vincent: Prize fighters', *The Mariner's Mirror*, 101:2 (May 2015), 135–155; a less detailed account is: Denis Orde, 'Nelson Goes to Law', *The Nelson Dispatch*, vol. 12, part 1, Winter 2015, 39–46.

[3]John Locker (d. 1843), third of Captain William Locker's five children (Nicolas, i, p. 23).

[4]Inserted without arrow from below.

[5]Written above the letter 'm'.

[6]John Hamilton, 1st Marquess of Abercorn (1756–1818).

Mr: S. is quite right thet thro' the medium of your influence is the surest way to get my interest, it is true and it will ever be whilst you hold your present conduct, for you never ask any thing that does not do honor to your feelings as the best woman as far as my knowledge goes that ever lived, and it must do me honor the complying with them, My Dear Lady old Daton is a chattering old fool what would the world say if you flirted it away with every coxcomb, all would despice [*sic*] you as they now envy you, for what can they say only thet you are kind and good to an old friend with one arm a broken head + no teeth, the Good must love you and I trust I am amongst the foremost if not the very first, The Princess C.[1] is not very wise and my Dear friend if you was to sett your understanding against her she would fall, and she ought to know by this time thet to gain my good will is not to neglect you, as for 'tother proud — she is ignorant of any thing like good manners, I go to the watering place if I do without your[2] consent May God inflict his punishment, I cannot serve God + Mammon. I long to get to Bronte for believe me this England is a shocking place a walk under the chesnut trees although you may be shot by a Banditti is better than to have our reputations stubbed in this Country. I have this day orders to be completed to my compliment [*sic*] of men, and could you think it possible with the very worst men in this port, not one seaman, do the superiors think thet my Name is a host of strength, or do they wish to see the San Josef only equal to other ships, but Hardy and myself will work and have her superior – Nelson shall be first, Let jealousy cabal + art. +c +c +c If the present Gale abates thet the people can be got on board tomorrow she shall sail on Saturday[3] for Torbay therefore my Brother has consented to stay with me. The Physician[4] has just been with me and has enjoin'd me not to touch wine + yesterday not even porter went near my mouth to my great mortification, he recommends if I had time an operation but all must wait till a peace with kindest regards to Sir Wm: Believe me Ever your faithful

Nelson + Bronte

Pray tell your friend Mrs: Thomson that I have deliverd her note to her friend and he desires me to say . . . your goodness, how sensible he is of her kindness as the very particular business he is engaged upon will not

[1]Castelcicala?
[2]Inserted.
[3]31 Jan 1801.
[4]Thomas Trotter.

be over for two or 3 days he defers answering her not till thet time,[1] what a hard case these poor peoples is but between your unpar[al]elled goodness and my attention I hope they will yet be happy and comfortable In my opinion neither of them can be happy as they are, may the Great god of Heaven protect comfort and assist you is the fervent wish of may Dear Lady once . . .[2]

Your affectionate friend

Nelson + Bronte

67. *To Lady Hamilton*

[Pettigrew, ii, p. 646][3]

Pray, tell your friend, Mrs. T., that I have delivered her note to her friend; and he desires me to say, through your goodness, how sensible he is of her kindness. As the very particular business he is engaged upon will not be over for two or three days, he defers answering her note till that time. What a hard case these poor people's is! But, between your unparalleled goodness and my attention, I hope they will yet be happy and comfortable. In my opinion, neither of them can be happy as they are. May the great God of Heaven protect, comfort, and assist you, is the fervent wish of, my dear Lady, ever your affectionate friend,

Nelson and Bronté.[4]

68. *To Lady Hamilton*

[Jean Kislak: 1989.037.00.0001] San Josef Torbay Feb^ry^: 1st: 1801.

My dear Lady,

I believe poor dear M^rs^: Thomsons friend will go mad with Joy, he cries prays and performs all tricks Yet dare not shew all or any of his feelings he has only me to consult with, he swears he will drink Your

[1]The words 'till that time' are inserted.

[2]After the word 'once' the paper was torn at opening the letter. Probably it read originally: 'once again'.

[3]Pettigrew introduced this letter: 'On the 29th:'.

[4]According to Pettigrew, ii, p. 646, this was written 'on the 29th'.

health this day in a Bumper, and damn me if I don't Join him in spite of all the doctors in Europe for none regards You with truer affection than myself, You are a dear good creature and Your kindness and attention to poor M^{rs}: T. stamps You higher than ever in my mind, I cannot write I am so agitated by this Young Man at my Elbow I believe he is foolish he does nothing but rave about You + her. I own I partake of his Joy and cannot write any thing, The San Josef left Plymouth Yesterday at 1 of clock + anchored here at 8 this morning where I found an order to hoist my flag in the S^{t}: George, as Lord Spencer says I must go forth as the Champion of England in the North, and my San Josef is to be held by Captain Wolseley[1] of the S^{t}: G^{e}: till my return when I hope to have a knock at the Republicans, in this instance they have behaved handsomely[2] could not be better, I trust I shall soon be at Portsmouth and every endeavour of mine shall be used to come to Town[3] for 3 days, + perhaps You + Sir William may like to ~~share~~ see Portsmouth, Capt: Darby[4] is just come in he desires me to say every thing which is kind and thet he wishes he could see you instead of Your picture which I have handsomely framed + glazed, the post is waiting + I have been 2 hours pulling from L^{d}: S^{t}: Vincents house[5] [It] is blowing fresh, may the heavens Bless You + Yours is the fervent prayer of Your unalterable and faithful

Nelson and Bronté.

best regards to Sir William,[6] Instead of under Cover direct as follows.

Lord N – + + +
to the care of Sir Thos: Troubridge B^{t}:
Brixham
Devon
which will give them to me 4 hours sooner.

[1]William Wolseley (1756–1842), 'Acting-Captain of the San Josef', which – according to Nelson in a letter to St. Vincent of 20 Feb 1801 – he neglected, leaving to 'attend his dying wife' (Nicholas, iv, p. 287).

[2]The word 'handsomely' stands at the end of a line.

[3]London.

[4]Henry D'Esterre Darby (d. 1823) had been with Nelson at Palermo (see introduction to Chapter I), so that it can be assumed that Lady Hamilton knew him personally.

[5]St Vincent had a house near (now in) Torquay: Torr[e] Abbey.

[6]After this phrase Nelson left the centre of the page empty, as it was the third page and likely to be torn on opening.

69. *To Lady Hamilton*

[Huntington: HM 34078] San Josef Feb^{ry}: 2nd: 1801.

My Dear Lady, All Your letters are so good so kind so like Yourself, thet had not Your last been so excellent and even far excelling all the others I should not have known which to have Selected, I have cut out two lines and never will part with them, I have no letters as yet to day except the return'd one from Plymouth therefore I shall not close this 'till after post is arrived I dined yesterday with Troubridge Darby Hardy my Brother + Parker,[1] who all drank a bumper to your health and I sett all the Doctors at Defiance 'till my Brother said I should hurt myself, and M^{rs}: Thomsons friend drank two because he said you had been so kind to his dear friend who he loved more than life such is the power of good + generous actions they do good to the doer + the receiver, I live entirely on board as the Ship is by Hardys excellent arraingements more comfortable than other ship[s] I have seen, I wish from my heart I could have Sir William + You on board, then indeed I should be truly happy I have this moment receiv'd Your letter of Saturday[2] + my brother is sorry Your have not been well but thanks You for having sent for Charlotte,[3] I rejoice to hear You say You are better I am afraid it was Your last going out with me + walking across M^{r}: Daniels Damp Yard, but pray my Dear friend get better I cannot bear the thoughts of Your being Sick, especially for Your goodness to me, I can only beg you to believe my friendship will do as much in return, only recollect the old nurses advice Nurse a Cold, Starve a fever, therefore pray be sure + nurse yourself If I was Sir William You should not get out of bed for a week nor out of the house for a fortnight, You ought to follow my advice as you know how exactly I follow Yours when I am sick.

Ever yours Nelson and Bronté.

that friend of our dear M^{rs}: T^{s}: is a good soul + full of feeling he wishes much to see her + her little one, if possible I will get him leave for two or 3 days when I go to Portsmouth and you will see his gratitude to You.

[1]Edward Thornborough Parker (1780–1801), at that time captain of the *Medusa*.

[2]31 Jan 1801.

[3]Nelson's niece by his brother William, Charlotte Mary (1787–1873), later Lady Bridport, wife of Samuel Hood, great-nephew of Admiral Sir Alexander Arthur Hood, Viscount Bridport.

The Earl is determined Davison writes me to carry on the law suit + is dreadfully a[1] angry with him for the part he has taken he would have been glad to have left me without a friend, well knowing my ignorance of money matters, may the Heavens bless + protect You my dear Lady and Believe me Ever for Ever Your Sincere obliged + attatched

Nelson + Bronte.

70. *To Lady Hamilton (alias 'Mrs Thomson')*

[Jean Kislak: 2004.006.00.0003][2]

My Dear M^{rs}: Thomson Your good and dear friend does not think it proper at present to write with his own hand ~~at present~~ but he hopes the time is not far distant when he may be united forever to the Object of his wishes, his only only love, he Swears before heaven that he will marry You as soon as it is possible which he fervently prays may be Soon he charges me to say how dear You are to him and that You must every opportunity kiss and bless for him his dear little Girl which he wishes to be called Emma out of gratitude to our dear Good Lady Hamilton but weither its from L^{d}: N^{n}: he says or Lady H. he leaves to Your judgement and choice, I have given Lord N. a hundred pounds this morning for which he will give Lady Hamilton an order on his agents and I beg that You will distribute it amongst those who have been useful to You on the late occasion, and Your friend my Dear M^{rs}: Thomson may be sure of my care of him and his interest which I consider as dearly as my own, and do You Believe me Ever Your most sincere + affectionate friend

Nelson + Bronte

M^{rs}: Thomson

Lady Hamilton must desire at the Back for it to be paid to the person who carries it.

[1]The 'a' appears to have been a first beginning of the word 'angry', which Nelson then decided to write further to the centre of the sheet of paper, thus ensuring that nothing of the text would be lost on being torn open. The seal was eventually placed on the other side of the piece of paper just under the letter 'a'; the paper is however just torn on the opposite side.

[2]Pettigrew, i, p. 647, introduced this letter: 'On the 3rd, though undated:'; Morrison, ii, p. 110, assumed similarly: 'No date (February 3rd, 1801)'.

71. *To Lady Nelson*

[Huntington: HM 34043] San Josef Torbay
febry: 3rd: 1801.

My Dear Fanny

I received Yesterday Your letter from Briton,[1] it never was my intention to find [fault] but the fact is I have nothing and every thing if I want a piece of pickle it must be put in Saucer if a pin of butter or an earthen plate, but I shall direct what things I want in future the stands for the large decanters I thought was to have been repair'd and sent me if they are not I shall desire Hancock[2] to send me two not one thing thet Mr: Dods sent but is ruined large nails drove thro [*sic*] the Mahogany table + Drawers to fasten the packing cases, if they had been sent so to a Gentlemans house + new of course they would have been returned, Mr: D. has only sent 3 keys, of the small table + chest of Drawers not of the wardrobe, Trunk, case of the Turkey cup +: +: by the bye the trident of Neptune is bent double from ill package I have six silver bottle stands but not one Decanter to fit them You told me six of the house ones should be sent, I beg my kindest regards to Josiah + Miss Locker[3] the Ellis's +: and Believe me your affectionate

Nelson

72. *To Lady Hamilton*

[*a)* Pettigrew, i, pp. 421–2, and ii, p. 647;
b) Morrison, ii, p. 111 (No. 507)]

[*a)*] San Josef,
February 4th, 1801.

My dear Lady Hamilton,

[*b)*] It blows so very hard that I doubt if it will be possible to get a boat on shore, either to receive or send letters; but if it moderates in time for the post, of course mine shall go, and I hope from my heart to hear you are better and it[4] has made my head ache stooping so much, as I have been making memorandums for my will, and, having regularly signed it, if I was to die this moment, I believe it would hold good. If I am not able

[1]*Sic*, see also Doc. No. 62, but different from spelling in address!

[2]Referred to in Nelson's letter to Davison of 31 Aug 1801 as 'Captain Hancock, of the Cruizer Sloop' (Nicolas, iv, p. 481).

[3]Lucy or Elizabeth (first and fourth daughters of William Locker).

[4]Pettigrew has here: 'better. It'.

to send it, as far as relates to you, this day, I will to-morrow. I have been obliged to be more particular than I would,[1] as a wife can have nothing, and it might be taken from you by will or the heirs of your husband. If you disapprove of any part say so, and I will alter it; but I think you must approve;[2] I have done my best that you should. I shall now go to work and save a fortune. Say, shall I bequeath the £2000, owing me from Sir William for the same purpose? You must keep this letter till you receive a copy of my m°.[3] What a pretty piece of history[4] letting out the French squadron.[5] I was laughed [at] by some wiseacres[6] in power, when I said if I was a French Admiral I would come out in spite of all the English fleet, as they kept close into Brest, and I would be outside of them before morning. Your dear kind letters of Monday,[7] are just come on board in a shore boat, and I shall try and get mine ashore, but it is barely possible. Sir William should say to the prince that, situated as you are, it would be highly improper for you to admit H.R.H. That the Prince should wish it I am not surprised at, and that he will attempt every means to get into your house and into any place where you may dine. Sir W^m should speak out, and if the Prince is a man of honour he will quit the pursuit of you. I know his aim is to have you for a mistress. The thought so agitates me that I cannot write. I had wrote a few lines last night, but I am in tears, I cannot bear it. Tell Mrs T. her friend is grateful for her goodness, and with my kindest regards to Mrs. Jenkins and Horatia, and ever believe me, your sincere, faithful, and affectionate

[*a)*] [8] Nelson and Bronté.

Make my respects to Sir William, the Duke, and Lord W. Gordon.

[1]Pettigrew has here: 'wished'.

[2]Pettigrew has here: '–'.

[3]Pettigrew has here: 'memorandum'.

[4]Pettigrew has '!' after 'history'.

[5]On 23 Jan 1801, Vice-admiral Ganteaume (Honoré Joseph Antoine Ganteaume, 1755–1818), with seven ships-of-the-line, escaped from Brest without detection and headed south. Like Bruix in 1799, he got into the Mediterranean but took refuge in Toulon instead of taking the clear route to Egypt to land his troops. Eventually he did get as far as the coast of Egypt, but fled at the sight of British sails and achieved nothing. (N. A. M. Rodger, *The Command of the Ocean* (London, 2004) [hereafter: Rodger], p. 466).

[6]Pettigrew has here: 'wise ones'.

[7]2 Feb 1801.

[8]The whole passage from 'Sir William should say to the prince' is not in Pettigrew. Pettigrew, i, p. 422, simply has after 'barely possible.' the finishing line: 'Believe me yours. &c.'.

[a)][1] . . . Make my kindest regards to Mrs. Jenkins and Horatia, and ever believe me,

Yours,
N. & B.

P. S. – We drink your health every day. Believe me your letters cannot be long or too minute of all particulars. My mind is a little easier, having perfect confidence.

73. *To Lady Hamilton (draft of will and letter)*

[BL: Egerton 1614 ff. 18–19, no. 10]

And as Emma Hamilton, the wife of the Right Hon'ble Sir Wm: Hamilton K. Bt: has been the great cause of my performing those services which have gained me honors and rewards I give unto her in case of the failure of male heirs as directed by my will, the entire rental of the Bronte Estate for her particular use + benefit, and in case of her death before she may come into the possession of the Estate of Bronte she is to have the full power of naming any child she may have In or out of wedlock or any child male or female which she the said Emma Hamilton wife of the Rt: Hble: Sr: Wm: Hn: may choose to adopt and call her child by her last will + testament or by deed declaring her Intent and the sword given by H. S. Mty:[2] is to be deliver'd on her coming to the Estate or to the person she may name as directed by my said will, and I likewise give to the said Emma wife of the Rt: Hble: Sr: Wm: Hn: K. Bt: a picture of H. S. Mty: sett in diamonds with the Queens cipher on the opposite side whom God preserve with all the Diamonds which surround it, as it is now lodged in a mahogony [*sic*] Box in the care of Alexr: Davison Esqr: St: James's square London, and I give all my other Boxes lodged in the aforesaid Box at Alexr: Dns: Esqr: in which Diamonds are placed viz one with the portrait of the Emperor Paul of Russia, one of the King of Sardinia[3] and the one said to have been sent me by the mother of the Grand Sign[i]or likewise to the said Emma Hn: wife of Sr: Wm: Hn: K. Bt: to be sold if she pleases and the Income to be for her use during her natural life, and

[1]After 'copy of my memorandum', Pettigrew, ii, p. 647, gave this different end to the letter.
[2]His Sicilian Majesty.
[3]Charles Emmanuel I (1751–1819); reigned 1796–1802.

at her decease it is to be given to a child called[1] in whom I take a very particular Interest and as Emma H^{n}: is the only person who knows the parents of this female[2] child I rely with the greatest confidence on her unspotted honor and Integrity that she will consider the child as mine and be a Guardian to it, shielding it from want and disgrace and bringing it up as[3] the child of her Dear friend Nelson + Bronte, and to this female child, of which Lady Hamilton shall only be the declarer that it is the one I mean I give and bequeath all the money I shall be worth above the sum of Twenty thousand pounds the Interest of it to be received by Lady H^{n}: for the maintenance + education of this female child, the principal to be paid her at the Death of Lady H^{n}: if she has attained the age of 21 years or thet she may marry; the Guardians of my adopted child to be namd by Lady H^{n}: in her will,

Such is [*sic*] my Ideas if you have no objection if you have I will endeavour to alter them to your wishes, I shall now begin and save a fortune for the little one[4]

Thursday[5] noon, I have this mom^{t}: received your letters of Tuesday[6] all that you have been so good as to write me have come safe. I have deliverd the letter to M^{rs}: Thomsons friend and he feels truly grateful for all your affectionate regards to poor dear M^{rs}: Thomson who you say + truly is a pattern for all wives + mothers, I write the note for him as he does not wish his hand to be known at present, We are here all in a bustle from this French squadron having got to sea, so much for our sharp look out, I have letters from Dumouir[7] + Sir B. Boothby.[8] D^{r}:[9] says pay my sincere comp^{ts}: to the Excellent Lord Hamilton + to his incomparable Lady, let her remember[10] the promise she made ~~me~~ to send me the portrait of my D^{r}: Nelson + her own, be so kind as to be the Interpreter of the Barronne [*sic*] de Bearent who pays to her the most tender compliments Sir B. B^{y}: says In the dreary times I have passed here, the passage of your party

[1]Between the words 'called' and 'in whom' Nelson left a gap.

[2]Inserted.

[3]The word 'as' is inserted below the end of the last line of the first page of this document. It is repeated at the beginning of the first line of the next page.

[4]The following letter is written in a much smaller handwriting than Nelson's usual handwriting.

[5]5 Feb 1801.

[6]3 Feb 1801.

[7]Dumouriez: Charles-François du Périer du Mouriez (1739–1823).

[8]Brooke Boothby (1744–1824), linguist, translator, poet and landowner, friend of Rousseau.

[9]Dumouriez.

[10]Inserted.

which I think it would be difficult to match seems like a bright dream in a long night, I beg of your Lordship to present my affectionate regards to Lady H^{n}: (certainly one of the most charming women in the world,) nothing can please me so much as to have Justice done you, Thank God you want not the Society of Princes or Dukes, If you happened to fall down + break your nose or knock out your Eyes you might go to the devil for what they care, but it is your good heart which attaches to you, your faithful and affectionate

Nelson + Bronte[1]

Troubridge desires his best regards so does Hardy, Darby. Signal is just made to sail. Send me back the first half-sheet of paper[2] as it is clearer worded than the original memorandum.

74. *To Lady Hamilton (alias 'Mrs Thomson')*

[Jean Kislak: 1989.037.00.0002][3]

My Dear M^{rs}: Thomson, Your dear and excellent Friend has desired me to say, that it is not usual to X'ten children[4] 'till they are a month or six weeks old, and as Lord Nelson will probably be in Town as well as myself before we go to the Baltic he proposes then if You approve to X'ten the child and that myself + Lady H^{n}: should be two of the Sponsors, it can be X^{t}:ened at S^{t}: Georges Hanover Square and I believe the parents being at the time out of the Kingdom if it is necessary it can be stated born at Portsmouth or at Sea, Its name will be Horatia Daughter of Iohem[5], + ~~Horatia~~ Morata[6] Etnorb,[7] If You read the sirname [*sic*] backwards and take the ~~names~~ letters of the other names, it will make very extraordinary the names of Your real + affectionate friends Lady H. and myself but my Dear friend consult Lady H^{n}: Your friend consults me and I would not

[1]The following postscript is added on the outside of the letter (upside down) on the part that was folded towards the inside on closing the letter, below the space for the address and the seal.

[2]This refers to the draft of a codicil to his will and the beginning of this letter until 'his hand to be known at'.

[3]Referring to Doc. No. 73, Pettigrew, ii, p. 649, stated: 'On this day, also, Lord Nelson writes about the christening of the child:'; Morrison, ii, p. 111, wrote: 'no date (February 5th, 1801)'.

[4]Separated 'chil/dren'.

[5]After the 'name' Iohem follows a blot of ink.

[6]'Morata' is added above the crossed-out '~~Horatia~~'.

[7]'Iohem + Morata Etnorb' is an anagram for 'Emma + Horatio Bronte'.

lead him wrong for the world he has not been very well I believe he has fretted but his spirit is too high to own it, but my Dear Madam both You him + Your little one, must always believe me Your affectionate

Nelson and Bronté.

The child if You like it can be named by any clergyman with[t] its going to church.

75. *To Lady Hamilton (alias 'Mrs Thomson')*

[*a)* Pettigrew, ii, p. 650; *b)* Morrison, ii, p. 113 (No. 510)][1]

[*a)*] My Dear M[rs]: Thomson [*b)*] Your good friend is very much obliged by your kind present of this morn[g]: it is very like what I remember his, he has put it[2] in a case with her dear mothers, for I almost love you as much as he does, he is sorry for the trouble You have had about the nurse but he says[3] children bring their cares and pleasures with them; but, however, you will rely on Lady Hamilton, her goodness and good advice cannot be too closely followed; she is the pattern I wish you to imitate. Respecting the naming and christening of the child he wrote to Lady Hamilton yesterday. He hopes to get leave for three days to come to town when the ship gets to Portsmouth. Ever your [*a)*] friend and unalterable friend,

N. & B.

76. *To Lady Hamilton*

[Houghton: MS Lowell 10]

San Josef
feb[ry]: 6th: 1801

It blows a Gale of Wind but which only affects me as it may deprive me of my Dear and much honor'd friends letters, Your letters are to me Gazettes for as yet I have not fixed upon any nor ~~th~~ can they be half so interesting to my feelings although you know I am not a little fond of a newspaper and we have often almost quarrelled for a first reading and I

[1]In referring to Doc. No. 74, Pettigrew, ii, 650, assessed that this letter was 'apparently written on the next day' (6 Feb 1801); Morrison noted: 'no date (February 6th, 1801)'.
[2]Pettigrew (ii, pp. 650) assumes that Nelson had received 'a portion of the child's hair'.
[3]Of this first passage there is also a transcript in Christie's 20 June 1990-sale, lot 225.

trust the time will soon arrive when we shall have those amicable squabbles again. I am now of course very much by myself for none ever come to me except at meals or I send for either Hardy or Parker and they are both so modest + well behaved thet it is really a pleasure to have them on board, Parker boast[s] whenever he drinks Your health which is at least once a day, thet he had the honor of being Your Aid de camp and thet he has given many messages by Your orders, ah those were happy times, would to God we were at this moment in the Bay of Naples and all matters for those good monarchs going on as well as it did at that time[1]

Noon this moment has brought me Your two kind letters You may rely I shall not open my mouth on poor dear M^{rs}: Thomsons business to any creature on this earth, You and I should be very unworthy if we did any such thing as[2] all the secret of these two people rests solely in our bosoms, He desires me to say thet he approves very much of the sum of money and submits it to your discretion if a small pension should not be promised if the secret is well kept, but desires thet nothing should be given under handwriting,[3] He also desires You will now and then give the nurse an additional guinea. He thinks it might be better to omit Xtening the child for the present, and even privately baptizing it the clergyman would naturally ask its parents names which would put poor dear M^{rs}: T. in some trouble or cause suspicion, but in all this matter he submits himself to Your prudence + friendship he will send You more money as M^{rs}: T. wants it only let him know every thing, He says poor fellow he would have given any thing to have seen the child especially in Your charming company, to say the truth this Lad seems to love you not a little but who does not I am sure I do, Capt: Williams nephew conducts himself very well and I shall take him into the S^{t}: George with me for which ship Capt: Hardy has got his commission but she is still at Portsmouth,[4] Saturday[5] noon, M^{r}: Davison came whilst I was at dinner yesterday + gave me Your letter, he says you are grown thinner but he thinks You look handsomer than Ever I know he is a very great admirer of Yours, he says You told him to tell me not to send You any more advice about seeing comp^{y}: for thet You are determined not to allow the world to say a word ag^{t}: You, therefore I will not say a word I rest

[1]This refers to the events in late June and early July 1799, when Nelson, accompanied by Lady Hamilton as his interpreter, helped to retake Naples for the royalists.

[2]Here Nelson first wrote 'all', but then wrote a bold 's' over the 'll'.

[3]'writing' is inserted.

[4]Continued on the same line.

[5]7 Feb 1801.

confident in your conduct I was sure you would not go to Mrs: Walpoles[1] it is no better than a Bawdy house, this morning brought me Your letter of Thursday,[2] I am sorry for all Your trouble but poor Mrs: Thomsons friend will never forget the obligation. Ever my Dear Lady Yours affectionately + for Ever amen

Nelson + Bronte

77. *To Lady Hamilton*

[CRC/28]

San Josef
Febry: 8th: 1801

My Dear Lady,

Mr. Davison demands the privilege of carrying back an answer to your kind letter and I am sure he will be very punctual in the delivery, I am not in very good spirits and except thet our Country demands all our services + abilities to Bring about an honorable peace nothing should prevent my being the bearer of my own letter, but my dear friend I know You are so true and loyal an Englishwoman thet you would hate those who would not stand forth in defence of our King Laws Religion and all which is dear to us, It is Your sex that make us go forth, and seem to tell us, none but the Brave deserve the fair, and if we fall, we still live in the hearts of those females You are dear to us. It is your sex that rewards us, it is Your sex who cherish our memories, and You my Dear honor'd friend are believe me the first the best of Your sex, I have been the world around and in every corner of it and never yet saw Your equal or even one which could[3] be put in comparison with You. You know how to reward virtue, honor and courage, and never to ask if it is placed in a Prince, Duke, Lord, or Peas~~xxx~~ant, and I hope one day to see You in Peace before I sett out for Bronte which I am resolved to do, Darby['s] is one of the ships sent after the French squadron I shall therefore give the print to Hardy, I think they might come by the mail coach as a parcel wrapt up round a stick any print shop will give you one, and direct it as my letters the coach stops for parcels at the White Bear I believe Piccadilly, pray have

[1]Maria, Countess Waldegrave, née Walpole (1736–1807), the secret wife of Prince William Frederick (1776–1834), son of Prince William Henry, Duke of Gloucester and Edinburgh.

[2]5 Feb 1801.

[3]Inserted.

you got my picture from Mr: Heads,[1] I hope Mr: Brydon has executed the frames to your satisfaction the Bill he is directed to send to me, Only tell me how I can be useful to you and Sir William and Believe nothing could give me more pleasure, being with the greatest truth my Dear Lady Your most obliged + affectionate Friend

Nelson + Bronté.

I am told the moment the St: George arrives thet I am to be tumbled out of this ship as the Ville de Paris is going to Plymouth to be paid, and the Earl will hoist his flag here[2] and if I am as fortunate in getting a fresh painted cabbin (which is probable) I shall be knocked up, at all events I shall be made very uncomfortable by this hurry,

It has been very good and friendly of Mr: Davison to travel upwards of 200 miles to make me a visit, I rather think[3] the Great Earl will not much like his not having called on him but his manner of speaking of Mr: Davison for his friendship to me in the matter of the Law Suit, Lord St: Vincent states to my Solicitors[4] as offensive to him, Why should it,[5] only thet Mr: Davison wishes thet I should have justice done me and not to be overpowered by weight of Interest + money. Once more God Bless You + Sir Wm:

N. & B.

Sir Isaac Heard[6] has gazetted Troubridge's Hoods +c: honors, but has no[t] gazetted mine + he has the Kings order for mine as much as the others[7]

[1]Guy Head (1760–1800); painted Nelson in 1798/99.

[2]This does not appear to have happened; St Vincent accepted the post of 1st lord of the Admiralty on 19 Feb 1801, taking his post with the rest of the cabinet in July.

[3]Inserted; in lighter ink than the surrounding text.

[4]Richard Booth and William Haslewood; for Nelson's cooperation with Booth see: Knight, p. 396, fn.

[5]Inserted, without an arrow from below the line; in lighter ink than the surrounding text.

[6]Sir Isaac Heard (1730–1822); from 1784 until his death senior Officer of Arms of the College of Arms in London.

[7]The honour referred to is the Order of St Ferdinand and Merit. The king's permission to Nelson to accept the dukedom of Bronte and to wear the grand cross of the Order of St Ferdinand and Merit, was not gazetted until 5 Sept 1801, though the royal licence had been granted in Jan 1801. Nelson asked Davison to intervene with Sir Isaac Heard in the post-script to the letter of 28 Jan 1801 (Nicolas, iv, p. cc) and he complained about this treatment in a letter to Addington of 18 July 1801 (Nicolas, iv, p. 424).

78. *To Lady Hamilton*

[Morrison, ii, p. 113 (No. 511)][1]

Mr. Davison will deliver this letter and its enclosure. He is very good and kind to me, and perhaps I can never repay the great and heavy obligation I owe him; but if it pleases God that I should retire into the country, I should not want a carriage, for I can walk, and my affairs would soon arrange themselves. I do not think I ever was so miserable as this moment. I own I sometimes fear that you will not be so true to me as I am to you, yet I cannot, will not believe you can be false. No, I judge you by myself; I hope to be dead before that should happen, but it will not. Forgive me, Emma, oh, forgive your own dear, disinterested Nelson. Tell Davison how sensible I am of his goodness; he knows my attachment to you, and I suspect he admires you himself. I cannot express my feelings. May God send me happiness. I have a letter from Sir William; he speaks of the Regency as certain, and then probably he thinks you will sell better – horrid thought. Only believe me for ever your

79. *To Lady Hamilton*

[Pettigrew, i, p. 423] Feb. 9th, 1801.

* * * The St. George is just arrived, but it blows so strong, and such a heavy sea, that my things cannot be moved, and yet I believe the Earl will order his flag to fly here, which is as much as to say *turn out*. You cannot think how dirty the St. George is compared to my own San Josef, and probably her inside is worse than her outside appearance. Hardy is just come on board. The ship is not fitted for a flag – her decks leaky, and is truly uncomfortable, but it suits exactly my present feelings.

N. & B.

[1]Morrison noted: 'no date (February 8th, 1801)'.

80. *To Lady Hamilton*

[NMM: WAL/1][1]

I may not be able to write to you tomorrow but, thou art present ever to my eyes I see hear no one else Parker sitts next me to cut my meat when I want it done, May God send us a happy meeting I am writing in[2] a room full of interruption therefore give me credit for my thoughts, You can guess them they are I trust like your own,

81. *To Lady Hamilton*

[NMM: WAL/2][3]

Your dear friend my dear and truly beloved Mrs. Thomson, is almost distracted he wishes there was peace ~~of~~ or thet if your uncle[4] would die he would instantly then come and marry you, for he doats on nothing but you + his child, and as it is my God Child I desire you will take great care of it, he has Implicit faith in your fidelity even in conversation with those he dislikes, and thet you will be faithful in greater thing he has not doubt, may God bless you both + send you a happy meeting is the wish of Yours N. + B.

82. *To Lady Hamilton*

[NMM: SUT/2]

San Josef
february 11th: 1801.

My dear Lady,

I was prepared on reading your first letter to have wrote a most affectionate letter but your last has been so truly unkind thet I can only recal [*sic*] to mind it is very easy to find [a] stick if you are inclined to beat your Dog, therefore it is no wonder you should endeavour from every word of mine to find cause for an excuse him who will never forget you

[1]Morrison, ii, p. 113 (No. 512) inserted this letter here in the chronological order of his edition, but merely noted: 'no date (1801)'.

[2]Inserted.

[3]Morrison, ii, p. 113 (No. 513) inserted this letter here in the chronological order of his edition, but merely noted: 'no date (1801)'.

[4]A reference to Sir William Hamilton.

but to the last moment of his existence pray to God to give you happiness and to remove from this ungrateful world your old friend

Nelson + Bronte

I would only [await] your order to write to M[rs]: Denis but you may believe I am too much disordered by the Ingratitude + nonsence of a very old friend.

83. *To Lady Hamilton*

[*a)* Pettigrew, i, p. 424; *b)* Morrison, ii, p. 113 (No. 514)]

[*a)*] Feb. 11th, 1801.
[*b)*] 3 o'clock.

Well, my dear friend, I only wish you could read my heart, then, I am sure, you would not write, or even think a hard thing of me. Suppose I did say that the West-country women wore black stockings, what is it more than if you was to say what puppies all the present young men are? You cannot help your eyes, and God knows I cannot see much. Only *don't admire*, you may detest as much as you please. I am glad you have found out Mrs. Kelly is so handsome; in that case you will give me credit for never going to make her a visit, but to say the truth, I think her quite the contrary: red hair, short, very fair, I believe, but her face beplaistered with red. Respecting Kingsmill's[1] friend, I declare solemnly that I know not if [it] is a man or woman, and could never bear the smallest idea of taking her out to the West Indies. It is now 17 years since I have seen her. I have no secrets, and never had but one, only one, love in my life, and damn me, if I lose her, if ever I well have another, for, let me be ever so much on my guard, she never can be content with me. Few woman, My dear Lady, have your sense to make a good selection and to be sure of your choice, to have implicit confidence in him, and that he is more particular in your absence than in your presence. I am sorry Mr Pitt[2] is out. I think him the greatest Minister this country ever had, and the honestest man. With every affectionate wish, believe me for ever your attached and

[1]Sir Robert Brice Kingsmill (1730–1805) was an old friend from Nelson's time in the West Indies.

[2]William Pitt the Younger (1759–1806); second son of Pitt the Elder (Earl of Chatham), served as Prime Minister of Britain in 1783–1801 and 1804–6; the reason for his resignation in 1801 was that George III would not agree to his plans for Catholic Emancipation; he was replaced by Henry Addington (1757–1844).

affectionate [&c][1] It blows a gale of wind and very heavy sea. If you see Mrs. Thomson, say her friend has been a little fretted at her nonsense, but is better, as he is sure it can only proceed from her affection for him, but he desires me to beg of you to tell her never to harbour a doubt of his fidelity, for that will make him doubt her, and to spit in the face of any one who speaks disrespect of him. Give my godchild a kiss and blessing from me. [*a)*] N. & B.

84. *To Lady Hamilton*

[Christie's sale, November 2014, lot 23] S^{n}: Joseph
1 oClock 1801[2]

My Dear Lady

my letter to You with two others was put into the Post office at Brixham at . . . 2 oClock on Sunday. (I began, wrote under the date + carried upwards) You may open my letter before [the one carried by] M^{r}: Davison, for when I wrote this part I had finished my letter to go by him[3] I have had the mid up to the post and he assures me that he untied the red tape and put the three letters into the post office, I therefore hope it is come to land if not it is intercepted which God knows is of no further consequence than the interruption of a free communication between 2 such dear friends, M^{r}: Thomson s friend desires you will assure her of his inalterable + affectionate regard, and begs she will be assured that all the world cannot either change or make him wish to change for a moment and that he is unalterably hers, Do this my Dear friend for this [*sic*] good young people I really pity them, kiss my God Child and believe me ever Your affectionate

Nelson + Bronte

85. *To Lady Hamilton*

[Pettigrew, i, p. 424] Feb. 12, 1801.

* * * * I suppose all this new Ministry will bring about a peace, or a more vigorous prosecution of the war. If the former, I shall very soon

[1]Inserted by Morrison.
[2]According to Christie's: 'dated on the address panel 12 February 1801'.
[3]End of line.

go to Bronté, and it is odd I have never heard from Graeffer, nor indeed have I wrote. * * The Earl is gone to London to consult, I suppose, with the new Administration. Do not forget me; consider I am a miserable fellow shut up in wood. I cannot get on board the St. George, the sea is so very high.

N. & B.

86. *To Lady Hamilton*

[*a)* Pettigrew, i, p. 425; *b)* Morrison, ii, p. 114 (No. 515);
c) Christie's, 3 Dec 2003, lot 139]

[*c)*] Friday[1] night 9 oclock.

I remember Your story of that M[r]: Hodges at Naples how he used to get suppers at this place and the other + pay for them on purpose for your company but I rest confident You will never admit him to any of your parties, as for the P. of W. I know his character + my confidence is firm as a rock 'till you try to irritate me to say hard things that you may have the pleasure of scolding me but recollect it must remain four days before it can be made up, not as before in happy times 4 minutes, consider my dear friend what You ought to say if I did not fire at Your scolding letters, + suppose me if it is possible for a mom[t] answering your scolds with a joke I know I should fire if I thought that of You, that You was indifferent, but firing like the devil with vexation anger and retorting can only proceed from conscious innocence, I defy the malice of any one, and my mind is as pure as my actions, I never intend if I can help it to set my foot out of the ship but she is so compleatly uncomfortable You can [*b)*] have no conception how miserable she is. By Hardy's account he[2] has been on board two days, endeavouring to make my place a little decent, but it is neither wind nor water tight; but I shall religiously stay on board, as you like me to do so, and I have no other pleasure. I cannot get on board, it blows so very hard, and a heavy sea; all our topmasts struck, and every thing as close as possible. The boat which went to Brixham cannot get off, therefore, if your letters had not been directed to Sir Thomas Troubridge, I should not have had them. I had a letter from Mr. Davison to tell me he had delivered my letter – can you ever scold me again? Recollect

[1]13 Feb 1801; the address panel reproduced in the facsimile of the outside of the letter in Christie's catalogue of 2003 gives the date '15 February 1801'.

[2]Pettigrew, i, p. 425, has here: 'is by Hardy's account. He'.

the answer to this letter is to be marked No. 1, therefore turn over a new leaf. Only rest quiet, you know that everything is arrainged in my head for all circumstances. You ought to know that I have a head to plan and an heart to execute whenever it is right and the time arrives. That person[1] has her separate maintenance. Let us be happy, that is in our power. Do you know how I am amusing myself this evening? Troubridge is gone to bed, and I am alone with all your letters except the cruel one, that is burnt, and I have scratched out all the scolding words, and have read them 40 times over, and if you were to see how much better & prettier they read I am sure you would never write another scolding word to me.[2] You would laugh to see my truly innocent amusement, therefore, again I entreat you never to scold me, for I have NEVER deserved it from you, you know. Troubridge is my guest during the absence of the *Ville de Paris*. He always says 'now[3] comes the fourth & old toast, all our friends – the King – success to the fleet, and, though last, not least, Lady Hamilton.' Then they do as they please. I am certainly much better for leaving off wine. I drink nothing but water at dinner, and a little wine and water after dinner. I believe it has saved me from illness. The smell of the paint has[4] gone. [*c)*] for half a farthing I would advertise him.

Pray tell me if Mr: Nepean sent You directly my letter + Troubridges they were both under the same cover + directed by Troubridge Good night and good night I could say it till to-morrow[5] I wish I was with you, that time shall come,[6]

May the heavens Bless You good night guess what my feelings and thoughts are, Ever for Ever Your attached

Nelson and Bronté.

Sir Isaac Heard has behaved very ill to Me[7]

[1]Lady Nelson.

[2]Christie's catalogue of 2003 renders this passage: 'alone with all your letters except the *cruel* one that is burnt, and I have scratched out all the scolding words and have read them 40 times over and if you was to see how much better and prettier they read I am sure you would never write another scolding word to me".

[3]Pettigrew, i, p. 425, has here: 'says, now' and does not give a closing quotation mark after 'Lady Hamilton'.

[4]Pettigrew, i, p. 425, has here: 'is'.

[5]Inspired by Shakespeare's Romeo and Juliet, act ii, scene ii, lines 185–6, where Juliet takes leave from Romeo, who has entered her family's garden: 'Good night, good night! Parting is such sweet sorrow / That I shall say good night till it be morrow'.

[6]Continued below the address.

[7]See end of Doc. No. 77.

87. *To Lady Hamilton*

[*a)* Pettigrew, i, p. 42; *d)* Sichel, p. 520] [*a)*]Feb. 14, 1801.

[*d)*] I doubt whether a boat can get on shore. But we are going to try. Trowbridge [*sic*] is just come to say it is impossible, therefore you must be content with my assurance that I write every day. Pray send the enclosed to Mrs. Thompson and assure her of my unalterable attachment to her and her friend. I trust my dear Lady to your doing me full justice and to make her dear mind at ease for ever, for ever and ever. Yours faithful . . .

Sunday[1] noon. It continues to blow so hard, and the sea is so very high, that I scarcely expect the possibility of getting a boat with this weather; she would be lost in an instant, [*a)*] The sea has come over the San Josef's forecastle, and in my after-cabin the motion is so great that I cannot sit down. We have only to trust to our cables, for the sea is breaking against the rocks mountains high. Since Friday[2] noon not a boat has been out; [*d)*] but in fair or foul weather, at sea or on shore, I am ever for ever yours, [*a)*] Nelson and Bronté.

88. *To Lady Hamilton*

[Pettigrew, i, pp. 425–6] February 15th, 1801.

My dear amiable friend, could you have seen the boat leave the ship I am sure your heart would have sunk within you. I would not have given sixpence for the lives of the nine men. A tremendous wave broke, and missed upsetting the boat by a miracle. Oh, God! how my heart jumped to see them safe. Then they got safe on shore, and I had given a two pound note[3] to cheer up the poor fellows when they landed, but I was so anxious to send a letter for you. I knew it was impossible for any boat to come off to us since Friday[4] noon, when the boat carried your letters, inclosed for Nepean, and she still remains on shore. The gale abates very

[1] 15 Feb 1801.

[2] 13 Feb 1801.

[3] The Bank of England started issuing paper money shortly after it was established in 1694, but settled two years later, not to issue notes for sums of less than £50. This policy was abandoned due to gold shortage after the Seven Years War, when the Bank started to issue notes of £10. The French Revolutionary War caused shortages of bullion, which made the Bank issue notes of £5 in 1793 and notes of £1 as well as £2 in 1797. Notes were still individually signed, however.

[4] 13 Feb 1801; this is why Docs Nos 87 and 88 were both sent on 15 Feb.

little, if any thing, and it is truly fortunate that our fleet is not in port, or some accident would most probably happen: but both St. George and this ship[1] have new cables, which is all we have to trust to; but I have no fear; I can take all the care which human foresight can, and then we must trust to Providence, who keeps a look our for Poor Jack.

I cannot, my dear friend, afford to buy the three pictures of the Battle of the Nile, or I should like very much to have them, and Mr. Brydon cannot afford to trust me one year; if he could, perhaps I could manage it. I have desired my brother to examine the four numbers of the tickets I bought with Gibbs. I hope he has told you, I dare say in the office. Here are the numbers of the tickets my agents have bought for the ensuing lottery. I hope we shall be successful. I hope you always kiss my god-child for me.

Monday Morning.[2] It is a little more moderate, and we are going to send a boat, but at present none can get to us, and therefore I send this letter to say that we are in being. I hope in the afternoon to be able to get letters, and if possible answer them. Kiss my god-child for me; bless it, and believe me ever yours,

Nelson and Bronté.

89. *To Lady Hamilton*

[NMM: CRK/19/8] San Josef
feb^{ry}: 16th: 1801.

N^{o}: 2.

My Dearest friend Your letters have made me happy to-day, and never again will I scold unless you begin, therefore pray never do, My confidence in you is firm as a rock, and thet you would direct the[3] to be kicked down stairs if he was to offer to make you a visit I wonder at Sir W^{m}: to think of asking such a Wretch to dinner, I cannot imagine who can have stopped my Sunday's letter, thet it has been is clear and the Seal of the other has been clearly opened, but this might have happened from

[1]The *St. Joseph.*

[2]16 Feb 1801.

[3]Here follows a small gap until the end of the line; in the original letter someone has added in pencil: 'Duke of Gloster?', which most probably refers to Prince William Frederick (1776–1834), son of Prince William Henry, Duke of Gloucester and Edinburgh, and his secret wife Maria, Countess Waldegrave, née Walpole (1736–1807), who was to succeed his father William (1743–1805) as Duke of Gloucester and Edinburgh in 1805, rather than to his elderly, but not less promiscuous father (see Doc. No. 218, in which Nelson explicitly refers to the son); though the gap in this letter could also refer to the Prince of Wales.

letters sticking together, Yours all come safe but the numbering of them will point out directly if one is missing I do not think thet any thing very particular was in that letter, which is lost. Believe me my Dear friend thet Lady A. is as damn'd a W—e as ever lived, and Mrs Walpole is a Bawd. M^rs: U.[1] a foolish pimp eat up with Pride thet a P— will condescend to put her to expences, Only do as I do and all will be well, and you will be every thing I wish I thank you for your kindness to poor dear M^rs. Thomson I send her a note[2] as desired by her dear good friend who doats on her, I send you a few Lines wrote in the late gale which I think you will not disapprove, how interesting your letters are you cannot write too much, or be too particular.

Though — s polish'd verse superior shine
Though sensibility grace every line
Though her soft Muse be far above all praise
And female tenderness inspire her lays
  Deign to receive, though un=adorn'd[3]
    By the poetic Art
  The rude expressions which bespeak
    A Sailors untaught heart.
An [*sic*] Heart susceptible, sincere and true
An Heart by Fate, and nature, torn in two,
One half to duty and his Country due
The other better half, to Love and You
  Sooner shall Britains Sons resign
    The Empire of the Sea
  Than Henry[4] shall renounce his faith
    And plighted ~~faith~~ vows[5] to thee
  and waves on waves shall cease to roll,
    and tides forget to flow
  Ere thy true Henrys constant Love,
    Or ebb, or change, shall know.

the Weather thank God is moderating, I have just got a letter from the new[6] Earl at the ad^y:[7] full of comp^ts: but nothing shall stop my Law Suit

[1]Udney? see Doc. No. 96.

[2]See Doc. No. 90.

[3]Nelson appears to have first written 'un=adorned', but then crossed out the 'e' and added the apostrophe.

[4]The name 'Henry' was used as a synonym for a sailor in a poem that Nelson referred to in his letter to lady Hamilton of 21 Jan 1801 ('Henrys anchors fixed in . . .').

[5]'vows' stands above the crossed-out word '~~faith~~'.

[6]Inserted.

[7]St Vincent had been offered the post of 1st lord of the Admiralty, which he accepted on 19 Feb 1801.

and I hope to cast him, I trust when I get to Spithead that[1] there will be no difficulty in getting leave of absence, the letters on Service are so numerous from three days interruption of the Post thet I must conclude with assuring you that I am for Ever Your attached + unalterably Yours

Nelson & Bronte.

I shall begin a letter at night.

90. *To Lady Hamilton (alias Mrs Thomson)*

[NMM: CRK/19/10][2]

I sit down my Dear M^rs^. T. by desire of poor Thomson to write you a line[3] not to assure you of his eternal love and affection for you and his dear child, but only to say that he is well and as happy as he can be seperated from all which he holds dear in this world, He has no thoughts seperated from your love and your interest, they are united with his One fate one destiny he assures me awaits you both, what can I say more only to kiss his child for him and love him as truly sincerely and faithfully as he does you, which is from the bottom of his Soul, he desires that you will more + more attatch yourself to dear Lady Hamilton.

91. *To Lady Hamilton*

[Jean Kislak: 1990.035.00.0001]

3.

Monday night[4] 9 oclock.

My dearest friend I have read all your letters over and over My Brother has a bluntness and want of fine feelings which we are not used to but he

[1]Nelson changed here an 'e' into an 'a'.

[2]1814-letters, I, p. 173, superscribe this letter: 'see letter x. Page 29.' (Doc. No. 89 in this collection).

[3]This appears to be the 'note' mentioned in Doc. No. 89.

[4]16 Feb 1801. Pettigrew, i, p. 426, and Morrison, ii, p. 115, claimed the letter was written on 17 Feb 1801, which was a Tuesday; this confusion of dates appears to have been caused by the date on the outside of the letter; it there bears the date of '17 February 1801', above the address (for the need to write the date on the outside of a letter, above the address, see General Introduction, 'C. Conditions under Which Letters Were Written').

means nothing, I dare say somebody had told him in the Street a squadron of 7 Sail is gone after the Enemy, and they naturally concluded I was sent to say the truth had I been Lord Spencer I should have detatched one Nelson as a much more likely man to come up with the Enemy + to beat them [than] the man they have sent Sir Robt: Calder,[1] but I am destined for the north, unless the Mediterranean command should become vacant in that case I should realize a fortune gain honor and if you came out not return to England for some years but Lord Keith I believe loves the good things in thet station too well, Supposing thet was to happen which is not likely I would take an oath, never to sleep out of the Ship unless absolutely forced by the Impossibility of not [*sic*] getting on board, but at present there is no prospect of my getting money, to the W^{t}: Indies I would not accept a command or to the East was if offered me to morrow altho' it is a sure fortune for I never will be far from you in case my presence should be necessary, Our friend Troubridge is to be a Lord of the ad^{ty}: and I have a Sharp Eye and almost think I see it, No poor fellow I hope I do him injustice he cannot surely forget my kindness to him, when I am at Sea I shall send my packets thro' him, whenever I get to Portsmouth I shall ask for 3 days leave of absence but time must be allowed for the answer and if another ad^{l}: is arrived to take charge of the Ships, which may be assembled, but at the worst my Dear friend can find a very good reason to come + see me altho' it would not be half so satisfactory as my going to see you in London, You cannot think how I long for our little innocent plan to be put in execution I cannot account for your receiving 5 letters in one day it is beyond my comprehension it may be some irregularity in the post office here or the carelessness of the midshipman sent to put them in the office,[2] Yours come perfectly regular + to the time they are wrote, one is lost clearly but I can hardly think by any body near you, it has been in some post office out of curiosity this is my opinion but God only knows, It is now got very moderate but recollect if a Gale of Wind comes from the East to South no boat can live in Torbay, Ah my Dear friend I did remember well the 12th: feb^{ry}: and also the two months afterwards[3] I shall never forget them and never be sorry

[1]Robert Calder (1745–1818).

[2]This letter itself is an example of delays in the post: it was written on Monday, 16 Feb, put into the post by Nelson on Tuesday, 17 Feb, and stamped on the outside on Thursday, 19 Feb, in the post office.

[3]This may refer to 1799 when Nelson was staying with Lady Hamilton at Palermo (until 19 May of that year). Before he had not been with her on any 12 Feb and in 1800 he was just leaving her on that day, sailing with Lord Keith to Malta, staying away for about a month.

for the consequences, Say whatever you please to M^rs: Denis for me,[1] for I fear saying too much, I admire what you say of my God Child if it is like its mother it will be very handsome for I think her one aye the most beautiful Women of the age, Now do not be angry at my praising this dear childs mother for I have heard people say she is very like[2] you, My Dear friend you will I hope never receive any more cross letters but always such as ought to be wrote by my Dear Lady your obliged unalterably attached + faithful

Nelson and Bronté.[3]

I would Steal White Bread sooner than my Godchild should want.

Forgive do You say, That I do from my soul and do you forgive me if I have offended.[4]

92 *To Lady Hamilton*

[Morrison, ii, pp. 116–17 (No. 518)] *San Joseph*, February (17th), 1801

I am so agitated that I can write nothing. I knew it would be so, and you can't help it. Why did you not tell Sir William? Your character will be gone. Do not have him *en famille*, the more the better. Do not sit long at table. Good God! He will be next you, and telling you soft things. If he does, tell it out at table, and turn him out of the house. Do not sit long. If you sing a song, I know you cannot help it, do not let him sit next you, but at dinner he will hob glasses with you. I cannot write to Sir W^m, but he ought to go to the Prince and not suffer your character to be ruined by him. Oh, God, that I was dead! But I do not, my dearest Emma, blame you, nor do I fear your inconstancy. I tremble, and God knows how I write. Can nothing be thought of? I am gone almost mad, but you cannot help it. It will be in all the newspapers with hints. Recollect that the villain said to Mr Nisbet, *how you hit his fancy*. I am mad, almost dead, but ever for ever yours to the last moment, your, only your [&c][5] I could not write another line if I was to be made king. If I was in town, nothing

[1]The letter is continued on the fourth page, upside down, below the address.
[2]Continued above the address.
[3]The postscript is written to the left of the signature.
[4]This sentence is added above a line across pages 2 and 3.
[5]Inserted by Morrison between the surrounding parts of the text that are given in quotation marks.

should make me dine with you that damned day, but, my dear Emma, I do not blame you, only remember your poor miserable friend, that you must be singing & appear gay. I shall that day have no one to dinner; it shall be a fast day to me. He will put his foot near you. I pity you from my soul, as I feel confident you wish him in hell. Have plenty of people, and do not [say] a word you can help to him. He wishes, I dare say, to have you alone. Don't let him touch, nor yet sitt next you; if he comes, get up. God strike him blind if he looks at you – this is high treason and you may get me hanged by revealing it. Oh, God! That I were. I have read your letter, your resolution never to go where the fellow is, but you must have him at home. Oh, God! But you cannot, I suppose, help it, and you cannot turn him out of your own house. He will stay & sup and sitt up till 4 in the morning, & the fewer that stay the better. Oh, God! Why do I live? But I do not blame you; it is my misfortune. I feel nobody uses me ill. I am only fit to be second, or third, or 4, or to black shoes. I want no better part than I have. I see your determination to be on your guard, and am as fixed as fate. If you'll believe me, don't scold me; I am more dead than alive, to the last breath yours. If you cannot get rid of this I hope you will tell Sir William never to bring the fellow again. I send a note for M^{rs} T.

93. *To Lady Hamilton (alias Mrs Thomson)*

[Huntington: HM 34082]

My Dear M^{rs}: Thomson Your most dear friend desires me to say that he sincerely feels for You and thet if Your Uncle is so hard hearted as to oblige You to quit his house thet he will instantly quit all the world and its greatness to live with You a domestic quiet life. Lady Hamilton will always give You good advice + You will always find an affectionate friend In

Nelson + Bronte

Love to my God child.

94. *To Lady Hamilton*

[BL: Egerton 1614 ff. 20–21, no. 11]

San Josef
feb^{ry}: 17th: 1801.

4

My Dear friend the Gale is coming on again but I am going to send our letters on shore but have no expectation of farther communication this day tomorrow I hope it may be better. I send you the numbers of the tickets bought for the next Lottery – 2951, 9308, 42002, 50416, they are quarters – I have not put in for the Diamond I cannot afford it, but never mind Diamonds do not constitute happiness. I expect Troubridge will be ordered to London today he will of course call upon you. I dare not longer defer sending my letter as the wind + sea increases. Tell Sir W^m^: I hope his Treasury business is settled to his satisfaction, M^rs^: Thomsons friend begs you will make his affectionate remembrances and assure her of his eternal love which she conducts herself so well, and Kiss my God child for your Ever faithful affectionate + attatched Nelson + Bronte.

Comp^ts^: to Lord W^m^: + the Duke.[1]

I send you a form for ruling paper to know if letters are missing.

95. *To Lady Hamilton*

[BL: Egerton 1614 ff. 22–23, no. 12] Tuesday night.[2]

5

I have my Dear friend burnt the memorandums of my will and have not yet wrote a word beyond the paper I sent you,[3] Do you approve of that as far as it goes, I know that for your advantage it must be left in trust as a wife can have no property except it be made over by her husband I am not clear how far it is right that a husband should be a Trustee I rather think not, in the next place would you like the Diamonds to be sold for I do not see how Diamonds can be in trust, and if they are not and Sir W^m^: was not to leave them to you His Heirs would have right to them in short it would be giving the Legacy to Him + his heirs – however I will do as you please, or if you leave the matter to me I will do it to the best of my abilities and judgement, The star I shall leave to you not in trust nobody would take that momento [*sic*][4] of friendship affection + esteem from you, May curses light on them if they did, the King's sword I always intended should go with the Dukedom + Estate of Bronte, the aigrette

[1]The following sentence is added in smaller writing than the rest of the letter in the bottom right-hand corner of the page, next to Nelsons signature and the postscript.

[2]17 Feb 1801.

[3]Nelson had sent drafts of a will with his letter of 5 Feb 1801 (Doc. No. 73).

[4]As the 'star' is mentioned together with Nelson's diamonds, it probably refers to the diamond star of the Order of the Crescent that Nelson had received from the Ottoman sultan; see will of 5 Mar 1801. Nelson bequeathed this 'Diamond Star' to Lady Hamilton in his will of 5 Mar 1801 (Doc. No. 118) and again settled the 'diamond star as a token of my friendship and regard' to Lady Hamilton in his will of 10 May 1803 (Doc. No. 259).

also to my heirs as a mem^{o}– thet I once gained a victory,[1] do you approve you are the friend I consult for I know you have my interest at heart, when I may have the inexpressible happiness of coming to London I had better lodge at an Hotel Lothians or any nearer, for recollect I must unless once it may be necessary at Lord S^{t}: V^{ts}: to hold a candle to the Devil however all matters shall be properly settled between us, I had a letter from thet person at Brighton[2] saying she heard from my Brother thet I was ill + offering to come and nurse me but I have sent such an answer thet will convince her she would not be received[3] I am almost afraid you will think I have gone too far for she must see there is some strong reason, but my intentions are in every thing to give you satisfaction, therefore do not be angry for the strength of my letter, It is not my intention to go on shore at Portsmouth but on duty to the admiral and nothing but a gale of wind shall keep me half an hour ashore – you know my word is my bond, I have received the greatest benefit in leaving off wine my sight of the one Eye is certainly much improved and my general state of health better, the boat which carried your letters this morning has not been able to get on board again and it now blows and such a heavy sea that there is no prospect of getting letters tomorrow, but I shall try hard. May the heavens Bless you my Dear amiable good friend and Believe me Ever for Ever your own attatch'd friend Nelson + Bronte Good Night, Good Night may God bless you for Ever remember me most kindly to my Dear M^{rs}: T. be good to her for my sake + kiss + bless my God child for me, Heaven will reward you when you write to the Queen you say I am sure every thing which is proper for me She will be doubtless very useful to both of us –[4]

Wednesday morn^{g}: a little more moderate am going to[5] send this letter and hope to be able to get yours + answer God bless you, N. + B.

N. & B.

[1]As to what became of these articles, see Appendix 3.

[2]Lady Nelson.

[3]Lady Nelson wrote on Tuesday, 24 Feb 1801, to Alexander Davison about this letter: 'I beg you will candidly give me your opinion of the following extract. "I have received Your letter of the 12th: I only wish People would never mention My Name to You, for weither I am blind, or not, it is nothing to any person, I want neither nursing, or attention, And had You come here, I should not have gone on shore nor would You have come afloat. I fixed as I thought a proper allowance to enable You to remain quiet, and not to be posting, from one end of the Kingdom to the other, Weither I live, or die, am sick or Well I want from no one, the sensation of pain or pleasure, And I expect no comfort till I am removed from this World" 17th of Feby I received this on Saturday [21 Feb 1801] You may suppose the consternation it threw me into . . .' (NMM, DAV/2/30).

[4]The letter is continued in the same line!

[5]The rest of the letter from here on is written on that part of the outside of the letter that would have been folded in for sealing and sending it.

96. *To Lady Hamilton*

[Jean Kislak: 1993.151.00.0005] Wednesday night.[1]

7 –

My Dearest Emma 'tis not that I believe that You will do anything which can injure me (that I am [*sic*][2] cannot help saying a few words on that fellows[3] dining with You for You do not believe it is out of love for Sir William no You know the contrary that his design is upon You) no that I will never believe, but You have been taken In, You that are such a woman of good sence put so often on Your guard by myself M^rs^: Udny, M^rs^: Spilsbury, M^rs^: Denis + M^r^: Nisbet, You that have declared only that very morning that You were upon Your Guard,[4] what shall we[5] say if a poor foolish woman had been so cajoled, I knew that he would visit You, and You could not help coming down stairs when the P was there and notwithstanding all Your declarations never to meet him, to receive him <u>and by his own</u> <u>invitation</u> <u>En famille</u>[6] but his words are so charming that I am told no person can withstand them If I had been worth 10 millions I would have betted every farthing that You would not have gone into the house knowing he was there and If You did which I would not have believed thet You would have sent him a proper message by Sir William and sent him to hell, and knowing your determined courage when You had got down I would have laid my head upon the Block with the axe uplifted + said strike If Emma does not say to Sir W^m^: before the fellow, My character cannot shall not[7] suffer by permitting him to visit, oh I wish I had been so placed then + there then my head my distracted Head would have been off, Hush hush my poor heart keep in my breast be calm, Emma is true but no one not even Emma could resist the serpents flattering tongue[8] + knowing that Emma suits him, thet even a stranger would not invite her to meet the fellow, what will they all <u>say</u>[9] + think that Emma is like other woman [*sic*] when I would have killed anybody who had said

[1] 18 Feb 1801.

[2] This is written at the end of the second line.

[3] The Prince of Wales's.

[4] A blot of ink is spilt over the last two letters of the word 'Guard'.

[5] Inserted.

[6] 'and by his own' (at the end of a line) is underlined thrice; 'invitation' (at the beginning of the new line) is also underlined thrice; 'En famille' is underlined once ordinarily and then with three loops (that is six more times).

[7] Inserted.

[8] Inserted.

[9] Underlined twice.

so must now hang down my head and admit it, forgive me I know I am almost distracted but I have still sense enough left to burn every word of Yours, therefore if I should be worse which is likely I have not a paper, all Your pictures are before me, what will M^rs^: Denis say an[d] what will she song [*sic*] be calm be gentle the Wind is Changed do You go to the Opera tonight, they tell me he sings well I have eat nothing but a little rice + drank water, but forgive me I know my Emma and dont forget thet You had once a Nelson a friend a dear friend but alas he has his misfortunes he has lost the best his only friend his only Love, dont forget him poor fellow he is honest, Oh I could thunder + strike dead with my Lightining [*sic*], I dreamt it last night, my Emma I am calmer reason I hope will resume her place please God. Tears have relieved me, You never will again receive the villain[1] to rob me but I will be calm + trust to providence but what will all the world say do modest women receive him You nor I think so may the heavens bless You I am better only tell me You forgive me dont scold me indeed I am not worth it, and Ever to my last breath Yours and if not Yours no ones in this world Ever Yours faithful affectionate + attatchd

Nelson + Bronte

You cannot now help the villains dining with You, get rid of it as well as You can, do not let him come downstairs with You, or hand You up. If you do Tell me + then [*sic*][2]

97. *To Lady Hamilton*

[Huntington: HM 34079]

8 Saint George
feb^ry^: 19th: 1801.

Forgive every cross word. I now live.[3]

My Dearest Emma forgive my letter wrote and sent last night, perhaps my head was a little affected, no wonder it was such an unexpected such

[1]The Prince of Wales.

[2]The word 'then' is at the bottom of the third page. The fourth page of the letter is empty.

[3]This line is underlined in a zigzag movement. The underlining begins at the end of the line, goes to its beginning, right in front of the word 'forgive' then, with the ink becoming paler (perhaps because of the angle of the pen) towards the right again. At the beginning of the word 'cross' the line is started afresh in dark ink, leading to the end of the line (though again becoming softer under the words 'I now'), then turning back and again going to the beginning of the line, where it turns again, weakening again towards the centre of the line, where the word 'cross' is underlined separately with new vigour. Morrison has put this phrase at the end of the letter, assuming that it was added after writing the whole letter.

a knock down blow, such a death, but I will not go on for I shall get out of my senses again, will You sing for the fellow, The Prince unable to conceal his pain,[1] +:[2] no, you will not I will say no more for fear of my head it was so good of You to send to thank Mr: Nisbet for his not asking You to meet the fellow as he knew his vile intent and yet the same morning to let him[3] come and dine with you En famille – but I know it was not my Emma Sir Willm: always asks all partys to diner, I forgive You, forgive I beseech You Your old and dear friend, tell me all every word that passes he will propose if You[4] no You will not try – he is Sir Wms: guest –

Thursday[5] I have just got your letter and I live again do not[6] let the Lyar [*sic*][7] come, I never saw him but once the 4th day after I came to London and he never mentioned Your name may God Blast him be firm, Go and dine with Mrs: Denis on Sunday do not I beseech You risk being at home does Sir William want You to be a whore to the rascal[8] forgive all my letter you will see what I feel and have felt, I have eat not a morsel except a little rice since yesterday morning and 'till I know how this matter is gone off but I feel confident of Your resolution and thank You 10,00000 [*sic*] of times, I write You a letter which may be said as coming from me if you like I will endeavour to word it properly did You sit alone with the villain[9] for a moment No I will not believe it, oh God – oh God, keep my sences, do not let the rascal In tell the Duke thet You never will never[10] go to his house if he admits the fellow Mr: G.[11] must be a scoundrel he treated You once ill enough + cannot love you or he would sooner die. Ever for Ever aye for Ever Your Your Your only Yours

Nelson + Bronte[12]

I have this moment got my orders to put myself under Sir Hyde Parkers orders, and suppose I shall be ordered to Portsmouth tomorrow or next

[1]Poem by Dryden (1697) put to music by Handel in his *Alexander's Feast or The Power of Music An Ode in honour of St. Ceclia's day* (1736).

[2]*Sic*, not '+c:'.

[3]Inserted.

[4]End of line and of first page.

[5]19 Feb 1801 was a Thursday, so it that appears that Nelson continued the letter on the same day.

[6]Underlined twice

[7]The Prince of Wales.

[8]The Prince of Wales.

[9]The Prince of Wales.

[10]*Sic*, 'never will' stands at the end of one line, the second 'never' at the beginning of the next.

[11]Charles Greville.

[12]After this signature on the third page, Nelson left a gap and only continued with the postscript below the central part of the page.

day and then I will try hard to get to London for 3 days – May heaven Bless us – but do not ~~better~~ let that fellow[1] dine with You, do not write here after you receive this I shall be gone, You can in Sir W^{ms}: name write a note to Sir H. Parker, asking if the S^{t}: George is ordered to Spithead, if so write to Portsmouth desiring my letters to be left at the Post Office 'till the ships arrival.

98. *To Lady Hamilton*

[Morrison, ii, p. 119 (No. 524)] *St George*, Torbay, February 19th, 1801

I have received your most affectionate letter, and I feel very much for the unpleasant situation the Prince, or rather Sir William, has unknowingly placed you, for if he knew as much of the P'^{s} character as the world does, he would rather let the lowest wretch that walks the streets dine at his table than that unprincipled lyar [*sic*]. I have heard it reported that he has said he would make you his mistress. Sir William never can admit him into his house, nor can any friend advise him to it unless they are determined on your hitherto unimpeached character being ruined. *No* modest man would suffer it. He is permitted to visit only houses of *notorious ill fame*. For heaven's sake let Sir William pause before he damns your good name. Mr Greville I take to be a man of strict honour, and he knows what I say of the Prince to be true. If *I have not mistaken my man*, which I shall be truly sorry to have done, I will answer with my head that Mr Greville would go down on his knees and beg Sir William to save your unspotted honour, for although I know you would send him to the Devil were he to propose such a thing to you, yet all the world have their eyes upon you, and your character, my amiable friend, is as much lost as if you was guilty. Let Sir William consult any man of honour. I am sure the Duke of Queensberry would agree with me. I have, my dear friend, perhaps, given too full an opinion, but you know, when I do give an opinion, it is generally to be understood, and, hitherto, seldom wrong. Make my affectionate regards to Sir William, and entreat him not to suffer such bad company into his house, and do you and him ever believe me your most attached and affectionate friend,

[1] The Prince of Wales.

99. *To Lady Hamilton (alias Mrs Thomson)*

[Morrison, ii, p. 119 (No. 523)][1]

Your friend is at my elbow, and enjoins me to assure you that his love for you and your child is, if possible, greater than ever, and that he calls God to witness that he will marry you as soon as possible, and that it will be his delight to call you his own. He desires you will adhere to Lady H.'s good advice and, like her, keep those impertinent men at a proper distance. He behaves, I can assure you, incomparably well, and loves you as much as man ever loved woman, and do you, my dear, believe me ever your dear friend.

100. *To Lady Hamilton (alias Mrs Thomson)*

[Huntington: HM 34083][2]

My Dear Mrs: Thomson I gave Your letter to Your friend who is much pleased with Your resolution he says he feels confident of Your conduct and begs You will follow the admirable conduct of our Dear Lady Hamilton who will send the Prince to the Devil he again begs me to be his bondsman and thet he will marry You the moment Your Uncle dies or it comes a peace, + he desires his blessing to his child and You will forgive my desiring You to kiss it for me, Your friend has not been very well but hopes to be better very soon, Ever Believe me Your + his sincere friend

Nelson + Bronte.

101. *To Lady Hamilton*

[Huntington: HM 34080] 9 St: George Thursday[3] night

My Dearest friend, here I am fixed in my new habitation which it is my firm intention never to sleep out of except from dire necessity[4] 'till the

[1]Arranged by Morrison between letters of 19 Feb 1801, but possibly written at a later date. According to Morrison: 'with superscription "Mrs Thomson, to the care of Lady Hamilton".'
[2]Without date; arranged by Morrison, ii, p. 120 (No. 525), between letters of 19 and 20 Feb 1801, but possibly written at a later date.
[3]Apparently 19 Feb 1801.
[4]For a similar promise, see letter of 16 Feb 1801, 9 pm (Doc. No. 92).

campaign is over except when I may get 3 days leave to go to London to settle many of my private affairs, and I hardly think it will be refused me Your good sence judgement and proper firmness must endear You to all Your friends and to none more than Your old + firm friend Nelson, You have shewn that you are above all temptation and not to be drawn into the paths of dishonor for to gratify any pride or to gain any Riches, how Sir William can assotiate [*sic*] with a person of a character so diametrically opposite to his own, but I do not chuse as this letter goes through many hands to enter more at large on this subject, I glory in Your conduct and in Your Inestimable friendship and good Sir William when he reflects must admire Your virtuous + proper conduct, I wish you were my Sister that I might instantly give You half my fortune for Your glorious conduct, be firm Your cause is that of honor against Infamy – May the Heavens bless you and let no consideration suffer You to alter Your Virtuous and Sensible resolution pardon all this from an old and Interested friend You know I would not in Sir Williams case have gone to Court without my Wife and such a wife never to be matched, It is true You would grace a Court better as a Queen than a visitor,[1] 11 oClock friday[2] I have this moment my orders to go to Portsmouth + expect to be there tomorrow noon, I again My Dear friend entreat both You and Sir William not to suffer the Prince to dine or even visit 'Tis what no real modest person would suffer and Sir William ought to know thet his views <u>are dishonourable</u>, May God bless You and make You firm in resisting this vile attempt on Your character and with best regards to Sir William Believe me Ever Your most Sincere + affectionate friend

Nelson + Bronte.[3]

You can my Dear friend write a line on Sunday[4] evening it can be made up as a small parcel and then I shall get it on Monday[5] morning although there is no regular post, it will make me so happy to be assured thet the fellow did not even see you on Sunday, The Portsmouth[6] mail coach setts out either from the Golden Cross Charing

[1]The letter is continued ('11 oClock' in the same line).
[2]20 Feb 1801.
[3]There is a gap left on the rest of this (the second) page. The rest of the letter is written on the third page.
[4]22 Feb 1801.
[5]23 Feb 1801.
[6]Inserted.

Cross, or Gloucester Coffee House Piccadilly anybody can tell You the direction as underneath Heavens bless you my own only dear friend – I write on this side that You may tear off the half sheet in case You chuse to read any part of it[1] – pray give the enclosed[2] to our Dear friend Your letters are just come heavens bless you do not let the villain into Your house dine out on Sunday,[3] Sir W^m^: will find out the Prince does not come to dine with him

Vice Ad^l^: Lord Nelson +c:

Portsmouth
To be left at the Mail Coach office 'till called for.

102. *To Lady Hamilton*

[NMM: CRK/19/9] friday[4] Night 9 O Clock S^t^: George

having my truly dearest friend got through a great deal of business I am enabled to do justice to my private feelings which are fixed ever on you and about you whenever the public service does not arrest my attention, I have read all all your kind + affectionate letters and have read them frequently over + committed them to the flames much against my inclination, there was one I rejoiced not to have read at the time it was where you consented to dine + sing with the Prince Thank God it was not so I could not have borne it, and now less than ever, but I now know he never can dine with you, for you would go out of the house sooner than suffer it, and as to letting him hear you Sing I only hope he will be struck deaf + you Dumb sooner than such a thing should happen, but I know it never now cannot, [*sic*] You cannot think how my feelings are alive toward you probably more than ever and they never can be diminish'd my hearty endeavours shall not be wanting to improve + to give us new[5]

[1]The text on the second half sheet, starts after the signature: 'You can my Dear friend write a line . . .'.

[2]It is not clear, what the enclosed may have been.

[3]22 Feb 1801.

[4]This letter was dated in the Croker Collection (pencilled note on the actual manuscript): '1801 March 18'. This date, however, is wrong. The letter must have been written in the Channel, before leaving for Copenhagen, before 22 Feb 1801 (date when Troubridge had left Nelson). Nelson was on board the *St George* from 19 Feb 1801 onwards. On 20 Feb he left for Spithead, where he arrived the following day, so that he could assume to be 'in the Downs' in the near future. I therefore suggest dating the letter Friday, 20 Feb 1801.

[5]'us new' is underlined twice.

ties of regard + affection, I have seen and talked much with Dear M[rs]: Thomson['s] friend[1] the fellow seems to eat all my words when I talk of her and his child, he says he never can forget your goodness and kind affection to her and his dear dear child, I have had you know the felicity of seeing it and a finer child never was produced by any two persons it was in truth a love begotten child, I am determined to keep him on board for I know if they got together they would soon have another, but after our two months trip I hope they will never be seperated and then let them do as they please, we are all bustle and activity, I shall sail on monday[2] after your letter arrives Troubridge will send it as an ad[ty] letter on tuesday[3] I shall be in the Downs, if we have any wind and Troubridge will send under cover to Ad[l]: Lutwidge.[4] It is not my intention to sett my foot out of the ship except to make my take leave Bow to Admiral Milbank.[5] I have been much pressed to dine ashore but, no never if I can help it, 'till I dine with you, 11 OClock, Your Dear letters just come on board, they are sympathetic with my own feelings + I trust we shall soon meet to part no more Monday[6] I shall be here[7] for letters Tuesday[8] at Deal, Recollect, I am for Ever Yours aye for Ever while life remains, yours, yours faithfully Nelson + Bronte I charge my only friend to keep well + think of her Nelsons Glory. I have wrote to Lord Eldon[9] the Chancellor as my Brother desired, pray as you are going to buy a ticket for the Pigot diamond, buy the right number or it will be money thrown away for Ever ever ever yours only yours

Kindest regards to my Dear M[rs]: Thomson + my God Child.'

[1]The word 'friend' is above the line between the words 'Thomson' and 'the'.

[2]23 Feb 1801; if the dating of the letter is correct, Nelson slightly misjudged the course of events, as he had not yet been granted the leave of absence he had applied for; as a matter of fact he arrived on Saturday at Spithead and proceeded on leave for three days to London on Monday, 23 Feb 1801.

[3]24 Feb 1801.

[4]Admiral Skeffington Lutwidge (1737–1814) had been captain of the *Carcass* on which Nelson had sailed to the Arctic in 1773 (see Knight, p. 652, for more information).

[5]Mark Milbank[e] (1724–1805).

[6]23 Feb 1801.

[7]At Spithead.

[8]24 Feb 1801.

[9]John Scott, 1st Earl of Eldon (1751–1838).

103. *To Lady Hamilton (alias Mrs Thomson)*

[Huntington Library, HM 34081]

Your friend my Dear M^{rs}: Thomson has been very unhappy at the ~~scho-~~ shocking conduct of your Uncle[1] but Your firmness and virtue has made his mind at ease and he desires me to tell You that if You are forced to quit his house by his shameful conduct that then nothing should make him go to sea even under my flag, nor if he could be made a Lord or a Duke with 40,000 £ a year and give You up he would reject them with disdain and be happy to live on 100 £ a year, I admire his spirit and he is close by me, I hope Lady Hamilton our dear + amiable friend send[s] You my letters immediately as she receives them, but I know her worth and thet she would scorn a mean or dirty action, but If You think there is any reason to suspect her of opening Your letters I will if You desire it direct them to another house perhaps You know some female friend they might be directed under cover to, I hope to get him to London in a very few days and You and he can settle every thing, dont tell Lady H^{n}: that I suspect her of doing either You or Your friend any injury – I declare to God I believe her conduct to be purity itself – by the bye, Sir W^{m}: must be mad to attempt giving his wife the reputation of w–e to the P.[2] I could not have believed if I had not been told it from most undoubted authority, I can assure You + Your friend that you are both sure of the fortune as far as is possible enough to content You + him and the unalterable regard of Your firm Friend

Nelson + Bronte

I beg you will be easy under all circumstances My old messmate Troubridge carries this to Lady H^{n}: You do not know him but Lady H. does – You

[1]A day before Nelson wrote this letter, the 'uncle', Sir William Hamilton, had reported to Nelson about Lady Hamilton having 'one of her terrible sick head-achs', adding: 'Among other things that vex her, is – that we have been drawn in to be under the absolute necessity of giving a dinner to ***** on Sunday next. He asked himself; having expressed his strong desire of hearing Banti's and Emma's voices together. I am well aware of the danger that would attend ****** frequenting our house. Not that I fear, that Emma could ever be induced to act contrary to the prudent conduct she has hitherto pursued; but the world is so ill-natured, that the worst construction is put upon the most innocent actions. As this dinner must be, or ****** would be offended, I shall keep it strictly to the musical part; . . . In short, we will get rid of it as well as we can, and guard against its producing more meetings of the same sort. Emma would really have gone any lengths, to have avoided Sunday's dinner. But I thought it would not be prudent . . .' (1814-letters, ii, pp. 200–201).

[2]Prince of Wales.

will receive a letter wrote this day under cover to M^{r}: Nepean directed to Lady H—

Off Portland, 10 o'clock, Friday, February 20th, 1801.

8 oClock Saturday[1] morning in a Gale of Wind at SW off the Isle of Wight.

I have been very unwell all night + horrid dreams If Your Uncle persists in having such bad company to dinner Your friend begs and I agree perfectly with him in opinion that You should dine out of the house and take especial care not to go home 'till you know the wretches are gone, but I dare say they will stay on purpose to torment You, You can dine with Lady Hamilton or some other friend, and after all If the beast turns You out of his house because You will not submit to be thought a w—e You know then what shall happen, but follow my advice, and I will support Your friend + Yourself If you think that Lady Hamilton or any one else opens Your letters Tell me where to direct them + then Your friend may write himself Ever your affectionate N. B. Kiss my God child for me her father sends his blessing to Your and it.

104. *To Lady Hamilton*

[Huntington: HM 34044]

St George at Sea off Portland
feb^{y}: 20th: 1801
10 oClock at night

My Dear Lady and excellent friend and [best] of Women Our friend Troubridge going to London has been so kind as to offer to take charge of this letter for you and I write one with pleasure for I never can or will forget all your kindness and goodness to me on various occasions I have reason to believe I owe my life to you and I declare to God I would lay it down to make you happy, I trust Sir William has long before this time found out the character of the Prince[2] and that on no consideration in the World will he suffer him to enter his Doors, Sir W^{ms}: Character would suffer[3] + Yours would be ruined, let him go to his Women of fashion they are good enough for him and the virtuous excellent Lady Hamilton let her remain so, forgive my writing so freely my opinion but Nelson would

[1]21 Feb 1801.
[2]Prince of Wales.
[3]Inserted.

ill deserve the name of a friend if he could be a[1] quiet Spectator of the Dishonor which is intended you and Sir William no at the Risk of never being spoke to I would bawl with my whole strength and my last breath should say do not suffer him into your house, may the Heavens Bless, protect + preserve you from all Injury is the fervent prayer of My Dear Lady Your attatched + affectionate Friend

Nelson & Bronte[2]

I have wrote for 3 days leave of absence I have much to settle, off the Isle of Wight 8 oClock

Saturday[3] Morng:

105. *To Lady Hamilton*

[*a)* Pettigrew, i, pp. 430–31; *b)* Morrison, ii, pp. 120, 121 (No. 527)]

[*a)*] St. George, Spithead, 8 o'clock, February 22nd, 1801.

[*b)*] I hope you will have seen Troubridge last night, and he will probably tell you that he did not leave me perfectly at ease. In short, when I have a letter for you it rushed into my mind that in 10 hours he would see you. A flood of tears followed – it was too much for me to bear. I could not help telling him what would I not have given to have been in his pocket. I am sure, my amiable friend, that you will on no consideration be in company with that ——, neither this day or any other. He is a false, lying scoundrel, what I wrote you. You know enough to my honour and resolution that I will fulfil even much more than I promised.

8 o'clock I am just going on shore to call on the Admiral and Commissioner, and shall be on board as soon as possible.

Noon. – On board again; have received your truly comforting letters. In doing what I wish, you win my heart for ever. I am all soul and sensibility; a fine thread will lead me, but with my life I would resist a cable from dragging me. I hope very soon to get a few days leave of absence, but Sir Hyde[4] does not come down till next Monday or Tuesday,[5] but

[1]Inserted.

[2]The following passage is in the upper part of the third page (the second page is empty).

[3]21 Feb 1801; Nelson was granted the leave of absence; he took it from Monday 23 Feb 1801.

[4]Parker.

[5]23 and 24 Feb 1801.

Troubridge can tell you. But perhaps that would be telling him or making him guess my business in Town. But whenever I am absent he will receive and send all my packets. After the letter I wrote *her*[1] the other day. I do not think she will attempt to either come here or go to London.[2] I will do as you please; but I do not believe she will venture without my orders; but *all* as your please. I have been pressed to dine ashore by the Admiral, an old man, eighty, with an old wife dressed old ewe lamb fashion. Admiral Halloway,[3] an acquaintance of twenty-five years, wanted me to dine with him as to-day, or Wednesday.[4] He has a wife and four children. Sir Charles Sexton,[5] the Commissioner, an acquaintance of near thirty years, was also very pressing; his wife, I am told, likes a drop, & looks like a cook-maid. But I will dine nowhere without your consent, allthough [*sic*] with my present feelings, I might be trusted with 50 virgins naked in a dark room. My thoughts are so fixed that not even the greatest strokes of fortune could change them, but I am, my dear friend, for ever, for ever, your faithful

[*a)*] N & B

[*b)*] I have answered Sir Wm's letter, but as he had not mentioned the Prince's name I could not bring it in, but if ever he does my heart, head, tongue and pen is ready to let out. I shall send to the mailcoach office in the morning. Heavens bless you. I have been obliged to bring in the whole Royal family, but not that eldest blackguard[6] in particular. You will approve I am sure, and I say God bless the King.

106. *To Lady Hamilton (alias 'Mrs Thompson')*

[William Clements: Hubert S. Smith, Volume 1 'Naval Affairs'][7]

My Dear Mrs: T. Poor Thompson seems to have forgot all his ill health and all his mortifications and sorrows in the thoughts that he will soon

[1]Lady Nelson.

[2]The text of this letter was copied by Lady Nelson in a letter to Davison: see fn. to Doc. No. 95.

[3]John Holloway (1744–1826), at the time port admiral at Portsmouth.

[4]25 Feb 1801.

[5]Pettigrew, i, p. 431, has here 'Saxton', which is the correct spelling of Sir Charles Saxton.

[6]Prince of Wales.

[7]Morrison, ii, p. 121 (No. 528), noted 'undated (February 23rd, 1801)'; this appears plausible, since Nelson went to London for three days' leave on 23 Feb and it appears from the contents of the letter that it was written just before he left for London.

bury them all in your dear dear bosom he seems almost beside himself I hope you have always mind'd what Lady H[n]: has said to you for she is a pattern of attatch[t] to her Love I daresay twins[1] will again be the fruit of Your + His meeting the thought is too much to bear, have the dear thatch'd Cottage[2] ready to receive him and I will answer that he would not change it for a Queen + a Palace Kiss Dear H for me.

107. *To Lady Nelson*

[Huntington: HM 34045] London February 24th: 1801.

As I am sent for to Town on very particular business for a day or two I would not on any account have you come to London but rest quiet where You are, nor would I have You come to Portsmouth for I never come on Shore, The King is reported to be more than very Ill, But I and every good subject must pray for his life, I hope Josiah may be able to get a ship now this change of ministers has taken place, as Ever Your affectionate

Nelson.

Josiah is to have the Thalia, and I want to know from him two good Lieutenants they must be of my approval I wish L[t]: Champion to be second would he like M[r]: Yule[3] to be first if I can induce him to quit the S[t]: George, he must return an answer by the Post directed to me Lothians Hotel.

108. *To Lady Hamilton*

[*a)* Pettigrew, i, pp. 431–2; *b)* Morrison, ii, pp. 121, 122 (No. 529)] [*a)*] Portsmouth, February 27th, 1801.

My dearest friend,

[*b)*] Parting from such a friend is literally tearing one's own flesh; but the remembrance will keep up our spirits till we meet. My affection is, if

[1]Knight has doubted this transcription (p. 354, note), suggesting 'theirs'. A transcription at the William Clements Library gave 'mine', but was corrected into 'twins', which is what I read. A theory that the second twin that Lady Hamilton gave birth to was given to the Foundling Hospital has been rightly rejected (see Roger Knight as quoted above and Terry Coleman, *Nelson* (London, 2001), p. 246).

[2]Contemporary slang for female genitals.

[3]Nelson discharged Lieutenant John Yule from the *St George* to the *Thalia* on 8 Mar 1801.

possible, stronger than ever for you, and I trust it will keep increasing as long as we both live. I have seen M[rs] Thomson's friend, who is delighted at my having seen his dear child. I am sure he will be very fond of it. I arrived here before noon, and have had my hands [*sic*] full of business. To-morrow we embark troops. I will write you a long letter to-night, and send it under cover to Troubridge; therefore you will have it on Sunday.[1] Hardy, Parker, and Fremantle,[2] desire their remembrances. [*a)*] For ever, aye for ever, believe me,

N. & B.

109. *Verses from Lady Hamilton to Nelson*

[Morrison, ii, p. 143 (No. 572)]

Silent grief and sad forebodings
(Lest I ne'er should see him more,)
Fill my heart when gallant Nelson,
Hoists Blue Peter at the fore.

On his Pendant anxious gazing,
Fill, with tears mine eyes run o'er,
At each change of wind I tremble
While Blue Peter's at the fore.

All the live-long day I wander,
Sighing on the sea-beat shore;
But my sighs are all unheeded,
When Blue Peter's at the fore.

For when duty calls my hero
To far seas, where cannons roar,
Nelson (love and Emma leaving),
Hoists Blue Peter at the fore,

Oft he kiss'd my lips at parting,
And at every kiss he swore,

[1] 1 Mar 1801.
[2] Thomas Fremantle (1765–1819), who had been with Nelson in the Mediterranean 1794–96 and had been wounded, like Nelson, at Tenerife in 1797.

Nought could force him from my bosom,
Save Blue Peter at the fore.

Oh, that I might with my Nelson,
Sail the wide world o'er and o'er,
Never should I then with sorrow,
See Blue Peter at the fore.

But (ah me!) his ship's unmooring;
Nelson's last boat rows from shore,
Every sail is set and swelling,
And Blue Peter's seen no more.

110. *To Lady Hamilton*

[*b)* Morrison, ii, p. 122 (No. 530);
c) Christie's, 19 Oct 2005, lot 19;
d) Christie's, 20 June 1990, lot 224] [*c)*] March 1st: 1801, 8 oclock, Morng:

My Dearest friend,

fearing that it may not be possible to get a boat on shore in the afternoon at [*sic*] it has the appearance of blowing hard, I send this line to apprize You of it that no little ruffle might take place in Your dear, good and exalted mind, only always rely thet I will never omit an opportunity of writing – therefore if at any time vessels should come from the fleet without letters You may be sure thet it is unknown to me, which may happen from my being detatched but I hope not from the same cause as Lord Keiths – not telling me, I have read over twenty times Your dear kind letters, and although I must naturally be happy thet Your affection is such as You describe and so exactly a counterpart of my own feelings, yet I must beg thet my friend will not be sick or grieve too much for a temporary but unavoidable absence [*b)*] of a few weeks, and if we were both differently circumstanced, that should not be – no, not for an hour. But recollect, all my exertions are to bring about a peace. No, I am sure you will not go anywhere but where it is right, and never suffer that fellow to enter your house. I assure you my very short trip to London has, if possible, given me an additional confidence, and I believe I never shall have cause to think otherwise than I do of you. You read, of course, my brother's letter; and if you like to have Mrs. Nelson up, say that I will pay their lodgings, and then you can have as much of her company as you please;

but Reverend Sir[1] you will find a great bore at times, therefore he ought to amuse himself all the mornings, and not always to dine with you, as Sir William may not like it. They can twice or thrice a week have a beef steak at home, [*d)*] for some people may say by and bye thet Sir W^m^: maintains the family of the Nelsons which would vex me, I am brushing these folks up and I do not find that activity which my mind carries with it, It would not be possible I fear for You + Sir Willm: to give me a visit at Yarmouth, it should be no expence to him, tomorrow if we can get our ships company paid today we are off for the Downs. Tell M^rs^: Thomson that her friend is more in love with her than ever, and I believe dreams of her, he is sorry that she was a little unwell when he was in London as it deprived him of much pleasure but he is determined to have full scope when he next sees her. Ever Yours for ever

Nelson + Bronte

Kiss my godchild for me + Bless it[2]

111. *To Lady Hamilton*

[Morrison, ii, pp. 122–3 (No. 531)] Sunday[3] noon

After my letter of 8 o'clock this morning went on shore, on board came Oliver,[4] and when he was announced by Hardy, so much anxiety for your safety rushed into my mind that a pain immediately seized my heart, which kept increasing for half an hour, that, turning cold, hot, cold, &c, I was obliged to send for the surgeon, who gave me something to warm me, for it was a deadly chill. This morning has brought me your three dear letters by the post, and as many from Troubridge. Parker being appointed to a fine ship,[5] I have charged him to deliver into your own

[1]Nelson's brother William.

[2]This postscript is added at the top of the space that Nelson left empty in the centre of the page in order to avoid parts of the text being torn on breaking the seal. Nelson has drawn a line around this postscript.

[3]1 Mar 1801.

[4]Francis Oliver, described by Kate Williams, *England's Mistress. The Infamous Life of Emma Hamilton* (London, 2006), p. 330, as 'Sir William's old secretary'.

[5]The *Medusa.*

hands, if possible, this letter. Oliver shall keep till to-morrow.[1] Why my dear friend, do you alarm yourself? Your own Nelson will return safe, and, under the hand of Providence, is as safe as if walking London streets. The troops are only 800, and are intended for the better manning our ships. Recollect the more force we have the less risk. You may rely we shall return in May – perhaps long before; the sooner we are off, the quicker we return, and the enemy much less prepared to receive us. I wish it was in my power to get leave of absence for James Dugdale, but not even an ad. or captain could get an hour's leave, and Sir Thomas Pasley[2] at Plymouth has no power to grant it. Amongst many cards, I think I saw somebody's rout, but as I cared for no rout, or the writers, I did not trouble my head about it. I am sure neither of us should have gone to Lady D's rout;[3] we could amuse ourselves better at home. Mr. Levington served that fellow[4] right, damn him. That Lady Aber[5]: is a damned bitch; she would pimp for her husband that she might get at her lovers,[6] for I dare say not one satisfies her, but no proper lover[7] but two that I know of. Would to God I had dined alone with you. *What a desert* [*sic*] *we would have had*. The time will come, and believe me, that I am, for ever, for ever, your own. Thanks for the account of my godchild. Heavens bless it! Our activity will make a peace, and then I would not call the King my uncle. Sir Charles Sexton, the Commissioner, who you & Sir William would have known had you come to Portsmouth is on board seeing the ship; he is charmed with your picture,[8] and says he did not believe such a handsome woman existed. I told him your equal did not, and that your

[1]From here on the Christie's Catalogue for 1989 transcribes the passage as follows: '... Why my dear friend do you alarm yourself your own Nelson will return safe and under the hand of Providence is as safe as if walking London streets, the troops are only 800, and are intended for the better manning our ships, recollect the more force we have the less risk, you may rely we shall return in May perhaps long before, the sooner we are off the quicker our return and the *enemy* much less prepared to receive us . . . I am sure neither of us should have gone to Lady H. rout – we could amuse ourselves better at home. Mr. Livingstone answered that fellow right damn him that Lady Aber. Is a damned bitch. She would pimp for her husband that she might get at her lovers for I dare say not one satisfies her, but no people love but two that I know of. Would to God I had dined alone with you, what a *Desert we would have had . . .*'

[2]Sir Thomas Pasley (1734–1808); an acquaintance of Nelson's from his years in the West Indies.

[3]Catalogue of Christie's sale of 3 Dec 2003, lot 138, has here: 'Lady H. rout –'.

[4]Prince of Wales.

[5]According to Christie's catalogue of 2003, this refers to 'the Marchioness of Abercorn', [second] wife of John James Hamilton, 1st Marquess of Abercorn (Lady Cecil Hamilton; 1770–1819).

[6]Catalogue of Christie's sale of 3 Dec 2003, lot 138, has here: '*her lovers*'.

[7]Catalogue of Christie's sale of 3 Dec 2003, lot 138, has here: 'no people love'.

[8]Christie's speculate here: 'a mention of Emma's picture (presumably the pastel portrait done by J. H. Schmidt in 1800, which hung in Nelson's cabin)'.

goodness, abilities, and virtues exceeded far away your beauty. He is a rough sailor, 70, and a very old friend of mine. He quite regrets you and Sir William did not come to Portsmouth with *me*.

112. *To Lady Hamilton*

[Houghton: MS Lowell 10] March 1st: 1801, 9 oclock.

Now my own Dear Wife for such you are in my Eyes and in the face of heaven I can give full scope to my feelings for I dare say Oliver will faithfully deliver this letter, You know my dearest Emma that there is nothing in this world thet I would not do for us to live together and to have our dear little child with us, I firmly believe that this campaign will give us peace and then we will sett of for Bronte, in 12 hours we shall be across the water and freed from all the nonsence of his friends or rather pretended ones, nothing but an event happening to him could prevent my going and I am sure you will think so, for unless all matters accord it would bring 100 of tongues and slanderous reports if I seperated from her, (which I would do with pleasure the moment we can be united, I want to see her no more) therefore we must manage till we can quit this country or Your uncle dies I love I never did love any one else I never had a dear pledge of love 'till You gave me one and you thank my God never gave one to any body else, I think before March is out You will either see us back or so victorious thet we shall insure a glorious issue to our toils think whet my Emma will feel at seeing [me] return safe perhaps with a little more fame her own Dear loving Nelson, Never if I can help it will I dine out of my ship or go on shore except duty calls me, let Sir Hyde have any glory he can catch I envy him not, You my beloved Emma and my country are the two dearest objects of my fond heart, a heart susceptible + true[1] only place confidence in me and You never shall be disappointed, I burn all Your dear letters because it is right for Your sake and I wish you would burn all mine, they can do no good and will do us both harm if any Seizure of them or the dropping even one of them would fill the mouths of the world sooner than we intend, my longing for You both person and conversation You may readily imagine what must be my sensations at the Idea of sleeping with you it setts me on fire even the thoughts much more would the reality I am sure my love + desires are all to you and[2] if any woman naked was to[3] come to me even as I am this moment ~~every~~ from thinking of You I hope it might rot off If I would

[1]Reference to his poem, sent with Doc. No. 89.
[2]The 'nd' is (partly) hidden under a stain of ink.
[3]The 'to' is partly hidden under a stain of ink.

touch her even with my hand no my heart person + mind is in perfect union of love toward my own Dear beloved Emma the[1] real bosom friend of her all hers all Emmas

Nelson + Bronte.

Oliver is gone to sleep he is grown half foolish I shall give him 10£ in the morning, and I have wrote a letter recommending a friend of his to the Chairman of the East India Company which he said you would be glad I should do for[2] him I have nothing to send my Emma, it makes me sorry, You + Sir W^{m}: could not come to Yarmouth, that would[3] be pleasant, but we shall not be there more than a week at farthest, I had a letter this day from the Rev^{d}: M^{r}: Holden who we met on the continent he desired his kind comp^{ts}: to You + Sir W^{m}: he sent me the letters of my Name + recommended it as my Motto – Honor est a Nilo Horatio Nelson[4] – may the Heavens bless you my love my Darling angel my heaven given Wife the dearest only true wife of her own 'till death

Nelson + Bronte.

I know you will never let thet fellow or any one come near you

Monday[5] morn^{g}: Oliver is just going on shore the time will ere long arrive when Nelson will land to fly to his Emma, to be for ever with her, let that hope keep us up under our present difficultys. Kiss and Bless our dear Horatia think of that

113. *To Lady Hamilton*

[Houghton: pf MS Eng 196.5 (22)][6]

My Dearest friend this moment receiv'd Your letter from Troubridge, my heart bleeds for you but I shall soon very soon return Damn al[l] those thet would make You false, but I know You will be true + faithful, send

[1]The letters 'E' and 'th' are partly hidden under a stain of ink.

[2]The letter 'f' is partly hidden (at the bottom) under a stain of ink.

[3]The letters 'ld' are hidden under a stain of ink.

[4]The name 'Horatio Nelson' is written above the Latin words 'Honor est a Nilo' (honour be to the Nile). There is again a stain of ink, here covering the letters 'tt' and 'H' (this time in a lighter shade of black).

[5]2 Mar 1801.

[6]According to Morrison, ii, 122 (No. 533): 'Dated *St. George* March 2nd, 1801' (probably on an envelope that is lost).

for M^rs: Nelson what signify's [*sic*] a few hundred pounds to make Your dear mind a little at ease, Troubridge will forward Your letter[s] If you are at a loss to know where I am

I shall hate M^rs: Denis if she does not take care, my mind is fixed thet if ever the Damn'd fellow is admitted into Your company then Your Nelson is rejected, and I would sooner believe the World to be at an End this week, Just sailing therefore do not say much, fancy what I would say, but this I will[1] say to the last moment of my Existance thet I am all all Your Nelson + Bronte

Sir W^m: wrote me in his letter thet if he could get over thet Sunday the —— should never come into his house, remind him of that.

Oliver went at 9 oclock this morning. Love to my god-child.

114. *To Lady Hamilton*

[Pierpont Morgan: MA321]

S^t: George thick fog off
Dungeness 8 in the
Morning March 3rd: 1801.

My Dearest friend the fog has been so very thick since our sailing yesterday noon that it may truly be said we have got thus far blindfolded and if it continues I fear we shall not be able to get into the Downs this day, and I shall be deprived of my greatest pleasure absent from all I hold dear, the [pleasure] of receiving Your kind and affectionate letters – they are always a balsam to my heart, this expedition cannot last more than two months and it is very possible not half the time therefore Cheer up fair Emma,[2] Your own will return safe + sound and with his heart devoted to You alone, I have got on board a Col^l: Stewart Brother to Lord Garlies[3] a very good active young man he commands the corps of troops we have on board, I have also a Cap^n: Thesiger[4] on b^d: he was in the Russian service and is now a Volunteer[5]

11 oclock I have wrote to my Brother about M^rs: Nelsons coming to London + that I will willingly pay the expence therefore I am sure if You like to ask her she will take her old Lodgings and be happy to be

[1]Not 'would', as Morrison has it (ii, p. 124).

[2]Beginning of a poem by Cornelia Knight; see fn to Doc. No. 63.

[3]George Stewart (1768–1834), naval officer and son of John Stewart, 7th Earl of Galloway (1736–1806), whom he was to succeed as 8th Earl.

[4]Frederick Thesiger, aide-de-camp to Nelson at Copenhagen.

[5]This word stands at the very end of a line. The letter is continued at the beginning of the next line.

with You, she can walk without fear of being run away with, + I have recommended my Brother to amuse himself in the mornings and to dine at home two or three times a week.[1]

2 oclock can just see the land + expect to be at an anchor by 3 when Hardy goes on shore with my excuses to the Admiral, I hope to sail at day light in the morn^{g}: for Yarmouth and[2] to be there on Thursday,[3] I must be upon Deck but ever ever ever for Ever Your and only Your Nelson and Bronte.

Give the note to M^{rs}: Thomson.[4]

½ p^{t}: 2 Just anchored and as probably I shall not be able to send again on shore Hardy carrys this Heavens Bless You.

115. *To Lady Hamilton*

[Huntington: HM 34084] S^{t}: George
March 4th: 1801

My dear Lady

Do try and persuade Sir Willm: to come with You + make me a visit, the change of air will do You good and I will try to make it pleasant to You both, we will[5] have none but Sailors near us, Tylers ship[6] has been

[1]Compare Doc. No. 110; finished at the end of the last line of the first page of the letter; the continuation starts at the top left-hand of the second page.

[2]Here Nelson apparently first wrote 'at', but then corrected it into 'and' by writing over the 't' the letters 'nd'.

[3]5 Mar 1801.

[4]The letter is continued in the same line.

[5]Inserted.

[6]Captain Charles Tyler (1760–1835), whom Nelson knew from the Mediterranean in 1793–94, was at that time in command of the *Warrior*. The *Warrior*'s logbook contains the following entry for 3 Mar 1801 noon until 4 Mar 1801 noon (in contemporary sea time: 4 Mar): 'Wednesday – 4 – West / WBN /NW – . . . – Mod^{te} + clowdy, Rec^{d} a Pilot from HMS Overyssel Arrived HMS S^{t}. George (L^{d}. Nelson) and the Russel Rec^{d} 2 flat Boats, 2 Carronades + shot for them, sail'd HMShip Defence at 5 ½ weighed + made sail + cross'd T.G^{t}.Yards – at 6 took the ground fired several guns + furl'd sails at 7 a Deal Pilot came on bd. down T.G^{t}.yd^{s}. + struck ye Masts, out Launch, struck lower yards + topmasts, Bent the stream Cable to the Anchor. with a new Messenger bent to it, + laid the stream Anchor out to the South^{d}. bro^{t} too the Messenger at 11 hove the ship off + let go the best B^{r} [Boat?] Anchor, HMS Pluto anchor'd to the West of us, bent 3 hawsers together, and run out to her, at 6 AM weighed + warp'd into deep water, at 8 came to with the best B^{r} in 9 ½ fm^{s} Sway'd up lower yards + topmasts at 10 fidded [*sic*] T.G^{t}.masts, + cross'd the yd^{s}. Noon weighed + made sail hove too, in Boats, sail'd HMShips S^{t}. George and Russel.' (TNA: ADM 51/1345, part 5, Journal of the Proceedings of His Majesty's Ship Warrior Chas

foolishly ashore all night but she is afloat again, do pray for charitys sake come and see Your old and attatch'd friend

Nelson + Bronte.

Just getting under sail shall be at Yarmouth I hope tomorrow night.

116. *To Lady Hamilton*

[Huntington: HM 34085]

St: George Downs 7 – Vs:[1]
4 oClock

My Dearest friend,

Your dear letter is just received this day I wrote to my Brother abt: Mrs: Nelson, therefore send and ask her without more ceremony, She will come, Damn thet fellow but You will be firm I am, It would grieve me to see Sir Wm: without You but if you approve I will ask, Davison will come down with the mail + with my Brother, but Sir William will not come without You, thanks for the Lock, I will write Sir Wm: this evening but even now am fearful I shall save post. Ever for Ever Your own

Nelson + Bronte.

Cannot find the numbers.[2]

117. *To Lady Nelson*

[*a)* NMM: AGC 17/10, Nelson's draft; b) BL: Add MS 28333, ff. 3–4, original with the beginning cut off and *c)* a comment added by Lady Nelson]

[*a)*] St: George March 4th: 1801.

Josiah is to have another ship + to go abroad If the Thalia cannot soon be got ready,[3] I have done all for him, + he may again as he has often

Tyler Esqr. Commander Commenceing the first day of April 1800 and ending the 31st day of March 1801).

[1]This may possibly, though rather strangely, refer to the seven valleys between the eight (not seven) sisters on the South Downs coast, west of Eastbourne.

[2]This refers to lottery numbers (those mentioned in Doc. No. 94 and again in Doc. No. 143).

[3]Naish, p. 580, fn 2: 'Josiah did not get the *Thalia*, nor was another ship given to him. His lieutenant from the *Thalia*, Samuel Colquitt, had brought various charges against him, which Nelson attributed to spite. But in spite of his intervention, Josiah had no further employment. Colquitt was made a rear-admiral in 1846.'

done before wish me to Break my neck, and be abetted in it by his friends who are likewise my Enemies but I have done my duty as an honest generous man, + I neither want or wish for any body to care ~~about me~~ what becomes of me, weither [*sic*] I return [*b)*] or am left in the Baltic, Living[1] I have done all in my power for you,[2] and If dead[3] you will find I have done the same,[4] therefore my only wish is to be left to myself, and wishing you every happiness Believe thet I am your affectionte [*sic*]

Nelson + Bronte

[c)] This is My Lord Nelson's Letter of dismissal which so astonished me that I immediately sent it to Mr. Maurice Nelson[5] who was sincerely attached to me for his advice, he desired me not to take the least Notice of it as his Brother seemed to have forgot himself

118. *Duplicate of Nelson's will*

[CRC][6]

Duplicate of Lord Nelsons Will

Whereas I Horatio Nelson of the Nile and of Burnham Thorpe in the county of Norfolk Duke of Bronte in Sicily +c: +c: +c: a Vice Adl: in His Majestys fleet being in sound health both in body + mind do declare first revoking all former wills made by me this to be my last will + testament, first I commend my soul unto God thet through the merits of His Son Jesous [*sic*] Christ it may be saved, my Body if my country choose not to pay the carcass of him who when alive devoted it to its service any honors, I desire if its in England thet it may be burried [*sic*] at Burnham Thorpe near where my mother[7] is and my father is to

[1]Not 'seeing' as in draft.

[2]Naish, p. 580, fn 3: 'On February 14 Nelson had written to Lady Hamilton, 'that person has her separate maintenance: let us be happy, that is in our power.' (see Doc. No. 87, of 13 Feb).

[3]Not 'Dead' as in draft.

[4]The day after this letter was written, Nelson left his wife £1,000 a year (see Doc. No. 118).

[5]Nelson's brother Maurice Nelson (1753–1801).

[6]To this last will Nelson later added two codicils on 6 and 16 Mar 1801 (Docs Nos 120 and 132); in his letter of 1 Oct 1801 (Doc. No. 228) he announced that he would make over his 'little estate' (Merton) to Lady Hamilton; these settlements were updated and added to in Nelson's will of 10 May 1803 (Doc. No. 259) with its codicils.

[7]Catherine Nelson (1725–1767).

be burried [*sic*] without any funeral pomp and thet whet the custom of the world would allow to a person of my rank I desire it may be given to the Poor of those paris[he]s[1] where my father is rector viz Burnham Thorpe Sutton + Norton, as to my worldly effects I dispose of them as hereafter mentioned, and I desire that my words may be interpreted in their plain common sence, When as I believe I am worth upwards of twenty thousand pounds placed in the public funds, in prize money due pensions +^{c}: +^{c}: from the Interest of this money I desire thet one thousand pounds a year may be regularly paid to my wife Frances Herbert Nelson till[2]

(2)

her Death, thet is I mean that if I am worth twenty thousand pounds in the funds and prize money due (but not to include any of my Boxes pictures + swords +^{c}:), then the interest of thet twenty thousand pounds to be paid to Lady Nelson during her natural life and I having in my lifetime made her a present of four thousand pounds I think I have done very handsomely ~~by~~ towards[3] her, and I dispose of all money which I may die worth above the sum of twenty thousand pounds (never calculating my estate in Sicily Diamonds +^{c}: which will be disposed of as hereafter mentioned) I give the first three thousand pounds above the aforementioned twenty thousand pounds, to Thomas Ryder Esqr: of Lincolns Inn and Alexander Davison Esqr: of St. James's Square London in trust for the use and benefit of Emma Hamilton wife of the R^{t}: Honble: Sir William Hamilton K. B^{t}: now residing at number 23 Piccadilly the interest and principal to be at her disposal either in her lifetime or at her death as she shall direct, I also give in trust to the gentlemen aforesaid in trust [*sic*] for Emma Hamilton +^{c}: as aforementioned three Boxes set with Diamonds viz one of His Imperial Majesty the Emperor Paul of Russia one of the King of Sardinia and one other said to be sent me by the mother of the Grand Signor, also a picture,

N. B finish as page 2nd: in the original

[1] The line finishes with 'paris', above which Nelson has added another 's'.
[2] End of page 1.
[3] 'towards' is written above the crossed-out '~~by~~'.

(3)

sett in Diamonds of his Sicilian Majesty and on the other side the cypher of Her Sicilian Majesty set in Diamonds all of which said Boxes she may direct to be sold and the interest applied to her use and according to her directions either in her lifetime or at her death, and I likewise give to the said Emma Hamilton but not in trust my Diamond Star[1] which I request she will wear either in its present form or in any other she may like best in remembrance of an old and sincere friend,

And whereas His Sicilian Majesty has granted unto me the estate of Bronte in the Island of Sicily, it is my intention and will to dispose of it as follows, first to my father the Revd: Edmund Nelson[2] and at his death to my eldest Brother Maurice and if he leaves male children then to his children but in failure of Issue shall then to my Brother William and in like manner to his male children and to their legitimate male children, to my sister Susannah Bolton[3] + her male children[4] in like manner then to my sister Catherine Matcham[5] and to her male children as before directed, and I farther [*sic*] direct thet whoever is the possessor of the Estate ~~if it is under 1200 pound a year~~ shall pay to the next successor the one quarter part of the net rental of the estate if it is under 1200 pounds a year, if above 2000 pounds a year, then never more than 500 pounds a year and I farther [*sic*] direct that the Diamond hilted sword given to me by His Sicilian Majesty[6] shall be delivered by my executors to my father if he be alive or to such heir to the Estate of Bronte as is directed by my will and –

N B finish page (3rd:)

(4)

the sword is to be left in succession to the possessor of the Dukedom and estate of Bronte provided they are those mentioned by my will or by any codocil or deed of mine, I give unto my Elder Brother the gold Box presented to me by the City of London, I give unto my Brother William the Gold Sword presented to me by the captains who fought with me at the battle of the Nile, I give unto my sister Bolton the silver cup presented

[1]See Doc. No. 95; probably the diamond star of the Order of the Crescent.

[2]Edmund Nelson (1723–1802)

[3]Susannah Nelson (1755–1813) had married Thomas Bolton (1752–1834).

[4]There was only one of Susannah's sons still alive: Tom (1786–1835), later to become 2nd Earl Nelson; George had died at sea in 1799.

[5]Catherine Matcham, née Nelson (1767–1842), Nelson's youngest sister, had married the East India merchant George Matcham (1753–1833) with whom she had eleven children.

[6]See Appendix 3.

to me by the Turkey company I give unto my sister Matcham the sword presented to me by the City of London, The Diamond aigrette the Collar of the Bath + the Medals + order of St: Ferdinand[1] I leave to the care of my hereditary heirs in order thet it may be recollected there was once such a person as myself living. It is my direction that all the money which I may die worth beyond the 20,000 £ appropriated to pay the interest of Lady Nelson's jointure and of the three thousand pounds given to Lady Hamilton, be equally divided between my father Brothers + Sisters and in case of any of their deaths then their children to stand in their place, all my other Effects to be equally divided between my Brothers + Sisters except such as I may dispose of by the codocil to my will or codocils which I may hereafter ~~make~~ execute.

Dated on board His Majestys ship St: George at sea, March fifth one thousand eight hundred and one.

Nelson + Bronte

Witness.

T M Hardy Captain H M Ship St: George,
Frederick Thesiger Captain the Royal Navy
Delivered by Lord Nelson as a Duplicate of his Will[2] wrote on four half sheets of paper, on board the St: George at Sea 1801 March 16th Witness our hands

T. M. Hardy Frederick Thesiger

119. *To Lady Hamilton*

[*a)* Pettigrew, i, p. 436; *b)* Morrison, ii, p. 125 (No. 537)]

[*a)*] St. George at sea,
March 6th, 1801.

My dearest Friend, how [*b)*] tiresome and alone I feel at not having the pleasure of receiving your dear, kind, friendly, and intelligent letters. I literally feel as a fish out of water. Calms and foul winds have already prolonged our passage, from what is often done in fourteen hours to

[1] See Appendix 3.
[2] Nelson added the following codicils to this will: one on 6 and two on 16 Mar 1801, all of which are also given in this volume.

three days, and yet no appearance of our arrival this day. It now snows and rains, and nearly calm. All day yesterday I was employed about a very necessary thing; and I assure you it gave me pleasure, instead of pain, the reflection that I was providing for a dear friend. I have given you, by will, £3000., and three diamond boxes, and the King of Naples's picture in trust, to be at your disposal, so that it is absolutely your own. By the codicil, I have given you the money owing me by Sir William, likewise in trust. The trustees are, Mr. Ryder, a very eminent law man, and Mr. Davison; they will be my executors. If you like any body else, say so, and it shall be done. The star I have given you to wear for my sake. You must not think, my dearest friend, that this necessary act hastens our departure, but it is a right and proper measure. Why should my friends be neglected, and those who I care nothing for have my little fortune, which I worked so hard and I think so honourably for?

Half-past eight. Just anchored in the sea, thick as mud. I am really miserable; I look at all your pictures, at your dear hair, I am ready to cry, my heart is so full. Then I think your may see that fellow. I should never forgive it. It would go near to kill me; but I never will believe it till I know it for certain.

Noon. Under sail, steering for Yarmouth, but cannot arrive before 5 o'clock. How I regret not being in time to save post, for I judge as of my own fleet.

Three o'clock – In sight of Yarmouth. With what different sensations to what I saw it before! Then I was with all I hold dear in the world; now, unless the pleasure I shall have in reading your dear, dear letters, how indifferent to the approach. Although we are too late for the post, yet Hardy will take this letter on shore. I shall put it under cover to Troubridge as I shall those of tomorrow. May the Heavens bless my own dear friend and let me read happy & good news from her. Kiss my dear, dear godchild for me, and be assured I am for ever, ever, ever, your, your, your, more than ever yours yours, your own, only your, [*a)*] Yours

N. & B.

I am wet through and cold.

120. *First codicil to Nelson's last will of 5 March 1801*

[CRC] Duplicate

Whereas the R[t]: Hon[ble]: Sir William Hamilton K B is in my debt the following sums Viz. nine hundred and twenty seven pounds lent him at Palermo in January 1799 also the sum of two hundred and fifty five pounds lent him between July + November 1800 also one thousand and and [*sic*] ninety four pounds pounds[1] being one half of our Expences from Leghorn to London in 1800, making in the whole the sum of two thousand two hundred and seventy six pounds, I give this debt aforementioned in trust to Thomas Ryder Esq[r]: of Lincolns Inn and to Alexander Davision Esq[r]: of S[t]: James's Square for the use + benifit [*sic*] of Emma Hamilton to be disposed of as she may direct, and likewise request thet my friends Thomas Ryder Esq[r]: + Alexander Davison Esq[r]: will execute the Office of Executors to my will made fifth March 1801 and thet they will each accept of one hundred pounds to buy a Ring, and it is my directions thet the Sum necessary to pay Lady Nelson the Sum of one thousand pounds a year (which I calculate will be twenty thousand pounds) be at her death equally divided as directed by will, given on board His Majestys ship Saint George at Sea March Sixth one thousand eight hundred and one Nelson + Bronte

I declare this a codicil to my last will and testament, March 6th, 1801.

Nelson & Bronte.

Witness

T. M. Hardy Captain of HM Ship S[t]: George
Frederick Thesiger Captain in the Royal Navy,
Delivered by Lord Nelson this 16th March 1801,
As a Duplicate to His codocil of March 6th: 1801.
T.M.Hardy Frederick Thesiger

121. *To Lady Hamilton*

[*a)* Pettigrew, i, p. 437; *b)* Morrison, ii, pp. 126–7 (No. 539)]

[*a)*] 10 o'clock,
March 6th, 1801, at night.

My dearest Friend,

[*b)*] I have received, I dare say, all your kind letters and newspapers. No one else sends me any thing. I am sorry you are not well, nor can

[1] *Sic*, twice 'pounds', once squeezed at the end of the line, once at the beginning of the next.

my mind be at rest, although I am obliged to keep up an appearance of alacrity. Nothing shall make me go on shore to any amusement or dinner. In the morning, if very fine, I shall go to make my bow to the Commander-in-chief,[1] but have asked some sailor folks to dinner. Our expedition must be very short. I don't think at most more than six weeks, probably not half so long. And if necessity[2] should call me to England, I will come directly. What a rascal that fellow must be. It shows, however, he has no real love – not like a person you & I know – and what bitches and pimps those folks must be. I have always been taught that a pimp was the most despicable of all wretches, and that chap who once treated Emma so infamously ill[3] ought to have, ever before Sir William, one of your rebukes in your best & most legible hand. He would never forget it. God forbid that I should deprive you of innocent amusements, but never meet or stay if[4] any damned whore or pimp bring that fellow[5] to you. Let no temptation make you deviate from your oath. I hope Mrs. Nelson will soon be with you; write to her, she will come. I have just received a letter from my brother to say he will be at Yarmouth on Monday, then I will make a point of it. Lord St. Vincent, I see, has carried his false suit against his own Secretary,[6] and I suppose I shall be cast, but try it I will. How infamous against poor Nelson! every body, except you, tears him to pieces, nor has he but only you, as a disinterested friend, that he can unbosom to. Aye would to God our fates had been different. I worship – nay, adore you, and if you was single and I found you under a hedge, I would instantly marry you. Sir W^{m} has a treasure, and does he want to throw it away? That other chap[7] did throw away the most precious jewel that God Almighty ever sent on this earth. You must be aware, my dear friend, that the letters cannot be answered by the same day's post, for the letters are delivered at 3 o'clock, and the post goes out for London at 2 o'clock, it arrives at one.

[1]Sir Hyde Parker. This project was not quickly carried out as Nelson wrote the following day (Doc. No. 122), in a passage commenting on Sir Hyde Parker's young wife: 'Sir Hyde wanted me to dine with him to day or to morrow my answer was My ship was my home'.

[2]Catalogue of Christie's sale of 21 June 1989 has here: '*necessity*'.

[3]This refers to Charles Greville, a nephew of Sir William Hamilton and former lover of Emma Hart (as she then was), who had passed her on to his uncle in Naples.

[4]Catalogue of Christie's sale of 21 June 1989 has here: 'in'.

[5]Catalogue of Christie's sale of 21 June 1989 suggests here: '[the Prince of Wales]'.

[6]Probably this refers to Benjamin Tucker (1762–1829).

[7]Probably this refers again to Charles Greville.

Just going to bed with much rheumatism. May God bless you for ever, says your truly affectionate, Ever Yours

Nelson and Bronté.

March 7. I am just going on shore with Hardy to pay my formal visit, there for I carry these letters. I hope Sir Hyde will be pushed on to sail. The sooner we go the less resistance, and, oh heavens grant it, the sooner I, your Nelson, will return to his own dear, good, only friend. Heavens bless you! I wrote to keep Sir Wm from the Downs, & sent you a letter inside of his, but how different to these. It kills me to write cold letters to you, ever for ever your

122. *To Lady Hamilton*

[CRC]

St: George,
March 7 9 oclock

Never my dearest only friend say do my letters bore me [*sic*], no they are the comfort of my life the only real comfort I feel seperated as I am from all I hold dear, I receiv'd Your affectionate letter by Davison and the profile, he said you would give him another, do if you please for he knows well our attatchment, and he did a thing to day that pleased me as he knew how it would distress me even to be on board when his wife came to visit the ship, he told me he had told her (for which she has brought some Miss with her[)]thet it must not interfere in his visit to me and thet she must not ask to come on board the St: George, he dined here to day and Hardy took me aside to say thet Davison had asked him to take his wife and Miss to see one of the ships, and as I had promised Davison to take a walk with him in the morng: to stretch my legs I desired Hardy to take a boat fetch her afloat show her the St: George and land them again, I could not do less and I hope you think so, Davison said I know your determination about women therefore I would not ask the favor of you, Sir Hyde wanted me to dine with him to day or to morrow my answer was My ship was my home, I saw her for a moment she is skinny and may be called ugly certainly very plain but all womenkind are so to me but one only one do I know thet is all my fond heart can wish, and when in any way I prove false to Her may Gods vengeance light upon me, We want neither Kings nor Regents to make us happy we have it thank God in ourselves, You have my Dear friend judged most of little Parker he was not one hour in London thet same day was at Sheerness and I expect him here fitted out in two days he know my love for you for who does not every body who dines with me, and to serve you I am sure he would run bare footed to London this is but an act of Justice or I am much mistaken, Thet fellow how I hate him would it where [*sic*] peace and we at Bronte thet Bitch Miss K.[1] go she be damned, it shall be the receptacle for Virtue + honer [*sic*], even if we go to the Baltic[2] our trip must be very short, six weeks I think the very outside at [*sic*] I wish I could fly to soon even to take look, but my Dear dear friend, you are present[3] wherever I go, all my prayers and vows are for our happy meeting and when we are to part no more, remember me most affectionately to Mrs. Thomson tell her he[r][4] dear friend is as well as can be expected and has a comfort in firmly believing her constant, he desires me to say he burns all her letters although it goes to his heart he is all astonishment at the conduct of her Uncle[5] how extraordinary, as to his Aunt[6] he dont care a fig for her, Kiss my god child for me + ever believe me my Dear friend your most affectionate + attatchd

Nelson + Bronte.

Shall I offer Sir William a sum of money for Madam Le Bruns picture of You,[7] but I fear he would think it a rub[8] off, Sunday morn^{g}:[9] like M^{r}: Beckford but I would explain thet to him, as I would not take such a dirty method of being paid, By what waggon did you send the china, Yesterday I tasted for the first time your cordials the very finest Noyau[10] I told Davison I opened it for him as he was a particular[11] friend. I am going to call on the Mayor thet is right, Ad^{l}: Dickson[12] has bought an estate in Norfolk I have not yet seen him no shall I trouble myself I have left my name, I suppose it is for his raw Miss of a wife, how the two things must must be jealous of each others greatness. May heaven Bless Us Yours for Ever

Nelson + Bronte

[1]Cornelia Knight.
[2]The words 'to the Baltic' are inserted.
[3]Underlined twice.
[4]Here the paper was torn on opening the letter.
[5]Sir William Hamilton.
[6]Lady Nelson.
[7]See p. 189 n. 3 and Appendix 3.
[8]The letter is continued on the following page below the address.
[9]The words 'Sunday morn^{g}:' are written above the words 'like M^{r}: Beckford'.
[10]Crème de Noyaux is an almond-flavoured crème liqueur made from apricot kernels.
[11]The letter continues on top of the page, above the address.
[12]Sir Archibald Dickson (d. 1803).

123. *To Lady Hamilton*

[Pettigrew, i, p. 439][1]

My dear Friend,

I have wrote a letter to Sir William. Reports say we are to sail on Friday. May God [send] us soon back and victorious, then how happy we shall be.

Yours,

N. & B.

124. *To Lady Hamilton*

[Morrison, ii, p. 127 (No. 541)][2]

I have wrote you fully by Mr. Davison, who will be with you on Wednesday[3] morning. Your letters to-day have made me miserable; there is a turn in them that I have noticed, it almost appeared that you liked to dwell on the theme that that fellow wished, and what he would give, to enjoy your person. But never, no never, will I credit that you will ever admit him into your presence, much less the other. The first drives me for ever from you, and probably out of the world. My senses are almost one to-night; I feel as I never felt before. My head! My head! But I will lay down and try to compose my spirits, miserable wretch that I am. Good night; all Mr Hodges after his messages to you. No, I will never believe anything against my friend's honour & faith to me. Good night, I am more dead than alive, but all your's till death – no, the thought of Horatia cheers me up. We will be yet happy. My God! My God! Look down and bless us; we will pray to thee for help & comfort, and to make our situation more happy. Good night, my own.

[1]Pettigrew did not give a date of the letter, but reproduced it immediately after the letter that is given as Doc. No. 122 in this collection; Doc. No. 122 was written on Saturday, 7 Mar 1801, and Nelson refers to a 'Friday' in this letter, he probably wrote the letter on Sunday, 8 Mar, and refers to Friday, 13 Mar 1801. He wrote: 'Reports say we are to sail on Friday'; they actually sailed on Thursday, 12 Mar, which appears to be another indication that the note was rather written five than less days before the supposed sailing, which eventually occurred a day earlier.

[2]According to Morrison: 'no date (Mar 9th, 1801)'.

[3]11 Mar 1801.

125. *To Lady Hamilton*

[Morrison, ii, p. 127 (No. 541)]

Monday morning[1] – If I have said anything too strong, my only friend, forgive me. I am sorry my brother is coming, I like to be alone and reflect; now I shall scarce have a moment to write to thee, my own dearest friend. I shall soon return, and than we will take our fill of love. No, we never can be satiated till death divides us. I wish you could have come down with Mrs Nelson, but that is not possible. May the great God comfort you, and believe me for ever your, your own

126. *To Lady Hamilton*

[*a)* Pettigrew, i, p. 439; *b)* Morrison, ii, pp. 127–8 (No. 542)]

[*a)*] St. George, March 10th, 1801.[2]

[*b)*] Your letter, my dearest Friend, of yesterday, that is of Sunday gave me infinite satisfaction, and, believe me, my feelings and affections keep pace with yours. I shall, please God, soon return to enjoy happiness, that is if with her who I hold most dear. The Commander-in-chief[3] has his orders, but I dare say it will be two or three days before he is off. I long to go that I may the sooner return. Troubridge will, I am sure, take care of all our packets, only every day or two make newspapers, letters, &c. in one packet, for the more packages, the more liable to be lost, and I would not have a line of yours lost for the riches of Peru. I devour, I feed upon them. What can Sir William mean by wanting you to launch out into expense and extravagance?[4] He that used to think that a little candlelight, and iced water would ruin him, to want to set off at £10,000. a year, for a less sum would not afford concerts and the style of living equal to it. Suppose you had set off in this way, what would he not have

[1]9 Mar 1801.

[2]In Clive Richard's collection (CRC 80) an envelope, dated by Nelson 'Yarmouth March Tenth 180' and addressed by him to 'Lady Hamilton / 23 Piccadilly / London' and signed 'Nelson' is preserved. This envelope probably contained this letter. The envelope has a free-stamp on it dated 'Mar 11 / 1801' and another stamp 'YAR / MOUTH'.

[3]Sir Hyde Parker.

[4]Catalogue of Christie's sale of 21 June 2003 comments: 'Sir William was at this time entertaining lavishly at 23 Piccadilly, his guests including his cousin, the Marquess of Abercorn, the elderly Duke of Queensberry and various singers of the day, but a projected dinner for the Prince of Wales to which Nelson objected particularly vehemently never took place.'

said? But you are at auction, or rather to be sold by private contract. Good God! My blood boils; to you that everything used *to be refused.* I cannot bear it. Aye, how different I feel! A cottage, a plain joint of meat, and happiness, doing good to the poor, and setting an example of virtue and goodliness, worthy of imitation even to kings and princes. My brother and Mr. Rolfe,[1] a cousin of mine, are on board – the former is prying, and a little of a bore. I long to be alone or with you. I hate company, it ill accords with my feelings. Damn Lord A.,[2] do not let him take libertys. I suppose I shall lose my cause against Lord St. Vincent, I have only *justice, honour, and the custom of the service* on my side; he has *partiality, power, money, and rascality* on his, but we are good friends, and I have the highest opinion of his Naval ability. You know, my dear Emma, that I would not detract from the merit of my greatest enemies. No, I am above that. You will have Mrs. Nelson with you. She will be company, and the little woman's tongue never lays still – she is a cheerful companion. You cannot write me too much, or too particularly, tell me everything, even your thoughts and feelings. When did you see Lord A.? You did not tell me. May the heavens bless and preserve you for your, your, yours and only yours, and for you alone, your own dear affectionate, sincere friend

[*a)*] Yours,

Nelson and Bronté

127. *To Lady Hamilton*

[BL: Egerton 1614 ff. 24–25, no. 13] S[t]: George
March 11th: 1801.

My Dearest Friend, After the receipt of this letter you must send no more letters but thro' Troubridge for I suppose we shall be off, on Friday[3] at furthest, Soon very soon I hope to return to all thet can make life desireable [*sic*] to me, you say my Dear friend why dont I put my Chief forward, he has put me in the front of the battle and Nelson will

[1]Robert Rolfe ('still living' in 1845; see: Nicolas, iv, 270), Nelson's cousin by his father's sister Alice and her husband the Rev. Robert Rolfe of Hillborough; Nelson's cousin Robert Rolfe was rector of Saham, Watton, Norfolk.
[2]Catalogue of Christie's sale of 21 June 2003 assumes this is meant to be Lord Abercorn.
[3]13 Mar 1801.

be first I could say much but I will not make your Dear mind uneasy, the St: George will stamp an additional ray of glory to Englands fame if your Nelson survives, and thet Almighty providence who has hitherto protected me in all Dangers and cover'd my head in the day of Battle will still if it be his pleasure support + assist me, In spite of all Malice, every thing relative to the Gods child I leave to your management and in perfect confidence in your goodness, therefore my mind is easy about her, never no never suffer thet fellow to come within your doors, a Villain what will Sir Wm: think of my letter but it is all true, my Brother is here + so prying thet I have been almost obliged to scold him, as to thet fool Oliver, I was certainly very wrong to write to the Chairman of the East India Compy:[1] and never will write to the Directors, do you know it is asking for 1000 £ Sterling which Mr: Oliver I dare say means to get by our Interest, a Director sells a Writership at Bengal for 1000 £ Sterling, We have rewarded him well, I have not been well all Night + have naturally been thinking and hoping for future happiness, I go God knows with a heavy heart, keep me alive in your remembrance, my last thought shall be fix'd on thee yes my last Sigh shall go to my own dear Incomparable Emma I ask nothing terrible in death but leaving thee, and should you be should you be false to me I only hope I shall be taken off, but I do not believe that is possible, your heart I judge it by my own, Say In thy Breast can falsehood ere be formed –

Ah no, ah no, ah no, I judge it by my own may the Great God of heaven preserve us for each other shall Ever be the fervent and constant prayer of my Dearest Emma Your own constant + faithful

Nelson + Bronte

Tell Mrs: Thomson her friend is miserable at parting with her + his dear child he desires me to beg you to be kind to her and to Bless his child for him and to comfort his afflicted Wife that is to be, and to make her cheer up agt: her uncle and his cruelty for neither he or I can call it by any other name.

[1]This letter (presumably in support of his brother's interests) is not in Nicolas' edition of Nelson's letters.

128. *To Lady Hamilton*

[Christie's Corporate Art: PH 431] St. George 9 oClock, 11 March,

My Dearest only friend You had said nothing thet ought to have offended me but You know my disposition what I must suffer in parting from all my Soul holds dear, If You do not tell me all of that fellow I shall be more miserable our trip cannot be long and If You are forced to extremities I must very soon arrive, nothing stops me You understand, this goes by Troubridge I shall endeavour to get it on board a ship in the Roads[1] in the morning, I am glad Mrs: Nelson is with You say how much I am obliged I have directed this night Davisen [*sic*] to give her 100 £ to pay expences, pray whet has Christie[2] done about Your picture[3] I have no letter from him, how can any man sell Your resemblance, to buy it many would fly, as for the original no price is adequate to her merits those of her dear mind + heart if possible exceed[4] Your[5] beauty, all this worlds greatness I would give up with pleasure, so be it amen Emma let me be the friend of your bosom I deserve it for my confidence is reciprocal, I see clearly my Dearest friend You are on Sale[6] I am almost mad to think of the Iniquity of wanting you to associate with a Sett of Whores, Bawds, + unprincipled Lyars [*sic*], can this be the Greet[7] Sir William Hamilton I Blush for him, be comforted You are sure of my friendship, and Mrs: Thompsons friend desires me to beg of You to tell her, thet he Swears eternal fidelity and if he does not say true he hopes the first shot from Cronenburgh Castle will knock his head off, my Brother is gone on Shore, and if the weather is moderate we are off at Day light, unless Vessels are left by Sir H. Parker I have directed all my letters to be returned to No: 23 Piccadilly so take care th[e]y get into Your possession, Ever for Ever Your own Dear loving friend till Death

Nelson + Bronte.

[1]Roads of (Great) Yarmouth.

[2]James Christie the Younger (1730–1803), who in 1794 had taken over the auction house, then still in Pall Mall, that his father, also James Christie, had founded in 1766.

[3]This refers to Sir William's sale of a picture of *Lady Hamilton as Bacchante (or Ariadne)* by Marie Louise Elisabeth Vigée le Brun (1755–1842); see postscript of Doc. No. 122 and Appendix 3.

[4]Inserted.

[5]*Sic*, not 'her'.

[6]Underlined twice.

[7]Clearly, the second 'e' is meant to be an 'a'.

129. *To Lady Hamilton (alias 'Mrs Thomson')*

[Morrison, ii, pp. 129–130 (No. 545)][1]

You may readily believe, my dearly beloved Mrs. T., how dear you are to me – as much as life, and that every thought and affection is devoted to you alone; and although I am much worn out since we parted, yet, I am sure that the sight of my heaven-given wife will make me again a happy father, and you a mother. Be assured that I love nothing but you in this world, and our dear child. Fancy what would happen, and will happen, when we meet. I can say no more; flattering fancy wafts me to your dear, dear arms.[2] When you see our dear mutual friend, L^{y} Ham^{n}, say every kind thing for your husband to her, and hug our dear child. God bless you.

130. *To Lady Hamilton (alias 'Mrs Thomson')*

[Morrison, ii, p. 130 (No. 546)][3]

My dearest Mrs T., – Poor T. is very well in health, and only feels the separation from his dear wife and child, but he bears it, as he is sensible that it is all for the best to make an independence for his family. He desires that you will love Lady Hamilton, and do everything which that most excellent woman desires you. Kiss his child for him; he gives you 10,000, and is for ever your faithful husband.

131. *To Lady Hamilton*

[BL: Egerton 1614 f. 26, no. 14] S^{t}: George March 13th: 1801

Ah my Dearest beloved friend I see I feel what the call of duty to our country makes me suffer, but we must recollect which is[4] the only comfort I can know the reflection at some future day of what we have both suffered In the cause of our country You have sent your dearest friend and I have left mine, the conduct of the Roman matron return with your

[1] According to Morrison: no date, bearing the superscription: 'To be delivered by Lady Hamilton'.

[2] Inspired by the line 'Still flattering fancy wafts him home' from the song 'The Wandering Sailor', published in [Robert] *Pocock's Everlasting Songster* (Gravesend: 1800), p. 11.

[3] According to Morrison: 'no date (March 1801)'.

[4] Inserted.

shield, or upon it,[1] so it shall be my study so to distinguish myself that your heart shall leap for joy when my name is mentioned, I know I see that I am not to be supported In the way I ought but the S^{t}: George is beginning to prepare this day for battle, and she shall be true to herself, Murray[2] who fortunately join'd since we sail'd is my supporter and desires me to tell you that he never will desert me, he sees as do every one what is meant to disgrace me but that is impossible, Even the Captain of the Fleet[3] sent me word that it was not his doing for thet Sir H.[4] had run the Pen through all that could do me credit or give me support, but never mind Nelson will be first if he lives, and you shall partake of all his glory, our Breeze is fresh, what our Neapolitan Princesses would say fresh gales, but quick quick quick + let ~~return~~ Nelson return to his Mate for he is disconsolate. March 14th: both yesterday and to day Six years I was in action in the Agamemnon, for these two Nights I have done nothing but dream of you, the first I saw your tears as plain as possible on your left cheek, and working with anguish I had wet your picture the Hair had broke, last night I thought thet poor Mira was alive and between us, what can this mean time can discover.

March 16th: All yesterday was such a dreadful nasty day, snow frost sleet, strong breezes that I could not put pen to paper, but all my thoughts where [*sic*] fixed on thee all night I dreamed of you, I saw you all in Black and thet fellow setting by you all this must mean something, before you receive this all will be over with Denmark either your Nelson will be safe and Sir Hyde Parker a victor or he your own Nelson will be laid low, in case of the latter I have this day added another codicil to my will[5] and given you my Pelisse,[6] I must try + copy my will therefore you must excuse my writing for if any accident was to happen to the ship, I have no will but one made some years ago when I had nothing,[7] well my task is done + I shall enclose the original + send it to the care of M^{r}: Davison by the first opportunity and I shall send this letter on board the

[1]According to Plutarch (*Moralia*, 241) a characteristic exhortation of a Spartan mother to her son, handing him his shield, would be: 'Η ταυ η επι τας' ('Either [with] it, or on it').

[2]George Murray (1759–1819), captain (later admiral) who had fought with Nelson at St Vincent; he would go on to fight with him at Copenhagen and serve with him in the Mediterranean from 1803.

[3]For Nelson's lack of closeness to Domett, see his letters to Troubridge of this period as given in John Knox Laughton's edition of *The Naval Miscellany*, Vol. 1 ([n. pl.], 1902), particularly letter 18 (of 29 Mar 1801) on p. 424.

[4]Sir Hyde Parker.

[5]See next document.

[6]See Appendix 3.

[7]The text continues in darker ink.

London that it may go when any vessel goes for England for I do not expect to be told any more than Lord Keith told me. I know nothing but by common report Sir H. has not told me officially a thing I am sorry enough to be sent on such an expedition but nothing can I trust degrade do what they will, reports say we are to anchor before we get to Cronenburgh Castle that our minister at Copenhagen may negotiate –, what nonsense how much better could he negotiate was our fleet off Copenhagen and the Danish Minister would seriously reflect how he brought the fire of England on his Masters fleet + capital but to keep us out of sight is to seduce Denmark into a war, which I as an Englishman wish to prevent by making that coxcomb Prince[1] see our machines, every good in the cause of humanity and of honor to our country must arise by spirited conduct + every ill to both from our, delicacy. If they are the plans of ministers they are weak in the extreme + very different to what I understood from Mr: Pitt, If they originate with Sir Hyde it marks him, in my mind, as[2] but never mind your Nelsons plans are bold + decisive all on the great scale I hate your Pen + Ink men a fleet of British ships of war are the best negotiators in Europe, they always speak to be understood + generally gain their point their arguments carry conviction to the Breasts of our Enemies. Ever for Ever my Dearest Emma to the last moment of my life my <u>last</u> sigh shell be to you from all your

Nelson + Bronte.

Wednesday night or Thursday[3] we shall be off Copenhagen if <u>we</u> please, as I said 8 days and all will be finishd but it was my way + not this.

132. *Duplicate of second codicil to Nelson's will of 5 March 1801*

[CRC] Duplicate

I give unto Emma Hamilton my Turkish Pelesse;[4] and also all pictures of herself which now do or may belong to me,[5] also a full length picture of the Queen of Naples painted by request at Vienna, to Capt: hardy my

[1]Frederick, Crown Prince of Denmark (1768–1839); regent since 1784, later King Frederik VI; son of the mad Christian VI (1749–1808) and Caroline Matilda of Great Britain (1751–1775), sister of George III, who had been expelled from Denmark in 1772.

[2]Nelson left an empty space between the words 'as' and 'but'.

[3]18 or 19 Mar 1801.

[4]See Appendix 3.

[5]This remark was inspired by Nelson's recent purchase of Madame Vigée Le Brun's painting of Lady Hamilton as Ariadne (normally referred to as 'Bacchante'); see Appendix 3.

worthy Captain I give except my Plate and table Linnen[1] all my Furniture at present on board the S^{t}: George with spying Glasses Wine, China + Glass ware, my silver cup marked EH to be return'd to Lady Hamilton, to Thomas Allen my servant fifty pounds and all my cloaths. Dated on Board the S^{t}: George at Sea March sixteenth one thousand eight hundred and one Nelson and Bronte.

I declare this as a codocil to my will March ~~16th~~ 5th:[2] 1800 Nelson + Bronte

Delivered by Lord Nelson as a Duplicate to codocil

Frederick Thesiger

133. *To Lady Hamilton*

[NMM: MON/1/18] March 17th: 1801.

My Dearest friend of heart I send you a Memorandum[3] of whet I have given you, If I die I like better you should have them than anybody else If I live they are all yours together with the donor, Even had I millions or an Empire you should participate it with me, I dreamt last night that I beat you with a stick on account of that fellow + then attempted to throw over head a tub of Boiling hot water, you may believe I woke in an agony and thet my feelings cannot be very comfortable I have no communication yet with <u>My</u> Commander In Chief,[4] Lord Spencer placed him here + Has compleatly thrown me in the Back Ground, thet Lord S^{t}: V^{t}: writes Ad^{l}: Dixon[5] so now I guess thet Lord S^{t}: V^{t}: recommend'd Sir H. P. in the strongest manner, because he wanted to get rid of him, they all hate me + treat me Ill I cannot my Dear friend recall to my mind any one real act of kindness but all of unkindness, but never mind We will be happy in spite of all they can do if it pleases God, why we are not this day off Copenhagen I cannot guess our Wind is fair but a frigate is Just sent away by

[1]The words 'and table Linnen' are inserted.

[2]Nelson crossed out '16th' fairly thoroughly and wrote underneath '5th:'; I assume from this correction that he accidentally wrote the current date and then noticed that he should refer here to the date of the will, instead; therefore I inserted this codicil here; on 16 Mar 1801 Nelson also got copies of the will of 5 May 1801 and the first codicil of 6 May 1801 made and signed (see Docs Nos 118 and 120), so that it appears likely that he noticed the need of adding a further codicil on this day.

[3]There is no memorandum preserved with this letter; Nelson is most probably referring here to his will of 5 Mar and the codicils of 6 and 16 Mar (Docs Nos 118, 120 and 132).

[4]Sir Hyde Parker.

[5]James William Taylor Dixon had been captain of the *Ramillies*, 74, at Copenhagen.

the Commander In Chief perhaps to say we are coming thet they may be prepared or to attempt to frighten at distance, palt[r]y the last + foolish the first but mine is all guess I have not communicated with a creature out of the Ship since I left Yarmouth <u>they see</u> I suppose it is not for their Interest. Never mind my dear friend I think of you + thet is company enough. May the Heavens Bless + preserve you for your own for Ever yours to His last sigh Your Nelson + Bronte.

134. *To Lady Hamilton*

[Christie's Corporate Art: PH 431]

St: George off the Scaw
March 19th:[1]
1801

My Dearest friend I have bought Your picture[2] for I could not bear it should be put up at auction and If it had cost me 300 drops of Blood I would have given it with pleasure I think the picture had better be delivered to Mr: Davison packed up and I have charged him not to mention it or to shew it to any Soul breathing I design it always to hang In[3] my Bed chamber and If I die it is Yours after we get Into[4] the Baltic it may be very dangerous writing for if the Vessel is taken which is very probable my correspondence will certainly be publish'd therefore I shall never sign my name in future,[5] Heavens Bless you, Send my letter + order to Mr: Christie, directly.

135. *To Lady Hamilton*

[Pettigrew, i, p. 447]

My dearest Friend, we are now eighteen miles from Cronenburg Castle, and if the wind is fair to-morrow, and the Danes hostile, you shall have more reason than ever to glory in the name of your ever faithful friend,

Nelson and Bronté

8 o'clock, March 20th, 1801.
Best remembrances to Sir William and all friends.

[1]This line starts only 4 cm left of the folding line and thus covers most of the width of the page.
[2]As Ariadne (or Bacchante), by Madame Vigée Le Brun, from Christie's.
[3]Nelson may have used a capital 'I' here, because the word 'In' stands at the beginning of a line.
[4]But then: 'Into' stands in the centre of the line.
[5]As many of the following documents prove, Nelson did not stick to this resolution.

136. *To Lady Hamilton*

[BL: Egerton 1614 ff. 28–29, no. 15] St: George at Anchor 18 miles from Cronenburgh March 21st: 1801.

My Dearest friend the wind and weather prevents us from giving peace to Denmark for one day which I am sorry for, as the coxcomb Prince[1] wants to be brought to his senses, and to the true Interest of his country, If the Neutrality[2] was acknowledgd by us as they wish it, Denmark would have much less trade with any trading Powers than at present, Russian Prussian Imperial, even Neapolitan flags would be used and Denmark from having at this time half the trade of france would be reduced to a sixth part of it, therefore it is really a great advantage to Denmark to abandon the wishes of Russia ~~+ Prussia~~ and to try to lower her naval power in the Baltic if she does not in a very few years the Baltic will change its name to the Russian Sea. Suppose this Prince is obstinate and says war with England let us lower her (and of course agrandize [*sic*] Russia,) a moments reflection if indeed he is capable of reflecting which I doubt, for I have seen him – he is very like Prince Esterhazys son[3] thet is he was twenty years back, would tell him I lose all my possessions in East and West Indies,[4] all my subjects property to an Immense amo[u] nt, my subjects can have no trade, what will Russia lose nothing, what can I gain, only a name of [*sic*] having assisted in lowering the pride of England, and do I not at the same moment raise the pride of Russia Yes, but I will for a moment suppose this gentleman fool still violent, Oh if we beat England she shall[5] repay all the val~~our~~ue[6] of our ships colony's + expences, suppose Mr. Foolham you + your dirty tribe beat England, where the devil do you think we can find money to pay you, our seamen will spew it up to please you Yes Yes, ~~and~~ the only chance of getting

[1]Frederick, Crown Prince of Denmark (later King Frederick VI).

[2]Russia, Sweden and Denmark had formed a Northern Convention, which is often referred to as an Armed Neutrality; the British government had learned of this convention in mid-Jan and as a consequence declared an embargo on the ships of the Baltic powers concerned (Knight, p. 351 n.).

[3]This probably refers to the youngest son of prince Nikolaus II Esterházy de Galantha (1765–1833) who probably suffered from a mental illness.

[4]In the West Indies Denmark possessed the islands of St Thomas and St John in the Virgin Islands and south of them the island of Sta Cruz; in the East Indies Denmark possessed the Nicobar Islands, Serampore in Bengal and Tranquebar, a sea port in India.

[5]Inserted.

[6]The letters 'ue' are above the crossed-out letters 'our'.

money from England is to ~~yet~~ let[1] her be[2] successful, then some day we may save you from Russia, will thet Power, allow you to cramp her trade with Sound Dues, which you claim as masters of that narrow sea, yet at the same moment you want to lower and to take away the rights of England as sovereign of her seas, however I will suppose you as victorious as your most sanguine hopes could wish you, you will have lost perhaps a million sterling, you will have not one fourth of the trade you had before this glorious campaign you will lose your great revenue for farewell Sound dues, and will you Mr: Prince have gaind any thing but real Enemies as Paddy[3] says you will have gain'd a loss and such a loss as must lose your country, these Ideas my sensible friend the vicinity of Denmark naturally gives rise to, and I let them out to you as one of the most sensible women of the age and if I was to add of men to[o] I should be more correct, your beauty which I own is beyond thet of all other women is still below thet of your understanding, for I believe that either Johnson or Burke would be struck with your excellent writings, and both these rare and most extraordinary qualifications are almost eclipsed by your goodness and gentleness of heart, there you shine with unequalled lustre the first make you the Envy of all the women ~~+ age~~ in this world (your wisdom they do not envy your for they know not the worth of it getting what their want of sence makes them call the honors of this world mistress to a Prince +c: +c: by their folly) But your goodness of heart your amicable qualities your unbounded charity will make you Envied in the world which is to come there will be your sure reward and where they can never hope to reach, you will not my dear friend at this moment consider these true thoughts of your worth can be with a view of adulation, for it is very possible they may be the last words ever wrote to you, by your old faithful + most affectionate friend till Death

Nelson + Bronte.

Your heart my friend may feel too much on reading this pray do not let it, for my mind is tranquil and calm ready and willing to stand in the breach to defend my country, and to risk whatever fate may await me in thet post of honor, but never mind perhaps I may laughing come back, Gods will be done Amen Amen.

[1]The word 'let' stands above the crossed-out word 'yet'.

[2]Inserted.

[3]This common diminutive of the name of the Irish patron saint Patrick is used in British slang for an Irishman.

137. *To Lady Hamilton*

[Morrison, ii, p. 131 (No. 549)] March 21st, 1 o'clock

May the great God of heaven and earth preserve you and your friend. He has no fear of death but parting from you. May God grant you a happy meeting and soon, and believe me ever yours,

138. *To Lady Hamilton*

[Pettigrew, i, p. 448] St. George,
March 23, 1801.

My dearest friend, now we are sure of fighting. I am sent for. When it was a joke I was kept in the background; to-morrow will I hope be a proud day for England – to have it so, no exertion shall be wanting from your most attached and affectionate friend, till death,

Nelson and Bronté.

139. *To Lady Hamilton*

[BL: Egerton 1614 f. 32, no. 17] Elephant at anchor
6 miles from Cronenburgh
March 26th: 1801.

My Dearest friend this afternoon I left the S^{t}: George for a few days as she draws too much water for the service it is intended I should perform, and our friend Foley has been so good as to receive me for a few days I have the faithful representation of you with me for as I cannot have the pleasure of looking at the original it ~~is~~ makes me happy even looking at the picture of the very dearest and best friend I have in the world You know I am more bigoted to your picture than ever a Neapolitan was to S^{t}: Januarious[1] and look upon you as my Guardian Angel[2] and God I trust will make you so to me His will be done Sir Hyde Parker has by this time found out the worth of your Nelson and thet he is a useful sort of man on

[1]St Januarius is the principal of the many patron saints of Naples.

[2]Nelson did not use the term 'Guardian Angel' coherently; here, as in Docs Nos 141 (poem), 153 and 174, he means to refer to Lady Hamilton herself; he also used the term to refer to paintings of Lady Hamilton (see Doc. No. 142).

a pinch,[1] therefore if he ever has thought unkindly of me I freely forgive him Nelson must stand amongst ~~stand amongst~~ the first or he must fall. I have receiv'd my dear good amiable friend all your letters except those by the Parson,[2] up to the 18th: and I receivd those which arrived at Yarmouth after I saild such friendly letters I always burn although it goes to my heart, We are waiting for a wind to pass Cronenburgh I long for it to arrive for the sooner this business is over the sooner we shall meet, ah that will be a happy day, You will get all my letters by the Kite,[3] who carried over Mr: Vansittart,[4] they are all March 28th:[5] March 28th: under cover to Sir Thomas Troubridge, I wrote you the night before we saild likewise under cover to Troubridge but being obliged put the packet on board the Agincourt Capn: Ryves[6] In the packet was a letter for Mr: Davison desiring him to send to Mrs: Nelson 100 £ and ~~a sum xxx xxx xxx xo~~[7] Mrs: Thomson, ~~xxx xxx xxx xxx xxx~~ xxx[8] If you have thet you have all I would not have our good friend Lord William[9] in too great a hurry with his songs, I beg we may deserve them first, we have the mortification to want a wind we see the Danes amusing themselves with preparations to resist us, but with God's blessing the Devil himself cannot stop us, March 30th: ½ pst: 5 The fleet is now under sail steering for Cronenburgh I have this moment made the signal for my division 10 Sail of the Line and if old Stricker for that is the Govrs: name attempts to strike me I shall try who can strike the hardest blow, Your friend Nelson will acquit himself as he has been used to do and the blessing of God will attend him to Him do I submit myself in the day of Battle and he has hitherto always supported me, There is a little Boy thet you beg'd Foley to take he was in the Lion but for drawing a knife was dismissed from her, I have made [him] come into the cabbin

[1] Nelson describes his meeting with Sir Hyde Parker in a letter to Davison of 25 Mar 1801 (now at the British Library, Egerton 1614, ff. 30–31, no. 16); see Nicolas, iv, p. 295, under the date of 24 Mar 1801.

[2] Nelson's brother William.

[3] A brig.

[4] Nicholas Vansittart (1766–1851); Knight, p. 675, reports: 'sent to Denmark by Addington as minister plenipotentiary on a special mission in 1800, leaving in March 1801'.

[5] The date of the continuation of the letter is written on top of a new page; below it the text of the previous page is continued. The date appears to refer to the text that follows after this sentence: 'I wrote you . . .'.

[6] George Frederick Ryves (1758–1826).

[7] Here a few words are crossed out with a set of narrow, nearly vertical lines of dark ink; in part the ink is spread out in blots, so that the words cannot be deciphered any more. The ink for the deletions is darker than the ink Nelson used; also, judging from the direction of the deletions, they appear to be made by a right-handed person. At the very end of the crossed-out passage an 'o' (of 'to'?) can be seen. Under the first block of deletions I assume the words 'a sum', the 'm' being fairly clearly visible.

[8] Here a few words are crossed out in the same fashion as the previous ones, before 'Mrs: Thomson'. The last word is underlined. The end of the passage possibly reads 'for all'.

[9] Gordon.

down on his knees touch your picture with his hand and then kiss it a Neapolitan castom [*sic*], I have hardly time to tell you thet the aide de camp of the Prince Royal of Denmark, has been on board Sir Hyde Parker a young coxcomb about 23. In writing a note in the Ad^{ls}: cabbin the Pen was bad he called out admiral, If your Guns are no better than your Pens you may as well return to England, On asking who commanded the diff^{t}: ships amongst others he was told Lord Nelson, he exclaim'd what is he here I would give a 100 guineas to see him, then I suppose it is no joke, if he is come, he said aye you will pass Cronenburgh thet we expect but we are well prepared at Copenhagen there you will find a hard nut to crack, I must have done for breakfast is waiting. and I never give up a meal for a little fighting, may the heavens Bless you for Ever is the fervent prayer of Your ~~Ever for~~[1] Ever attatchd + affectionate till Death

Nelson + Bronte.

Monarch[2]	Moss[e]
Bellona	Thompson
Elephant	Foley
Ardent	Bertie[3]
Isis	Walker[4]
Polyphemus	Lawford[5]
Agamemnon	Fancourt[6]
Defiance	R. A. Graves[7] – Cap^{n}: [Retalick][8]
Russell	[Cuming][9]
Glatton	Blith[10]

[1]Here a word is crossed out in the same thorough fashion as above in the same letter, using dark ink, as above; probably 'Ever for'. The top of the 'E' can be seen and the top of the 'or', too. The 'f' would fit in size and the length of the deletion also matches the length of the (for Nelson, fairly common) expression.

[2]This list of ships is not (yet) complete. According to a list in BL Add. MS. 34,918 ff. 48–49 the British ships were gunned as follows (*Edgar* and *Ganges* are ships-of-the-line that are not in Nelson's list): *Elephant* 74, *Defiance* 74, *Monarch* 74, *Bellona* 74, *Edgar* 74, *Russel* 74, *Ganges* 74, *Glatton* 54, *Isis* 50, *Agamemnon* 64, *Polyphemus* 64, *Ardent* 64, Frigates: *Amazon* 36, *Desirée* 40, *Blanche* 36, *Alcmene* 36, Sloops: *Dart* 24, *Arrow* 24, *Cruizer* 24, *Harpy* 24, Total Number of Guns 1058; The Carronades are not counted in the number of Guns – nor the Bomb Vessels, + Gun Brigs.

[3]Albemarle Bertie.

[4]James Walker.

[5]John Lawford.

[6]Robert Devereux Fancourt (d. 1826).

[7]Rear Admiral Thomas Graves (1747–1814).

[8]Nelson was rather careless here with his spelling, so that I preferred to give the actual name (sometimes also spelt: Retallick) – instead of trying to render what he actually wrote.

[9]Nelson's spelling rather resembles 'Cummins'; William Cuming.

[10]*Sic*, this should be 'Bligh'.

140. *To Lady Hamilton*

[*a)* Pettigrew, i, p. 452; *b)* Morrison,
ii, p. 132 (No. 551)]

[*a)*] Elephant,
March 30th, off Copenhagen,
9 o'clock at Night.

My dearest Friend,

[*b)*] We this morning passed the fancied tremendous fortress of Cronenburg, mounted with 270 pieces of cannon. More powder and shot, I believe, never were thrown away, for not one shot struck a single ship of the British fleet. Some of our ships fired; but the *Elephant* did not return a single shot. I hope to reserve them for a better occasion. I have just been reconnoitring the Danish line of defence. It looks formidable to those who are children at war, but to my judgement, with ten sail of the line I think I can annihilate them; at all events, I hope to be allowed to try. I am not very well, and tired, but Foley is very good to me. I have much to do here, exactly what you said in London. May God whom I worship, protect and send me victorious. Amen, if it be His good pleasure. May the Heavens bless you. My best regards to Sir William. I hope his pictures have sold well. Recommend to Lord William not to make *songs* about *us*, for fear *we* should not deserve his good opinion. Once more, adieu, and may God bless you shall be my last word.

141. *To Lady Hamilton*

[BL: Egerton 1614 ff. 34–35, no. 18 (letter),
and CRC/33 (poem)][1]

S^{t}: George
April 2nd: 1801. 8 o'clock. at night.

My Dearest friend that same Deity who has on many occasions protected Nelson has once more crowned his endeavours with compleat success, the difficulty of getting at the Danes from sand banks was our greatest enemy for from that event it took us between 4 + 5 hours to take all their floating batteries this made the battle severe, the Prince Royal of

[1]Letter and poem are here reproduced together, because that is how Pettigrew, ii, 16–18, with the originals at his disposal renders them (a facsimile of the poem is between pages 16 and 17); it also appears likely that the poem was included in the letter, because they both bear the date of 2 April 1801. It needs to be noted, however, that they are written on pieces of paper with different watermarks; the watermark of the letter cannot be entirely read, but finishes with the year 1798, whereas the watermark of the poem is 'F FINCHER / 1796'.

Denm^{k}:[1] was a spectator and nearly killed, when all the flower of the Danish marine was in the possession of your friend I sent a flag of truce on shore with a kind note which instantly brought off the Adjutant General of H. R. H^{gs}:[2] with a civil message only wishing to know the precise meaning of my flag of truce and ~~to say~~ to say thet the fire of the State of Denmark was stopped and thet the officer sent would agree to any cessation of hostilities I pleased, this was not very inconvenient to me as the Elephant had run on shore alongside a 74 and two or three floating batteries, all our ships behaved well and some of them have lost many men, Poor Cap^{n}: Riou[3] has lost his life a better officer or better man never existed, in short of 18 sail large + small, some are taken some sunk some burnt, in the good old way I do not know how soon Sir Hyde Parker may send to England and I must write to several persons and am not a little tired for I have scarcely slept one moment from the 24th: of last month, may the heavens bless you remember me kindly to Sir William the Duke Lord William and all our friends for Ever your affectionate and attatch'd friend

Nelson + Bronte.

Lord Nelson to his guardian angel.[4]
From my best cable tho' I'm forced to part
I leave my anchor in my Angels heart
Love like a pilot shall the pledge defend
And for a prong his happiest quiver lend
Answer of Lord Nelson's guardian angel.
Go where you list, each thought of Angel's soul
Shall follow you from Indus to the Pole
East, West, North, South, our mind shall never part
~~And~~ ~~glad~~ Your[5] Angel's loadstone ~~shell~~ shall[6] be Nelson's heart.
Farewell and oer the wide wide sea
Bright glorys course pursue

[1]Frederik, Crown Prince of Denmark (later King Frederik VI), who was governing as regent of Denmark (since 1784).

[2]Commander Hans Lindholm; see: Ole Feldbæk, *The Battle of Copenhagen 1801. Nelson and the Danes*, trans. Tony Wedgwood (first published in 1985 under the title *Slaget på Reden*; Barnsley: Leo Cooper, [2001]), p. 200.

[3]Edward Riou (1762–1801).

[4]For another poem, see Doc. No. 90.

[5]The word 'Your' stands below the crossed-out word '~~And~~'; between '~~And~~' and 'Angels' Nelson had inserted with an arrow from below, above the line the word: '~~glad~~'.

[6]The word 'shall' stands above the crossed-out word '~~shell~~'.

And adverse winds to Love and me
Prove fair to fame and you,
And when the dreaded hour of battles nigh
Your Angels heart which trembles at a sigh
By Your superior danger bolder grown
Shall dauntless place itself before your own
Happy thrice happy should her fond heart prove[1]
A shield to Valour Constancy + Love[2]

S^{t}: George April 2nd: 1801 9 oclock at night very tired after a hard fought Battle.

142. *To Lady Hamilton*

[BL: Egerton 1614 ff. 36–37, no. 19] Ap^{l}: 5th: 1801.

My dearest friend I am really tired out would to God it was all over and I safely landed in England, on the 3rd: I was sent on shore to talk to the Prince Royal I believe I told him such truths as seldom reach the Ears of Princes,[3] the People receiv'd me as they always have done and even the stairs of the Palace were crowded huzzaing + saying God Bless Lord Nelson[4] I rather believe these kind salutations were not very pleasing to

[1]The word 'prove' is added above the word 'heart' at the end of the line.
[2]There is a line left free after the text of the poem.
[3]See Appendix 5 for a Minute of a Conversation with the Prince Royal of Denmark on 3 April 1801.
[4]Colonel Stewart gives a different account of Nelson's reception in Copenhagen: 'On the 4th of April, his Lordship left the Ship, accompanied by Captains Hardy and Fremantle, and was received with all possible attention from the Prince. The populace showed a mixture of admiration, curiosity, and displeasure. A strong guard secured his safety, and appeared necessary to keep off the mob, whose rage, although mixed with admiration at his thus trusting himself amongst them, was naturally to be expected. The events of the 2nd had plunged the whole Town into a state of terror, astonishment, and mourning; the oldest inhabitant had never seen a shot fired in anger at his native Country. The Battle of that day, and the subsequent return of the wounded to the care of their friends on the 3rd, were certainly not events that could induce the Danish Nation to receive their conqueror, on this occasion, with much cordiality. It perhaps savoured of rashness in Lord Nelson thus early to risk himself amongst them; but with him, his Country's cause was paramount to all personal consideration' (Nicolas, iv, p. 326, copying from Clarke & M'Arthur, ii, pp. 275). Judging of how Addington and Sheridan were reported to have commented the event, Nelson's version appears to have reached Britain at the time; these politicians spoke of 'loudest and most general acclamations' and 'plaudits and acclamations' (Pettigrew, ii, p. 20).

the Royal Ears nor count Bernsto[r]ffs[1] who I gave a pretty broad hint that his proceedings where [*sic!*] very foolish however he was very civil the Prince upon many points seem'd to quake for on his question for what is the British fleet come into the Baltic, my answer was not to be misunderstood, To crush the formidable armament of which Denmark is to contribute her part preparing against Great Britain, however it has brought forward a negotiation and if they have not enough we must try and get at their arsenal + city thet will sicken them if they have not had enough the carnage was dreadful on board all their vessels I saw on shore a Cap[n]: Biller[2] now a Commodore who commanded a Danish frigate at Naples he enquired kindly after you and Sir Will[m]: he had often been at your house, aye who had not that happiness for you[3] ever was and ever I am sure will be good, You must know you have been in the battle for your two pictures one done by Miss Knight[4] crowning the Rostral Column, the other done at Dresden[5] I call them my Guardian Angels and I believe there would be more virtue in the prayers of Santa Emma than any saint in the whole Calendar of Rome, I carried on board the Elephant with me and they are safe + so am I not a scratch, today I have been obliged to write a letter to Lord S[t]: Vincent which I hope will touch his heart, God knows it has mine it was recommending to his protecting hand the widows + orphans of those brave men who lost their lives for their King + Country under my orders,[6] It has truly made my heart run out of my Eyes it brought fresh to my recollection that only when I spoke to them all + shook hands with every Captain wishing them all with Laurel crowns alas too many are covered with cypress, The Commander In Chief has just told me thet the vessel goes to England this night if

[1]The Danish Minister for Foreign Affairs, Christian Günter count of Bernstorff (1759–1835).

[2]Steen Bille (1751–1833).

[3]Inserted.

[4]Cornelia Knight; so far we only know of this picture's existence from this passage in Nelson's letter.

[5]A pastel by Johan Heinrich Schmidt (1757–1821), done in Dresden in 1800, now at the National Maritime Museum, London; see Appendix 3.

[6]No letter of this contents can be found in Nicolas. Nicolas, iv, p. 336, however, gives a letter to St Vincent of 'apparently about April 5th, 1801, which has a similar subject: what 'actuates me to address this letter to you . . . [is the] justice to the brave Officers and men who fought on that day. . . . in my conscience I think that the King should send a gracious Message to the House of Commons, for a gift to this Fleet; for what must be the natural feelings of the Officers and men belonging to it, to see their rich Commander-in-Chief burn all the fruits of their victory, which, if fitted up and sent to England, as many of them might have been by dismantling part of our Fleet, would have sold for agood round sum? . . .'.

possible May the heavens bless you my best friend and believe me Ever your attatched

Nelson + Bronte.

My best regards to Sir William The Duke Lord William + all my friends. Kindest regards to M[rs]: Nelson if she is with you which I hope she is.[1]

Dates of letters send by the Cruizer
March 31st: 2
Ap[l]: 2 – 1
5 – 1
4

143. *To Lady Hamilton*

[Huntington: HM 34086]

My dearest Friend,

I have just got hold of the ~~paper~~ verses wrote by Miss Knight they belong to You the latter part is a little applicable to my present situation, it is dreadfully cold, I am sure from our communication with the shore yesterday thet it is only fear of Russia thet prevents all our disputes being settled, these people must sooner or later submit and I long to get to Revel before the Russian fleet can join thet of Cronstad but my dear friend we are very lazy, we Mediterranean people are not used to it, some farther [*sic*] propositions are to come off this day but I fear it blows too hard, May the Great God of heaven + Earth bless + protect You is the constant prayer of Your old and attatch'd friend

Nelson + Bronte.

Ap[l]: 6th: 7 In the morn[g]: I am obliged to stop as I know not exactly the moment of the vessels sailing

N[o]: of our Lottery tickets:[2] –
2951
9308 You can send and
42002 inquire our luck.
50416.

[1]The following overview is on the last page (page 4) of the letter.
[2]See also Docs Nos 94 and 116.

144. *To Lady Hamilton*

[BL: Egerton 1614 ff. 38–39, no. 20] Ap[l]: 9[th]: 1801.

My Dearest and best friend you will perceive thet I am become a negotiator, a bad one no doubt but perhaps as upright a one as any England could send, Count Bernsto[r]ff has taken to his bed and was not able (willing) to make me a visit Yesterday, he had sent off some vague notes to Sir Hyde Parker and I sent him a message thet I was ashamed of his conduct did he take Sir Hyde Parker for a fool, to leave off his ministerial Duplicity for ~~they~~ it would not suit a British Admiral who came to treat with their hearts in their hands, my object is to make Denmark our friend by conciliation now we have[1] shewn ~~them~~ we can beat them, In mercy spare, in my[2] opinion nations like Individuals are to be won more by acts of kindness than cruelty, we could burn Copenhagen would thet win an affection towards England, the Armistice has tied up Denmark and let us loose ag[t]: her Allies, for which I think Russia will go to war with her. If our Ministry do not approve of my humane conduct I have begged they would allow me to retire and under the shade of a chesnut-tree at Bronte[3] where the din of war will not reach my Ears do I hope to solace myself, make my people ~~and~~ happy and prosperous[4] and by giving my advice (if asked) enable His Sicilian Majesty my Benefactor, to be more than ever respected in the Mediterranean, and to have peace with all the Barbary States, this my dear friend you may write to the Queen + tell Prince Castel[c]icala I hope the King + Acton will teke care of my Estate, yesterday I was shut up in a room in the Palace half wet throug[h]– it was a hard task to make them in plain terms suspend the treaty of the famed confederacy ag[t]: England, whet will Paul[5] say to all this, I am worn out no words can express the horror of my situation, The Prince has been very kind in expressions towards me, and said the world would think my humane conduct on the late melancholy occasion placed me higher than all my

[1]The letter 'h' in 'have' is written over an 's'.

[2]The letter 'y' in 'my' is written over something else (perhaps 'opi').

[3]The word 'Bronte' is underlined three times. Another reference to chestnut trees at Bronte can be found in Doc. No. 66: 'I long to get to Bronte for believe me this England is a shocking place a walk under the chesnut trees although you may be shot by a Banditti is better than to have our reputations stubbed in this Country.'

[4]For information about Nelson's ideas concerning Bronte and how he got them pursued, see Jane Knight, 'Nelson and the Bronte Estate' in *Trafalgar Chronicle*, vol. 15, 2005, 133–44.

[5]Tsar Paul, regarded as the driving force behind the Northern Convention, was already dead by the time this letter was written.

victories Brilliant as they had been, I dined with the Prince as did Col[l]: Stewar[t] Cap[n]: Foley + Fremantle[1]

9 oclock at night.

having concluded the Treaty of Armistice with Denmark, I got on board between 6 + 7 + found to my Inexpressible satisfaction all your truly kind + affectionate Letters, my honord respec'd[2] dearest friend you are too good to me, but indeed my friendship is reciprocal and I would sooner die by torture than abandon a little of it Colonel Stewart is going home with the Armistice and I have wrote M[r]: Addington[3] thet If he does not approve of it, I beg to be superseded and to be allowed to retire[4] for God knows I want rest and a true friend to comfort me, Your virtue [Your good][5] conduct is admirable and I could not wish to consider you as my friend If you kept sure scandalous company as the P. W. how Sir W[m]: can bear to associate with such wretches I cannot think I wish you had sent me a copy [I have it thanks][6] of the Letter which Guiseppe gave you, I have scarcely time to turn round all here hang on my shoulders but I am trying to finish + hope to be home next month[7] my health will not allow me to remain here all the summer I hope I assure you to retire why should I fag my life out I am not Commander In Chief[8] none of my Gallant Lieutenants are promoted but I enjoy thet reward the approbation of such a friend as you + S[r]: William which is all I require, I hope to get Sir Hyde to let me pass the Channel the moment the wind suits for we are losing time + I want to be home and to receive the sincere affectionate

[1]Continued on next page; at the top of third page of letter.

[2]This word stands at the end of a line, which is perhaps the reason why it is so awkwardly abbreviated.

[3]Henry Addington, 1st Viscount Sidmouth (1757–1844); Prime Minister 1801–4.

[4]See Nicolas, iv, pp. 339–41 for the letter to Addington.

[5]These words have been assumed, merely judging from a possible 'y' at the beginning and the lower part of what may have been a 'g', the rest being torn away on opening the letter.

[6]The words 'I have it thanks' have been inserted above the words 'copy of'. At the bottom of the page Nelson has again inserted 'I have it'.

[7]The following passages are written on the outside of the letter (upside down, judging from the text on the inside of the letter) on the two parts that were folded towards the inside on closing the letter. The text from 'my health' until 'which is' is below the space for the address and the seal. The text from 'all I require' until the signature is above the space for the address and the seal.

[8]Nelson acknowledged the receipt of his appointment as commander-in-chief in his letter to the secretary of the Admiralty of 5 May 1801 (Nicolas, iv, p. 352); see Doc. No. 157.

friendly congratulations of you my best devoted, I am Ever and for Ever your sincere affectionate + attached

Nelson and Bronté.

best regards to the Duke, L^{d}: W^{m}: D^{r}: B^{d}: +: +:

145. *To Lady Hamilton (alias Mrs Thomson)*

[William Clements: Hubert S. Smith,
Volume 1 'Naval Affairs']

S^{t}: George Ap^{l}:
9th: 9 oclock at night.

I have receiv'd my dear M^{rs}: Thomson all your truly kind and affectionate letters which I have read over to Your own dear friend, really between Your goodness and our dear amiable Lady Hamilton my mind is kept easy Your friend was on shore with me to day to receive the ratification of the treaty of armistice, I receiv'd as a warrior all the praises which could gratify the ambition of the vainest man, and the thanks of the nation from the King downwards for my humanity in saving the town from destruction, Nelson is a Warrior, but will not be a Butcher I am sure could you have seen the adoration + respect[1] You would have cried for joy, there are no honer[s] can be conferr'd equal to this, having done my duty not all the World should get me out of the ship, No I owe it to my promise and not all the world shall make me ever in the smallest article break it, You are my dearest M^{rs}: Thomson so good so right in all you do thet I will teke care your dear friend shall do no wrong he has cried on account of his child, he begs for heavens sake you will take care thet the nurse had no bad disorder[2] / for he has been told that Captain Hamond[3] before he was 6 weeks old had the bad disorder which has ruined his constitution to this day, he desires me to say he has never wrote his aunt[4] since he saild + all the parade about a house is nonsence he has wrote to his father but not a word or message to her, he does not nor cannot care about her, he believes she has a most unfeeling heart, I only recommend

[1]See note above to Doc. No. 142.
[2]Probably the smallpox.
[3]Graham Eden Hamond (1779–1862), who had commanded the fifth-rate *Blanche* at the Battle of Copenhagen; he was son of Andrew Snape Hamond (1738–1828), comptroller of the navy 1784–1806.
[4]Lady Nelson.

the example of Dear Good amiable Lady H^{n}: she is a pattern + do not let your uncle persuade you to receive bad company when you do your friend hopes to be killed, I have receiv'd all your + Lady H^{s}: Letters to April 1st: I have such short notice + so many letters to write thet is to Lord Minto Ł Lord Carysfort,[1] M^{r}: Add^{n}: + Lord S^{t}: Vincent with a Line to Troubridge Believe me my dearest excellent M^{rs}: Th^{n}: thet I am for Ever because I know your worth most affectionate + devoted till death

Nelson + Bronte.

146. *To Lady Hamilton*

[BL: Egerton 1614 ff. 40–41, no. 21] April 11th, 1801.

My Dearest Friend I have answer'd the King of Naples's Letter[2] and have told him thet in six weeks after the Peace I hope to be at his feet, for thet it is my intention to go to Bronte, I can assure you thet I am fixed to live a country[3] life and to have many (I hope) years of comfort, which God knows I have never yet had only moments of happiness,[4] but the case shall be altered, I tell you my dear good friend all my little plans for I know you did, and I hope always will take a lively interest in my happiness, nor do I believe it is in the power of any persons however dignified their stations to corrupt your truly Innoc^{t}: Mind, then even Nelson humble as he is would coment thet his dear friend Emma was lost although alive for he could never see her more, but I know your heart is as firm [as] a rock and thet it would be much easier to remove Peligrini[5] than meke you do a wrong thing, Gold Silver + Jewels may be presents from Royalty, I can only send you a sprig of Laurel + the friendship of an humane + generous heart, which I believe you would prize more than all the Riches of this World, what little I have is honestly come by, earn'd by my Blood, and therefore I may eat my morsel of bread in Peace without a sting of conscience, The death of Paul may prevent the shedding of more human blood in the North the moment thet is clear I shall not remain one minute and at all events I hope to be in England in May, We have reports

[1]John Proby, 1st Earl of Carysfort (1751–1828), at that time Envoy to the King of Prussia at Berlin.
[2]The letter referred to is not to be found in Nicolas.
[3]The word 'country' is underlined twice.
[4]*Sic* ('never' and 'only').
[5]Giovanni Antonio Pellegrini (1675–1741), famous for having painted murals in several English country houses.

thet the Swedish fleet is above the Shallows distant 5 or 6 Leagues, all our fellows are longing to be at them, and so[1] do I , as great a Boy as any of them for I consider this as being at school and going to England, as going home for the holidays, therefore I really long to finish my task, I am glad to hear that Sir Williams Pictures sold so well, but believe me before I would have sold a Picture of you I would have starved, I wonder Sir W^{m}: could do it, I cannot write Politicks as my letter probably will be read, but I have to beg you will remember me most affectionately to our friends of all ages + sexes therefore I cannot mention names, I will endeavour and know tomorrow if you may safely write to Copenhagen, Ever yours affectionately.

147. *To Lady Hamilton*

[BL: Egerton 1614 ff. 42–43, no. 22] Ap^{l}: 13th: Copenhagen.

My Dearest friend,

all your letters up to the 4th: April I received with Inexpressible pleasure last night, by this occasion of the Post I only acknowledge them I wrote you yesterday but as they go around it may be a day later before you receive them, as soon as we are over the grounds in ab^{t}: 2 days I shall write you fully, I love you for your attatchment to your dear Queen[2] and your resolution to live + die with her, she deserves it all for her faithful affection to you is beyond all description I expect to be in England in may [*sic*] let what will happen, for I do not believe we shell fire another shot in the Baltic, you will hear thet I have been so careful not to encrease the strength of our opponents who certainly died hard thet I have only put down six Sail of the Line instead of seven, but a ship more or a ship less cannot add to my reputation and it might injure a poor Danish officer which I do not thank God want to do, I have been astonish'd at several pieces of news you tell me, but I know your worth, honor modesty + good sence is superior to thet of any woman my Eyes ever beheld. May the God of heaven bless and protect you, I cannot write Politicks, many thanks for the song, John Bull has always had faith in me, and I am grateful, I have deliver'd your message and the young[3] says thank God

[1]Inserted.

[2]The Queen of Naples.

[3]Referring to the invented friend (alias Nelson) of the invented Mrs Thomson (alias Lady Hamilton). A pencilled note in the original has here 'Connor?' which does not appear to make sense.

his aunt[1] has done writing to him, so best for she only tormented him I shall write you more by the Brig, Cap^{n}: Fancourt desires his regards as I do mine to Sir W^{m}: the Duke Lord William all our real friends.

148. *To Lady Hamilton*

[Pettigrew, ii, pp. 31–2] April 14th, 1801.

My dearest Friend,

I was in hopes that I should have got off some Copenhagen china to have sent you by Captain Bligh,[2] who was one of my seconds on the 2nd. He is a steady seaman, and a good and brave man. If he calls , I hope you will admit him, I have half promised him that pleasure, and if he can get hold of the china he is to take charge of it. I have this day pressed on Lord St. Vincent my leave to retire, and told him I hoped it would be before April was out. If we have peace with Russia, nothing shall keep me a moment, and to prepare for it I have sent to the Prince to request that he will give a general order for my free passage through his dominions in case I land at Lubeck, which is only thirty-eight miles from Gluckstadt on the Elbe.

Yours,

Nelson and Bronté.

I shall write by the brig Sir Hyde Parker is going to send home. Best regards to Sir William, the Duke, &c. &c. I have wrote by the post. Rev. Mr. Comyn[3] has not joined. I hope he was not in the Invincible.[4]

149. *To Lady Hamilton*

[BL: Egerton 1614 ff. 44–45, no. 23] S^{t}: George Ap^{l}: 15th: 1801.

My Dearest invaluable Friend I can get nothing here worth your acceptance, but as I know you have a valueble collection of china, I send you some of the Copenhagen manufacture it will bring to your recollection

[1]Lady Nelson.

[2]William Bligh (1754–1817).

[3]Comyn had been Chaplain on board the Vanguard at the Battle of the Nile. According to Pettigrew (ii, p. 32), Nelson solicited of the Lord Chancellor, and obtained for him the Rectory of Bridgeham, in Norfolk.

[4]Rear-Admiral Totty's ship, wrecked going out of Yarmouth Roads (Pettigrew, ii, p. 32).

thet here your attatched friend Nelson fought and conquered, Cap^{n}: Bligh has promised to teke charge of it and I hope it will reach you safe, our guns are all out of the ship in order to get her over the shallow water, my Commander In Chief has left me but if there is any work to do I dare say they will wait for me, Nelson will be first who can stop him I have much to say and before one month is over I hope to tell you in person, you may get out by management from Troubridge weither my leave is come out if it is not I will go without it for here I will not stay, I have just got a passport from the Prince which I shell use when occasion requires, Ever yours most faithfully

Nelson and Bronte.

150. *To Lady Hamilton*

[Huntington: HM 34087] Elephant Baltic April 17th: 1801.

My Dearest friend,

once more I am shifted to the Elephant + Cap^{n}: Foley is so good as to be plagued with me, S^{t}: George cannot yet be got over the shallows and as the Swedish fleet was at sea the 14th: Sir Hyde desired me to shift my flag, for my part I do not expect to fire another gun the Swedes cannot be such fools as to wait for us, my mind is fixed to be in England the latter end of May I hope much sooner, nothing shall keep me here I cannot write Politicks therefore can only assure You thet I am Ever Your most affectionate + faithful

Nelson and Bronté.

151. *To Lady Hamilton*

[Huntington: HM 34088] Elephant
April 20th: 1801. off Carlscroona[1]

Yesterday my Dearest friend we saw the Swedish Squadron not at sea but shut up very snug in their harbour inside of their Batteries and what

[1] Karlscrona.

is worse for us their numerous rocks, thus all our hopes of getting alongside them is at an end they will not trust themselves out again this summer, We are, at least I am anxiously[1] waiting for news from England and expect thet we shall be ordered to abstain from hostilities ag^{t}: Russia, in that case if a ship cannot be given me to go to England I shall land at Lubec[2] only one days journey to Hamburgh and take a packet to carry me over, should the worst happen and thet we have no cessation with Russia all must be finish'd by the middle of May and then I will not stay half an hour, why should I, no real friend would advise me to it, and for what others say I care not a farthing, my health and other circumstances imperiously demand it, I have given up in reason every thing to my country but the late ministers have done less for me than any other man in my situation the Commander In Chiefs made fortunes by their Victories for which ministers gave them 1000 £ a year more than poor Nelson, higher title in the Peerage[3] + promoted their followers, whilst mine were all neglected, and now what even the custom of the service and common justice gives me is attempted to be witheld [*sic*] from me by force of Money and Influence, the 25th: of May is fixed for the day of trial[4] and it is seriously my interest to be in England on thet day, I hope you will not be gone into Wales for thet would afflict me very much what signify the dirty acres[5] to you, and Sir William + M^{r}: Greville will not consult you on the granting new leases, I want a real friend to comfort me and I know none so sincere and affectionate as Yourself, I have this day wrote more pressingly if possible to Troubridge about my leave for home I will go that is certain, may the God of heaven Bless and protect Your from all harm is the fervent prayer of Your sincere attatch'd + affectionate friend 'till Death,[6]

kindest regards and affections administered to those of our friends + acquaintances as the case requires.

[1]Nelson appears to have added the letters 'ly' later, as they are squeezed into the text in smaller handwriting.

[2]Lübeck.

[3]This may refer particularly to St Vincent, who received an additional pension voted for him by the (in 1797 still existing) Irish parliament and who was created Earl instead of merely Baron and then Viscount, as Nelson had been after the battles of the Nile and Copenhagen.

[4]Against St Vincent, on the issue of prize money.

[5]Sir William's real estate, inherited from his first wife.

[6]The letter is not signed.

152. *To Lady Hamilton*

[Huntington: HM 34089] S^{t}: George April 23rd: 1801

My Dearest amiable friend this day twelve months we sail'd from Palermo on our tour to Malta, ah those were happy times, days of ease and nights of pleasure how different, how forlorn alas no wonder I so severely feel the difference but as we are returning to the anchorage near Copenhagen I hope a Very short time will place me in London, Yesterday Sir Hyde Parker wrote me word that the Russian minister at Copenhagen had sent him a letter saying the Emperor had ordered his fleet to abstain from all hostilities, therefore[1] Sir H. P. was determined to return to the anchorage near Copenhagen, I am truly anxiously looking out for my leave of absence or that the whole fleet may be ordered home, stay I will not if the Ad^{y}: would make me Lord High Admiral of the Baltic, don't You think I am perfectly right, If was[2] to think the contrary it would break my heart for I have the very highest opinion of Your judgement, I hope you have had no more plagues and thet You have lived quiet as You like if not I hope you have had spirit enough to act properly and decidedly, I will tell You a curious thing I received a few days ago a present of some ale + Dried fish from a person who is naval[3] officer at Leith, he spells his name different[ly][4] from all Thompsons I have seen except one he spells his Thomson, however, hi[s][5] ale is excellent and all the Thomsons who spell their name this way thet I know are all excelent [*sic*] people may God bless You my deares[t][6] friend God knows how this letter goes or one which is aboard the London under cover to Troubridge wrote 3 days ago, I dare say they are all read who cares I glory in Your regard and affection and Your friendship has been and will ever be I hope the greatest comfort of my life

read the enclosed and send it if You approve who should I consult but my friends.[7] remember me in the most affectionate manner were [*sic*] proper and respects and compl^{s}: as the person deserves to whom you give them.

[1]The letters 'ore' are written above the letters 'theref' at the end of a line.
[2]Sic, not 'you were'; 'was' is the first word on the second page of the letter.
[3]The 'l' is glued in at the end of the line, which is at the centre of the letter.
[4]Here the letter is glued into a volume so as not to allow the end of the line to be read.
[5]See previous footnote.
[6]Again, the end of the line is glued into the volume.
[7]Pettigrew assumes this 'alludes to the paper on the Armistice', probably meaning Nelson's letter to Lindhom of 22 April 1801 (Nicolas, iv, pp. 343–6).

153. *To Lady Hamilton*

[BL: Egerton 1614 ff. 46–47, no. 24] S^{t}: George Koige[1] Bay
Ap^{l}: 25th: 1801.

My Dearest Friend,

Sir Hyde has just sent word thet the Arrow sloop sails for England this day, therefore I have only ~~times~~ time to say thet I hope in a fortnigh[t][2] to be in London, I am in expectation every moment for the removal of the fleet from the Baltic, be thet as it may I will not remain, no not if I was sure[3] of being made a Duke[4] with 50,000 £[5] a year, I wish for happiness[6] to be my reward,[7] and not titles or money Tomorrow is the birthday of Santa Emma.[8] She is my[9] Guardian Angel and sure she has more Divinity about her than any other human form now alive, It is not in my power to do much honor to it in this place but I have invited the Admirals, and all the Captains who had the happiness of knowing you[10] and of course experiencing your kindness when in the Mediterranean, they are invited to assist at the fete of Santa Emma, in the morning I have Divine Service then as good a dinner and wine as money can purchase, you may rely my saint is more adored in this fleet than all the saints in the Roman Cal~~l~~ender, but my Dear friend you are so good so ~~virtous~~ virtuous, there is certainly more of the angel than the human being about you, I know you pray'd for me both at the Nile and here, and if the prayers of the Good, as we are taught to believe are of avail at the Throne of Grace, why may

[1]Usually transcribed 'Kioge', meaning Køge Bay.
[2]The word 'fortnigh' finishes at the very end of the sheet.
[3]Underlined twice.
[4]Underlined twice.
[5]Underlined twice.
[6]Underlined three times.
[7]Underlined five times.
[8]The words 'Santa Emma' are underlined five times each.
[9]Underlined six times.
[10]According to Doc. No. 154, Nelson had 24 people for dinner. Colin White (ed.), *Nelson. The New Letters* (Woodbridge, Suffolk, 2005), pp. 46–7, gives invitations to Captains Fremantle ('If you don't come here on Sunday to Celebrate the Birthday of Santa Emma Damn me if I ever forgive you, so much from your affectionate Friend as you behave on this occasion'), Dixon ('I hope you will have no objection to Celebrate the Birth day of Lady Hamilton which will be kept on board the St: George on Sunday next the 26th: Dinner on table at ½ pt: 3 oclock and in dining here you will truly oblige') and Tyler ('Sunday the 26th being Santa Emma's birth day I beg you will do me the favour of dining on board the St: George as I know you are one of her votarys and you will oblige your affectionalte friend'). The Rev. Alexander Scott noted down in his diary on 24 April 1801: 'Lord Nelson has invited me to Dinner on Sunday, and asked me to preach' (*Recollections of the Life of the Reverend A. J. Scott, D.D. Lord Nelson's Chaplain*, London, 1842, p. 76).

not yours have saved my life, I own myself a Believer in God,[1] and if I have any merit in not fearing death it is because I feel thet his power can shelter me when he pleases, + thet I must fall whenever it is his good pleasure, may the God of heaven and Earth the protector of those who truly worship him Bless and preserve you my Dearest Friend for the greatest happiness which you can wish for in this world is the constant prayer of your real sincere + affectionate Friend till Death,

Nelson + Bronte.

Best regards to Sir William + all friends.

154. *To Lady Hamilton*

[Huntington: HM 23635] S^{t}: George April 27th: 1801.

All Your letters my Dearest best friend to the 17th: came safe on the eve of Your natal Day You will readily conceive the pleasure they must have given me to know You my Dear Amiable still take an interest in my Glory,[2] I transfer it all to my guard^{n}: angel Santa Emma, Yesterday, I had 24 at Dinner and drank at Dinner in a Bumper of Champaine [*sic*] Santa Emma, The 4th[3] toast after dinner came as usual Your mortal part, without a compliment for I scorn to say what I do not believe, it is thet you are an angel upon earth I am serious, Sir Hyde said he had seen You at the opera and so said his parsun [*sic*] secretary[4] who was at Hamburgh when we were there, I told them I was sure they were mistaken for I did not believe you had been there, but they were positive, so You see how little fame is depended upon, poor T. is also very angry thet his wife should suspect him of infidelity, Damn me if I do not believe he would die 10,000 deaths sooner, or have even the idea, but my Dear friend there are those who love to do mischief as they are incapable of doing good, I hope if the fleet is not ordered home to go in the Blanche for both my mind and body are required in England, therefore unless You are sure thet we are ordered to attack the Russian fleet it is of no use writing any

[1]The word 'Believer' is underlined three times and the words 'in God' four times.

[2]Sir William Hamilton described his wife's reaction to Nelson's victory at Copenhagen: 'You would have laughed to have seen what I saw yesterday! *Emma* did not know whether she was on her head or heels – in such a hurry to tell your great news, that she could utter nothing but tears of joy and tenderness' (1814-letters, ii, pp. 212–13).

[3]*Sic*, without ':'.

[4]Alexander Scott (1768–1840); later served with Nelson as chaplain and translator on board *Victory* in 1803–5, when Nelson send him on special missions.

more letters, I hope to be in London as soon as this letter, and I should like a good lodging[1] in an airy situation, I have directed Hardy to take care of all my letters and return them to England, I have so much to tell You thet I cannot tell you where to begin, I trust we shall have a general peace and then nothing shall stop my going to Bronte, May the God of Heaven bless and preserve You for the sake of Your affectionate + attatch'd friend till Death

Nelson + Bronte.

If You are got acquainted again with that B—h[2] You may say what you please but T. never shall answer her or any other womans letter except Yours my best + only true friend, but you are above mortal nothing ever did or ever can equal Your excellent head, heart, person + Beauty, Bless you for ever, Curse them thet treat You unkindly, poor T. is gone to Petersburgh with Cap^{n}: Fremantle but I can answer that his wife may have the child Inoculated[3] and for his sake I hope it will do well for his life is wrapt up in the mother + child.

155. *To Lady Hamilton*

[from copy in Michael Nash's archive; the copy is taken from Manuscript Collection Relating to Admiral Horatio Nelson – US Naval Academy Museum, Annapolis, Maryland, USA]

St. George, April 28th, 1801.

My dearest Friend

I had last night one of my dreadful attacks and this day I have applied to Sir Hyde Parker, and he tells me the Blanche shall carry me to England. I have several letters ready wrote for you, but I do not send them, as it is more than probable this will never reach England ~~bef~~ Write no more, I hope to be sail'd within a Week keep this to yourself, Ever your most attatchd and affectionat

A small vessel sails with letters in two days

[1]Underlined twice.

[2]Lady Nelson?

[3]This most probably refers to inoculation against smallpox; the subject is dealt with again in Docs Nos 184 and 335.

156. *To Lady Hamilton*

[*a)* Pettigrew, ii, p. 50; *b)* Morrison, ii, pp. 143–4 (No. 573)]

[*a)*] St. George, May 2nd, 1801.

My dearest Friend,

[*b)*] I am waiting for the sailing of the *Blanche* frigate, which is destined to carry the answers of the next vessel to England, and the vessel we have been expecting every day for this week. I have been so very indifferent, and am still so weak, that I cannot take the journey to Hamburgh by land, or I should have been off long ago. I shall get on shore the first land we make in England, but as it is likely to be Yarmouth, I should rejoice to find a line of your friendly hand at the Wrestlers. I dare not say much, as most probably all my letters are read. May the God of Heaven bless you, my dearest friend, ever your [*a)*] Ever your faithful and affectionate.

157. *To Lady Hamilton*

[Pettigrew, ii, p. 50; *b)* Morrison, ii, p. 144 (No. 575)][1] [*a)*] 2 o'clock

My dearest Friend, from [*b)*] all I now see it is not possible that this fleet can be much longer kept here, and I find that although from others, there may be much self, yet Mr. Addington wishes me to have the sweets of seeing this business finish'd. It must soon happen, & I will live to see you once more, and that once will last, I hope, till time, as far as relates to us, shall be no more. We must cheer up for the moment. At present we are in the hands of others; we shall be masters one day or other.

Blanche just going. Damn that *fellow* and Lord ——. Never see them; may God's vengeance light upon them. I am like the rock of Gibraltar.

158. *To Lady Hamilton*

[BL: Egerton 1614 ff. 48–49, no. 25, and ff. 51–52, no. 27] Last Word.

My Dearest Friend, again + again I thank you for all your goodness, thanks for your sentiments and thanks for not one scold in them indeed

[1]Pettigrew gave this letter directly after Doc. No. 158, which was dated 2 May 1801, so that it would appear that this letter, too, was written on 2 May; Morrison suggests that it was written on 5 May 1801, which appears likely, because Nelson received the news of being appointed commander-in-chief in the Baltic to which the passage 'Mr. Addington wishes me to have the sweets of seeing this business finish'd' seems to refer.

I never deserve to be either scolded or even suspected of deserving it, I cannot say any thing my heart is full + big, Hardy + Parker are at work sealing up, I hope this will be the last packet I send off the next shall be myself + directed for you, in the meantime I send you six bottles of Old Hock[1] 200 years of age if you believe it, so says the Prince of Denmarks Aide-de-camp, only 10 bottles came so they stole two, I send you the Danish line of defence correct in the minutest degree,[2] Have a good glass + frame put to it I shall repay you the expence when we meet tis to add to the Nelson Room, there is a print coming out something similar, I have wrote M^r^: Beckford[3] pray give him the letter, you may shew the Line of defence to Troubridge, it is perfect to one gun + shape of vessel, Ever for Ever for Ever your Nelson + Bronté.

Provenstein[4] 15 ports on the Lower Deck 16 on the upper. Quarter Deck + forecastle cut off small Cabbin left on the Quarter Deck

Wagren – 13 poerts lower deck 14 upper Cut down the same way
Jutland[5] same as Wagrin[6]
Dannenburgh[7] – regular 64 – 13 + 14 Ports
Zealand[8] regular 74 – 15 Ports lower deck 16 upper deck
Holstein regular 64 – 13 + 14 Ports
Infrodosten[9] regular 64 – 13 + 14 Ports
Ca Ira – 80 – 18[10] lower deck – 16 upper
Franklin 80 – 16 D^k^: – 16 D^k^: 2o Quart^r^: Deck Forecatle 2 side
Tonnant – like Franklin
Spartiate – Acquillon Alcide, Censeur Timolion Genereaux 15 Ports lower deck – 15 upper, 8 Quarter deck, 2 Forecastle – Guerier Conquerant People Sovereign, Heureaux[11]

[1]German sweet wine from Hockenheim.

[2]A print of the 'DISTRIBUTION OF THE ENEMYS FORCE BEFORE COPENHAGEN: MARCH 30th 1801' by 'Robinson Kittoe, del^t^', showing images of the ships and boats with names attached to them, appears to have been enclosed in the letter (the folding lines allow for it); it is now bound in with it; BL: Egerton 1614 f. 50; it lists ships of the line, gun brigs, batteries, bomb, floating batteries, Frigates or small ships, a small sloop, small vessels of different descriptions.

[3]Not published in Nicolas.

[4]*Prøvestenen.*

[5]*Jylland.*

[6]*Sic*, not as before '*Wagren*' (it should be '*Wagrien*').

[7]*Dannebrog* (name of the Danish flag).

[8]*Sjælland.*

[9]*Infødsretten.*

[10]A '16' is here corrected to be an '18'.

[11]*Sic*, as all the names before listed.

Mercure – 14 lower deck – 15 upper – 72^{r}: Deck 2. Forecastle
L'Orient. 17 Ports on each of the 3 Decks – 10 2^{n}: Deck 6 Forecastle
S^{t}: Joseff [*sic*] – 16 Ports ~~Lower deck~~, each deck, 5 2^{n}: Deck 2 Forecastle
– S^{n}: Nicholas – 15 Lower D^{k}: 16 upper
D^{n}:[1] Isidro – 13 Lower 14 upper

The Name of each ship to be wrote between the Main + Foremast, – The Portrait disapproved only to be like the outlines formerly sold by M^{r}: Brydon.[2]

The ships to be put in rotation as captured, L'Orient will then be placed as at present,

159. *To Lady Hamilton*

[BL: Egerton 1614 ff. 53–54, no. 28] S^{t}: George
May 5th: 1801.

My Dearest and only friend All my things were on board the Blanche and Sir Hyde was to have dismissed me this day but alas in the night arrived Colonel Stewart which has overturn'd all my plans Sir Hyde has revoked[3] his leave of absence, he is orderd home + I am appointed Command^{r}: In Chief, to paint or describe my grief is impossible, I have this day wrote to the Admiralty thet my health is in[4] such a state thet they must send out some person who hes strength enough to get on with the business, Sir Hyde setts off in the Blanche for heavens sake keep up your spirits believe me every thing you can wish or desire me, I will write fully by way of Hamburgh to-morrow, for God [*sic*] sake do not scold me I cannot bear it as I do not deserve it, I dare say if I did write to Castelcicala[5] the 17th: it was thet Stewart was waiting for a boat being manned + thet I should be thought about not to answer his letter which I had never thought of I am very very ill and any untowardness from you will kill

[1] *Sic*, not 'S^{n}:'.

[2] This refers to an engraving, showing Nelson in profile, published in London on 1 Jan 1801, after the drawing by Simon de Koster, done in 1800 (Richard Walker, *The Nelson Portraits*, Portsmouth, 1998, illustration on p. 249).

[3] *Sic*, Pettigrew has changed this into 'worked'.

[4] Inserted.

[5] Fabrizio Ruffo di Bagnara Prince Castelcicala (1763–1832); Neapolitan diplomat, ambassador to London 1789–95 and 1801–15; in between these postings he was minister of foreign affairs and distinguished himself as member of the 'giunta di stato' (council of state) in the pursuit of Jacobins.

me much sooner than any shot in Europe may deliver the enclosed and believe me forever your most attatch'd and affectionate Friend till Death

Nelson + Bronte.

160. *To Lady Hamilton*

[BL: Egerton 1614 ff. 55–56, no. 29]

My Dearest Friend, As both my friends and enemies seem not to know why I sent on shore a flag of Truce[1] the former many of them thought is [*sic*] was rue[2] de guerre and not quite justifiable, the latter I believe attributed it[3] to a desire to have no more fighting, and few very few to the cause that I[4] felt, +[5] which I trust in God I shall[6] retain to the last moment, humanity, I know it must to the world be proved and therefore I will suppose you all the world to me first no ship was on shore near the Crown batteries or any where else within reach of any shore when my flag of truce went on shore, the Crown batteries and the batteries on Amack + in the Dockyard were firing[7] at us, one half their shot necessarily striking the ships who had surrendered and our fire did the same and worse for the surrendered ships had four of them got close together and it was a massacre, this caused my note It was a sight which no real man could have enjoy'd, I felt when the Danes became my prisoners, I became their protector, and if that had not been a sufficient reason, the moment of a compleat victory was surely the proper time to make an opening with the nation we had been fighting with, when the Truce was settled and full possession taken of our Prizes the ships were ordered except two to proceed and Join Sir Hyde Parker, and in performing this service the Elephant and Defiance grounded on the middle ground, I give you verbatim an answer to a part of a[8] letter + ~~person~~ from a person[9] high in rank about the Prince Royal which will bear testimony to the

[1]The words 'a flag of Truce' inserted.
[2]*Sic*, not 'a ruse'.
[3]Inserted.
[4]Inserted.
[5]Inserted.
[6]Inserted.
[7]Nelson added the 'n' before the 'g'.
[8]The words 'letter +' are inserted.
[9]The words 'from a person' are added on the third page of the letter, immediately behind '~~person~~', which is written on at the end of a line on the second page of the letter.

truth of my assertions, viz[1] – As to your Lordships motives for sending a flag of truce to our Government it never can be misconstrued, and your subsequent conduct has sufficiently shewn that humanity is always the companion of true Valour you have done more, you have shewn yourself a friend of the reestablishment of peace and good harmony between this country and Great Britain –

If after this either pretended friends or open enemies say any thing upon the subject, tell them they be Damned.[2]

get Mr: East[3] or some other able man to put these truths before the Public.[4] Envious men, + Enemies wish to hurt me, but truth will stand its ground + I feel as firm as a rock I have wrote strongly to Mr: Nepean to come home, why should I stay.

May 8 2 oclock

All my only friend for such I feel you and be so for Ever to your true and faithful Nelson + Bronte.

161. *To Lady Hamilton*

[Huntington Library, HM 34090]

Much having been said relative to the bad terms of the Armistice made with Denmark I wish to observe, first thet the Armistice was only intended a military one and thet all political subjects were left for the discussion of the ministers of the two powers – Peace Denmark could not in the moment make with you, as the moment she made it with you, she would lose all her possessions except the Island of Zealand, and that also the moment the frost sett in; therefore there was no Damage we could do her equal to the loss of every thing, our destruction would have been Copenhagen + her fleet, then we had done our worst, and not much nearer being friends. By the Armistice we tied the arms of Denmark for 4 months from assisting our enemies + her allies, whilst we had every part of Denmark + its provinces open to give us every thing we wanted, Gt. Bt: was left the power of taking Danish possessions[5] and ships in all

[1]The following lines until the line 'this Country and Great Britain –' all begin with an '='.

[2]Underlined three times.

[3]Morrison, ii, p. 145 (No. 579) gives here 'Este'.

[4]I have not found a contemporary publication of this declaration.

[5]See note to letter of 21 Mar 1801 (Doc. No. 137) about Danish possessions.

parts of the world, whilst we had lock'd up the Danish navy + put the key in our pocket, time was afforded the two countries to arrainge matters on an amicable footing, besides to say the truth, I look upon the Northern league to be like a tree, of which Paul was the Trunck [*sic*] + Sweden + Denmark the Branches, If I can get at the Trunk and hew it down the branches fall of course, but I may lop the branches + yet not be able to fell the tree, + my power must be weaker when its greatest strength is required, If we could have cut up the Russian fleet thet was my object, Denmark + Sweden deserved whipping but Paul deserved punishment, I own I consider it as a wise measure + I wish my reputation to stand upon its merits.[1]

best regards to Sir William + all our friends, to my Brother M[rs]: Nelson +[c]: Hardy Colonel +[2] Stewart desire their remembrances.

[*text in secretary's handwriting with parts written by Nelson in bold:*]

May 8th: 1801

My Dearest Friend,

As both my friends and Enemies seem not to know why I sent on shore a Flag of Truce the former many of them thought it was **rue de guerre** and not quite justifiable, the latter I believe attributed it to a desire to have no more fighting, and few very few to the cause that I felt, and which I trust in God I shall retain to the last moment, humanity. I know it must to the world be proved and therefore I will suppose you all the world to me, first no ship was on shore near the Crown batteries or any where else within reach of any shore when my Flag of truce went on shore, the Crown batteries, and the batteries on Amack and in the Dock Yard were firing at us, one half their shot necessarily striking the ships who had surrendered and our fire did the same and worse for the surrendered ships had four of them got close together + it was a massacre, this caused my note It was a sight which no real man could have enjoyed, I felt when the Danes became my prisoners, I became their protector, and if that had not been a sufficient reason, the moment of a compleat victory was surely the proper time to make an opening with the nation we had been fighting with, When the Truce was settled and full possession taken of our Prizes the ships were order'd[3] except two to proceed and join Sir Hyde Parker, and in performing this service the Elephant, + Defiance

[1]The bottom part of the second page is left empty. The text continues on the third page.
[2]*Sic*. The '+' stands at the end of a line.
[3]The word is squeezed in at the end of the line.

grounded on the middle ground, I give you verbatim an answer to a part of a letter from a person high in rank about the Prince Royal which will bear testimony to the truth of my assertions, viz[1] – As to your Lordships motives for sending a flag of truce to our Government it never can be misconstrued, and your subsequent conduct has sufficiently shewn that humanity is always the companion of true Valour you have done more, you have shewn yourself a friend of the re-establishment of peace and good harmony between this country + Great Britain –[2]

On the Armistice

Much having been said relative to the bad terms of the Armistice made with Denmark I wish to observe first that the Armistice was only intended a military one and that all political subjects were left for the discussion of the ministers of the two powers.

Peace Denmark could not in the moment make with you, as the moment she made it with you, she would lose all her possessions except the Island of Zealand, and that also the moment the frost sett in, therefore there was no damage we could do her equal to the loss of every thing, our destruction would have been Copenhagen and her fleet, then we had done our worst, + not much nearer being friends. By the Armistice we tied the arms of Denmark for 4 months from assisting our enemies + her allies, whilst we had every part of Denmark and its provinces open to give us every thing we wanted, Great Britain was left the power of taking Danish possessions and ships in all parts of the world whilst we had locked up the Danish Navy + put the key in our pocket time was afforded the two countries to arrainge matters on an Amicable footing, besides to say the truth I look upon the Northern league to be like a tree, of which Paul was the Trunk + Sweden and Denmark the Branches If I can get at the Trunk and hew it down the branches fall of course, but I may lop the branches and yet not be able to fell the tree, + my power must be weaker when its greatest strength is required, If we could have cut up the Russian fleet that was my object, Denmark, + Sweden deserved whipping but Paul deserved punishment, I own I consider it as a wise measure + I wish my reputation to stand upon its merits. **Duplicate – originals sent by way of Rodstock[3] this day, Heavens bless you + all our friends, a letter goes this day also by the Danish Post and also by Rods^{k}:**

[1]The following lines only until the line '[Govern]ment it never can be misconstued' all begin with a double quotation mark (in Nelson's original more lines are marked '=').

[2]The rest of the letter to Lady Hamilton ('If after this either pretended friends or open enemies say any thing upon the subject, tell them they be Damned. . . .') is not copied. Instead the enclosure is copied immediately below.

[3]Rostock.

162. *To Lady Hamilton*

[Pettigrew, ii, pp. 54–55] May 8th, 1801.

My dearest Friend,

I hope you have received my numerous letters sent by the post since April 10th, say six or seven or more, but perhaps they never will arrive. The Post Office in Denmark may stop them, although an English merchant, Mr. Balfour, said he would take care and send them under cover to his merchant. The Cruizer arrived yesterday, and Sir Thomas Troubridge had the nonsense to say, now I was a Commander-in-chief I must be pleased. Does he take me for a greater fool than I am, for if I had ever such good health, that I must soon be a complete beggar if I staid, I will explain to you. Sir Hyde Parker, when he had the command in the Baltic given to him, had the chance of great honours and great riches from the prizes to be taken; but that was not enough for such a great officer; he had the emolument of the whole North Sea command given to him, and taken from Dickson, and of course I had then the honour of sharing one-fifth part as much as Sir Hyde Parker, Dickson, Totty,[1] &c. will share for the Danish battle, and Sir Hyde, I dare say, will get near £5000. Now, what is done for me? Orders not to make prizes in the *Baltic*. My commission as Commander-in-chief does not extend to the North Sea, therefore I can make no prize-money here, and am excluded from sharing with Dickson what may be taken in the North Seas. He shares for my fighting; but if the Dutch come out, and he fights, I am not to have one farthing. I have now all the expenses of a Commander-in-chief, and am stripped even of the little chance of prize-money, which I might have had by being in a subordinate situation. This is the honour, this is my reward – *a prison for debt*. I see no other prospect. I have wrote very strongly by the Arrow,[2] which left us your birth-day. I wrote by Sir Hyde, desiring they would send out another Commander-in-chief, and I have wrote it again this day.[3] Why should I die to do what pleases those who care not a damn

[1]Thomas Totty (1746–1802).

[2]A letter Nelson may be referring to here is that to St Vincent of 9 April 1801: '… if I have deserved well, let me retire; if ill, for heaven's sake supersede me, for I cannot exist in this state' (Nicolas, iv, p. 341). His letters became more outspoken, however, after having received his appointment as commander-in-chief; to Evan Nepean on 5 May 1801: 'I will endeavour to execute the high trust reposed in me, as well as my abilities, and a most wretched state of health, will allow' (Nicolas, iv, p. 353); to St Vincent on 5 May 1801: 'I am, in truth, uable to hold the very honourable station you have conferred upon me'; to Addington on 5 May 1801: 'My health is gone, and although I should be happy to try and hold out a month or six weeks longer, yet death is no respecter of persons.'

[3]In Nicolas, iv, p. 359, is a letter to St Vincent of the previous day (7 May 1801), which brings up the subject of Nelson's lack of health again: 'I shall either soon go to Heaven, I hope, or must rest quiet for a time.'

about me? I will try and bear up and return; but it breaks my poor heart. My conduct is surely different, or I know not myself.

Your truly affectionate,

Nelson and Bronté.

163. *To Lady Hamilton*

[Pettigrew, ii, p. 56]

St. George,
May 8th, 1801. Baltic

My dearest Friend,

Under your kind care I might recover, and I trust in God I shall be supported till that time arrives. You understand every thing in what I have said, for this letter will be read ten times at least before you get it. I trust another Admiral is on his way to supersede me, for it is downright murder to keep me here. If I could fight a battle, the smell of powder and exertion might cheer one for the moment. Had the command been given me in February, many lives would have been saved, and we should have been in a very different situation; but the wise heads at home know every thing. I have wrote this day a packet for you with all my public letters, by way of Rostock and Hamburgh; therefore if you see Troubridge, say I have wrote to him, Nepean, and the Earl,[1] that way. I have wrote you more letters by the Danish post, but I have not heard of one getting to you, therefore I must not say a word. How are all our friends? They may depend I am firm as a rock – 'tis not a Dukedom and £50,000. a year could shake me. Whilst I live my honour is sacred.

Yours truly.

Damn our enemies – bless our friends.

Amen – Amen – Amen.

I am not such a hypocrite as to bless them that hate us, or if a man strike me on the cheek to turn the other – No, knock him down, by God.

Some cruel remarks have been made in some of the papers relative to the first flag of Truce and the Armistice. All false, for I feel all honourable for me. I have answered them by way of Rostock, and you must get some able friend to fit them out for the public eye, for I will not sit down quietly and have my public character pulled to pieces. Colonel Stewart

[1]Nicolas, iv, p. 358 and p. 359 to Nepean and St Vincent.

is now my guest; Hardy, &c. are all well. Thank Lady Malmesbury[1] for her congratulations. George Elliot[2] is very well, but cannot be expected to write. May the heavens bless you.

164. *To Lady Hamilton*

[BL: Egerton 1614 ff. 57–58, no. 30] May 11th: 1801.

My Dearest Friend If I had staid [*sic*] in Kioge[3] bay I should have been dead before this time, for what with ill health + the terrible disappointment of not going home it would have overpower'd me but I trust that long before this time you will know thet ~~no~~ somebody is coming out to superseed [*sic*] me, I have wrote so strongly that they cannot avoid it, I have as much right to have my health taken care of (you understand me) as any other person in the fleet, and if they would make me Lord High Admiral of the Baltic I would not stay, but my Dear Friend you know enough of my attention to my duty thet whilst I do hold the command every thing[4] which is active shall go on, but being stopped fighting, I am sure thet any other man can as well look about him as Nelson, I am now far on my way to Russia where I shall be able to form a pretty decisive opinion as to the views + plans of the new Emperor[5] I have my dear friend taken it into my head that within these few days your picture has turn'd much paler than it used to be, it has made me quite uneasy I hope to God you have not been unwell, or any thing happened which could make you look differently on me If it has I care not how soon I leave this world of folly and nonsense but why should I think so, Innocent myself I feel I deserve and shall have a Just return, without friendship this life is but misery and it is so difficult to find a true friend thet the search is almost needless but if ever you do it ought to be cherish'd as an exortic [*sic*] plant you will not forget to remember me most kindly to Sir William, The Duke who I shall always regard because you tell me he is your god friend and supports your honor against all rascals, Apropos M^{r}: Comyn has not yet join'd I suppose he is with Sir Edward Berry, he has several letters for me from you, you allude to a story of Lady S. I cannot

[1]Harriet Maria Mayand (1761–1830) married the diplomat James Harris (1746–1820), who was later created 1st Earl of Malmesbury.

[2]George Elliot (1784–1863), son of Gilbert Elliot, Lord Minto.

[3]Køge. The bay stretches south-west of Copenhagen.

[4]Inserted.

[5]Alexander I. (1777–1825), who succeeded as Emperor of Russia after the murder of his father Paul I (reigned 1801–25).

comprehend it but[1] I shall if ever the Parson Joins, I defy my dear friend[2] only the malice of my enemies, they may do their worst I do not believe thet you will credit them and then I care not,

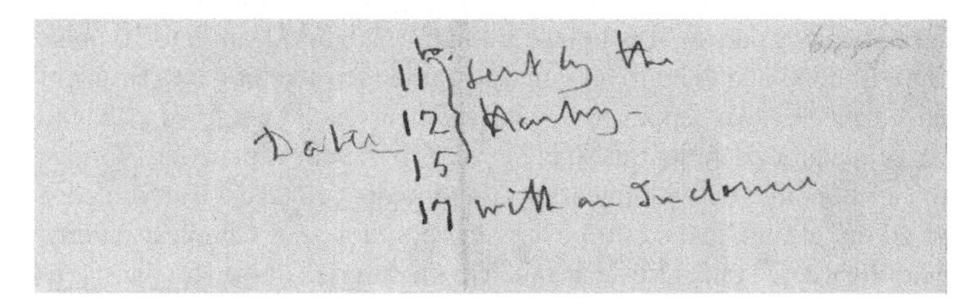

Dates 11 } sent by the
12 } Harpy-
15
17 with an Inclosure

List of letters sent on 11, 12, 15 and 17 May 1799[3] by Nelson in his letter to Lady Hamilton of 11 May 1801 (Doc. No. 164) [BL Egerton MS 1614, detail].

165. *To Lady Hamilton*

[BL: Egerton 1614 ff. 59–60, no. 31] May 12th: Gulph of Finland off Pakerot Ligh[t]house[4] 6 o'clock.

My Dearest and only friend here I am very near the Latitude of 60° degrees North the air like a fine January day, but my heart as warm towards you as the sincerest friendship can make it, and as if I was upon the Equator, You deserve every mark of kindness from me and by the living God you shall always experience it whilst I draw breath which notwithstanding the unkindness of some folks I hope will be yet some years I did not my dear friend come to the Baltic with a design of dying

[1] The following passages are on the outside of the letter, on the sides that were folded inside for the sending of the letter. The part from 'I shall' until 'I care not' are a continuation of the inside also in writing-direction. The rest is upside down on the other side of the address.

[2] The words 'dear friend' are inserted.

[3] These dates appear to have been added later, when the *Harpy* left the fleet; they correspond to the letters we know about, although we do not know of an enclosure to the letter of 17 May 1801 (Doc. No. 168).

[4] The lighthouse on the cliff of Pakri/Pakerordi (from German Packerort, which again was derived from the placename 'Packer/Packar' of an 15th-century village, combined with the German word 'Ort' for a ledge on a coastline), at the top of the Pakri peninsula, west of Revel/Tallinn, near the then Russian naval port, called Baltiski Port, which has changed in Estonian into Paldiski.

a natural[1] death who will thank me,[2] those who care not one farthing for me, our friend[3] Troubridge has felt[4] so little for my health thet I have wrote him word I should never mention it again to him by the 12 of June or before I hope to be in London[5] wher[e] I am fixed as to the plan of life I mean to pursue, it is to take a small neat house from 6 to 10 miles from London and there to remain till I can fix for ever or get to Bronte. I have never known happiness beyond moments[6] and I am fixed as fate to try if I cannot attain it after so many years of labour and anxiety, forgive me tormenting you with my affairs, but I know you take a lively interest in all my affairs, and so do I every day pray for your compleat felicity, May 13th: here I am at Revel as much to the surprize of the Russians as to most in the squadron, expresses are gone to Petersburgh and I have wrote to Count Pahlen the Prime Minister[7] and I dare say we shall be ordered a very friendly reception, I have ordered very fine beef + soft bread for our ships but there is not a sign of vegetation the Russian fleet sail'd from hence on the 2nd: to Join the Cronstat[8] fleet at Caskna Gorku,[9] where they are moor'd 43 Sail of the Line, but with 25 if we were at war I should not hesitate trying what stuff they are made ~~of~~ on,[10] in abt: a week I shall return from hence and by the time I get down I hope a new Adl: will be arrived, when I shall proceed direct for England, may the heavens bless

[1]Underlined twice; Nelson had written to Addington on 5 May 1801 in a similar vein: 'I own, at present, I should not wish to die a natural death' (Nicolas, iv, p. 355).

[2]Inserted.

[3]Underlined twice.

[4]Underlined twice.

[5]In fact it would take until 2 July 1801 for Nelson to come back to London.

[6]Nelson had written in a similar vein to Lady Hamilton on 11 April 1801 'God knows I have never yet had only moments of happiness' (*sic*, as to 'never' and 'only').

[7]'Prime Minister' does roughly describe the position(s) Peter von der Pahlen (1745–1826) held; he enjoyed the favour of Paul I, for three years (1798–1801), serving as the military governor of St Petersburg, the governor of the Baltic provinces, the inspector of six military districts, the Grand Chancellor of the Maltese Order, the chief director of mail, a member of the Imperial Council and of the Board of Foreign Affairs; as a consequence of his being implicated in Paul's murder, he was discharged on 1 April 1801, of which Nelson probably did not know.

[8]'Cronstat' was the contemporary spelling of 'Cronstadt'.

[9]This may refer to one of the following bays on the southern side of the Gulf of Finland between Revel (now Tallinn) and Kronstadt (near St Petersburg), from west to east: Kasper, Kunda or the huge Narva Bay on which lays the village Kohtla (now part of the town of Kohtla-Järve), which is spelt in Russian Кохтла (=Caskna?); город (gorod = Gorku?) means town.

[10]The word 'on' appears above the crossed-out word 'of'. The correction is in much darker ink.

you + grant us a meeting a happy one I am sure it will be for I know not such true friends as we are,[1]

To the Duke Lord William +[c]: say everything, Troubridge has not been kind, but never mind. I have sent Galuchi, the child on board Foley a pres[t]: in your name, he is a fine boy but a Pickle remember me most affectionately to all our friends and to those I love most, say you what is proper. I will soon be in England.

166. *To Lady Hamilton*

[BL: Egerton 1614 ff. 61–62, no. 32] S[t]: George
May 15th: 1801 Revel Bay

My Dearest Friend After 17 days not out of my cabbin I was forced to row 7 miles to make the formal visit to the Governor, General[2] + head of the Ad[ty]: here it cost me about 3 hours, they wanted me to dine on shore but if I had been ever so well I would not it is a horrid nasty place and nothing less than the arrival of the Emperor[3] shall get me ashore again, As usual I receiv'd all the compliments to which I have been used and which have spoilt me except to your good heart,[4] the crowd was of course all the Town, this morning the Governor and Admiral will be on board the S[t]: George and tomorrow morning I shall get answers to my letters from Petersburgh, I have wrote a line my dear Friend by the post but as the post is a month going and my letter will assuredly be read, it is only a date to say where I am, I have wrote to Lord S[t]: Vincent to say I expect to find another Admiral when I return, or probably he will never see me again, I cannot I will not stay here thet you may rely upon why should I[5] when my health + happiness can I hope be perfect by going to England May 16th: Yesterday I had all the world on board on ~~baord~~ board[6] not less than thirty officers + nobles of Rank except to you my own friend I should not mention it, 'tis so much like vanity but hundreds come to look at Nelson, that is him, that is him in short 'tis the same as

[1]The following passage is written upside down (judging from the direction within the letter).

[2]Pettigrew, ii, p. 62, suggests here 'Governor-General'.

[3]Alexander I.

[4]Compare passages in Docs Nos 8 ('You and Sir William have spoiled [me]'), 29 ('You and Good Sir William have spoilt me for any place but with you') and 44 ('you and Sir William have so spoiled me that I am not happy anywhere else but with you').

[5]The word 'I' appears to have been inserted later.

[6]The first 'on board' appears at the end of a line; then it is repeated at the beginning of the next line.

in Italy + Germany and I now feel that a good name is better than riches, not amongst our great folks in England, but it has its fine feelings to an honest heart, All the Russians have take[n] it into their heads that I am like Sowaroff, Le Jeune Sowaroff.[1] this evening I expect the return of the courier from Petersburgh, I have increas'd my cough very much by going round the ship with the Russian officers and my trip on shore, I only hope the first land I next set my foot upon will be Old England and the first house will assuredly be yours, As you will know when an Ad[l]: is coming out to superseed [*sic*] me or that permission is come out for my return home, I hope to find you my only friend in London for I have much to say to you

167. *To Lady Hamilton*

[Pettigrew, ii, p. 68] St. George, Revel Bay,
May 15th, 1801.

My dearest Friend,

The Harpy brig sails to-morrow for England. You will not receive this line for a fortnight after her arrival I cannot say a word on politics. I expect to find a new Admiral on my return, which will be in a very few days.

Yours, &c.

Nelson and Bronté

Most probably you will never receive this letter. I have three wrote for you now lying by me. Finish of eight lines to Lord St. Vincent: – 'I expect to find a new admiral when I return off Bornholm, or most probably you will never see again

Your affectionate,

N. & B.'[2]

[1]Alexander Vasilyevich Suvorov (1729 or 1730–1800).

[2]No such letter is to be found in Nicolas' edition of *The Dispatches and Letters of Lord Nelson*, but on 17 May 1801 Nelson finished a letter to St Vincent: 'In four days I hope to join Admiral Totty, off Bornholm' (Nicolas, iv, p. 373).

168. *To Lady Hamilton*

[Pettigrew, ii, p. 68][1]

St. George,
May 17 th, 1801. 7 o'clock in the Evening.
Last letter.

My dearest Friend,

I sailed from Revel this morning, and feel I am now steering for England for the recovery of my health. I expect to be there a few days after this letter; for if the Admiralty have any bowels of compassion, an Admiral must have long since sailed to supersede me. I have wrote a very strong letter to the Board[2] in case none is sailed. I shall keep by Rostock and Lubeck in case I am to go by land; it is only one day's journey to Hamburgh. This day I reckon, if Sir Hyde Parker had not been ordered home, I should have arrived perhaps in London. What a thought! But the time *shall* soon come in spite of all the world, and all my enemies, damn them. I cannot obey the Scriptures and bless them.[3]

I am rather inclined to believe that the Emperor of Russia had some fears for his fleet of forty-three sail of the line, for he seemed very anxious to get rid of my small squadron. I have much to tell you – the boat is waiting – night coming on. Adieu.

Yours, &c.

Nelson and Bronté.

169. *To Lady Hamilton*

[BL: Add. MS 34,274, f. 61]

St: George off Rostock
May 24th: 1801
1 – under Davisons cover +c to Troubridge +c to Nepean.[4]

My Dearest beloved friend Yesterday I join'd Adl: Totty where I found little Parker with all <u>all</u> my treasures your dear kind friendly letters, Your picture as 'Santa Emma[5] for a Santa you are if ever there was one in this world, for what makes a saint the being so much better than the rest of the human race therefore as truly as I believe in God do I believe

[1]According to Doc. No. 164, this letter was sent 'with an Inclosure'.
[2]of the Admiralty; see letter to Evan Nepean of 17 May 1801 (Nicolas, iv, 374).
[3]Compare Doc. No. 163.
[4]This line appears to have been added later, since it is written in smaller letters between the line above and the address to Lady Hamilton.
[5]*Sic.* There is no closing quotation mark after the words 'Santa Emma'.

you are a Saint and in this age of Wickedness you sett an example of real Virtue and goodness which if we are not too far sunk in Luxury and Infamy ought to rouse up almost forgot Virtue and may Gods curse alight upon those who want to draw you my dearest friend from a quiet home into the company of men + women of bad Character, and I am one of those who believe that in England the higher the class the worse the company, I speak generally I will not think so bad of any class but that there may be some good individuals in it, how can I sufficiently thank you for all your goodness + kindness to me a for~~xx~~lorn[1] outcast except in your generous soul,[2] My health I have represented to the Admiralty in such terms thet I have no doubt but an Admiral has sail'd to take my place, the Harpy has carried a stronger letter than any of the former, this vessel stetes thet I do not know thet I shell go to sea again, as my health requires the shore + gentle exercise and so it does, and really if the Admiralty had allowed me to go home and in the event of hostilities being renewed in the Baltic I might perhaps in thet case have been able to command the fleet but the Baltic folks will never fight me if it is to be avoided, In my humble opinion, we shell have peace with the northern powers, If we are Just in our desires Will you have the goodness to carry the inclosed after you have sealed it to M^{rs}: Maurice Nelson and your own dear generous [heart] will say every kind thing for me, She shell be fixed where she pleases and with every comfort in this world, and ever be considered as my honor'd sister-in-law I feel my dear Brother's confidence and she shall feel he has not mistaken me,[3] tell M^{rs}: W^{m}: Nelson how much I esteem her for all her kindness, and thet[4] I shell never forget her complying with my request in staying with you although I hope it has been truly pleasant to herself, to M^{rs}: Denis say every kind thing you please for her letter, tell her I want not to conquer any heart if that which I have conquered is happy in its lot, I am conf[id]ent, for the conqueror

[1]At the centre of the word, between 'for' and 'lorn', Nelson crossed out one or two letters that cannot be deciphered any more.

[2]Compare Doc. No. 85: 'Do not forget me; consider I am a miserable fellow shut up in wood.'

[3]Pettigrew, ii, p. 79, comments: 'He gave to his brother's widow an annuity of £100. *per annum*, which she received until his death, and she was afterwards assisted by Lady Hamilton. She died about 1810 or 1811'.

[4]The following passages are written on the outside of the letter (upside down, judging from the text on the inside of the letter) on the two parts that were folded towards the inside on closing the letter. The text from 'I shell' until 'is happy' is below the space for the address and the seal. The text from 'in its' until the signature is above the space for the address and the seal.

is become the conquered, I want but one true heart, There can be but one Love although many real well-wisher[s], Ever for Ever your Dear + truly affectionate Friend

Nelson + Bronte.

Best regards to Sir William

170. *To Lady Hamilton*

[*a)* Pettigrew, ii, p. 80; *b)* Morrison, ii, pp. 149–150 (No. 589)][1] [*a)*] St. George, Bay of Rostock

My dearest Friend,

[*b)*] Although I wrote you late last night by the Speedwell all my proceedings to that time, I yet should think myself a great beast if I was to omit an opportunity of writing to you a line by way of Hamburgh, where I am sending off an express to Sir James Crawfurd. I wrote to the Admiralty yesterday that I did not think I should be able to write any more letters to them, for the stooping so many hours hurts me very much. I trust yet to being in London before June 12th. If the new Admiral would arrive, I should certainly sail in two hours. I have directed the *London* to be the show ship, for I will have no visitors here that I can help. It is said that the Duke or Prince of Mecklenburg[2] intends to come here to see the fleet, but nothing, you may rely, shall force me to go on shore. There is but one person, and to that person the Devil himself should not keep me afloat. May God bless and protect you, my dearest, best, most amiable, virtuous friend. The hock I ordered to be sent by the wagon. The Harpy will arrive, I hope, to-morrow. The Speedwell will have a good passage. I have ten millions of things to say to you, and I long so to let all out. If Ministers had really thought highly of me they should have given me the command in February, not in May, when I can do no good. I am sure you will comfort poor blind Mrs. Nelson. Whatever you do, I will confirm; and there is an old black servant, James Price, as good a man as ever lived, he shall be

[1]According to Morrison: 'no date (May 26th, 1801)'.
[2]Frederick-Francis (Friedrich-Franz) I of Mecklenburg-Schwerin (1756–1837).

taken care of, and have a corner in my house as long as he lives. My uncle[1] left him £20. a-year.

Ever yours,

[*a)*] Nelson and Bronté.

[*b)*] This day comes on my great cause against the Earl.[2] May the just gain it. Thomson will be very well when he gets home, and is nursed by his wife, and so you may tell her from me. I am so glad to hear of your determination not to leave London 'till my arrival. If Mrs. Denis' young man comes out we will take care of him.

171. *To Lady Hamilton*

[Monmouth: volume 320 E321] St: George Rostock May 27th: 1801.

My Dearest Friend, a Russian Lugger having this moment brought me a letter from the Russian Minister announcing that the Emperor to mark the effect of my letter of the 16th: of May[3] had instantly taken off the embargo from the English Shipping in all the Ports of Russia, this my dear friend is such a strong proof of peace in the Baltic thet this fleet must be home in a very short time, but I trust thet another admiral is arrived or nearly so by this time, when I shell sett off in two hours, all the world is come to Rostock to see me and are much disappointed at the finding that I do not either go on shore or permit them to come on board the St: George, No never I have said so and would not break my word for all the world, The London is the Show Ship, The General of the Troops sent off to desire to make me a visit my answer was thet I had no right to expect thet honor as I was unable to return his visit, however yesterday the old General + 3 Aid de Camps [*sic*] came walked over the ship such a one as they had never seen + went on shore again, the old General said your picture was the greatest and rarest curiosity he had ever seen, I have announced to the Duke of Mecklingburgh[4] the impossibility of my going on shore therefore he may come or not as he pleases for nothing shall

[1]William Suckling (c. 1729–98).

[2]Nelson's lawsuit about prize money against St Vincent.

[3]To the Russian 'prime minister' Count Pahlen, declaring that his fleet sailed nowhere without consent of the Russian authorities and announcing that he was about to 'sail immediately into the Baltic' (Nicolas, iv, pp. 371–373).

[4]Frederick-Francis (Friedrich-Franz) I of Mecklenburg-Schwerin.

make me go on shore unless to sett off for England if the Admiralty are unkind enough to refuse me a ship of war to carry me home as the late Board did,[1] but never mind may the heavens bless you, If you approve give the enclosed to Mrs: Denis if not burn it, I don't like thet part of her letter, I have an opinion of her similar to yours, Ever for Ever your most faithful

Nelson and Bronté.

best regards to Sir William the Duke, Mr: Beckford, + all our friends + damn all our Enemies,

I heve just had a deputation of the Senate[2] to invite me on shore, but No

172. *To Lady Hamilton*

[Pettigrew, ii, p. 83] St. George, Rostock, June 1st, 1801.

My dearest Friend,

I was in hopes my successor would have been arrived long before this time, and why he is not I cannot imagine, unless it is wished to kill me; for a pistol put to my head would be charity to keeping me here dying a lingering death. I feel the cruelty of the measure, for everybody knows my readiness to serve when I am able, and there is anything to be done, but in the Baltic there can be nothing, and in fourteen days I believe we shall not have a ship in the Baltic, for all will be peace. May God send me safe amongst my friends, who will nurse and cherish me. I am going to Kioge Bay, there to wait my successor's arrival, for he cannot be many hours. Two days ago I had sailed from this place for Kioge Bay, when, being obliged to anchor with a fine wind, I received a letter from his Highness the Duke of Mecklenburg Strelitz,[3] brother to the Queen,[4] saying that he was arrived at Rostock to see me, and desired I would appoint the time for his coming on board the St. George. I was therefore obliged to return to this anchorage, and wrote, expressing my sorrow that my ill health would not allow of the possibility of my going on shore to

[1]An allusion to the end of his trip through continental Europe, when he had to arrange his return from Hamburg with the Hamiltons on a packet boat.

[2]The council of the city was called a 'Senate', originating from the republican roots of Rostock as a Hanseatic town.

[3]Charles II, Duke of Mecklenburg (1741–1816, reigned 1794–1816), father of the popular queen Luise of Prussia.

[4]Charlotte of Mecklenburg-Strelitz (1744–1818), wife of George III.

wait upon him. Yesterday was a bad day, to-day fine, and I hope the old gentleman will come off, sixty-one years of age, and the moment he his gone the anchor shall be at the bows. Not all the princes in Europe should make me go on shore. I have said it, and that is sufficient. My word is my bond. There is one comfort, my dearest friend, they cannot keep this fleet when it comes peace, which will take place in ten days at farthest. I do not write all I could, as my letter goes by way of Hamburgh, and will most probably be read.

Believe me ever yours,

Nelson and Bronté.

Best regards to Sir William, Hardy, Parker, Stewart, all desire their respects.

173. *To Lady Hamilton*

[consulted at Sotheby's, 19 May 2010] S^{t}: George June 1st: 8 A M

My Dearest best amiable friend, I have been annoy'd to death for an hour this day the Duke of Meclenburgh[1] with his whole Court Men Women + children to the amount of 100 I am told came on board at 2 oclock, but I got rid of them before three He is a respectable venerable Man made 10,000 apoligys [*sic*] for the Liberty he had taken in bringing so many persons for he knew thet I had forbid it, to which I could only reply thet he commanded and having given him two salutes of the whole fleet of 21 guns each he went off quite happy, he admired Your picture most exceedingly but who does not, for where can your resemblance be, not in the World and my heavens keep You a non pareil[2] at day light I sail for Kioge to wait the arrival of the new admiral may the God of heaven + Earth soon give us a happy meeting being for Ever + more then Ever your

[Nelson and Bronte][3]

[1]Probably referring to the Duke of Mecklenburg Schwerin (not Mecklenburg Strelitz).
[2]End of line.
[3]The signature was cut out of the letter.

174. *To Lady Hamilton*

[Pettigrew, ii, pp. 84–85] St. George, Kioge Bay, June 5th, 1801.

My dearest Friend,

Little potatoe Harris has this moment given me your letter. I can only assure you that he brought the best recommendation in Europe, for if he had brought letters from all the Kings and Queens, &c. &c. in Europe, they would have all sunk as they ought before the orders of my guardian angel. When I consider how my saint Emma has protected me, I am always full of gratitude. However, my devotion ended, as the boy cannot live upon prayers, I have asked him to dinner, and Hardy has put him in a mess, and you may rely on my care of him whilst I remain, which I trust will not be many days. Hardy says our youngsters amount to thirty-five, and none of them can now be shot at in the Baltic, if Lord St. Helens[1] manages well. Apropos, you know him, did you dine with him? He seems a very mild, good man, but all our diplomatic men are so slow. His Lordship told me that he hoped in a month he should be able to tell me something decisive. Now, what can take two hours I cannot even guess, but Ministers must do something for their diamond boxes. I gained the unconditional release of our ships, which neither Ministers nor Sir Hyde Parker [achieved], by showing my fleet. Then they became alarmed, begged I would go away, or it would be considered as warlike. On my complying, it pleased the Emperor and his Ministers so much, that the whole of the British shipping were given up in the following words: 'Je ne saurais donner à votre Excellence un témoignage plus éclatant de la confiance que l'Empereur mon maître lui accorda qu'en lui annonçant l'effet qu'a produit sa letter de 16 de ce mois. Sa Majesté Impériale a ordonné sur le champ la lever[2] de l'Embargo mis sur les Navires Anglais'. I must stop, for old Mr. Sheppard, Purser of the Vanguard, is just come on board to dine with me. I never forget our old friends, and Mr. S. is really a good old man, but who is obliged to go to sea from the extravagance of his children. Old Sheppard has made his bow to your picture: so I made Harris, and every one I make do the same, that has the pleasure of knowing Santa Emma. I am anxious in

[1]Alleyne FitzHerbert, 1st Baron St Helens (1753–1839); newly appointed British ambassador to Russia.

[2]This should be: 'levée'.

the extreme at not getting letters from England, nor any notice of the speedy arrival of an Admiral.

Ever yours,

Nelson and Bronté.

Best regards to Sir William, the Duke, Lord William, Mr. Beckford and all friends. Hardy and Parker desire their regards.

175. *To Lady Hamilton*

[BL: Egerton 1614 ff. 63–64, no. 33]

S^{t}: George
June 8th: 1801

My dearest Friend I may now tell you that I have been since April 15th: rapidly in a decline But am now thank God I firmly believe past all danger On the 15th: of April I row'd 5 hours in a bitter cold night in a boat as I fancied Sir H. P^{r}: was going after the Swedish fleet, a cold struck me to the heart, on the 27th: I had one of my terrible spasms or heart stroke which had near carried me off, and the severe disappointment of being kept in a situation where there can be nothing to do before August almost killed me, from thet time to the end of May I brought up whet every one thought was my lungs and I was emaciated more than you can conceive but Parker came and brought me all your truly affectionate letter[s], in particular thet of May 5th: it roused me, made me reflect thet I had still one dear friend who would not desert me although all the world might it gave a turn to my disorder I have been mending ever since firmly relying on your goodness, and am perhaps as well this day as ever I was in my life, I am in momentary expectation of the arrival of an Admiral for I must not remain here probably I have lost my cause ag^{t}: Earl S^{t}: V^{t}:[1] by it, indeed after the letters I have wrote unless the Admiralty have a desire to see me Dead they cannot allow me to remain but God Almighty has protected me, in spite of all the little Great men, it is this day 34 days since I have had a scrap of a pen from England, so little do the Admiralty think of us, merch^{t}: ships from London bring papers of the 23 May, but the Admiralty not a Line dont you recollect how I got scolded, because I sent letters to them only three ways, and a fourth offered it happened

[1]About prize money.

at Palermo[1] when I was slaving and for which the present first Lord of the Ad^y:[2] is trying to Rob me of my honourable right, but if I am poor by such unjust means, whet I have will wear well for it is honestly got at the expence of my blood therefore never mind them[3] my happiness thank God does not rest either on their smiles or frowns, I keep a fast-sailing Brig ready to carry me off the moment my successor arrives, may the Heavens Bless + preserve you my only true friend, I rejoice that M^rs: W^m: Nelson is still with you, I am sure of your goodness to poor Blind M^rs: N. whatever you promise her I will most punctually perform, best regards to all friends, Ever for Ever your

Nelson + Bronte

176. *To Lady Hamilton*

[BL: Egerton 1614 ff. 65–66, no. 34] St. George
June 10th: 1801, Kioge[4] Bay

My dearest Friend,

It is now 36 days since I receiv'd the scrap of a pen from England although the Wind has blown fair these 4 days what it means is beyond my comprehension, we have newspapers to the 25th: by which I see no movements of a new Admiral. I duly appreciate the kindness of the Admiralty, and nothing I believe but Gods protection hes saved my life, and thank God but not them I am perfectly recover'd and as far as relates to health I dont think I ever was stronger or in better health, it is odd but after severe illness's I feel much better, I continue my warm milk every morning at 4 oclock, In 10 days the fleet must be ordered home for no power in the Baltic will fight us this year, I shall not forget all these

[1]Nelson wrote to Evan Nepean, the Secretary of the Admiralty on 26 Nov 1799 from Palermo: 'It was with extreme concern that I read your letter of October 11th, being perfectly conscious that want of communicating where and when it is necessary, cannot be laid to my charge. I find on looking at my letter book that I did write . . . I own I do not feel that if Cutters and Couriers go off the same day, that it is necessary to write by a Convoy . . . As a Junior Flag Officer of course without those about me, as Secretaries, Interpreters, &c., I have been thrown into a more extensive correspondence than ever, perhaps, fell to the lot of an admiral . . .' (Nicolas, iv, 110).

[2]St Vincent.

[3]After the word 'them' the letter is continued on the outside, upside down (seen from the writing in the inside of the letter) below (until 'you my') and above the address (from 'only true friend').

[4]With a strange bent line over the 'o', an attempt at writing 'ø'?

things yesterday I had the Prince Royal['s][1] Adju[t]: on board to dinner with a civil message from the Prince, the Danes have a great confidance in my opinion and we had much confidential conversation, therefore you may rely thet Denmark fights no more ag[t]: me, but I find the whole country is in a ferment at the unusual + hard capitulation forced upon their West India Island[s],[2] and so I think them, such as even the French under monarchy never imposed when they took our Islands last war,[3] June 11th: this day 22 years I was made a Post Captain by Sir Peter Parker[4] as good a man as ever lived if you meet him again say thet I shall drink his health in a bumper this day for I do not forget thet I owe my present exalted rank to his partiality, although I feel if I had even been in an humbler sphere thet Nelson would have been Nelson still, my Eyes are almost stretch'd out looking at [the] Point of Land where ships come from England but alas not a thing to be seen, I begin to be very uneasy, Little Harris has begged thet he may have a full dress suit of uniform, which I have promised him when we get to Engl[d]: If he is kept in order he will be a good young man + with 35 there is no great danger of his being spoilt, but he is too much[5] for his age, when will any thing arrive may she bring me as kind affectionate letters as the last, and I shall bear 'till our arrival which cannot be many days.

177. *To Lady Hamilton*

[Pettigrew, ii, p. 98]

St. George, Kioge Bay,
June 12th, 1801.

My dearest Friend,

I am writing a last line as the Pylades is getting under sail, and in the moment a cutter is reported to be in sight. I am all now anxiety, therefore cannot get on, so you must excuse my short letter of this day, but since I wrote yesterday not a piece of news nor a boat has been on board. Let

[1]Frederik, Crown Prince of Denmark (later King Frederik VI), who was governing as regent since 1784.

[2]In the West Indies Denmark possessed the islands of St Thomas and St John in the Virgin Islands, and south of them the island of Sta Cruz.

[3]This may refer to the taking of Tobago in 1781 (Rodger, p. 349) and St Kitts in 1782 (ibid., p. 353) during the American War of 1777–1783; Rodger also explains, why the French were not pursuing any strong interests in the naval campaign (pp. 340–41).

[4]Sir Peter Parker (1721–1811) had been influential in furthering Nelson's early career in the West Indies.

[5]The end of the letter is written on the outside, upside down (in relation to the writing in the inside) below the address (seen from the outside writing).

me have good, good news, it cannot be too good. Yes, then it would distract me with happiness – if bad from you it would so grieve me that I should become melancholy. Thirty-seven days, not a scrap of a pen. Bear me up.

Ever your faithful,

Nelson and Bronté.

My dearest Friend,

I am overjoyed. I shall be better and happier than ever, and be as soon in England as possible. I have sent off four letters this day, two by Troubridge, and two by Davison – this makes five.

Ever yours,

Nelson and Bronté.

11 at night.

June 12th. Have only read the Admiral's letter, and that Admiral Pole[1] is coming. Will write to-morrow if I keep my senses.

178. *To Lady Hamilton*

[NMM: WAL/47]

My Dearest only true friend and you are true because I am and I am because you are we have no dirty interest, I was so overcome yesterday with the good and happy news thet came about my going home thet I believe I was in truth scarcely myself, the thoughts of going do me good yet all night I was so restless thet I could not sleep, it is nearly calm therefore Ad[l]: Pole cannot get on I whish I had a rope fast to him, I believe I should pull myself to pieces, but I will have a little more patience but my nails are so long not cut since february thet I am afraid of their breaking but I should have thought it treason to have cut them as long as their [*sic*] was a possibil[it]y of my returning for my old dear

[1]Charles Morice Pole (1757–1813); for details, see Pettigrew, ii, pp. 98–9, fn. F53.

friend to do the job for me,[1] how is Sir W^m: better I shall do as you please about going into the country, but in the party to Wales there will be Mr. Greville who I am sure will be [a] stop to many of our conversations for we are used to speak our mind freely of Kings + beggars, + not fear being betray'd, do you think of all this against my arrival, June 14th: looking out very sharp for Admiral Pole, if he was not to come I believe it would kill me, I am ready to start the moment I have talked with him one hour, this day I am going to invest Sir Thos: Graves with the ensigns of the order of the Bath, he will be Knighted with the sword given me by the Captains of the Nile.[2] Your green chair is to represent the Throne placed under a canopy made of the Royal standart [*sic*] + Elevated, Your Blue sattin [*sic*] Pillow is to carry the Ribbon, Star, + Commission, and Hardy has trimmed out the Quarter [deck] in his usual style of Elegance,[3]

Sunday evening June 14th: 9 oclock.

Our parade is over I have acted as King as well as I could I have letters from Tyson of Ap^l: 12th: he seems poor fellow very unhappy about his wife, The wind is fair for Ad^l: Pole he must be here tomorrow, and I shall sail next day, at day light, Ever for Ever your faithful

Nelson + Bronte.

How could the Duke torment himself with such company, June 15th: the Wind is fair for Ad^l: Pole he must arrive in the course of the day how slow he moves at least in my Idea, I shall move faster homewards, best regards to all our friends My Brother scolds me because I do not write to him, If he knew as you do what I have [to do][4] for near 80 sail of Pendents he would not think so, but he hes[5] no patience and now thinks thet what would has [*sic*] satisfied him before, and which he has neither got or is likely to get to get,[6] is not worth[7] his acceptance, best regards to M^rs: Nelson,

[1]Lady Hamilton appears to have regarded the cutting of fingernails as an expression of motherly care; see her letter of 27 Oct 1798 to Nelson, where she writes: 'my dear little fatherless Fady tell him to keep his head clean + when he comes back I will be his mother as much as I can comb work + cut his nails for with pleasure I cou'd do it all for him, in London'.

[2]See Appendix 3 for the later history of this sword.

[3]The rest of the line is left empty. The letter is continued on the next (=third) page.

[4]The letter continues on the outside, on the parts that were to be folded inside.

[5]*Sic*. Clearly an 'e' and no 'a' as in the 'has' of the following line!

[6]*Sic*, twice 'to get'.

[7]The letter is here continued above the address.

179. *To Lady Hamilton*

[NMM: PST/83, 'Photostate' (kind of photocopy) apparently in diminished size]

My dearest friend,

I hope in God to be with you long before this letter, but neither I am or no Believe me Ever aye for Ever your faithful

Nelson + Bronte

Best regards to Sir William I have neither seen or heard of any thing like you since we parted, what consolation to think we tread on the same Island,

June 30th: ½ p^{t}: 1 running in for Yarmth:

CHAPTER III

THE CHANNEL CAMPAIGN, JULY–OCTOBER 1801

Back in England, on 30 June 1801, Nelson pursued a busy and rather unsettled schedule. On arriving at Yarmouth, he first visited wounded sailors in hospital and then immediately went on to London, where he reported to the First Lord of the Admiralty, Earl St Vincent, in the morning of 1 July. He spent a few days at Boxhill in Surrey with the Hamiltons and picked up old contacts, among them with Prince Castelcicala, the Neapolitan ambassador to Britain, who pressed him to write to the Prime Minister, Henry Addington.[1] After another meeting with St Vincent he 'was so unwell with pain in my stomach that I have been forced to get again into the country', this time to Staines.[2] There he received an invitation from the Prime Minister to meet him alone. The result of the meeting appears to have been an agreement according to which on the one hand Nelson's barony was allowed to be perpetuated and on the other hand he was prepared to take command of a squadron of small ships, ordered to defend the English coast against an attempt of invasion by the French.[3] Apparently Addington hoped to calm fears of an invasion by employing Nelson for this rather unusual task for a Vice-Admiral. Nelson, however, appears to have identified immediately with this new command. When he received his orders, on 25 July, he had already finished a lengthy memorandum 'on the defence of the Thames'.[4] Two days later, Nelson hoisted his flag on board the *Unité* frigate at Sheerness.

During the first eight days of his new command, between 27 July and 3 August 1801, stationed at Sheerness, Deal and then in the Downs, Nelson wrote daily to Lady Hamilton [180–186].[5] The contents of the letters reflect how much his time was taken up by naval matters. He embraced them energetically and joyfully, even jokingly claiming that Admiral Graeme, who had also lost his right arm, and the Commander of the Troops, who had lost a leg, together with him should 'be caricatured as the lame defenders of England' [180]. He proudly reported that he had 'found thet reception which I have been so used to' [183] and interspersed his letters with assurances of affection [mostly 182–185]. After a few days, however, he started to enquire about Lady Hamilton's search for a house [183] and to complain about what a strain his tasks are placing him under [184 and 185].

[1]Roger Knight, *The Pursuit of Victory. The Life and Achievement of Horatio Nelson* (London, 2005) [hereafter: Knight], p. 403; Nicolas, iv, pp. 421–2.

[2]Nicolas, iv, p. 423.

[3]Knight, p. 403.

[4]Nicolas, iv, pp. 425–8.

[5]Doc. No. 185 was written on two days, 1 and 2 Aug.

On 4 August 1801 he wrote two rather matter-of-fact accounts of his proceedings and acknowledged the receipt of letters from Lady Hamilton [187 and 188], before receiving a letter from Lady Hamilton that quite upset him. Apparently the problem was related to finding a home for them together, as the letter starts with an emphatic decision: 'buy the House at Turnham Green'. The irregular spread of ink in Nelson's writing betrays great emotional upheaval as he continues: 'how can You be angry with me I do not deserve it'; he complains about her 'reproaches . . . I took it as you desired + now to be abused . . . my heart is almost broke' [189]. The shock lasted until the following day: 'Your scolding letter has almost killed me for godsake write no more such for they are worse than death'. Apparently Lady Hamilton was envious of the attention, Nelson paid his father, since he defended himself: 'I know not thet I wrote to my father more news than to You'. In his first letters from Sheerness, Nelson had still wished Lady Hamilton to pass his regards to his father [180, 182 and 183]. Now he had to recognise that his father would have to be treated as having taken sides with Lady Nelson. Nelson never again was to send regards to his father in a letter to Lady Hamilton . Trying to calm her now, he stressed again: 'I really wish you would buy the House at Turnham Green'. His regards went to the trio of his sister-in-law 'M^rs: Nelson the Duke [of Queensberry] + Lord William [Gordon]', partisans of Lady Hamilton [190].[1] Although Lady Hamilton now sent 'dear kind letters' that made him feel 'much better', he pushed the subject of the purchase of a house [191, 195, 196, 198, 201 and 203] until he could affirm, on 20 August: 'I approve of the house at Merton' [207].

During the night of 4 August, while Nelson was troubled by Lady Hamilton's reproaches, his men attacked French gun vessels at Boulogne. Nelson admitted: 'sometimes the exertion of my mind is beyond the strength of my body' [191]. He did not appear to have force left, to mentally support somebody else. To news from Lady Hamilton that she was not well he reacted by recommending her to 'get well' or helplessly stating: 'would I could do any thing to comfort You' [191 and 192]. He even demanded: 'I hope by your next letters I shall be made better' [193]. Instead of rejoicing at being admired, Nelson started complaining from the *Medusa*, to which ship he had moved his flag: '50 boats are rowing I am told about her this mom^t: to have a look at the one armed man'; 'I hate to be praised except by you'; 'I came from Harwich yesterday noon not having set my foot on Shore although the Volunteers +^c:

[1]These three were the usual addressees of Nelson's regards in his next letters to Lady Hamilton; see Docs Nos 191, 192, 195, 196, 207 and 209.

were drawn up to receive me and the people ready to draw the Carriage'; 'Oh how I hate to be stared at' [192, 194 and 196]. Nelson longed to be with Lady Hamilton, but this proved difficult to arrange, as he stated in his 'vagabond state' in a letter from Harwich of 10 August [195]. Two days later he was 'pushing for the Downs', annoyed that his servant, Tom Allen, had not managed to get all his luggage on board [197]. On his arrival in the Downs a day later Nelson was happy about receiving Lady Hamilton's 'truly kind and affectionate letters', but not able to give her equally comforting news. As to her lack of health he merely advised her to 'cheer up', commented that he could not 'be in good health', while she was 'sick', and went on to complain about his own lack of well-being: 'I have had a fever all night'. Similarly he dispersed her worries about his safety, first by assuring her that as a 'Vice-Admiral' he was not likely to be in danger, but then by discarding the justification of her worries: 'you would naturally hate me if I kept back when I ought to go forward' [198]. Nelson continued complaining about his head being 'split' and 'much swelled' [199 and 200], a problem that only appears to have abated on 15 August, when his 'fingers itch[ed] to be at' the French boats off Boulogne [201].

This second attack that he ordered, executed in the night of 15 August, was a failure, because 'the damn'd French had their vessels chain'd from the Bottoms to the Shore and also to each other'. As a result many British sailors were killed or wounded; among the later was Nelson's young supporter Captain Edward Parker [202]. Parker's state of health was a subject in nearly all the letters Nelson wrote in the days to come until Nelson joined Sarah Nelson, Sir William and Lady Hamilton at Deal on 28 August [203–207 and 210–212, written on 17–20 and 22–24 August]. Nelson arranged private accommodation for Parker, 'that the ship may be cleaned and purified, for the wounds smell very bad' [203]. On one of his visits ashore Parker 'got hold of my hand, and said he could not bear me to leave him, and cried like a child' [205]. Nelson also attended a funeral and repeatedly went 'to the hospital to see my poor fellows' [204 and 205], of which he wrote that 'together it has almost upset me' [205].

Nelson himself now clearly was in need of comfort. In most of the ten letters he wrote during the eight days between 17 and 24 August, he gratefully acknowledged the receipt of letters (often several at a time) from Lady Hamilton [203–206 and 209–210] or commented on their contents [207 and 208]. He was longing to meet his lover, arranged for her to come to Deal with Sarah Nelson and Sir William Hamilton, and suffered, when the fulfilment of his duty threatened to oblige him to leave Deal [203–207 and 210–212]. He rejoiced at Lady Hamilton's having found a 'house at Merton', in Surrey, close to London [207–210]. In his longing for homely intimacy with Lady Hamilton he strongly resented being visited by 'a Lady Somebody, and a Mrs. Somebody', 'Lady this that and t'other' who 'came alongside', but Nelson resolutely decided: 'I was stout + will not be shewn about like a Beast' [207 and 209]. To Lady Hamilton's repeated worries about his own safety he again replied by reminding her of her interest in his fulfilment of duty [204 and 205],[1] which mellowed into comforting words that 'there is no risk for my rank', promising 'no more boat work' [205, 209 and 210]. As a result of bad weather, communications with the shore (read: receiving letters from Lady Hamilton) were made difficult and Nelson was troubled with severe sea sickness [209 and 210].

Before they could meet, however, Nelson spent a few days going to the Dutch port of Flushing (Vlissingen in Dutch), in order to explore the possibilities of an attack there. On his return to Deal on 27 August he was convinced that within reason no such opportunity offered.[2] For nearly three weeks Nelson was now able to spend time ashore with the Hamiltons and his brother William's wife, Sarah. The women used the time for sea bathing. Nelson introduced Lady Hamilton to the Lutwidges.[3] He knew Admiral Lutwidge, now commander-in-chief in the Downs, since his teenage participation in a polar expedition in the *Carcass* under Lutwidge's command. Lady Hamilton got on particularly well with his wife. Unpleasant moments were a blackmail note written to Nelson and the visit paid by Nelson's stepson Josiah Nisbet, who managed to meet his stepfather, though nothing is known about the contents of the former or the subject of conversation with the latter.[4] A constant worry remained the state of health of the wounded Captain Edward Parker.

When the Hamiltons returned to London on 20 September, Nelson was in 'silent distraction' [213 and 214]. The 'fate of poor Parker' remained a major reason for concern until, on 27 September 1801, 'Dear Parker left this world for a better at 9 o'clock' [213–217 and 219–224]. Sadness at Edward Parker's death was mingled with annoyance at having to pay for the funeral, settle his debts and – worst of all – having to deal with his father, who turned out to be a 'swindler' [238; see also 225–227 and 243].

The 44 letters Nelson wrote to Lady Hamilton in the period between 20 September and 23 October 1801 [213–256], when he gave up his

[1]See also an earlier appeal to Lady Hamilton's patriotism in Doc. No. 198.
[2]Knight, p. 415.
[3]Skeffington Lutwidge and his wife Catherine, née Harvey.
[4]Knight, pp. 413, 415.

command, were dominated by complaints about his lack of health and by complaints about his command. One of the major ailments he was complaining about was sea-sickness, which he was more prone to on small ships [217, 221, 234 and 246]. He also frequently complained about having a or feeling 'cold' [223, 235, 247, 248, 252 and 256], a 'violent head ache' [223], troubles with his heart [224 and 239], generally being 'seriously unwell' [230, 238, 241 and 243], a 'complaint in my stomach + bowells' [244–246, 252 and 256] and a 'tooth ache [that] torments me to pieces' [247 and 248]. In letters of 8 and 14 October Nelson attributes his ailments ('attack on my heart' and 'complaint [in his stomach]') to 'fretting at being kept here doing nothing' [239 and 246]. Nelson was clearly unhappy with his command and expressions of frustration at his command occupy a similar space in his letters of the period to complaints about lack of health: 'I would give the universe was I quit of my present command', longing to be 'liberated[,] for cooped up on board ship with [my] head for ever leaning over paper has almost blinded me' [220 and 243; similarly 218, 227, 228, 232, 233, 236, 238–241, 244–246, 248 and 249]. Since Nelson addressed similar complaints to the Admiralty at the time, Roger Knight summarises: 'Nelson was essentially an aggressive admiral who was always going to be uncomfortable at being used by Addington's government as a military icon to achieve diplomatic ends. . . . For the Admiralty he was an irritable subordinate, one who took up an unreasonable amount of the board's time in encouraging and restraining him.'[1]

Feeling unwell both physically and in his professional situation, Nelson's despondency about being 'cooped up on board' small ships, with nothing to do, meant that he was in need of mental support. Writing to Lady Hamilton he demanded letters from her for his 'comfort' [222, 225, 226 and 246]. A recurrent theme in his letters was how to make arrangements so that he could send letters to his lover and receive them from her [215, 217, 220, 228, 229, 231, 233, 234, 238, 239, 243, 247 and 248]. Sometimes he acknowledged that receiving her letters made him 'feel better' or even 'cheered [him] up' [226, 234 and 252]. He was also pleased that she forwarded letters or even sent a 'packet' [244 and 254]. When a letter that Lady Hamilton had sent saddened or even depressed him, however, he made her responsible for his lack of well-being: 'Your first letter almost broke my heart'; 'I am by no means so well as I could wish Your letter has agitated me not a little' [236

[1]Knight, p. 418.

and 241]. The heartbreaking effect of the letter in case may have been caused by another of Lady Hamilton's attempts to make him jealous,[1] since a day earlier he had reacted to an account of hers: 'I am vexed but not surprised my Dear Emma at that fellows wanting You for his mistress' [234]. Lady Hamilton may simply have wished to attract Nelson's attention. Another similarly motivated attempt may have been telling Nelson about her own ailments. Nelson, however, simply outdid her in matters of suffering and self-pity: 'I am sorry to hear thet You have been Ill and my cold is so dreadfully bad thet I cannot hold up my head' [247]. If Nelson showed an interest in her health at all, it was mostly by giving advice in a way that came close to a reproach: 'Wrap Yourself up warm when You go out of the house + for Gods sake wear more cloaths when winter approaches' [229, similarly 234]. Overall it thus appears that Nelson needed more reassurance from Lady Hamilton than he was able to give her.

Nelson's letters of this period are markedly lacking in outbursts of passion and assurances of affection such as are so characteristic of the early stage of their affair [see for example 42 and 43] and the weeks after the birth of their daughter [see for example 80, 81, 83, 86, 99, 102, 108, 110 and 125]. Their daughter is now rarely mentioned [only in 213, 223, 228 and 230]. Rather than expressing how attractive Lady Hamilton was for him, Nelson simply longed to be with his lover [223, 224, 230, 232, 243 and 244] and he now stressed his admiration for Lady Hamilton's virtue [230 and 234], kindness [249], and skill in letter-writing and singing [217 and 244].

As before [43], he assured her of his obedience [229]. This obedience to Lady Hamilton's wishes was put to the test regarding Nelson's contact with his father. As we have seen, due to Lady Hamilton's pressure, Nelson had already had to recognise that his father would have to be treated as having taken sides with Lady Nelson. On 26 September 1801, the day of Parker's death, Nelson wrote to Lady Hamilton how uneasy he felt about his father's loyalty to Lady Nelson. He also made sure his lover knew he would not do anything without her consent:

> I had yesterday a letter from my father, he seems to think that he may do something which I shell not like, + I suppose, he means, going to Somerset S^{t},[2] shall I to an old man enter upon the detestable subject

[1]For an earlier example, see Doc. No. 86.

[2]The words '+ I suppose, he means, going to Somerset S^{t},' are given at the top of the page, above the line 'do something which I shell not like, +'. Somerset Street was where Lady Nelson stayed at the time.

> it may shorten his days, but I think I shall tell him thet I cannot go to Somerset Street to see him, but I shall not write till I hear your opinion If I once begin you know it will all out, about her and her ill treatment to her son, but you shell decide [223]

Although Nelson announced three days later that he would write to his father 'to-morrow', pointing out the he would not take 'the smallest notice of how he disposes of himself' [225], he seems still to have been doubting as to how to proceed. On 5 October he wrote to Lady Hamilton: 'I have not yet wrote to my father but I shall' [234]. It is possible that because of Nelson's hesitation, Lady Hamilton lost her nerves and herself wrote to Nelson's father. This 'anonymous letter' is what Edmund Nelson refers to in a letter to his son, in which he expressed his sorrow about 'severe reproaches I felt from an anonymous letter for my conduct to you which is such it seems as will totally separate us'.[1] Nelson remained insecure, writing to Lady Hamilton: 'I have one from my Father which has hurt me, I shall not answer it 'till I hear from You, on Monday, but more of this to morrow' [241]. In another letter Nelson continued the subject:

> I think of writing my poor old father to this effect – that I shall live at Merton with Sir William and Lady Hamilton – that a warm room for him and a cheerful society will always be there happy to receive him – that nothing in *my conduct* could ever cause a separation of a moment between me and him, for that I had all the respect and love which a son could bear toward a good father – that going to Burnham was impossible, as my duty, even if I was inclined, would not permit it – that as to anonymous letters, they made no impression where they did not fit, and that I should ever conduct myself towards him as his dutiful son. Tell me, my friend, do you approve? If he remains at Burnham he will die, and I am sure he will not stay in Somerset Street,[2] Pray let him come to your care at Merton. Your kindness will keep him alive, for you have a kind soul. [242]

In this case, however, Lady Hamilton's kindness was not to prevail, as Nelson conceded on 13 October: 'I am sorry I sent You my Fathers letter I shell not answer it' [245]; although two days later, he tried to mellow the severity of her judgment: 'My Poor Dear Father is wrong' [247].

[1]NMM, WAL/13 (also to be found in: Pettigrew, ii, pp. 210–11, and Morrison, ii, p. 133, no. 632); for text of the letter, see fn. to Doc. No. 241.

[2]Where Lady Nelson was living at the time.

With the purchase of a home for his new family, Nelson was now rearranging his family allegiances. As to the members of this new family, Nelson positively asserted: 'whatever . . . You do for my little charge [their daughter Horatia] I must be pleased with' [223]. First, however, the technicalities of moving into Merton Place were dominating Nelson's thoughts. After having arranged the actual purchase, it still took a while for the previous owner, Mrs. Greaves, to move out [223, 229 and 234]. Even when that was achieved, moving in took some more days, accompanied by Nelson's impatient comments [238, 241 and 246]. In the meantime the question of how the estate would be managed took up some space in the correspondence between Nelson and Lady Hamilton. Apparently Lady Hamilton was now taking up the classic role of an upper-class naval officer's wife.[1] She developed Nelson's idea of a 'farm' [214 and 217] by suggesting to buy an adjoining 'Duck Close + field' [223 and 237] and to let 'Pigs + Poultry, Sheep . . . eat off the grass' [249 and 252]. Nelson happily accepted her managing the affairs of Merton. He sometimes asked her to arrange specific things, such as transferring his furniture and other belongings to the house [216 and 226], receiving sherry that he had ordered [232] or hanging up pictures [254, 256 and 257]. The general management of Merton, however, he left to her, insisting 'It is as much Yours as if You bought it' [218 and 228]. He repeatedly praised her 'excellent' management [223, 224, 226, 229, 230, 240, 246 and 252] and he declared : 'You are to be[,] recollect, Lady Paramount of all the territories and waters of Merton' [237, similarly 243]. A part that Lady Paramount had to take was also to arrange for the house to be insured [227] and to deal with servants [226, 229 and 249]. Significant as such decisions were, legally Lady Hamilton was still merely acting as Nelson's representative.[2] When Nelson wrote 'I agree with you, that nothing but what is mine should be there [at Merton]' [225, also 227], it appears that she herself had suggested this arrangement in order to guarantee their independence from others, notably Sir William Hamilton. The option of any furniture or paintings or even the

[1]For a general introduction into this subject, see the section 'Running the home' in the chapter 'The Aristocracy and the Gentry' in Margarette Lincoln's, *Naval Wives & Mistresses* (London, 2007) [hereafter: Lincoln], pp. 73–7.

[2]Nelson thus had to instruct his lawyer, Haslewood: 'Lady Hamilt^{n} will be in Town on Sunday night or Monday morning early and If you will have the goodness to call on her at Noon on Monday she will have the goodness to give directions to M^{r}: Dods the uppolsterer, relative to the appraising such furniture as her Ladyship may chuse to keep for me in the house' (NMM: SUT/2, letter from Deal of 18 Sept 1801).

house itself belonging to Lady Hamilton simply did not arise. She could merely be the 'whole + sole commander' of the house [243] by the grace of Nelson – like Nelson was commander by the grace of the government. Any impression that would undermine this set-up needed to be avoided: 'for heaven's sake never do you talk of having spent any money for me. I am sure you never have to my knowledge', placating: 'and my obligations to you can never be repaid but with my life' [230].

As long as Nelson himself had not yet been at Merton, the idea of settling down with Lady Hamilton remained fragile. He repeatedly mentioned going to his Sicilian duchy Bronte and even suggested 'Merton may become a dead weight on our hands' [218, 234 for 'dead weight', 235 and 243]. In this uncertain situation social contacts mattered. In respect to networking for Nelson ashore, Lady Hamilton was again adopting the role of a 'naval wife'.[1] As with Captain Gore[2] before [197], Lady Hamilton was now asked to supply Nelson with an inscribed silver item to present to Dr Baird [220, 224, 227 and 235]. Her services went beyond the merely technical, in that Nelson used her Neapolitan contacts, namely to the Neapolitan ambassador to Britain, Castelcicala, as well as to the King and Queen of Naples, in order to pass on messages [231, 244 and 258]. He also kept sending her regards from captains in his squadron as well as passing hers to them [220, 232, 236, 237, 240 and 244]. She even kept in touch with them herself [252]. The most intense link of the kind developed with Admiral and Mrs Lutwidge with whom Nelson and the Hamiltons had spent much time when ashore together during the first three weeks of September at Deal [215, 227, 231, 234, 236, 240, 244, 249 and 254]. Besides maintaining contact with men he was with at sea, Nelson expected Lady Hamilton to keep in touch with naval officers ashore [217, 234 and 250]. At the same time he reinforced links with friends and relations of Lady Hamilton, most obviously by exerting his patronage for a young cousin of hers, Charles Connor,[3] and the son of a singer friend, Brigida Banti [217, 218, 220, 229, 244, 249 and 255], but also by simply passing his regards to 'the Duke' of Queensberry in nearly all of his letters. Apart from naval and private contacts, Nelson even involved Lady

[1]Lincoln, pp. 56–65 (section about 'Patronage and influence').

[2]John Gore (1772–1836).

[3]Son of Mrs Cadogan's sister Sarah Connor (Flora Fraser, *Beloved Emma. The Life of Emma Lady Hamilton* (London, 1986) [hereafter: Fraser], p. 311).

Hamilton in his political contacts, for example by passing on a letter he had received from the then Home Secretary, Lord Pelham[1] [252].

Towards the end of the month of separation between 20 September and 23 October 1801, political issues moved into the foreground of Nelson's letters to Lady Hamilton. During most of the letters he had predominantly been occupied with his ailments and Lady Hamilton's management of his house at Merton. When, at the beginning of October, she considered being allowed to wear her Maltese Order, Nelson at first discarded the issue: 'What you want with all the Heraldry I know not' [230]. Two days later, however, he wrote encouragingly: 'as the Order of Malta will be restored I suppose now You and Ball will have permission to wear the order' [234]. On 19 October, a few days before giving up his command, Nelson saw Lady Hamilton emphatically as a politically active person: 'I know although You can adapt your language + manners to a child yet thet You can also, thunder forth such a torrent of Eloquence thet Corruption + Infamy would sink before Your voice in however exalted a situation it might be placed' [254]. At the same time, Nelson started considering a political career for himself, while he could observe others' 'long faces' at peace approaching and naval occupation decreasing [251; similarly: 237 and 243; about peace approaching in general: 228, 230, 232, 234 and 237]. Nelson used the opportunity to meet William Pitt, who had resigned as Prime Minister earlier the same year, at his home, Walmer Castle, near Deal, commenting: 'he may perhaps be useful to me one day or other' [243]. He hinted 'I shall . . . let them see that I may be useful in council as I have been in the field' [252] and specified two days later that he meant 'thet I could be as useful in the cabinet as in the field' [255].

With the prospect of giving up his command, Nelson's mood was clearly improving. He now felt 'much better' [253] and consoled Lady Hamilton: 'the Ad^ty: will not always be there' [254]. He was now relaxed enough to paint a humorous self-image of their long hoped-for encounter: 'how I should laugh to see you my Dear friend rowing in a boat, the Beautiful Emma, rowing a one armed Admiral in a boat, It will certainly be caricatured' [256].

[1]Lord Thomas Pelham (1756–1826); Whig politician who was Home Secretary from July 1801 until August 1803 under Addington; he would succeed his father to become 2nd Earl of Chichester in 1805.

180. *To Lady Hamilton*

[NMM: MON/1/19]

Sheerness
July 27th: 1801

My dearest Emma[1] My flag is flying on board the Unitè [*sic*] frigate She will probably go to the Nore tomorrow, as the Wind is Easterly it is lucky I follow'd my plan of coming by land instead of water, for it would have taken me two days if I have any ship fit to sail with me on Wednesday[2] certainly I shall go either for Margate or towards Hosely bay, Coffin[3] does not return 'till Wednesday therefore Parker + myself are alone, and we have enough to do today I dine with Ad^{l}: Greme,[4] who has also lost his right arm, and as the Commander of the Troops has lost his Leg, I expect we shall be caricatured as the lame defenders of England, under all circumstances which you know I am tolerable, resting confidently on our right + honorable intentions to [cast other][5] remember me affectionately to my charge[6] to my Father, Brother +^{c}: say all thet is proper to them, and also to the good Duke + Lord Willm: and ever Believe your only Yours affectionat[el]y

Nelson + Bronte.
A little tired.

181. *To Lady Hamilton*

[Pettigrew, ii, pp. 131–2]

July 28th, 1801.

My dearest Emma, Ten thousand thanks for your affectionate letter. At this moment I could do nothing with volunteer Captains, having no post to give them. Should the enemy really approach, the country must have their services, and I should be glad to have on that occasion our friend Bowen, I have many offers on that head, but Bowen may rely, if any

[1]The address 'Dearest Emma' had been used before to address Lady Hamilton; see for example Lord Bristol's letter of 18 April 1800, Morrison, ii, p. 99 (No. 483).

[2]29 July 1801.

[3]Admiral Sir Isaac Coffin (1759–1839), 'aggressive officer who could not serve afloat after an injury in 1794; commissioner of the naval dockyard at Ajaccio in Corsica [1796]' (Knight, p. 628), Lisbon (1797–98) and 1799–1804 at Sheerness.

[4]Admiral Alexander Graeme (1741–1818).

[5]I have not been able to decipher these words. The 'to cast' could also be interpreted as 'to last', but that seems to make no sense either.

[6]His daughter Horatia.

come to me, that he shall. My time is so fully employed, that I am not able to get off my chair I can only say, that I am as ever,

Yours,

Nelson and Bronté.

I dine at the Admiral's,[1] who seems a good man. it blows hard. If the Dutch mean to put to sea, this is their time. How vexed I am at the Spaniards being able with impunity to come before Gibraltar, and to protect the French ships. Parker desires his compliments, and shall expect your letter to-morrow.

182. *To Lady Hamilton*

[Monmouth: E 95] July 29th: 1801

My Dearest Emma, Your letter of yesterday naturally called forth all those finer feeling[s] of the soul which none but those who regard each other as you + I do can conceive although I am not able to write so well and so forcibly mark my feelings as you can yet I am sure I feel all the affection which is possible for man to feel towards w<u>omen</u> and such a woman, not one moment I have to myself and my business is endless at noon I sett off for Faversham to arreinge the Sea Fencibles on thet part of the coast, at 9 oclock I expect to be at Deal to arrainge with Adl: Lutwidge various matters,[2] and tomorrow evening or next day morning to sail for the coast of France thet I may judge from my own Eye and not from those of others. be where I may, you are always present to my thoughts – not another thing, except the duty I owe my country ever interferes with you, you absorb my whole soul, whether I write little or much never mind I am yours for Ever and ever

Nelson + Bronté

In abt: 5 days I hope to be again upon some part of the English coast, you shall hear from me every day if possible.

I have not rose from my chair since 7 this morning a post chaise is at the Door, for Ever yours best regards to my father, Brother, Mrs: Nelson the Duke of Queen[s]berry, Lord William +c:

[1]Graeme.

[2]Nelson's letter to Lutwidge of 3 Aug 1801 (Nicolas, iv, p. 436) gives an indication of what they conversed about: positioning of boats and ships.

183. *To Lady Hamilton*

[BL: Egerton 1614 ff. 67–68, no. 35] Deal July 30th: 1801.

My dearest Emma having finish'd all my business at Sheerness yesterday at one oclock I sett off for Deal calling on my way at Faversham in order to examine into the state of our Sea fencibles at thet place and on thet part of the coast, I found thet reception which I have been so used to and it seemed the general opinion thet If I was authorised to say to the seamen on thet coast thet it was necessary for them to Embark on board our floating batteries thet they would go, on the assurance thet when the danger was passed thet they should be landed at their homes again for the expression was thet they never believed the thing serious 'till I was appoint^{d}: to this command, however unless the matter comes closer I hope the Ad^{ty}: will not make me speechifyer but the fact is the men are afraid of being tricked,[1] at 9 oclock I got to Ad^{l}: Lutwidge not having tasted a morsel since 7 in the morning at 10 we supped the Ad^{l}: + his wife Parker myself + Cap^{n}: Bazeley,[2] my flag was hoisted this morn^{g}: in the Leyden 64, which ship if the surf will allow me I shall be on board of to-morrow morning.[3] I have no bed but thet does not matter, although I shall doubtless have much envy ag^{t}: me yet I wish to shew good people thet they have not mistaken their man, this service must soon be over, I have sent for the Medusa frigate in which ship I mean to go over to the coast of France, it is W^{m}: ~~Chatch~~ Cathcarts[4] ship you know Cap^{tn}: Gore, the Amazon is not yet arrived in England, reports are so vague that it is difficult to say whence this host of Thieves is to Issue forth, your letters are gone to Sheerness and I shall be deprived of the pleasure of receiving them 'till tomorrow they are my dear Emma the only comfort I can have or desire to have during our seperation being for Ever Your faithful

[1]On the same day Nelson wrote to St Vincent about a conversation he had had with the Captain in command of the Sea Fencible at Feversham: 'He thought if the Admiralty, through me, gave the men assurances that they should be returned to their homes, when the danger of the Invasion was passed, that the Sea-folk would go; but that they were always afraid of some trick: this service, my dear Lord, above all others, would be terrible for me. to get up and harangue like a Recruiting Serjeant! I do not think I could get through it' (Nicolas, iv, p. 432).

[2]John Bazeley (d. 1828); for a detailed biography, see Pettigrew, ii, 133–4.

[3]The words 'I shall be on board of tomorrow morning' are above the line, inserted by an arrow from below the line between the words 'allow me' and 'I have'.

[4]William Cathcart (1782–1804); The name 'Cathcart' is written above a crossed-out first attempt at spelling his name.

Nelson + Bronte.

when you write to Sir William say every thing which is kind, also to my Father, M^{rs}: Nelson the Duke Lord W^{m}: Gordon who I shall always esteem amongst my truest friends.

pray have you heard of any House from M^{r}: Christie I am very anxious to have a home where my friends might be made welcome, Coffin charged me to say how sorry he should be to lose your good opinion, and thet he never faild calling

184. *To Lady Hamilton*

[NMM: CRK/19/11]

Deal – Shall be on board the Medusa before this letter go [*sic*] from the Town July 31^{t}: 1801.

My Dearest Emma, did not you get my letter from Sheerness on Thursday morn^{g}:[1] telling you I was just setting off for Deal as I have no letter from you of yesterday only those of Wed^{y}[2] which went to Sheerness, it has been my damn'd blunder and not yours for which I am deservedly punish'd, by missing one of your dear letters they are my comfort joy + delight, My time is truly fully taken up and my head aches before night comes, I got to bed last night at ½ p^{t}: 9, but the hour was so unusual thet I heard the clock strike one to say thet I thought of you would be nonsence, for you are never out of my thoughts, at this moment I see no prospect of my getting to London but very soon the business of my command will become so simple, thet a child may direct it what rascals your post-chaise-people must be They have been paid every thing Capt: Parker has one receipt for 7: £ odd, and I am sure thet every thing is paid therefore do not pay a farthing, the Cart-Chaise I paid at Dartford, You need not fear all the women in this world for all others except Yourself are posts[3] to me I know but one for who can be like my Emma I am confident you will do nothing which can hurt my feelings, and I will die by torture sooner than do any thing which could offend you, Give 11,000 kisses to my dear Horatia yesterday the subject turn'd on the Cowpox a gentleman declared thet his child was Inoculated with the cowpox and afterwards remain'd in a house where a child had the smallpox the natural way and

[1]30 July 1801; Doc. No. 183.
[2]29 July 1801.
[3]Though 'pests', as 1814-letters, i, p. 41, have it, appears to make more sense.

did not catch it therefore here was a full trial with the Cowpox, the child is only feverish for 2 days, and only a slight inflammation of the arm takes place instead of being all over scabs[1] but, do you what you please, I did not get your newspapers therefore, do not know what promise you allude to, but this I know I have none made me, the extension of the patent of peerage is going on but ~~my~~ the wording of my Brothers note they have wrote for a meaning to,[2] the petent must be a new creation, first to my father if he outlives me then to William, + His Sons, then to Mrs: Bolton + her sons, and Mrs: Matcham + hers, farther than thet I care not it is far enough, but it may never get to any of them for the old patent may extend by true male [issue] of my[3] own Carcase, I am not so very old + may marry again a Wife more Suitable to my genious [*sic*]. I like the Morning Chronicle,[4] Ever for Ever yours only your

Nelson + Bronte.

best regards to Mrs: Nelson the Duke + Lord William, I have totally fail'd for poor Madame Bruyes,[5] Bonapartes wife[6] is one of Martinique + some plan is supposed to be carried on.

185. *To Lady Hamilton*

[*a)* Pettigrew, ii, pp. 137–8; *d)* Sotheby's, 13 Dec 1990]
[*d)*] Medusa at Sea between Calais +

Bolonge, Augt: 1st: 1801

When I reflect my dearest Emma thet for these last two years on this day we have been together the thoughts and so many things rush into my mind that I am really this day very low indeed even Parker could not help noticing it by saying on this day you should be cheerful but who can tell what passes in my mind Yes You can for I believe You are feeling as I do,

[1]For an earlier mention of the subject, see Doc. No. 154. For a description of the results of the actual inoculation of Nelson's daughter Horatia, see Doc. No. 335.

[2]Inserted.

[3]Inserted.

[4]Nelson or the Hamiltons may at this time have already been acquainted with the proprietor of the *Morning Chronicle*, Perry. He is referred to several times in Nelson's letters from the Mediterranean and in one of his last letters to Lady Hamilton before the Battle of Trafalgar.

[5]The 'u' is inserted. The person referred to here may be the widow of Nelson's opponent at the Battle of the Nile, François-Paul Brueys d'Aigalliers, comte de Brueys (1753–98).

[6]Josephine de Beauharnais, née: Marie Josephe Rose de Tascher de La Pagerie, (1763–1814).

when I was in the bustle perhaps I did not feel so strongly our separation or whether being at sea makes it appear more terrible, for terrible it is My heart is ready to flow out of my Eyes, but we must call fortitude to our aid, I did not intend to have sailed 'till this morning but at 10 last night, we had an [*a)*] intelligence that the enemy were come out of Boulogne. I put to sea of course, but as yet have not been able to get off Boulogne. I send you one receipt for money paid Mr. Dean, and although I have no receipts for the other journey, you may rely that by James,[1] Captain Parker says, they were each paid before I ever took a chaise a second time. It only shews what rascality there is moving – always get a receipt, and every now and then a receipt in full, or one day or other you will be ruined. Consider how you are at the mercy of all your servants.

August 2nd. I am going this morning to take a look at Boulogne, and shall then send over a cutter with this letter. Many of the officers here think that the enemy are afraid we have some design of invading their coast, for they are erecting many new batteries on this part of their coast. Be that as it may, in a very short time we shall be so well prepared, that our sea officers wish they may come forth. I have not had a letter from you since Wednesday[2] – I only mention this to shew you, that although we may write every day, yet they cannot always be as regularly received. I am not unwell, but I am very low. I can only account for it by my absence from all I hold dear in this world. Captain Gore is very good and kind to me, and your nephew Cathcart bears a very high character as a seaman and an officer, although he certainly does not possess the graces. To Mrs. Nelson say every thing which is kind, and to the Duke and Lord William.

Yours,

Nelson and Bronté.

186. *To Lady Hamilton*

[NMM: RUSI/203] off Boulogne Aug^{t}: 3rd: 1801.

My dear Emma,

The wind is too far to the northward to allow our Bombs to go on the coast this morning or some of the rascals should repent their vaporing nonsence, I believe my head will be turn'd with writing so much as I am

[1] James Price?
[2] 29 July 1801.

forced to do, You may assure our friends thet between Dieppe + Dunkirk I will ensure them from any invasion for the present, the French had better be damn'd than to allow us to catch them 3 miles from their own ports. Your dear letters of the 1^{t}: I rec^{d}: at 8 o clock last night, best regards to all our friends + believe me Ever your affectionate

Nelson + Bronté.

When you write to Sir W^{m}: say every thing which is kind.

187. *To Lady Hamilton*

[BL: Egerton 1614 ff. 69–70, no. 36] Medusa off Bologne Aug^{t}: 4th: 1801.

Two more are gone since I wrote this letter.[1]

My Dearest Emma,

Bologne is evidently not a pleasant place this morning three of their floating batteries are sunk what damage has been done to the others and the vessels inside the Pier I cannot say but I hope and believe thet some hundreds of French are gone to Hell this morning for if they are dead assuredly they are gone there, In fire or out of fire I am for ever your own affectionate

Nelson and Bronte.

Tell the Duke and Lord William thet the embarkation of the French army <u>will not</u> take place at Bologne, beyond this I cannot say, In my visits to the Bombs in my barge my friends think the French have been very attentive to[2] me for they did nothing but fire at the boat + the diff^{t}: vessels I was in but God is good.

188. *To Lady Hamilton*

[Pettigrew, ii, p. 139] Medusa, off Calais, 7 o'clock, August 4th, 1801.

My dearest Emma,

Your kind and affectionate letters up to yesterday are all received. Ten times ten thousand thanks for them, and for your tender care of my dear little charge Horatia. I love her the more dearly, as she is in the upper part

[1]This sentence is squeezed between date and beginning of text of letter. It was apparently added later and probably refers to Docs Nos 188 and 189, which were written the same day.
[2]Inserted.

of her face so like her dear good mother, who I love, and always shall with the truest affection. I am on my way to Ostend and Flushing, and shall probably be off Margate on Friday.[1] Captain Gore is very kind and good to me, for I must be a great plague to him. I have to thank him even for a bed. I have only one moment to write this, as Admiral Lutwidge sent his own boat with my letters of this day's post. Best regards to Mrs. Nelson, kind love to Horatia, and believe me,

Yours,

Nelson and Bronté.

This goes through my kind friend, Admiral Lutwidge. I wrote to you to-day through Troubridge.

189. *To Lady Hamilton*

[Houghton: pf MS Eng 196.5 (22a)] Medusa Aug^{t}: 4th:
off Boulogne

My Dearest Emma, buy the House at Turnham Green I can pay for it how can You be[2] angry with me I do not deserve it, conscious of[3] thet I think no more of Your reproaches,[4] respecting the seal, it is Your pleasure[5] thet I have it. You said She[6] has no right to it, none has a right[7] to use[8] but Yourself I took it as you desired + now to[9] be abused, but I forgive You although my heart is almost broke, Damn thet Christie how negligent he has been, for ever Your

Nelson + Bronte.
I have not a moment
10000 kisses were due.

[1]7 Aug 1801.
[2]In the words 'can You be' the ink weakens visibly and the pen appears to start writing in two lines. The following words 'angry with me I do' are by contrast in dark black ink.
[3]Again, the words 'deserve it, conscious of' appear to weaken and split into two lines, whereas 'thet I think no more' are in dark black ink, forming a bold line.
[4]Here again Nelson appears to have taken up ink.
[5]The letters 'sure' are again in two lines, whereas the following words are in dark black ink.
[6]Lady Nelson.
[7]'none has a right' is written in double lines.
[8]Not 'me', as Morrison has it.
[9]Again: '+ now to' in double lines and the following words 'be abused' in bold black ink.

190. *To Lady Hamilton*

[BL: Egerton 1614 ff. 71–72, no. 37]

Medusa
Aug^{t}: 5th: 1801

My Dearest Emma,

There is not in this world a thing thet I would not do to please my dearest friend but you must not take things amiss thet never were intended, I know not thet I wrote to my father more news than to You in fact I know not my own movements they are as uncertain as the wind I can always tell You were [*sic*] I am when I write but at what spot when letters may find me is impossible [to say] I intend going towards Flushing from thence towards Margate Hosely or Harwich but if I was to die for it I cannot tell which, Your scolding letter has almost killed me for godsake write no more such for they are worse than death however it is passed the seals +^{c}: You had in Your own possession but only tell me how to please and You know I will do it with pleasure, I really wish you would buy the House at Turnham Green I have 3000 £ which I pay in a moment and the other I can get without much difficulty, it is my dear friend extraordinary but true thet the man who is push'd forward to defend his country has not from thet country a place to lay his head in, but never mind happy truly happy in the estimation of such friends as You I care for nothing, how great has been Sir James Saumarezs success[1] from my heart I rejoice the Spaniards will never surely go to sea again, my command is only ag^{t}: small craft therefore small must be my services in the taking + destroying way but you know I will not be inactive I hope soon to be able to get to London for a day or two at least I will try, make my best regards to M^{rs}: Nelson the Duke + Lord William, what a shocking accident of Lord Abercorn. For Ever my Dearest best friend

Your affectionate
Nelson and Bronte.
Pray send the enclosed.

[1]Saumarez, freshly promoted to rear-admiral of the blue on 1 Jan 1801, had found a French squadron anchoring off Algeziras in the Bay of Gibraltar. He at first unsuccessfully attacked this squadron on 6 July 1801. When his ships had been quickly repaired at Gibraltar, Captain Keats arrived with reinforcements, followed by a Spanish squadron. On the afternoon of 12 July 1801 Saumarez started a second attack, this time on the combined squadron, which resulted in a night action in the course of which two Spanish ships sunk each other and the British captured a French ship without any losses of their own.

191. *To Lady Hamilton*

[Pierpont Morgan: MA321]

Medusa back of [*sic*] the
Godwin [*sic*] Sands[1]
Aug^{t}: 6th: 1801.

My Dearest Emma,[2]

The wind being Easterly and the Sea fencibles not being so forward as I could wish them I have deferred my visit to Flushing 'till they are embarked and our floating batteries plac'd in the places assign'd them, All Your dear kind letters receiv'd yesterday made me much better for I was not quite so well as when in London I could not drink Champaigne a sure sign thet all is not right, but indeed I am not to call ill, but sometimes the exertion of my mind is beyond the strength of my body, I hope You will be able to get the house at Turnham Green either to hire or buy, shall I desire my Lawyer to call + talk to You if you think it will suit me + he shall hire or purchase it, Messrs: Booth + Hazlewood[3] N^{o}: 4 Craven Street Strand I really want a House, I am grieved to hear You complain keep well get well for the sake of all Your friends and for the sake [of] none more my dear Emma than Your faithful and for ever attatch'd

Nelson + Bronte.

The guardian Angels[4] although laying by me in their cases are not hung up in this ship, best regards to M^{rs}: Nelson the Duke + Lord William

192. *To Lady Hamilton*

[Huntington: HM 34091]

Medusa Margate Roads
Aug^{t}: 7th: 1801.

My Dear Emma,

pray send the enclosed for me,[5] I arrived here yesterday Evening and received your kind letters from the Downs of the 5th: I am vexed

[1]The Goodwin Sands are off Deal.

[2]The address 'My Dearest Emma,' appears to have been added later by Nelson, because there is not really enough space for it and in comparison to the date and the beginning of the text it is written in a lighter shade of black ink.

[3]Richard Booth and William Haslewood.

[4]Inserted. The expression 'Guardian Angels' refers here to paintings of Lady Hamilton (see note to Doc. No. 139 for use of the term).

[5]That is, what Lady Hamilton appears to have done, as there is nothing kept with this letter.

thet such a racket should be made of these trifling things, consider thet when I do my utmost they are boats of 50 or 60 tons, but I ever have done my best, I grieve my dear Emma to hear you are unwell would I could do any thing to comfort You try and get well we shall all meet at Naples or Sicily one of theses days I thank Castelcicala for his aff^{te}: note and send him an answer, tomorrow morning I go over to Hosely bay or Harwich to see whet is to be done with the Sea fencibles on thet coast I have given directions to cap^{n}: Gore (or rather requested) not to let any body[1] come into the ship but who had business with me for the Medusa would be full from morning 'till [night] 50 boats are rowing I am told about her this mom^{t}: to have a look at the one armed man I hope Rev^{d}: Sir[2] will be satisfied with the new petent as it is taken from Hilborough on purpose to please him and if I leave none he must breed stock from His own place, a letter tomorrow will find me at either Hosely or Harwich perhaps Troubridge will send it for you, with my best regards to M^{rs}: Nelson + the Duke + Lord William Believe me Ever your most affectionate + faithful

Nelson + Bronte

Cap^{n}: Gore is very good to me for I must be a great plague to him, + Parker is very well + much to do I delivered Your message to Allen, he says he has no fear for his wife whilst she is with you.

193. *To Lady Hamilton*

[Pettigrew, ii, p. 145] Medusa,
August 7th, 1801.

My dear Emma,

Pray send good Castelcicala's letter. My mind is not so perfectly at ease as I wish it, but I hope by your next letters I shall be made better. To our friends say every thing which is kind.

Ever yours,
Nelson and Bronté.

[1]Both words are underlined twice.
[2]Nelson's brother William.

194. *To Lady Hamilton*

[Pettigrew, ii, p. 147] Medusa, Harwich,
August 9th, 1801.

My dearest Emma,

I find from Lord St. Vincent that even my quitting my post at this moment would create an alarm, therefore I must give it up; but, my dear friend, the time will come when I am more at liberty. I hope that you and Sir William will come and see me when I can get a little more stationary, for at present I am running to every port. To-morrow I intend to go to the Nore, and from thence to Margate, perhaps the Downs, or over the water, not to fight, I have no such thing at this moment in my head. Times are when it is necessary to run risks: I do not mean myself, for I should be very sorry to place any one where I would not wish to be myself; but my flotilla must not be wantonly thrown away, I reserve them for proper occasions. I wish, my dear Emma, that my name was never mentioned by the newspapers; it may create poor Nelson enemies, not that I care, only that I hate to be praised except by you. My conduct at this time of service, is not to be altered by either praise, puffs, or censure. I do my best, and admit that I have only zeal to bear me through it. Thank our excellent friend, Lord William, for his new song – the last seems always the best. How is the Duke? I saw Sir Edward Berry last night: he inquired after you kindly. We only got the Medusa into Harwich at noon. I have been in a cutter since six o'clock; apropos, I have seen Captain Dean, late of the King George packet. You may remember the other cutter which conveyed us over; she was dismasted on the Sunday, and very near sinking. We had a good escape. Make my best regards to Mrs. Nelson, and believe me,

Yours, &c.
Nelson and Bronté.

I passed close to our Baltic friends yesterday; sent a boat aboard the St. George, got a letter from Hardy, a nod from George Murray, &c. &c.

195. *To Lady Hamilton*

[Huntington: HM 34092] Medusa Harwich
Aug^{t}: 10th: 1801.

My Dearest Emma,

Your letter from Mar^{te}: I received last night and those from the Downs yesterday morning I have them all, admire them all, and when You do not scold me I am the happiest man alive, and only rely thet I never deserve it, You know my quick temper and cannot bear false accusations although I cannot get to London yet I hope thet the business of the house will go on I should think the purchase would be the best, then I should collect all my little matters together, having arraingd all my business here, at noon I am going to the Nore I may be there two days but it is impossible to say I wish I could fix any time or place where I could have the happiness of meeting You but in my vagabond state I fear it is impossible I think I could have come to London for a day to arrainge about the house without any injury to the Kings service but patience my dear Emma and Ever for ever be assured thet I am Your faithful + affectionate

Nelson + Bronte.

best regards to the Duke Lord Wm: Mrs: Nelson[1] and all our real friends.

196. *To Lady Hamilton*

[NMM: CRK/19/12] Sheerness
Augt: 11th: 1801

My dearest Emma,

I came from Harwich yesterday noon not having set my foot on Shore although the Volunteers +c: were drawn up to receive me and the people ready to draw the Carriage Parker had very near got all the honours, but I want none but whet you my dear Emma confer You have sence to discriminate whether they are deserved or no, I came on Shore for my business lays with the Admiral[2] who lives in a Ship hauled on Shore and the Commissioner, Slept at Coffins and having done all[3] thet I can, am off for the Downs to day if possible, as far as Sepr: 14th: I am at the Adtys: disposal but if Mr: Buonaparte do [*sic*] not chuse to send his miscreants before that time my health will not bear me[4] through Equinoctial Gales, I wish thet Sir William was returnd I would try and persuade him to come to either Deal Dover or Margate, for thus cut off from the Society of my dearest friends tis but a life of sorrow and sadness, but patienza per forca[5]

[1]The ink of this line was not dry, when the letter was folded, so an imprint of it was left on the opposite page.
[2]Skeffington Lutwidge.
[3]Inserted.
[4]Inserted.
[5]'Patienza per forza' (Italian) roughly translates here into 'we must be patient'.

I hope you will get the House, if I buy, no person can say this shall or shall not be altered and you shall have the whole arraingement, remember me most kindly to M[rs]: Nelson, the Duke + Lord William write to me in the Downs May the Heavens bless and preserve you for Ever + Ever is the constant prayer[1] of my Dear Emma your most affectionate + faithful

Nelson & Bronte

The Mayor + Corporation of Sandwich when they came on board to present me the freedom of thet antient [*sic*] town, requested me [to] dine with them I put them off for the moment, but they would not be let off, therefore this business <u>dreadful</u> to me stands over + I shall be attacked again when I get to the Downs, but I will not dine there without you say approve, nor perhaps then if I can gett off Oh how I hate to be stared at.

197. *To Lady Hamilton*

[BL: Egerton 1614 ff. 73–74, no. 38] Aug[t]: 12th: 1801.

My dearest Emma,

You must know me well enough thet even when I cannot fully repay an obligation yet I always wish to do something which at least may mark my gratitude, so is my situation with Cap[n]: Gore, I therefore wish you to order for me a peice [*sic*] of plate value 50£ in order thet I may leave it as a momento [*sic*] thet I am not insensible of his kindness to me, he is very rich therefore I must teke care not to offend, he has every thing except a silver Urn or Tea Kettle and lamp I think the latter a useful peice [*sic*] of plate and will come to about the sum I propose, to have wrote on the Kettle, From Vice Ad[l]:[2] Viscount Nelson Duke of Bronte to Captain John Gore of His Majestys ship Medusa in gratitude for the many acts of kindness shewn him ~~whilst~~ when[3] on board the Medusa in August 1801. and let it be done as soon as possible as I expect ab[t]: next tuesday[4] to leave this ship and go into the Amazon, have it directed for me at deal + a Bill sent with it, but if my Dear Emma you think anything else more suitable of the same value be so good as to order it, That Beast Allen has left behind or lost all my papers but I have sent him after them and he is

[1]The letters 'er' are in a lighter shade of black ink than the surrounding words and they hardly fit into the gap between 'pray' and 'of', so that it appears they were added later.

[2]The words ,Vice Ad[l]:' are inserted.

[3]The word 'when' is written above the word '~~whilst~~'.

[4]18 Aug 1801.

such a notorious lyar [*sic*] thet he never says truth no such is his delight in lying thet even to do himself good he cannot resist the pleasure he has in telling a Lye for I askd him in the boat for my red case as I did not see it, his answer [was] Sir I put [it] in the stern locker, I then desired him to teke particular care in handing the case up the side, when he knew perfectly [well] thet he had not put it in the boat and as all my things were brought by him from Coffins house to the landing place I never expect to see It more, There is 200£ in it and all my papers, huzza huzza what a beast he is but I trust more to other peoples honesty than his cleverness, he will one day ruin me by his Ignorance Obstinacy + Lies, I am pushing for the Downs but whether I can stay one day or two, is impossible to say but it shall not be long before we meet as for going out of the kingdom without seeing you nothing shall prevent me I would sooner give up my command.

We are just off Margate + I think[1] one of my vessels may save post, I send it under cover to Sir T. T.[2] Ever for Ever yours most truly + faithfully

Nelson + Bronte

Nothing can or shall shake me, cann[ot][3] write M^{rs}: Th. today as it may be read.

198. *To Lady Hamilton*

[Pettigrew, ii, pp. 150–51] Medusa, Downs, August 13th, 1801.

My dearest Emma,

I have received all your truly kind and affectionate letters, and you may rely it is not my fault that I cannot get to London to see you and Mrs. Nelson; but I believe it is all the plan of Troubridge, but I have wrote both him and the Earl my mind. But 'Cheer up fair Emma',[4] cheer up, then I shall be better to hear you are so, for I would not give a farthing for friendship that could be in good health when the friend of my heart is sick. I have had a fever all night, and am not much better this morning.

[1]There is a blot of ink, appropriately placed over the letters 'ink' that, however, can still be read.

[2]Thomas Troubridge.

[3]The end of the word disappears under the piece of paper to which the letter is glued at the edge.

[4]First line of Cornelia Knight's poem; see Appendix 4.

I am going to-morrow morning over to the French coast, therefore you may be one day without hearing from me; but I assure you, my dear friend, that *I* am going into no danger. The services on this coast are not necessary for the personal exertions of a Vice-Admiral, therefore, I hope that will make your dear good friendly heart easy, you would naturally hate me if I kept back when I ought to go forward – never fear, that shall not be said of me. I find both at Harwich and Margate that they are disappointed at my not going on shore; the whole gentry of the country came to see me just as I came away, but a Sir George Murray, a very loyal gentleman, related to Princess Augusta,[1] came near Margate in a Custom house cutter to see me. I was in hopes to have seen Lord William Respecting Banti's son[2] I will ask Captain Gore to take him, and I should hope he would not refuse me, or I will take him into the Amazon, and fix him with Captain Sutton,[3] and under Robert Walpole's eye, who is Lieutenant of her. Get the lad ready and send him to me. Whatever I can do you may command, for yours are acts of kindness. Look out for a house for me (to buy, if you like it), but have a dry situation.

Yours,
Nelson and Bronté.

I have received, I believe, every letter and paper. Never ask the question, do they bore me?[4] All others do most damnably. Yesterday I received more than one hundred. Pray write me everything and of everybody – all you say must be most interesting to your,

Nelson and Bronté.

Allen is returned with my case...[5]

[1]Lady Augusta Murray (1768–1830), daughter of John Murray, 4th Earl of Dunmore and Lady Charlotte Stewart, secretly married in Rome, in contravention of the Royal Marriages Act 1772, the sixth son of George III, Prince Augustus Frederick, who was to be created Duke of Sussex on 27 Nov 1801.

[2]Bridiga Banti, née Giorgi (1757?–1806) was an Italian opera singer, at the time living and performing in London, who often performed duets with Lady Hamilton. She had a son, named Giuseppe, who published a short biography of his mother in Bologna in 1869 (*Vita di Brigida Banti nata Giorgi*), but I have not been able to find out whether he is the son mentioned here.

[3]Samuel Sutton (1765–1833).

[4]See beginning of Doc. No. 122: 'Never my dearest only friend say do my letters bore me, no they are the comfort of my life the only real comfort I feel seperated as I am from all I hold dear.'

[5]For Nelson complaining about his servant Allen having misplaced the case and lied about it, see Doc. No. 197.

199. *To Lady Hamilton*

[Pettigrew, ii, pp. 151–2]

Downs,
August 13th, 1801.

My dearest Emma,

Your letters to-day make me happy. Thank Mrs. Nelson for the perusal of Mrs. White's letter. She is a woman of sense. I send you a letter from Mrs. Cannon. I suppose I must give her the money. What can I do, but it must be as you please. Keep it secret, I will send an order by return of post, if you choose, and you shall write her a kind letter. My head is split.

Ever yours,
Nelson and Bronté.

Send me a translation of the Queen's letter. Must I write? I shall write to General Jerningham.

200. *To Lady Hamilton*

[*a)* Pettigrew, ii, p. 153–4;
b) Morrison, ii, p. 161 (No. 614)]

[*a)*] Medusa, at sea,
August 14th, 1801.

My dearest Emma,

[*b)*] The fever which I had seems fallen in my head, which is much swelled,[1] and my poor teeth pain me very much. I fear my letter will not be in time for the post to-day, and tomorrow likewise, the winds and tides fall out so cross that the vessels cannot get over the same day, therefore, do not expect one; you know I will write and send over if it is possible, but we cannot command the winds & the waves. Do not be uneasy about me, as I told you yesterday there is at this moment no service for a Vice-Admiral; but, my dear Emma, your good heart fancies danger for your friend, and a more truehearted one does not exist than

Your faithful,

[1]Christie's 1989-sale, lot 247, transcribed here: 'swell'd'.

[*a)*] Nelson and Bronté.

[*b)*] I am obliged to send off the cutter, and have not a moment. The cheese arrived safe and[1] excellent. Send to some good wine merchant for three dozen[2] of the best champagne, and order to the Downs by wagon,[3] directed on board the *Amazon*, or I shall[4] have nothing to give you, and that[5] would be shameful in me who receive[6] all good things from you.

201. *To Lady Hamilton*

[*a)* Pettigrew, ii, p. 154–5;
c) Christie's, 21 June 1989, lot 248,
partial transcription]

[*a)*] Medusa, off Boulogne,
August 15th, 1801.

My dearest Emma,

From my heart I wish you could find me out a good comfortable house, I should hope to be able to purchase it. At this moment I can only command £3000; as to[7] asking Sir William, I could not do it, I would sooner beg. Is the house at Chiswick furnished? If not, you may fairly calculate at £2000 for furniture,[8] but if I can pay, as you say, by little and little,[9] we could accomplish it. Be careful how you trust Mr. —;[10] all must be settled by a lawyer. It is better to pay £100,[11] than to be involved in law. I am very anxious for a house, and I have nobody to do any business for me [*c)*] but you my dear friend. If Davison was in town I would get him to look about and settle all the Law universally for me,[12] [*a)*] but as to a house, you are an excellent judge, only do not have it too large, for the

[1]Christie's 1989-sale, lot 247, has nothing between 'safe' and 'excellent'; probably the transcription at Christie's again missed out a '+' here, as in the transcription of lot 244 which is given as a facsimile in the catalogue (Doc. No. 236).

[2]Christie's 1989-sale, lot 247, transcribed here: '3 dozn.'.

[3]Christie's 1989-sale, lot 247, transcribed here: 'Down [*sic*] by waggon'.

[4]Christie's 1989-sale, lot 247, transcribed here: 'shall I'.

[5]Christie's 1989-sale, lot 247, transcribed here: 'this'.

[6]Christie's 1989-sale, lot 247, transcribed here: 'receives'.

[7]Christie's sale 2003, lot 143, has here: '3000£ and'.

[8]Christie's sale 2003, lot 143, has here: 'furnish'd if not you may fairly calculate at 2000£ for furniture'.

[9]Christie's sale 2003, lot 143, has here: 'pay as you say by little & little'; Christie's sale 1989, lot 248, has the same, except: 'little and little'.

[10]Christie's sale 1989, lot 248, has here: 'Christie'.

[11]Christie's 1989-sale, lot 247, transcribed here: '100£' and no commas in this sentence.

[12]This passage is missing in Pettigrew's transcription; it appears that in copying he missed a line between the first and the second 'but'.

establishment of a large house would be ruinous.[1] As you may believe, my dear Emma, my mind feels at what is going forward this night; it is one thing to order and arrange an attack, and another to execute it; but I assure you I have taken much more precaution for others, than if I was to go myself – then my mind would be perfectly at ease, for after they have fired their guns, if one half the French do not jump overboard and swim on shore, I will venture[2] to be hanged, and our folks have only to go on, never think of retreating. This will not go away till to-morrow. Many poor fellows may exclaim, *Would it were bed-time, and all were well*; but if our people behave as I expect, our loss cannot be much. My fingers itch to be at them. What place would you like to come to, Margate or Deal? Dover, I fear, would be inconvenient; Hosely Bay would be also the same. As for having the pleasure of seeing you, that[3] I am determined upon. I am fagging here, and perhaps shall only get abuse for my pains to be half ruined in my little fortune, but rich or poor, believe me,

Ever yours,

Nelson and Bronté.[4]

202. *To Lady Hamilton*

[BL: Egerton 1614 ff. 78–79, no. 40] Medusa
Aug[t]: 16th: 1801.

My dearest Emma

You will be sorry to hear that dear little Parker is wounded but the Doctors assure me he will do well, Langford[5] has his leg shot thro' but will do, the damn'd French had their vessels chain'd from the Bottoms to the Shore and also to each other, therefore although several of them were taken yet they could not be brought off, they will not unchain them for us to catch them at sea, the enemy have lost many men, so have we about 100 killed and wounded, Nobody acquitted themselves in every respect better[6] than Cathcart, he saved Parker from being a prisoner, Parker

[1]Christie's 1989-sale, lot 247, transcribed here, rather unconvincingly: 'serious'.
[2]Christie's 1989-sale, lot 247, transcribed here 'venture', too, but Christie's sale 2003, lot 143, has here: 'return'.
[3]Christie's 1989-sale, lot 247, has not got the word 'that' in this passage.
[4]Christie's sale 2003, lot 143, gives the autograph letter as signed: 'ever for ever my dear Emma your most faithful and affectionate Nelson & Bronte'.
[5]Frederick Langford (d. 1815), a lieutenant in the *Medusa* at the time.
[6]Inserted.

shew'd the most determined courage so did Langford you will believe how I am suffering and not well into the bargain, Troubridge hes wrote me such letters thet I do not know if I shall ever write to him again[1] it is all his doing my not coming to London I shall be 2 days in the Downs but it is just on[2] Sir William's arrival how I envy him the sight of your blessed face and probably I shall be gone before you can come I have no friend but <u>one</u> as I wrote Troubridge thet is you Good dear disinterested Emma, I am agitated but believe me Ever for Ever yours

Nelson + Bronte

This letter will be opened to a certainty to hear news from Boulogne.

203. *To Lady Hamilton*

[Pettigrew, ii, pp. 157–8] Medusa, Downs, August 17th, 1801.

My dearest Emma,

Your kind letter of Saturday[3] I received last night, and I regret that I cannot find a house and a little piece of ground, for if I go on much longer with my present command, I must be ruined. I think your perseverance and management will at last get me a home. I am now likely to be here till Thursday.[4] I wish Sir William had been either at home or not coming. Perhaps you, my excellent friend, and Mrs. Nelson, might have come down to Deal; how happy you would have made me, but I hope to get in again somewhere after this next trip, and by that time Sir William will have arranged his affairs in London. As for Troubridge, never send a letter through him. I shall never write to him again unless his letters are done away.[5] I am no longer useful, and we know, 'No longer pipe, no longer dance'. The Admiralty are beasts for their pains; it was only depriving me of one day's comfort and happiness, for which they have my hearty prayers. Parker will do well, I hope, but he must be kept very quiet; his thigh is broken in three places, but as he has youth, the doctors hope it will unite; it is the only chance he has. Langford is suffering very much. I have sent and taken lodgings for them both, and I trust they will

[1]Two days later Nelson reported having done so; see Doc. No. 204.

[2]Inserted.

[3]15 Aug 1801.

[4]20 Aug 1801.

[5]Nelson was furious, because Troubridge had not allowed him to go ashore to see Lady Hamilton; see: Knight, p. 409.

get well as fast as I wish them. Now we shall see whether the Admiralty will again neglect me, or whether officers and men who serve under me are to be neglected. We all dine at the Admiral's[1] to day, and sleep on shore, contrary to my inclination; but Captain Gore has requested it, that the ship may be cleaned and purified, for the wounds smell very bad, and they cannot begin to wash till Parker and Langford are removed out of the cabin. To-morrow morning I will be on board again. Mr. Pitt is coming to Walmer Castle. If he asks me to dinner, I shall go to Sandwich; at present I shall not think of it. What pleasure can I derive from it? Remember me to Sir William. I wish you were here.

Ever yours,

Nelson and Bronté.

To Mrs. Nelson, the Duke, and Lord William, say every thing which is kind. How can the Duke think you would take his house? Never.

204. *To Lady Hamilton*

[NMM: CRK/19/13] Deal
August 18th: 1801

My dearest Emma Your dear good kind and most affectionate letters from Saturday[2] to last night are arrived and I feel all you say, and may heavens bless me very soon with a Sight of your dear angelic face, You are a nonpareil no not one fit to wipe your shoes I am ever have been and always will remain your most firm fixt and unalterable friend, I wish Sir William had come home a week ago then I should have seen you here, I have this morning [been] attending the funeral of 2 young Mids a Mr: Gore, cousin of Capt: G. + a Mr: Bristow[3] one 19 [the] other 17 years of age, last night I was all the evening in the hospital, seeing thet all was done for the comfort of the poor fellows, I am going on board for nothing should keep me living on shore without you were here I shall come in the morning to see Parker + go on board again directly I shall be glad to see Oliver I hope he will keep his tongue quiet abt: the Tea-Kettle[4] for I shall

[1]Skeffington Lutwidge.

[2]15 Aug 1801.

[3]Pettigrew, ii, p. 160, informs in a fn. that these two Midshipmen were of the *Medusa*, Gore only 16 years of age, killed by 'no less than five musket balls. They were buried at Deal in one grave, . . . His Lordship's sensibility was freely expressed on this occasion by a flow of tears.'

[4]For Captain Gore, see Doc. No. 197.

not give it 'till I leave the Medusa You ask me whet Troubridge wrote me there was not a syllable about you in it it was about my not coming to London at the importance of which I laughed and then he said he should never venture another opinion, on which I said then I shall never give you one, this day he has wrote a kind letter and all is over,

I have however wrote him in my letter of this day as follows_Viz and I am this moment as firmly of opinion as ever thet Lord St. Vincent + yourself should have allowed of my coming to town for my own affairs for every one knows I left it without a thought for myself,[1] I know he likes to be with you but shall he have thet felicity and he deprive me of it No thet he shall not but this business cannot last long and I hope we shall have peace and I rather incline to thet opinion, but the Devil should not get me out of the kingdom without being[2] some days with you, I hope my Dear Emma you will be able to find a house suited for my comfort I am sure of being happy[3] by your arraingement, I have wrote a line to Troubridge about Darby, Parker will write you a line of thanks if he is able I trust in God he will yet do well, You ask me my Dear friend if I am going on more expeditions and were [*sic*] If I was to forfeit your friendship which is dearer to me than all the World, I can tell you nothing, for I go out [the moment] I see the enemy and can get at them it is my duty and you would naturally hate me if I kept back one moment. I long to pay them, for their tricks t'other day the debt of a drubbing which surely I'll pay, but where when or how, it is impossible your own good sence must tell you for me or mortal man to say, I shall act not in a rash or hasty manner, thet you may rely and on which I give you my word of honor Just going off. Ever for ever your faithful

Nelson & Bronte.

Every kind thing to M^rs: Nelson

205. *To Lady Hamilton*

[Pettigrew, ii, pp. 161–2]

Deal,
August 19th, 1801.

My dearest Emma,

Oliver came on board about two o'clock this morning with young Banti, who you may be assured I will take every possible care of. I have

[1]At the beginning of each line of the quotation Nelson gives an '='.
[2]The 'ing' in 'being' is added, rather squeezed between the words 'be' and 'some'.
[3]The word 'happy' is underlined twice.

all your truly kind and affectionate letters by Oliver, and also those by the post to-day. You may rely, that as soon as I can with honour get clear of this business, I shall resign it with pleasure; but if I was to give it up at this moment, you would hate me. The whole history must be over by the 14th of September, if not, I will certainly think of giving the command up; but as I have had all the fag, and what is to come must be playful compared to what has passed, I may as well have the credit of finishing this business. I think it very probable I shall never personally be engaged, therefore, my dear Emma, do not let your disinterested friendship make you uneasy. How often have I heard *you* say, that you would not quit the deck if you came near a Frenchman.[1] Would you have your attached friend do less than you purpose for yourself? That I am sure you would not. In these bombardments there is no risk for my rank, therefore I pray be quiet. I have wrote Sir William a letter, which you will see; he was so good as to write me one from Milford on the 12th, by a Revenue cutter, which arrived this morning. I had a note from Mr. Trevor;[2] he is at Ramsgate; he was sailing about with Mrs. T., but did not, he says, come near the ship, as he heard I had been *unfortunate*. I write a line to Mrs. Nelson. I am sure she will not leave you. I will entreat it of her. I am sure the kettle[3] is all right, and as it should be; I shall leave it packed with a letter to-morrow. I expect the Amazon; but all my movements are uncertain; but this is the most likely place to find me. The Three Kings I am told is the best house (it stands on the beach), if the noise of the constant surf does not disturb you. dear Parker is much better. I am sure he will be much gratified with your uniform kindness. When I left him to go on board yesterday, for I would not stay on shore, he got hold of my hand, and said he could not bear me to leave him, and cried like a child. However, I promised to come on shore this morning to see him, and nothing else could have got me out of the ship, for this beach is very uncomfortable to land upon. Oliver will tell you that I have been to the hospital to

[1]G. S. Parsons, *Nelsonian Reminiscences. Leaves from Memory's Log* (London, 1843), pp. 63–4, recalls the following occurrence at Malta in 1799 that Nelson may have had in mind: '"Anchor a-hoy!" resounded fore and aft; and we hove short to the music of the shot, some of them going far over us. / Lord Nelson was in a towering passion, and Lady Hamilton's refusal to quit the quarter-deck did not tend to tranquillize him. . . . a shot from Long Tom of Malta . . . struck the unfortunate fore-topmast, inflicting a deadly wound. His Lordship then insisted upon Lady Hamilton's retiring, who did not evince the same partiality for the place of "de safety" as our illustrious friend the Prince of *****, and leaving them in high altercation, I proceeded to his Majesty's frigate Success.'

[2]John Trevor, 3rd Viscount Hampden (1748–1824) had been British Minister to Sardinia, at Turin, 1783–98.

[3]The present for Captain Gore; see Docs Nos 197 and 204.

see my poor fellows, and altogether it has almost upset me, therefore I have not wrote so much as I should. Forgive me, and believe me,

Yours,

Nelson and Bronté.

Your interest with Sir William is requested to come and see a poor forlorn sailor.

206. *To Lady Hamilton*

[Christie's, 3 Dec 1986, lot 315] [Deal],
19 August 1801

My dearest Emma [... I have] pocketed one of your letters but have not read it [he longs to see his friends and asks her to entreat Sir William Hamilton to come with her and Mrs. Nelson on a visit] it will be a charity to me and Parker & Langford [expressing concern for her health] you can Bathe in the Sea that will make you strong & well[1] [saying that if she were to write to him her letter would be taken to him at sea and he could come on shore at short notice, and sending his regards to the Duke of Queensberry and Lord William Gordon, concluding] Ever for ever your faithful friend

Nelson & Bronte

[*Nelson was also at this time oppressed by financial worries. He felt his presence in the Channel was unnecessary, but his request for leave to come to London for consultation with the Lords of the Admiralty to settle his affairs was discouraged*]

I would come and see you all in London if the Ad.^{m} would allow me [*His gloom and frustration are evident from his longing for distraction:*] I shall never be long at Sea and if you send off a letter Adm. Lutwidge will forward it by a Cutter and I can come into the Downs in a few hours, and although I hate the Downs I feel if my friends come it will be paradise

[1]The 'benefits of sea bathing' for Lady Hamilton was also subject of a letter that Nelson wrote on the same day to Sir William Hamilton (Huntington Library, HM 34052), in answer to his letter of 12 Aug 1801 that is given in 1814-letters, ii, 216–19. Nelson appeals directly to Sir William in a similar way as to Lady Hamilton: 'for charitys sake come down'.

207. *To Lady Hamilton*

[Pettigrew, ii, pp. 162–3]

Medusa, Downs,
August 20th, 1801.

My dearest friend,

I approve of the house at Merton; and as the Admiralty are so cruel (no, I never asked the Board of Admiralty), as Troubridge and the Earl are so cruel as to object to my coming to London to manage my own matters, I must beg and entreat of you to work hard for me. Messrs. Booth and Haslewood[1] will manage all the law business. I have £3000. ready to pay to-morrow, and I can certainly get more in a little time if the people will have patience, therefore pray, dear Emma, look to it for me. I shall approve your taste. How often have I, laughing, said I would give you £5000. to furnish a house for me – you promised me, and now I claim it; and I trust to your own dear good heart for the fulfilment of it. I wrote Sir Thomas Troubridge[2] that I had but one real friend; his answer was, that he knew I had a hundred, but I do not believe the ninety-nine. It is calm, and our men are not arrived, therefore cannot go to sea this day. How happy I shall be to see you, Sir William, and Mrs. Nelson here, and how dear Parker will be delighted. He is much better to-day. I went on shore one minute to see him, and returned instantly on board. Captain Gore told me that Mr. and Mrs. Trevor[3] had been alongside, inquiring for me; that he had asked them to dinner, and that they would call again, so alongside they came. Captain Gore told them he was afraid he had done wrong, for that I was very busy; upon this Mr. Trevor came into the cabin, and begged pardon, but asked for Mrs. Trevor and two ladies to come in. My answer was, for being acquaintances of yours, Yes, if they wished to see the ship; but that I really could not allow them to stay dinner, for that every moment of my time was taken up. I did not go upon deck to receive them. They stayed ten minutes, inquired after you and Sir William, hoped you would come down and stay at Ramsgate, and away they went, making many apologies. I told him no other person should have come in, but for old acquaintance sake I could not refuse him. The other ladies were a Lady Somebody, and a Mrs. Somebody. I neither

[1]Nelson's solicitor who handled his prize money claim against St Vincent.

[2]C. Rachel Jones, *Some Norfolk Worthies* (London, 1899), p. 18, writes: 'the packets which Lord Nelson so often mentions were letters to and from Lady Hamilton, which Troubridge undertook to convey between these friends. Letters from Nelson to Troubridge on the subject of Lady Hamilton were many, but these have all been recently destroyed.'

[3]See Doc. No. 205.

know or care for their names. Make my kindest regards to Sir William, Mrs. Nelson, the Duke, and Lord William. I think if you will take the trouble for my house you will have country employment enough without going to Richmond, where you never can do as you please.

Ever yours,

Nelson and Bronté.

208. *To Lady Hamilton*

[Pettigrew, ii, p. 166] August 20th, 1801.

My dear Friend,

I am very much flattered by Mr. Greville's kindness, and the great honour he has done me, but independent of that, I admire his description of the rising prosperity of Milford,[1] and the rising of its industrious inhabitants, which will make proprietor and tenant rich in time, and not like many fools be like the boy with the *golden egg*.[2] I hope Graeffer is going on so at Bronté; I am sure I take nothing from that estate.[3] I entreat, my good friend, manage the affair of the house for me, and believe me, yours,

Nelson and Bronté.

Furniture and all fixtures must be bought.

209. *To Lady Hamilton*

[NMM: CRK/19/14] Medusa Downs
Aug^{t}: 21^{t}:[4] 1801.

My Dear Emma dearest best friend of Nelson, Sir William is arrived and well, remember me kindly to him, I should have had the pleasure of

[1]Charles Greville had convinced his uncle, Sir William Hamilton, to invest in the development of Milford Haven (in south-west Wales).

[2]Referring to Aesop's fable of the 'Goose That Laid the Golden Eggs'. In this fable the keepers of a goose that lays a golden egg every day slaughter their goose in order to get at all the gold at once – with the result that they do not find any gold at all inside the dead goose; the moral of this fable being, that being too greedy in the short term can ruin long-term benefits.

[3]A lengthy report by Graefer of 26 Sept 1801 about the state of affairs at Bronte can be found in Pettigrew, ii, pp. 196–8.

[4]1814-letters and the catalogue of the National Maritime Museum have misdated this letter 31 Aug 1801; it is clearly dated 21st.

seeing him but for one of my Lords + Masters Troubridge therefore I am sure neither You [n]or Sir William will feel obliged to him

the weather is very bad and I am very sea sick I cannot answer your letters probably, but I am writing a line to get on shore if possible, indeed I hardly expect thet your letters can get afloat,

I entreat you my dear friend to work hard for me and get the house and furniture and I will be so happy to lend it to you and Sir William therefore if you were to take the Dukes house a cake house open to everybody he pleases you had better have a booth at once you never could rest one moment quiet, why did not the Duke assist Sir Willm: when he wanted his assistance why not have saved you from the distress which Sir William must every day feel in knowing thet his excellent wife[ha]s sold her jewels to get a house for him whilst his own relations great as they are in the foolish World's Eye would have left a man of his respectability and age to have lodged in the streets did the Duke or any of them give him a house then, forgive me you know if anything sticks in my throat it must out, Sir William owes his life to you which I believe he will never forget, to return to the house, the furniture must be bought with it + the sooner it is done the better I shall like it, Oh how bad the weather is – the devils here want to plague my sold[1] out, yesterday just after dinner but I would have seen them damn'd before they should have come in, The Countess Montmorris, Lady this that and t'other came alongside a M^{r}: Lubbock with them to desire they might come in I sent word I was so busy that no person could be admitted as my time was employ'd in the Kings service, then they sent their names which I cared not for + sent Capt: Gore to say it was impossible + that if they wanted to see a ship they had better go to the Overyssel \a 64 in the Downs\ they said no they wanted to see me, however I was stout + will not be shewn about like a Beast and away they went, I believe Capt: Gore wishes me out of his ship for the Ladies admire him I am told very much, but however no Captain could be kinder to me than he is, these Ladies he told me afterwards were his relations I have just got your letters many thanks for them You do not say in the end Sir W^{m}: is arrived I am glad that you approve You may rely my dear friend that I will not run any unnecessary risk no more boat work I promise you, but ever your attatched + faithful

Nelson + Bronte.

To the Duke + Lord William, say everything which is kind + to M^{rs}: Nelson I am so dreadfully sea sick thet I cant hold up my head.

[1]*Sic*, Nelson appears to mean 'soul' here.

210. *To Lady Hamilton*

[Houghton: MS Hyde 77, 7.111.7]

Medusa
Aug^{t}: 22nd: 1801

My Dear Emma I shall try and get this letter through Troubridge but one day he is angry and another pleased that to say the truth I do not wish to trouble any of them, I have been sea sick these last two days and I should die to stay here one quarter of the winter, God knows whether these fellows will try and come over I can hardly think thet they are fools enough, You may rely my Dearest friend thet I will run no unnecessary risk therefore let Your friendly mind be at ease, would to God it was peace and then I would go to Sicily and be happy, I cannot get on shore and afloat again the surf is so great and yet I could have wish'd to have seen Parker but nothing but necessity should have made me remain on shore, and If I was to go I could not get off I expect the Amazon today and shall get on board her, but in a very wretched state for I have nothing in reality fit to keep a table and to begin and lay out 500£ is what I cannot afford, therefore in every respect I shall be very miserable, I know not why, but today I am ready to burst into tears pray God Your friendly letters may arrive and comfort me, I am sure I get not one Scrap of comfort from any other quarter, Banti seems stout and will I dare say do very well he is not sea sick, which I am that is very odd and I am damn'd sick of the sea, this moment I have Your letters and although I rejoice[1] from my heart thet You are coming yet I am fearful I shall not be here by Wednesday night but I hope on Thursday or Friday[2] at farthest, The three rooms next the sea are all Sitting Rooms[3]

1	2	3

---

are all sitting rooms. with a gallery before them next the sea I will desire two of the Rooms if possible for I believe except a dark sitting room they are the only rooms in the House and I will desire ~~the~~ good Bedchambers, to be kept for You at an inn You cannot take rooms with^{t}: being in the

[1]Inserted.
[2]Wednesday, Thursday and Friday were 26, 27 and 28 Aug 1801.
[3]Repeated at the beginning of the next line.

House for it is the eating and drinking that is charged + not the Rooms but I am sure the House will give You accommodation and I will send to say so this day, I will lose no time in returning for the meeting of You and Sir William and M^{rs}: Nelson will be the joy of my life, being for Ever Your most affectionate

Nelson + Bronte.

I send this under cover to Nepean, Your letters for Parker had better be directed for me at Cap^{n}: Parkers but explain this to him but the postage is nothing therefore direct to him the cost is nothing + he pays nothing You understand me for I should not like my letters to be opened therefore do away to him the direction you sent today, I hear he is much better today he will rejoice to see You, remember me kindly to Sir William + M^{rs}: Nelson I am glad she is coming down with You, but I fancy you will hate the town of Deal at least I do at this moment but I shall think it paradise[1] when my Dear only friends come to it, pray get the house + furniture.

I have sent to pay M^{r}: Salter[2] but I have not got the other bills.

211. *To Lady Hamilton*

[Pettigrew, ii, p. 171] Medusa, Downs, August 23rd, 1801.

Six in the morning.

My dearest Emma,

I am ready to run mad, I have been at this horrid place one whole week, and now on the approach of my dearest friends am forced to go to sea and am fearful that I cannot be here by Wednesday night, or before Thursday or Friday[3] at soonest, and I am more fearful that you will hate Deal and be as tired of it as I am without you. if you were here we would drive to Dover Castle and Ramsgate if you pleased. Poor little Parker cannot occupy much of your time, and Sir William may be so tired as to shorten his visit when I arrive, therefore had it not better be Friday, by which I hope to be able to get back, but for two or three days, when we are once afloat you know no one can answer, witness our voyage to

[1]For similar use of the word, see end of Doc. No. 206.

[2]According to Pettigrew, ii, p. 171, fn.: 'The respected Silversmith in the Strand, well known to all Naval Officers'.

[3]Wednesday, Thursday and Friday were 26, 27 and 28 Aug 1801.

and from Malta.[1] We are just getting under sail. May God bless you and believe me,

Your most faithful,

Nelson and Bronté.

If you are here before my arrival, and choose to be known to Admiral Lutwidge, he is as good a man as ever lived. I know very little of her; she is a very good woman, but her figure is extraordinary. Oh that I could stay. How I hate going to sea. The rooms are taken, and the master of the inn sends me word everything shall be done. I shall send a cutter in two days.

212. *To Lady Hamilton*

[Pettigrew, ii, pp. 171–2] Medusa at sea, August 24th, 1801.

My dearest Emma,

So little is newspaper information to be depended upon, that on Thursday[2] although with a + I was not a quarter of an hour on shore. I went to Parker, from him to the Admiral, from the Admiral to Parker, did not stay five minutes, was very low, did not call upon any of the wounded, nor at the Three Kings, got into the boat, and have not since been out of the Medusa. If I had staid ashore, I should not have had Trevor[3] on board. The information I have received about Flushing is not correct, and I cannot get at the Dutch; therefore, I shall be in the Downs I trust on Wednesday evening, ready and happy to receive you. Whatever Sir Thomas Troubridge may say, I feel I have no real friends out of your house.[4] How I am praying for the wind to carry me and to bring me to your sight. I am tired at not being able to get at the damned rascals; but they are preparing against me in every quarter, therefore they cannot be preparing for an invasion. I agree with you, fight them if they come out, so I will and reserve myself for it. I believe

[1]Nelson and the Hamiltons left Palermo on 24 April 1799 for Syracuse, and Syracuse for Malta on 3 May 1799, from where they returned to Palermo on 1 June 1799 – all this about nine months before the birth of Lady Hamilton's and Nelson's daughter Horatia.

[2]27 Aug 1801.

[3]See Docs Nos 205 and 207 (the latter about Trevor visiting Nelson on board).

[4]Sichel, p. 514, renders this sentence as underlined, in Italics: '*Whatever Sir Thomas Troubridge may say, I feel I have no real friends out of your house.*'; see Doc No 207 for what Troubridge said about the number of Nelson's friends.

the enemy attaches much more importance to my life than our folks, the former look up to me with awe and dread, the latter fix not such real importance to my existence. I send this under cover to Parker in case you are not come, that he may send it to London. I am making some arrangements and shall be across directly. With my kindest regards to Sir William believe me,

Yours,

Nelson and Bronté.

213. *To Lady Hamilton (alias Mrs Thomson)*

[*b)* Morrison, ii, p. 165 (No. 621); *c)* Christie's, 21 June 1989, lot 252, and 3 Dec 2003, lot 145][1]

[*c)*][2] I came on board but no Emma, no no my heart will break I am in silent distraction, The four pictures of Lady H^{n}: are hung up but alas, I have lost the original but we part only to meet very soon again, it must be it shall be

Turn over

[*b)*] My dearest wife, how can I bear our separation? Good God, what a change! I am so low that I cannot hold up my head. When I reflect on the many happy scenes we have passed together, the being separated is terrible, but better times *will* come, *shall* come, if it pleases God. And to make one worse the fate of poor Parker. But God's will be done. Love my Horatia and prepare for me the farm. If the furniture will suit, we must get other; there are sales every day. My head is almost turned. Continue to love me as Lady Hamilton does; she knows my thoughts, and although this letter is incoherent, yet she will explain it all. May the heavens bless[3] you. Amen, amen, amen.

[1]Morrison, ii, p. 165, suggested as date of the letter 'end of September' and arranged it between letters of 15 and 21 Sept; Christie's catalogues of 2003 (lot 145) suggested 'circa 29 September 1801'; I follow Morrison's suggestion, because Nelson wrote in a letter of 20 Sept 1801 to Alexander Davison: 'Lady Hamilton with her party went to London this morning' (Nicolas, iv, p. 492).

[2]The following passage is on the address panel, which bears the address: 'M^{rs}: Thomson care / of Lady Hamilton'; usually text that was written on the address panel was added at the end of the letter, but as the passage finishes 'turn over' I have followed Morrison in giving this passage before the main part of the letter.

[3]Christie's catalogue of 2003, lot 145, transcribed this, rather unconvincingly, as 'keep'.

214. *To Lady Hamilton*

[Pettigrew, ii, pp. 181–2]

Amazon,
Sept. 20th, 1801.

My dearest Emma,

Although I ought to feel grateful for Sir William, you, and Mrs. Nelson's goodness incoming to see a poor forlorn creature at Deal, yet I feel at this moment only the pain of your leaving me, to which is added, the miserable situation of our dear excellent little Parker. Dr. Baird[1] is in great distress about him, and it can hardly be said that he lives at this moment, and before night will probably be out of this world, and if real worth and honour have a claim to Divine favour, surely he stands a fair chance of happiness in that which is to come. I will not say what I feel because I know that your feelings are similar. We might have comforted each other, but the Fates have denied us that comfort. Sir William's business forces him to London, and mine irresistibly forces me to remain on this miserable spot. I got on board at seven o'clock, and found what a difference! I must not think of it. My sailing to-morrow depends on poor Parker. If he dies he shall be buried as becomes so brave and good an officer. Mr. Wallis[2] is just come on board; he says, there are no hopes. I am sick to death, but

Ever yours,

Nelson and Bronté.

I send you Mr. Haslewood's letter about the furniture. Do what you think best, I shall be content. We must not sink under the will of Providence. The valuation had better be, probably, by Mr. Haslewood's man – it can make no difference to Mr. Dods;[3] but do as you please, and see it right.

215. *To Lady Hamilton*

[*a)* Pettigrew, ii, pp. 183–4;
b) Morrison, ii, pp. 165–6 (No. 622)]

[*a)*] Amazon, Sept. 21st,
1801, [*b)*] ½ past 7.

[*a)*] My dear Emma,

[*b)*] My letter from Dr. Baird last evening, and from the Assistant-Surgeon at 4 this morning, again revive my hopes of our dear little Parker.

[1]A physician in the Royal Navy (d. 1843).
[2]Who had been purser of the *Elephant* when Nelson was on her in the Baltic.
[3]An upholsterer.

He is free from fever, and his stomach got rid of the sickness. He can speak, therefore I hope the blood is forming again, and if the ligature can hold fast he may yet do well. Pray God he may, in which I know you and all with you most heartily join; but I dare not be too sanguine. We have a good deal of swell, and it blows strong, so that I cannot go under Dungeness, indeed, I know of no use I am, either there or here. We can do nothing in future but lay at anchor and wait events. I have wrote Lord St. Vincent strongly on the subject this day. A gale of wind is brewing, and I think our communication with the shore will be cut off. The moon is also eclipsed to-morrow.[1] Would to God I was on shore at the farm. I have sent to Mr. Dods to carry you a list of my things at his house, and to receive your orders what is to go to the farm. I have not yet any answer from the Admiralty on the subject of my last letter. Make my best regards to Sir William, Mrs. Nelson, Mrs. Cadogan, &c. &c. to the Duke, and all friends of ours, and believe me ever, your

[*a)*] Nelson and Bronté.

[*b)*] Yesterday, if I could have enjoyed the sight, passed through the Downs 100 sail of West Indiamen. If Sir William had accepted Mrs. Lutwidge's bribe of the ginger,[2] I suppose he would now have got it, for captain Beresford[3] is arrived. I send you verbatim a postscript of Admiral Lutwidge's letter: viz. 'Remember us to your friends who have just left you, when you write, with the sincere regret we felt in parting with them'.[4] I shall keep my letter open to the last moment.

Noon. I have this moment your kind line from Rochester. I grieve at your accident. I am obliged to send my letters now, for I doubt if a boat can go at 3 o'clock.

[1]An eclipse of the moon causes a spring tide that leads to strong currents in straits (such as the Strait of Dover).

[2]Mrs. Lutwidge wrote on 23 Sept 1801 from Deal to Lady Hamilton: 'Tell Sir William, with my best regards, that had he waited one day longer, I would have had an opportunity of presenting him with the ginger, as Captain Beresford and two hundred sail of ships arrived on Sunday. However, the ginger is safe in the closet, whence it shall be conveyed to Piccadilly by the first safe opportunity, only that I should have been much more happy in presenting it myself.' (Pettigrew, ii, pp. 185–6).

[3]John Poo Beresford (1766–1844).

[4]Mrs Lutwidge expressed similar feelings in a letter to Lady Hamilton, written two days later, on 23 Sept (Pettigrew, ii, pp. 185–6).

216. *To Lady Hamilton*

[NMM: CRK/19/15] Sep^{t}: 21st: ¼ p^{t}: 10 Oclock [1801].[1]

My dear Emma,

I wish you would send the letter to M^{rs}:[2] Dods directly for otherwise he may inadvertently If done + it comes to London deliver some of the things, The wardrobe is hers,[3] + If any of her cloaths are at M^{r}: Dods they had better be seperated from mine, and indeed whet things are worth removing to have them directly sent to Merton, a Bed or two I believe belong to my Father but am not sure, I send you D^{r}. Bairds comfortable note this moment rec^{d}: You will [find] Parker is treated like an Infant, poor fellow I trust he will get well + take possession of his Room at the Farm, Ever your affectionate

Nelson + Bronte.

217. *To Lady Hamilton*

[Pettigrew, ii, pp. 184–5] Amazon,
September 23rd, 1801.

My dear Emma,

It blows so fresh to-day that I almost doubt whether a boat will be able to get on shore with our letters, therefore, if you ever miss receiving letters, you may be sure that it is either from bad weather, or that I am gone out of the Downs. I shall write you every day if it is possible, and you may always be assured that if you do not get a letter from me, that no person in London does. At six this morning, I received a letter from Dr. Baird, saying, dear Parker had a bad night, and he was afraid for him, he was so very weak, therefore, we must not flatter ourselves, but hope the best. I am more than half sea-sick. I can tell you no news, for we can at present hold no communication; the surf is very high on the beach. I shall try if it is possible at three o'clock, but I do not expect your letters off to-day although I am most anxious to hear of your safe arrival in town, with all the news. Your letters are always so interesting that I feel the greatest disappointment when I do not receive them. Have you seen Troubridge? I dare say he came the moment you arrived. I hope you have seen Mr.

[1]According to the address panel posted in Deal.
[2]*Sic*, this should be 'M^{r}:'.
[3]Lady Nelson's.

Haslewood and Mr. Dods, and that you will be able to get to Merton long before the 10th of October, before which I hope the Admiralty will remove me from my command; much longer than that, I assure you, I will not stay.[1] I leave the letter open in hopes I may get a communication with the shore. Charles[2] is very well, is a very good boy. So is Banti; but the latter is initiated into the vices of London; I fancy, at least, he loves to spend money. Make my best regards to all your party, and believe me,

Yours,

Nelson and Bronté.

What a difference to when you was here. A boat that sells things to the people is the only boat that has come to us since six this morning. He says, he will get on shore, therefore, I send my letters. Captain Sutton desires his best compliments. I am very sick.

218. *To Lady Hamilton*

[Monmouth: E 107]

Amazon
Sepr: 23rd: 1801.

My Dear Emma I receivd your kind letters last evening and in many parts they pleased and made me sad so life is chequered and if the good preponderates then we are called happy I trust the farm will make you more so than a dull London life, make what use you please of it, It is as much yours as if you bought it, therefore if your Relation[3] cannot stay in your house in Town surely Sir William can have no objection to your taking her to the farm The pride of the Hamiltons surely cannt: be hurt by sitting down with any of your Relations you have surely as much a right for your Relations to come into the house as his could have It has vexed [me][4] as I know it must give you great pain meke use of me for your happiness, The vagabond thet stole your medal will probably be hanged unless Mr: Varden will swear it is not worth 40 shillings which I dare say he may do with a safe conscience, I should not wish it to be brought into a Court of Law as the extraordinary nature of the medallion will be noticed, I am sure you

[1]As a matter of fact he stayed until 21 Oct, arriving at Merton on 22 Oct 1801.

[2]Connor; see also Doc. No. 220, where he is mentioned as being on board Sutton's ship, the *Amazon*, with Nelson.

[3]According to Kate Williams, *England's Mistress* (London, 2006), p. 281, this is a reference to Emma Carew, Lady Hamilton's daughter by Harry Fetherstonhaugh.

[4]Here the first page ends, which could explain the lack of coherence in the sentence.

will not let any of the Royal blood into your house they have the impudence of the Devil, his mother was a bastard of my relations Sir Edward Walpole,[1] but let us turn our thoughts to the Dear farm whatever you do about it will be right and proper, make it the interest of the man who is there to take care I am not cheated more than comes to my share and he will do it poco poco[2] we can get rid of bad furniture and buy others, all will probably go to Bronte one of these days I shell certainly go there whenever we get peace, I have had odd letters from Troubridge about what Cap^{n}: Bedford[3] told me of the conversations ab^{t}: officers,[4] whether it is intended to quarrel and get rid of me I am not clear but do not take any notice if you see him which I dare say you will for he likes to come to you (but do not let him unless Sir William is there,) Remember me kindly to M^{r}: Este,[5] I hope we shell have peace Ever yours faithfully

Nelson + Bronte.

219. *To Lady Hamilton*

[Pettigrew, ii, p. 187]

Amazon,
September 23rd, 1801.

My dear Emma,

I send Dr. Baird's note, just received; it will comfort you. Captain Bedford says he[6] is thought better since the report.

Ever yours,

Nelson and Bronté.

If he lives till Thursday[7] night I have great hopes.

[1]Here Nelson appears to be referring to Prince William Frederick (1776–1834), who was to succeed his father (brother of George III) in 1805 as Duke of Gloucester and Edinburgh, and whose mother, Maria, Duchess of Gloucester (1736–1807), was an illegitimate daughter of Edward Walpole (1706–84), son of the prime minister Sir Robert Walpole (1676–1745) and brother to Nelson's maternal grandmother.

[2]Italian for 'little by little'.

[3]William Bedford (c. 1764–1827), a captain since 1794, had been 'present at the raids on Boulogne on 15 August 1801, on which occasion he offered to serve as a volunteer under the junior officer in command of the boats. The offer, however, was declined by Lord Nelson' (Wikipedia, 17 July 2019; see also: Pettigrew, ii, p. 187).

[4]In a letter to St Vincent of the same day (23 Sept 1801) Nelson describes how 'The Boat service . . . is got very unpopular' (Nicolas, vii, p. ccxxx*).

[5]Dr Lambton Este, physician and private secretary to Charles Lock, former consul at Naples.

[6]Captain Edward Parker.

[7]24 Sept 1801.

220. *To Lady Hamilton*

[Pettigrew, ii, pp. 187–8]

Amazon,
September 24th, 1801.

My dear Emma,

This morning's report of Parker is very favourable indeed, and if he goes on well this day I think he will recover. I should have gone out of the Downs to look about me this morning, but I wish to leave Parker in a fair way. Sutton is gone on shore to make inquiries, and if Dr. Baird will allow me to see him for a few minutes, I intend to go on shore to assure him that I love him, and shall only be gone a few days, or he might think that I neglected him; therefore, my present intention is to sail in the morning at daylight; therefore you will not probably get a letter on Saturday,[1] but you shall if I can, but do not expect it. I would give the universe was I quit of my present command, and in October, one way or other, I will get clear of it. The wind is now freshing, and I do not think I shall be able to land, but I will write him a line. Dr. Baird is very unwell, and I should not be surprised if he is seriously ill from his attention to the wounded under his care. Whether I can afford it or not, you must have made for me a silver cup, gilt inside, price about thirty guineas, with an inscription, "As a mark of esteem to Doctor Andrew Baird, for his humane attention to the gallant officers and men who were wounded at Boulogne, August 16th, 1801, from their commander-in-chief, Vice-Admiral Lord Viscount Nelson, Duke of Bronté, &c. &c. &c." What do you think of this? Will you order it? I must find money to pay for it. Never mind the newspapers, they cannot say we are saving of our money. We give it where it is wanted Even Troubridge writes me, he wished you had stayed at Deal. What can you do in London? I have already got cold, but I hope it will go off; I long to hear the result of your visit to Merton. I hope Mr[s]. Greaves[2] will give up sooner than the 10th. Mr. Dods will do anything for you, and have them removed to Merton as soon as you can: I long to see you at work. I hope Mrs. Nelson will stay with you as long as possible. Make my best regards to Sir William. I hope he has had plenty of sport. To Mrs. Nelson say every thing which is kind, to the Duke, &c. &c. and be assured I am

[1]26 Sept 1801.

[2]The previous owner of Merton Place, a widow, according to Fraser, p. 292, 'showed some reluctance to move out'.

Yours,

Nelson and Bronté.

All the Captains regret your absence. Charles is a very good boy, and so is Banti: Captain Sutton is very kind to them.

221. *To Lady Hamilton*

[NMM: AGC/17/11] 2 oclock.[1]

Allen has given the enclosed for his wife, Cap^{n}: Sutton is this mom^{t}: come from the shore, Parker's stump has been dressed looks very well he has taken port wine, has Eat [*sic*], and is asleep I have now great hopes, a gale of wind I believe is coming on, Ever my Dear Emma your faithful

Nelson + Bronte.

I am very low bad weather,

222. *To Lady Hamilton*

[Pettigrew, ii, p. 189] Amazon, off Folkstone,
September 25th, 1801.

My dearest Emma,

I got under sail this morning at daylight, intending to return to the Downs on Sunday or Monday,[2] but receiving a note from Dr. Baird of our dear Parker's being worse, and requesting me to stay a day or two longer, and as it is calm, so that I can neither get to the coast of France or to Dungeness, I am returning to the Downs. My heart, I assure you, is very low; last night I had flattered myself, I now have no hopes. I dare say Dr. Baird will write you a line, but we must bear up against these misfortunes. I have not had your letters to-day; they are my only comfort. Yesterday the Calais flat boats, &c. came out. Captain Russel[3] chased them in again, but they can join at any time, as the season approaches when we cannot go on their coast. You must, my dear friend, forgive me,

[1]According to the address panel, this was sent 'Deal September Twentyfourth / 1801'.

[2]27 or 28 Sept 1801.

[3]John Russel(l); Pettigrew, ii, p. 189, adds: 'of the *Gier*, he was Post Captain in 1802, commanded the Sea Fencibles in Argyllshire, and died on half-pay in 1813'.

for I cannot write any thing worth your reading except that I am at all times, situations, and places,

Yours,

Nelson and Brontë.

223. *To Lady Hamilton*

[NMM: CRK/19/16] Amazon
Sep^{t}: 26th: 1801. 8 OClock

My Dearest Emma Your kind letters came on board ab^{t}: 6 OClock, You may rely upon one thing that I shall like Merton therefore do not be uneasy on thet account I have that opinion of your taste + judgement that I do not believe it can fail in pleasing me, We must only consider our means and for the rest I am sure you will soon make it the[1] prettiest place in the World, I dare say M^{r}: Haselwood acted like all Lawyers whose only consideration was for their client but I am sure you will do for me all the civil things towards M^{rs}: Greaves, If I can afford to buy the Duck Close + the field adjoining It would be pleasant but I fear it is not in my power but I shall know when my accounts are settled at New Year's Year [*sic*], to be sure we shall employ the tradespeople of our village in preference to any others in what we want for common use, and give them every encouragement [to] be kind + attentive to us, from my heart do I wish thet I was with you and it cannot be long for today I am far from well violent head ache and very cold , but it[2] may be agitation whatever my Dear Emma you do for my little charge[3] I must be pleased with, probably she will be lodged at Merton at least in the spring when she can have the benefit of our Walks, it will make the Poor mother happy I am sure I do not write to her today as this goes through the Admiralty but tell her all I would say, You know my unchangeable thoughts about her, I shall have the child christened when I come up, have we a nice church at Merton, We will set an example of goodness to the under Parish[4] Would to God I was with you at Laleham I shall never forget our happiness at that place M^{r}: Davison will pay M^{rs}: Nelson 50£ Octr 1st I dare say M^{r}: Shakespeare has some orders about it, I had yesterday a letter from my

[1]Inserted.
[2]Inserted.
[3]Their daughter.
[4]Not 'underparishioners', as 1814-letters have it.

father, he seems to think that he may do something which I shell not like, + I suppose, he means, going to Somerset S^{t},[1] shall I to an old man enter upon the detestable subject it may shorten his days, but I think I shall tell him thet I cannot go to Somerset Street to see him, but I shall not write till I hear your opinion If I once begin you know it will all out, about her and her ill treatment to her son, but you shell decide Our accounts of Dear Parker I fear preclude all hopes of his recovery, it was my intention to have gone ashore this morning to have called on Ad^{l} Lutwidge but the wind is coming fresh from the SW, I have declined it for I doubt if I could get off again, at 10 OClock with your letters came off D^{r}: Bairds note to say every hope was gone I have desired thet his death should be sent by Telegraph to the Admiralty, they will[2] surely honor his memory although they would not promote him, What are our feelings, my Dear Emma, but we must cheer up, + with best regards to M^{rs}: Nelson believe me Ever for Ever your most affectionate

Nelson + Bronte.

best regards to Sir W^{m}: I send you the last report, who knows[3]

224. *To Lady Hamilton*

[Pettigrew, ii, pp. 190–91][4]

My dearest Emma,

I had intended to have gone on shore this morning, to have seen dear Parker, but the accounts of him are so very bad, that the sight of his misery poor fellow would have so much affected me, and if he had been in his senses must have given him pain, that I have given up the idea, unless he feels better and expresses a wish to see me, then dear fellow I should

[1]The words '+ I suppose, he means, going to Somerset S^{t},' are given at the top of the page, above the line 'do something which I shell not like, +'. Somerset Street was where Lady Nelson was staying at the time.

[2]The passage starting with 'surely' (and finishing with 'Ever for Ever') is written on the outside of the letter on one of the parts that where folded towards the inside on closing the letter, finishing at the end of the paper. The last passage of the letter, starting 'Your most affectionate', is written on the other part to be folded towards the inside, starting at the top end of the page and finishing above the address.

[3]The words 'I send you the last report, who knows' are written in a lighter shade of black ink than the words 'best regards to Sir W^{m}:', so it appears that they were added later.

[4]Pettigrew, ii, 190 claimed that Nelson wrote 'on the same day' to Davison, 'My dear Parker left this world for a better at nine o'clock this morning'; this letter to Davison was dated 'September 27th, 1801' (Nicolas, iv, p. 497).

be too happy to go. I slept not a wink all night, and am to-day very low and miserable. Captain Sutton is gone to see how he is, and should he express a desire to see me, I will go whatever I may suffer from it, but he will soon be at a place of rest, free from all the folly of this world.

Sutton is returned. Dear Parker left this world for a better at 9 o'clock; I believe we ought to thank God. He suffered much, and can suffer no more. I have no one to comfort me. I shall try and keep up, and I beg you will. We can now do no good. I shall leave the Downs as soon as the funeral is over.

Your management of my affairs at Merton, are like whatever else you undertake, excellent. I shall write this day to Mr. Haslewood to order £1000. to be paid for the furniture, and what you bargained for. Mrs. Nelson's quarter is to commence October the 1st. If Davison has left no directions I must pay it. I know not who else to desire. Would to God I was with you, then I might cheer up a little. I have wrote to Mr. Haslewood and desired him to call on you at noon. You will see my letter, it is more regular for me to desire my agents to pay Mr[s]. Greaves, I can do it by Tuesday's post,[1] but these lawyers know how to take a regular receipt, which we do not. Remember me most kindly to Mrs. Cadogan, Oliver, &c. Sir William gone to Newmarket! well wonders will never cease. Believe me,

Ever yours,

Nelson and Bronté.

My heart is almost broke, and I see I have wrote nonsense, I know not what I am doing. Send down Dr. Baird's cup[2] as soon as you can. I shall not write or say any thing about it.

225. *To Lady Hamilton*

[*a)* Pettigrew, ii, pp. 192–3; *b)* Morrison, ii, p. 168 (No. 625)]

[*a)*] Amazon, September 28th, 1801.

My dearest Emma,

[*b)*] We are going this noon to pay our last sad duties to dear good Parker. I wish it was over for all our sakes, then we must endeavour to cheer up, and although we cannot forget our Parker, yet we shall have the

[1]Tuesday was 1 Oct 1801.
[2]See Doc. No. 220.

comfortable reflection how we loved him, and how deserving he was of our love. I am afraid his father is but in very indifferent circumstances; but I doubt if the Admiralty will assist him, however, they shall be tried. I hope the Admiralty will direct all the expenses of the lodgings, funeral, &c. to be paid – if not, it will fall very heavy upon me. Pray write me when I am to direct my letters to Merton. Is it a post town, or are the letters sent from the General Post Office? I wish I could see the place, but I fear that is impossible at present{.}[, and if I could you would not, perhaps, think it right for me to come now Sir William is away.] I entreat I may never hear about the expenses again. If you live in Piccadilly or Merton it makes no difference, and if I was to live at Merton I must keep a table, and nothing can cost me one-sixth part which it does at present, for this I cannot stand, however *honourable* it may be. God bless you and believe me,

Yours,

Nelson and Bronté.

If the wind is to the westward, I shall go to Dungeness, but you must not, by Gore's account, which I send, be surprised at not hearing from me regularly, but you know I always shall write and send when it is possible. I only send this that your dear friendly mind should be easy.'

'*Half past one*. – Thank God the dreadful scene[1] is past. I scarcely know how I got over it. I could not suffer much more and be alive. God forbid I should ever be called upon to say or see as much again. Your affectionate letters are just come, they are a great comfort. The worst, thank God, is past. I must have plate, &c. at Davison's, and I agree with you, that nothing but what is mine should be there, and that Sir William should always be my guest. I told you so long ago. I will find out what spoons, &c. I have, and send you a list to-morrow, but to-day I am done for, but ever

Yours,

[*a)*] Nelson and Bronté.

[*b)*] I will write to my Father to-morrow, and take not the smallest notice of how he disposes of himself.[2]

[1]Captain Edward Parker's funeral.

[2]In his letter of 26 Sept 1801 (Doc. No. 223) Nelson had written: 'I had yesterday a letter from my father, he seems to think that he may do something which I shell not like, + I suppose, he means, going to Somerset S^{t}'.

226. *To Lady Hamilton*

[CRC]

Amazon
Sep^{r}: 29th: 1801

My Dearest Emma,

I send by the coach a little parcel containing the Keys of the Plate chest + the case of the Tea urn, and there is a case of Colebrook Dale[1] Breakfast sett, and some other things, M^{r}: Dods had better go to the house for he is Davisons man, will you have your picture carried to Merton I should wish it, and mine of the Battle of the Nile, I think you had better not have Sir Williams Books or any thing but what is my own, I have sent in the parcel by the coach this day, 2 salt sellers [*sic*] 2 ladles, which will make 4 of each as 2 are in the chest, You will also find spoons + forks sufficient for the present, If sheets are wanting for the Beds will you order some and let me have the bill, I also think that not a servant of Sir William, I mean the cook should be in the house, but I leave this and all other matters to your good management, Would to God I could come and take up my abode there, and if such a thing should happen thet I go abroad, I can under my Land [*sic*] lend you the house thet no person can molest you, not thet I have at present any idea of going anywhere but to Merton, do you take Black James,[2] do as you please I have no desire one way or the other,[3] Our Dear Parkers circumstances are a little out of order but I have undertaken to settle them if the creditors will give me time, for the poor [Father][4] is worse than nothing, I have given him money to buy mourning + to pay his passage home again, I trust in God that he will never let me want for I find no man who starts up to assist me I can with a quiet conscience when all is gone, live on bread + cheese, Never mind as long as I have your friendship warm from the heart, I have got some of Dear Parkers hair which I value more than if he had left me a Bulse of Diamonds I have sent it in the little Box, keep some of it for poor Nelson

[1]China from the Coalport Porcelain Works (John Rose & Co), in Coalport, Shropshire, from 1795; for an illustration of this service (decorated with Nelson's coat of arms in the centre surrounded by a wreath of oak leaves on the edge), see: Rina Prentice, *The Authentic Nelson* (London, 2005), p. 142.

[2]James Price.

[3]In his letter of 26 May 1801 (Doc. No. 170) Nelson was more determined: 'there is an old black servant, James Price, as good a man as ever lived, he shall be taken care of, and have a corner in my house as long as he lives. My uncle left him £20. a-year.'

[4]Someone inserted the word 'Father' in the original manuscript. The word is in the text of Pettigrew's edition.

Noon blows strong I have just receiv'd your kind letters They indeed comfort me, and I hope we shall live to see many many happy years, + Ever Your faithful

Nelson + Bronte

to the Duke say every thing which is kind.

227. *To Lady Hamilton*

[Pettigrew, ii, p. 195]

Amazon,
September 30th, 1801.

My dearest Emma,

I well know by my own feelings that you would think of my birth-day with a degree of pleasure and pain. I am sensible of all your goodness. Respecting the farm and all the frugality necessary for the present to be attached to it, I know your good sense will do precisely what is right. I only entreat again that everything even to a *book* and a cook at Merton may be mine. The house should be insured for three or four thousand pounds, including the furniture, that all may not be lost in case of fire. The Admiralty have refused to bury Captain Parker. He may have stunk above ground, or been thrown in a ditch; the expense of that and lodgings, &c. has cost me near £200, and I have taken, poor fellow, all his debts on myself, if the creditors will give me a little time to find the money. Dr. Baird has been very, very good indeed. I wish the cup had arrived, for I have taken leave of him with only thanks much against my inclination. You are very good, my dear Emma, about poor Parker's father. If he calls you will of course see him, but he is a very different person from his son. He has £72. more in his pocket than when he came to Deal. I wish for his own sake that his conduct had been more open and generous like mine to him, but never mind.

As I shall go under Dungeness to-morrow for three or four days, I went on shore at nine to call on the Admiral (Lutwidge), and to thank him and her for their attentions to dear Parker, and I presented your regards, &c. I called on poor Langford, who has got full possession of your chaise. He removed from the other lodgings to where Captain Bedford's officers are – much more airy. Dr. Baird is in great wrath with the methodist. – He gave her six guineas as a present from me, and she was not satisfied. I shall endeavour, in a very little time, to get a few days leave of absence, if not, to get rid of my command. The business of G. is over, it is gone to

Dickson.[1] I wish I could with propriety have undertaken it, it could not fail, if well managed, and it would have made me an Earl. You asked me did I see Parker after he was dead? I believe if I had it would have killed me. I intend Flaxman[2] to prepare a little monument, about fifty pounds, for him, on a column or pyramid. I shall use Sir William's or your taste on the occasion. I cannot afford one, or it should be handsomer, but the will must be taken. Remember me kindly to Mrs. Cadogan, Oliver, and all friends. Langford desires me to say everything which is kind. To the Duke say all that is kind, and ever believe me,

Yours,

Nelson and Bronté.

228. *To Lady Hamilton*

[Pettigrew, ii, p. 199] Amazon,
October 1st, 1801.

My dearest Emma,

From various causes it is as well for me to leave the Downs for a few days to change the scene a little, and also it is right to look a little at my squadron under Dungeness. I left the Downs at day-light, and am now writing off Folkestone. I shall have Hardy to dine which will be a pleasure to me, for he is a good man. Captain Sutton has just been giving me such instances of want of feeling in Mr. Parker, that I am quite disgusted with him; he is a dirty dog. How unlike his worthy son! But I have done with him. I shall send this letter on shore to New Romney, but I think you had better, after a day or two, direct your letters to Deal, for longer than three or four days I shall not remain here. At this moment I fancy you setting forth to take possession of your little estate,[3] for this very day I shall make a codicil to my will, leaving it in trust for your use, and

[1]Edward Stirling Dickson (1765–1844) had been ordered to attack the West African island of Goree (now part of Senegal's capital Dakar). Nelson had written to St Vincent on 23 Sept 1801: 'You will easily believe that I should have liked to have tried the business at Goree, but the objections to it were innumerable you would have Dickson and all of us, *the Service*.' (Nicolas, vii, p. ccxxx*). According to Wikipedia, it was only 'in 1804, commanding HMS *Inconstant*, [that Dickson] led a force which captured the West African island of Gorée'.

[2]John Flaxman (sculptor, 1755–1826); Nelson had suggested in a letter to Edward Berry of 26 Jan 1801, that Flaxman should be commissioned to execute a monument to captain Miller (Nicolas, iv, p. 276).

[3]Merton in Surrey.

to be at your disposal until you wish me to leave it to my *nearest and dearest* relation.[1] We die not one moment the sooner by doing those acts, and if I die, my property may as well go to those I tenderly regard, as to those who hate me; but I trust to live many years with those who love me. I send you a very handsome letter from Lord George Cavendish.[2] I must return his visit when I get back to Deal, but shall not dine there or anywhere else. I hope soon to be done with this command. I am yet of opinion it will be Peace before this month is out. Pray God send it calm, and we shall hardly save post as it goes out at one o'clock. The French have all gone into Boulogne, but probably they will be out to-day. Dr. Baird has been very attentive and good to me, and he gave your good things to Langford.

Ever yours,

Nelson and Bronté.

229. *To Lady Hamilton*

[Houghton: MS Lowell 10] Amazon Dungeness
Oct^{r}: 2nd: 1801

My Dearest Emma,

I am sorry the Lawyers should have been the cause of keeping You one moment from Merton and I hope You will for ever love Merton sure nothing shall be wanting on my part, from me you shall have every thing you want, I trust my Dear friend to your economy [*sic*] for I have need of it, to You I may say my soul is too big for my purse, but I do earnestly request thet all may be mine in the house even to a pair of sheets, towels +^{c}: +^{c}: You are right my Dear Emma to pay Your debts to be in debt is to be in misery and poor tradespeople cannot afford to lay out of their money, I beg you will not go too much on the Water for the boat may upset or you may catch an autumnal cold which cannot be shook off all the Winter, Wrap Yourself up warm when you go out of the house + for Gods sake wear more cloaths when winter approaches, or you will have the Rhumatism [*sic*], I hope You are this moment fixed, Damn the lawyers, I am not surprized at M^{rs}: Greevis's[3] loving You, who does not,

[1]Their daughter Horatia.

[2]George Cavendish, 1st Earl of Burlington (1754–1834); according to Pettigrew (ii, p. 199), he had attended the funeral of Captain Edward Parker with Nelson.

[3]Probably 'Mrs. Greaves', the widowed previous owner of Merton Place.

for Your heart shows itself in Your face, and such a face who must not love, If black James[1] has no particular desire to come, I can have none to have him, he must be a dead expence, You will do what is right + I shall be happy in leaving every thing to your management, I dont wonder Sir William is tired of Warwick Castle how could he expect to find anything equal to what he left, he might as well have searched for the Philosophers Stone[2] poor M^{rs}: Nelson I pity her she never was so happy in her life, but the little woman will try + be with You again very soon and she will succeed, tell me how I can do anything for You at this distance You command me my Dear Emma + I obey with the greatest pleasure, Your letters for the next two or 3 days may be directed for me here after thet to Deal I have had Dear Hardy onboard all the morning he is a good man + attach'd to me indeed so is Bedford, Sutton, Gore + others but these from no interested motives make my best regards to Sir William when You write, + to M^{rs}: Cadogan say every kind thing + I hope Emma You take care of your Relation[3] when You can get her well married or[4] settled We will try + give her something, Ch^{s}: is a good boy + Your relations are ever those of Your affectionate + faithful

Nelson + Bronte

230. *To Lady Hamilton*

[*a)* Pettigrew, ii, pp. 202–3;
c) Christie's, 9 Dec 1998, lot 40, facsimile;
e) Christie's, 1998, lot 40, transcription]

[*c)*] Amazon Dungeness
Oct^{r}: 3rd: 1801

My Dearest Emma,

Your kind letters of Wednesday night + Thursday[5] morning I have just received and I should be too happy to come up for a day or two but thet will not satisfy me and only fill my heart with grief at separating, very soon I must give in for the cold weather I could not bear besides to say

[1]Price; for Nelson's changing attitude towards him see Docs Nos 170, 226.
[2]According to legend, this stone, once ground could turn base metals into gold or give eternal life; thus it was very much sought after, particularly in the Middle Ages and early modern times.
[3]See Doc. No. 218; there Kate Williams, *England's Mistress: The Infamous Life of Emma Hamilton* (London, 2007), p. 281, claimed 'your relation' to be a reference to Emma Carew, Lady Hamilton's daughter by Harry Fetherstonhaugh.
[4]Not '&' as Pettigrew, ii, p. 200, has it.
[5]30 Sept and 1 Oct 1801.

the truth I am one of those who really believe we are on the Eve of Peace as mine can be only guess from various circumstances do not give it as my opinion I think we are almost signing, You may ask do you know any good reason for this joyful Idea, I can answer No but my mind tells me it must be, I shall long to have the picture of the little one[1] You will send it me, and very soon I shall see the original and then I shall be happy, do not think I am seriously unwell, but I am naturally [*a)*] very low. What have I to raise my spirits? Nothing. The loss of my friend, the loss of Parker, The surgeon recommends me to walk on shore, but that I cannot do, we lay so far off, and surf, and what is to become of my business – but it cannot last long. What you want with all the Heraldry[2] I know not – they are devils for running up a bill. I shall not agree to Sir William's[3] keeping house whenever I come, that is impossible. I hope Mr. Haslewoood has done every thing to get you into the possession,[4] and for the rest and management I give all up to you. I have had a letter from Lieutenant Turner – he has got the gout, and desires his kind regards. I have had rather a begging letter from Norwich, but I cannot at present do any thing, for I have nothing; [*e)*] . . . to say my dear Emma how I love, honor, and respect your virtues is impossible .. the old . . . world may be damned as they deserve . . . Would that Sir Wm had stayed . . . he would have been happier with his friends than his great relations. I wonder not at his desire to return and I know all attempts will be made to get at you . . . be firm . . . and by your trust you keep it in trust for me and if such a misfortune was to happen that it [the affair][5] was got heard of I believe it would kill me, but I know your care of my interest . . . [*a)*] for heaven's sake never do you talk of having spent any money for me. I am sure you never have to my knowledge, and my obligations to you can never be repaid [*e)*] but with my life. Ever for ever your faithful till death.

[*a)*] Nelson and Bronté.

Make my kind regards where proper. Captains Sutton, Bedford, and Gore, all inquire after you. Are there any images standing in the grounds?

[1]Their daughter Horatia.

[2]Tsar Paul, as the Grand Master of the Order of St John, had made Lady Hamilton 'Dame Petite Croix' for her exertions to procure supplies for the Maltese (Carola Oman, *Nelson*, London, 1947, p. 384); in his letter of 5 Oct (Doc. No. 234) Nelson mentions that the order was about to be restored and therefore the orders of Lady Hamilton and Ball (who had been created 'Commandeur Grande Croix') soon be recognised.

[3]Christie's catalogue of 1998 transcribes here: 'William'.

[4]Of the house at Merton.

[5]The Christie's-additions appears to refer to the affair of Nelson and Lady Hamilton, but I think this refers to the approaches of the Prince of Wales.

Gore says there are. If so you will take them away – they look very bad *Patienza*. Pray is our Belmonte dead at Baden?[1] Tell me.

231. *To Lady Hamilton*

[Pettigrew, ii, p. 203] Just anchored,
October 4th, nine o'clock.

My dear Emma,

You are right, *no* champagne till we can crack a bottle together. Your letter with the papers I suppose are gone to Romney. I shall have them in the evening.

Yours,

Nelson and Bronté.

Send to Castelcicala that from my heart I congratulate him, and beg to present my duty to his and mine august Sovereign. The Lutwidges' have sent off congratulations for you, and I always send your regards and respects.

232. *To Lady Hamilton*

[BL: Egerton 1614 ff. 80–81, no. 41] Amazon off Fo[l]k[es]tone
Oct[r]: 4[th]: 1801.

My Dearest Emma Although Preliminary articles[2] are signed yet I do not find thet such lengths are gone towards peace as to point out a time when hostilitys shall cease, and I am directed to be particularly vigilant, and the Earl says[3] the country has receiv'd so many proofs of my Zeal in its service as leaves no doubt of my remaining at ~~my~~[4] the head of the squadron 'till peace is proclaimed,

I was in hopes thet at least all my feeble services might be dispenced with, this has fretted me a good deal for they would perhaps glad[l]y get Rid of my claim at least for Poor Langford, I have wrote the Earl saying

[1]No, Gennaro Ravaschieri Fieschi Pinelli Pignatelli (1777–1829), 9th Prince of Belmonte (since 1798), whom Nelson had taken on board the *Foudroyant* from Palermo to Leghorn (9–16 June 1800), was to outlive Nelson.

[2]Of the Peace of Amiens.

[3]Inserted.

[4]The following word 'the' is written in darker ink, so that it appears that Nelson had a short break, before he continued writing.

thet I was in hopes my humble services were no longer wanted, but at least I hoped that I might have 4 or 5 days leave of absence for thet I wanted rest, and could not stay in the Channell when the cold Weather sett In. I shall try the Effect of this letter, and although my whole soul is devoted to get rid of this command yet I do not blame the Earl for wishing to keep me here a little longer it is probable disturbances may break out in these squadrons when I am gone, I am of some consequence, If I can I should like to come on shore good friends with the Administration or my brother will stand no chance probably he does not much at present, I have wrote congratulations to M^r: Addington, but if Ministers can shake off those who have a claim on[1] them they are glad of the opportunity, If I am forced into this measure for a month you + Sir William might come down and I would hire a house + have our own things on shore + not cost 1/8 part of the other cheating fellows expence.[2] I hear he hes been fool enough to say as nobody goes twice to his house he takes care to make them pay enough the first time what a fool, but he did not know if it had been 50 times as much I should have paid it with pleasure for the happiness of my Emmas company, I think I shall get off this staying here but I hope you will agree with me thet a little management may not be amiss, Sir Ch^s: Pole has sent the two pipes of sherry I have wrote to Portsmouth this day to have them sent to Merton, therefore the wine cellar must be prepared, as to M^r: Duncan he is a Blackguard I gave Sutton the letter to Read, he says he is ready to subscribe something for her distress but I have done nothing 'till I know whether you[3] you [*sic*] would like it, nor shall I dine on shore as it is impossible to get on board in a dark night heavy surf +^c: therefore I shell stay on board altogether unless it is a very fine day which is not to be expected, the surf seldom is little at this season, make my best regards to M^rs: Cadogan + all friends + Believe me Ever for Ever your faithful

Nelson + Bronte

To the Duke Sir W^m: +^c: say every thing which is proper, Yawkins[4] desires to be rem^d:

[1]The 'n' is written over an 'f'.

[2]This probably refers to Lady Hamilton and Nelson's joint stay at Deal between 28 Aug and 20 Sept 1801, when they stayed at the 'Three Kings'.

[3]The letter is continued on the outside, upside down from the writing direction of the inside, first below the address and then above it.

[4]Master of the *King George* hired cutter (Pettigrew, ii, p. 204); see also Doc. No. 194: 'I have seen Captain Dean, late of the King George packet'.

233. *To Lady Hamilton*

[Pettigrew, ii, p. 205]

Amazon,
October 5th, 1801.

My dearest Emma,

give the inclosed to Allen's wife. I have been expecting the pleasure of hearing from you by the coach, and when the tide turns, I shall send on shore and examine the coach office. Your kind letters are my only consolation.

Yours,

Nelson and Bronté.

When does Sir William return? Say every thing which is kind to Mrs. Cadogan, &c.

234. *To Lady Hamilton*

[Huntington: HM 34093]

Amazon
Oct^{r}: 5th: 1801.

My Dearest Emma,

The Weather is getting so very bad that I doubt whether the letters can be got on shore, I am half sea sick and much vexed but still if the Ad^{ty}: would send me leave by telegraph[1] it should go hard but I would get on shore, at Ramsgate or some where nothing should keep me, it is hard to be kept here but I should be sorry to quarrel the last few days, Ad^{l}: Lutwidge has offered to dine at 3 oClock, but If I dined it would almost be impossible to get afloat, and all my wish is to get ashore for good as the folks say, I am vexed but not surprised my Dear Emma at that fellows[2] wanting You for his mistress but I know Your virtue too well to be the [3] of any Rank stinking Kings Evil, the meanness of the titled pimps does not surprize me in these degenerate days, I suppose he will try to get at Merton as it lays in the road I believe to Brighton,[4] but I am sure You will never let them into the premises. Your Virtue deserves a Throne or

[1] A semaphore line (visual telegraphy using signal arms or shutters) existed for example between London and Deal.

[2] The Prince of Wales or the Duke of Gloucester (Doc. No. 218)?

[3] Space left blank by Nelson.

[4] Where the Prince of Wales was at that time extending his pavilion.

a Peageant [*sic*], as they may be the children of honor, not of Infamy + disease, Do You think we shall soon get to Bronte I should be very happy, but I must first settle all my affairs in this country + Merton may become a dead weight on our hands, but more of this hereafter, Thank God it is peace may the heavens bless us, say every thing kind to Charlotte hers is a nice Innocent letter, and to M[rs]: Nelson + my brother you know what to say, as to M[r]: Addingtons giving him any thing I do not venture to believe he ever will, I never had a kind thing done for me yet, as the Order of Malta will be restored I suppose now You and Ball will have permission to wear the order,[1] however You shall abroad, I am vexed thet you are so much troubled to get into the house, I wish we were all in it, I shall only come to town on particular business or to give a vote in some interesting question + that in order to get something for my Brother, I have not yet wrote to my father but I shall today it rains dreadfully pray take care + do not catch cold, You have not told me if You have seen Troubridge, Hallowell will call of course or he will behave very Ill M[r]: Turner desires his thanks for Your kind enquiries (for I always say those things for You as I am sure You do for me) and he will certainly come + see you when he comes to London, + Believe me my Dear Emma Ever

Yours faithful

Nelson + Bronte[2]

Your kind letter just arrived, it has quite cheer'd me up, may the heavens bless You, I always send Your remembrances to the Ad[l]: + M[rs]: L.[3] We must think about Charles + Banti, Ch[s]: says he should like to get into a Public Office but I shall do everything You wish me for him, pray God I may soon see you.

235. *To Lady Hamilton*

[Jean Kislak: 1987.004.00.0001][4] 2 oClock, just going on shore.

My Dearest Emma,

I did not pay M[r]: B.[5] for the drawing of the San Josef – 10 £ is the price pay him out of the 300 £ have You bought any cows, I wish You were

[1]Of St John of Malta; see Doc. No. 230.

[2]Continued on the fourth page, upside down, starting at the top of the page (what is the bottom of the first three pages).

[3]Ludwidge. The text is continued on the other side of the address field.

[4]Pettigrew, ii, p. 206, gives this letter between those of 5 and 6 Oct 1801 without any explanation as to the dating.

[5]This may refer to Thomas Baxter (1782–1821), painter who was to draw Merton Place.

got in and I with You it is dreadfuly [*sic*] cold to day, Good Admiralty let me get on shore, I shall not give M^{rs}: D.[1] a sixpence damn her, never fear I am firm as a rock, I have settled with Lutwidge for them to forgive my [not] Dining with them, I would not do a thing to hurt Your feelings for the World for Your friendship is what I value beyond all the World, how the Lawyers torment You but my Dear Emma I hope very soon to be in the place You wish to be Your faithful

Nelson and Bronte.

I have just got a letter from a surgeon of the Navy begging for money If I do not get away very soon I shall be ruined.

236. *To Lady Hamilton*

[BL: Egerton 1614 ff. 82–83, no. 42]

Amazon
Oct^{r}: 6th: 1801.

My dear Emma,

To my astonishment Cap^{n}: Sutton of thc (Romulus) send [*sic*] me word last night that he was arrived and ordered to hoist a Broad Pendant on board the Isis and he came on board this morning at 7. it being a very fine beach I went on shore with him, Sutton[2] + Bedford to call on Ad^{l}: Lutwidge for the first time since my return from Dungeness + for the second time since your departure, I expected I own + had prepared Allen +^{c}: with my trunk and directed M^{r}: Wallis to make out the necessary orders to leave with Sutton when lo came the letters and one from Troubridge, of which I send you an extract[3] "The Earl desires me to beg of you to remain untill the time for hostilities ceasing in the Channell is fixed, + then if you wish it you can have leave of absence I think without striking your flag if that is your wish in short every thing thet can be done to meet your wishes will, but pray remain for the ~~very~~ few days, the ratification is expected tomorrow + the time for hostilities ceasing will be settled directly, and in the Channell very soon indeed", Under all these desires I cannot help staying 14 days is the outside but by complying I hope to get rid of it long before that time your first letter almost broke my heart but the latter made up in some measure for it. When have I walked

[1]Denis.

[2]*Sic*, Sutton is mentioned here again.

[3]The following lines begin with an '=' until the line 'in the channel very soon indeed, under'.

up if I did walk could I walk with but Sutton + Bedford, at Dungeness I never thought of going on shore, however although I intended to have walked with Sutton + Bedford our old round what thoughts would have rushed into mind, but your letter determined me to go on board again and I shall <u>not</u> set my foot on shore again 'till I go for good Cap^{n}: Sutton has brought his wife down with him + is going to take a house at Deal, she is niece to Lord Hotham, skin + bone, with red nose, C^{tn}: Sutton enquired much after you so did M^{rs}: Lutwidge she + the Ad^{l}: are quite in raptures with you, I have had a letter from Parker's uncle at Durham of thanks, I shall be glad the cup is coming[1] Dr. Baird dines on board today what a curious letter of M^{rs}: N. + my brother's how I regret this fortnight at all events Suttons being here will be ready for me to start when the Board will give me leave or otherwise I want no assistance, I shall[2] perhaps go to Dungeness where we lay 5 or 6 miles from the shore then you are sure I cannot walk, M^{r}: Boltons is a very foolish letter I can do nothing how lucky his son has been. [as][3] to permissions he is a fool + I dare say we need not carry that article to Bronte, M^{r}: Scott[4] who writes Italian + all Languages and is a very clever man would be truly useful + wants to go, but more of this when we meet which pray God may be soon, I shall come strai[gh]t to Merton.[5]

I did not pay M^{r}: B.[6] for the Drawing 10£

237. *To Lady Hamilton*

[*a)* Pettigrew, ii, pp. 207–8;
b) Morrison, ii, pp. 172–3 (No. 631)] [*a)*] Amazon, Oct. 6th, 1801.[7]

My dearest Friend,

[*b)*] I have just got your letter of yesterday, and am very angry with Mr Haslewood for not having got you into possession of Merton, for I was in hopes you would have arranged everything before Sir William came home. I shall write Mr. Haslewood to-day on the subject. The Peace seems to make no impression of joy on our seamen, rather the contrary,

[1]Reference to Nelson's present for Dr Baird (see Docs Nos 197, 204, 220, 224 and 227).
[2]The letter is continued on the outside, upside down, first below (until 'son has been'), then above the address.
[3]The beginning of this line is under the piece of paper to which the letter is glued.
[4]Alexander Scott.
[5]The following words are added on the right-hand margin of the two additional passages on the outside of the letter.
[6]Probably Thomas Baxter (see Doc. No. 235).
[7]Morrison claims that this letter was dated 'October 7th, 1801'.

they appear to reflect that they will go from plenty to poverty. We must take care not to be beset by them at Merton, for every beggar will find out your soft heart, and get into your house.[1] Lord George Cavendish has just been on board to make me a visit before he leaves Walmer to-morrow; if the weather is moderate, I shall return his visit and call on Billy Pitt, as they say he is expected to-day. I intend to land at Walmer Castle. But for this visit I should not have gone ashore till all was finished. Make my best regards to Sir William. I hope he will be able in bad weather to catch fish in the water you so beautifully describe. You must take care what kind of fish you put into the water, for Sir William will tell you one sort destroys the other. Commodore Sutton has been on board all the morning, but dines with Admiral Lutwidge. Bedford says his wife is an ugly likeness of Mrs. Lutwidge, so you see that ugly women do get husbands, and Sutton is certainly a very good looking man; I recollect S.'s[2] wife is niece to Lord Hotham. You will see amongst my things return the round table and the wardrobe – extraordinary that they should return again into your possession. You are to be recollect, Lady Paramount of all the territories and waters of[3] Merton, and we are all to be your guests, and to obey all lawful commands. What have you done about the turnip field, duck field, &c.? Am I to have them?[4] I wish I could get up for four or five days. I would have roused the lawyers about. The Isis is just coming in – Sutton's broad pendant is to be in her. Yawkins has just been on board, and I delivered your compliments as directed. He always inquires after you and Sir William, and he desires me to say that he wishes Sir William was now here, for there were never so many fish in the Downs. The beach for two days has been remarkably smooth – not a curl on the shore. I shall send to Mr. Turner; you will win his heart by your goodness. Your going away made a blank in our squadron. Dr. Baird is very much affected at receiving the cup; it made him really ill, so that he could not come to dinner, but he deserved it for his humanity. Lord St Vincent, never, I dare say, gave him a sixpence. Best regards to Sir William, Mrs. Cadogan, and all our friends,

Yours,

[*a*)] Nelson and Bronté.

[1]Christie's 21 June 1989-sale, lot 253, has transcribed here, rather unconvincingly: 'purse' (for the use of 'purse', see Doc. No. 229).

[2]Sutton's.

[3]Christie's 21 June 1989-sale, lot 253, has transcribed here: 'at'.

[4]Christie's 21 June 1989-sale, lot 253, has transcribed here no question marks and generally much less punctuation.

238. *To Lady Hamilton*

[NMM: CRK/19/17]

Amazon
Oct^{r}: 8th: 1801.

My Dearest friend I do not expect although I am writing thet any boat can communicate with us today, What can be the use of keeping me here for I can know nothing such weather, and, whet a change since yesterday it came on in one hour from the water like a mill pond to such a sea as to make me very unwell, If I had gone to make my visit I could not have got off again I rejoice that I did not go, Until I leave the station I have no desire to go on shore for Deal was always my abhorrence, that Parker[1] is a swindler Langford owed our dear Parker 25 £ of which there was no account but Langford desired his agents to pay M^{r}: Parker, Langford req^{d}:[2] that he would wait 2 or 3 months as it would be more convenient to him, to which the other agreed, aye as long as you please he got 1:11,6[3] from Samuel by casting his account wrong, the first thing he does is to desire Langfords agents to pay 34 £ for Langford 9£ more than the debt, he is worse than a Public Thief His conduct to me was absolutely the worst species of thieving, for it was under false pretences, He sent Doctor Baird on board to me to say that in London his pocket book was stole in which was 20 £ and begged my assistance to get him home + that he had not a farthing to buy mour[n]ing for his dear son, at this time he had 47£ in his pocket, besides whet he had sold of his sons, he has behaved so unlike a gentleman but very like a Blackguard to both Capt: Sutton Bedford + Hardy, I am now clear thet he never lost one farthing + that the whole is a swindling trick, so you see my dear friend how good neture is imposed upon, I am so vexed that he should have belonged to our Dear Parker, I have now done with the Wretch for ever, I hope he has got nothing from you + If you have promised him anything do not send it.[4]

Ten OClock Your kind letters are arriv'd I rejoice thet you have got into Merton. I hope to get the letter on shore but it is very uncertain, Ministry my Dearest friend think very differently of my services from you, but never mind I shell soon have done with them afloat,

Make my kindest regards to Sir William and all our friends + Believe me Ever your faithful + affectionate

Nelson + Bronte.

[1]The father of Captain Edward Parker.
[2]requested.
[3]1814-letters have transcribed here: 'one pound eleven shillings and sixpence'.
[4]In the next line Nelson continued '10 OClock . . .'.

I have just got a very kind letter from Capt Read he says he will come + see me be where it will, he enquir'd after you and Sir W^{m}:[1]

239. *To Lady Hamilton*

[Pettigrew, ii, pp. 212–13]

Amazon,
October 8th, 1801. Half-past seven.

My dearest Friend,

I send on shore one line by the boat which goes for our letters, to tell you not to be surprised if you get no other letter to-morrow, for it now blows very hard, and every appearance of an increasing gale. How I am praying for the Admiralty. Last night I had one of the attacks on my heart, which some day will do me up;[2] but it is entirely gone off. I know it has been brought on by fretting at being kept here doing nothing. I shall write late, and if possible get it on shore, but you must not expect. Make my best regards to Sir William, and believe me,

Yours,

Nelson and Bronté.

240. *To Lady Hamilton*

[BL: Egerton 1614 ff. 84–85, no. 43]

Amazon
Oct^{r}: 9th: 1801.

My dearest Friend,

how provoked I am at the slowness of thet Damn'd rascal Buonaparte in ratifying the treaty, I hope he will for if we are involved in a War again, our fools who rejoiced thet the French could not come to eat them up will frighten themselves to death and our country become an easy prey, there is no person in the world rejoices more in the peace than I do but I would burst sooner than let a damn'd Frenchman know it let them rejoice that the English Rod (its navy) is taken from them the Rod that has flogged and would continue to flog them from one End of the world to the other, We have made peace with the French Despotism, and we will I hope

[1]The postscript is added on the outside of the letter on one of the parts that were folded towards the inside on closing the letter, upside down, judging from the text on the inside of the letter.

[2]Compare Doc. No. 54 ('severe pains of the heart').

adhere to it, whilst the French continue in due bounds but whenever they overstep that and usurp a power which would degrade Europe then I trust we shall join Europe in crushing her ambition, then I would with pleasure go forth and risk my life for to pull down the overgrown detestable power of France, The country has so foolishly called out for peace that I almost wonder we had not to make sacrifices, It has been the cowardice + treachery of Europe thet has elevated France and certainly not her own courage, or ability but I long to get on shore, and why am I troubling either you or myself with all this stuff, from my heart I wish I was at Merton and you showing me the place and your intended improvements for I have the very highest opinion of your taste and œcconemy [*sic*], I have not had an opportunity of sending to M^r^: Turner your kind message + probably he has got the trumpet before this time, but you are good + thoughtful to every body, I am going to send Sutton under Dungeness to watch the fellows thet they do not pick up any of our trade for the few days thet remain,

Letters just come off Lutwidge has sent me word thet the vessel with the ratification arrived at 8 this morning, M^rs^: Lutwidge has sent me Partridges + a pine apple and always enquires for you + Sir Willm. Troubridge writes me thet I may be assured. We will not keep you longer than I have before stated thet is I suppose 14 days and he hopes the exercise ashore will quite restore me, Now I never will go on shore but only per force[1] I hate Deal and from my heart wish I was out of sight of it, remember me kindly to Sir Willm: The Duke and all our friends and none but real friends shall come to Merton, but you are to manage every thing. Ever your affectionate.

Nelson + Bronte.[2]

The wine from Portsmouth is on its journey is there a good wine cellar, I have a good deal at Davisons, We will eat plain but will have good wine, Good fires + a hearty welcome for our friends, but none of the Great shall enter our peaceful abode I hate them all, I have had a real kind letter from Davison such a one as is scarce in these degenerate times. God Bless you

[1]This is adapted from the Italian expression 'per forza' which can mean 'necessarily', 'of course' or against one's will, willy-nilly' (the last option appears to be the most appropriate here); compare 'Patienza per forza' in Doc. No. 196.

[2]The following postscript is on the outside of the letter, upside down below (until 'but none of') and above the address.

241. *To Lady Hamilton*

[NMM: MAM/7]

Amazon
Oct^{r}: 10th: 1801.

My Dearest Friend,

Your letters I have just received and am sorry thet you cannot go to a Public place without being tormented by thet fellow[1] who has not the smallest regard for Sir William, I hate and detest all the Great and I would not associate with such company for the World, I have had a letter from M^{r}: Addington he says[2] =I owe it to my regard for your Lordships high Character and to my public Duty to declare it to be my opinion that it is of the utmost Importance to the Interests of the country thet your flag should be flying 'till the Definitive treaty is signed, you will then have seen the ship safe into Port and may close with honor ~~+ glo[ry~~ a][3] career of unexampled success + glory.) I shall mo[s]t assuredly not stay one hour after hostilitys cease which must be the 22nd: and I hope the Admiralty will release me before I can only offer if it is necessary to come down again, you see how I am situated and I must not on my brothers account fly in these peoples faces, but I am by no means so well as I could wish your letter has agitated me not a little, an[d][4] I have one from my Father[5] which has hurt me, I shall not answer it 'till I hear from

[1]Most likely the Prince of Wales (for the Duke of Gloucester, see Docs Nos 218 and 234).

[2]After the word 'says' a new line starts that begins with '=', as do the following lines until the line '=unexampled success + glory.) I shall mo[s]t'.

[3]The rest of the word beginning with '~~glo~~'(at the bottom of the page) is torn.

[4]The 'd' at the end of 'and' is missing at the end of the line, where the paper was torn under the seal on opening the letter.

[5]Nelson had received a letter from his father, in which his father hinted at someone (Lady Hamilton) trying to separate him from his son, Horatio. The manuscript of the letter is to be found at NMM, WAL/13; it is dated 'B^{m} [Burnham] Ot 8 1801' and reads as follows: 'My Dear Horatio, Upon the happy return of peace I may with a little variation, address you in the words of an apostle, and say you have fought a good fight, you have finished your military career with glory, + honor, henceforth there is laid up for you, much Happiness, subject indeed in this present time to uncertainty, But in [a] future State, Immutable + incorruptible, [as] a publick character I could be acquainted only with what was made publick respecting you, now in a private station possibly you may tell me where it is likely your generall place of Residence may be, so that sometimes we may have mutuall happiness in each other notwithstanding the severe reproaches I felt from an anonymous letter for my conduct to you which is such it seems as will totally separate us. This is unexpected indeed. Most likely the Winter may be too cold for me to continue Here, and I mean to spend it between Bath + London if Lady N. is in a Hired house and by Her self, Gratitude requires that i should sometimes be with Her if it is likely to be of any Comfort to Her. Every where age and my many infirmities are very troublesome and require every mark of respect at present I am in the parsonage, it is warm and comfortable I am quite by my self except the Gentleman who takes care of the Churches He is a worthy sensible sober man,

you, on Monday, but more of this to morrow, I am sending off many of our ships to Sheerness to be paid off, would to God my turn was come I am glad you are going to Merton and I hope Sir William will like it I am sure I shall, I am very full of business today therefore you must excuse a short letter, Sutton Bedf[d]: Hardy +[c]: are all on sh[o]re[1] it being a very fine day, but I shall n[ot] [2] probably go out of the ship 'till I have done with her say everything kind for me to Sir Will[m]: and all our friends and Believe me Ever your most faithful

Nelson + Bronte

242. *To Lady Hamilton*

[Pettigrew, ii, p. 211][3]

I think of writing my poor old father to this effect – that I shall live at Merton with Sir William and Lady Hamilton – that a warm room for him and a cheerful society will always be there happy to receive him – that nothing in *my conduct* could ever cause a separation of a moment between me and him, for that I had all the respect and love which a son could bear toward a good father – that going to Burnham was impossible, as my duty, even if I was inclined, would not permit it – that as to anonymous letters, they made no impression where they did not fit, and that I should ever conduct myself towards him as his dutiful son.

N. & B.

Tell me, my friend, do you approve? If he remains at Burnham he will die, and I am sure he will not stay in Somerset Street,[4] Pray let him come to your care at Merton. Your kindness will keep him alive, for you have a kind soul.

---

in all respects and as far as rest with Him, makes me very Happy. I cannot do any publick Duty nor Even walk to the next House But my Dearest Son, Here is still Room eno: to give to you a warm a joyfull and affectionate reception, if you could feell an inclination to Look once more at me in Burnham parsonage I pray God to Continue placing his Blessings in all stations and undertakings Edm: Nelson' (also to be found in Pettigrew, ii, pp. 210–11, and Morrison, ii, p. 133, no. 632).

[1]The paper is torn here at the centre of the line.

[2]The paper is torn here at the centre of the line.

[3]Pettigrew inserted this letter as if it had been written on 8 Oct. Judging from the subject covered (how to deal with Nelson's father), I suggest a different chronology in the introduction to this part.

[4]Where Lady Nelson was living at the time.

243. *To Lady Hamilton*

[NMM: PBE2591]

Amazon
Oct^{r}: 11th: 1801.

My dearest Friend,

I ought and do beg you 10,000 pardons for not having sent the mem^{m}: for Davisons house but I was really so unwell thet I could not would to God I was liberated for cooped up on board ship with [my] head for ever leaning over paper has almost blinded me and it is impossible to be sure of a beach for one hour together, Cap^{n}: Bedford + Sutton say they will not go any more unless it is perfect calm for they got wet with all their care and activity, and yet I ought to return L^{d}: George Cavendish's visit, and I see Billy Pitt has arrived as the colors are hoisted, I will see him before I leave the station he may perhaps be useful to me one day or other We have now cold fogs and you cannot conceive how truly uncomfortable I am, A Boy Master + Commander is just come made Post, never performed a jot of service, whilst dear Parker, Somerville[1] Langford + others smarting dying of their gallant wounds cannot get a step You cannot conceive how full every bodys mouth is, As to Merton you are the whole + sole Commander, I wish naturally thet every thing in the place should be mine but as to living we will settle thet matter very easily. I only wish I was with you, I agree with you no great folks they are a public nuisance how odd thet the King has had no Levèee [*sic*], I hope he is well but should almost fear it, I have had a very affectionate letter from Colonel Stewart, on the Death of Dear of [*sic*] Parker, he desires something as a remembrance of him. I have secured a book and a chart, The newspapers are not come I am out of patience a damn'd rascally Frenchman to be drawn by Englishmen[2] I blush for the degraded state of my country, I hope never more to be dragged by such [a] degenerate set of People, would Our ancestors have done it, So the villains would have drawn Bonaparte If he had been able to get to London to cut off the Kings head, and yet all our Royal family will employ Frenchmen. Thanks to the navy, they could not, 11 oclock Your letters are just come but now we cannot get newspapers, they cannot come the same day to and from Merton, soon very

[1]Philip Somerville.

[2]The French ambassador's coach had been drawn through London in joy at the Peace of Amiens.

soon I hope to be with you, fo[r there][1] can be no use in keeping me here, Sutt[on,[2]] Bedford +^{c}: all enquire after you, Old Yawkins I always give your + Sir W^{ms}: remembrances, Ever my Dear Friend your most faithful + affectionate.

Nelson + Bronte[3]

The Boy will come of course and stupid De Goulds men but not my steward he is too fine for me, Our navy is all blank at the Peace, If you see the Duke say every kind thing, Best regards to M^{rs}: Cadogan, Oliver +^{c}:

244. *To Lady Hamilton*

[NMM: CRK/19/18] Amazon
10 OClock Oct^{r}: 12th: 1801

My dearest Friend,

This being a very fine morning and smooth Beach, at 8 OClock I went with Sutton and Bedford + landed at Walmer but found Billy[4] fast asleep so left my card, walked the same Road thet we came when the carriage could not come with us thet nicht [*sic*] and all rushed into my mind and brought tears into my eyes, ah how diff^{t}: to walking with such a friend as You Sir William + M^{rs}: Nelson, called at the Barracks on L^{d}: George[5] but he is gone to London, from thence to the Ad^{ls}:[6] found him up and waiting half an hour to see M^{rs}: Lutwidge who entreated me to stay dinner I came directly on board I did not even call to see poor Langford who has been worse these few days past and God knows when he will be Well, I am afraid it will be a long time for several pieces of bone is [*sic*] lately come away and more to come, but Troubridge has so completely prevented my ever mentioning any bodys service, thet I am become a cipher + he has gain'd a victory over Nelsons spirit I am kept here for what he may be able to tell I cannot but long it cannot shall not be, Sutton + Bedford are gone a

[1]The letters in square brackets were added by Pettigrew. In the original this part of the text was torn on tearing the seal.

[2]See previous footnote.

[3]The following passage is added on the outside of the letter, on the parts that were folded away before sealing the letter.

[4]William Pitt.

[5]Cavendish.

[6]Ludwidge.

tour till dinner time but nothing shall make me but almost force go out of the ship again 'till I have done and the Admiralty in charity will be pleased to release me, I am in truth not over well I have a complaint in my stomach + bowells but it will go off, If you was here I should have some Rhubarb but as you are not I shall go without, Sutton has sent into Yorkshire for a cow thet in the spring will give 14 lb^s:[1] of butter a week, and he has given Allen the finest goat I ever saw the latter I am afraid will be troublesome, Just as I was coming off I received your packet and thank you from my heart for all your kindness, what can Rev^d: Sir[2] want to be made a Doctor for he will be laughed at for his pains. I thank you for the Kings[3] letters I shell write a kind line to Castelcicarla [*sic*],[4] and answer the Kings very soon + write to Acton for he can make Bronte every thing to me If he pleases I dare say I did wrong never to write to him but as he treated Sir Willm: Unkindly I never could bring myself to it, I am glad the Duke has been to see you and taking plants from him is nothing, make my kindest remembrances to him I would have every body like your choice for I am sure you have as fine a taste in laying out Land as you have in music I'll be damn'd if M^rs: Billington[5] can sing so well as you, She may have stage trick but you have pure nature.[6] I always say every thing for you + Sir William I wish you had translated the Kings + Actons letter[s], Banti cannot, I may be able to dispose of Charly[7] but not of the other + he would corrupt Ch^s: for Ever yours

NELSON + BRONTE

M^rs: L.[8] enquires always particularly after you, We all laugh + say she is more fond of soldiers than ever since Genl: Don[9] has shewn her how he would keep off the French.

[1]Pounds.
[2]Nelson's brother William.
[3]The King of Naples' letters.
[4]This should be Castelcicala.
[5]Elizabeth Billington (1765–1818), famous opera singer.
[6]The following passages are written on the outside of the letter (upside down, judging from the text on the inside of the letter) on the two parts that were folded towards the inside on closing the letter. The text until the signature is above the space for the address and the seal, the postscript is below the space for the address and the seal.
[7]Charles Connor.
[8]Lutwidge.
[9]Sir George Don (1756–1832).

245. *To Lady Hamilton*

[Monmouth: E 112]

Amazon
Oct[r]: 13th: 1801.

My Dearest Friend,

Sutton and Bedford would fain persuade me thet by the Post today the Admiralty will give me leave to go on shore I own I do not believe it, or I should not begin this letter for I should certainly be at Merton tomorrow at Breakfast but they have no desire to gratify me thank God there is no more than 9 days to the cessation of hostilities after that they can have no pretence, my complaint is a little better and you cannot think how vexed I am to be unwell at a time when I desire to come on shore and to enjoy a good share of health but at this season and in this place it is impossible that I can be free from colds, the wind is set in very raw from the westward M[r]: Turner came and dined with me yesterday, and brought the trumpet with him and he has charged me to say how much he feels obliged by your kind remembrance of him, this is the first time for 5 years thet he has been on board,

11 oclock the letters are arrived and Troubridge tells me not to think of leaving my station so here I shell stay miserable shut up for I will not stir out of the ship, I am sorry I sent you my Fathers letter I shell not answer it, I told D[r]: Baird yesterday thet I was determined never to mention to Troubridges unfeeling heart whether I was sick or well, I wish to my heart I could get to Merton I had rather be sick there than well here, but in truth I am so disgusted that this day I care but little what becomes of me, I have this day received a curious letter from the Order of S[t]: Joachim, in Germany desiring to elect me Knight Grand Commander thereof, I shell send it to M[r]: Addington thet he may give me his opinion + obtain if proper the Kings approbation,[1] this is very curious, D[r]: Baird is just come on board thet although I am not confined to my bed thet I should be much better out of a frigates cold cabbin but never mind my Dear friend I see + feel all kindness's [*sic*] + unkindness towards me, make my kindest regards to Sir W[m]: M[rs]: Cadogan + all friends + Believe me Ever your faithful + affectionate

Nelson + Bronte[2]

M[r]: Pitt has just been on board and he thinks it is very hard to keep me now all is over, he asked me to dine at Walmer but I refused I will

[1]Nelson passed this letter on to the king in order to ask permission to accept it. This permission granted, Nelson finally accepted the order in a letter of 9 June 1801 (see Pettigrew, ii, pp. 665–6, appendix no. 3).

[2]The postscript is added on the outside of the letter, upside down, starting (in reading direction) from below the address and ending 'above' it.

dine no where till I dine with you + Sir William, for Ever my Dearest only friend your Most aff^{te}: N + B – Sutton + Bedford desire their best respects.

If I am cross you must forgive me I have reason to be so by Great Troubridge.

N. B.

246. *To Lady Hamilton*

[author's collection] Amazon
Oct^{r}: 14th: 1801.

I have wrote to Sir William at Merton it goes on shore with this[1]

My Dearest Friend

To morrow Week all is over no thanks to Sir Th^{s}:[2] I believe the fault is all his, and he ought to have recollected that I got him the medal of the Nile who upheld him when he would have sunk under grief + mortification,[3] who placed him in such[4] situation in the Kingdom of Naples that he got by my Public letters, titles the Colonelcy of Marines, Diamond Boxes from the King of Naples, 1000 ounces in money for no expenses that I know of, who got him 500 £[5] a year from the King of Naples and however much he may abuse him, his pension will be regularly paid,[6] who brought his character into notice look at my Public letters, Nelson thet Nelson that he now Lords it over, so much for gratitude, I forgive him but By God I shell not forget it, he enjoys shewing his power over me, never mind altogether it will shorten my days, the day is very bad blows rains + great sea, my complaint has return'd from absolutely fretting, and was it not for the kindness of all about me

[1]This note is written in a slightly lighter shade of ink than the rest of the first page, so that it appears that it was added after finishing writing the main part of the letter.

[2]Troubridge.

[3]Reference to Troubridge having stranded his ship on a sandbank at the entrance of the Bay of Aboukir and therefore not being able to take part in the battle. Nelson had ensured that Troubridge's ship was treated equally to the others in getting praise and honours.

[4]Pettigrew has inserted before the word 'situation' the article 'a'.

[5]*Sic*, not '£500' as Pettigrew has it.

[6]Nelson himself, by contrast, did not receive any income from his estate in Bronte until late 1803; in the late summer of 1803 he complained: 'I had rather the King gave me a sum of money in lieu' (quoted in Jane Knight, 'Nelson and the Bronte estate' in *Trafalgar Chronicle*, 2005, 133–44, 138).

they damn them would have done me up long ago I am anxiously waiting for your letters they are my only comfort for they are the only friendly ones I receive, Poor Cap^{n}: Somerville is on board, Himself wife + family makes 20 without a Servant and has only 100 £[1] a year to maintain them, he has been begging me to intercede with the Ad^{ty}: again but I have been so rebuffed that my Spirits are gone + the Great Troubridge have [*sic*] what we call cowed the Spirits of Nelson[2] but I shell never forget it, he told me If I asked any thing more thet I should get nothing I suppose alluding to poor Langford, no wonder I am not well,

noon Your kind letters are Just come and have given me great comfort, pray tell Sir Willm: thet If I can I will write to him this day but certain tomorrow I have much to do from Admiralty orders letters +^{c}: I rejoice at your occupation I have only heard live pretty + keep a pig have you done anything ab^{t}: the turnip field say every thing thet is kind for me to Sir W^{m}: M^{rs}: Cadogan +^{c}: I have deliver'd your message to Sutton + Bedford You may rely on a visit Ever my Dear Friend your affectionate

Nelson + Bronte

half sea sick[3]

I thank you for Rev^{d}: D^{rs}:[4] letter + M^{rs}: N^{s}: her going to Swaffham is mentioned seven times + in the Postscript It puts me in mind of the directions for the Cardinal[5] I have laughed but she is [a] good wife for him or he[6] would have been ruined long ago his being a Doctor is nonsense, but I must write tomorrow + congratulate him or else the fat will be in the fire, for Ever Yours to the Duke say every thing,

N + B

[1] *Sic*, as to the position of the '£'.

[2] See also Doc. No. 244.

[3] This is added to the left of the signature. The text is continued on the outside of the letter, below the address field.

[4] His brother William.

[5] This is a reference to Cardinal Ruffo (1744–1827), who was pretty lost as to what to do at Naples in 1799.

[6] The text is continued above the address field.

Letter from Nelson to Lady Hamilton of 14 October 1801 (Doc. No. 246) [Author's Collection]

247. *To Lady Hamilton*

[NMM: CRK/19/19]

Amazon
Oct^{r}: 15th: 1801

I have wrote a line to Merton
excuse my letter.[1]

My dearest Friend,

I have receiv'd all your letters of yesterday + the one sent from the post at Merton and also one Missent to Poole but I do not write direct to Merton 'till I hear thet mine to Sir William sent yesterday gets to you before those by London, The Admiralty will not give me leave 'till the 22nd: and then only ten days what a sett of beasts My cold has now got into my head and I have such dreadful pain in my teeth thet I cannot hold up my head but none of them cares a damn for me or my sufferings, therefore you see I cannot discharge my Steward, and yet think upon consideration thet I will send up all my things + take my chance as to their sending me down again what do you think, at all events every thing except my bed, I have Ladle spoons forks everything at least I shell have soon 2000 £ worth, What a Bitch thet Miss Knight is as to the other I care not what she says

[1]The passage 'I have wrote a line to Merton excuse my letter.' appears to have been added later by Nelson, because it is written in a lighter shade of black ink than the surrounding text.

My Poor Dear Father is wrong, but more of this when we meet which will be Friday the 23rd: at farthest If possible the 22nd: But the Admiralty are hard upon me, I am sorry to hear thet you have been Ill and my cold is so dreadfully bad thet I cannot hold up my head and am so damn'd stupid thet you must my Dear friend, forgive my letter, Adl: Lutwidge is going to Portsmouth Sir Wm: Parker[1] is going to be tried for something Make my kindest regards to Sir William + Believe me Ever yours most faithfully

Nelson + Bronte

248. *To Lady Hamilton*

[Huntington: HM 34094] Amazon
Octr: 15th: 1801.

My dearest Friend,

I have wrote by the way of London but as Your letter came regular mine may go most likely, the Adty: will not let me move till after the 22nd: and I have got a dreadful cold, I send you a letter for my father when read send to London to be put in the Post, I could not say less I hope you will approve, forgive my short letter but the tooth ache torments me to pieces, Ever Yours most faithfuly [*sic*]

Nelson + Bronte.

Sutton + Bedford desire their best respects + will certainly come + eat Your Brown Bread + Butter.

249. *To Lady Hamilton*

[NMM: CRK/19/20] Amazon
Octr: 16th: 1801.

My Dearest Friend,

It being a very fine morning and the beach smooth I went to call on Adl: Lutwidge and return'd on board before 10 O'Clock,[2] Mrs: L. is delighted with your present[3] Sutton +c: were called forth to admire it. She joins in abusing the Admiralty, She pressed me very much to dine with them at 3 o clock but I told her I would not dine with the angel Gabriel If he was to ask me to be dragged through a night surf, her answer was thet she

[1]Sir William Parker (1743–1802).
[2]Here, unusually for Nelson, the apostrophe is clearly visible.
[3]See also Doc. No. 254.

hoped soon I should dine with an angel for she was sure you was one, In short She adores you, but who does not You are so kind so good to every Body old, Young Rich or Poor it is all the same thing, I called on Poor Langford who has a long time to look forward to for getting well, he told me of your goodness in writing him a line and I called upon D^{r}: Baird he disapproves of Rhubarb + has persribed [*sic*] Magnesia + Peppermint, + I call'd on M^{r}: Lawrence so you see I did much business in one hour I was on Shore, Civility to Lutwidge was proper for me and indeed my duty the moment I got your letters off I came and have read them with real pleasure They have made me much better I think at least I feel so, I admire the Pigs + Poultry, Sheep are certainly mo[st][1] beneficial to eat off the grass, Do <u>you</u> get paid for them and take care thet they are kept on the premises all night, for thet is the time they do good to the Land They should be folded, Is your head man a good person and true to our Interest I intend to have a farming book I am glad to hear you get fish not very good ones I fancy, It is thank God only 6 days before I shall be with you, and to be shewn all the beauties of Merton I shell like it leaves or no leaves, No person there can take amiss our not Visiting, the answer from me will always be very civil thanks but thet I wish to live retired, We shell have our sea friends and I know Sir Willm: think[s] they are the best, I have a letter from M^{r}: Trevor begging me to recommend a youngster for him, but none before your Charles, Banti I suppose must return but at present we know not what ships are to be kept in commission, I have a letter from a female relation of mine, She has had 3 husbands and he M^{r}: Sherstone 3 wives, Her Brother a Nelson I have been trying ever since I have been in England to get promoted, the last + present Ad^{ty}: promised I never saw the Man he is in a ship in the North Seas, 45 years of age. I have a letter from Troubridge recommending me[2] to wear flannell [*sic*] shirts, Does he care for me <u>No</u> but never mind Only Six Days they shell work hard to get me back again, Remember me kindly to Sir William the Duke and all friends + Believe me Ever your most affectiona^{te}:

Nelson + Bronte

Do you ever see Castelcicala, he is a good man + faithful to his master + mistress.

[1]The 'st' has been torn with the seal.

[2]Here the inside of the letter is finished and the text continues on the outside of the letter (upside down, judging from the text on the inside of the letter) on the two parts that were folded towards the inside on closing the letter. The text from 'to wear' until 'all friends' is below the space for the address and the seal, the text from '+ Belive me' to the end of the letter is above the space for the address and the seal.

250. *To Lady Hamilton*

[NMM: CRK/19/21]

Amazon
Oct^{r}: 16th: 1801.

My dearest Friend,

I send you a letter for Allens wife, and one for Germany which I wish you would make Oliver put in the foreign post office and pay what is necessary, I would send you the letter to which it is an answer but it would be over weight, It is all compliments + the man says its all truth, the wind is freshened cold but very fine day, best regards to Sir William M^{rs}: Cadogan M^{r}: Oliver + all friends for Ever Yours faithfully

Nelson + Bronte.

I have a letter from Rev^{d}: Doctor[1] he is as big as if he was a Bishop, and one from the Bedel of the University to say how well he Preached I hope you ordered something good for him, for these big wigs love Eating + Drinking.

251. *To Lady Hamilton*

[NMM: CRK/19/22][2]

My Dearest friend,

The two letters would have been over weight so I send you the letter I have answerd, pray take care of it, it is a curiosity, Ever your faithful

Nelson + Bronte

Amazon 2 PM

Yawkins [is] in great distress his cutter paid off + he like many others very little to live upon, he begs his best respects to Sir William he breakfasted here this morning many very long faces at Peace.

[1]His brother William; for the importance of the doctorate see Doc. No. 246.

[2]Someone added in pencil: '16 Octr 1801'; on the outside the letter is postmarked 17 Oct 1801.

252. *To Lady Hamilton*

[1814-letters, ii, pp. 84–7, no. XXIV]

Amazon,
October 17th, 1801.

My dearest Friend,

Although my complaint has no danger attending it, yet it resists the medicines which Dr. Baird has prescribed; and I fancy, it has pulled me down very much. The cold has settled in my bowels, I wish the Admiralty had my complaint: but they have no bowels; at least for me. I had a very indifferent night, but your and Sir William's kind letters have made me feel better. I send you a letter from Lord Pelham;[1] I shall certainly attend, and let them see that I may be useful in council as I have been in the field. We must submit; and perhaps, these Admiralty do[2] this by me, to prevent another application. You may rely, that I shall be with you by dinner on Friday,[3] at half past three or four at farthest. I pray that I may not be annoyed, on my arrival; it is retirement with my friends, that I wish for. Thank Sir William kindly for his letter; and the inclosure, which I return. Sutton is much pleased with your letter; and, with Bedford, will certainly make you a visit. They are both truly good and kind to me. Our weather has been cold these two days, but not bad. I have got a fire in the cabin; and, I hope my complaint will go off.

My heaven bless you! I send this through Troubridge, direct in Piccadilly. I shall, you may rely, admire the pigstye, ducks, fowls, &c. for everything you do, I look upon as perfect. Dr. Baird has been aboard to see me. He thinks I shall be better; and that a few days on shore will set me up again.

Make my kind remembrances to Sir William, the Duke, and all friends; and believe me, ever, your most affectionate

NELSON & BRONTE.

Bedford has made me laugh. Mrs. Lutwidge has been babbling, that she will go to Portsmouth with the Admiral; who says, he shall be so fully employed that he cannot be much with her. She whispered Bedford – 'I have many friends in the army there!' She will certainly marry a soldier, if ever she is disposable. But, perhaps, you will agree with me, that no good soldier would take her. I am sure, the purchase would be dear, even

[1]At that time Home Secretary.
[2]Pettigrew, ii, p. 222, has here: 'the Admiralty does'.
[3]23 Oct 1801; see also Doc. No. 247.

if it was a *gift*. Don't call this a bull. Sutton's man was on the farm; and the sheep, when not belonging to the farm, always paid so much sheep, so much lambs: but, I dare say, you manage well. Sir William's letter has delighted me, with your activity and prudence.[1]

253. *To Lady Hamilton*

[BL: Egerton 1614 ff. 86–87, no. 44] Amazon
Oct^{r}: 18th: 1801.

My Dearest Friend,

I am to day much better than I have been for several days past and I believe my cold has taken a favorable turn, and I trust to being perfectly stout + strong before Friday,[2] no thanks to the Adm^{ty}: we have had and it still blows a very heavy gale of Wind from yesterday 5 oclock, I doubt whether any boat will be able to get to us today with your letters and less do I believe that mine will get on shore for the wind blows partly from

[1] 'We have now inhabited your Lord$^{p's}$ premises some days, & I can now speak with some certainty. I have lived with our dear Emma several years. I know her merit, have a great opinion of the head & heart that God Almighty has been pleased to give her; but a seaman alone could have given a fine woman full power to chuse & fit up a residence for him without seeing it himself. You are in luck, for in my conscience I verily believe that a place so suitable to your views could not have been found, & at so cheap a rate, for if you stay away 3 days longer I do not think you can have any wish but you will find it compleated here, & then the bargain was fortunately struck 3 days before an idea of peace gat abroad. Now every estate in this neighbourhood has increased in value, and you might get a thousand pounds to-morrow for your bargain. The proximity to the capital, and the perfect retirement of this place, are, for your Lordship, two points beyond estimation; but the house is so comfortable, the furniture clean & good, & I never saw so many conveniences united in so small a compass. You have nothing but to come and enjoy immediately: you have a good mile of pleasant dry walk around your own farm. It would make you laugh to see Emma & her mother fitting up pig-sties and hen-coops, & already the Canal is enlivened with ducks, & the cock is stutting with his hens about the walks. Your L$^{p's}$ plan as to stocking the Canal with fish is exactly mine. I will answer for it, that in a few months you may command a good dish of fish at a moment's warning. Every fish, if of any size, has been taken away, even after the bargain was made, for there are many *Troubridges* in this world, but Nelsons are rare. I think it quite impossible that they can keep you at Deal more than 3 or 4 days longer; it would be *ridiculous*. This neighbourhood is anxiously expecting your L$^{dp's}$ arrival, and you cannot be off of some particular attention that will be shewn you, of which all the world know that you have merited above all others. I enclose a letter which I have received from Count Dillon O'Kelly, who supped with me at Coblenzell's [fn: Louis, Count von Cobentzel, 1753–1808, an Austrian diplomatist, who took a leading part in the most important negotiations of the period.] at Prague. See how your merit is estimated on the Continent, and shame be it that so little justice is done you at home. Be so good as to bring or return the letter, as I must answer it. Adieu, my dear Lord & most sincere friend I have in this world, yours,'(Morrison, ii, pp. 175–6, no. 638)

[2] 23 Oct 1801.

the Land, I could not write all my thoughts through the Admiralty for I should not be surprized if now + then for curiosity['s] sake they wish to know our truly Innocent correspondence I think it probable that I shall be obliged for a week perhaps to return to Deal for I find and there they are right to put by all superfluous expences, and only to keep what I call clean men-of-war in commission 'till the Definite Treaty is signed, what has been done already in the Naval department will reduce our expenses 150,000£ a month, We shall make a better treaty with arms in our hands, I am very angry at the great rejoicings of the military and in some Ports our naval men at Peace, Let the rejoicings be proper to our several stations the manufacturer because he will have more markets for his goods, but seamen + soldiers ought to say, Well, as it is peace we lay down our arms and are ready again to take them up If the French are Insolent, there is a manly rejoicing and a foolish one We seem to have taken the latter and the damn'd French will think it proceeds from fear, I hope to manage so thet I shall get something for my Brother[1] for myself it is out of the Question they can give me nothing as a pension at this time but good things may fall, I shall talk and be much with Mr: Addington If he wishes it, If not I can have no desire to go to the House[2] + give myself trouble, Lord St: Vincent says two days ago, When you my Dear Lord hold my place you will be obliged as I am to act on the defensive against such presumptuous claims

I am in hopes the Weather will moderate after 12 oclock for you will fancy I am ill, but recollect in the Winter it is often a week has been 14 days without any communication with the shore, I recd: all your letters yesterday but you need not direct them to the care of Adl: Lutwidge, Wednesday[3] will be your last day of writing, have you thought of the turnip field can we get it, We will If possible + in any reason of price.[4]

I finish my letter thet if it is possible it may get on shore but I have no expectation at present, Make my kindest regards to Sir William Mrs: Cadogan, The Duke when you see him + all our friends I am certainly In luck not to be ordered to these court-martials they will altogether take a fortnight at least, Ever my Dearest friend your most faithful + affectionate

Nelson + Bronte

What a gale does it blow with you.

[1]William.

[2]House of Lords.

[3]21 Oct 1801.

[4]The following passage is written on the outside of the letter, upside down, below (until 'court martials') and above the address.

254. *To Lady Hamilton*

[NMM: CRK/19/23]

Amazon
Oct^{r}: 19th: 1801.

My Dearest Friend,

What a gale we have had but Ad^{l}: L.[1] boat came off and as your letter was wrote it got on shore at least I hope so for the boat absolutely seemd swallowed up in the sea none of our boats could have kept above water a moment therefore I could not answer all the truly friendly things you told me in your letter[s] for they were not opened before the boat was gone, I am sure[2] you did well to send M^{rs}: L.[3] a gown and she loves you very much, but there is no accounting for taste She admires entirely Red Coats you, true blue[4] they dine with Billy Pitt to-day, or rather with M^{r}: Long; for Pitt does not keep house in appearance although he asked me to come + see him, and thet I shall do out of Respect, to a great man although he never did anything for me or my relations. I assure you my Dear friend thet I had rather read + hear [*sic*] all your little story of a white hen getting into a tree an anecdote of Fatima[5] or hear you call Cupidy Cupidy that [*sic*] any speech I shall hear in parliament, because I know although you can adapt your language + manners to a child yet thet you can also, thunder forth such a torrent of Eloquence thet Corruption + Infamy would sink before your voice in however exalted a situation it might be placed. Poor Oliver what can be the matter with him, I must leave my cot here Till my discharge when it shall come to the farm, and cotts are the best things in the world for our sea friends why not have the picture from Davisons and those from Dods, especially my Fathers and Davisons, apropos, Sir Willm: has not sat I fear to Beechy,[6] I want a half length the size of my Fathers + Davison's, I wonder your picture is not yet come from Hamburg you have not lost the directions for unfolding them, nor the measure thet I may have frames made for

[1]Lutwidge's.

[2]Inserted.

[3]Lutwidge.

[4]Representing soldiers and sailors respectively; for Mrs. Lutwidge's interest in soldiers; see postscript in Doc. No. 252.

[5]Fraser, p. 265, describes her as 'the nubian maid whom Nelson had brought to Emma from Egypt'.

[6]William Beechey (1753–1839), had painted Nelson in 1800/1801 and also his father in the same period.

them for up they shell go up[1] as soon as they arrive What have your picture + not hang it up, no I will submit in the Farm to every order but that, the weather today is tolerable but I do not think I could well get on shore but Thursday[2] I hope will be a fine day I shall call on M^{r}: Pitt make my visit at the hospital and get off very early on Friday[3] morning, my cold is still very troublesome I cannot get my Bowels in order In the night I had not a little fever but never mind, the Ad^{ty}: will not always be there, Every one has their[4] day, God Bless you my Dear friend and believe me ever yours most faithfully

Nelson and Bronte.

Write on Wednesday[5]

Your Letters of yesterday are receiv'd, Rev^{d}: D^{r}: would like to be a Bishop, I have sent poor Thompsons letter + the distressed M^{rs}: Brist[ys?] to the Earl. Kindest regards to Sir William.

255. *To Lady Hamilton*

[NMM: CRK/19/24] Amazon
Oct^{r}: 20th: 1801.

My Dearest Friend how could you think for a moment that I would be a time server to any minister on Earth and If you had studied my letter a little closer you would have seen thet my intention was to shew them thet I could be as useful in the cabinet as in the field My Idea is to let them see thet my attendance is worth soliciting, for myself I can have nothing but for my Brother something may be done, living with M^{r}: Addington a good deal never in your sense of the Word shell I do it, what leave my dearest friends to dine with a Minister damn me if I do, beyond what you yourself shell judge to be necessary perhaps it may be once and once with the Earl but thet you shall judge for me, If I give up all Intercourse

[1] Inserted.
[2] 22 Oct 1801.
[3] 23 Oct 1801.
[4] Pettigrew has here 'their' as well, while 1814-letters put 'his'.
[5] 21 Oct 1801. The following passage was added on those outside parts of the paper that were folded inside before sealing the letter. Seen from the earlier part of the letter, these words are upside down on the part above the address. The following words are written on the other part of the outside of the letter that gets folded inside for sealing the letter, under the address.

you know enough of Courts thet they will do nothing, make yourself of consequence to them and they will do whet you wish in reason and out of reason I never should ask them, It must be a great bore to me to go to the house, I shell tell M^{r}: A^{n}:[1] thet I go on the 29th:[2] to please him and not to please myself, but more of this subject when we meet, D^{r}: Baird is laid up with the Rhumatism [*sic*] he will now believe thet the cold may effect [*sic*] me, this is the coldest place in England most assuredly, Troubridge writes me, thet as the Weather is sett in fine again he hopes I shell get walks on shore, he is I suppose laughing at me. but never mind I agree with you in wishing that Sir William had a horse why dont you send to the Duke for a Poney [*sic*] for him, I am just parting with four of my ships, Cap^{ts}: Conn,[3] Rowley,[4] Martin, + Whitter[5] who are proceeding to the Nore in their way to be paid off, The surf is still so great on the beach thet I could not land dry if it was necessary today, but I hope it will be smooth on Thursday[6] If not I must go in a boat to Dover, and come from thence to Deal, Sutton says he will get the Amazon under sail and carry me down for thet I shell not take cold, Bedford goes with a squadron to Margate, so thet all our party will be broke up, I am sure to many of them I feel truly obliged, make my kind[c]st respects to Sir William + believe me Ever your most faithful + affectionate

Nelson + Bronte.[7]

I wish Banti was seperated from Charles for he is a knowing one I wish I could get him with a good Capt: who would keep him strict to his duty, Hardy cannot get paid 100 £ he advanced for M^{r}: Williams s nephew.

Many thanks for M^{rs}: Nelsons letters the Rev^{d}: D^{r}: likes going about, only think of his want^{g}: to come up with an address of thanks, Why [the] King will not notice him although he is a Doctor + less for being my Brother. for they certainly do not like me

[1]Addington.
[2]To take his seat as a Viscount in the House of Lords.
[3]John Conn (c. 1773–1810).
[4]Charles Rowley (1770–1845).
[5]Header Whitter.
[6]22 Oct 1801.
[7]The following passages are added upside down (seen from the earlier parts of the letter) on the outside of the letter on those parts that will be folded inside before sealing the letter. The first passage (above the address) ends with the words 'Williams s, nephew'. The second passage starts with the words 'Many thanks'.

256. *To Lady Hamilton*

[NMM: CRK/19/25] Amazon,
October 20th, 1801.

My Dearest Friend Only two days more the Admiralty could with any conscience keep me here, not that I think they have had any conscience I dare say Master Troubridge is grown fat, I know I am grown lean with my complaint which but for their indifference ab^{t}: my health would never have happened or at least I should have got well long ago in a warm room good fire + sincere friends, I believe I leave this little squadron with sincere regret + with the good wishes of every creature in it, how I should laugh to see you my Dear friend rowing in a boat, the Beautiful Emma, rowing a one armed Admiral in a boat, It will certainly be caricatured, ~~when~~ well[1] done farmers wife I'll bet your turkey ag^{t}: M^{rs}: Nelsons, but Sir William + I will decide Hardy says you may be sure of him, + that he has not lost his appetite, You will make us rich, with your Œcconemy, I did not think tell Sir William that Impudence had got such deep root in Wales, I send you the letter as a curiosity and to have the impudence to recommend a Midshipman, it is not long ago a person from Yorkshire desired me to lend him 300 £ as he was going to sett up a school, Are these people mad or do they take me for quite a fool, however I have wisdom enough to laugh at their folly and to Be myself your most obliged + faithful friend

Nelson + Bronte.

best regards to Sir William M^{rs}: Cad^{n}: + all friends.

257. *To Lady Hamilton*

[NMM: CRK/19/26] Amazon
Oct^{r}: 21st: 1801

My dearest Friend,

It blows strong from the westward and is a very dirty day with a good deal of surf on the Beach but Hardy and Sutton recommend my going on

[1]The word 'well' is written above '~~when~~'.

shore this morning as they believe it may blow a heavy Gale tomorrow, but what comfort could I have had for two whole days at Deal I hope the morning will be fine but I have ordered a Deal Boat as they understand the beach better than ours, + If I cannot land here I shall go to Ramsgate Pier, and come to deal in a carraige, has M^rs: Cadogan got my Peers robe for I must send for M^r: Webb and have it altered to a Visc^ts: Lord Hood wrote to me to-day and he is to be one of my introducers, he wanted me to dine with him the 24th: but I'll be damn'd if I dine from Home that day, and it would be as likely we should dine out the 23rd: If you + Sir William ever wish me to dine with his Brother[1] it must be the time of a very small party, for it would be worse than death to me to Dine in so large a Party, I expect that all the animals will increase where you are for I never expect thet you will suffer any to be killed, I am glad Sir William has got the Dukes Pony riding will do him much good, I am sorry to tell you that D^r: Baird is so ill thet I am told it is very probable he may never recover[2] this place is the Devils for dreadful colds and I do not believe I should get well all the Winter, for both cough + Bowels are still very much out of order, You are now writing your last letter for Deal so am I for Merton from Deal at least I hope so for If I can help it I will not return to it, I have much to do being the last day on board, but Ever my Dearest friend Believe me your truly affectionate

Nelson + Bronte.

I am literally starving with cold but my heart is warm, I suppose I suppose [*sic*] I shall dine with Lutwidge but I am not very desirous of it for I shall have Sutton Bedford + Hardy with me, You must prepare Bantis mother as it is a peace for some other line of life than the navy Yesterday he sold a pair of silver buckles he would soon ruin poor Charles, who is really a well disposed Boy I never shall get warm again I believe I cannot feel the Pen Make my kindest regards to Sir William M^rs: Cadogan Oliver +c Sutton Hardy + Bedford all join in kind remembrances.[3]

As Monday[4] is Horace's[5] birth day I suppose I must send him a one Pound note.

[1]Frederick Hamilton (1728–1811), a minister of religion.

[2]Dr Baird was to live on until 1843.

[3]The additional postscript ('As Monday is . . .') is added on the outside of the letter on one of the parts that were folded towards the inside on closing the letter, upside down, judging from the text on the inside of the letter, below the address.

[4]26 Oct 1801.

[5]Nelson's nephew by his brother William.

258. *To Lady Hamilton*

[NMM: CRK/19/27][1]

My Dearest friend,

Hardy begs you will send the enclosed to Naples, I wish Tyson would come home for many are pulling at him + I want to pay him I will not be in his debt 48 hours after his arrival, Hardy is Just anchored and his commodore gone on shore, Ever your most faithful

Nelson + Bronte.

M[rs]: Nelson had better direct her letters to me unless I am on the spot, You see you paid postage and it lays me open to their Post office conversation

[1]On the top of the page someone (not Nelson) pencilled: 'Deal Octr 29 1801'.

CHAPTER IV

SETTLED, MAY 1803–AUGUST 1805

It is doubtful whether Nelson experienced the idyll at Merton that he had hoped for. Instead of being rowed about in a boat by Lady Hamilton, he suffered from exhaustion. Lady Hamilton wrote to his sister-in-law, Sarah Nelson: 'I am sorry to tell you I do not think our Dear Lord well. He has frequent sickness, and [is] Low, and he throws himself on the sofa tired and says, I am worn out, but yet he is better, and I hope we shall get him up.'[1] Considering that he had regarded himself 'as useful in the cabinet as in the field' [255], he did not show much political skill in the weeks to come. On 20 November he reminded the Lord Mayor that the City of London had not yet honoured those 'who [had] fought and so profusely bled under my command' at the battle of Copenhagen.[2] On having informed the Prime Minister, Addington, about his attempt to gain honours for his subordinates, he was discouraged that a letter to the Lord Mayor 'could be productive of no good, and might, and (I firmly believe) would, lead to serious embarrassments'.[3] As a consequence Nelson wrote again to the Lord Mayor: 'By the advice of a friend, I have now to request that your Lordship will consider my letter as withdrawn.'[4] Nelson's speech in the House of Lords, on 21 December 1801,[5] was similarly lacking in political astuteness. Even if he might have been right in pointing out that Malta, Minorca and the Cape were 'of no sort of consequence' to Britain,[6] it was exceedingly undiplomatic to advocate this view in a debate about peace negotiations with France, in which these assets were at issue. William Huskisson,[7] former Under-Secretary for War, remarked in a private letter to the War Minister, Lord Dundas:[8] 'How can Ministers allow such a fool to speak in their defence?'[9]

Things did not go smoothly in respect to family affairs, either. Nelson's father, Edmund, stayed in touch with Lady Nelson and came to Merton in November 1801, only after having visited his daughter-in-law at Somerset Street, her London residence.[10] Family relations remained

[1]Sichel, p. 503, dating the letter 'Mid-November, 1801'.

[2]Nicolas, iv, p. 524 (BL Egerton 1614, ff. 88–89).

[3]Nicolas, iv, pp. 525–6 (letter to Addington of 20 Nov 1801) and fn. 7 (Addington's answer of 27 Nov 1801).

[4]Nicolas, vii, p. ccx (letter of 28 Nov 1801).

[5]Roger Knight, *The Pursuit of Victory. The Life and Achievement of Horatio Nelson* (London, 2005) [hereafter: Knight], p. 441.

[6]Edgar Vincent, *Nelson. Love & Fame* (London, 2003), p. 468, quoting from Hansard.

[7]William Huskisson (1770–1830); son-in-law of Admiral Mark Milbanke.

[8]Henry Dundas (1742–1811), later Lord Melville.

[9]Quoted in Tom Pocock, *Horatio Nelson* (London, 1994), p. 267.

[10]Knight, p. 428.

strained, even after the visit. Lady Nelson wrote a letter that would be her last attempt at reconciliation:

> My dear husband, – It is some time since I have written to you. The silence you have imposed is more than my affections will allow me and in this instance I hope you will forgive me in not obeying you. One thing I omitted in my letter of July[1] which I now have to offer for your accommodation, [is] a comfortable warm house. Do, my dear husband, let us live together. I can never be happy till such an event takes place. I assure you again I have but one wish in the world, to please you. Let every thing be buried in oblivion, it will pass away like a dream. I can now only intreat you to believe I am most sincerely and affectionately your wife, Frances H. Nelson.[2]

This letter was returned with a note: 'Opened by mistake by Lord Nelson, but not read. A. Davison'.[3] At about the same time Lady Hamilton addressed a letter to Edmund Nelson that provoked this reply, on 21 December: 'The intelligence you have trobled [*sic*] y[r] self to communicate to me respecting the lad Cook, vexes me more than a little, as I am concerned that any act of mine should have given any[one] the least anxiety, or for a moment interrupted the domestick quiet of my good son, who is every day so affectionately showing marks of kindness to me'.[4] It appears there was no more contact between Edmund and his famous son until the father's death on 26 April 1802, on which the son commented in a rather self-centred way: 'Had my father expressed a wish to see me, unwell as I am, I should have flown to Bath.'[5] Without a sign of personal grief Nelson corresponded with his sister, Catherine Matcham, and her husband about the arrangements for the funeral at Burnham Thorpe, at which he himself did not participate.[6] With the last supporter of the case of Lady Nelson gone, the relationship between Lady Hamilton and

[1]An unfinished draft of this letter has come down to us; Naish, p. 588: 'My dearest Husband, – Your generosity and tenderness was never more strongly shewn than your writing to Mr. Marsh yesterday morning for the payment of your very handsome quarterly allowance, which far exceeded my expectation, knowing your income and had you left it to me, I could not in conscience have said so much. Accept my warmest, my most affectionate and grateful thanks. I could say more but my heart is too full. Be assured every wish, every desire of mine is to please the man whose affection constitutes my happiness. God bless my dear husband. (*unfinished*).'

[2]Naish, pp. 596–7.

[3]Naish, p. 596, fn. 4.

[4]Morrison, ii, p. 179, no. 645.

[5]Knight, p. 429.

[6]Knight, p. 429.

Nelson's sisters, Catherine Matcham and Susannah Bolton, and their families improved.[1]

In the course of the year 1802 Nelson's and Lady Hamilton's life at Merton stabilised into a family life with countryside amusements. Lady Hamilton wrote a letter for Nelson to John Broadbent, a merchant at Messina:[2]

> It would make you laugh to see Emma and her mother fitting up pig sties and hen coops and already the canal is enlived with ducks, and the cock is strutting with his hens about the walks. Your L^{ps} plan as to stocking the canal with fish, is exactly mine, and I will answer for it that in a few months you may command a good dish of fish at a moments warning.[3]

It appears that both Nelson and Lady Hamilton liked to have guests in their house. The proximity to London and position on the road to Portsmouth was an advantage for being visited both by family and by naval and other friends. They seem to have generally followed their earlier resolution: 'I agree with you no great folks they are a public nuisance' [243]. One of the few visitors who may have fitted into the range of 'great folk' was Lord Minto, who was back in England after having resigned his post of ambassador at Vienna. He commented: 'The whole establishment and way of life is such to make me angry, as well as melancholy . . . If it was Lady H's house there might be a pretence for it; to make his own a mere looking-glass to view himself all day is bad taste'.[4]

Merely entertaining lots of various visitors at home did not satisfy Nelson's and Lady Hamilton's desire for activity. It was decided that they would go on a journey to Wales with Sir William Hamilton. The tour had the useful side effect of promoting Sir William's venture in Milford Haven on the south-western tip of Wales, which he tried to develop as a merchant port. Sir William had inspected the place a year earlier, in August 1801, and reported to Nelson about the favourable 'harbour', the entrance into which was protected by 'the two light-houses lately erected'.[5] How better to convince possible investors of this maritime enterprise than by having the foremost admiral of the day promote it?

[1]Flora Fraser, *Beloved Emma. The Life of Emma Lady Hamilton* (London, 1986) [hereafter: Fraser], p. 294.

[2]Knight, p. 467; Broadbent is also mentioned in Nelson's letters during the blockade of Toulon 1803–5 (Nicolas, v, 164; vi, pp. 141–2) and Nelson asked him to send a letter to Lady Hamilton in 1805 (Doc. No. 360).

[3]Catalogue of Christie's sale of 21 June 1989, lot 251; Morrison, ii, p. 176, no. 638.

[4]Knight, p. 422; about range of guests in general: Knight, pp. 426–7.

[5]1814-letters, ii, p. 217 (Sir William to Nelson on 12 Aug 1801).

The journey, undertaken during the summer months of July and August 1802, was something of a triumphal procession. The route was even extended, because some towns desired to be visited by the famous admiral on his tour.[1] Nelson may have been distracted by the attention paid to him, but in his speeches he still acknowledged the part his sailors had played in his professional success.[2] He even thought of naval needs in the middle of the country. Passing through the forest of Dean induced Nelson to note down a memorandum on the usefulness and importance of sustainable forestry management for shipbuilding.[3]

The eventful trip and active lifestyle appear to have been a little stressful for Sir William, who was already 73 years of age. Morrison's edition of *Hamilton & Nelson Papers* reproduces a written exchange between husband and wife which he dates from about this time, but which may have been written in 1801 when the couple were staying at Deal and Lady Hamilton was enjoying sea-bathing and Nelson's company:

> Lady Hamilton: 'As I see it is a pain to you to remain here, let me beg of you to fix your time for going. Weather I dye in Picadilly or any other spot in England, 'tis the same to me; but I remember the time when you wish'd for tranquillity, but now all visiting and bustle is your liking. However, I will do what you please, being ever your affectionate & obedient'
>
> Sir William Hamilton: 'I neither love bustle nor great company, but I like some employment and diversion. I have but a very short time to live, and every moment is precious to me. I am in no hurry, and am exceedingly glad to give every satisfaction to our best friend, our dear Lord Nelson. The question, then, is what we can best do that all may be perfectly satisfied. Sea bathing is usefull to your health; I see it is, and wish you to continue it a little longer; but I must confess that I regret, whilst the season is favourable, that I cannot enjoy my favourite amusement of quiet fishing. I care not a pin for the great world, and am attached to no one so much as to you'
>
> Lady Hamilton: 'I go when you tell me the coach is ready'
>
> Sir William: 'This is not a fair answer to a fair confession of mine.'[4]

[1]Marianne Czisnik, 'Nelson and the Nile: The Creation of Admiral Nelson's Public Image', in: *The Mariner's Mirror*, 88:1 (Feb 2002), 41–60 [hereafter: Czisnik, 'Nelson and the Nile'], 53 with further references. For the details of the route, see Knight, pp. 430–32.

[2]Czisnik, 'Nelson and the Nile', 53.

[3]Nicolas, v, pp. 24–8.

[4]Morrison, ii, pp. 195–6 (nos 679 and 680 with fn.).

Sir William summarised the marital disagreements in another, undated note to his wife, suggesting that they should try to compose their differences:

> I have passed the last 40 years of my life in the hurry & bustle that must necessarily be attendant on a publick character. I am arrived at the age when some repose is really necessary, & I promised myself a quiet home, & altho' I was sensible, & said so when I married, that I shou'd be superannuated when my wife wou'd be in her full beauty and vigour of youth. That time is arrived, and we must make the best of it for the comfort of both parties. Unfortunately our tastes as to the manner of living are very different. I by no means wish to live in solitary retreat, but to have seldom less than 12 or 14 at table, & those varying continually, is coming back to what was become so irksome to me in Italy during the latter years of my residence in that country. I have no connections out of my own family. I have no complaint to make, but I feel that the whole attention of my wife is given to Ld N. and his interest at Merton. I well know the purity of Ld N.'s friendship for Emma and me, and I know how very uncomfortable it wou'd make his L^{p}, our best friend, if a separation shou'd take place, & am therefore determined to do all in my power to prevent such an extremity, which wou'd be *essentially detrimental* to all parties, but wou'd be more sensibly felt by our dear friend than by us. Provided that our expences in housekeeping do not increase beyond measure (of which I must own I see some danger), I am willing to go on upon our present footing; but as I cannot expect to live many years, every moment to me is precious, & I hope I may be allow'd sometimes to be my own master, & pass my time according to my own inclination, either by going my fishing parties on the Thames or by going to London to attend the Museum, R. Society, the Tuesday Club, & Auctions of pictures. I mean to have a light chariot or post chaise by the month, that I may make use of it in London and run backwards and forwards to Merton or to Shepperton, &c. This is my plan, & we might go on very well, but I am fully determined not to have more of the very silly altercations, that happen but too often between us and embitter the present moments exceedingly. If realy one cannot live comfortably together, a *wise* and well *concerted separation* is preferable; but I think, considering the probability of my not troubling any party long in this world, the best for us all wou'd be to bear those ills we have rather than flie to those we know not of. I have fairly stated what I have on my mind. There is no time for nonsense or trifling. I know and admire your talents & many excellent qualities, but I am not blind

> to your defects, & confess having many myself; therefore let us bear and forbear for God's sake.[1]

We do not know how they managed to bear each other's weaknesses and whether there were many more 'very silly altercations', but we can gather from surviving accounts that worries about 'expences in housekeeping' never quite left them. For appearances' sake Sir William kept the house in Piccadilly, although at the same time his Welsh possessions did not generate sufficient income.[2] An elaborate calculation of September 1802 that took into consideration the joint expenses of the tour to Wales as well as the journey home from Naples overland in 1800 showed that Sir William still owed Nelson well over £ 1,000.[3]

Nelson himself was not free from monetary worries, either. At the end of the year 1801 he wrote to his agents that after he had 'sold Diamonds' he could still use the 'money in the funds (and I think I have India Stock)' to pay his debts; in order to pay his agents themselves he announced that he would have to 'trespass on your indulgence', but added calmly that he could count with 'arrears of pay' and prize money: '(even if I lose my cause with L^{d}: S^{t}: V^{t}:) 5000 £ from the Alcmene, Prizes, and near 3000 £ from the Lima Convoy'; he summarised: 'I take no shame to be poor,[4] never for myself have I spent 6^{d}: it has all gone to do honor to my country and in a way which whether the persons have deserved it or no, is for their consideration not for mine'.[5] The 'cause with L^{d}: S^{t}: V^{t}:', referred to in this letter, was about prize money for two Spanish treasure ships taken in late 1799, when Nelson was acting as senior flag officer in the Mediterranean after St Vincent's return home to England. Nelson had challenged in court the opinion St Vincent should receive the 'flag eighth' of the prize money, but had lost in the Court of Common Pleas in March 1801.[6] He had brought the case before the King's Bench, which would only decide in the autumn of 1803 (in his favour), but at this stage during the long-drawn-out case Nelson was pessimistic as to his chance of success: 'I find it very hard to fight against the first Lord. I much doubt if Justice ought to be painted blind, for I see her eyes always turned to the

[1]Morrison, ii, p. 197, no. 684; Sir William had written in a similar vein to his nephew, Charles Greville, earlier in the year (on 24 Jan 1802), Morrison, ii, p. 182, no. 651.

[2]Knight, p. 423.

[3]Morrison, ii, pp. 401–5; the originals of these accounts are at the Huntington Library, HM 34057 and HM 34058.

[4]Underlined twice with very straight lines.

[5]BL Egerton 1614, f. 90, no. 46 (also in Pettigrew, ii, 241).

[6]See above, Docs Nos 65, 77 and 95.

rich & powerful'.[1] His Italian possessions in Bronte, on Sicily, did not generate any income either,[2] but rather required investment. The income that his estates in England generated was rather modest; in April 1803 Nelson wrote to Mr. Patenson: 'The cow sold well, The Hay I sold for 100 Guineas I have now 6 Pigs five weeks old do you buy pigs for your farm if you do I wish You would take them + give me the price which You may think proper '.[3] Nelson's monetary preoccupations continued during his time ashore between October 1801 and May 1803, since he had to support his wife, pay off and keep house at Merton,[4] while living on half-pay during the peace with France.

Being ashore did not stop Nelson keeping up his naval and political contacts – in part jointly with Lady Hamilton. Although Nelson's overall correspondence shrank dramatically during his time ashore between October 1801 and May 1803,[5] among the little correspondence he was keeping up there is some proof of Nelson and Lady Hamilton cooperating. She translated into Italian[6] a letter of his to the Queen of Naples and copied (co-wrote?) other parts of Nelson's correspondence.[7] She also added postscripts to letters that Nelson wrote to Captain Sutton, inviting him to Merton[8] and she kept up a correspondence of her own with

[1]Christie's sale of 2003 (Spiro-sale), lot 147 (letter to Duckworth, who also claimed a share, of 13 Feb 1802); quoted by Knight, p. 424, from a copy at the NMM; for the details of the case, see Grahame Aldous QC, 'Lord Nelson and Earl St Vincent: Prize fighters', in *The Mariner's Mirror*, 101:2 (May 2015), 135–55.

[2]Knight, p. 425.

[3]Huntington Library, HM 34188.

[4]Nelson's accounts of the period can be found in Morrison, ii, pp. 394–400.

[5]For the development of Nelson's correspondence, see Marianne Czisnik, 'Nelson's Circles. Networking in the Navy during the French Wars', in Gordon Pentland and Michael T. Davis (eds), *Liberty, Property and Popular Politics. England and Scotland, 1688–1815. Essays in Honour of H. T. Dickinson* (Edinburgh, 2016), pp. 194–206, esp. pp. 195–8.

[6]Clive Richards' Collection, letter dated 'Merton Dec^{r}: 24th: 1801', starting: 'Madam, an Expression in Your Majestys letter that I had said in Parliament something thet you could not approve has forcibly struck my feelings, as I can assure your Majesty thet neither in Parliament or out of it (and I defy any person to assert it) have I ever mentioned your name but in the manner I know it deserves as one of the greatest Monarchs in Europe in point of abilities, and as a person of the greatest honor, and when I cease for a moment to speak of Your Majestys greatness + goodness may the curse of God light upon me, [...]'.

[7]For example, a letter of Nelson's to St Vincent of 28 Jan 1803 (Morrison, ii, 205; see Nicolas, v, p. 41) and a draft of letter to Alexander Stephens (author of *A History of the Wars of the French Revolution*, published in 1803), dated 23 Piccadilly, 10 Feb 1802 (Morrison, ii, p. 206, no. 702; longer final version in Nicolas, v, p. 43).

[8]William Clements Library, Ann Arbor, University of Michigan, Smith collection, 'Letters of Horatio Lord Nelson to Captin S. Sutton, R.N with Memorabilia of the Battle of Trafalgar'; letters by Nelson to Sutton of Nov 1801 (Lady Hamilton's postscript: 'I wish you were all free + comfortable with us at Merton tell Hardy + Bedford so love to Charl[es Connor]') and 21 Jan 1802 (Lady Hamilton's postscript: 'My Dear friend, Sir Wm + Mrs Nelson beg their compliments + I hope you will soon come to Merton'); both letters can be found in Nicolas, iv, pp. 522–3 and v, p. 3, but without Lady Hamilton's postscripts (although Nicolas, vii, p. 48, gives the addition by Hardy to a letter from Nelson to Sutton of 25 Sept 1805).

Captain Ball. He informed her 'Entre nous, the Cabinet Ministers are of opinion that I am fitted for the station of Minister at Malta', but that he would not 'accede to the terms they first proposed', finishing his letter: 'Adieu, my dear sister, be assured of my unalterable regard'.[1] Once at his post in Malta, Ball confided to Lady Hamilton on 8 November 1802: 'our business here is a jumble'.[2] It is not clear, whether this letter had reached Merton on 4 December 1802, when Lady Hamilton wrote Nelson's memorandum on Malta for Addington. In this memorandum Nelson continued to insist on his opinion about Malta: '*England does not want it*'.[3]

Nelson's relationship with his former mentor, St Vincent, who was now First Lord of the Admiralty, had cooled. This was due to St Vincent's disapproval of Nelson's relationship with Lady Hamilton and also to their legal dispute about prize money. This personal distance, however, was not to Nelson's disadvantage as St Vincent's policies were antagonising many members of the navy. In order to reduce expenses in peacetime St Vincent applied rigorous measures without any consideration for working structures. Roger Knight summarises the methods and effects:

> He very soon picked a permanent quarrel with the Navy Board under its comptroller Sir Andrew Snape Hamond,[4] and personal relations became so fraught that the two officers, on whom the efficient working of the navy most depended, communicated only by letter. Contracts were cancelled. Dockyard officials were summarily dismissed, while, in an atmosphere of fear, droves of restless and dissatisfied skilled workers were turned out of the gates of the various dockyards.[5]

Nelson supported the setting up of the Commission of Naval Inquiry to look into the abuses in the naval departments and he pointed out some problems in the current system of prize agents, but he did not support the measures St Vincent eventually applied. Instead, he focused on alerting the prime minister to problems of manning and supply of timber.[6] If he had ever seriously entertained political ambitions [as 252 and 255

[1]Morrison, ii, p. 187, no. 662; the salutation 'sister' derives from both of them having received the order of Malta from Ferdinand IV of Naples and III of Sicily (see Doc. No. 234).

[2]Morrison, ii, p. 201, no. 691.

[3] Morrison, ii, p. 202, no. 693

[4]Andrew Snape Hamond (1738–1828), comptroller of the navy board 1784–1806.

[5]Knight, p. 438.

[6]Knight, p. 439.

might indicate], he appears to have given them up. Instead of a political occupation another employment in the navy became likely, when international tensions rose at the beginning of 1803 and war appeared imminent. On 9 March he sent a note to Addington, the prime minister: 'Whenever it is necessary. I am your admiral.' Indeed, the cabinet had singled out Nelson for the command in the Mediterranean.[1]

Amidst these political and naval developments, Sir William Hamilton died, on 6 April 1803. The pension of £700 that he had left his wife,[2] would not suffice to keep up her living standards. Sir William himself had unsuccessfully tried to secure a state pension for her.[3] In order to pursue this aim, a week after her husband's death, Lady Hamilton addressed a letter to the prime minister in order to put forward her claim for a state pension. She argued that what he had left her would allow her merely to live 'below those [circumstances] becoming the relict of such a public minister' and she went on to claim how she herself, 'too, strove to do all I could towards the service of our King and Country'. She elaborated:

> The fleet itself, I can truly say, could not have got into Sicily, but for what I was happily able to do with the Queen of Naples, and through her secret instructions so obtained: on which depended the refitting of the fleet in Sicily; and, with that, all which followed so gloriously at the Nile.[4]

As Lady Hamilton could neither maintain the house at 23 Piccadilly nor acceptably move in with Nelson at Merton, she moved to cheaper accommodation in Clarges Street.[5] In view of Lady Hamilton's insecure finances and his own imminent departure on another mission Nelson wrote his last will on 10 May [259] and added a first codicil to it three days later [260]. The texts of these two documents clearly follow a traditional legal style and were probably composed by a lawyer or clerk.[6] Nelson repeated much of the contents of his previous will, of 5 March 1801 [118]. He again laid down that, 'unless His Majesty shall signify it to be his pleasure that my body shall be interred elsewhere' (which he expected), he wished to be buried in Burnham Thorpe. He also repeated

[1]Knight, p. 445.

[2]Knight, p. 435.

[3] Morrison, ii, p. 193, no. 673, letter of 2 July 1802 to the Marquess of Douglas, afterwards 10th Duke of Hamilton.

[4]1814-letters, ii, pp. 131–3, esp. 132.

[5]Knight, p. 435.

[6]Because of the elaborate style I have decided to reproduce only those passages that are in some way or other relevant to Nelson's relationship to Lady Hamilton and his wife.

the settlement of an annuity of £1,000 on his wife. Unlike in his will of March 1801, Nelson did not assume any more that he would 'die worth above the sum of twenty thousand pounds'. This was no longer the case, because most of his wealth was now invested in real estate. As promised in a letter of 1 October 1801 [228], Nelson left the house at Merton to Lady Hamilton. Together with the house itself he left her its contents ('all the household furniture implements of a household wines plate china linen pictures and prints which shall be in and about my house at Merton') and surrounding grounds ('my grounds farms lands tenements and hereditaments in the several parishes of Merton, Wimbledon, and Mitcham . . . shall not exceed seventy acres as shall be selected by the said Emma Lady Hamilton within six months after my decease'). Thus, lacking in monetary funds to dispose of, he now had to arrange for a sufficient number of his possessions to be sold so that his executors would be able to purchase 'bank annuities . . . with the residue of my personal estate', which would guarantee the annuity for Lady Nelson. As a consequence he no longer left to Lady Hamilton a fixed sum ['three thousand pounds' in 118] nor 'three Boxes set with Diamonds' for her to dispose of and sell, if need be. He merely maintained the bequest of his 'diamond star as a token of my friendship'.[1] His estate in Bronte and the revenue thereof as well as a number of valuable items were meant to go to his brother and sisters. The first codicil revoked the will in respect of leaving 'my capital messuage at Merton' to Lady Hamilton [260]. This surprising move was apparently meant to protect the bequest from a possible new husband, since Nelson now settled Merton on his executors, who were to leave it to the disposal of Lady Hamilton 'notwithstanding her coverture by any husband with whom she may happen to intermarry' [259].

Now events followed in quick succession. On 16 May 1803 Nelson received his 'appointment from the Lords Commissioners of the Admiralty, as Commander-in-Chief of his Majesty's ships and vessels employed and to be employed on the Mediterranean Station'.[2] He left immediately for Portsmouth and merely sent a short note of comfort to Lady Hamilton from Kingston on his way south [261]. On 18 May 1803, Nelson received his orders from the Admiralty. He was to proceed to Malta, where he would have to take the squadron of Sir Richard

[1]In Doc. No. 118 Nelson had been more specific: 'which I request she will wear either in its present form or in any other she may like best in remembrance of an old and sincere friend'; see also Doc. No. 95 ('momento [*sic*]').

[2]Nicolas, v, p. 66.

Bickerton[1] under his command and to make arrangements with Alexander Ball, now Commissioner of the island, about its 'protection and security'. On arrival at his station off the French naval port of Toulon Nelson would have to 'take, sink, burn, or otherwise destroy, any Ships or Vessels belonging to France, or the Citizens of that Republic'. Next to that main task Nelson was given a set of additional duties with different degrees of urgency and importance: 'detaining and sending into Port any Ships or Vessels belonging to the Batavian Republic' (French dominated Netherlands), 'to be attentive to the proceedings of the French at Genoa, Leghorn, and other Ports on that side of Italy', thus protecting or assisting 'Egypt, or any other part of the Turkish Dominions, or . . . the Kingdoms of Naples and Sicily or the Islands of Corfu', 'be watchful of the conduct of the Court of Spain' by obtaining 'all the intelligence you may be able to collect'. With regard to Spain Nelson's task was quite intricate, because he was to avoid insult by infringing Spanish neutrality, while at the same time he was instructed 'not to suffer any Squadron of Spanish Ships of War to enter a French Port, or to form a junction with any Squadron, or Ships or Vessels of that, or the Batavian Republic'. He also was 'to be careful not to infringe the Neutrality of other Powers'. Apart from his tasks relating to foreign states, Nelson had to arrange convoys for British merchantmen and, of course, he was ordered: 'you are to transmit to our Secretary, for our information, frequent accounts of your proceedings, and every intelligence you may have obtained, proper for our knowledge'.[2]

The Admiralty had made sure that the *Victory*, which had undergone extensive repairs, was made ready for service. Though smaller than, for example, the *St Josef* that Nelson had commanded before, she was an efficient fighting ship and sea-kindly.[3] She was commanded by Sutton, whom Nelson knew well from his command in the Channel in 1801. When Nelson arrived at Portsmouth, 'almost smothered with dust' he quickly consulted with Sutton and Hardy (then in command of the *Amphion*) and decided to join the *Victory* immediately, while he noticed that his 'things only begin to arrive' [262]. Once on board the *Victory*, Nelson was 'examining the list of things which are coming' and noticed that matters were in a 'pretty state of confusion' [263]. The problem of getting his own things

[1]Sir Richard Bickerton (1759–1832) had remained in the Mediterranean during the Peace of Amiens as commander-in-chief and then served there as second-in-command under Nelson from 1803 until 1805 (shortly before the Battle of Trafalgar; see Knight, pp. 622–3).

[2]Nicolas, v, pp. 68–9.

[3]Knight, p. 447.

sorted did not cause the same annoyance as when he had joined the fleet destined for the Baltic in early 1801 [see 57 and 58]. Even after having found something missing, Nelson did not complain to Lady Hamilton as he had done to his wife, but rather suspected his own inefficiency: 'I have left my silver seal at least I cannot find it' [267].

Going on board ship and sailing[1] evoked feelings of separation so that Nelson wrote about the 'Sweet hope of again returning', his wish 'that we may meet again' and that 'being afloat makes me now feel that we do not tread the same element . . . My heart is full to bursting!' [262, 264 and 265]. After two days at sea this sense turned into a more optimistic and reassuring vein: 'I feel a thorough conviction that we shall meet again with Honor Riches + health and remain together 'till a good old age . . . be assured that my attatchment + affectionate regard is unalterable nothing can shake it'. He added, resorting in a confused way to the alias of Mrs Thomson: 'and pray say so to my Dear M[rs]: T. when you see her, tell her that my love is unbounded to her + her dear sweet child and if she should have more it will extend to all of them, in short my Dear Emma say every thing to her which your dear affectionate heart + head can think of' [267]. This barely veiled passage is the first indication of Lady Hamilton expecting another child of Nelson's.

While en route to the Mediterranean Nelson's mind turned to practical professional matters. As if writing a logbook he reported to Lady Hamilton about taking 'a Dutch ship from Surinam, of some value' [266], approaching Ushant in the hope of seeing 'admiral Cornwallis[2] in an hour' [267], then, continuing the same letter on the next day, commenting on not finding Cornwallis: 'it blows strong, what wind we are losing', and the great disappointment of having to leave the *Victory* behind for Cornwallis: 'I am just Embarking in the Amphion' [267], which at least was captained by his old companion Thomas M. Hardy. Nelson's next letters again consist of a series of entries that cover the period between 25 May and 4 June and report: 'foul wind', 'Our wind has been foul blowing fresh and nasty sea', then, off Lisbon, 'a gentle fair wind', 'fresh breeze + fair', 'entering the Streights of Gib[r]:', 'we captured a Brig from the West Indies yesterday' [268], 'we took a French brig from Cette,[3] and a Dutch one from the same place. We have had foul winds . . . and at present our wind is favourable, but with a nasty sea' [269]. The apparent luck in taking prizes on the way into the Mediterranean at first

[1]Nicolas, v, p. xvii, claims that Nelson hoisted his flag on 18 May, while Knight, p. 583, says he did so on 19 May; both agree on the date of sailing: 20 May 1803.
[2]William Cornwallis (1744–1819), a friend from the West Indies in the 1770s
[3]Since 1928: Sète.

induced Nelson to predict optimistically: 'I think it cannot be a long War Just enough to make me independant in pecuniary matters' [267]. His seeming strain of luck, however, was rather due to the advantage of surprise, as Nelson himself noted: 'I am much hurried for they know nothing of the war' [268]. Bad luck soon set in. Just after passing the Straits of Gibraltar Nelson complained that he would have taken an attractive prize, 'if we had proceeded direct in the Victory' [269].

On his passage to Malta, off Algiers, Nelson found time to ponder different subjects [269]. His mind wandered back to Lady Hamilton who might find his letter when 'returning from Hilborough, where my fancy tells me you are thinking of setting out'. His own current situation was not as secure so he decided to write of himself in the third person singular, particularly as he was referring to where and how he wanted to proceed: 'The Admiral does not mean to stay at Malta more than twenty-four hours'. In fact, Nelson's stay at Malta was as short as could be. The chaplain, Alexander Scott recorded in his diary of 16 June 1803: 'At half past three, I accompanied the Admiral to the house of Sir Alexander Ball . . . We returned on board just as they were beginning to illuminate the city, in honour of Lord Nelson.'[1] This time Nelson did not write to Lady Hamilton how he was feted.[2] Instead, four days later, he merely sent a note about passing Messina [270], and another five days later told her that 'it was so hot [at Malta] that I was glad to breath [*sic*] the sea air again' [271]. Off Capri, where he had stopped to let ashore Hugh Elliot,[3] the new British envoy to Naples, Nelson wrote a short letter as he did not dare 'by this conveyance' to say much more than that 'Lord Nelson' was 'very anxious to join the fleet off Toulon' [271].

Having passed Cape Corse, sailing towards his station off Toulon, Nelson's means of sending letters would most probably be by ships. As a consequence he no longer saw the danger that his letters 'would all be read'. He seized the opportunity to give Lady Hamilton an account of the situation in Naples. His valet Gaetano Spedilo, a former servant of Sir William's, had told him what had become of acquaintances of Lady Hamilton. To this account Nelson added his own pessimistic assessment

[1] [Anon.], *Recollections of the Life of the Rev. A. J. Scott, D.D. Lord Nelson's Chaplain* (London, 1842) [hereafter: Scott's *Recollections*], p. 107.

[2] For such accounts, see Docs Nos 54, 56, 142 and 166.

[3] Hugh Elliot (1752–1813), brother to Sir Gilbert Elliot, Lord Minto, whom Nelson knew well from his positions as civil governor of Toulon (in 1794) and viceroy of Corsica (1794–96) and who had helped him to get the command of the Mediterranean fleet in 1798; they met in Vienna in 1800, where the then Lord Minto was British Minister between 1799 and 1801; Nelson took his son George with him as midshipman to the Mediterranean in 1803.

of the political situation at Naples, summarizing: 'Naples will be conquered sooner or later' [272]. Although Nelson kept trying to gain support from the Queen of Naples for the pension Lady Hamilton craved [272, 328 and 340], during his time in the Mediterranean he frequently reaffirmed his assessment of the rotten state of affairs in the kingdom of Naples [274, 275, 296, 299, 323, 326–329, 339, 342, 345 and 350] and he criticised the Queen in person: 'I fear that she is a time-serving woman, and cares for no one except for those at the moment who may be useful to her' [277; similarly, 323, 327]. Even though this assessment may have been unfair, since the fragile power of the Bourbon kingdom was under constant pressure from French supremacy on land, Nelson was correct in assuming that neither naval nor personal support could be gained from Naples.

On 8 July 1803 Nelson arrived in the *Amphion* at his station off Toulon [272]. His letters were now no longer dominated by the constant change of scene, but rather the contrary: the uniformity of daily routine. He now wrote as himself, usually signing his name as 'Nelson and Bronte' or 'Nelson + Bronte' and he stuck more calmly to specific subjects. A letter written on 12, 18 and 21 July set out some of the main subjects that – apart from shifting political topics – would occupy his mind during the long blockade awaiting him: his affection for Lady Hamilton, worries about money, receiving news and enduring bad weather [273]. Nelson described the conditions that he found and had to expect during the blockade: 'We have just had a 3 days Gale but we are close off Toulon looking at them, [...] the happiness of keeping a station is always to have a foul wind and never to hear the delightful sound Steady' [273; similarly, 276, 287, 290 and more, dealt with below]. Under such unstable conditions Nelson complained that he had not 'heard the least bit of English news' that would give him some orientation and that he had 'not received one farthing of Prize Money' [273]. Nelson's main comfort was thinking of Lady Hamilton. His first letter written on his station off Toulon starts: 'My Dearest Emma, To whom can we write so readily as to those Dear friends who occupy our whole attention' [273].

After arriving off Toulon, Nelson's greatest preoccupation was for the *Victory* joining him as they were 'almost eating salt beef' [273]. When she arrived on 30 July 1803 Nelson transferred to her together with his trusted captain, Thomas Masterman Hardy. He decorated his cabin with pictures [274] and was relieved after 'two days pretty strong gales' that 'Victory is so easy at sea' [276]. Another relief was the arrival of the *Phoebe* with 'the only scrap of a Pen which has been received by any person in the fleet since we sail'd from England'. Nelson commented: 'You will readily conceive my Dear Emma the sensations which the sight and reading even your few lines [caused] they cannot be understood but by those of such mutual and truly sincere attatchment as yours and mine, although you said little I understood a great deal' [274]. Nelson continued to express his love for Lady Hamilton: 'I am ever for ever, with all my might, with all my strength, yours, only yours. My soul is God's, [...] my body is Emma's' [292; see also 271–274, 276, 281, 283, 284, 286, 287, 291–293 and 298 until the end of the year 1803 alone]. Apart from expressing emotional attachment, Nelson was also concerned with his lover's practical concerns. He arranged, for example, that those of her 'cases' with 'furniture + linen' that had been taken to Malta would be shipped home to England [293 and 288]. Apparently securing their material possessions was of considerable significance to Lady Hamilton, since Nelson admonished her: 'for a few hundred pounds you will not fret yourself' [269; similarly, 272]. His assurance betrays what she was worried about: 'whether I live or die you will be better off than ever' [269].

Lady Hamiltons's material worries, however, do not appear thoroughly unjustified, considering how much Nelson's financial resources were tied up in administering his possessions in real estate. The mortgage for his house at Merton still had to be paid [273 and 274] and Nelson still owed the previous owner, the widowed Mrs Greaves, part of the price for the house [278]. While he was keen on Lady Hamilton living at Merton, as it was cheaper than London [299], he also continually thought about what still needed to be invested in the house. His thoughts about a 'new entrance', 'the subterraneus [*sic*] passage . . . the kitchen door and windows', as well as other alterations and improvements filled many lines in his letters [292, 341 as well as 296, 306, 322, 323, 328, 337, 343, 345 and 347]. He even thought of purchasing adjoining land [296, 342 and 348]. These considerations appear to have been motivated by a desire to settle his relationship with his lover. The idea of his 'soul [being] at Merton' [287; similarly, 276, 280, 291 and 325] extended into an expectation towards Lady Hamilton: 'I would wish you, my Emma, to remain at Merton' [347]. He was generous enough to assure his lover that she should determine what would be changed [323 'as you like I am content'; similarly, 329], but he also reminded her: 'we need be great œeconimicsts [*sic*] to make both ends meet and to carry on the little improvements' [306]. These improvements, Nelson tried to convince himself and his lover, would serve as an investment into her future: 'If [. . .] Addington ever means to give You the pension it is done before this time if he does not never mind you have a good house and Land at Merton which he cannot take from you, and I do not believe the French will' [297]. Despite having made his will before leaving for the

Mediterranean, Nelson was aware, however, that he had not yet been able to provide sufficiently for Lady Hamilton to be able to maintain the house at Merton and her lifestyle in general in the event of his death. He therefore, on 9 February 1804, left her a pension out of the 'Rental of my Estate at Bronte' [303; also: 306]. This provision was made to calm his conscience rather than to provide for Lady Hamilton's needs, since his estate at Bronte was in fact an additional strain on his finances [269, 272, 275, 276, 278, 280, 287, 290, 293, 306, 324, 329, 339, 340, 342 and 345]. As late as November 1804 he had to accept that 'I shall get nothing from Bronte . . . till 8 years are expired' [350].[1]

Apart from future prospects of income, present separation appears to have been on Lady Hamilton's mind. To this worry, common to naval wives,[2] Nelson responded in different ways. He expressed his 'love and affection' to her, his 'wife in the eye of God' [284], for: 'my love for you is as unbounded as the ocean' [283; see also above]. In order to make their separation more bearable to her he tried to reconcile the conflict between fulfilling his duty and being with his lover by claiming that all his 'honors reflect on you' [284, similarly 291 'are you not a sharer of my glory', 293]. Lady Hamilton would have to stay content as sharer in Nelson's fame, since he continued destroying her letters, apparently leaving only a rather insignificant note and a love poem [279 and 357], thus depriving posterity to judge her by her letters to him. After arriving at his station off Toulon, Nelson jokingly remarked: 'I have not a thought except on you and the French fleet – all my thoughts, plans, and toils tend to those two objects, and I will embrace them both so close when I can lay hold of either one or the other, that the devil himself should not separate us' [276]. Such an approach to the problem was not always appropriate to the strength of Lady Hamilton's feelings. In his letter of 18 October 1803 Nelson appealed to his lover that she should let 'reason have fair play' in order to understand that 'absence to us is equally painful' [293; similarly, 291 and 292].

For Nelson, absence from home did not only mean absence from Lady Hamilton, but also absence from their daughter Horatia. She appears to have been nearly as much on his mind as Lady Hamilton. Throughout his absence at sea he sent kisses to her in his letters to Lady Hamilton [262, 307, 308, 310, 320, 324, 327–329, 331, 332, 342, 343, 348, 354, 357, 370, 371, 373 and 377 'my angel Horatia'] and he wished to be with

[1]See also: Jane Knight, 'Nelson and the Bronte Estate' (*Trafalgar Chronicle*, vol. 15, 2005, 133–44, at 138), who quotes from a letter by Gibbs to Nelson of 30 July 1803 (NMM CRK/17/30) that no regular income was to be expected in the near future from the estate.

[2]Margarette Lincoln, *Naval Wives & Mistresses* (London, 2007), pp. 100–105.

her: 'she must be grown very much how I long to hear her prattle' [297; similarly, 296]. On 6 September 1803 he left the 'Sum of Four Thousand Pounds Sterling Money of Great Britain' in a codicil to his will to her, 'who I acknowledge as my adopted Daughter'. In this codicil he also settled that until her eighteenth birthday the interest on the bequest would 'be paid to Lady Hamilton for her Education and maintenance' [285]. Until October 1804 he kept appealing to Lady Hamilton to take Horatia to Merton [286, 293, 324, 328, 329, 336, 343 and 347]. He repeatedly told her to take care that Horatia might not fall into a pond or brook on his grounds [306 and 323]. Nelson's concerns appear to have clashed with the difficulty of wringing Horatia from the hands of her nurse, Mrs Gibson. Nelson wrote to Lady Hamilton: 'you may if you like tell Mrs: G.[1] that I shall certainly settle a small pension on her' [310]. On 13 August 1804 Nelson was insisting on the well-being of his daughter: 'She is become of that age when it is necessary to remove her from a mere nurse and to think of educating her' [336]. Two weeks later, about a year after he had settled this bequest to his daughter, he informed Lady Hamilton rather bluntly: 'the moment I get home I shall put it out of your power to spend dear Horatias money I shall settle it in trustees hands and leave nothing to chance' [339].

Nelson expected Lady Hamilton not only to have Horatia separated from her nurse and thus possibly attracting attention to herself as her possible mother, but also to deal with unpleasant things that he himself had not taken or would not take upon himself to arrange or execute. One of these was ensuring that Horatia was inoculated against smallpox. Nelson had already suggested the vaccination when in the Baltic and in the Channel in 1801, putting the consequences into perspective: 'the child is only feverish for 2 days, and only a slight inflammation of the arm takes place instead of being all over scabs' [155 and 185]. Nelson himself had apparently not arranged anything himself during his time ashore. Now receiving the mere account of the consequences caused him a nightmare: 'I wish I had all the small-pox for her, but I know the fever is the natural consequence. I dreamt last night I heard her call papa, and point to her arm just as you described' [335]. Another unpleasant task that Nelson expected Lady Hamilton to perform was being strict to their daughter: 'she is like her mother will have her own way or kick up a devil of a dust, but you will cure her, I am afraid I should spoil her' [293]. Among the educational 'cures' that Nelson apparently regarded as necessary was to threaten withdrawal of love in case of disobedience. He thus expected

[1]Gibson.

Lady Hamilton to 'kiss dear Horatia for me and tell her to be a dutiful + good child and if she is that we shall always love her' [310; similarly, 300 and 301]. The belief in the necessity of punishment was probably common at the time and it was clearly part of Nelson's naval set of values, since he said about a sailor who had been a 'bad boy' that 'good floggings I hope will save him from the gallows' [323; similarly, 300].

Despite this, Nelson saw himself as a caring parent. Apart from his worries about his daughter's safety at Merton he sent her presents from the Mediterranean: a watch [293, 296, 300 and 301] and some books of Spanish dresses [314]. He also tried to establish a link with her through the writing of letters [294, 301 and 314], although the first of these was probably more meant to be read later, since at the time Horatia was only two years of age and it dealt with what he had settled on her in the codicil to his will [294]. In order to secure financial means for her future, Nelson even hoped to limit his own influence on what he had settled on her: 'our dear H[a]: how I long to settle what I intend upon her and not leave her to the mercy of any one or even to any foolish thing I may do in my old age' [365].

Nelson's insecurity was less about his own old age than about what was currently going on. On 26 August 1803, more than three months after leaving England, he noted with relief: 'I have received all your truly kind and affectionate letters from May 20th: to July 3rd: (with the exception of one dated May 31st: sent to Naples)[1] this is the first communication I have had with England since we sail'd' [283]. Nelson continued complaining for some time: 'I never hear from England' [290; similarly, 291 and 293]. In the course of the blockade he had to maintain, he appears to have got used to slow and varying flows of information from Britain. On 2 October 1804 he reported about receiving a letter from Lady Hamilton 'of July 1st, it having travelled in a Spanish smuggling boat to the coast of Italy and returned again to Spain, the boat not having met any of our ships' [344]. Since news from Britain did not arrive regularly and reliably, Nelson had to make his own efforts in order to secure information. One source of information were French papers, which he took some trouble to secure. In August 1804 he wrote: 'the Childers is going to Roses[2] to get us some news from Paris which is the only way I know of what is passing in England' [333; similarly, 274, 278, 290, 327 and 331].[3] The *Victory*'s polyglot chaplain, Alexander Scott, whom Nelson

[1]See Doc. No. 274: 'the only scrap of a Pen which has been received by any person in the fleet since we sail'd'.

[2]Port town on the Catalan coast near the French border.

[3]See also Knight, p. 451.

usually referred to as 'Doctor Scott'[1] in order to distinguish him from his secretary, John Scott,[2] then had to 'wade through numberless ephemeral foreign pamphlets . . . encumbering rubbish', since 'nothing was too trivial for the attention of this great man's mind, when there existed a possibility of its being the means of obtaining information'.[3] Lady Hamilton, too, understood the importance of information, for example when she 'very much obliged' John Scott by writing to Nelson the 'news of M^{rs}: S^{ts}: being brought to bed' [299].

Apart from maintaining a flow of information, Lady Hamilton also participated in the exertion of patronage. This could be through asking favours for her friends, on which Nelson optimistically commented: 'I shall you know always feel too happy in obeying your commands for you never ask favors but for your friends in short in every point of view from Ambassatrice[4] to the duties of domestic life I never saw your equal, that Elegance of manners accomplishments and above all your goodness of heart is unparalleled' [281]. Lady Hamilton may also have had a hand in placing some old Neapolitan acquaintance under Nelson's care: Sir William's old valet, Gaetano Spedilo [267–269, 272, 287, 291, 299, 324, 340 and 363][5] and Faddy [280, 295, 306 and 339], whom Lady Hamilton had already recommended to Nelson's care in 1798, when she referred to him as 'my dear little fatherless Fady' [17; similarly, 13] and who managed to advance in his career in the navy [339]. Some attempts to secure patronage for Lady Hamilton did not turn out to be such happy undertakings. A Mrs Voller, who had 'shown uniform kindness' to Lady Hamilton, had sent out her son, about whom Nelson remarked: 'what can I do for a child who has never been at sea?' [334]. Supporting Lady Hamilton's relative, Charles Connor, turned out to be even more difficult. After encouraging reports that he 'behaves well' [270; similarly, 271, 278 and 298], at the end of the year 1803 Nelson gave a first indication of a traumatic reaction: 'He had about three months ago, something wrong in his head. The killing a Lieutenant and some men belonging to the Phoebe, made such an impression, that he fancied he saw a ghost, &c. but Dr. Snipe[6] thinks it is gone off. Was any of his family in that

[1]Although he received his doctorate only after the Battle of Trafalgar; see: Scott's *Recollections*, p. 123.

[2]John Scott, Nelson's secretary 1803–5, killed at the Battle of Trafalgar.

[3]Scott's *Recollections*, p. 120–21.

[4]Italian for 'ambassadress'. On marrying Sir William Hamilton Lady Hamilton was not allowed to use the English title.

[5]'Gaetano Spedillo' was registered as supernumerary onboard *Victory* (Knight, p. 617).

[6]Dr John Snipe (d. 1805); physician of the fleet in 1803–5.

way?' [298]. Throughout the first half of 1804 Nelson continued asserting that there was 'something very odd about him' [316] and that he had 'a kind of silly laugh when spoken to' [323]. Although in June 1804 he seemed 'very much recovered' [325; similarly 327], the joint efforts of captains Capel, Hillyar[1] and Hardy in the second half of the year 1804 [334, 342 and 357] could not quite compensate for Charles' lack of ability: 'he was rated Midshipman, and forced by Captain Hillyar to study, which he was not very fond of' [357].

Patronage invested in members of Nelson's extended family could turn out similarly disappointingly. Young William Suckling[2] had to be looked after by getting him a new uniform made [295], by arranging him to be in a frigate 'with a very good man who has a school master' [299] and by seeing that he wrote home [340: 'William says he has wrote twice I suppose he thinks that enough']. Nelson encountered grown-up problems with Sir William Bolton, the nephew of his brother-in-law, Thomas Bolton.[3] Lieutenant Bolton was given the command of the *Childers* sloop and Nelson was at first prepared to attribute his inability to make any prize money to bad luck [299], continued to try to use his influence for his advancement [334, 342, 345 and 357] and kept charging him with special tasks in order to give him opportunities to take prizes [326, 349 and 353]. In 1805, however, Nelson got annoyed at Bolton's inability to join him, cursing his 'lethargic disposition' [361]. While waiting for him, he judged him as too 'lazy' to take any prizes and he complained: 'he has no activity' [364]. Nelson got very impatient, when 'that goose Sir William Bolton' was so much delayed that Nelson had to appoint somebody else to the frigate *Amphitrite* [365].

Although Nelson may have allowed himself in his letters to Lady Hamilton to pass a quick and perhaps unfair judgement on William Bolton, his assessments of his subordinates were generally positive. He repeatedly praised those he most closely cooperated with: Captain Hardy [293, 297, 334 and 343], his secretary John Scott [273, 287, 293 and 343] and Reverend Alexander Scott [297, 340 and 355 'my friend']. He also acknowledged men from the lower ranks and even threw a midshipmen's party [297]. At such events, Dr Scott observed that 'Lord Nelson

[1]James Hillyar (1769–1843).

[2]William Benjamin Suckling, went out to the Mediterranean in 1803 with Nelson on board *Amphion* and transferred with him to *Victory* on 30 July 1803 (Knight, p. 617); in January 1804 Nelson 'put Suckling into a frigate with a very good man who has a school master' (Doc. No. 299); in early March 1805, he wrote: 'I have got Suckling placed in the Ambuscade, with Captain Durban' (Doc. No. 361).

[3]A biographical sketch of Sir William Bolton can be found in Knight, p. 614.

was constantly studying the characters of those whom he had about him, and would lead them into discussions in which he afterwards took no part, for the mere purpose of drawing out their thoughts and opinions'.[1] He clearly had the well-being of all men in the fleet at heart and he proudly reported that the ship and even the whole fleet were 'kept in the most perfect state of health' [306 and 349]. Generally he was pleased to find: 'we all draw so well together in the fleet' [343].

Drawing together was useful, if not necessary, since the nearest British base was 'that out of the way place' Malta [290; similarly, 276, 287, 293 and 343]. Malta was not only too far away from Nelson's station off Toulon to be of much use for supplying the fleet, 'it became a short-term liability, for the island could not feed itself'.[2] As this became clear, Nelson was starting to complain about Ball, who 'appears to forget that he was a seaman, he is bit with the dignity of the Corps Diplomatique', 'and even an ad^{l}: must not know what he is negotiating about' [276 and 293]. Whatever the reason for these disparaging comments, Nelson did not make any comparable remarks after October 1803. In October 1804 he even wrote: 'Your Brother Ball desires to be remembered to his Sister Emma' [345], referring to the fact that both, Alexander Ball and Lady Hamilton, had received the Maltese Order of St John. Nelson thus alluded to the relationship that the three – Ball, Nelson and Lady Hamilton – had cultivated in the Mediterranean in 1799 when they maintained a three-sided correspondence [27, 36 and 39].[3]

Mistrust of diplomatic activities appears also to have affected Nelson's relationship to the British envoy at Naples, Hugh Elliot. He remarked sarcastically to Lady Hamilton: 'M^{r}: Elliot who knows more of Naples than any of us' [293]. If Nelson felt annoyed by diplomatic activities, this was probably also due to the fact that he himself preferred to correspond directly with important actors on the Mediterranean scene, rather than through an envoy, governor or other person not answerable to himself. Thus, Nelson deliberately bypassed Hugh Elliot: 'I believe M^{r}: E. had rather that Acton + the King + Queen looked to him for my services than applying to myself, but circumstanced as I have been and am with that Court Sir William Hamilton gave it up and no other person shall deprive me of the immediate communication, No my dear Emma what I do for them shall be from myself and not through him' [300].

Nelson's own diplomatic efforts were mostly conducted in writing, but at the beginning of 1804 he decided to intervene in a delicate issue.

[1] Scott's *Recollections*, pp. 123–4.
[2] Knight, p. 464.
[3] See also the introduction to Chapter I.

The Dey of Algiers had expelled the British envoy, John Falcon, charging him with having received 'Moorish women into his house'.[1] On 9 January 1804 Nelson sent Captain Keats[2] with *Victory*'s trusted chaplain, Alexander Scott [299], and a set of dispatches to Algiers.[3] About a week later he followed himself. When he arrived off Algiers on 17 January, he approved of Keats' conduct and maintained that he would not give up an iota of my original modest demand'.[4] As he had to acknowledge his own inability to waste effort on such a relatively minor issue he concluded: 'nothing I suppose but a flogging will put him in order, and with the French fleet ready to put to sea that I have not time for' [300].

Focusing time and energy on the French fleet at Toulon was enough to drain his resources. A recurring theme in Nelson's letters to Lady Hamilton was the wearisome harsh weather conditions: 'one day precisely like the other except the difference of a gale of wind or not . . . and if the french do not come out soon I fear some of my ships will cry out' [293; similarly: 297, 298, 302 'snow storm', 305 and 307]. At the end of December 1803 the weather was so bad, that the fleet had to sail to the archipelago of La Maddalena on the north-eastern coast of Sardinia for unloading [298]. The sound between the archipelago and the Sardinian mainland, called Agincourt Sound by the British, was to become an important winter station and victualling base.[5] In February 1804, with the winter not yet over, indications increased that the French fleet was preparing to move. Nelson reported to Lady Hamilton: 'so many troops are prepared for embarkation and a general Embargo at Genoa Leghorn + reports say at Civita Vecchia and the Ships seized for transports . . . We saw the French fleet in Toulon on the 22nd: perfectly ready, I have heard very lately from Naples the French army is ready for Service and have baked a months bread for their army, The Stroke is ready, where will it fall, but this fleet is prepared for all events and for our numbers it cannot [be equ]alled, our only wish is to meet [the]m' [304]. During the following weeks Nelson continued to hope that the French fleet would come out [306–309]. It finally left Toulon on 5 April 1804, but 'in the evening they stood inshore again' and 'went in again the next morning' [312 and 313; see also 324]. Without any specific indication of a positive French move, Nelson had to resort to mere hoping: 'My only wish is for the coming out of the French fleet to finish all my uneasinesses' [318].

[1]Nicolas, v, p. 348.
[2]Sir Richard Goodwin Keats (1757–1834).
[3]Nicolas, v, pp. 345–51.
[4]Nicolas, v, pp. 376–7.
[5]Knight, pp. 460–61.

Such preoccupations about naval developments in early 1804 were accompanied by private worries. As Lady Hamilton was expecting to give birth, Nelson was 'anxious in the extreme' about her 'recovery' [305; similarly, 304 and 306–308]. Only in one letter did he become explicit as to what Lady Hamilton would have to recover from: 'call him what you please if a girl Emma' [307]. The suspense was released, but Nelson 'upset' when he had to learn 'that you was recovering but that dear little Emma was no more' [310; similarly, 313]. In the period of suspenseful expectation Nelson had in some cases returned to referring to himself and to Lady Hamilton as 'the admiral' and 'Mrs. T.' [302, 304 and 305].[1] This indicates that Nelson again worried about the insecure means of conveying their correspondence. More gravely, he had to respond to an example of Lady Hamilton's jealousy. At the height of her pregnancy Nelson was annoyed: 'with respect to the lady, *my* friend at Gib^r^. I cannot barely guess what you mean' [308]. Lady Hamilton appears to have again attempted to make Nelson jealous by teasing him with how she was admired by other men,[2] to which Nelson coolly reacted: 'I am dull of comprehension believing you all my own' [323]. Usually, however, receiving letters from Lady Hamilton provoked Nelson to even more intense declarations of love, such as: 'Dear wife, good, adorable friend, how I love you, and what would I not give to be with you this moment, for I am for ever all yours' [335; similarly until the end of the year 1804: 299, 302, 304, 308, 310, 313, 315, 318, 319, 321, 322, 328, 332, 334, 335, 339, 341, 343, 345–349, 352–354 and 356).

Worries about gaps in the flow of information were reinforced in April 1804, when the *Swift* cutter was taken by a French privateer on its way to the British Mediterranean fleet. Nelson's anger about sending dispatches and letters 'in a vessel with 23 men not equal to cope with any row boat privateer' was mixed with anxiety about a possible publication [315 and 321]. He learned that the French consul was 'bragging' about pictures of Lady Hamilton [323; similarly 321] and defiantly declared his love of Lady Hamilton: 'Read that whoever opens this letter and for what I care publish it to the world' [321; similarly, 346 and 356]. However Nelson handled the possibility of their liaison being published, his concern was based on a misconception of the workings of French politics. Without reading the dispatches or examining their contents, the French consul had sent on the letters to the Minister of the Navy, Decrès. Decrès had

[1]For earlier examples since leaving England in May 1803, see Docs Nos 267, 269, 270, 271 and 275; another later example can be found in Doc. No. 353 of 23 Nov 1804.

[2]For earlier attempts to make Nelson jealous, see introduction to Chapter II and Doc. No. 86.

deemed them so important that he had merely ordered them to be collected at the post office and passed from there directly to the office of the First Consul, Napoleon Bonaparte. What Napoleon made of them remains unknown, but lacking in parliamentary control, let alone a public discourse on government policies, he clearly did not see any need to publish diplomatic details that might induce French citizens to form their own opinions.[1]

Even though the contents of the letters lost in the *Swift* do not appear to have been used against Nelson in particular or the British in general, the loss of part of the correspondence aroused Nelson's concern. Nelson had to repeat questions as he assumed 'the answers came out in the Swift' [322]. The risk of further losses caused Nelson to start listing the letters he had sent [particularly in 328 and 331; see appendix 7 for this new practice, starting in May 1804] and to mention how he had sent them. His various lists and references lacked bureaucratic precision, however, as he referred to the letters he had written in different categories. One obvious category was by date. But Nelson sometimes varied his use of a letter's date between the date it was written and the date it was sent, as in: 'I wrote you my dearest Emma on the 8th: a letter dated June 27th:' [332; similarly, 328 and 346 refer to the date of sending rather than of composition, but without saying so]. In other cases Nelson referred to places through which he had sent letters. This kind of reference was sometimes complicated, when letters passed through several places, as a letter 'to Madrid' that he later referred to has having gone 'by Barcelona' [320, 328 and 331]. In compiling lists of his letters to Lady Hamilton he sometimes grouped letters by the places he had sent them through, but in doing so confused the exact places. For example, of Doc. No. 307 which he had planned to send via Gibraltar, he later claimed that it was sent 'safe thro' Spain' [308], 'by Gibraltar' [328] and 'by Barcelona' [331].[2] Some place-names were virtually interchangeable with a person's name, so that letters that went via Roses (or Rosas) could also be referred to as having passed through 'friend Gayner['s]'[3] hands [297, 306, 308, 313, 322, 324, 325, 328, 329 and 337] and those via Naples through the hands of the French banker Falconet[4] [331 and 356–358]. Similarly Nelson did not follow a strict system as to whether to refer to names of

[1]For a detailed analysis of what the French did with the captured documents, see Appendix 6.

[2]See Appendix 7.

[3]Edward Gayner (1764–1846); Nelson describes him in Doc. No. 297 as 'an honest Quaker who lives at Roses in Spain'.

[4]Knight, p. 636, describes him as a French 'Merchant in Naples and banker in partnership with Abraham Gibbs until the later moved to Sicily' in June 1803; see also Doc. No. 329.

captains carrying letters or the names of their ships [ships' names can be found in 298, 306, 313, 324, 328, 333, 337, 339, 342 and 356; and captains' names in 292, 312, 315, 317, 318 and 328]. The decision to send a letter by a certain means, as his announcement on 27 August 1804 that 'this goes by Triumph' [339], must not be confused with the letter actually being sent, as Nelson only wrote on 22 September: 'I can no longer defer sending off my dispatches to catch the Triumph at Gibraltar' [342].[1] Although it is at times difficult to assign letters listed by Nelson to specific documents, these lists mostly served a more general purpose, which was to convey the message: 'you must only rely my own Emma that I omit no opportunity of writing' [332].

The fact that the link between Nelson and Lady Hamilton depended entirely on letters that arrived irregularly if at all also affects the contents of their exchange in writing. Even if letters arrived fairly quickly, it was difficult to respond and exchange thoughts or ideas. For example, Nelson had received letters from her on 10 May 1804 up to '5 April' [325], to which he only replied on 27 May 1804 by asking: 'I do not understand what you mean or what plan' [323]. This question, which he appears to have sent at the end of the month,[2] thus may have reached Lady Hamilton about two months after her having mentioned the plans to which Nelson was now referring. Even if she then understood what he was referring to and if she actually answered it, Nelson did not take up the subject again. Instead of communicating via post in any meaningful way, their correspondence consisted more of a monologue for an imagined reader. When Nelson was not writing about his own situation, he dealt with a variety of subjects that linked him to home, such as family, friends, material needs and politics. As Nelson put it: 'I can only touch hastily upon several subjects' [345]. He thus wrote about the mistress his brother Maurice had left behind on this death, settled a bequest for 'poor blind Mrs Nelson' [310 and codicil in 311] and referred to passing on money to 'poor Mrs. Bolton' [330]. In other letters he gave his opinion about joint acquaintances [for example, in 293 and 310] or passed on regards to Lady Hamilton from someone in his fleet [331 and 343; from Admiral Campbell][3]. Only on rare occasions did he actually react to what she had written and then rather curtly: 'I am glad that You have had so pleasant a trip into Norfolk' [350].

[1]For another example of a confusing use of present tense, see Nelson's announcement on 7 April 1804 of sending a letter with Captain William Layman (1768–1826) and Layman's actual leaving on 14 April 1804 (Docs Nos 312 and 328).

[2]See Appendix 7.

[3]Sir George Campbell (1759–1821).

The only way of adding to letters was to send presents. This became even more complicated than some of the difficulties they encountered in sending letters. For example, Lady Hamilton sent a box on 18 May 1804 and repeatedly asked about its arrival. After several disappointing replies from Nelson [333, 334 and 341], he could confirm the box's arrival only a year later [361]. This bad experience, however, did not discourage Nelson from sending presents to his lover and child. Naturally he avoided sending anything that could decay; an attempt by Macaulay in Malta to treat Nelson with some milk by sending him a sheep failed: 'unfortunately they get dry before they arrive' (297). Consequently, Nelson treated his and Lady Hamilton's daughter to a watch [300] and sent his lover 'Chains + Earings + Bracelets' [297; similarly: 287], a comb, gloves and a muff [300, 307, 337], Palermo silk [339], Spanish dresses, Naples shawls and 'Armoisins' [342], wine [299 and 317], honey [315] and at least one 'case of macaroni' [324, announcing a second; the first was mentioned before in 310] or simply money [330].

Lady Hamilton's financial situation was a recurrent theme in Nelson's letters. For a woman in her position there were no other respectable means of achieving income than through male benefactors. Lady Hamilton at one time was hoping for a legacy from the Duke of Queensberry; following her request, Nelson wrote to the old duke, but distanced himself from the morality of the venture: 'I like the Duke + hope he will leave you some money but for myself I can have no right to expect a farthing nor would I be a legacy hunter for the world I never knew any good come from it' [310]. By contrast, Nelson vigorously supported Lady Hamilton's claim to a pension in her own right, although he was aware that it would be difficult to achieve. As first he offered to solace: 'never mind you have a good house and Land at Merton' [297], but he realised about a month later: 'I wish M^{r}: Addington [the then prime minister] would give you 500 £ a year then you would be better able to give away than at present' [299]. Consequently, on 19 February 1804, he bequeathed some (probably rather fanciful) income from his estates in Brontë to her [303; see 306 about the compensatory purpose of the bequest]. Probably being aware that this bequest would be insufficient, he continued supporting his lover's claim to a pension by writing about the issue to Acton, the 'prime minister' of Naples, [322] and the Queen of Naples herself [328], asking her to write to the new Prime Minister, Pitt, although he doubted 'her constancy of real friendship to you' [329] and concluded: 'I wish M^{r}: Ad^{n}: had given you the pension. P[i]tt + hard hearted Grenville never will' [323, similarly: 328 'all their promises are pie-crusts, made to be broken' and 350].

Seeing that the hoped-for state pension would not be forthcoming and his bequests to Lady Hamilton would not be sufficient to support her financially, he began to urge her not to spend too much money. At first, he merely wrote that both of them would have to be careful not to spend too much, reminding them both to be 'œconimicists' [306] and stating: 'we shall do very well with prudence' [328; similarly, 329 and 339]. By the end of August 1804, however, it became apparent that Sir William Hamilton's nephew (and former lover of Lady Hamilton), Charles Greville, in executing Sir William's will, interpreted the husband's bequest to his wife in such a way that income tax had to be deducted from the amount. Nelson commented on this transaction: 'M^{r}: Greville is a shabby fellow it never could have been the intention of Sir William but that you should have had 700 £ a year Net money for when he made the will the income Tax was double to what it is at present, and the estates which it is paid from is increasing every year in value it may be law but it is not just nor in equity would I believe be considered as the will and intention of Sir William' [340]. Nelson tried to calm Lady Hamilton's worries by reminding her of the £ 500 he had settled on her in the third codicil to his will [339 and 350, referring to 303]. He then went on to cloak his admonition of frugality with praise of her generosity [345: 'if you have a fault it is that you give away much more than you can afford']. Eventually, on 13 October 1804, he bluntly stated: 'You give away too much' [348]. As it became apparent that all their attempts to secure a pension for Lady Hamilton had failed, Nelson realised that demanding a frugal lifestyle alone would not do and, in December 1804, settled in a fifth codicil another bequest (of £ 2,000) on his lover [355].

Notwithstanding his doubts as to Lady Hamilton's ability to manage her personal finances, Nelson relied upon her ability to represent his interests in England. He frequently asked her to arrange matters for him, be it passing on a letter [289], organising a present [325], passing on information [337] or communicating with his lawyer [278] and even with Melville,[1] now First Lord of the Admiralty, [356] and Addington, then Prime Minister [326]. When a quarrel between his agents and at one time also with his lawyer broke out [282, 322, 338 and 339], he not only referred the matter to her, but entrusted her with informing the quarrelling parties that he could not answer their letters [348]. Even in matters in which she would not be able to play an active part, Nelson kept her informed. Much as her opinion mattered to him, Nelson did not easily change his own view, when Lady Hamilton found fault in someone.

[1]Henry Dundas, Viscount Melville (1742–1811).

Nelson had, for example, clearly supported Hamond in his conflict with St Vincent [293]. This did not prevent Lady Hamilton from criticising Hamond for some unkindness, but only to learn that Nelson defended him [340], an embarrassment which made her try to delete Hamond's name from the letter.[1] Equally, Nelson was not prepared to criticise St Vincent, apparently unlike Lady Hamilton, whom he reminded: 'Your disposition is too generous to insult a fallen man, . . . and I am sure nine-tenths of those who now abuse the Earl and Troubridge were, and would be again, their most abject flatterers were they again in office – for me, I feel myself above them in every way, and they are below my abuse of them' [342]. As a loyal supporter of government, he was annoyed at Lord Moira[2] having used Nelson's proxy vote in the Lords against Addington [338 and 344]. More generally, however, he felt that a 'change of Ministry can do us no harm' [328; similarly, 341].

Nelson's worries evolved around his situation in the Mediterranean, politically as well as personally. Having noticed that 'the French have no trade'[3] Nelson became resigned to the fact that 'Prize Money does not seem my lot' [273; similarly, 272, 278, 293, 306 and 361]. He complained that the little prize money he made merely covered his expenses [310 and 329] and that the Admiralty deprived him of any possible chances to make any by appointing Sir John Orde to command a squadron off Cadiz [354 and 362]. Nelson had already assessed the situation correctly in January 1804: 'unless we have a Spanish war I shall live here at a great expence' [299]. The question now was whether he would maintain his command long enough.

The weather conditions were draining Nelson's energy. In April 1804, when spring might have brought relief from the harsh winter conditions, he remarked: 'I never saw such a continuation of bad weather' [316]. 'Gales of wind' continued through the following months and made Nelson comment: 'we have had no summer here' [331; see also 326, 327, 329, 333, 337, 343 and 347]. These harsh conditions were also mentally exhausting. Nelson repeatedly complained about monotony on board: 'here I am one day precisely like the other except the difference of a gale of wind or not . . . our days pass so much alike that having described one you have them all', 'the same faces, and almost the same conversation' [293 and 331; similarly, 324 and 327].[4] Not surprisingly Nelson's health

[1]See note to Hamond's name in Doc. No. 340.

[2]Francis Rawdon Hastings, 2nd Earl of Moira (1754–1826), general to whom Nelson gave his proxy in the House of Lords.

[3]Knight, p. 460.

[4]For the effects of the monotony on the crews, see Knight, p. 475.

suffered. Complaints about colds, fever, spasms, coughs, head-aches, 'pains in my breast' and rather vague diagnoses, such as 'my health is so so' [313], are recurrent themes in his letters [269, 298, 300, 305, 309, 318, 320, 324, 326, 328, 329, 331, 343, 350, 351, 353, 356 and 357].

As a result of his continuing bad health Nelson considered applying for leave, but hesitated, because he did not want to give up his command [332]. After another month of bad weather, he eventually wrote, on 15 August 1804, to the Admiralty applying for leave.[1] Although he had suggested that a winter's rest in England would restore his health, he doubted that he would get back the Mediterranean command, adding: 'The more likelihood of a Spanish war, the less chance for me' [338]. Meanwhile, the Neapolitan court urged him to stay in the Mediterranean [345] and Nelson repeatedly doubted the wisdom of leaving his command at a time when there were 'strong indications of a Spanish war' [348]. As Nelson waited for 'permission or refusal for my return to England' [349 and 351], he started to worry: 'I should not much like to arrive in the very depth of Winter I hardly think my shattered constitution would stand such a shock' and that at a time, when 'I am now for the first time in my life likely to pick up some Money' [352; similarly 353]. As it turned out, Admiral Campbell was forced to leave the fleet on account of bad health before Nelson [354] and it was only at the very end of the year 1804 that Nelson finally 'received the Admiralty's permission to go to England for the re-establishment of my health' [357, of 30 December]. The news rather than relieving him of his doubts, increased them: 'I shall most likely never serve again. The winter has been quite different to the last. We have not had a cold day, nor near so many gales of wind, but my cough is very troublesome, particularly from two in the morning until I have had my breakfast; but a little of your good nursing will set me up again', but he would be allowed some time to decide: 'The going home of George Campbell has protracted my departure till another Admiral comes out, which may very well be in January, then unless the French fleet is actually at sea, nothing will keep me two hours' [357].

The delay in being able to return home resulted in Nelson's being in the Mediterranean, when the political situation was about to change. Throughout the year 1804 Nelson had followed what had been going on in France, observing political instability [320], assessing 'what a capricious nation those French must be' [325] and hoping that the French fleet would leave Toulon [332]. At the same time he had (rightly) dedicated much more time to observing the fragile situation in Spain. As

[1] Nicolas, vi, p. 157.

early as 26 September 1803 he sensed 'that we are almost shut out from Spain for they begin to be very uncivil to our ships' [290]. In March 1804 he suspected that the Spanish fleet would join the French [307] and generally worried at the time that it was 'very uncertain how we stand with Spain' [309]. In October 1804 Nelson registered 'strong indications of a Spanish War' [348], which he felt confirmed a month later: 'My last letters having been sent back from Roses not suffered to be landed assures me that we are at War with Spain' [352; similarly, 353]. The situation had become so tense by November that Nelson did not even mention to Lady Hamilton, when Spain formally declared war on Britain on 12 December 1804.

War with Spain did not only carry the prospect of prize money, but also the likelihood of joint Franco-Spanish operations. On 19 January 1805, when Nelson lay with his fleet in the protected Agincourt Sound in the north of Sardinia, he learned that the French fleet had left Toulon. As his task was to protect British allies and trading routes in the Mediterranean, Nelson immediately set sail towards the south-east, passing the Straits of Messina on 31 January and reaching Alexandria a week later. Not having encountered the French fleet, he return west. On 18 and 20 February, as he was passing Malta, he wrote a letter to Lady Hamilton that reflects the strain he remained under. Although he still did not know where the French fleet had gone, he rightly suspected that 'they got crippled, and returned to Toulon, for they were not used to encounter a Gulf of Lyons gale, which we have been in the practice of for these twenty months past', a view which was confirmed when he was off Malta. From now on Nelson had to expect another attempt by the French fleet to leave port. He was torn between returning to England and maintaining on station, determined: 'but it shall never be said of me, as it has been of another Commander-in-chief, that I gave up the command, when the enemy's fleet was actually at sea' [360].

For the next two months, until 19 April, Nelson cruised with his fleet between Sardinia, Corsica, Toulon, Majorca and Sicily.[1] During this period the subjects he covered in his letters to Lady Hamilton started to narrow to naval matters and his love for her. At first, he still dealt with health issues and kitchen arrangements [361 and 362], but then he returned to expressions of love and affection that he had not used for months in his letters to his lover, as on 16 March 1805: 'The Ship is just parting and I take the last moment to renew my assurances to My Dearest beloved Emma of my eternal love affection and adoration, you

[1]For details, see Knight, pp. 482–6 with map on pp. 484–5, 584.

are ever with me in my Soul, your resemblance is never absent from my mind, and my own dearest Emma I hope very soon that I shall embrace the substantial part of you instead of the Ideal, that will I am sure give us both real pleasure and exquisite happiness' [363; similarly, 358 and 360–366]. Knowing that the French fleet was 'ready for Sea and the Troops embarked and I am in momentary hopes of their putting to Sea' [362], Nelson continued covering the different areas of the western Mediterranean that they might aim for.

On 19 April, when off the coast of Sicily, Nelson learned that the French fleet had again left Toulon, heading westwards. As the French had sailed on 30 March they were twenty days ahead of Nelson, who immediately made sail for Gibraltar. On his arrival in Tetuan, on 3 May 1805, he learned that the French had passed through the Straits, that is, outside the sphere of his command. Consequently, Nelson felt 'very very unwell, after a two years hard fag it has been mortifying the not being able to get at the Enemy' [368]. Having decided that the Mediterranean was not under immediate threat and having victualled his ships, Nelson ventured out into the Atlantic, hoping to 'get hold of the French fleet' [369]. Suspense was not only mounting for Nelson. Lady Hamilton was desperately trying to get information about his whereabouts. William Marsden,[1] the Secretary to the Admiralty, wrote to Nelson on 17 April 1805: 'Even to Lady H's repeated enquiries I thought myself obliged to give obscure answers'.[2] Thus starved of information, Lady Hamilton reproached Nelson for not having used all possible channels to send letters to her. Nelson's defence against these allegations punctuated his letters to her during this period [362, 367 and 371], but did not affect the intensity and frequency of his expressions of affection and love [368, 369, 371, 374, 377, 378 and 380].

Having learned that the French fleet was heading for the West Indies, Nelson decided to follow. Considering how much the ships had been exposed to harsh conditions and how badly 'St Vincent's ill-judged and savage attempts at reform' had endangered 'efficiency, sailing performance and, in some cases, safety',[3] his crossing of the Atlantic was amazingly quick. During the 24 days (instead of the 34 the Franco-Spanish fleet needed)[4] Nelson had time enough to ponder his personal situation. In mid-Atlantic he penned down his thoughts on his daughter's future,

[1]William Marsden (1754–1836) was second secretary to the Admiralty since 1795 and succeeded Evan Nepean (1751–1822) in 1804 as secretary to the Admiralty.

[2]Knight, p. 482.

[3]Knight, p. 481.

[4]Ernle Bradford, *Nelson. The Essential Hero* (London, 1979), p. 318.

financially securing her as well as determining her education by Lady Hamilton, rather than a nurse [372 and 373]. While in-fighting at home had resulted in a change at the head of the Admiralty from Melville to Middleton, now Lord Barham,[1] Nelson chased the French fleet that had been joined by the Spanish squadron at Cadiz. At Barbados, where he arrived on 4 June, he received information from the governor of St Lucia, General Brereton, that 'the Enemys fleet and army are supposed to have attacked Tobago and Trinidada' [374]. His frustration at not finding them and his anger towards General Brereton pervade the letters he wrote on his way back [375 and 377–379]. He tried to console himself with having saved the West Indian islands' commerce and with the hope of at least catching Gravina, the Spanish admiral [375 and 376].[2] Running dangerously low on water supplies,[3] the *Victory* reached Gibraltar on 19 July 1805. It took another month for Nelson to get to Spithead, arriving on 18 August. Marsden alerted Lady Hamilton of Nelson's arrival, so that she could return from Southend, where she had been sea bathing, to Merton in time to receive him.[4] While spending a day in quarantine, Nelson, who had 'not heard from my own Emma since last April' [380], arranged to see her again and, just before leaving the *Victory*, received a note from Lady Hamilton 'of last night from Merton' and a 'letter of August 10th' [381].

[1]Knight, p. 482; Sir Charles Middleton hat just been made Lord Barham (1723–1813).
[2]Federico Carlos Gravina y Napoli (1756–1806).
[3]Knight. p. 493.
[4]Knight, p. 496.

259. *Nelson's last will and testament (extract)*

[TNA: Prob. 1/22][1]

[*written in a secretary's hand, except what is printed in bold letters; signed on each page 'Nelson + Bronte'*]

This is the last will and testament of me Horatio Viscount Nelson of the Nile and of Burnham Thorpe in the county of Norfolk and united kingdom of Great Britain and Ireland and Duke of Bronte in the kingdom of Farther Sicily.

First in the event that I shall die in England I direct my executors hereinafter named (unless His Majesty shall signify it to be his pleasure that my body shall be interred elsewhere) to cause my body to be interred in the parish church of Burnham Thorpe in the county of Norfolk aforesaid near the remains of my deceased father and mother and in as private a manner as may be and I direct that the sum of one hundred pounds shall be divided amongst the poor of the several parishes of Burnham Thorpe Sutton and Norton all the county of Norfolk that is to say one third part to the poor of each of the said parishes the same to be distributed at the discretion of the respective curates or officiating ministers of those parishes and in such manner and proportions and to such objects as they respectively shall think fit And I give and bequeath to Emma Lady Hamilton widow of the right honourable Sir William Hamilton knight of the most honourable order of the Bath my diamond star as a token of my friendship and regard I likewise give and bequeath to the said Emma Lady Hamilton the silver cup marked E.H. which she presented to me I give and bequeath to my brother the reverend William Nelson doctor in divinity. The gold box presented to me by the city of London Also I give and bequeath to the said William Nelson the gold sword presented to me by the Captains who fought with me at the battle of the Nile. Also I give and bequeath to my sister Catherine Matcham the sword presented to me by the city of London Also I give and bequeath to my sister Susannah Bolton the silver cup presented to me by the Turkey company Also I give and bequeath to Alexander Davison of S[t]. James's Square in the country of Middlesex esquire **my Turkish Gun Scymitar + Canteen** Also I give and bequeath to my late captain and worthy friend Captain Hardy all my telescopes and sea-glasses and one hundred pounds in money to be paid three months after my death

[1]To this last will Nelson later added codicils on 13 May and 6 Sept 1803 (Docs Nos 260 and 285), 19 Feb, 7 June and 19 Dec 1804 (Docs Nos 303, 311 and 355) and 11 Sept and 21 Oct 1805 (Docs Nos 382 and 402).

And I give and bequeath the sum of one hundred pounds to each of my executors hereinafter named to be paid or retained at the end of three months from my ~~decease~~ death and I give and bequeath to my before-named brother William Nelson and William Haslewood of Craven Street in the Strand in the county of Middlesex esquire all the residue and remainders of my goods chattels and personal estate whatsoever and wheresoever (except the household goods and furniture wines plate china linen pictures and prints which shall be in my house at Merton at my decease and also except my diamond sword and jewels hereinafter bequeathed and also except any other articles which I do or shall or may by this my will or by any codicil or codicils hereto otherwise bequeath and dispose of) To hold to them their executors administrators and assigns upon the trusts and for the ends intents and purposes hereinafter limited expressed declared and contained of and concerning the same vis. Upon trust that they the said trustees and the survivor of them and the executors and administrators of such survivor do and shall as soon as may be after my death convert into money such parts of the same personal estate as shall not consist of money and do and shall lay out and invest in the purchase of three pounds per cent consolidated bank annuities so much and such part of the same money and also of the money which shall belong to me at my death as by the dividends interest and income thereof will produce the clear yearly sum of one thousand pounds and do and shall stand and be possessed of the said bank annuities upon trust that from time to time during the natural life of Frances Herbert Viscountess Nelson my wife they the said trustees and the survivor of them and the executors or administrators of such survivor do and shall permit and suffer or authorize and empower the said Viscountess Nelson my wife and her assigns to receive and take the dividends interest and income of the same bank annuities when and as the same shall become due and payable in addition to all other provisions made by me at any time heretofore for her and in addition to the sum of four thousand pounds lately given by me to her and which sum of four thousand pounds it is my will that she shall retain I direct and declare that the provision made for her by this my will and also the said four thousand pounds shall be accepted and taken by her in lieu and full satisfaction of all dower right and title of dower and free bench of her the said Viscountess Nelson my wife of and in all or any of the freehold and copyhold lands and hereditaments of which I am now seized or possessed or of which I have been or shall be seized or possessed at any time during her coverture by me and I also declare and direct that in case the annual income to arise or be produced from the bank annuities to be purchased with the residue of my personal estate shall be insufficient to answer and pay the sum of one thousand pounds a year then the deficiency shall be answered to the said Viscountess Nelson my wife out of the rents, issues and profits of my barony town and feud lands and hereditaments in Farther Sicily, hereinafter devised and I charge the rents issues and profits thereof with the payment of the said yearly sum of one thousand pounds or such part thereof as the bank annuities to be purchased with the residue of my personal estate shall be insufficient to answer and pay so that in all events the said Viscountess Nelson my wife shall be entitled to receive a clear annual income of one thousand pounds during her natural life provided always that nothing contained in this my will shall extend or be construed to subject my real estates in England to the payment of the said annuity of one thousand pounds or any part thereof. And upon further trust that my said trustees or the survivor of them or the executors or administrators of such survivor do and shall on my decease pay and divide the surplus of my residuary personal estate which shall remain after investing such part thereof in three per cent consolidated bank annuities as shall be sufficient to produce one thousand pounds a year as aforesaid and also on the decease of the survivor of me and my said wife do and shall pay transfer assign and distribute the said bank annuities to be purchased as aforesaid to answer the said sum of one thousand pounds a year unto and amongst the said William Nelson, Susannah Bolton and Catherine Matcham, or such of them as shall be living as those respective periods and the issue of such of them as shall have departed this life in the mean time having issue then living to be divided between them in such manner that they may take their respective shares as tenants in common and so and in such manner and in such proportions that the issue of deceased parents may as between themselves take as tenants in common and per stirpes and not per capita and so as no person or persons may take under the description of issue unless his her or their parent or parents repectively shall have departed this life as to the said bank annuities in the lifetime of the survivor of myself and my said wife and as to the said surplus of my residuary personal estate in my life time provided always and in case a pension or pensions to the amount or value of one thousand pounds a year or upwards shall in my life time be granted to the said Viscountess Nelson my wife by His Majesty or by parliament then and in that case the said sum of one thousand pounds a year to be granted to her as aforesaid shall be in lieu of the provision of one thousand pounds a year hereby made for her and then and in that case the same provision shall cease and be void[1] and in that case the whole of my residuary personal estate shall be divisible and distributable on my death in

[1]Naish, p. 610, adds a fn. here: 'It has been stated that when Lady Nelson was voted a pension of £2,000 a year by Parliament in February 1806, this clause took effect. The letters which follow show this was not so and she enjoyed the annuity and the pension.'

the same or the like manner and to the same persons and in the same proportions as if the death of my said wife had taken place at the instant of my death And in pursuance and in exercise and execution of all and every power and powers authority and authorities enabling me in this behalf I nominate and appoint the said William Nelson and William Haslewood and their heirs and assigns to succeed on my death to the duchy of Bronte in the kingdom of Farther Sicily and the town and estate of Bronte in the same kingdom and all and singular the messuages lands tenements jurisdictions immunities franchises and hereditaments situate[d] in the kingdom of Farther Sicily which were granted to me by His present Majesty Ferdinand by the grace of God King of Both Sicilies and of Jerusalem, Infant of Spain, Duke of Parma, Piacenza, Castro, &c, Great Prince of Tuscany &c. by letters patent or other instrument bearing date on or about the tenth day of the month of October in the year one thousand seven hundred and ninety nine and all other [*sic*] the dutchies towns estates messuages lands tenements jurisdictions immunities franchises and hereditaments situate[d] in the said kingdom of Farther Sicily of which I am seized or over which I have any power of nomination or appointement [*further elaborate arrangements for Bronte follow*[1]] . . . And I give and devise unto the said Emma Lady Hamilton her heirs and assigns my capital message at Merton in the county of Surry and the outhouses offices gardens and pleasure-grounds belonging thereto and such and so many and such parts of my grounds farms lands tenements and hereditaments in the several parishes of Merton, Wimbledon, and Mitcham or any of them as together with and including the scite [*sic*] of the said message outhouses offices gardens pleasure-grounds shrubbery canal and mote shall not exceed seventy acres as shall be selected by the said Emma Lady Hamilton within six months after my decease such election [*sic*] to be testified by some deed or instrument in writing under her hand and seal And I further direct that all money due on the security of the same message and other hereditaments at my death shall be paid and satisfied out of my personal estate and out of the money arising from the sale of the residue of the said farm under the directions herein after contained in exoneration of the said message and other hereditaments so devised to and for the benefit of the said Emma Lady Hamilton as aforesaid And I give and devise unto the said William Nelson and William Haslewood their heirs and assigns all the residue of my lands and grounds situate[d] in the parishes of Merton, Wimbledon and

[1]These are to be found on sheets 5–10 of the will, transcribed by Nicolas, vii, pp. ccxxiv–ccxxix.

Mitcham aforesaid or so much thereof as shall not be by me sold and conveyed or otherwise disposed of in my life time and also in the mean time till selection thereof as aforesaid by the said Emma Lady Hamilton as to such part or parts thereof as are to be or may be selected by the said Emma Lady Hamilton as aforesaid to hold the same unto and to the use of the said William Nelson and William Haslewood their heirs and assigned for ever upon trust that they, the said William Nelson and William Haslewood and the survivor of them and the heirs and assigns of such survivor do and shall as soon as conveniently may be after my decease sell and dispose of the same lands and hereditaments either together and in one lot or in parcels and several lots and either by public auction or private contract as to the said William Nelson and William Haslewood and the survivor of them his heirs and assigns shall seem meet and convey the same when sold unto the person or persons who shall agree to become the purchaser or purchasers thereof and to his her and their heirs and assignes for ever or to such person or persons and for such uses ends intents and purposes as he she or they shall direct or appoint [further technical arrangements follow][1] And I give and bequeath all the household furniture implements of a household wines plate china linen pictures and prints which shall be in and about my house at Merton at my decease and not otherwise disposed of by this my will or any codicil or codicils which I may hereafter make to the said Emma Lady Hamilton for her own use and benefit . . .

[*further arrangements about the administration of Nelson's estate follow; the will is signed by Nelson and three 'Clerks to Messrs. Booth and Haslewood' on 10 May 1803*]

260. *First codicil to Nelson's last will and testament*

[TNA: Prob. 1/22]

[*written in a secretary's hand, except what is printed in* ***bold letters****; signed on each page 'Nelson + Bronte'*]

I Horatio Viscount Nelson of the Nile and of Burnham Thorpe in the county of Norfolk and united kingdom of Great Britain and Ireland and Duke of Bronte in the kingdom of Farther Sicily to my last will and testament bearing date the tenth day of this instant May do make and publish a

[1]On sheets 11 and 12 of the will, transcribed by Nicolas, vii, pp. ccxxx–ccxxxi.

codicil in manner following (that is to say) Whereas in and by my said last will and testament I did give and devise (among other things) unto Emma Lady Hamilton therein named her heirs and assigns my capital messuage at Merton in the county of Surry with the appurtenances and such and so many and such parts of my grounds farm lands tenements and hereditaments in the several parishes of Merton Wimbledon and Mitcham as any of them as together with and including the site of the said messuage outhouses offices gardens pleasure grounds shrubbery canal and mote shall not exceed seventy acres as should be selected by the said Emma Lady Hamilton within six months after my decease Now I do hereby revoke and annul the gift and devise so made of the said capital messuage and premises in and by my said last will and testament And in lieu thereof do give devise and dispose of the same in manner following that is to say I give and devise unto William Nelson and William Haslewood in my said will named their heirs and assigns my said capital messuage at Merton in the county of Surry and the outhouses offices gardens and pleasure grounds belonging thereto and such and so many and such parts of my grounds farm lands tenements and hereditaments in the several parishes of Merton Wimbledon and Mitcham in the said country of Surry or any of them as (together with and including the site of the said messuage outhouses offices gardens pleasure-grounds shrubbery canal and mote) shall not exceed seventy acres as shall be selected by the said Emma Lady Hamilton within six months after my decease such election [*sic*][1] to be testified by some deed or writing under her hand and seal To the use of such person or persons and in such parts shares or proportions and for such estate and estates and interest and interest and charged and chargeable in such manner with any sum or sums of money annuities legacies rent charges or otherwise and either absolutely or conditionally and subject to such power of revocation and new appointment as the said Emma Lady Hamilton from time to time as well when covert as sole and notwithstanding her coverture by any husband with whom she may happen to intermarry by any deed or deeds writing or writings to be sealed and delivered by her in the presence of two or more credible witnesses and to be attested by the same witnesses or by her last will and testament in writing or any writing purporting to be or to be in the nature of her last will and testament or any codicil or codicils thereto to be signed and published by her in the presence of and to be attested by three or more credible witnesses shall direct limit give or appoint the same And in default of such direction limitation and appointment and in the mean time and from

[1]For this choice of word, see the actual will (Doc. No. 259), from which Nelson apparently copied.

time to time until such direction limitation or appointment shall be made and take effect and from time to time as to so much and such parts of the said capital messuage and premises of which no such direction limitation or appointment shall be made To the use of the said Emma Lady Hamilton for and during the term of her natural life without impeachment of or for any manner of waste and from and after the decease of the said Emma Lady Hamilton To the use of my own right heirs In all other respects I ratify and confirm my said last will and testament In witness whereof I the said Horatio Viscount Nelson and Duke of Bronte have to this codicil to my last will and testament contained in three sheets of paper set my hand and seal and my seal also to the first sheet where the sheets are fastened together and have also executed a duplicate thereof this Thirteenth day of May one thousand eight hundred and three.

Nelson + Bronte

261. *To Lady Hamilton*

[Morrison, ii, p. 210 (No. 712)]

Kingston[1] ¼ before 6[2]

Cheer up, my dearest Emma,[3] and be assured that I ever have been, and am, and ever will be, your most faithful and affectionate Nelson & Bronté.

262. *To Lady Hamilton*

[Houghton: pf MS Eng 196.5 (33)] May 18th: 1803.

My Dearest Emma,

I wrote you a line from Kingston by the Dukes Servant, and having breakfasted at Liphock[4] arrived here almost smothered with dust exactly at one oclock. I found Hardy + Sutton waiting for me they both agreeing with me, my flag is hoisted in the Victory to prevent without the service absolutely requires it the indelicate removal of an Admiral to-morrow night or friday[5] morning at daylight she sails, my things only begin to

[1]Kingston-upon-Thames, about 4 km (= 2.5 miles) from Merton.
[2]Morrison added in brackets: May 16th, 1803.
[3]Possible reference to 'Cheer up fair Emma' (see Appendix 4).
[4]Liphook.
[5]20 May 1803.

arrive this evening and till noon tomorrow Lord Gardner[1] dining out I have Hardy Sutton + M^{r}: Scott +[2] Murray to dine with me, but what a change it will not bear thinking of, except in the Sweet hope of again returning to the Society of those we so sincerely love, Either my Ideas are altered or Portsmouth it is a place the picture of desolation + misery but perhaps it is the contrast to what I have been used to Hardy is in good health + spirits, the Victory lays so far off that I can hardly see her, and the Amphion is beyond my vision, I am writing to the Admiralty must keep them in good humour, I hope Your Marraige is gone off well for the Girl may thank you (if it is worth thanking) for Her Husband when you see my Eleve[3] which you will when you receive this letter give her a kiss for me and tell that I never shall forget either her or Her Dear Good Mother and do you believe me for ever my Dear Emma Your most faithful + affectionate

Nelson + Bronte.

Write to the Duke of Queensbury[4] and say how truly sensible I am of all his kindness, when I am on board I will write him a Line + say every thing for me to the Duke of Hamilton[5] + Marquis of Douglas,[6] M^{r}: Este +^{c}: and to the D$^{r:}$[7] + my sisters[8] you will say every thing that [is] Kind and never forget me to Your good mother[9]

I beg that You will let M^{r}: Booth manage Your accounts + never mind the loss of a few Hundred Pounds.

263. *To Lady Hamilton*

[NMM: MAM/26, photocopy] May 19th: 1803.

My Dearest Emma,

I have been examining the list of things which are coming down this Evening and what comes tomorrow the latter will of course not

[1]Admiral Lord Alan Gardner (1742–1809), whom Nelson had met in the West Indies, was at that time commander-in-chief at Portsmouth.

[2]This '+' replaces a ',' that Nelson appears to have put before.

[3]Their daughter Horatia.

[4]Queensberry.

[5]Archibald Douglas-Hamilton, 9th Duke of Hamilton (1740–1819).

[6]Alexander Douglas-Hamilton (1767–1852), 6th Marquess of Douglas, later to become 10th Duke of Hamilton.

[7]Nelson's brother William.

[8]Susannah Bolton and Catherine Matcham.

[9]Mary Cadogan.

go with me, my sopha + the large chair are not in any of the list therefore I fear for them my Linnen I am like wise not sure of as it was not marked Linnen, my Wine will go to the Custom House and come to me as it can. M^{r}: Turner of Portsmouth the factotum of a Sea Officers will take charge of what may come after my departure M^{r}: Crighton not sending me a List nor have I M^{r}: Burgess's at least I cant find the latter although I think to have seen it, the Victory is in a pretty state of confusion, and I have not moved my cot from the Amphion I shall take my chance + get it tomorrow Lord Gardner made such appoint of my . . .[1]

264. *To Lady Hamilton*

[Pettigrew, ii, p. 300]
By messenger May 20th, 1803.

My dearest Emma,

The boat is on shore, and five minutes sets me afloat. I can only pray that the great God of heaven may bless and preserve you, and that we may meet again in peace and in true happiness. I have no fears. Your dear kind letters are just come.

Yours,
Nelson and Bronté.

265. *To Lady Hamilton*

[Morrison, ii, pp. 210–11 (No. 713)] *Victory*, noon,
May 20th, 1803.

You will believe that although I am glad to leave that horrid place, Portsmouth, yet the being afloat makes me now feel that we do not tread the same element. I feel from my soul that God is good, and in His due wisdom will unite us, only when you look upon ~~our dear child call~~[2] to your remembrance all you think that I would say was I present, and be assured that I am thinking of you every moment. My heart is full to bursting!

[1]The rest of the letter (part of which can be seen through the hole created when the seal was torn) was not photocopied.

[2]Morrison, ii, p. 211 (No. 713) comments here: 'words have been scored over, but can be deciphered'.

May God Almighty bless & protect you, is the fervent prayer of, my dear beloved Emma, your most faithful, affectionate

266. *To Lady Hamilton*

[Pettigrew, ii, p. 300]

Victory,
May 21st, 1803.

My dearest Emma,

This morning we stopped a Dutch ship from Surinam, of some value. Hardy carries her into Plymouth. We have a fine wind. I have only a moment to say, God in heaven keep you.

Yours,
Nelson and Bronté.

267. *To Lady Hamilton*

[NMM: CRK/19/28]

May 22nd: 8 oclock in the morning

My Dearest Emma,

We are now in sight of Ushant and shall see admiral Cornwallis in an hour I am not in a little fret on the idea that he may keep the Victory + turn us all into the Amphion it will make it truly uncomfortable but I cannot help myself, I assure you my Dear Emma that I feel a thorough conviction that we shall meet again with Honor Riches + health and remain together 'till a good old age + look at your and my Gods childs Picture but till I am sure of remaining here I cannot bring myself to hang them up be assured that my attatchment + affectionate regard is unalterable nothing can shake it, and pray say so to my Dear Mrs: T. when you see her, tell her that my love is unbounded to her + her dear sweet child and if she should have more it will extend to all of them, in short my Dear Emma say every thing to her which your dear affectionate heart + head can think of We are very comfortable Mr: Elliot[1] is happy quite recover'd his spirits he was very low at Portsmouth Geo Elliot is very well say so to Lord Minto Murray Sutton in short every body in the ship seems happy and if we should fall in with a French man of war I have no fears but they will do as we used to do Hardy is gone

[1]Hugh Elliot.

into Ply^{s}:[1] to see our Dutchman safe, I think she will turn out a good prize, Gaetano desires his duty to Miledi he is a good man and I dare say will come back for I think it cannot be a long War Just enough to make me independant in pecuniary matters If this wind stands on Tuesday we shall be on the coast of Portugal and before next Sunday in the Mediterranean,[2] To M^{rs}: Cadogan say every kind thing to good M^{rs}: Nelson The Docter +^{c}: +^{c}: If you like you may tell him about the entailing of the Pension but perhaps he will be so much taken up with Canterbury that it will do for some dull evening at Hilborough I shall now stop till I have been on board the Admiral,[3] only tell M^{rs}. T. that I will write her the first safe opportunity I am not sure of this I shall direct to Merton after June 1st: therefore as you change make Davison take a direction to Nepean but I would not trouble him with too many directions for fear of embroil May 23rd: We were close in with Brest yesterday and found by a frigate that ad^{l}: Cornwallis had a rendezvous at at[4] sea, thither we went, but to this hour cannot find him it blows strong, what wind we are losing, If I cannot find the ad^{l}: by 6 oclock we must all go into the Amphion and leave the Victory to my great mortification so much for the wisdom of my superiors[5] I keep my letter open to the last for I still hope as I am sure there is no good reason for my not going out in the Victory, I am just Embarking in the Amphion cannot find ad^{l}: Cornwallis may God in Heaven Bless you prays your most sincere

Nelson + Bronte.[6]

Stephens's publication,[7] I should like to have, I have left my silver seal[8] at least I cannot find it.

[1]Plymouth.

[2]24 (Tuesday) and 29 May 1803 (Sunday); actually, because of the then imminent change of ships, Nelson's progress was delayed and on 30 May he was 'still off Cape Finisterre' (see Doc. No. 268).

[3]Lord Gardner.

[4]The first 'at' is at the bottom of the fourth page of the letter; the text continues on the fifth page of the letter with another 'at'.

[5]For the state of the inexperienced crew on board *Victory*, see Knight, pp. 449–50.

[6]The postscript is inserted at the top of the fifth page of the letter, between 'rendezvous at' and 'at sea', and separated from the text below by a line.

[7]Alexander Stephens, *History of the Wars of the French Revolution*, 2 vols (London, 1803). Nelson had written to him about his actions at Naples in 1799 (see Nicolas, v, p. 43).

[8]Information about Nelson's seals can be found in Rina Prentice's *The Authentic Nelson* (London: National Maritime Museum, 2005), pp. 151–2, though a silver seal is not mentioned there.

268. *To Lady Hamilton*

[CRC/46] May 25 1803.

My Dearest Emma,

Here we are in the middle of the Bay of Biscay nothing to be seen but the sky and water I left the Victory at 8 oclock last night a reflection I think on those who ordered me for I am sure she is not wanted off Brest, Hardy takes good care of us, and the Amphion is very comfortable May 26th: we have now got a foul wind thanks to the Admiralty + our not finding Adl: Cornwallis off Brest for we could with ease have been round Cape St: Vincent when this would have been a fair wind not a vessel is to be seen on the face of the waters May 30th: Our wind has been foul blowing fresh and a nasty sea we are still off Cape Finisterre we have seen some Spaniards but not one Frenchman we speak nothing for I am very anxious to get to my station this is all lost time and the sooner I get to work the sooner if it pleases God I shall return, perhaps by my being delay'd much harm may arise and even Sicily may fall into the hands of the French but we are carrying sail + doing our utmost patience is a virtue at sea, Your Dear picture and H.[1] are hung up it revives me even to look upon them Your health is as regularly drank as ever the third toast + that is all we drink Sutton was in desperation when we left the Victory as to news you will not expect after what I have told You that we have not spoken a vessel Gaetano has been tolerable William very sea sick, June 2nd: We have just passed the Rock of Lisbon + with a gentle fair wind If it holds we shall be off Cape St: Vincent in the night June 3rd: We have had a fresh breeze + fair at this momt: 2 oclock[2] we are entering the Streights of Gibr: having run more than 100 Leagues since 8 oclock yesterday morning I have caught a little cold but am otherwise very well I am anxious to hear what is passing + hope that we shall anchor at Gibraltar by 8 oclock, June 4th: I am sailing at 1 oclock having just been to pay my respects to the Govr:[3] we capturd a Brig from the West Indies yesterday[4] and our boats another this [morning][5] Buonaparte's brother

[1]Horatia's.

[2]After the previous line finished with 'momt:', '2 oclock' starts a new line.

[3]Sir Thomas Trigge (c. 1742–1814), acting in 1803–1804 for the Prince Edward, Duke of Kent (1767–1820; nominally Governor of Gibraltar from 1802 until 1820, but replaced by an acting governor from May 1803; son of George III and father of the future Queen Victoria).

[4]The word 'yesterday' can merely be guessed at, since several letters have been damaged or torn away on opening the letter.

[5]The word 'morning' that Pettigrew gives here is completely cut away.

Jero[me,[1] passed][2] a few days ago in a ship of the Line[3] from Martinique, May Heaven[s][4] Bless + preserve You my Dear Emma for the sake of Your most faithful affectionate + attatched

Nelson + Bronte.

I am much hurried for they know nothing of the war.

269. *To Lady Hamilton*

[*a)* Pettigrew, ii, pp. 304–5; *b)* Morrison, ii, p. 213 (No. 718)]
[*b)*] June 10th, 20 leagues east of Algiers.

[*a)*] My dearest Emma,

[*b)*] We left Gibraltar at three o'clock, June 4th. The next day we took a French brig from Cette,[5] and a Dutch one from the same place. We have had foul winds, but by exertion are got so far on our voyage, and at present our wind is favourable, but with a nasty sea. The Admiral has had a severe cold and is a little feverish. I really believe from anxiety to get on his station. Mr. Elliot,[6] if this wind continues, leaves us to-morrow, as he passes over to Sardinia, and we inside the island of Galeta, passing Tunis[7] and Cape Bon. Gaetano will go in the Maidstone, and I hope return in her; but I think that very doubtful, when he once gets with his wife and family. I shall write to Mr. Gibbs to tell me about your things,[8] and if I ever get hold of them I will send them home. How this letter will get home I know not. It will be read by every post office from Naples to London. Be assured, my dear Emma, of my most affectionate regard and esteem, & for all belonging to you.[9] The Admiral does not mean to stay at Malta more than twenty-four hours, for he is very anxious to get off Toulon. News I can tell you none, except from vessels spoke. We find that it was the *Jemappe*,

[1]Jérôme Bonaparte (1784–1860).
[2]This, again, can only be found in Pettigrew.
[3]Parts of the word are cut away, but it can still be deciphered.
[4]The paper after the letter 'n' is cut away, but there appears to be the trace of another letter at the bottom, next to the 'n'.
[5]Since 1928: Sète.
[6]Hugh Elliot, about to take his post as British envoy in Naples.
[7]Pettigrew has here 'Turin', but the island of Galeta or Galita is about 80 km off the northern coast of present-day Tunisia, Cape Bon is the north-eastern tip of present-day Tunisia and Tunis is situated between the two (island and cape).
[8]Left behind at Naples; see also Docs Nos 276 and 288 ('furniture and linnen').
[9]Reference to their daughter Horatia.

seventy-four, passed the Straits[1] a little before us, she was in a calm off Majorca, the 31st of May, so that if we had proceeded direct in the *Victory*, we should have had her to a certainty. This letter will probably find you returning from Hilborough, where my fancy tells me you are thinking of setting out, for it will amuse you by change of scene. I pray Heaven preserve you & yours[2] in health and happiness, & send us a happy meeting. I have wrote Gibbs a long letter to know something about Bronté – this is a matter I am determined to settle as speedily as possible, for the Admiral says it is shameful the way it has been managed. I have also wrote about your things at Malta. You forgot to give me the order, but I suppose they will believe me. Ld N. will send them home, but it is not for the value, which, please God, you can never want, but for the pleasure of getting your own things. I hope to hear that all your affairs are settled. All I beg is that for a few hundred pounds that you will not fret yourself. Let them do what they will, whether I live or die you will be better off than ever.

June 11th. Mr. Elliot just leaving us, but this letter I send to Gibbs to send by the post, therefore I cannot write all I wish, but when the Admiral gets off Toulon, he intends sending a vessel direct to England.

Yours,

270. *To Lady Hamilton*

[Pettigrew, ii, p. 310] June 20th, 1803.

My dear Emma,

I am now in the passage of the Pharo.[3] Charles is with me, and Captain Capel says behaves very well. I dare not say more, for I never expect you will ever receive this letter from

Yours.

271. *To Lady Hamilton*

[Huntington: HM 34095] June 25th: off Capre.[4]

My Dearest Emma,

Close to Capre the view of Vesuvious [*sic*] calls so many circumstances to my mind thet it almost overpowers my feelings I do not believe that I shall have any opportunity of sending this letter to Naples and if I did

[1]Of Gibraltar.
[2]Another reference to their daughter Horatia.
[3]of Messina.
[4]Capri.

Lord Nelson does not believe that Mr: Elliot would have any opportunity of sending it safely to England therefore I can tell You little more than here we are, We arrived at Malta June 15th: in the afternoon and saild Thursday[1] in the night Lord Nelson being so very anxious to join the fleet off Toulon Sir A. Ball is very well but I think he looks melancholy, it was so hot that I was glad to breath [*sic*] the sea air again I saw the Marquis Testefatte I think that is the name he enquired after You, what is going on in Italy I cannot tell You, and if I could dare not by this conveyance, The Admiral tells me that very soon he shall have a good + safe opportunity only therefore My Dear Emma Believe all the kind things I would say and your fertile imagination cannot come up to them for I am ever and if possible more than Ever Your faithful[2]

Charles is very well The Maidstone is just in sight from Naples where she went with Mr: Elliot, reports say by the Maidstone that all at Naples have great confidence in Lord Nelson

272. *To Lady Hamilton*

[NMM: CRK/19/29][3]

My Dearest Emma,

although I have wrote letters from various places merely to say here I am and there I am Yet as I have no doubt but that they would all be read, it was impossible for me to say more than here I am and well, and I see not [*sic*] prospect of any certain mode of conveyance, but by sea which with the means the Admiralty has given me of small vessels can be but seldom, our passages have been enormously long, from Gibr: to Malta we were 11 days arriving the 15th:[4] in the evening and sailing in the night of the 16th: that is 3 in the morning of the 17th: and it was the 26th:[5] before we got off Capre,[6] where I had ordered the frigate which carried Mr: Elliot to Naples to join me, I send you copys of the King and Queens[7] letters I am vexed that she did not mention you I can only account for it by hers being a Political letter, when I wrote to the Queen I said 'I left Lady Hamilton the 18th: May, and so attatch'd to your Majesty that I am

[1]23 June 1803.
[2]No signature follows here, but an empty line.
[3]As this letter was finished on 'July 8th:', it must have been begun before that date.
[4]of June 1803.
[5]Here Nelson appears to have changed a 5 into a 6.
[6]Capri.
[7]Of Naples.

sure she would lay down her life to preserve yours your Majesty never had a more sincere attatched and real friend than your dear Emma, You will be sorry to hear that Good Sir William did not leave her in such comfortable circumstances as his fortune would have allowed, He has given it amongst his relations, But she will do honor to his memory, although every one else of his friends call loudly against him on that account.'[1]

I trust my dear Emma she has wrote you, if she can forget Emma I hope God will forget her, but you think that she never will or can, now is her time to shew it, You will only shew the King + Queens letters to some few particular friends, The King is very low lives mostly at Belvidire[2] Mr: Elliot had not seen either him or the Queen from the 17th: the day of his arrival to the 21st: on the next day he was to be presented I have made up my mind that it is part of the plan of that Corsican Scoundrel[3] to conquer the Kingdom of Naples he has marched 13,000 men into the Kingdom on the Adriatic side and he will take possession with as much shadow of right of Gaeta + Naples and if the Poor King remonstrates or allows us to secure Sicily He will call it war and declare a conquest, I have cautioned Genl: Acton[4] not to risk the Royal family too long, but Naples will be conquered sooner or later[5] as it may suit Buonaparte's convenience, The Morea + Egypt are likewise in his eye, an army of full 70,000 men are assembling in Italy, Gibbs[6] + Noble[7] are gone to Malta, I am you may believe very anxious to get off Toulon to join the fleet Sir Richd: Bickerton went from off Naples the day I left Gibr:

We passed Monte Christo[8] Bastia + Cape Corse yesterday, and are now moving slowly direct for Toulon what force they have I know not indeed I am totally ignorant, some say 9 Sail of the Line some 7, some 5. if the former they will come out for we have only the same number including 64s: and very shortly manned however I hope they will come out and let us settle the matter You know I hate being kept in suspence,

[1]From the beginning of this quotation ('I left Lady Hamilton . . .') Nelson has marked the beginning of each line with a '='. The last line marked like this is: 'on that account, I trust my Dear Emma'.

[2]Probably Belvedere Marittimo, about half way between Naples and Messina on the Calabrian coast.

[3]Napoleon Bonaparte.

[4] 'Prime minister' of Naples under Ferdinand IV.

[5]Napoleon conquered it in 1806.

[6]Abraham Gibbs (*fl.* 1799–1804) was a merchant from Naples who moved to Palermo in 1799 and lived with the Hamiltons in the Palazzo Palagonia; later looked after Nelson's business affairs, including the administration of his estate at Bronte.

[7]Edmund Noble (*fl.* 1799–1805) was a merchant from Naples who accompanied the Hamiltons to Palermo in 1799 and moved to Malta on 14 June 1803.

[8]Nowadays: Montecristo (island south of Elba).

July 8th: I left this hole, to put down what force the French have at Toulon. 7 Sail of the Line ready, five frigates + 6 corvettes. 1 or two more in abt: a week, We to day 8 Sail of the Line – tomorrow 7 – including two 64 gun ships.[1]

You will readily believe how rejoiced I shall be [to] get one of your dear excellent letters, that I may know every thing which has passed since my absence, I sincerely hope that Mr: Booth[2] has settled all your accounts, never mind my Dear Emma a few hundred pounds[3] which is[4] all the rigid gripe of the Law not justice can wrest from you, I thank God that you cannot want (although that is no good reason for its being taken from you) whilst I have 6 pence you shall not want for five pence of it, but you have bought your experience that there is no friendship in money concerns, and your good sense will make you profit of it, I hope the minister has done something for you, but never mind we can live upon Bread + Cheese[5] independance is a blessing, and although I have not yet found out the way to get prize money, what has been taken has run into our mouths, however it must turn out very hard if I cannot get enough to pay off my debts and that will be no small ~~xxx~~ comfort, I have not mentioned my Bronte affairs to Acton as yet, but if Naples remains much longer I shall ask the question, but I expect nothing from them, I believe even Acton wishes himself well + safely removed, I think from what I hear that the Kings spirits are so much depressed that He will give up the reins of Naples at least to his son,[6] and retire to Sicily Sir William you know always thought that he would end his life so, certainly His situation must be heart breaking, Gaetano return'd in the frigate I believe he saw enough of Naples, He carried his family money and Mr: Falconet (Gibbs being absent) will pay Mr: Grevilles pension to Gaetano's family, I have now [sent] Gato: to the post and he desires to present his duty + to tell you that Mr: Ragland from Sir Williams death will not pay any more pensions without orders from Mr: Greville, Vincenzo has had none paid he is very poor keeps a shop his son wanted I find to come in the frigate

[1]This passage from 'I left this hole' until '64 gun ships' appears to have been added later. The date 'July 8th:' is at the bottom of the page and at the end of a line. The next three lines are written in smaller writing; the end of the paragraph is squeezed on top of the following page, separated by a line from the rest of the page. The text in normal size writing starts: 'You will readily . . .'.

[2]Of Messrs: Booth and Haslewood.

[3]Compare Doc. No. 269 at the end.

[4]Inserted.

[5]See 'I can with a quiet conscience when all is gone, live on bread + cheese, Never mind as long as I have your friendship warm from the heart' (Doc. No. 227).

[6]Francesco.

to me, I cannot afford to maintain him therefore I shall give no encouragement, old Antonio was allowed a carline[1] a day that is now not paid, Sabitello[2] lives with Mr: Elliot Nicolo + Mary Antonio have left Mr: Gibbs for some cause Gato: says he believes for amore, Francesca has two children living and another coming She lives the best amongst them, like Gallant Homme, Pasqual lives with the Duke Montelione[3] and Joseph with the old Russian, Your house is a Hotel the upper apartments are kept for the Marquis the owner, Mr: Elliot has taken the House of the Baille Franconi[4] on the Chaia,[5] Dr: Nudi enquired kindly after us and all the women at Santa Lucia[6] expected when they saw Gaetano that you was arrived, Bread never was so dear every thing else in plenty, the Wages not being raised Go: says the Poor of England are a million times better off, so much for Gaetano's news he desires his duty to Signora Madre,[7] + remembrances to Mary Ann[8] Fatima +c:

July 8th: we join'd this morning the fleet the men in the ships are good but the ships themselves are a little the worse for wear and very short of their compliments [*sic*] of men, We shall never be better there[fore] let them come the sooner the better, I shall write a Line to the Duke that he may see I do not forget my friends and I rely my Dearest Emma on your saying every kind thing for me to the Dr: Mrs: Nelson Mrs: Bolton Mr: + Mrs: Matcham Mrs: Cadogan whose kindness and goodness I shall never forget, You will have the goodness to send the enclosed as directed and be assured that I am to the last moment of my life your most attatched faithful and affectionate

Nelson + Bronte.

[1] Carlino, a Sicilian coin. One carlino was worth ten grana and twelve carlini were equivalent to one Sicilian piastra.

[2] Sabatello.

[3] Diego Pignatelli Aragona Cortés 10. Principe di Noia, Duca di Monteleone (1774–1818), married to a member of the Caracciolo family.

[4] This probably refers to the Neapolitan noble family Francone; the founder of the dynasty in the 13th century had been Balì di Santo Stefano.

[5] The Via Chiaia is a major street in the city of Naples, stretching westwards from the Royal Palace; in the 18th century several Neapolitan noble families (among them the Francone) built their palazzi along this street, outside the old city centre, close to the royal palace; Sir William and Lady Hamilton's residence had been about 200 m south of the Chiaia.

[6] Part of Naples, between the Royal Palace to the north and the Castel dell'Ovo to the south.

[7] 'Mrs. Mother' referring to Lady Hamilton's mother, Mary Cadogan.

[8] 1814-letters, i, p. 122, put a comma here, so as to show that 'Mary Ann' is one person.

273. *To Lady Hamilton*

[BL: Egerton 1614 ff. 94–95, no. 49] Amphion July 12th: 1803.

My Dearest Emma,

To whom can we write so readily as to those Dear friends who occupy our whole attention, that to me you are that person I will not assert, for if I could believe that it could be doubted I should feel that I had reason to think the same, but that I hold to be impossible, it is now near two months since my departure and thanks to the Admiralty nothing is yet arrived nor have I heard the least bit of English news, It is my intention the first money I get to pay off M^{rs}: Graves 2000£ mortgage which is due 1st: of October next, and after that M^{r}: Davison then I shall have M^{r}: Matchams mortgage money lodged, after which I shall send you some to begin next spring our alterations, but first I will if I can get out of debt, I am talking as if I had made a fortune and God knows as yet I have not received one farthing of Prize Money[1] some vessels are taken but they even if they are condemned will not give me much, Prize Money does not seem my lot, however time must give me something handsome, and I shall keep every body alive and on the look out, for although money may not absolutely constitute the whole of happiness yet we <u>both</u> know that happiness sets [*sic*] much more easy when we have a purse of money to resort to, and we must allow that there is great comfort in it, July 18th: off Toulon We have just had a 3 days Gale but we are close off Toulon looking at them, I have not seen a single vessel these five days except our own fleet, therefore I neither can tell you news nor have received any, the happiness of keeping a station is always to have a foul wind and never to hear the delightful sound St<u>ea</u>dy Victory I hope will soon join I have heard Sutton has made 8 thousand pounds in her in his way to join me but I fear with my usual prize luck I shall not share for his prizes, but perseverance will do wonders and some day I shall get very rich, Hardy has been very unwell indeed I was afraid that he would have been obliged to go home but he is much better, his loss would have been a most serious one to me, Rev^{d}: D^{r}: Scott is very busy translating his health is much recovered,[2] Murray Hardy + M^{r}: Scott are on a Court Martial so I have all the ship to myself, My Secretary I esteem a treasure he is not only a clever man but indefatigable in his business and an extraordinary

[1]Inserted.

[2]Probably a reference to the stroke of lightning that had hit him on his way to the West Indies in 1801 (see Doc. No. 293 with fn.).

well behaved modest man, in short I feel very well mounted at present and I trust shall have no reason to wish for any alteration I long to hear of your Norfolk excursion and everything you have been about for I ever am most warmly interested in all your actions July 21st: we have not seen a vessel these many days the Medusa and Termagant have been up the Gulph of Lyons they spoke some Spaniards from Marsailles [*sic*] who tell them that all the seamen are sent to Toulon and the mercht: ships laid up, We are anxious for the Victorys joining as we are almost eating salt beef, make my kind regards to Mrs: Cadogan and all our friends and Be assured I ever am my Dearest Emma your most faithful + affectionate

Nelson and Bronte.

274. *To Lady Hamilton*

[NMM: CRK/19/30]

Victory off Toulon
Augt: 1st: 1803.

I dont know that you will get this letter.

My Dearest Emma,

You letter of May 31st: which came under cover to Mr: Noble of Naples enclosing Davison's correspondence with Plyh:[1] arrived by the Phœbe two days ago, and this is the only scrap of a Pen which has been received by any person in the fleet since we sail'd from England. You will readily conceive my Dear Emma the sensations which the sight and reading even your few lines [caused] they cannot be understood but by those of such mutual and truly sincere attatchment as yours and mine, although you said little I understood a great deal and most heartily approve of your plan and society for next Winter, and next spring I hope to be rich enough to begin the alterations at Dear Merton it will serve to amuse you and I am sure that I shall admire all your alterations, even to planting a gooseberry bush, Sutton joined me yesterday and we are all got into the Victory, and a few days will put us in order, every body gives a very excellent character of Mr: Chevalier[2] the servant recommended by Mr: Davison, and I shall certainly live as frugal as my station will admit, I have known the pinch and shall endeavour never to know it again, I want to send 2100 £ to pay off Mrs: Graves[3] on Octr: 1st: but I have not

[1]Plymouth.
[2]William Chevalier (*fl.* 1803–5).
[3]Greaves.

received one farthing, but I hope to receive some soon, but M^{r}: Haslewood promised to see this matter kept right for me, Hardy is now busy hanging up your + Horatias picture and I trust soon to see the other two safe arrived from the Exhibition I want no others to ornament my cabbin I can contemplate them + find new beauties every day and I dont want any body else You will not expect much news from us We see nothing,[1] I have great fear that all Naples will fall into the hands of the French and if Acton does not take care Sicily also, however I have given my final advice so fully and strongly[2] that let what will happen they cannot blame me, cap^{n}: Capel says M^{r}: Elliot cannot bear Naples I have no doubt but that it is very different to your time, the Queen I fancy by the seal has sent a letter to Castelcicala her letter to me is only thanks for my attention to the safety of the Kingdom if D^{r}: Scott has time and is able he shall write a copy for you, The king is very much retired, He would not see the French General S^{t}: Cyr[3] who came to Naples to settle the contribution for the paymt: of the French army,[4] The Queen was ordered to give him + the French Minister a dinner but the King staid at Belvidere[5] I think he will give it up soon and retire to Sicily if the French will allow Him, Acton has never dared give M^{r}: Elliot or one Englishman a dinner, The fleet are ready to come forth but they will not come for the sake of fight^{g}: me, I have this day made Geo: Elliot Post[6] L^{t}: Pettit[7] a Master + Commander and M^{r}: Hindmarsh[8] Gunners son of the Bellerophon who behaved so well this day 5 years a Lieu^{t}: I reckon to have lost two french 74^{s}: by my not coming out in the Victory but I hope they will come soon, with interest, this goes to Gib^{r}: by Sutton in the Amphion, I shall write the D^{r}:[9] in a day or two I see by the French papers he has kissed hands,[10] With kindest regards to your good mother and all at Merton +^{c}: +^{c}: +^{c}: I am Ever yours most faithfully + affectionately

Nelson + Bronte

[1]Probably meaning 'no ships'.

[2]This probably refers to a letter to the Queen of Naples, given in Nicolas, v, pp. 142–3.

[3]Laurent de Gouvion Saint-Cyr (1764–1830), at that time in command of the French occupying force in the Kingdom of Naples.

[4]In the treaty of the Peace of Florence, of 28 Mar 1801, Naples had been forced to accept French garrisons to their ports on the Adriatic Sea.

[5]Probably Belvedere Marittimo.

[6]Post-captain.

[7]Robert Pettet.

[8]John Hindmarsh (1785–1860).

[9]Nelson's brother William.

[10]He has been received by the king in order to get his appointment as Prebendary of Canterbury confirmed.

275. *To Lady Hamilton*

[NMM: CRK/19/31; *a)* Pettigrew, ii, p. 326]

Victory off Toulon
Aug^{t}: 10th: 1803

My Dearest Emma,

I take the opportunity of M^{r}: A'courts[1] going through Spain with M^{r}: Elliots dispatches for Engl^{d}: to send this letter, for I would not for the world miss any opportunity of sending you a line, by Gibralter I wrote you as lately as the 4th[2] but all our ways of communicating with England are very uncertain, and I believe the Admiralty must have forgot us for not a vessel of any kind or sort has joined us since I left Spith^{d}: News I absolutely am ignorant of, except that a schooner belonging to me put her nose into Toulon + 4 frigates popt [*sic*] out and have taken her and a transport loaded with water for the fleet, however I hope to have an opportunity very soon of paying them the debt with interest, M^{r}: Acourt says at Naples they hope that the mediation of Russia will save them, but I doubt if Russia will go to war with the french for any kingdom, and they poor souls relying on a broken reed will lose Sicily, As for getting any thing for Bronte I cannot expect it for the finances of Naples are worse than ever, patienza[3] however I will[4]

[*a)*] I see many Bishops are dead is my brother tired of Canterbury, I wish I could make him a Bishop if you see him or write say that I have not 10 minutes to send away M^{r}: Acourt who cannot be detained

I hope L^{d}: S^{t}: V^{t}: has sent out Sir W^{m}: Bolton as soon as I know who is first Lord I will write him.

276. *To Lady Hamilton*

[Pettigrew, ii, p. 331] August 21st, 1803.

We have had, my dearest Emma, two days pretty strong gales. The Canopus has lost her fore-yard, but we shall put her in order again. This is the

[1]William A'Court, had been Chargé d'affaires at Palermo from Drummond's departure for Naples late Dec. 1801 until the Court removed from Palermo to Naples July 1802, and at Naples from Drummond's departure shortly after 8 March 1802 until Elliot's arrival 18 June 1803.

[2]This probably refers to Doc. No. 274, which was written on 1 Aug 1803.

[3]'Pazienza' is Italian for 'patience'.

[4]Here the page ends and a continuation of the letter is missing.

fourth gale we have had since July 6th, but the Victory is so easy at sea, that I trust we shall never receive any material damage. It is never my intention, if I can help it, to go into any port – my business is to be at sea, and get hold of the French fleet, and so I shall by patience and perseverance. As for Malta you know what I said about it in Parliament[1] – it is useless to us for the blockade of Toulon, and nothing but an action, and probably not that, can ever make me go there – it takes upon the average seven weeks to get an answer to a letter. Malta and Toulon are entirely different services. It struck me that it was a horrid place, and all the captains who have been laid up there detest it. Our friend Ball, if I am not mistaken, wishes himself afloat, but he is too proud to own it. *He* is, I can assure you, a great man, and on many occasions appears to forget that he was a seaman, he is bit with the dignity of the Corps Diplomatique; but I differ with no one, however I can think a little, and can see *a* little into a mill-stone.

I entreat that you will let nothing fret you, only believe me, once for all, that I am ever your own Nelson. I have not a thought except on you and the French fleet – all my thoughts, plans, and toils tend to those two objects, and I will embrace them both so close when I can lay hold of either one or the other, that the devil himself should not separate us. Don't laugh at my putting you and the French fleet together, but you cannot be separated. I long to see you both in your proper places, the French fleet at sea, you at dear Merton, which in every sense of the word, I expect to find a paradise. I send you a copy of Gibb's letter, my answer, and my letter to Mr. Noble about your things, and I will take all care that they shall get home safe.[2]

277. *To Lady Hamilton*

[Pettigrew, ii, p. 332]

I see that Graeffer[3] has pensioned some man that is said to have gained my cause, 65 ounces a year, and Gibbs recommends me to buy him off. This is one thing that I never heard of before, however I have sent Gibbs an order to receive this year's rents,[4] and to sell the stock on the farm, that the debts may be paid as soon as possible. You may rely that I shall take care and settle something, if possible, *solid* before I leave this

[1]See introduction to this chapter.
[2]See also Docs Nos 269 and 288.
[3]This should be: Graefer.
[4]From his estate in Bronte.

country. It is more than two months since I have heard from Naples, and till yesterday five weeks since I heard from Malta. I had a letter from poor Macaulay, he desires to be most kindly remembered to you. I hear Mr. Elliot does not like Naples, indeed I can conceive it is very different to what it was in our time. Do you ever hear from the Queen? I fear that she is a time-serving woman, and cares for no one except for those at the moment who may be useful to her. However, *time will shew*. I am every day taking care of them. It is seven weeks since I heard from Gibraltar, for I have no small vessels to send about. We are cruising here in hopes some day to get hold of the French fleet, and that will repay us for all our toils.

278. *To Lady Hamilton*

[Pettigrew, ii, p. 332]

They say the house[1] which is fitted up is ridiculous. Instead of a farm house it is a palace – quite a folly in Græffer.

I had yesterday Charles on board to dine with me; he is not much grown, but Captain Capel says he behaves very well. I want to know what changes have taken place at the Admiralty – the French papers have announced Lord Castlereagh.[2] I have wrote to Mr. Booth, and to Mr. Haslewood, and ordered home from Gibraltar £2100. to pay off Mrs. Greaves, and I hope it will arrive before the 1st of October, but if it should not, I trust that Haslewood will manage that I get into no scrape. It is the first-fruits of prize-money, not much you will say, but I am not over fortunate in that respect. Be so good as to write a note to Haslewood. I long to be out of debt. I see by the papers that my cause has been argued and judgment deferred,[3] I hope I shall get it, I long to know Haslewood's opinion. You will be sorry but not surprised to hear of Lord Bristol's death.[4] We are all well, and with kindest regards to Mrs. Cadogan, and all friends, believe me,

Yours,

Nelson and Bronté.

[1]At Bronte.

[2] Robert Stewart, Viscount Castlereagh (1769–1822).

[3]This refers to Nelson's court case against St Vincent; for details see fn. to Doc. No. 65.

[4]Frederick Augustus Hervey (1730–1803), 4th Earl of Bristol and Bishop of Derry, father of Elisabeth Foster, died on 8 July 1803, in Lazio.

279. *Lady Hamilton to Nelson*

[Houghton: MS Lowell Autograph]

Merton Mondy Morning[1]

I can only my beloved Nelson send you my friend Mrs Johnsons letter[2] to me all that I can say you will do every thing that's kind god bless you my Love my all of good ever believe me your most affectionate Emma Hamilton

280. *To Lady Hamilton*

[Houghton: MS Lowell Autograph] Victory
Aug^{t}: 24th: 1803.

My Dearest Emma, (5)[3]

Yesterday brought me letters from M^{rs}: Græfer via Malta as far as my own private concerns can occupy my attention in these times they have made me angry, but I have done, I am glad I wrote to Gibbs[4] if I have time I will send You copies in one part she says that if I had been there I should have spent more, that might be[5] and yet very improper for them she says the House cost so much, why did it, it was not my ordering. Græfer thought that I approved giving to the Poor so I am to be held forth as angry at a few ounces given to the Poor but I have done what I promised shall be pun[c]tually + regularly paid, from some expression in her letter I think she means to say that she cannot live for 200£ a year, I suppose she will say something of it to you, She intends to reside at Palermo and she wants me to apply to the Court for a pension, do you know the King never knew of my wish to resign Bronte it is said Acton dare not tell him, and now I fear the french will have Sicily so that I shall be well off, if that does not happen I shall hope to get regularly 2000£ a year that will be a pretty addition to our housekeeping What I have is Yours, what You have is Your own if it will keep Your carraige + buy

[1]Nelson referred to this note of Lady Hamilton's in Doc. No. 280, so that it was placed here.

[2]Referred to by Nelson in Doc. No. 280.

[3]Apparently Nelson numbered his letters at this stage. Probably three of the letters 1–4 are Docs Nos 276–278, taken from Pettigrew, the originals of which I have not been able to find.

[4]One letter of 11 Aug 1803 and two letters of 13 Aug 1803 are in Nicolas, v, pp. 159–60, 164–5 and 167, but none of them contains a reference to how to deal with Mrs Graefer.

[5]The word 'be' is written above another (beginning of a) word; 'n'?

cloaths and make a few presents to Your poor relations it will do well, we shall be rich for we will have no debts and but few wants I want only at dear Merton Your blessed society and our own family, I send You a letter from Syracuse in answer to one I sent the Baron Bosic from the Baron S^{t}. Guseppe,[1] it is very odd. I cannot account for it, surely he cannot be an impostor,

M^{r}: Acourt told me that Castelcicala was as great a favorite as ever with the Queen + that if Acton went away she would try + have him Prime Minister then I believe the Kingdom would be well governe'd [*sic*] if she has not wrote you she is an ungrateful B:[2] one word for all You did right in giving the Pianoforte and I am sure what You do will always be so, Ad^{l}: Campbell is on board + desires his best compliments. He has made a large fortune in the Channell fleet so much the better the more we take from the French the less they have + the sooner I hope we shall have peace. I have given M^{rs}: Johnsons letter[3] to the Lad South and have promised him my protection if he is a good boy whenever young Faddy comes he shall be promoted Ever for Ever Yours + only my Dearest Emma Yours Nelson + Bronte

281. *To Lady Hamilton*

[NMM: CRK/19/32]

My Dear Lady Hamilton,

Your friends godson arrived safe yesterday afternoon and I shall you know always feel too happy in obeying your commands for you never ask favors but for your friends in short in every point of view from Ambassatrice[4] to the duties of domestic life I never saw your equal, that Elegance of manners accomplishments and above all your goodness of heart is unparalleled, and only Believe me for Ever and beyond it your faithful + devoted

Nelson + Bronte.

Victory Aug^{t}: 24th: 1803

[1]Both barons (also searching for 'Giuseppe') I could not trace.

[2]Bitch?

[3]See note from Lady Hamilton to Nelson from Merton, on 'Mondy morning' (Doc. No. 279).

[4]Italian for 'ambassadress'. On marrying Sir William Hamilton Lady Hamilton was not allowed to use the English title.

282. *To Lady Hamilton*

[Pettigrew, ii, pp. 336–7]

To say the truth, I am so situated between Davison and Mr. Marsh[1] that I do not think I ever can name an Agent again. I have had many and great obligations to both of them, and I never put a sixpence into Mr. Marsh's pocket – to Davison it has been twice in my power. Say he has touched (besides the use of the money, which you may lay at £10,000), full 15,000, and when I told Davison how I was situated with Mr. Marsh, and that I wished to name them together, Davison declined it, and said, 'Whatever you do, let me stand alone'. I may never have the power of naming one alone, for Secretaries and other Admirals will naturally look to the compliment being also paid them of joining together; therefore, if Davison will never be joined, I see but little chance of my being able to name him alone, and indeed, Captains have naturally so many friends of their own, that it is not to be expected. I have wrote Davison pretty near as much some time ago,[2] but he may be assured that I shall never omit an opportunity when it can be done with propriety, and I am sure he is too much my friend to wish to place me in difficulties; but keep this to yourself. I will for a moment suppose a case which may happen: We take the French fleet, the Captains name the three Secretaries, and pay me, perhaps, the compliment of asking me to name a person in England to do the business. I should, of course, wish to join Mr. Davison and Mr. Marsh; it would hurt me for him to refuse to be joined to Mr. Marsh and the Secretaries here, and yet he would do it. I know he would give up the proportion, and only ask to have his name stand alone, but neither the captors nor the other parties would agree to it; therefore, I know of no other way but not taking the French fleet, and that would be very hard upon me; but I have done with that subject. What is it that Mrs. Denis thinks that I can be useful to Mr. Denis in at[3] Cività Vecchia; no prizes can be carried in there; even if the Pope[4] would allow it, nobody would trust their property under the Pope's care, therefore, I know of nothing. I shall never have any communication with that place now Lord Bristol is dead. It cannot be an object for them to go out, the pay will not hire their lodgings, and there can be no trade till the Peace.

N. & B.

[1]William Marsh (1755–1846), senior partner in the banking firm Marsh and Creed (Knight, p. 654).

[2]In a letter of 27 July 1803 (Nicolas, v, p. 143).

[3]The words 'in' and 'at' are both given by Pettigrew.

[4]Pius VII (formerly Count Barnaba Niccolò Maria Luigi Chiaramonte, 1742–1823; Pope, 1800–23).

283. *To Lady Hamilton*

[NMM: CRK/19/33][1] Aug[t]: 26th: 1803.
Wrote several days past

My Dearest Emma (1)

By the Canopus[2] ad[l]: Campbell I have received all your truly kind and affectionate letters from May 20th: to July 3rd: (with the exception of one dated May 31st: sent to Naples)[3] this is the first communication I have had with England since we sail'd, all your letters my dear letters are so entertaining and which paint so clearly what you are after that they give me either the greatest pleasure or pain, it is the next best thing to being with you I only desire my dearest Emma that you will always believe that Nelsons your own Nelsons Alpha + Omega is Emma I cannot alter my affection + love is beyond even this world, nothing can shake it but yourself, and that I will not allow myself to think for a moment is possible, I feel that you are the real friend of my bosom + dearer to me than life and that I am the same to you, but I will neither have P[s]: nor Q[s]:[4] come near you no not the slice of Single Gloster,[5] but if I was to go on it would argue that want of confidence which would be injurious to your honor, I rejoice that you have had so pleasant a trip into Norfolk, and I hope one day to carry you there by a nearer tie in law[6] but not in love + affection that [*sic*] at present, I wish you would never mention that persons[7] name it works up your anger for no useful purpose, her good or bad character of me or thee no one cares about, this letter will find you at dear Merton where we shall one day meet and be truly happy I do not think it can be a long war and I believe it will be much shorter than people expect, and I shall hope to find the new room built the grounds laid out neatly but not expensively new Piccadilly gates kitchen garden +[c]: only let us have a plan and then all will go on well it will be a great source of amusement to you, and H.[8] shall plant a tree I dare say she will be very busy M[rs]: Nelson or

[1]Nicolas, vii, p. 380, doubts the authenticity of this letter and adds, in fn. 5, an account of where this letter came from (sent by Duchess of Devonshire in 1815 to Mr Coutts, a banker, who passed it on to Nelson's sister, Mrs Matcham, with whom Horatia lived at the time).

[2]Nicolas, v, p. 182, fn.: 'The Canopus joined the Fleet on the 17th of August.'

[3]See Doc. No. 274.

[4]'Princes nor Queens'.

[5]This refers to Prince William Frederick, who was to succeed his father William Henry in 1805 as Duke of Gloucester and Edinburgh; among his nicknames were 'Silly Billy' and 'Slice of Gloucester'.

[6]Marriage.

[7]Lady Nelson's.

[8]Their daughter Horatia.

M[rs]: Bolton +[c]: will be with you and time will pass away till I have the inexpressible happiness of arriving at Merton even the thoughts [*sic*] of it vibrates thro' my nerves,[1] for my love for you is as unbounded as the ocean, I feel all your good mothers[2] kindness and I trust that we shall turn rich by being œcconymists [*sic*] spending money to please a pack of people is folly and without thanks I desire that you will say every kind thing from me to her + make her a present of something in my name,[3]

284. *To Lady Hamilton (alias Mrs Thomson)*

[NMM: CRK/19/34]

My Dearest beloved ~~Mrs. T~~ to say that I think of you by day night and all day and all night but too faintly express[es] my feelings of love and affection towards you ~~and our dear little girl the first fruit of our~~ unbounded affection, our dear excellent good ~~Lady Hamilton~~ is the only one who knows any thing of the matter + she has promised me, when you ~~are in the Strains~~[4] again to take every possible care of you as a proof of her never failing regard for your own dear Nelson, Believe me that I am incapable of wronging you in thought word or deed no not all the Wealth of Peru[5] could buy me for one moment it is all yours and reserved wholly for you and ~~you will~~ certainly ~~be with child again~~ from the first moment of our happy dear enchanting [*sic*] blessed meeting. The thoughts of such happiness my dearest only beloved makes the blood fly into my head, The call of our country is a duty which you would deservedly in the cool moments of reflection reprobate was I to abandon, and I should feel so disgraced by seeing you ashamed of me, no longer saying this is the man who has saved his country, this is He who is the first to go forth to fight our battles and the last to return, and then all these honors reflect on you, Ah they will think, what a man what sacrifices has he not made to secure our homes + propertys even the society + happy union with the

[1]Compare: 'You may readily imagine what must be my sensations at the Idea of sleeping with you it setts me on fire even the thoughts much more would the reality' (Doc. No. 113).

[2]Mary Cadogan.

[3]Here a sheet of paper finishes. The sheets that are kept with this letter bear the numbers (3) and (4); apart from the fact that sheet number (2) is missing, the watermark of the first sheet differs from that of the second and third sheet and the contents of the sheet numbered (3) shows that it was written after 9 Jan 1804 (reference to mission to Algiers). The sheets (3) and (4) of CRK/19/33 have therefore been inserted in this edition after the letter that has no end and is dated 13 Jan 1804 (Doc. No. 299).

[4]A possible reference to Lady Hamilton being in labour before childbirth.

[5]Regarded as a treasure trove because of its silver mines at Potosí (formerly 'Alto Perú', Upper Peru, nowadays Bolivia).

finest + most accomplishd woman in the world, as you love how must you feel, My heart is with you cherish it, I shall my best beloved return if it pleases God a victor and it shall be my study to transmit an unsallied [*sic*] name, there is no desire of wealth no ambition that could keep me from all my soul holds dear, no it is to save my country, my wife in the Eye of God and ~~my children talk with Dear Good Lady Hamilton She~~ will tell you that it is all right, and then only think of our happy meeting, Ever for Ever I am yours only yours even beyond this world,

Nelson + Bronte.

Aug^{t}: 26th: for Ever for Ever your own Nelson.

285. *Second codicil to Nelson's will*[1]

[TNA: Prob. 1/22/1][2]

I Horatio Viscount Nelson of the Nile and of Burnham Thorpe in the County of Norfolk and United Kingdom of Great Britain and Ireland and Duke of Bronte in the Kingdom of Farther Sicily having to my last Will and testament which bears date on or about the tenth day of May in the Year of our Lord one thousand eight hundred and three made and published a codicil bearing date the Thirteenth day of the same Month Do make and publish a further codicil to the same last will and testament in manner following that is to say I give and bequeath to Miss Horatia Nelson Thompson (who was Baptized on the thirteenth day of May last in the Parish of S^{t}: Marylebone in the County of Middlesex by Benjn: Lawrence curate and John Willock Ap^{t}: (Ck)[1] and who

[1]See Doc. No. 259.

[2]This codicil is accompanied by a letter to Haslewood: 'Private for yourself + most secret. / My Dear Haslewood / I send You home a codicil to my will which You will not communicate to any person breathing as I would wish You to open read it and if not drawn up properly send me a copy and I will execute it. it is possible that my personal Estate after the disposure of the furniture at Merton may not amount to 4000 £ and sooner than this Legacy or any other should go unpaid I would saddle Bronte or any other Estate with the Legacys, I only mention this as a thing that might happen, and I want to give several other small Legacys and to continue the annuity of one hundred pounds a Year to poor blind M^{rs}: Nelson. / I may congratulate you on the favorable termination (I hope) of my Law Suit You have acted not only as able Lawyers but a most friendly part thro' the whole business I begt you will express my Compliments and thanks to Serg^{t}: Shepherd who have [*sic*] done so much Justice to my cause, and be assured I am Ever My Dear Haslewood your obliged friend / Nelson + Bronte / I have pretty near settled all my Bronte matters and although I shall not probably at present be able to get the Value of it Yet I shall secure to be regularly paid my 3000 £ a year net. / Burn it when read.'.

I acknowledge as my adopted Daughter) The Sum of Four Thousand Pounds Sterling Money of Great Britain to be paid at the expiration of Six months after my decease or sooner if possible, and I leave my Dearest friend Emma Lady Hamilton sole Guardian of the said Horatia Nelson Thompson until she shal[l][2] have arrived at the age of Eighteen Years and the interest of the said four thousand pounds to be paid to Lady Hamilton for her Education and maintenance, this request of Guardianship I earnestly make of Lady Hamilton knowing that She will educate my adopted child in the Paths of Religion and Virtue and give her those accomplishments which so much adorn herself and I hope make her a fit Wife for my Dear Nephew Horatio Nelson who I wish to marry her if he proves worthy in Lady Hamiltons estimation of such a treasure as I am sure she will be.

farther I direct that the legacies ~~of~~ by this my codicil as well as the one by my last will and testament given and bequeathed shall be paid and discharged from and out of my personal estate only and shall not be charged or chargeable upon my real estates in the United Kingdom of Great Britain and Ireland and in the Kingdom of farther Sicily or any or either of them or any part thereof In[3] all other respects I ratify and confirm my said last will and testament and former codicil In witness whereof I the said Horatio Viscount Nelson and Duke of Bronte have to this codicil all in my own handwriting and contained in one sheet of paper sat my hand and seal this sixth day of September in the Year of our Lord one thousand Eight hundred and three

Nelson + Bronte [*seal follows*]

Signed Sealed + published
By the Right Honorable
Horatio Viscount[4] Nelson Duke of
Bronte as and for a Codocil
to his last will + testament
in the presence of,

Geo Murray – First Captain of the Victory
John Scott – Secretary

[1]Transcribed by Nicolas, vii, p. ccxxxvi, as 'Assistant Clerk'.
[2]The second 'l' may be hidden under the binding of the manuscript.
[3]The word 'In' stands at the beginning of the third page.
[4]Inserted.

286. *To Lady Hamilton*

[BL: Egerton 1614 ff. *97–**97, no. *50] Victory off Toulon
Sep^{r}: 8th: 1803.

I have my Dearest Emma done what I thank God have had the power of doing left four thousand pounds to my dear Horatia and desired that she may be acknowledged as my adopted Daughter and I made you her sole Guardian the interest of the money to be paid you untill she is 18 years of age, I trust my Dearest friend that you will (if it should please God to take me out of this world) execute this great charge for me and the dear little innocent for it would add comforts to my last moments to think that she would be educated in the paths of Religion + virtue and receive as far as she may be capable some of those brilliant accomplishments which so much adorn you my dearest friend, you must not allow your good heart to think that although I have left you this important charge that I fancy myself nearer being knocked off by the French Ad^{l}: I believe it will be quite the contrary that God Almighty will again and again bless our just cause with Victory and that I shall live to receive your kind and affectionate congratulations on a brilliant victory, But be that as it may I shall support with Gods help my unblemish'd character to the last and Be ever my Dearest Emma your most faithful attatched and affectionate

Nelson + Bronte.
Lady Hamilton.

287. *To Lady Hamilton*

[NMM: CRK/19/35] Victory Sep^{r}: 10th: 1803.

My dearest Emma what can I send you buffetting [*sic*] the stormy Gulph of Lyons nothing but my warmest affection in return for all your goodness to me and mine,[1] I have sent to Naples to try and get some shawls from the Kings manufactory and have requested M^{r}: Falconet to ask his wife to choose some for you and also some fine Venetian chains, I only wish my Dear Emma that I knew what you would like and I would order them with real pleasure therefore pray tell me We have so very little communication with the Med^{n}: world. Malta and Toulon are in seperate worlds, It takes on the [average][2] 6 or 7 weeks to get an answer to a letter and in 15 to 20 days by the french papers which we get from Paris we

[1]Their daughter, Horatia.
[2]Where the word 'average' is missing, the letter continues on a new page.

have news from London, not the best side of any question you may be sure but enough to give us an idea of how matters go on, I am of opinion that we shall have a Peace much sooner than is generally expected and that will be to me the very highest pleasure in this world to return to Dear Merton and your dear beloved society then I agree with you that I would not give sixpence to call the King my uncle, I have wrote again to Gibbs about my Bronte affairs and to M^{rs}: Greafer I will send you [a copy of this letter], if I can but you must preserve it for I have no other it may be necessary situated as I am to keep her in good humour for 1000 £ may be easily sold off the Estate and I never the wiser, however you will see what I have said. I have wrote to M^{r}: Elliot ab^{t}: Sabatello[1] what a rascal he must be Gaetano is going to Naples and I shall tell him but of course he would rather favor Sab^{to}: his Brother In Law than Julia, I send you my Dearest Emma a 100 £ which you will dispose of as follows, a present for yourself and if you like a triffle [*sic*] to the servants, something to the Poor of Merton, something for M^{rs}: Cadogan Miss Connor, Charlotte +^{c}: +^{c}: I only send this as a triffling remembrance from me whose whole Soul is at Merton Sep^{r}: 16th: the day after I wrote the former part of this letter, M^{r}: Scott received from Venice and desired to present to you two very handsome Venetian chains received from Venice this I would not suffer for I allow no one to make my own Emma presents but her Nelson therefore he will be paid for them but your obligation is not the less to him. He is a very worthy excellent, modest man and an excellent secretary. D^{r}: Scott is at times wrong in the head absolutely too much learning has turn'd him,[2] but we all go on very well I had a letter from Gibbs ab^{t}: Bronte[3] and from Noble which will begin another letter only Believe me at all times sides + ends most faithfully yours for Ever

Nelson + Bronte

[1]In a letter of 8 Sept 1803: 'I had a letter lately from Lady Hamilton, wherein she says Sabatello Sabitino denies having Julia's money. He had near seventy pounds in money and valuables belonging to her, and now he refuses to pay her. Now, I know that Julia said in my presence, that Sabitino had taken her money, &c, and if he does not return it, I desire to withdraw my character of him, and so does Lady Hamilton; for he may serve others in the same manner: therefore, in behalf of a poor, injured woman, who he knows he has otherwise injured, I beg you will speak to him, and if he does not instantly pay the money to you to be sent home, Lady Hamilton desires not to be considered as recommending him, and I do the same; for I cannot bear such a monster of ingratitude' (Nicolas, v, p. 199).

[2]Being 'wrong in the head' may also have been caused by Scott's head-wound caused by a stroke of lightning that hit him on a passage to the West Indies; Nelson himself attributed Scott's problems to both causes in Doc. No. 293.

[3]Jane Knight, 'Nelson and the Bronte Estate' (*Trafalgar Chronicle*, 2005, 133–44, at 138), quotes from a letter from Gibbs to Nelson of 30 July 1803 (NMM CRK/17/30) that no regular income was to be expected in the near future from the estate.

288. *To Lady Hamilton*

[Nicolas, v, p. 206] Victory, off Toulon,
September 18th, 1803.

My dear Lady Hamilton,

The furniture and linen which was left behind at Palermo and Naples, when you came to England,[1] is, I hope, by this time, safe at Malta. I have desired Mr. Noble to unpack, dry them, and send you a list of the contents, which you must send to the Treasury, in order to obtain an order for their being allowed to come direct to you, without passing through the Custom-House. I believe the cases are eighteen in number. I have requested the favour of Mr. Brown, Commander of the Prévoyante Store-Ship, who will carry them either to Portsmouth or the Nore, to whichever place he may be ordered. If you will apply by letter to my friend, Mr. Vansittart,[2] of the Treasury, I am sure he will send an order directly for their delivery. Only tell me, my dear Friend, in what manner I can be useful to you in this Country, and, believe me, I shall be truly proud in obeying your commands, being for ever, your most obliged, faithful, and affectionate,

Nelson and Bronte.

289. *To Lady Hamilton*

[Morrison, ii, p. 218 (No. 730)] September 19th, 1803

I write, my dearest Emma, the letter sent herewith, in order that you send it to Mr. Vansittart.[3] Ever yours most faithfully [&c.] As this ship goes by Malta, I do not write a line by her unless she should pick them up at Gib^r, for I have not a small vessel belonging to me.

290. *To Lady Hamilton*

[NMM: CRK/19/36] Sep^r: 26th: 1803

My dearest Emma,

We have had for these 14 days past nothing but gales of Wind and a heavy sea however as our ships have suffer'd no damage I hope to be

[1]See letter of 10 June1803 (Doc. No. 269), in which Nelson had promised: 'I shall write to Mr. Gibbs to tell me about your things, and if I ever get hold of them, I will send them home'.

[2]Nicholas Vansittart (1766–1851), Joint Secretary of the Treasury (whom Nelson came to know in 1800, when Vansittart was British minister plenipotentiary in Copenhagen).

[3]See Doc. No. 288.

able to keep the sea all winter, nothing but dire necessity shall force me to that out of the way place Malta, if I had depended on that island for supplies for the fleet we must all have been knocked up long ago, for Sir Rich[d]: Bickerton sail'd from Malta the same day I left Portsmouth so that we have been a pretty long cruise, and if I had only to look to Malta for supplies our ship's companys would have been done for long ago. however by management I have got supplies from Spain and also from fr<u>an</u>ce but it appears that we are almost shut out from Spain for they begin to be very uncivil to our ships, however I suppose by this time something is settled, but I never hear from England, my last letters are July 6th: near three months, but as I get french newspapers occasionally we guess how matters are going on, I have wrote M[r]: Gibbs again a long history about Bronte and I hope if Gen[l]: Acton will do nothing for me that he will settle something, but I know whatever is now settled I shall be the loser, till next year the debt will not be paid off how . . .[1]

291. *To Lady Hamilton*

[BL: Egerton 1614 ff. 96–97, no. 50] Victory off Toulon
Oct[r]: 5th: 1803

My Dearest Emma,

By a letter from Davison of the 15th: Aug[t]: sent by Lisbon which reached me on the 1st: of this month I was made truly happy by hearing that my Dearest Emma was at Southend and well, and last night I had the happiness of receiving your own dear letters of June 26th: from Hilborough and of Aug[t]: 3rd: from Southend and most sincerely do I thank God that it has been of so much service to your general health,[2] for believe me my Dear Emma that my life is wrapt up in your welfare, you desire to know my opinion of your coming to Malta or Sicily +[c]: +[c]: +[c]: I will tell you as I have told you before[3] my situation here, therefore you must let your own good sense have fair play, you may readily believe how happy I should be to have peace and to live quietly at Merton with all my soul holds dear, at this moment I can have no home but the Victory and wherever the French fleet may go there will the Victory be found, As to Malta or Sicily or Naples they are places which I may see from some extraordinary occasion, such as[4] an action a landing in Sicily and then probably only for a few days,

[1]The next page of the letter is not preserved in the Croker/Philips collection. As it was neither printed in the 1814–letters nor in Pettigrew, one can assume that it was separated from the first part of the letter at an early stage.

[2]Reference to Lady Hamilton's pregnancy.

[3]The words 'you before' are inserted.

[4]Inserted.

but should the French fleet travel Westward then I shall never see either Malta or Sicily, I assure you my Dearest Emma that Merton has a greater chance of seeing me sooner than Malta, how would you feel to be at that nasty place Malta with nothing but soldiers and diplomatick nonsence, and to hear that the fleet is gone out of the Streights the time will come must come that I shall see Merton if God spares me Malta it is possible I never may see unless after a battle and then that is not certain for if it takes place down the Med^{n}: it would be Gibralter in short my Dearest Emma I can see nothing but uncomfortableness for you by such a voyage, and however much we feel and I believe mutually the pain of being seperated yet the call of our country makes it indispensible [*sic*] for both our honors, the country looks up to the services of the poorest individual much more to me and are you not a sharer of my glory, these things must have their due weight in your mind and therefore I shall only assure you that my attatchment love and affection for you is what no time place or distance can shake I am for Ever + Ever your only yours my Dearest Emma

Gaetano is staying at Naples,[1]
Nelson and Bronte.

remember me kindly to my Brother M^{rs}: Nelson Horace[2] Charlotte and M^{rs}. Cadogan + all friends.

292. *To Lady Hamilton*

[*a)* Pettigrew, ii, p. 346; *b)* Morrison, ii, p. 219 (No. 733)]

[*a)*] October 6th, 1803.
[*b)*] My dearest, beloved Emma,

only believe that I should be far too happy to embrace my own dear Emma, but I see so many obstacles in the way of what would give us both such supreme felicity, that good sence is obliged to give way to what is right, and I verily believe that I am more likely to be happy with you at Merton than any other place, and that our meeting at Merton is more probable to happen sooner than any wild chase into the Mediterranean. I am ever for ever, with all my might, with all my strength, yours, only yours. My soul is God's, let him dispose of it as it seemeth fit to

[1]The phrase 'Gaetano is staying at Naples' is inserted between the end of the main part of the letter ('my Dearest Emma') and Nelson's signature.
[2]Nelson's nephew by his brother William, Horatio Nelson (1788–1808), Viscount Trafalgar.

his infinite wisdom, my body is Emma's. I have had a letter from Mr. George Moyston, who is at Naples, and a very kind one. He has been to the Cataracts in Upper Egypt, through Syria, Palestine, Greece, &c. but has nearly died two or three times, and is now a prisoner on parole to the French, being in quarantine at Otranto when the French went there.

I beg that you will not give credit to any reports which will reach England of the battle – trust to Providence that it will be propitious to your most sanguine wishes, and I hope that Captain Murray will be the bearer of a letter from me to you. Never fear, our cause is just and honourable. From Davison's letter of August 15th, I expect a ship of war every moment; it is now three months I see by the papers that Bolton[1] has got the *Childers*. Had he been here he would have been Post. The Admiralty will send him out of course, and if I know how, I must try and put £5000 in his pocket. Don't you laugh. How I talk of thousands when I do not know how, or rather have not tried, to put money in my own pocket, but they will come. I wish you would have the plan made for the new entrance at the corner. Mr. Linton should give up that field this winter, and in the spring it should be planted very thick to the eastward, and a moderate thickness to the north. The plan for filling up the water on the south and east sides of the house [is good], but care must be taken that the house is not made damp for want of drains. A covered passage from *Downings* must be made beyond the present trees, and rails, and chains, in a line with it to keep carriages from the house. An opening can be left with a post, that foot-passengers may go to the kitchen. This may be done even before you begin the room, it will amuse you, and be of no great expense. I am ever for ever, my dear Emma, yours most faithfully & affectionately

[*a)*] Yours,
Nelson and Bronté.

[*b)*] Best regards to Mrs. Cadogan.

293. *To Lady Hamilton*

[NMM: CRK/19/37] Victory off Toulon
Oct^{r}: 18th: 1803

My Dearest Emma,

Your truly kind and affectionate letters from July 17th: to Aug^{t}: 24th: all arrived safe in the Childers the 6th: of this month, believe me my

[1]William Bolton.

beloved Emma that I am truly sensible of all your love and affection which is reciprocal, You have from the variety of incidents passing before you much to tell me and besides you have that happy knack of making every thing you write interesting, here I am one day precisely like the other except the difference of a gale of wind or not since Sep^r: 1st: we have not had 4 fine days and if the french do not come out soon I fear some of my ships will cry out, You are very good to send me your letters to read M^rs. D.[1] is a damned pimping bitch what has she to do with your love She would have pimped for L^d: B.[2] or Lord L^le:[3] or Capt: M^c:Namara Prince of Wales or any one else She is all vanity fancies herself beautiful witty in short like you, She be damn'd as I wrote you the consulship at Civita Vecchia will not in itself pay their lodgings and the bad air will tip her off. there will be no Lord Bristol's table, he tore his last will a few hours before his death it is said that it was giving every thing to those devils of Italians about him, I wish he may have given M^rs: Denis any thing but I do not think it, and as for you my Dear Emma as long as I can I dont want any of their gifts as for old Q.:[4] he may put you into his will or scratch you out as he pleases I care not, if M^r: Addington gives you the pension it is well, but do not let it fret you, have you not Merton it is clear[5] \the first purchase\ and my Dear Horatia is provided for, and I hope one of these days that you will be my own Duchess of Bronte and then a fig for them all I have just had a letter from Gibbs of which I send you a copy You see what interest he is taking about Bronte I begin to think without some assistance like his that I never should have touched a farthing, it will be 1805, before I touch the estate neither principal or interest of the 7000 ounces have been paid and it is now <u>8000</u> ounces debt

You will see Gibbs at last has fixt on sending his daughter home and I shall be glad of so good an opportunity of obliging him as it will naturally tie him to my interest he was a great fool not to have sent the child with you as you wish'd, I am glad to find my Dear Emma that you mean to take Horatia home, <u>aye</u> she is like her mother will have her own way or kick up a devil of a dust, but you will cure her, I am afraid I should spoil her for I am sure I would shoot any one who would hurt her, She was always fond of my watch and very probably I might have promised her one indeed I gave[6] her one which cost 6 pence, but I go nowhere to

[1]Mrs. Denis?
[2]Lord Bristol?
[3]Lord Lonsdale? Probably referring to the Earl of Lonsdale who died in 1802.
[4]Queensberry.
[5]Of debts?
[6]The word 'gave' is written over another word.

get any thing pretty therefore do not think me neglectful,[1] I send you Nobles letter[2] therefore I hope you will get your cases in good order they have had some narrow escapes,

I am glad you liked South End how that Coffin could come over and palaver, Rowley Keith +^{c}: and Coffin to abuse the Earl,[3] now I can tell you that he is the Earls spy it is Coffin who has injured Sir Andrew Hamond so much, and his custom is to abuse the Earl to get people to speak out and then the Earl takes his measures accordingly to me it is nothing thank God there can be no tales told of my cheating or I hope neglecting my duty whilst I serve I will serve well and closely, when I want rest I will go to Merton, You know my Dear Emma that I am never well when it blows hard therefore imagine what a cruize off Toulon is even in summer time, we have a hard gale every week, and two days heavy swell, it would kill you and myself to see you, much less impossible [*sic*] to have Charlotte Horatia +^{c}: onboard ship, and I that have given orders to carry no women to sea in the Victory to be the first to break them, and as to Malta I may never see it[4] unless we have an engagement and perhaps not then for if it is compleat I may go home for 3 months to see you, but if you was at Malta I might absolutely miss you by leaving the Med^{n}: without warning, the other day we had a report the french were out + seen steering to the westward, We were as far as Minorca when the alarm proved false,[5] therefore my dearest beloved Emma although I should be the happiest of men to live and die with you, yet my chance of seeing you is much more certain by your remaining at Merton than wandering where I may never go, and certainly never to stay 48 hours–, You cannot I am sure more ardently long to see me that [*sic*] I do to be with you, and if the war goes on it is my intention to get leave to spend the next winter in England, but I verily believe that long before that time we shall have peace, as for living in Italy that is entirely out of the question, nobody cares for us, there, and if I had Bronte which thank God I shall not, it would cost me a fortune to go there and be tormented out of my life, I should never sittle [*sic*] my affairs there, I know my own dear Emma if she will let her reason have fair play will say I am right, but she is like Horatia very angry if she cannot have her own way, Her Nelson is

[1]As Nelson writes in Doc. No. 296, he wrote to Mr Falconet to get him a watch for Horatia; with Doc. No. 301 he sent the watch.

[2]This may refer to the letter from Edmund Noble from Malta of 27 Sept 1803 about 'Cases from Girgenti' (BL 34,920, f. 301).

[3]St Vincent?

[4]The words 'I may never see it' are inserted.

[5]Judging from the map given in Knight, p. 452, they went much further westward and did not even get close to Barcelona.

called upon in the most honorable manner to defend his country absence to us is equally painful, but if I had either stayed at home or neglected my duty abroad would not my Emma have blushed for me, She could never have heard of my praises and how the country looks up, I am writing my Dear Emma to reason the point with you and I am sure you will see it in its true light, but I have said my say on this subject and will finish, I have receiv'd your letter with Lord Williams + M^{r}: Kemble's about M^{r}: Palmer he is also recommended by the Duke of Clarence[1] + he says by desire of the Prince of Wales. I have without him 26 to be made Captains and list every day increasing, it is not <u>one</u> whole french fleet that can get thro' it, I shall probably offend many more than I can oblige such is always the case like the tickets – those who get them feel they have a right to them and those [who] do not get them feel offended for ever but I cannot help it, I shall endeavour to do what is right in every situation, and some ball may soon close all my accounts with this world of care + vexation, but never mind my own dear beloved Emma if you are true to me I care not and approve of all my actions however as you say I approve of them myself therefore probably I am right.

Poor Rev^{d}: M^{r}: Scott is I fear in a very bad way, his head had been turn'd by too much learning[2] and the stroke of lightning[3] will never let him be right again. The Secretary Scott is a treasure and I am very well mounted Hardy[4] is every thing I could wish or desire, our days pass so

[1]Prince William Henry (1765–1837), from 1788 Duke of Clarence, later William IV, befriended Nelson in the West Indies and was best man at his wedding in 1787; Nelson kept corresponding with him throughout his life; Knight, p. 677, describes him as a 'baleful influence'.

[2]For Nelson's idea about the effect of 'too much learning' on Alexander Scott, see fn. to Doc. No. 287 with further references.

[3]Scott's *Recollections*, pp. 85–86, record the event of summer 1801 as follows: 'he was . . . returning to Jamaica, in the frigate, when on the passage, the ship, soon after midnight, was struck by lightning in a severe thunderstorm. The electric fluid rent the mizzenmast, killing and wounding fourteen men, and descending into the Captain's cabin, in which Mr. Scott was sleeping, communicated with some spare cartridges and powder horns, which lay on a shelf immediately over his head. By this means he sustained a double shock, the electric fluid struck his hand and arm, passing along the bell wire, with which they were in contact, and the gunpowder exploding at the same time knocked out some of his front teeth, and dreadfully lacerated his mouth and jaw. The lightning also melted the hooks to which the hammock was slung, and he fell to the ground, receiving a violent concussion of the brain. His cabin was found in flames, himself a sheet of fire, and he was taken up senseless, and apparently not likely to live. On landing, he was lodged in a convent, at Kingston, and by the excellent skill of Dr. Blair, Physician to the fleet in the West Indies, he soon recovered from his external injuries; but one side of his body was paralyzed for a length of time – his sight, hearing, and the powers of his mind were also impaired – the last so much so, as to cause general apprehension that he would never regain them; and the nervous system was so completely shattered by the accident, that he suffered from it for the remainder of his life.' For another description of the late effects of the stroke of lightning, see Doc. No. 297.

[4]Inserted.

much alike that having described one you have them all, we now breakfast by candle light and all retire, at eight oclock to bed,

Naples I fancy is in a very bad way in regard to money they have not or pretend not to have enough to pay their officers, and I verily believe if Acton was to give up his place that it would become a province of France, only think of Buonaparte's writing to the Queen to desire her influence to turn out Acton, She answer'd properly at least so says M[r]: Elliot who knows more of Naples than any of us, God help him, and Gen[l]: Acton has I believe more power than ever, by Gibbs letter I see he has sent over about my accounts at Bronte, he can have no interest in being unfriendly to me why should he I want no great matters from him and he can want nothing from me that it is not my duty to give his Sovereigns therefore why should he be against us, for my part my conduct will not alter whether he is [in office] or not, our friend Sir Alex[r]:[1] is a very great diplomatick character and even an ad[l]: must not know what he is negotiating about, although you will scarcely believe that the Bey of Tunis sent the man at my desire, You shall judge, viz– 'The Tunisian Envoy is still here negotiating he is a moderate man and apparently the best disposed of any I ever did business with.'[2] could even the oldest diplomatick character be drier I hate such parade of nonsense, but I will turn from such stuff. You ask me Do you do right to give Charlotte things I shall only say my Dear Emma whatever you do in that way I shall always approve I only wish I had more power than I have but somehow my mind was not sharp enough for prize money L[d]: Keith would have made 20,000 £ and I have not made 6000 £

Poor M[r]: Este how I pity him but what shall I do with him however if he comes I shall shew him all the kindness[3] in my power Oct[r]: 22nd: the vessel is just going off I have not a scrap of news, only be assured of my most affectionate regard, remember me kindly to Charlotte I Shall always love those that are good to Horatia I will write her by another opportunity[4] remember me to M[rs]: Cadogan you may be sure I do not forget Charles, who has not been well. Cap[n]: Capel is very good to him.

I am Ever for ever my Dearest Emma your most faithful + affectionate

Nelson + Bronte.

[1]Ball.

[2]Nelson has marked the quotation only at the beginning of lines with an '='. The first line that is thus marked starts 'still here' and the last of the marked lines runs: 'with. could even the oldest diplomatick'.

[3]This may refer to Lambton Este having been appointed consul-general in Egypt.

[4]He obviously planned to send the letter he had written to Horatia (Doc. No. 294) by another means of conveyance than this one to Lady Hamilton.

294. *To Horatia Nelson Thompson*

[Pettigrew, ii, p. 352] Victory, off Toulon,
Oct. 21, 1803

My dear Child,[1]

Receive this first letter from your most affectionate father. If I live, it will be my pride to see you virtuously brought up; but if it pleases God to call me, I trust to Himself, in that case, I have left Lady Hamilton your guardian. I therefore charge you, my child, on the value of a father's blessing, to be obedient and attentive to all her kind admonitions and instructions. At this moment I have left you, in a Codicil dated the 6th of September, the sum of £ 4000. sterling, the interest of which is to be paid to your guardian for your maintenance and education. I shall only say, my dear child, may God Almighty bless you and make you an ornament to your sex, which I am sure you will be if you attend to all Lady Hamilton's kind instructions; and be assured that I am, my dear Horatia, your most affectionate father,

Nelson and Bronté.

295. *To Lady Hamilton*

[CRC] Oct[r]: 23rd: 1803.

My Dearest Emma,

Will You have the goodness to order Wright the Taylor to make me a uniform coat, and a suit of Livery and undress for William he must recollect that he is grown taller and not to have them too tight over the Breast which the last were, and Davison will contrive and send them out to me, I have sent to Davison to beg him to order me some things from Burgess, and some Brown Stout for ever I am my Dear Emma most faithfully Yours + only Your [*sic*]

Nelson + Bronte.

If young Faddy had been here I could have promoted him, but let him be told to pass his Examination in England, or he may not get confirmed,

[1]Pettigrew, ii, p. 352, states: 'his first letter to his child, addressing it to Miss Horatia Nelson Thomson'.

Closing my letter to you is like taking a long farewell but the Ship is on the Wing + this is the last moment to say may God almighty Bless + protect You for Your most faithful

Nelson + Bronte.

296. *To Lady Hamilton*

[Morrison, ii, pp. 219–20 (No. 734)]

[1]perhaps it had better remain till next year. Mr. Haslewood will do what is right about Linton, and he must take care that I am not taxed for the house when it is quitted more than is necessary, and I should like to have that part which we propose to take in, including Linton's house, *paled* round, and to make a new pathway to the extent of, from the field on Halfhide's side our house round Linton's house (of course, it shuts up the present footpath through the yard), and to cross just beyond the orchard, where the old footway will be as usual. There are contractors for park-paling, & if Mr. Newton and Mr. Leach are friendly we shall find no difficulty; but a good gravel pathway till it reaches the old must be made before we turn the one through the farmyard. I don't mean to pale immediately the whole premises, as I can't afford it. At Michaelmas you will be able to give up Mr. Bennett's premises, and that will be a great expense saved, for after all, my dear Emma, we are not rich. I have wrote to Haslewood fully about the land; I look upon him not only as my surveyor, but my friend. If Mr. Matcham wants his 4000l. he had better take it now I have it, not that I have any fears of Buonaparte's taking it from me. He be damned, and so he will. Amen.

Mr. M. can't take the money, it is trust; what a sad thing for poor old Unwin. I pity him most sincerely.

You have sent me, in that lock of beautiful hair, a far richer present than any Monarch in Europe could if he were so inclined. Your description of the dear angel makes me happy. I have sent to Mr. Falconet to buy me a watch,[2] and told him if it does but tick, and the chain *full* of trinkets, that is all which is wanted. He is very civil, and Mrs. Falconet has sent word that she will do her best in chusing any thing I may want; I believe they are very good people. I had a letter from Mr. Warrington, but I did not chuse to have anything to say to them – we know her of old.

[1]Morrison, ii, pp. 219–20 (No. 734) describes this letter as 'imperfect'; Pettigrew, ii, p. 371, who renders only part of it, refers to the letter in a footnote as 'fragment'.

[2]As promised in Doc. No. 293.

Our friend Acton flatters us much as ever in time of danger; however, it is well to be looked up to, and if he was to quit Naples the kingdom is lost, and I almost fear it will if he stays. Buonaparte threatens that if he[1] will not dismiss Acton, disarm his subjects, and get rid of English influence, that he[2] would march another army to Naples. *The King*, with his own hand, has refused and order'd *Gallo* to demand the withdrawing of the present French troops. Will Russia & the Emperor allow these good loyal sovereigns to be sacrificed?

297. *To Lady Hamilton*

[NMM: MAM/28, photocopy] Victory
Dec[r]: 7th: 1803.

My Dearest Emma,

Friend Gayner an honest Quaker who lives at Roses in Spain has taken charge of a letter for you he will enclose it to his correspondant at Bristol, this good Man having supplied our Ships who I sent to Roses had a mind to see me, therefore he embarked in a small Spanish vessel and luckily join'd next day off Toulon, I was of course attentive to him and he is gone back quite delighted with our regularity and he went to our church on Sunday he had never before been on board a Man of War at Sea, he is to get me Seges[3] and other good Spanish Wines for our cellar at Merton for there if it pleases God I shall spend next Xtmas, My dear Emma how easy peoples characters are blasted what can poor D[r]: Scott have done to injure any one, instead of the character you have heard of him, hear mine, He is a very sober unassuming man, very learned, very Religious and very Sickly, and he reads which is more I dare say than any of our proud churchmen, the lessons for the day, in German, Latin, Greek and English every Day, and even was he disposed to be irregular in his conduct it is not catching, and although I am good friends with all yet I am intimate with none, beyond the cheerful hours of meals, as you may judge from D[r]: Scotts letter, poor fellow once or twice every moon his head is gone at this moment he is abed not scarcely knowing any one, owning to the dreadful stroke of Lightning,[4] as for Hardy I am sure he cares not 3 straws for Troubridge or any at the same time he is too wise to say any thing against

[1]The king of Naples.
[2]Buonaparte.
[3]Most probably Sitges, which is a coastal town about 35 km south-west of Barcelona. Sitges has the winegrowing region of Penedès in its hinterland.
[4]See Doc. No. 293 with fn.

them, Murray is the intimate friend of both but I care not there is nothing thank God my Dear Emma to tell of me, but what you may judge of from Geo. Campbells letter of this day I have but one object in view to them, to find the French fleet and to beat them soundly, and then all the reward I shall ask is to be allowed to come to England, for this constant wearing of the wind must shake any constitution, but some happy day I doubt not I shall be amply repaid, We are very healthy and very unanimous but nearly all the fleet were perfect strangers to me and therefore I can expect no particular marks of private friendship.

(2)
and they have all their own friends as agents, who they will appoint, some of them have as a compliment named my secretary as a past agent, I am sometimes vexed as Good Davison thinks that I can appoint who I please,[1] what I can do he may be sure of, and if I am offered in case of our success ag[t]: the French fleet to name an agent He will be the Man, I am glad you have kept Bones picture[2] at Merton although the other is arrived safe and they all hang in my Bed room, The Watch String came in the right time for the other was very rotten, and as it comes from H[a]: it is of more value to me than if it was covered with diamonds, she must be grown very much how I long to hear her prattle Heavens bless her I am sure she will be mistress, If but Addington ever means to give You the pension it is done before this time if he does not never mind you have a good house and Land at Merton which he cannot take from you, and I do not believe the French will, for although I hear of their blustering at Bolounge [*sic*] and of Buonapartes being there parading, I can never believe that they can succeed beyond getting a few thousands on shore to be massacred, when he has tried and fail'd I think we shall have peace, I will write a line to the old Duke

(3)
I have got a little box of Chains + Earings + Bracelets which M[r]: Falconet writes me M[rs]: Falconet was so good as to chuse for you as he says they are nicely packed I have not open'd them but I donot [know] whether I can send them in the Admiralty packet, I have few opportunitys of getting any little thing for you and must trust to the taste of our friends but my beloved Emma will take my intentions as well meant, Dec[r]: 13th:[3] although I have not been ill yet the constant anxiety I have

[1]See Doc. No. 282.

[2]Henry Bone's copy of Elisabeth Vigée LeBrun's painting of *Lady Hamilton as Bacchante (or Ariadne)*; for more information, see Appendix 3.

[3]The date is inserted above the line.

experienced have shook my weak frame and my rings will hardly keep upon my finger, and what grieves me more than all is that I can every month perceive a visible (if I may be allowed the expression) loss of sight, a few years must as I have always predicted render me blind, I have often heard that Blind people are cheerful but I think I shall take it to heart, however if I am so fortunate as to gain a great Victory over the Enemy the only favor I shall ask will be for permission to retire, and If the contrary I sincerely pray that I may never live to see it, we must all have an end, but my dearest Emma let us hope the best my last thought will be for you and those we hold most dear, but I will have done this triste[1] subject, Ad^{l}: Campbell desires me to make his kind regards, I had his Nephew on board yesterday and to meet him Cap^{n}: Conns Son not 3 feet high, M^{rs}: Lutwidges Eleve young Dalton who is a very fine Lad Sir John Sinclair Lord W^{m}: Gordons Nephew and M^{r}: Bulkeley[2] the last grown one of the finest and active young men I ever saw I only regret that he has not served his time,[3] all the Grandees dined with Campbell + I had a Midshipmans party we are refitting some of our shattered Barks but we cannot even get one Cask of Water a river is found[4] but it is a fine anchorage[5] I am waiting for our Victuallers from Malta which have sail'd more than 14 days but you remember our beat round Maritimo in the Foudroy^{t}:[6] Hardy is well and the Victory in high order, Dec^{r}: 25th: off Toulon here we are and there (in Toulon) are the French I have not heard a scrap of news from any a master except Malta and Constantinople, I am as popular there as Ever so M^{r}: Drummond[7] writes me you know the Turkish mode of writing the Grand Vizir begins his letter, To the Model of Lords believing in the Messiah, The support of the Grandees of the T^{n}: Nations, +^{c}: +^{c}: and the Captain Pashas is in the same style, Good people they want my help to protect the Morea, + Egypt, Macaulay is still living he has sent me out a Milck sheep but unfortunately they get

[1]Italian (and other Romance languages) for sad.

[2]Richard Bulkeley; Nicolas, v, p. 184, fn.: 'Richard Bulkeley, the son of an old friend of Lord Nelson, who was with him at St. Juan . . . and from whom there are numerous letters in the Nelson Papers. Mr. Bulkeley was a Midshipman of the Victory, was wounded at Trafalgar, was made a lieutenant in 1806, and died between 1809 and 1814.'

[3]Enabling him to be promoted.

[4]The words 'a river is found' are inserted.

[5]Gulf of Palma or Pula Roads, both at the southern end of Sardinia.

[6]This probably refers to the return journey from Malta to Palermo at the end of May 1801 that took eleven days (20–31 May). The island of Marettimo is the outermost of the Aegadian Islands, off the western tip of Sicily.

[7]William Drummond of Logiealmond (1769–1828) served 1801–3 as Envoy to the court of Naples.

dry before they arrive, remember me Dear Emma to all our kind friends M^{rs}: Cadogan, Charlotte, Miss Connor +^{c}: +^{c}: I have wrote to the D^{r}: + to Horace and be assured I am to the last moment of my life yours only yours faithfully

Nelson + Bronte.

I have had a very kind letter from Tyson he took the opportunity of Cap^{n}: Duncan of the Serapis[1] to send me some good things.[2]

298. *To Lady Hamilton*

[Pettigrew, ii, p. 359] Victory, Madalena,
December 26th, 1803.

My dearest Emma,

After closing my dispatches the weather was so bad, that we could not unload our transports at sea, therefore I anchored here on Saturday, and hope to get to sea on Wednesday.[3] The Phoebe joined me here, and carries my letters to Gibraltar. I had Charles on board yesterday to dinner. Capel gives a very good account of him, and I have impressed upon his mind that if he behaves well, he will never want a protector in you and me. He had about three months ago, something wrong in his head. The killing a Lieutenant and some men belonging to the Phoebe, made such an impression, that he fancied he saw a ghost, &c. but Dr. Snipe thinks it is gone off. Was any of his family in that way? He is clever, and I believe Capel has been kind to him. I have had violent colds, and now and then a spasm, but Dr. Snipe takes care of me, and would give me more physic, but he says I am a bad patient; but I trust I shall do very well till the battle, and after that, if it pleases God I survive, I shall certainly ask permission to go home to recruit, and in this world nothing will give me so much pleasure as to see my dear Emma, being most faithfully,

Nelson and Brontë.

[1]The *Serapis*, under Charles Duncan as Master since Jan 1796, served as a storeship at Deptford from Jan 1802 to June 1803, but was recommissioned in May 1803 to sail under Commander Henry Warin, for the Leeward Islands; see Rif Winfield, *British Warships in the Age of Sail 1793–1817. Design, Construction, Careers and Fates* (London, 2005).

[2]The postscript is added upside down on the top of the last page.

[3]Saturday was 24 Dec and Wednesday 28 Dec 1803.

299. *To Lady Hamilton*

[NMM: CRK/19/38 and 33][1]

Victory under Majorca
Jan^{ry}: 13th: 1804

My own dear beloved Emma I rec^{d}: on the 9th: your letters of Sep^{r}: 29th: Oct^{r}: 2, 7, 10, 12, 17th: 21 Nov^{r}: 8th: 5th: to the 24th:[2] and I am truly sensible of all your kindness and affectionate regard for me which I am sure is reciprocal in every respect from your own Nelson, If that Lady Bitch knew of that persons[3] coming to her house it was a trick but which I hope you will not subject yourself to again, but I do not like it, however it is passed and we must have confidence in each other and my dearest Emma judging of you by myself it is not all the world that could seduce me in thought word or deed from all my soul holds most dear, indeed if I can help it I never intend to go out of the ship but to the shore of Portsmouth and that will be if it pleases God before next Xt^{s}:[4] indeed I think long before if the French will venture to sea, I send you a letter from the Queen of Naples they call out might + main for our protection and God knows they are sure of me. M^{r}: Elliot complains heavily of the expence and says he will retire the moment it is Peace he expected his family when they would sett down 11 Elliots. if my Dear Emma you are to mind all the reports you may hear you may always be angry with your Nelson in the first place instead of 8 days M^{r}: Acourt[5] he came on board one day just before dinner and left me next morning after breakfst: what pleasure people can have in telling lies but I care not what they say I defy them all,

You may safely rely that I can for ever repeat with truth these words for Ever I love you and only you my Emma and you may be assured as long as you are the same to me that you are never absent a moment from my thoughts, I am glad you are going to Merton You will live much more comfortable and much cheaper than in London, and this spring if you like to have the House altered you can do it, but I fancy you will soon tire of so much dirt and the inconvenience will be very great the whole summer, all I request if you fix to have it done [is] that M^{r}: Davisons architect

[1]The beginning of the letter is in CRK/19/38; the part of the letter, starting with the sheet number (3) is in CRK/19/33; for the reason of this assignment see fn.at number (3) below.

[2]It appears that Nelson had originally left a gap between 'letters of' and 'and I am truly sensitive' in order to fill in the dates of the letters sent. The impression that he filled in the dates later is caused by the fact that the dates are written in a narrow handwriting and '24th:' is written above the word 'and'.

[3]The Prince of Wales?

[4]Christmas.

[5]The words 'M^{r}: Acourt' are inserted.

~~you~~ who[1] drew the plan may have the insfection [*sic*] and he must take care that it does not exceed the estimate If it is done by contract you must not alter, or a bill is run up much worse than if we had never contracted, therefore I must either buy the materials and employ reputable workmen under the architect, or contract, I rather believe it would be better for me to buy the materials and put out the building to a workman, but you must get some good advice, with respect to the New Entrance . . .[2]

(3)[3]
Dr: Scott is gone with my mission to Algiers[4] or I would send you a copy of the King + Queens letter, I send you one from the Queen, both King Queen + Acton were very civil to Sir Wm: Bolton[5] he dined with Acton, Bolton does very well in his Brig but he has made not a farthing of Prize money if I knew where to send him for some he should go but unless we have a Spanish war I shall live here at a great expence although Mr: Chevalier takes every care and I have great reason to be satisfied, I have just asked Willm: who behaves very well whether he chooses to remit any of his wages to his father it does not appear he does at present he is paid by the King 18 £ a-year as one of my retinue therefore I have nothing to pay I have told him whenever he chooses to send any to tell Mr: Scott or Capt: Hardy and he will receive a remittance bill, so he may now act as he pleases, apropos of Mr: Scott he is very much obliged to you for your news of Mrs: Sts: being brought to bed, no letters came in the cutter but to me and he was very uneasy he is a very excellent good man and I am very

[1]The word 'who' stands above the crossed-out 'you'.

[2]Here the sheet is finished and no continuation of the letter is preserved in NMM, CRK/19/38.

[3]A sheet of paper numbered (2) is not in NMM, CRK/19/33. The printed versions of this letter in the 1814-letters and in Pettigrew continue at the end of Doc. No. 283, but as the beginning of the text on this sheet (numbered '(3)') refers to an event of Jan 1804 (the 'mission to Algiers') and bears the same watermark as CRK/19/38, I have chosen to insert this second part of the letter after that of 13 Jan 1804.

[4]On 9 Jan 1804 Nelson sent Captain Richard Goodwin Keats on a mission to Algiers in order to resolve the conflict with the Dey over local women in the house of the British consul, John Falcon (Nicolas, v, pp. 345–51); there is a short note about the issue in Scott's *Recollections*, p. 120.

[5]Nicolas, v, p. 183 (who gives the three sheets of CRK/19/33 as one letter, dated 26 Aug 1803, see Doc. No. 283, whereas pages (3) and (4) are here attributed to the unfinished letter in CRK/19/38), comments in a footnote: 'Sir William Bolton was not sent to Naples until the 8th of October 1803, (vide "Order-Book", and p. 238, post.) and other passages shew that if this letter [Doc. No. 283 in this collection] was begun on the 26th of August 1803, it was not continued until long after that date.'

fortunate in having such a one, I admire your kindness to my Dear sister Bolton I have wrote her that certainly I will assist Tom Bolton at College It is better as I tell her not to promise more than I am sure I can perform It is only doing them an injury I tell her If vacancys please God should happen that my income will be much increased, with respect to M^{r}: Bolton every body knows that I have no interest nobody cares for me but if he will point out what he wants I will try what can be done but I am sure he will not be half so well off as at present supposing he could get a place of a few hundreds a year he would be a ten times poorer man than he is at present I could convince you of it in a moment but if I was to begin then it would be said I wanted inclination to render them a service. I should like to see Sir H. P.'s book[1] I can not conceive how a man that is reported to have[2] been so extravagant of Governments money to say no worse[3] can make a good story I wrote to the old Duke no long since I regard him but I would not let him touch you for all his money no that would never do.

I believe M^{r}: Bennetts bill to be correct but it was not intended you should pay that out of the allowance for Merton and how could you[4] afford to send M^{rs}: Bolton 100 £ it is impossible out of your income. I wish M^{r}: Addington would give you 500 £ a year then you would be better able to give away than at present but your purse my Dear Emma will always be empty your heart is generous beyond your means.[5]

(4)
Your good mother is always sure of my sincerest regard pray tell her so Connor is getting on very well but I cannot ask Cap^{n}: Capel to rate him that must depend upon the Boys fitness and Capels kindness, I have placed another years allowance of 30 £ in Capels hands + given Connor a present.

What a story about Oliver and M^{r}: Matchams buying an Estate in Holstein and to sell out at such a loss I never heard the like I sincerely hope it will answer his Expectations it is a fine country but miserably cold.

[1]Home Popham, *A Concise Statement of Facts Relative to the Treatment Experienced by Sir Home Popham since his Return from the Red Sea* ([n.d., according to Nicolas, v, p. 184, fn.: 1803; according to the BL catalogue: 1805]).

[2]Inserted.

[3]In order to purge the naval administration of malpractice, St Vincent had created a Commission of Naval Enquiry, which accused Sir Home Popham – among others – of incurring unnecessary expenses in the repair of his ship in the East Indies. A parliamentary inquiry later settled that the evidence for this case against this supporter of Pitt had been fabricated by St Vincent's secretary, John Tucker. Unlike in the case of Sir Home Popham, where Nelson trusted St Vincent's evidence, Nelson supported Andrew Snape Hamond against St Vincent's eagerness in purging the navy.

[4]Inserted.

[5]Here a sheet of paper finishes and the letter is continued on a new one.

How can Tyson be such a fool I sincerely hope he will never want money, I am not surprised at Troubridges abuse but his tongue is no scandal, you make me laugh when you imitate the D^{r}:[1]

I am quite delighted with Miss Yonges goodness and I beg you will make my best respects to[2] her and her good Father and assure M^{r}: Yonge how much obliged I feel for all his kind attentions to you, those who do that, are sure of a warm place in my esteem

I have wrote to Dumourier[3] therefore I will only trouble you to say how much I respect him, I fancy he must have suffered great distress at Altona[4] however I hope he will now be comfortable for life. He is a very clever man + beats our Generals out and out dont they feel his coming advice [*sic*] him not to make Enemies by showing he knows more than some of us, Envy knows no bounds to its persecution – he has seen the World and will be on his Guard.

I put Suckling into a frigate with a very good man who has a school master he does very well, Bulkley[5] will be a most excellent sea officer it is a pity he has not served his time[6] I have answered M^{r}: Suckling's[7] letter,

Gaetano is very well and desires his duty I think sometimes that he wishes to be left at Naples but, I am not sure,

M^{r}: Denis['s] relation has been long in the Victory but if the ad^{ty}: will not promote my Lieut^{ts}: they must all make a retrog[r]ade motion but I hope they will not do such a cruel thing. I have had a very affectionate letter from Lord Minto. I hope George[8] will be confirmed but the Earl will not answer his application,[9] I shall send you some sherry and a cask

[1]William Nelson.

[2]Inserted.

[3]Charles François Du Perrier Dumouriez.

[4]Town situated on the river Elbe. Biggest town of the duchies of Schleswig-Holstein. Since 1938 incorporated into the city of Hamburg.

[5]Richard Bulkeley.

[6]In order to be promoted.

[7]This probably refers to Lieutenant-Colonel William Suckling, who was, according to Nicolas, iii, p. 1, a 'natural son' of Nelson's uncle William Suckling and father to young William Benjamin Suckling.

[8]Probably Elliot.

[9]Nicolas, v, p. 184, fn: 'This is explained by a Letter from Lord St. Vincent to Lord Minto, in Tucker's Memoirs (ii, p. 248), dated 2nd January 1804, whence it appears that Lord St. Vincent had desired Lord Nelson to promote Captains Durban and Hillyar, to Post vacancies, and as Lord Nelson had not written to inform the Admiralty of his having given Captain Elliot an Acting Order in the Maidstone, Lord St. Vincent said, "I was under the necessity of waiting an explanation, before I could recommend a commission to be made out for my young friend: a satisfactory one is now arrived and the needful will be done forthwith." Captain Elliot's commission bore date on the 2nd of January 1804, instead of on the day which he received his Acting Order'. –The following passage from 'I shall send you' until 'to the carraige' is crossed out with one big cross.

of Paxaretti,[1] by the convoy perhaps it had better go to ~~Davis~~ Merton at once or to Davisons cellar where the wine cooper can draw it off, I have two pipes of sherry that is bad but if you like you can send the Dr: a Hogshead of that which is coming. Davison will pay all the Dutys send it entirely free even to the carraige you know doing the thing well is twice doing it for sometimes carraige is more thought off than the prime cost.[2]

The Paxoretti I have given to Davison and ordered one Hogshead of sherry to Canterbury[3] and one to dear Merton.

300. *To Lady Hamilton*

[*a)* Pettigrew, ii, p. 372; *b)* Morrison, ii, pp. 222–3 (No. 742); *c)* Christie's, 3 Dec 2003, lot 150]

[*a)*] Victory, January 20th, 1804.

My dear Emma,

[*b)*] I send a very neat watch[4] for our god-child, and you will see it is by a good maker, that is I suppose it will *tick* for a year instead of a month or two. You will impress her that it is only to be worn when she behaves well and is obedient. I am very sorry that your comb is not arrived, the brig is at Malta, but I daresay it will arrive sometime and you shall have it the first opportunity. I send you Mr. Falconet's letter. You will see how very civil both of them are. Mr. Elliot is a great Minister, but I doubt whether the [*c)*] Queen has much real friendship for him Acton has him fast, but I believe Mr: E.[5] had rather that Acton + the King + Queen looked to him for my services than applying to myself, but circumstanced as I have been and am with that Court Sir William Hamilton gave it up and no other person shall deprive me of the immediate communication, No my dear Emma what I do for them shall be from myself and not through him, They are in very great fears at this moment.

[1]1814-letters have here 'Paxoretti', as has Nelson further down in the letter; a contemporary text of 1807 gives 'Paxaretti', however: 'From the Portuguese dominions we admit port and Madeira; and from the Spanish sherry and paxaretti' (*The Director*, 1807, 265). The name derives from the town of Pajarete (x and j used to be interchangeable in many Spanish words and names), which is situated East of Jerez de la Frontera and where Sherry wines (from the region of Jerez de la Frontera, near the Atlantic coast) and Malaga wines (from the Mediterranean coast) were mixed to make a sweet wine.

[2]The following additional note appears on the top of the page, where there was still some empty space left.

[3]To his brother William.

[4]See Docs Nos 293 and 296 and letter to Horatia of the same day (Doc. No. 301).

[5]Hugh Elliot.

I have been towards Algiers[1] where I sent a ship with Mr: Falcon our Consul who The Dey turn'd away but the Dey has been made so insolent by Mr: Norths conduct in giving him 30,000£ that nothing I suppose but a flogging will put him in order, and with the French fleet ready to put to sea that I have not time for,[2] I have been my own Emma but very indifferent a violent cold upon my breast Asses milk would have done me much service but I am better and I hope to continue so 'till the battle is over then I hope my business here will be finishd that it may be soon is the sincere wish of my Dearest Emma your Ever most faithful + affectionate

Nelson + Bronte.

I send You the Queens last letter Dr: Scott I fear will not have time to copy the other

301. *To Horatia Nelson Thompson*

[Monmouth: E 161] Victory
Janry: 20th: 1804

My Dear Horatia,
I send you a Watch which I give you permission to wear on Sundays, and on very particular days when you are dressed and have behaved exceedingly well and obedient I have kissed it and send it with the affectionate Blessing of Your[3]

Nelson + Bronte

Victory Janry: 20th: 1804[4]

302. *To Lady Hamilton*

[BL: Egerton 1614 ff. 98–99, no. 51] Victory
febry: 10th: 1804 Madalena

My Dearest best and only beloved friend We were blown in here on the 8th:[5] in the heaviest gale of Wind at NE and snow storm that I almost ever

[1]Nelson was off Algiers 17–19 Jan 1804.
[2]On 9 Jan 1804 Nelson had sent Captain Keats on a mission to Algiers (see Doc. No. 299). About a week later he followed himself and stayed off Algiers between 17 and 19 Jan, when he sailed north again.
[3]The words 'Blessing' and 'Your' are underlined thrice each with very thick lines of ink.
[4]The date is written at the bottom of the letter again.
[5]The words 'on the 8th:' are inserted.

felt, but all your letters to Dec[r]: 27th: I found just arrived they warmed me with the proof of your continued regard love and true affection it is be assured reciprocal I have not a thought wish or desire seperated from you I cannot tell you all I wish as Lord Nelson has enjoined the fleet not to write politicks, We are on the eve of a battle and I have no doubt but it will be a glorious one at least it shall be such a one that shall never bring a blush on the cheeks of my dearest best beloved friend when my name is mentioned our fleet is healthy, our men spirited, our Commanders brave + judicious, and for our numbers the finest fleet in the world, I only hope our dearest friends are well and happily past all danger,[1] may God in heaven bless and protect you my last sigh will be my dearest Emma for your felicity for I am to the last moment yours and only your faithful

---

best regards to all friends. I have received all letters + papers.

303. *Third codicil to Nelson's will*[2]

[TNA: Prob. 1/22/1]

I Horatio Viscount Nelson and Duke of Bronte +[c]: +[c]: +[c]: do hereby give and bequeath to my Dearest friend Emma Lady Hamilton Widow of the Right Honorable Sir William Hamilton K. B[th]: the net yearly sum of five hundred pounds to be[3] paid and consider'd as a tax upon the Rental of my Estate at Bronte in Sicily, to be paid every six months the first to be paid in advance and so continued for and during the term of Her natural Life, and however I may in my will have disposed of Bronte I declare this as a codicil to my said will and it is my intent notwithstanding any want of Legal forms of which I am ignorant that the allow[ed][4] net sum should be paid the said Emma Hamilton as I have before wrote, Dated on board His Majesty's Ship Victory at Sea this nineteenth day of February, one thousand Eight Hundred and four.

Nelson + Bronte,

Witness our hands the date as above written.
T.M.Hardy Cap[n]: of HMS. Victory
John Scott, Secretary[5]

[1]Allusion to birth of second child.
[2]See Doc. No. 259.
[3]Inserted.
[4]The letter is damaged at the margin.
[5]Hardy's and Scott's signatures are in their respective handwritings.

N B. The aforementioned sum of five hundred pounds a Year to be first paid after the Rent is received.

Nelson + Bronte.

304. *To Lady Hamilton*

[CRC]

Victory
febry: 25th: 1804

God knows whether you will ever get this letter my Dearest Emma for Lord Nelson tells me it is very probable never to reach you, Lord N. has been very anxious about your recovery and charges me to say every kind thing for him You kno[w][1] him and how sincerely he is devoted to [you],[2] nothing will probably leave th[e][3] fleet 'till after the battle, Lord N. thin[ks][4] (so I hear) that as so many troops are prepared for embarkation and a general Embargo at Genoa Leghorn + reports say at Civita Vecchia and the Ships seized for transports that the French will certainly try and get more Ships into the Medn:

We saw the French fleet in Toulon on the 22nd: perfectly ready, I have heard very lately from Naples the French army is ready for Service and have baked a months bread for their army, The Stroke is ready, where will it fall, but this fleet is prepared for all events and for our numbers it cannot [be equ]alled,[5] our only wish is to meet [the]m,[6] may God in heaven bless an[d] preserve you and those I hold most dear is my dearest Emma the fervent prayer of your most faithful + attatched —

Kind regard to all friends.

305. *To Lady Hamilton*

[Morrison, ii, p. 225 (No. 747)]

February 25th, 1804

As Lord Nelson tells me that it is very probable this letter may not only be read, but never arrive to your hands, I only write this line to say, here

[1]The last letter is at the end of the line, where the letter is torn.
[2]This word was torn with opening the seal.
[3]Here the end of the line was torn with the seal.
[4]Here again the end of the line was torn with the seal.
[5]The beginning of the line was torn with the seal.
[6]Again the beginning of the line was torn with the seal.

we are, and have for the whole of this month experienced such a series of bad weather, that I have seldom seen the like. I am anxious in the extreme to hear that you are perfectly recovered from your late indisposition.[1] Lord Nelson has heard very lately from Naples. The French army is prepared for service, and have a month's bread baked in readiness; an embargo is laid at Genoa and Leghorn, and all the vessels seized as transports; so that we must have some work very soon. I only hope to keep my health till the battle is over, but my spasms have been very bad lately. We saw the French fleet very safe on the 22nd, at evening. Lord Nelson rather expects the ships from Ferrol in the Mediterranean. With my kindest love and affection to all I hold dear, believe me for ever, my dearest Emma, your most faithful and attach'd.

This goes by Spain.

306. *To Lady Hamilton*

[NMM: CRK/19/39] Victory
March 14th: off Toulon.

Young Faddy my dearest Emma brought me two days ago your dear and most kind letter of Nov^{r}: 26th: and you are sure that I shall take a very early opportunity of promoting him and he appears to be grown a fine young man, but vacancys do not happen very frequently in this station however if he behaves well he may be sure of me, with respect to M^{r}: Jefferson I can [neither] say nor do any thing, The surgeon of the Victory[2] is a very able excellent man and the ship is kept in the most perfect state of health and I would not if I could but thank [God] I cannot do such an unjust act as to remove him, he is my own asking for and I have every reason to be perfectly content, M^{r}: Jefferson got on by my help and by his own misconduct he got out of a good employ=[3] and have [*sic*] seen another person at Malta hospital put over his head he must now begin again and act with much more attention and sobriety than he has done to ever get forward again but time may do much and I shall rejoice to hear of his reformation, I am not surprized my Dearest Emma at the enormous expences of the watering place but if it has done my own Emma service it is well laid out, a 1000 £ a year will not go far and we need be great œeconimicsts [*sic*] to make both ends meet and to carry on the little improvements as for making one farthing more prize-money I do not expect it, except by taking the French fleet and the event of that day who

[1]The expected birth of 'young Emma'. See also 'All I long for just now is to hear that you are perfectly recovered' in Doc. No. 306.

[2]Dr George Magrath.

[3]The word 'employ=' stands at the end of a line, so that it appears that Nelson had planned to continue in the next line with '=ment'.

can foresee, with respect to M^rs: Graefer what she has done God and herself knows but, I have made up my mind that Gibbs will propose 100 £ a year for her if so I shall grant it and have done I send you M^rs: G^s: last letter, whilst I am upon the subject of Bronte, I have one word more and your good dear kind heart must not think that I shall die one hour the sooner on the contrary my[1] mind has been more content ever since I have done, I have left you a part of the rental of Bronte to be first paid every half year and in advance,[2] it is but common Justice and whether M^r: Addington gives you any thing or not you will want it, I would not have you lay out more than is necessary at Merton the Rooms and the new entrance will take a good deal of money the entrance by the corner I would have certainly done, a common white gate will do for the present[3] and one of the cottages which is in the Barn can be put up as a temporary lodge, the Road can be made so

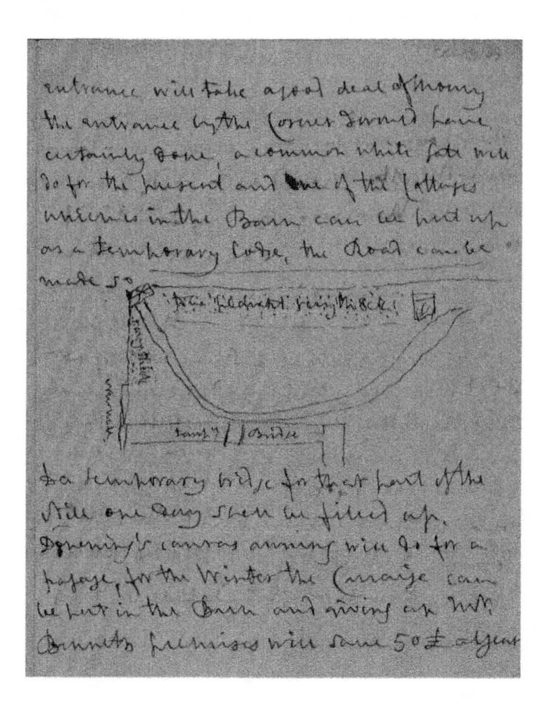
entrance will take a good deal of money
the entrance by the Corner I would have
certainly done, a common white gate will
do for the present and one of the Cottages
which is in the Barn can be put up
as a temporary Lodge, the Road can be
made so

& a temporary bridge for that part of the
[illegible] one day shall be filled up.
Downing's canvas awning will do for a
passage, for the Winter the Carriage can
be put in the Barn and giving up Mr
Bennett's premises will save 50 £ a year

Sketch of how Nelson wished his garden at Merton to be laid out,[4] in letter to Lady Hamilton of 14 March 1804 (Doc. No. 306) [NMM CRK 19 39, detail].

[1]Inserted.

[2]See Doc. No. 303.

[3]Nelson had written about the gate in Doc. No. 283.

[4]Nelson's explanations in the drawing are: of the hedges 'to lie [?]ted very thick!', 'very thick'; 'new wall'; 'temp^y: Bridge'.

to a temporary bridge for that part of the Nile one day shall be filled up. Downing's canvas awning will do for a passage, for the winter the carraige can be put into the Barn and giving up M^{r}: Bennetts premises will save 50 £ a year and another year we can fitt up the coach house + stables which are in the Barn The footpath should be turn'd, I did show M^{r}: Haslewood the way I wished it done, and M^{r}:[1] will have no objections if we make it better than ever it has been and I also beg as my dear Horatia is to be at Merton that a strong netting ab^{t}: 3 feet high may be placed round the Nile that the little thing may not tumble in and then you may have ducks again in it I forget at what place we saw the netting and either M^{r}: Perry[2] or M^{r}: Goldsmid[3] told us where it was to be bought, I shall be very anxious untill I know this is done I have had no very late opportunitys of sending to Naples but via Malta I wrote to Gibbs to desire he would send over and purchase the armosins[4] they will arrive in time, I hope the watch is arrived safe,[5] the British fair cutter I hope is arrived safe She has three packets from me to England,

The expences of the alterations at Merton you are not to pay from the income, let it all be put to a seperate account and I will provide a fund for the payment. All I long for just now is to hear that you are perfectly recovered[6] and then I care for nothing all my hopes are to see you and be happy at dear Merton again but I fear this miscarraige of Pichegru's[7] in france will prolong the War, It has kept the french fleet in Port which we are all sorry for Sir W^{m}: Bolton was on board yesterday he looks thin the fag in a Brig is very great and I see no prospect of his either making prize money or being made Post at present but I shall omit no opportunity I wrote to M^{rs}: B^{n}: a few months ago and gave her letter yesterday to Bolton he conducts himself very well indeed, Ever my Dearest Emma for Ever I am your most faithful + affec^{te}:

Nelson + Bronte

[1]Nelson left a gap after 'M^{r}:' which he never filled.

[2]James Perry (1756–1821), editor of the *Morning Chronicle*.

[3]Abraham Goldsmid (1756–1810); Knight, p. 640, describes him as: 'Financier and benefactor of naval charities'.

[4]Thick, plain silk.

[5]Nelson sent a watch with his letters to Lady Hamilton and Horatia of 20 Oct 1804 (Docs Nos 300 and 301).

[6]A reference to Lady Hamilton's confinement. See also 'I am anxious in the extreme to hear that you are perfectly recovered from your late indisposition' in Doc. No. 305.

[7]Charles Pichegru (1761–1804), formerly General in the French Revolutionary Army, had travelled in Aug 1803 from his English exile to Paris in order to head a royalist uprising. The plan was betrayed, Pichegru imprisoned in Feb 1804 and found strangled in prison in April 1804.

307. *To Lady Hamilton*

[Huntington: HM 34096]

(2)[1]

We have been expecting the french fleet at sea to relieve me from some anxiety but many think (but I do not) that the Spanish fleet is to join them,[2] but let us meet them in any reasonable numbers and You shall my dear Emma have no reason to be ashamed of Your own Nelson, I send You the comb which looks handsome, and a pair of curious gloves they are made only in Sardinia of the beards of mussles,[3] I have ordered a muff, they tell me they are very scarce, and for that reason I wish You to have them, I must write a line to M[rs]: Denis but in truth say although I am much obliged by her kind letter and good wishes that I can do nothing more and barely that to acknowledge the receipt, I do not think I can answer my brother by this opportunity I will write him soon remember me most kindly to the Duke of Queensberry I love the old man and would give up any thing but you to him, and to all our joint friends for I can have none seperate from being yours say every thing that is kind, never mind M[r]: Addington if he does not do what is right the more shame for him thank God I have both the power and inclination I shall not close this till the last, The destination of the Enemy has as many opinions as there are countrys, Sir Alex[r]: Ball is sure they are bound again to Egypt – time will shew, I send You my beloved Emma a note in order that You may upon Your birthday make some little presents and if you do not[4] give it all away it will look in bank notes very pretty in your pocket

[1]The beginning of the letter is missing.

[2]This may be a surprising idea, as Spain declared war on Britain only on 12 Dec 1804 (although the threat of war with Spain was present throughout the year 1804; see Doc. No. 309). I have not changed the dating of the letter, which is continued on 19 Mar, to the only possible alternative of 1805, however, because of two reasons: (1) Later in the letter Addington is mentioned in a way that refers to his political influence, which was certainly lost after the fall of his government in May 1804; (2) Nelson refers to a letter sent on 19 Mar 1804 in several later letters (see Appendix 7).

[3]Sea silk is an extremely fine, rare and valuable fabric produced from the long silky filaments of byssus secreted by a gland in the foot of several bivalve molluscs by which they attach themselves to the seabed. Sea silk was produced in the Mediterranean region from the large bivalve mollusc, *Pinna nobilis* until early in the 20th century. The shell, which is sometimes almost a metre long, adheres itself to rocks with a tuft of very strong thin fibres, pointed end down, in the intertidal zone. These byssus or filaments (which can be up to 6 cm long) are then spun and, when treated with lemon juice, turn a golden colour which does not fade. The cloth produced from these filaments can be woven even finer than silk and is extremely light and warm (Wikipedia, 21 Feb 2011).

[4]Inserted.

book, Kiss dear Horatia for me + the other call him what you please if a girl Emma, Kindest regards to Your good mother affection to Charlotte and all our friends, it now blows a gale of wind.[1]

March 19th: the gale seems abating and I shall get off the vessel for Gibralter, I have been very restless my dearest Emma for these several days + nights and shall not be better till I hear You are quite recover'd[2] I am Yours for Ever and Ever

Nelson + Bronte.

Hardy is well and desires his best respects.

308. *To Lady Hamilton*

[*b)* Morrison, ii, p. 225 (No. 749); *c)* Christie's sale of 2003, lot 151][3]

[*b)*] I take my chance of a letter I wrote you yesterday going safe thro' Spain, to say I recd last night your two letters of Janry 15th and 28th,[4] with respect to the lady, *my* friend at Gibr. I cannot barely guess what you mean, unless Mr Cutforth[5] is a married man, which I do not know is the case. I never saw him but once, and that was on board the *Amphion*. He is agent victualler. I never saw his house, but his character is excellent. Not all the world's goods or charms could shake my love and affection from my own dearest Emma; that, Horatia's being so ill and you so much indisposed, gave me a raging fever all night. I shall [*c)*] write in a few days by Gibr: but I would not miss the trial of friend Quaker Gayner, I am sure the french would have been at sea long ago but for the commotions in france they are perfectly ready, and seemingly ~~well~~ full manned and so are we ready to meet them,

remember me kindly to the Duke of Hamilton I respect him very much indeed, and to the good old Duke of Qy: say what you please I care not for all those nonsensical letters of Mr: Mockton[6] or your titled offers. I have confidence in Your love + affection and so ought You in the fidelity love and affection of Ever yours for ever

Nelson + Bronte

[1]This part of the letter ends at the bottom of the third page; Nelson continued it on 19 Mar 1804 on the fourth page.

[2]Reference to Lady Hamilton's expected confinement.

[3]Morrison states that this letter bears 'no date' and assumes it was written in 'March 1804'.

[4]Christie's catalogue has here, more convincingly: '15th and 28th'.

[5]James Cutforth (*fl.* 1803–5), agent victualler at Gibraltar.

[6]The name cannot be clearly made out in the centre, but this appears to be the most likely option for a transcription.

Kiss dear Horatia for me and the other,[1] I approved of the name you intended, best regards to Davison I shall write by Gib[r]: to him what changes.

309. *To Lady Hamilton*

[Huntington: HM 34065][2]

I do not write more as it is very uncertain how we stand with Spain we have odd reports of M[r] Frere[3] + the Prince of Peace[4] people are so fond of writing that You may hear I have not been very well but I am quite recovered it was a kind of rhumatick fever in my head I wish the french would come out and let us settle our matters I should then certainly ask to go home for rest I must have, Ever for Ever Yours faithfully, remember me most kindly to all friends Dear mother[5] Ad[l]: + M[rs]: L.[6] Charlotte Miss Connor +[c]: +[c]: +[c]:, God in heaven bless you Amen. Amen

310. *To Lady Hamilton*

[NMM: CRK/19/40]

Victory
April 2nd: 1804

I have my dearest beloved Emma been so uneasy for this last month desiring most ardently to hear of your[7] well doing,[8] Cap[n]: Capel brought me your letters sent by the Thisbe from Gibralter I opened opened found none but Dec[r]: + early in January I was in such an agitation, at last I found one without a date which thank God told my poor heart that you was recovering but that dear little Emma was no more and that Horatia had been so very ill it all together[9] upset me but it was just a [*sic*] bed time and I had time to reflect and be thankful to God for sparing you and our dear Horatia I am sure the loss of one much more both would have drove me mad, I was so agitated as it was, that I was glad it was night and that I could be

[1]Reference to the child Lady Hamilton was expecting (and by that time: must have given birth to) from Nelson.

[2]Only the last part of the letter is preserved.

[3]John Hookham Frere (1769–1846), Minister to Madrid 1802–4.

[4]Manuel Godoy (1767–1851), Principe de la Paz (since 1795); Godoy, Spanish prime minister, received the title 'Principe de la Paz' (Prince of Peace) in acknowledgement of his part in the settling of the Peace of Basle in 1795.

[5]Mary Cadogan.

[6]Lutwidge.

[7]Inserted.

[8]Referring to her pregnancy.

[9]'all together' could also be read as 'alltogether'.

by myself kiss dear Horatia for me and tell her to be a dutiful + good child and if she is that we shall always love her, you may if you like tell Mrs: G.[1] that I shall certainly settle a small pension on her it shall not be large as we may have the pleasure of making her little presents and my dearest Emma I shall not be wanting to everybody who has been kind to you, be they servants or gentlefolks Admiral Lutwidge is a good man and I like Mrs: Lutwidge and shall always more because she is fond of you, never mind the great Bashaw[2] at the Priory he be damn'd, If he was single and had a mind to marry you he could only make you a Marchioness,[3] but as he is situated and I situated I can make you a Duchess and if it pleases God that time may arrive Amen Amen As for your friend Ly: Harrington[4] she is in her way as great a pimp as any of them what a set, but if they manage their own intrigues is not that enough I am sure neither you or I care what they do much less Envy them their chere amèrs[5] as for Lord Sn: and the other I care nothing about them for I have every reason by my own feelings towards you to think you care only for your Nelson, I have not heard of your receiving the little box from Naples. Bracelets I fancy but I did not open them, I wish the amosins[6] may come in time for the conveyance of Capn: Layman[7] who has most unfortunately lost his sloop[8] he is strongly recommended by the Governor[9] + Garrison of Gibralter, but perhaps he may not be able to obtain it ~~but~~ we have such reports about the Kings health[10] that the present ministry may be out and for what I know or care another set may be not better for you or me, as for the Admiralty let who will be in they can neither do me any great good or harm, they may vex me a little but that will recoil upon themselves, I hope however they will confirm capn: Layman for he is attatched not only to me but is a very active officer but it was his venturing to know more about India than Troubridge that made them look shy upon him, and his tongue runs too fast I often tell him not to let his tongue run so fast, or his Pen write so much.[11]

[1]Gibson.

[2]Contemporary transcription of the Turkish title paşa (Pasha).

[3]This appears to refer to John Hamilton, 1st Marquess of Abercorn, who lived at Bentley Priory, Stanmore.

[4]Jane Stanhope, Countess of Harrington, née Fleming (1755–1824), lady of the bed-chamber to the British queen Charlotte of Mecklenburgh-Strelitz, wife of the 3rd Earl of Harrington, with whom she had ten children.

[5]This probably is meant to be 'chère amies' (French for: dear friends). There is no noun 'amèr' in French; 'amer' or 'amère' means 'bitter'.

[6]Armosins, thick plain silk.

[7]William Layman (1768–1826).

[8]The *Weasel*.

[9]Sir Thomas Trigge, acting Governor for the Duke of Kent.

[10]Early in 1804 there had been signs of the recurrence of the king's mental illness.

[11]Here a new sheet of a slightly smaller size (but same size as Doc. No. 306) starts. The contents of this second sheet is added to that of Doc. No. 306 in the 1814-letters (ii, pp. 16–20).

Although I cannot well afford it yet I could not bear that poor blind Mrs: Nelson should be in want in her old days and sell her plate therefore if you will find out what are her debts if they come within my power I will certainly pay them,[1] many I dare say if they had commanded here would have made money but I can assure you for prizes taken within the Mediterranean I have not more than paid my expences however I would rather pinch myself that [*sic*] she poor soul should want, your good angelic heart my dearest beloved Emma will fully agree with me, every thing is very expensive and even we find it, and will be obliged to œconemizes [*sic*], if we assist our friends and I am sure we should feel more comfort in it than in loaded tables and enter=[taining][2] a sett of people who care not for us, an account is this moment brought me that a small sum is payable to me for some neutral taken off Cadiz in May 1800, so that I shall not be poorer for my gift it is odd is it not.

I shall when I come home settle 4000 £ in trustees hands for Horatia for I will not put it in my own power to have her left destitute for she would want friends if we left her in this world she shall be independant of any smiles or frowns. I am glad you are going to take her home, and if you will take the trouble with Eliza + Ann[3] I am the very last to object, Tom[4] I shall certainly assist at college and I am sure the Dr:[5] expects that I should do the same for Horace but I must make my arraingements so as not to run in debt. April 9th: I have wrote to the Duke but by your account I fear he is not alive I write because you wish me and because I like the Duke + hope he will leave you some money but for myself I can have no right to expect a farthing nor would[6] I be a legacy hunter for the world I never knew any good come from it.

I send you a letter from Mr: Falconet I am afraid they have made a Jumble about the amosins, and I send you a very impertinent letter from that old cat,[7] I have sent her a very dry answer and told her I should send the sweetmeats to you. I always[8] hated the old Bitch but was[9] she

[1]See also Doc. No. 311.

[2]After 'enter=' the page finished and the next page starts with 'a sett of people'. It appears Nelson wanted to write 'entertaining' (this is what 1814-letters give here), but forgot to finish the word after having turned the page. For a similar forgetfulness, see letter of 14 Mar 1804 (Doc. No. 306).

[3]Eliza (1789–1861) and Anne (1791–1830) were the youngest daughters of Nelson's sister Susannah Bolton.

[4]Tom Bolton.

[5]His brother William.

[6]Inserted.

[7]His wife Fanny.

[8]The first two letters of the word 'always' are not easy to read and appear to be written over other letters.

[9]Inserted.

young and as beautiful as an angel I am engaged I am all soul + body my Emmas nor would I change[1] Her for all this world could give me, I would not have H.[2] think of a dog I shall not bring her one and I am sure she is better without a pet of that sort but she is like her mother would get all the old dogs in the place about her. April 14th: I am so sea sick that I cannot write another line except to say God Almighty bless you my Dearest Beloved Emma prays Ever your faithful Nelson + Bronte.

311. *Fourth codicil to Nelson's will*[3]

[TNA: Prob. 1/22/1]

I desire that the sum of one hundred Pounds Sterling money of Great Britain may be annually paid unto The reputed Widow of my Brother Maurice Nelson by whatever name she may assume be it S. Nelson or S. Field or any other name, and if I have not the means to pay this sum exclusive of my other Legacys I then trust that my friend Alexander Davison will pay it for me Regularly every Year and to be paid Quarterly as it is paid at present I declare this a codicil to my will this Seventh day of april one thousand Eight hundred and four.

Nelson + Bronte

Witness
T.M.Hardy
John Scott.[4]

312. *To Lady Hamilton*

[Pettigrew, ii, p. 382] Victory
[April] 7th, 1804.

My dearest Emma,

I send this by Captain Layman; he is a good man, and an excellent officer, and he is attached to me. I have given him a strong caution not to say too much at the Admiralty. If he was dumb, and could not write, it would, upon the whole, be better for him. Do you caution him not to talk too much. He will tell you of my determination not to be *absent* from

[1]The first letter of the word 'change' is written over another letter.
[2]Their daughter Horatia.
[3]See Doc. No. 259 and also fn. to Doc. No. 303.
[4]Signed in Hardy's and Scott's handwriting, respectively.

Merton on Christmas-day. Nothing, I can assure you, but events which I cannot foresee, can prevent me, and if I have the pleasure of meeting the French fleet, which I expect every hour, I shall certainly ask for *rest*, let who will be at the Admiralty, it is the same thing to me.

April 9th. Whilst I was writing, a frigate communicated to me that, thirty-four hours before, she saw the French fleet outside Toulon, standing off; that in the evening they stood inshore again. Yesterday we saw some French ships of war, and they are now in sight, working into Toulon. Captain Layman will tell you my anxiety. I was in great hopes that all my fag was near being brought to a close, and that I should visit dear Merton.

Yours.
Nelson and Bronté.

313. *To Lady Hamilton*

[NMM: CRK/19/41] Victory off Toulon
Ap^{l}: 10th: 1804

My dearest Emma,

I have received all your truly kind and affectionate letters to Jan^{ry}: 25th: by the Thisbe and last night your letter of Jan^{y}: 13th: by Naples. The amosins[1] will go under the care of Cap^{n}: Layman who unfortunately lost his sloop but with much credit to himself he has been acquitted of all blame I rejoice that dear H.[2] is got well and also that you my dearest Emma are recov'd of your severe indisposition,[3] in our present situation with Spain this letter probably may never reach you I have wrote fully and intend to send them by the Argo who I expect to join every minute, Elphi Bey I hear has had all his fine things taken from him he escaped into the Desert and is persued [*sic*] probably his head is off long before this time.[4] The french fleet came out on the 5th: but went in again the next morning, Yesterday a Rear Admiral and 7 sail of ships includ^{g}: frigates

[1]Armosins, thick plain silk.

[2]Their daughter Horatia.

[3]Reference to childbirth.

[4]After the British had defeated the French in Egypt a power vacuum ensued which resulted in a struggle between Ottoman Turks, Egyptian Mamluks (who had ruled Egypt for centuries) and Albanian mercenaries. Amidst these struggles a Mamluk chief, Elphy Bey, returned from exile in England. It appears he got entangled within inter-Mamluk competition and was murdered. Eventually, in 1805, the Albanian Muhammad Ali Pasha seized power in Egypt and founded a dynasty.

put their nose outside the harbour if they go on playing this game some day we shall lay salt upon their tails and so end the campaign of my Dearest Emma[1] your most faithful + affectionate[2]

I am glad to hear that you are going to take my dear H. to educate her she must turn out an angel if she minds what you say to her, and Eliza + Ann[3] will never forget your goodness.

My health is so so I shall get through the summer and in the winter shall go home

You will readily fancy all I would[4] say and do think, my kind love to all friends.

314. *To Horatia Nelson Thompson*

[1814-letters, ii, pp. 107–8] Victory,
April 13th, 1804.

MY DEAR HORATIA,

I send you twelve books of Spanish dresses, which you will let your guardian angel, lady Hamilton, keep for you, when you are tired of looking at them. I am very glad to hear, that you are perfectly recovered; and, that you are a very good child. I beg, my dear Horatia, that you will always continue so; which will be a great comfort to your most affectionate

NELSON & BRONTE.

315. *To Lady Hamilton*

[NMM: CRK/19/42] Victory April 19th: 1804

My Dearest Emma I had wrote you a line intended for the Swift cutter but instead of her joining me I had the mortification not only to hear that she was taken but that all the dispatches and letters had fallen

[1] Parts of the ink for the 'E' of Emma have left a mirror-image on the opposite (the right hand) page of the folded letter, so that it appears as if Nelson had folded the letter after finishing the page and that he decided only later to continue the letter on the right hand page.

[2] Here the page ends without a signature. The letter is continued on the next page.

[3] Nelson's nieces by his sister Susannah Bolton.

[4] The letters 'I wou' are on the piece of paper that was torn with the seal. Nelson did not leave any empty space for the seal to be torn in this letter.

into the hands of the enemy,[1] a very pretty piece of work I am not surprized at the capture but am very much so that any dispatches should be sent in a vessel with 23 men not equal to cope with any row boat privateer, as I do not know what letters of yours are in her I cant guess what will be said I suppose there will be a publication, the loss of the Hindostan was great enough but for importance it is lost in comparison to the probable knowledge the Enemy will obtain of our connections with foreign countrys, Foreigners for ever say and it is true we dare not trust England one way or other we are sure to be committed, however it is now too late to launch out on this subject, not a thing has been saved out of the Hindostan not a second shirt for any one and it has been by extraordinary exertions that the peoples lives were saved.

Captain Hollowell[2] is so good as to take home for me wine as by the enclosed list, and if I can some honey the Spanish Honey is so precious that if [any one has] a cut or sore throat it is used to cure it I mention this in case you should wish to give the Duke a Jar. the smell is wonderful It is to be procured no where but in the mountains near Roses, the Cyprus wine one hogshead was for Buonaparte I would recommend the wine cooper drawing it off and you can send a few dozens to the Duke who I know takes a glass every day at 2 oclock I wish I had any thing else to send you, but my dearest Emma, you must take the will for the deed I am pleased with Charlottes letter and as she loves my dear Horatia I shall always like her, what hearts those must have who do not, but thank God she shall not be depend^{t}: on any of them, your letter of feb^{ry}: 12th: thro' M^{r}: Falconet I have received I know they are all read therefore never sign your name I shall continue to write thro' Spain but never say a word that can convey any information except of eternal attatchment and affection for you and that I care not who knows for I am for Ever + Ever your only your Nelson + Bronte.

Poor Cap^{n}: Le Gros[3] had your note to him in his pocket-book and that was all he saved M^{r}: Este left him at Gib^{r}: and went to Malta in the Thisbe, Cap^{n}: Le G. is now trying. I think it will turn out that every person is obliged to his conduct for saving their lives she took fire 13 Leagues from the land.

[1] For details of the capture, see Appendix 6.
[2] Benjamin Hallowell.
[3] John Le Gros.

316. *To Lady Hamilton*

[Pettigrew, ii, p. 384]

Victory,
April 21st, 1804.

My dearest Emma,

We have had a hard gale of wind for two days, and it is now lulling for a moment, I am getting Hallowell on board to give him my dispatches. We shall be under Corsica to-morrow morning. I never saw such a continuation of bad weather. I received the inclosed from Charles. I did not, you may believe, let him go to the hospital There has been, several times within this year,[1] something very odd about him. Capel has been always very kind to him. I have had Dr. Snipe to examine him; he complains of a violent pain in the back of his head; it comes on occasionally. Has any of his family been so? He does not at other times, Capel says, want for abilities, and he is as well kept in money and clothes as any Mid. In the fleet. It has vexed me upon your account, for I know you will be sorry. I hope he will grow out of it. Remember me kindly to good Mrs. Cadogan, and believe me,

Yours,
Nelson and Bronté.

317. *To Lady Hamilton*

[NMM: CRK/19/43]

Victory
April 23rd: 1804

My Dearest Emma,

Hollowell[2] has promised me if the Admiralty will give him leave to go to London that he will call at Merton His spirit is certainly more independant than almost any mans I ever knew but I believe he is attatched to me I am sure he has not reason to be so to either Troubridge or any one at the adty: I have sent last night a box of Marischino Veratable[3] of Zara, which I got Jemmy Anderson to buy for me and 12 bottles of Tokay, I have kept none for myself being better pleased that you should have it, I am ever and for Ever your most faithful + affectionate

Nelson + Bronte.

[1] See Docs Nos 265, 278 and 298.
[2] Benjamin Hallowell.
[3] 1814-letters, ii, p. 34, have here 'Veritabile'.

Hollowell parted last night but being in sight I am sending a frigate with a letter to the Admiralty. May God Almighty bless you and send us a happy meeting.

318. *To Lady Hamilton*

[*a)* Pettigrew, ii, pp. 389–90;
b) Morrison, ii, pp. 229–30 (No. 758)] [*b)*] Victory, April 28th, 1804

I do not, my dearest Emma,

pass over the 26th[1] without thinking of you in the most affectionate manner, which the truest love and affectionate regard of man to a dear beloved woman, which could enter into my mind. I have been for some days, and am still, very unwell, without being seriously ill, but I fret absolutely like a fool for the faults of others. It was not fault of mine that the dispatches were taken, but of those who sent them in a vessel not fit to trust my old shoes in; nor is it my fault that the Kent, the finest ship in the fleet, is kept so long from England, notwithstanding my representations that she is now obliged to leave the fleet, to lay as guard-ship at Naples, and more will very soon be in as bad a plight. My only wish is for the coming out of the French fleet to finish all my uneasinesses. But I yet trust that the reign of Buonaparte will be soon over, and then that we shall have a few years of peace and quietness.

Remember me kindly to all we hold most dear, and be assured, my dear Emma, that I am for ever and ever, and if possible more than ever, yours most faithfully,[2]

[*a)*] Nelson and Bronté.
[*b)*] Captain Layman, Captain Hallowell, and I believe another packet of letters for you, are now at Gibraltar.

319. *To Lady Hamilton*

[Morrison, ii, p. 230 (No. 759)] May 3rd, 1804

I am much better, my dearest Emma, than yesterday. The ship is this moment going off. May heavens bless and preserve my own dear Emma & H.,[3] fervently prays your most affectionate

[1]Lady Hamilton's birthday.
[2]Instead of 'and be assured, my dear Emma, that I am for ever and ever, and if possible more than ever, yours most faithfully,' Pettigrew, ii, 390 has here: 'and believe me, Yours'.
[3]Their daughter Horatia.

320. *To Lady Hamilton*

[BL: Egerton 1614 ff. 100–101, no. 52]

Victory
May 3rd: 1804

Since I wrote you on the 28th: April we have not had the smallest communication with any vessel but as I am sending a letter to Madrid I cannot let the opportunity slip of saying we are alive this day, events my dearest Emma and great ones must very soon take place, france seems prepared in all quarters, and if they do not attempt something they must feel their own disgrace and as Buonaparte cares not for the lives of Frenchmen something must be done to keep up his Government which notwithstanding all that is said abroad I believe is in very great jeopardy at home, God send a finish to it for the benifit [*sic*] of mankind, I have not been very well latterly and I have only to wish for a battle with the french fleet when probably my career will be finish'd, I only ~~save~~ serve[1] you know for the pleasure of fighting them, that over, I shall ask for rest for a little time, but I most sincerely hope that by the destruction of Buonaparte that Wars with all nations will cease Sir Willm: Bolton is now on board very well, may God in heaven Bless and preserve my Dearest Emma for Her most faithful + affectionate.

Kiss H. for me.

Adl: Campbell is on board and desires his kind regards, so does Lord Nelson.

321. *To Lady Hamilton*

[NMM: CRK/19/44]

Victory
May 5th: 1804

I find my dearest Emma that your picture is very much admired by the french Consul at Barcelona[2] and that he has not sent it to be admired which I am sure it would be by Buonaparte they pretend that there was three pictures taken I wish I had them but they are gone[3] as irretrivably [*sic*] as the dispatches unless we ~~xxx~~ may read them in a book as we

[1]The word 'serve' is above the crossed-out 'save'.
[2]Pancôme Louis Adélaïde Viot.
[3]Taken in the *Swift* cutter.

printed their correspondance from Egypt,[1] but from us what can they find out that I love you most dearly and hate the french most damnably D^r: Scott went to Barcelona to try to get the private letters but I fancy they are all gone to Paris the Swedish + American Consul[s] told him that the french consul had your picture + read your letters and D^r: thinks one of them probably read the letters, by the masters account of the cutter I would not have trusted a pair of old shoes in her[2] he tells me she did not sail but was a good sea boat,

I hope M^r: Marsden will not trust any more of my private letters in such a conveyance if they chuse to trust the affairs of the Public in such a thing I cannot help it, I long for the Invasion being over it must finish the War and I have no fears for the event. I do not say all I wish and which my Dearest beloved Emma (Read that whoever opens this letter and for what I care publish it to the world) your fertile imagination can readily fancy [what] I would say but this I can say with great truth that I am for ever yours.[3]

322. *To Lady Hamilton*

[CRC]

Victory
May 22nd: 1804

My Dearest Emma,

Your two letters via Lisbon arrived the same day with those in the Leviathan I do not deserve Your scolding I have looked at my Log and I find that the Phœbe saild for Gibralter with the English letters on Dec^r: 27th: and that all the English letters went in her therefore no signal for English letters could be flying on the 28th: as you state, Your letter was Dated the 26th: The Camelion went to Naples but I never have or intend to write by such a very uncertain rout when I could write by a better at the same time, and we may be sure that all my letters would be read not that I care for they are filled with affection to You and I shall be more careful how I write a word of the fleet as I see that extracts from my letters get into the newspapers, Davison is very wrong ever to quote a word I write but I shall not scold him now as I fear poor fellow he is in

[1][Anon.] (ed.), *Copies of Original Letters from the Army of General Bonaparte in Egypt, Intercepted by the Fleet under the Command of Admiral Lord Nelson. With an English translation* (London, 1798).

[2]See letter of 28 April 1804 (Doc. No. 318).

[3]The word 'for' is underlined four times; the word 'ever' six times and the word 'yours' nine times.

the Kings bench[1] I am quite hurt about his getting into such a scrape, He always told me[2] oh I know my ground let me alone I cannot be deceived, it often turns out that these very clever men are oftener deceived than other people, now let me put you right about Mr: Marsh he did what was most perfectly right and it was very hard upon me to force the money out of his hands You know how 4000 £ was meant to be disposed off [*sic*], but never mind, I never meant but to pay Davison and with many many thanks and a due sence of the Obligations I owe him I had hopes if we got the Dutch ship given to the Victory but that with a little more I should be out of his debt and I do assure You my dearest Emma that I should have ordered the money to have been paid him but that he begged me not to think of it, I feel it all, I would not have acted so by him had I been as rich so finishes that matter,

with respect my dearest Emma to the improvements at Merton I never meant that they should be paid out of the 1200 £ a year and I send you an order that Davison will pay the bills, as I wish to know exactly what the alterations cost with respect to the Room I hardly know how to find the money but if it is to be done this year it is begun before this time It is too late to say a word now, I have wrote to Sir John Acton on the subject You wished me[3] but that Person[4] is now so much French that I doubt the effect if she does write so it is said but I cannot believe it I have not heard of the arrival of the watch for H.[5] or a little box for You but I suppose they went in the British Fair cutter and the answers came out in the Swift[6] I shall write by Gibr: in a few days this goes thro' Spain by the care of friend Gayner only be assured that I am for Ever + Ever Only Yours –

323. *To Lady Hamilton*

[NMM: CRK/19/45] Victory
May 27th: 1804

My Dearest Emma Yesterday I took Charles Connor on board from the Phœbe to try what we can do with him, at present poor fellow he has got a very bad eye and I almost fear that he will be blind of it owing to an olive stone striking his eye but the surgeon of the Victory[7] who

[1]Prison in Southwark (London).
[2]Inserted.
[3]Apparently helping to get a pension for Lady Hamilton.
[4]Queen of Naples.
[5]Their daughter Horatia.
[6]Which was taken in April 1804; for details of the capture, see Appendix 6.
[7]Dr George Magrath.

is by far the most able medical man I have ever seen and equally so as a surgeon [so] that if it can be saved he will do it, the other complaint in his head is but little more I think than it was when he first came to Deal a kind of silly laugh when spoken to, he always complains of a pain in the back part of his head but when that is gone I do not perceive but that he is as wise as many of his neighbours, you may rely my dear Emma[1] that nothing shall be wanting on my part to render him every service, Capel although I am sure very kind to younkers I do not think has the knack of keeping them in high discipline he lets them be their own master too much

I paid Ch[s]: account yesterday since he has been in the Phœbe £ 155 : s 14 – s[2] however he must now turn over a new leaf, and I sincerely hope poor fellow he will yet do well,

I wrote you on the 22nd: through Roses in[3] Spain and I shall write in a few days by Barcelona this goes by Gibralter I have wrote ad[l]: Lutwidge M[rs]: Lutwidge must wait for I cannot get through all my numerous letters, for whoever writes although upon their own affairs are offended if they are not answer'd I have not seen young Bailey I suppose he is in the Leviathan[4] + By the parcel I see he is in the Canopus and I can at present be of no use to him,

May 30th: Charles is very much recover'd I write you this day by Barcelona, Your dear phiz[5] but not the least like you on the cup is safe but I would not use it for the world for if it was broke it would distress me very much. Your letters by Swift[6] I shall never get back the french Consul at Barcelona is bragging that he has three pictures of you from the Swift,

I do not believe him but what if he had a 100 Your resemblance is so deeply engraved in my heart that there it can never be effaced and who knows some day I may have the happiness of having a living picture of you old Mother L. is a damn'd bitch but I do not understand what you mean or what plan. I am not surprised at my friend Kingsmill admiring you + forgetting Mary he loves variety and handsome women you touch upon the old Duke but I am dull of comprehension believing you all my own I cannot imagine any one else to offer in any way, we have enough

[1]The 'a' of 'Emma' is written on the other side of the folding line, so that it appears that Nelson folded the letter only after finishing writing it.

[2]The '£' and 's' are written above the first figures of the corresponding numbers. The 's' appears again after '14 –'.

[3]The words 'Roses in' are inserted.

[4]Nelson added a '+' after the word 'Leviathan'. Upside down on the top of the left-hand page he wrote '+ By the parcel I see he is in the Canopus'.

[5]Physiognomy.

[6]See Docs Nos 315, 318 and 321 and Appendix 6.

with prudance and without it we should soon be beggars if we had five times as much I see L^{d}: Stafford[1] is going to oppose M^{r}: Addington the present ministry cannot stand, I wish M^{r}: Ad^{n}: had given you the pension. P[I]tt + hard hearted Grenville[2] never will, what a fortune the death of L^{d}: Camelford[3] gives him, every thing you tell me about my dear H.[4] charms me I think I see her, hear her and admire her but she is like her dear dear mother, I am sorry if your account of Geo: Martins wife[5] is correct he deserved a better fate but he is like Foley gave up a great deal to marry the relation of a great man[6] although in fact she is no relation to the Duke of Portland,[7]

I wish I could but be at dear Merton to assist in making the alterations I think I should have persuaded you to have kept the Pike and a clear stream and to have put all the carp tench and fish who muddy the water into the Pond but as you like I am content only take care that my darling does not fall in + get drowned I begged you to get the little netting along the edge and particularly on the bridges. I admire the seal and God bless you also Amen.

The Boy South is on board another ship[8] learning to be a musician. He will return soon when he shall have the letter + money. I hope he will deserve it but he has been a very bad boy but good floggings I hope will save him from the gallows.

M^{r}: Falcon is a clever man he would not have made such a blunder as our friend Drake + Spencer Smith[9] I hear the last is coming via Trieste

[1]Stafford, George Granville Leveson-Gower (1758–1833), 1st Duke of Sunderland, The Marquess of Stafford (since 1803).

[2]William Wyndham Grenville, Baron Grenville; Nelson obviously assumes that on a change of government Grenville will get a ministry or even become prime minister; in fact, he only returned to politics after Pitt's death and then became prime minister (in 1806).

[3]Thomas Pitt, 2nd Baron Camelford (b. 1775) died on 10 Mar 1804; leaving his wealth to his sister Anne, William Wyndham Grenville's wife.

[4]Their daughter Horatia.

[5]Harriet, née Bentinck; sister of Vice-Admiral William Bentinck, granddaughter of William Bentinck, 1st Earl of Portland (1649–1709), married George Martin on 3 April 1804.

[6]On 31 July 1802 Foley had married Lady Lucy Anne Fitzgerald, daughter of the Duke of Leinster and Lady Emily Lennox, daughter of the Duke of Richmond, with whom he lived mostly in South Wales. Foley had rejected Nelson's offer to join him in the Mediterranean on the grounds of ill heath. It appears that Nelson attributed the rejection to Foley feeling obliged to please his wife.

[7]William Henry Cavendish Cavendish-Bentinck, 3rd Duke of Portland (1738–1809).

[8]Inserted.

[9]Francis Drake (1764–1821), then Envoy Extraordinary and Minister Plenipotentiary at the court of Bavaria, left Bavaria on 27 April 1804, when the prince elector 'refused to hold further communication with him', and did not return. In the same period Drake summoned John Spencer Smith, who had just taken his post as Envoy Extraordinary to the court of Württemberg in Feb, to Salzburg; Smith left Stuttgart on 3 April 1804 and 'remained in Upper Austria until recalled by dispatch of 6 July 1804'. As a consequence diplomatic relations were suspended to both courts from 1804 until 1814. See: S. T. Bindoff, E. F. Malcolm Smith and C. K. Webster (eds); *British Diplomatic Representatives 1789–1852* (London, 1934), pp. 22, 23 and 194.

to Malta perhaps he wants to get to Constantinople and if the Spencers get in[1] the Smiths[2] will get any thing Mr: Elliot I hear is a candidate for it, he complains of the expence of Naples I hear and that he cannot make both ends meet although he sees no company the historys of the Queen are beyond whatever I have heard from Sir Willm: Prince Leopolds establishm'd[3] is all french the Queens favorite Lt: Coll: St: Clair[4] was a subaltern, La Tour the Captain in the navy + another however I never touch on these matters for I care not how she amuses herself it will be the upset of Acton or rather he will not I am told stay. The King is angry with her his love is long gone bye[5]

I have only one word more Do not believe a syllable the newspapers say or what you hear mankind seems fond of telling Lies, remember me kindly to Mrs: Cadogan and all our mutual friends and be assured I am for ever my dearest Emma your most faithful and affectionate Nelson + Bronte.

Geo: Campbell desires me always to present his best respects, and make mine to good Mr: Yonge what can I write him I am sure he must have great pleasure in attending you, and when you see Sir Wm: Scott make my best regards acceptable to him there is no man I have a higher opinion of both as a Public + private character.

You will long ago have had my letter with one to Davison desiring he will pay for the alterations at Merton,[6] I shall send you a letter of the 100 £ a month to the Bank.

324. *To Lady Hamilton*

[BL: Egerton 1614 ff. 102–103, no. 53] Victory
May 30th: 1804

My Dearest beloved Emma I am writing this day by way of Gibralter + Barcelona[7] to take both chances I wrote you on the 22nd: thro' friend Gayner, the Quaker at Roses, We have nothing in the least new here we cruize, cruize and one day so like another that they are hardly distinguishable, but H<u>opes</u> blessed <u>hope</u>s keeps us up that some happy day the french may

[1]Into government? Earl Spencer, however, did not return into government after his resignation as First Lord of the Admiralty in 1801 until 1806, and then as Home Secretary.

[2]Referring to the brothers John Spencer (1769–1845) and William Sydney Smith (1764–1840); the latter is characterised by Knight, p. 669, as 'impulsive, egotistical but talented, who irritated all his fellow officers'.

[3]This probably means 'establishment'.

[4]Carlo Saint Clair?

[5]It is doubtful whether there ever was any: Maria Carolina was sent to Naples to marry Ferdinand as a replacement for her sister who had died just before leaving for Naples.

[6]This probably refers to Doc. No. 306.

[7]The 'B' of Barcelona is written above an 'E'.

come out then I shall consider my duty to my country fulfilled, I have been but so so and am not so well as I could wish a slow nasty fever hangs upon me but I have a good medical man in the Surgeon of the Victory[1] Dr: Snipe being absent at Malta, I am not seriously ill but am not quite in rude health, for Gods sake and my sake my dearest Emma do not believe any thing that newspapers may tell you I can tell my own tale, or conn over every word in my letter my saying we are on the eve of a battle could only be intended to convey my belief that the french intended to put to sea and so they did on April 5th: and had we not been near probably they would have push'd for their destination therefore my dearest Emma do not fancy this that, or [the] other, as how, where, when I can get at them, I cannot do impossibilitys or go into Toulon, but all that man can do shall be done and the sooner it is done the sooner I shall certainly be at dear dear Merton, kiss my dear H for me I shall hope to see her at Merton on my arrival I think the Election of Buonaparte to be Emperor will give us peace and the ministry seems going I hope Mr: Addington has given you a pension it is shameful if[2] he has not, however nothing shall be wanting from me I will give you 2/3s of the last bit of bread I have I have wrote Adl: Lutge: by Gibr: but [say] every kind thing for me to all friends I cannot say all I wish but you will readily fancy all I think towards[3] you I have sent you a case of macaroni by the Agincourt and will send for ~~me~~ more[4] from Naples this very day I have not heard from Gibbs this age nor of Bronte but I hope he will do well for me.[5]

Gaetano desires his duty he says he is afraid you have forgot him. I do not hear of Willm:[6] having any inclination to send home any part of his wages, dont you give any for it will come out of my pocket which is not necessary as[7] his pay is 18£ a year

325. *To Lady Hamilton*

[NMM: CRK/19/46] Victory
June 6th: 1804

Since I wrote you my dearest Emma on the 30 and 31st: May[8] nothing new has happened except our hearing the feu de Joie[9] at Toulon for the

[1]Dr George Magrath.

[2]The text continues on the last page, above the address, this time not upside down!

[3]The text continued below the address, upside down.

[4]The word 'more' is written above the word '~~me~~'.

[5]The text is continued inside the letter, upside down on page 2.

[6]Bolton. The letter is continued, still upside down, at the top of page 3.

[7]The text continues on page 2, below the addition that has been inserted there (upside down) already.

[8]Nelson wrote twice on 30 May (part of Doc. No. 323 and Doc. No. 324), but no letter of 31 May has come down to us.

[9]French for fireworks (literally translated: 'fire of joy').

declaration of Emperor, what a capricious nation those French must be however I think it must in any way be advantageous to England, there ends for a century all Republicks, by vessels from Marsailles[1] the french think it will be a Peace and they say that several of their merchant ships are fitting out I earnestly pray that it may be so and that we may have a few years of Rest, I rather believe my antagonist at Toulon[2] begins to be angry with me at least I am trying to make him so and then he may come out and beat me as he says he did off Bolonge,[3] he is the Admiral that went to Naples in Dec^{r}: 1792, La Touche Treville, who landed the Granadier,[4] I owe him something for that, I am better my dear Emma than I have been and shall get thro' the summer very well, and I have the pleasure to tell you that Charles is very much recover'd there is no more the matter with his intellects than with mine quite the contrary he is very quick, M^{r}: Scott who has overlooked all his things says his cloaths +^{c}: are in the highest order he has ever seen,[5] I shall place him in the Niger with Captain Hilliar[6] when she joins but all our ships are so full that it is very difficult to get a birth for one in any ship, could you conceive it possible but it is now from April 2nd: since I have heard direct from Ball The avarage time for a frigate to go and return is from 6 to 7 weeks from you I had letters April 5th: and the papers to April 9th: receiv'd May 10th with a convoy, this goes thro' friend Gayner Sir W^{m}: Bolton joined last night and receiv'd his Letters announcing his being called Papa he is got a very fine young man and good officer, Lord S^{t}: Vincent has desired he may have the first Admiralty vacancy for Post, but nobody will die or go home, apropos I believe you should buy a piece of plate value ~~XX~~ 50[7] £

[1]Marseilles.

[2]Admiral Louis René Madelaine Le Vassor, comte de La Touche-Tréville (1745–1804).

[3]Boulogne (in Aug 1801).

[4]Grenadiers. The Republican government of France had sent La Touche-Tréville on an expedition to Naples in Dec 1792 in order to force the Neapolitan government to distance themselves from a letter that the Neapolitan prime minister, Acton, had sent to the Court of the Ottoman Sultan. According to the French Republic, this letter was 'directed against the ambassador of the Republic [to the Ottoman Porte], citizen Sémonville, and it contained comments that were injurious to the French nation and its new government'. If the Neapolitan government should not be prepared to distance itself from this letter, La Touche Tréville was given orders to take Acton as a hostage until the Neapolitan government would 'solemnly notify the Porte' that they respected the French ambassador and Sémonville had been received at the Porte. The expedition, threatening as it was, had to be called off, when the French Mediterranean fleet under Truguet had to counter a threat from the Genovese. (Nicola Nicolini, *La spedizione punitiva del Latouche-Tréville (16 decembre 1792) ed altri saggi sulla vita politica napoletana alla fine del secolo XVIII* (Florence, 1939), pp. 13 and 23).

[5]It appears that Nelson started the letter with 'cloaths' as a verb and a different end in mind, like: 'he clothes orderly'; but changed the grammatical structure of the sentence, by changing 'he clothes' into the plural noun 'his clothes'.

[6]James Hillyar.

[7]The number '50' is inserted below a crossed-out number at the bottom of the page.

for our God daughter of Lady Bolton[1] and something of 20 or 30 £ value[2] for Colonels Sucklings, but my Emma you are not to pay for them, let it rest for me or if the amount is sent me I will order payment, remember me most kindly to H.[3] good M^rs: Cadogan Charlotte Miss Connor and all our friends at dear dear Merton where from my soul I whish I was this moment then I sincerely hope I should have no cause for sorrow, You will say what is right to M^r: Perry, Newton Patterson M^r: Lancaster +^c: you know all these matters [*sic*] God in heaven bless + preserve you for Ever prays ever yours most faithfully —

326. *To Lady Hamilton*

[NMM: CRK/19/47]

Victory
June 10th: 1804

My Dearest Emma,

I wrote to you on the 6th: via Roses this goes by Barcelona to which place I am sending Sir W^m: Bolton to fetch D^r: Scott who is gone there poor fellow for the benefit of his health

I have just had very melancholy Letters from the King + Queen of Naples on account of Genl: Actons going to Sicily, the insolence of Buonaparte was not to be parried without a war for which they are unable if unassisted I have letters from Acton May 28th: on board the Archimedes just going into Palermo, he will probably return to Naples unless new events arise and that may be for a minister once out may find some difficulty in renewing his Post, He has acted with great + becoming spirit, I am better but I have been very unwell it blows here as much as ever yesterday was a little hurricane of wind, I dare say Prince Castelcicala knows it by express if not you may tell him with my best Respects, He and every one else may be sure of my attatchment to those good Sovereigns, by this rout I do not chuse to say more on this subject with my kindest regards to H.[4] and your good mother Charlotte Miss C.[5] and all our friends Believe me my Dear Emma for ever your most faithful + affectionate _

[1]Nelson's niece, Kitty (1781–1850), daughter of Susannah, who had married her cousin Sir William Bolton.

[2]The rest of the letter is written on the top end of the outside of the folded sheet (until 'I wish I was') and – upside down – on the bottom end of it.

[3]Their daughter Horatia.

[4]Their daughter Horatia.

[5]Connor.

I fear Sardinia will be invaded from Corsica before you get this letter I have not small ships to send there,[1] or any where else not in the proportion of one to five.

You may communicate this to M^{r}: Addington if you think that he does not know it but to no one else except Castelcicala, of what relates to Naples.

I have very flattering letters from the Grand Vizir in the name of the Sultan + from Cadir now Capitan Pacha.

327. *To Lady Hamilton*

[Pettigrew, ii, pp. 397–8]

Victory,
June 17th, 1804.

Not the least alteration has taken place in the fleet since I wrote you last on the 10th *viâ* Barcelona. By the French accounts I see therefore almost a total change of Administration. I sincerely wish that Mr. Addington may have rendered you justice in granting the pension before he left office, if not, I fear it will never be done, for although Dundas would express his wishes for your success, when he had but little, if anything, to say, yet you will find now he has much to say that he will say less. My last letters from England are April 5th, going on for three months in total ignorance of what is passing, but as Doctor Scott has continued through Spain to get the Paris papers, we know all the great events which are passing. I still think that we have a fair prospect of Peace. Pitt can have no objection to treat with a French Monarchy, and I should think that the new Emperor would wish very much for one. My friend Monsieur La Touche has got his fleet fully manned – he sometimes plays bo-peep in and out of Toulon, like a mouse at the edge of her hole; but as these playful tricks, which mean nothing serious, may be magnified by nonsensical letters, of which too many are wrote, I desire and beg that you will never give any credit to them. You are sure that when any one can write from the fleet that I can, and you are sure that I should to you. I very much doubt now your female friend at Naples[2] has got Acton removed, whether he will be able to return. The male friend of ours[3] says he will go to Sicily, and as neither Russia nor

[1]The letter is continued on the outside, above the address (until 'to five'.), then below it (until 'Naples'), to finish above the first addition above the address.

[2]The Queen of Naples.

[3]The King of Naples.

England can trust either Gallo or Micheroux[1] who want the place, and who, we know, are both French in heart; this is the only chance he has at seventy-three of being again Prime Minister,[2] and the Queen cannot, I fancy, do now so well without him as formerly. My state of health is such that if I could fight the French fleet to-morrow, I should certainly solicit permission to come home for a few months rest, and I must do it before the winter, or I shall be *hors de combat*,[3] and they ought to make some allowance for my maimed carcass. Kiss dear Horatia for me, and remember me to all our friends. Charles is very near perfectly recovered, and he behaves very well. I long to hear how poor Davison gets on. I hope he is out of prison, for I fear he has been in one before this time.[4] Again and again bless you.

June 18. Dr. Scott has just brought me from Barcelona one of your dear prints, the French Consul[5] had it framed and glazed, the other he sent to Paris.

Yours,
Nelson.

328. *To Lady Hamilton*

[Morrison, ii, pp. 232–3 (No. 764)] *Victory*,
June 27th, 1804.

Last night, my dearest Emma, I received your three letters of April 13th and 22nd, and May 13th, by way of Naples. It is the only scrap of a pen we have had from England since April 5th, by Leviathan. You must not complain of my not writing, for I never miss an opportunity, as the following list will shew. February 25th by Barcelona,[6] March 2nd, 15th,

[1]Antonio Micheroux (1735–1805), Neapolitan diplomat with whom Nelson had to deal during the Neapolitan revolution of 1799.

[2]Acton at that time was 'only' 68 years of age (Gallo was 51).

[3]French for 'out of action'.

[4]Alexander Davison (government contractor and Nelson's old acquaintance and prize agent) had been found guilty in April 1804 of bribing voters. He had tried to purchase a parliamentary seat at Ilchester in Somerset by buying properties and offering money to those moving into them for voting for him. Although he withdrew from the contest, he was eventually convicted of bribery in 1804 and imprisoned for a year in the Marshalsea prison. Davison's imprisonment is also subject of Docs Nos 329 and 338; see there for further details.

[5]Pancôme Louis Adélaïde Viot.

[6]Docs Nos 304 and 305 both appear to have been of 25 Feb 1804.

by Rosas;[1] 19th, by Gibraltar;[2] April 10th, by Rosas;[3] 14th by Captain Layman;[4] 19th, 21st, 23rd, by the *Argo*;[5] 28th, by Rosas;[6] May 3rd, by Barcelona;[7] 5th, by Rosas;[8] 12th, by Rosas;[9] 30th, 31st, by Gibraltar;[10] June 6th, by Rosas;[11] 10th, by Barcelona;[12] 19th, by Rosas;[13] and be assured, my own Emma, that my fond attachment to you is greater if possible than ever. You will see, and I have wrote Davison to pay every bill relating to the alterations at Merton, and that nothing is to be touched on that business from the £100. a month. I also wrote to him to pay, if I can afford it, poor blind Mrs. Nelson's debts. The change of Ministry can do us no harm, and if Lord Melville is a true friend he may now get it[14] for you; but my dear Emma, all their promises are pie-crusts, made to be broken. I hope to get out of debt and to have my income clear, and then we shall do very well with prudence. I am not surprised at the time poor Davison is to be confined, after what passed in Parliament, I did not expect so little, and I fear he has a heavy fine to pay besides. He would only consult Lord Moira and such clever folks, but an ignoramus like me, could only warn him not to touch Boroughs.[15] He has, poor fellow, been completely duped, and who cares? Not one of those great folks. I am most sincerely sorry for him, but a year will soon pass away. Have not I been shut up in a ship without any one comfort? He is ashore, with his friends round him, and even you to go to see him. I would change with him with much pleasure. I shall write him a line, he must not kill

[1]A letter of 2 Mar is not in this collection; with the letter of '15 March' Nelson may be referring to the letter of 14 Mar (Doc. No. 306), which may have been sent on 15 Mar. Rosas is the Castilian form of Roses (which is Catalan).

[2]Doc. No. 307 was begun before 19 Mar and finished on 19 Mar. Nelson may be referring to this letter.

[3]Doc. No. 313.

[4]I have not been able to trace a letter of 14 April 1804. At the same time it is surprising that Nelson does not list Docs Nos 308, 309, 310 and 312 which he wrote at the end of Mar and beginning of April 1804.

[5]Docs Nos 315, 316 and 317.

[6]Doc. No. 317.

[7]Doc. No. 320.

[8]Doc. No. 321.

[9]It may be possible that Morrison made an error in transcription here, as I have only been able to trace a letter of 22 May (Doc. No. 322), not of 12 May.

[10]Doc. No. 323 was begun on 27 May, but finished on 30 May; Doc. No. 324 was dated 30 May; Nelson may here be referring to these two letters.

[11]Doc. No. 325.

[12]Doc. No. 326.

[13]This probably refers to Doc. No. 327, which was begun on 17 June and finished on 18 June.

[14]The pension Lady Hamilton was hoping and applying for.

[15]See fn. to Doc. No. 327.

himself, that his enemies would rejoice at, and I hope he will live to plague them. Acton being gone to Sicily, the Queen had authority to open his letters. Mr. Elliot explained the one relative to her writing to Mr. Addington. She said, as Mr. Elliot writes me, as Mr. Addington is out of office the application to him from her would no longer meet your purpose, and as to a letter to his successor, she must be regulated in that by your future explanation upon the subject. I can think a great deal. Mr. Elliot likes to class you in such a way as may make a precedent – that you recollect was always his plan, but I shall write Acton and the Queen to say, that there can be no harm in her writing to Mr. Pitt.[1] Your eminent services, and her personal obligations to you, &c. &c. But you know enough of the world not to be surprised at the forgetfulness from even great folks. How delighted I shall be with Merton, and I shall hope to find Horatia fixed there. Why not? Kiss her for me, and may God bless her. I am always glad to hear that Charlotte behaves well to you. She would be very ungrateful if she did not. Remember me kindly to Mrs. Cadogan and all our friends. I shall, if it pleases God, eat my Christmas dinner at dear Merton. My health absolutely requires a few months rest, even if my services are required again. Pray God in heaven bless and preserve you.

Yours.

329. *To Lady Hamilton*

[NMM: CRK/19/48] Victory
July 1st: 1804

Although I have wrote you my Dearest Emma a letter by Roses of June 27th:[2] not yet gone the weather being so very bad that ships cannot get across the Gulph of Lyons yet I will [not] miss the opportunity of writing by Gibr: You must not my Emma think of hearing from me by way of Malta it takes as long to send a letter to Malta as to England The Monmouth which you complain of not hearing by I knew nothing of her movements for some months before, The ships from Malta with the convoys pick up our letters at Gibralter therefore do not hurt my feelings by telling me that I neglect any opportunity of writing, Your letters of Apl:

[1]He did not quite recommend writing to Pitt, but insisted on the matter in his letter to the Queen of Naples of 10 July 1804 (Nicolas, vi, p. 105); the first letter on the subject can be found in Nicolas, vi, p. 31, and is quoted in a footnote to Doc. No. 329.
[2]Doc. No. 328.

13th: 22nd: + May 13th: through M^{r}: Falconet came safe a few days ago. M^{r}: Falconet is the French Banker and he dare not buy a little macaroni for me or let an Englishman into his house, Gibbs is still at Palermo I fancy he will make a good thing of my estate[1] however I wish it was settled he wrote me a short time since that he wished I would give him a hint (but without noticing that it came from him) that I thought M^{rs}: Græfer + her child had better go to England on pretence of educating her daughter $+^{c}$: but I would have nothing to do with any such recommendation it would end in her coming to me in England and saying that she could not live upon what she had and that I adviced her to come to England or she should not have thought of it, in short Gibbs wants to remove her he is afraid of his pocket I fancy and the daughter is I fancy now in some seminary at Palermo at Gibbs's expence I wrote him word fully I would advice no such thing she was to form her own Judgement, What our friends are after at Naples they best know, The poor King is miserable at the loss of Acton, The Queen writes me about Honest Acton $+^{c}$: +: + I hear that she has been the cause of ousting him and they say her Enemies that her conduct is all french that I do not believe although she is likely to be the dupe of french Emigrees [*sic*] who always beset her, I doubt much my dear Emma even her constancy of real friendship to you although in my letter to Acton[2] which M^{r}: Elliot says he read to her I mentioned the obligations she was under to you $+^{c}$: $+^{c}$: in very strong terms what could the name of the minister signify it was the letter which was wanted to the Prime minister,[3] but never mind with prudence we shall do very well I have wrote to Davison by land[4] who I am very sorry for[5] but he never would take a friends caution and he has been severely bit, Your accounts of Merton delight me and you will long ago have known that I have directed the bills for the alterations to be paid I never could have intended to have taken it from the 100 £ a month You will not hear of my making prize money I have not paid my expences these last nine months I shall expect to eat my X^{t}:mas dinner at Merton unless

[1]At Bronte.

[2]Nicolas, vi, p. 31, written in French: 'cette pension est due, et a été bien meritée. / La Reine de Naples est, j'en sui convaincu, aussi sincerement attachée à Lady Hamilton que'elle le doit, puis qu'Elle n'a jamais eu une amie aussi sincère et aussi désinteressée. Ainsi si Sa Majesté vouloit avoir la condescendance [*sic*] d'écrire une ligne à Monsieur Addington, . . .'.

[3]This refers to the Queen of Naples' excuse not to be able to write in favour of a pension for Lady Hamilton, as she did not know to whom to address it, since Addington was now out of office (see Doc. No. 328).

[4]The words 'by land' are inserted.

[5]This refers to Davison's imprisonment for bribery in a parliamentary election (see note to Doc. No. 327).

those events happen which I can neither foresee nor prevent I am not well and must have rest for a few months even should the country [want me] which is very likely they will not news I can have none

April 9th: [L]eviathan sail'd so Government dont care much for us, kiss my dear Horatia for me I hope you will have her at Merton and Believe me my Dear Emma that I am much as ever your attatch [*sic*] faithful + affectionate

Nelson + Bronte.

330. *To Lady Hamilton*

[*a)* Pettigrew, ii, p. 409;
b) Morrison, ii, p. 233 (No. 765)]

[*a)*] Victory,
July 1st, 1804.

My dearest Emma,

[*b)*] I have a moment, and but a moment, to write you a line through Spain. I wrote you yesterday by Gibraltar,[1] and sent you the first Bill of Exchange for £100. for you, and £100. for poor Mrs. Bolton. I take this opportunity of sending the second, as I dare say that this will be home months before the other. Nothing from England since April 5th. May God in Heaven bless and preserve you, my beloved Emma, for your ever most faithful & affectionate[2]

All my public dispatches go for Gibraltar this day.

331. *To Lady Hamilton*

[Morrison, ii, pp. 234–5 (No. 768)]

Victory,
July 9th, 1804

Last night, my dearest Emma, I received your most kind letter of May 24th, and I feel very much distressed that my numerous letters do not get quicker to your hand, but I can write and send off, and indeed, I dare say, if I was the carrier, they would not be so long in travelling. I have mentioned the date of every letter, and how they went, in a letter sent a few days ago by Barcelona; in March, three; in April six; in May, five; in June to the 19th, three; June 27th, July 1st.[3] I must not write a word of

[1]Doc. No. 329.
[2]Instead of 'May God in Heaven bless and preserve you, my beloved Emma, for your ever most faithful & affectionate' Pettigrew has here merely 'Yours'.
[3]For where these letters can be found in this edition see Appendix 7.

any political matter, for as I send this through Mr. Falconet, I have assured him in his employ with the French Government, shall be put in the letter. This, I am sure I may say, that we have had no summer here. For the last four days not a boat could pass. Before many months I shall certainly see all your improvements, and if government, after some rest, want my services, they shall have them, but I must have a change of air, for always shut up in the *Victory*'s cabin, cannot be very good for the constitution. I think you will find me grown thin, but never mind. Your trip to Canterbury I should suppose the very worst you could take; for, on any alarm, there you must stay, and in a town filled with soldiers; but if you like it I am content. However, we know to June 18th, all was safe. What a long letter Sir Sidney Smith has wrote. Well, this is an odd war – not a battle! Admiral Campbell always inquires after you, and desires to be kindly remembered. I have little to say – one day is so like another, and having long ago given you one day there is no difference but the arrival of a letter or newspapers; the same faces, and almost the same conversation. As for the great man at the P^y,[1] I care nothing about him or her. She is a deep one.

Remember me kindly to all our friends, and be assured, I am,

Yours.
Kiss dear Horatia for me.

July 11th. – We have the French news to June 28th. I have wrote to the q^n & lady[2] at Naples about your pension. I think she must try & do something. God bless you.

July 12th. We have Paris papers to June 27th. I believe we are never to hear from England again.

332. *To Lady Hamilton*

[BL: Egerton 1614 ff. 104–105, no. 54] Victory
July 14th: 1804

I wrote you my dearest Emma on the 8th: a letter dated June 27th: + July 4th: by way of Barcelona and 9th: and 12th: by way of Naples[3] I begin very much to suspect that my letters from Roses go directly into france you

[1]This appears to refer to John Hamilton, 1st Marquess of Abercorn, who lived at Bentley Priory, Stanmore; compare mention in letter of 2 April 1804: 'the great Bashaw at the Priory'.

[2]Instead of 'q^n & lady' Pettigrew, ii, pp. 408–9, has here 'great lady'.

[3]For where these letters can be found in this edition, see Appendix 7.

must only rely my own Emma that I omit no opportunity of writing for my truly affectionate regard can never never be diminished, although it will be frost and snow when I see dear Merton yet good fires and your charming society will make my heart warm and asses milk will set me up again, in due time I shall write to the Admiralty but this you will keep to yourself rest I ought to have for a few months even should they want my poor services, but there will be so many desirous of getting the Med^{n}: command that I cannot expect they will allow me to return to it, but all this keep to yourself it is time enough for the multitude to know of my movements by my arrival, whether it will be in frigate Brig or leaky 74 I cannot say that will depend on the Admiralty, but I yet hope before my departure that the french fleet will come out indeed I expect the Brest fleet into the Med^{n}: and that this will be the great scene of action this autumn + winter All I beg my dearest Emma that you will not believe any idle stories in newspapers I am perfectly prepared how to act with either a superior or inferior force My mind is firm as a Rock and my plans for every event fixt in my mind may God in heaven bless and preserve my own dear Emma for Her most affectionate + faithful – Kiss dear H^{a}: for me and remember me to all our joint friends

333. *To Lady Hamilton*

[NMM: CRK/19/49] Victory
Aug^{t}: 12th: 1804

Although my Dearest Emma from the length of time my other letters have been getting to you I cannot expect[1] that this will share a better fate, Yet as the Childers is going to Roses to get us some news from Paris which is the only way I know of what is passing in England I take my chance of the Post but I expect the Kent will be in England before this letter, and by which ship I write to the Admiralty relative to my health, therefore I shall only say that I hope a little of your good nursing with asses milk will set me up for another campaign, should the Admiralty wish me to return in the spring for another year, but I own I think we shall have Peace the Ambuscade arrived this day fortnight with our victuallers +^{c}: and very acceptable they were, By her I receiv'd your letters of May 14th: 22nd: + 30th: via Lisbon, and of April 9th:, 18, 15th: May 10th: 18th: 29th: June 1st: 5th:[2] thro' I suppose the Ad^{ty}:, the box you mention is

[1]The words 'I cannot expect' are inserted.
[2]The words 'June 1st: 5th:' are inserted.

not arrived,[1] nor have I a scrap of a Pen from Davison, the weather in the Med[n]: seems much altered in July 17 days the fleet was in a gale of wind, I have often wrote to Davison to pay for all the improvements at Merton the not building the chamber over the dining-room, you must consider, the stair window we settled was not to be stopped up, the underground passage will I hope be made but I shall please Good [*sic*] soon see it all I have wrote you my Dear Emma about H[a]: but by the Kent I shall write fully[2] may God Bless you my dearest best beloved Emma + Believe me ever your most faithful + affectionate. Kind love + Regards to M[rs]: Cadogan + all friends God Bless you again + again.

334. *To Lady Hamilton*

[Morrison, ii, pp. 238–9 (No. 777)] *Victory*,
August 13th, 1804

If I could tell when to begin a letter to my dearest, beloved Emma, I could never tell when to stop. I want and wish to tell you all my thoughts and feelings, but that is impossible; for thoughts so rush upon thoughts, that I cannot, as I said before, know where to begin a letter. The jog-trot of [that] I have receiv'd, &c., &c., but ill accords with my feelings. The *Ambuscade* brought me your letters to June 5th, *viz.* April 9th, 15th, 18th, May 14, 22, 30, *viâ* Lisbon. May 10, 18, 29, June 1, 4, 6,[3] by sea. The box you mention is not arrived,[4] nor have I a scrap of a pen or newspaper from Davison. What can be the meaning of all this? I do not understand it. Mrs. Voller has sent out her son, but what can I do for a child who has never been at sea? for although he may have been borne upon ship's books, that will not make him a seaman. With all those advantages, or rather disadvantages, it must be some years before he can qualify himself to be a Lieut. Capt. Hardy has been so good as to rate him Mid. Here, and lent him to Capt. Durban,[5] where, if he chuses, he may learn his profession. I know Mrs. Voller's uniform kindness to you and her goodness to the

[1]Nelson reports on 31 Mar 1805 (Doc. No. 361) that it 'is just arrived'.

[2]See Doc. No. 337.

[3]In Doc. No. 333 Nelson did not list letters of 4 and 6 June.

[4]Nelson made a similar remark in Doc. No. 333; he eventually wrote that he had received the box on 31 Mar 1805 (Doc. No. 361).

[5]Captain William Durban (d. 1837), of the *Ambuscade* frigate. Nelson had made him post-captain in 1803, because he was 'so pleased with [him] for . . . wise conduct on several occasions [and gave] him the command of the Ambuscade Frigate' (Nicolas, v, pp. 236–7; the promotion was probably given at St Vincent's instigation, see: Nicolas, v, p. 184, fn.; it was only formally confirmed on 17 January 1804; see also note to Doc. No. 299).

children upon every occasion, and therefore I should certainly be glad to do what I can to oblige her & good Mr. Voller; but I cannot, my dear Emma, do what is absolutely impossible. I have wrote her a civil letter. I have had the lad to diner, and I have requested Cpt. Durban, who is a very clever man, to keep him. I am equally obliged to good Hardy about Charles; if Capt. Hillyar cannot rate him, Hardy will.[1] Capel could do nothing for him in that way, therefore, from all circumstances, I have removed him entirely from the *Phoebe* and placed him in the *Niger* with a most excellent Captain,[2] and who, I hope, will keep him until his time is served. I do not think he has yet learnt much of his business as a seaman, but I will answer his intellects are good enough. His eye is saved, and I do not think there will be a blemish. Mr. Magrath, the surgeon of the *Victory*, has been very kind and attentive to him. Mr. Scott had him every day to read and write. In the *Phoebe* he was allowed to do as he pleased, and to throw away money. Only think of 11pr. of boots, half boots and shoes. We shall now sett him off again, and he shall have 30l. a year, and that, I am sure, is abundance. The lad is well disposed, and I have no fears about him; nothing, my own Emma, shall be wanting on my part to be useful to him.

I do not believe one syllable of the intention of the late Admiralty to remove me without my own application. I verily believe so much the contrary, that I much doubt that they would have suffered me to come home without much contesting the point. I have every reason to believe that as a Board, my whole conduct met their entire approbation, and to say the truth, the old Earl[3] was led wrong ag[t] his better judgement many a time. I am not so vex't with him as with the others. I am sure he would have promoted Bolton[4] if they had mentioned him, but never mind, the late Admiralty have the execrations of the service for destroying as much as in them lay *the Navy*.

335. *To Lady Hamilton*

[Morrison, ii, p. 239 (No. 778)][5]

My beloved, how I feel for your situation and that of our dear Horatia, our dear child. Unexampled love, never I trust to be diminished, never;

[1]A few days later Hillyar agreed to rate Charles Connor as Midshipman. This induced Nelson to write to Charles Connor on 20 Aug 1804, admonishing him how to behave and promising him an annuity of £30 (Pettigrew, ii, pp. 418–19).

[2]That again was James Hillyar.

[3]Earl St Vincent.

[4]Sir William Bolton.

[5]Morrison added a fn.: 'The following words are added in another hand: "The enclosed found in a letter to Lady H., dated *Victory*, August 13, 1804".'

no, even death, with all his terrors, would be jubilant compared even to the thought. I wish I had all the small-pox for her, but I know the fever is the natural consequence. I dreamt last night I heard her call papa, and point to her arm just as you described.[1] Give Mrs. Gibson a guinea for me, and I will repay you. Dear wife, good, adorable friend, how I love you, and what would I not give to be with you this moment, for I am for ever all yours.

336. *To Lady Hamilton*

[Morrison, ii, p. 239 (No. 779)] *Victory*, August 13th, 1804

I am now going to state a thing to you and to request your kind assistance, which, from my dear Emma's goodness of heart, I am sure of her acquiescence in. Before we left Italy I told you of the extraordinary circumstance of a child being left to my care and protection. On your first coming to England I presented you the child, dear Horatia. You became, to my comfort, attached to it, so did Sir William, thinking her the finest child he had ever seen. She is become of that age when it is necessary to remove her from a mere nurse and to think of educating her. Horatia is by no means destitute of a fortune. My earnest wish is that you would take her to Merton, and if Miss Connor[2] will become her tutoress under your eye, I shall be made truly happy. I will allow Miss Connor any salary you may think proper. I know Charlotte loves the child, and therefore at Merton she will imbibe nothing but virtue, goodness, and elegance of manners, with a good education, to fit her to move in that sphere of life she is determined to move in. I shall tell you, my dear Emma, more of this matter when I come to England, but I am now anxious for the child's being placed under your protecting wing. Perhaps I ought to have done this before, but I must

[1]It appears from this passage that Horatia had been inoculated (as usual in the arm) and was suffering from the fever that often followed the inoculation. Nelson himself had described the consequences of the inoculation in his letter of 31 July 1801 (Doc. No. 184): 'yesterday the subject turn'd on the Cowpox a gentleman declared thet his child was Inoculated with the cowpox and afterwards remain'd in a house where a child had the smallpox the natural way and did not catch it therefore here was a full trial with the Cowpox, the child is only feverish for 2 days, and only a slight inflammation of the arm takes place instead of being all over scabs'.

[2]Fraser, p. 311, explains: 'Mrs Cadogan's sister Sarah had married a Mr Connor from Ferry, near Hawarden, and "Miss Connor" was one of a gaggle of children who now came to their aunt and distinguished cousin for support – there were Mary and Cecilia and Ann and Sarah and Charles. . . . In fact, the Connor girls were surprisingly well educated, and Nelson made a good choice in them as governesses for Horatia. Mary and Cecilia and Ann Carbet Connor seem to have alternated in the position.'

not, in justice to my charge defer it for any consideration longer. May God bless you, my dear Emma, and reward you tenfold for all the goodness you have already shewn Horatia, and ever be assured that I am,

337. *To Lady Hamilton*

[NMM: CRK/19/50] Victory
Aug^{t}: 20th: 1804

My Dearest Emma the Kent left us 3 days ago and as the wind has been perfectly fair since her departure I think she will have a very quick passage and arrive long before this letter, but as a[1] ship is going to Roses I will not omit the opportunity of writing thro' Spain as you say the letters all arrive safe, We have noth^{g}: but gales of wind and I have had for two days fires in the cabbin to keep out the very damp air, I still hope that by the time of my arrival in England that we shall have Peace God send it I have not yet receiv'd your muff I think probably I shall bring it with me, I hope Davison has done the needful in paying for the alterations at Merton, if not it is now too late and we will fix a compleat plan and execute it next summer, I shall be clear of debt and what I have will be my own, God Bless you Amen, Amen, Geo. Elliot goes to Malta for a convoy to England this day if you ever see Lord Minto say so.

338. *To Lady Hamilton*

[Pettigrew, ii, pp. 419–20] Victory,
August 22nd, 1804.

My dearest Emma,

The ship was gone for Rosas, when the Spencer yesterday, nineteen days from Plymouth, joined us, by whom I had the happiness of receiving your letters of *viâ* Lisbon, June 28th, and one without a date through Mr. Marsden, July 4th, 7th, 10th, and 19th. I think it impossible that my friend the banker, I don't mention names,[2] would allow me to be distressed by loss of money in his banking house. I cannot believe it, and why Haslewood in some measure forced the £5000 from Marsh and Creed's hands, who lay out every farthing as they get it in the funds, never keeping more than £50 in hand; but I hope the best, and I am sure,

[1]Inserted.
[2]Goldsmid?

poor as I am, if the money I have in the house would save my friend, he should be welcome to it, but why should my all go to serve a parcel of people that I never saw or care one farthing about. I sincerely hope that the bathing has quite set you up again. The Kent will, I have no doubt, have a very short passage, and as she carries my request to come home for the restoration of my health,[1] which a few months may set up, and fit me, if the Admiralty pleases, to return to this command; but there are so many my seniors who are using every exertion for employment, that when once it is gone from me I stand no chance of getting it back again.[2] The more likelihood of a Spanish war, the less chance for me. You will know from Mr. Marsden what the Admiralty intend.

I wish my proxy had never been given.[3] I am not clear I should have voted on that side, but I have not read the debate. I hate the Grenvilles[4] – cold-hearted. If Lord Moira was to be First Minister, and I First Lord of the Admiralty, it would be my duty to support, but I am to expect nothing from them; and to make enemies of those who are in, I'll be damned if I do. I will stand upon my own bottom, and be none of their tools. When I come home I shall make myself understood. I like both Pitt and Lord Melville, and why should I oppose them? I am free and independent. I have not heard from Davison more than six months. I shall write him a line, poor fellow; I wish his time was out.[5] My kindest love to those we hold most dear – Horatia; and regards to good Mrs. Cadogan, Charlotte, &c. &c. &c. Don't forget old Oliver. God bless you. Amen, Amen, Amen. In a few days I shall write by Gibraltar.

339. *To Lady Hamilton*

[Houghton: pf MS Eng 196.5 (39)] Victory

Aug^{t}: 27th: 1804

My Dearest Emma,

Your dear kind letter by friend Gayner of June 22nd: + July 10th: are just receiv'd and those by Spencer to July 19th: I do not my Dear Emma

[1]Nicolas, vi, p. 157.

[2]See Doc. No. 332.

[3]Nelson had given his proxy vote in the House of Lords to Earl Moira, who disregarding Nelson's wishes (Nicolas, v, pp. 371–2; letter of 13 Jan. 1804 to Davison with note) had used it to vote against government. Nelson expressed his annoyance also in Doc. No. 344 and again in Sept 1805 in a letter to Davison (Nicolas, vii, p. 39).

[4]William Wyndham Grenville had two elder brothers: Thomas (1755–1846) and George, Marquess of Buckingham (1753–1813).

[5]Reference to his imprisonment in the Marshalsea prison.

believe that there is any danger of Davisons failure I mean the House, for if they sett off with a Capital of 500,000 £ no speculations [*sic*] could have injured them, especially last winter by the time the house was formed, as I wrote You Marsh + Creed were the only authorized persons to receive the Prize money from M^r^: Tucker, and neither Davison or Haslewood had a right to bully my agents, nor do I believe that they ever said I was in their debt, unless it was to save the money for me, when that was receiv'd I was 3800£ in D^s^: debt he had wrote me never to think of his debt for if it was never paid it was nothing to him, my agents put every farthing out to interest God knows it is not much, I dare say the Banking house has done no such thing for me but I shall be soon at home and settle all my affairs, and if I[1] do serve again for an expedition or another Year I shall be able to leave all my affairs in a better plight than at present, I am settling my Bronte affairs and next Year my net income from thence will be as sure as any estate in England, but I have very much to weed away, the gross amount is large but the salaries for Governor Campierios, the college fees +^c^: +^c^: +^c^: with M^rs^: Græfers pension will not be less than 800£ Sterling, a Year, I am now working to know why all this expence, if I allow M^rs^: G^r^: 100£ a Year I think I shall do well although I dare say[2] not half satisfy her, in case of any accident happening to Me I have given You 500£ Sterling a Year out of the Estate, but I hope we shall live many Years and spend it together the very thoughts of such bliss delights me the moment I get home I shall put it out of your power to spend dear Horatias money I shall settle it in trustees hands and leave nothing to chance, if Horace[3] behaves well he shall marry her,[4] M^r^: Elliot seems to think they will all go to the devil at Naples that it is perceptibly getting to be french I do not see things in so black a light as he does, M^r^: E. says both King + Queen are in desperation at my going away, they say that I have so uniformly protected them and never in the smallest instance committed them, notwithstanding what Castelcicala said, I have letters from Acton of Aug^t^: 9th: The lady I hear wishes to go to England and Acton says so, but I am sure that he has no such intention and that

(2) he will die in Italy, he longs to get to his house at Castle Mare[5] in short that he may be near the Court, and He thinks he can direct Circello,[6]

[1]Inserted.

[2]Inserted.

[3]Son of his brother William.

[4]See also Docs Nos 285 and 286.

[5]Castellammare, south of Naples.

[6]Tommaso Maria Somma, Marquis of Circello (1737–1826), who had been Neapolitan ambassador to France during the years 1786–93, but – according to contemporary judgement – 'unqualified' (the Italian entry for Circello in Wikipedia, 21 July 2019, quotes

but I doubt whether the Queen will permit him even to come to the Kingdom of Naples unless she finds that she is involved in difficultys and cannot get out of them, respecting Your business[1] He says, "I see what you tell me my Lord on Lady Hamiltons settlement by Sir William, I think [it] very just that she should be helped, I have wrote to Her Majesty on the Subject and she is pleased to answer me that she will do whatever is in her power on the subject and has acquainted your Lordship lately by one of her letters"[2]

I suppose my Dear Emma that letter is the one which I sent you and if her application thro' Castelcicala is as cold I do not expect much from it, never mind We shall never want with prudence

The letters You send with Yours are many of them interesting what a fool Sir E. H.[3] must be to tell but tittle-tattle is almost all that the men of the present day can talk about, to marry into the family of the Macnamaras, what a prospect, as for Cap^{n}: M^{c}namara it is not difficult to foresee that he will be shot he seems to lay himself out for it, and after what has happened no one will pity him,[4] our friend M^{r}: D.[5] seems to think him a nonesuch, every scrap of Your letters are so interesting that flattering fancy for the moment wafts me home,[6] Triumph + Narcissus leave the fleet this day to join the Maidstone therefore do not expect letters by those two this goes by Triumph, Gibbs sends you a piece of Palermo Silk which I have requested Sir Robt: Barlow[7] to send up from Portsmouth, he says there is nothing else worth Your acceptance he appears full of gratitude for your unremitted goodness to his daughter, If Davison has not paid poor M^{rs}: Nelsons debts which you say are 90£ I shall be very sorry, if he has not I will do it when I come home, M^{rs}: Cadogans account of

---

William Drummond, British minister to Naples in 1801–3 and to Palermo in 1806–8, having described him as 'inadatto').

[1]of getting (support for) a pension.

[2]All lines of this quoted passage start with '=' at their beginning.

[3]Probably Sir Edward Hamilton (1772–1851).

[4]Captain James Macnamara (not to be confused with the Captain James Macnamara with whom Nelson went to France in late 1783) had served with Nelson as a young captain in the Mediterranean; Nelson appeared for him as a character witness after he had killed an army officer in a duel over a quarrel over their dogs.

[5]Davison.

[6][Robert] *Pocock's Everlasting Songster, containing a selection of the most approved songs, which have been, and are likely to be sung for ever, with universal applause. . . .* (Gravesend, 1800), pp. 10–11, gives the poem 'The Wandering Sailor' which describes in three stanzas the adventures of a sailor who keeps thinking of home: 'The wind blows hard and mountains roll, / And thunder shakes from pole to pole, / The dreadful waves surrounding foam, / Still flattering fancy wafts him home;'.

[7]Sir Robert Barlow (1757–1843), whose daughter Hilare was to marry Nelson's brother William in 1829.

your dress made me laugh God in heaven bless you my own dear Emma and be assured that my only attatchment is to You and at present my dear Horatia, You will not have time to answer this letter before You will see Your own dear Nelson + Bronte remember me to Good M^{rs}: Cadogan, love to Charlotte +^{c}: +^{c}:

We have just reports from a vessel spoke that our fleet has gained a great victory God send it may be true and give us peace. Faddy is confirmed he is lucky + Sir R. Barlow speaks highly of him

340. *To Lady Hamilton*

[NMM: CRK/19/51]

Victory Aug^{t}: 31st: 1804 say 30th:
at Evening therefore I wrote in fact
this Day through Spain.

My Ever dearest Emma yesterday I wrote to you thro' Spain this goes by Naples M^{r}: Falconet I think will send it although I am sure he feels great fear from the french minister for having anything to do with us, M^{r}: Greville is a shabby fellow it never could have been the intention of Sir William but that you should have had 700 £ a year Net money for when he made the will the income Tax was double to what it is at present, and the estates which it is paid from is increasing every year in value it may be law but it is not just nor in equity would I believe be considered as the will and intention of Sir William never mind thank God you do not want any of his kindness nor will he give you Justice I may fairly say all this because my actions are different even to a person who has treated me so ill, as to ~~Hamond~~[1] I know the full extent of the obligation I owe him and he may be useful to me again but I can never forget his unkindness to you, but I guess many reasons influenced his conduct in bragging of his Riches, and my honorable poverty, but as I have often said and with honest pride, what I have is my own it never cost the widow a tear

[1]The name has been crossed out very thoroughly. Close examination on a document preservation tablelit from below by cold light makes it most likely that Nelson had written '[Andrew Snape] Hamond'. Examination of the crossed-out name under a microscope at the National Maritime Museum showed that before the (last layer of) crossing-out with ink was applied someone had tried to scratch the ink of the name away; this can be deduced from the fact that the fibres on the surface of the paper are forced into one direction. Infra-red light did not help in uncovering the crossed-out name. Since the ink that had been used for the deletion contained as much iron as that Nelson had used for writing, this shows that the name must have been crossed out with (near-)contemporary ink. A possible reason for crossing out the name may have been that Hamond got on well with Lady Nelson (Knight, p. 643).

or the nation a farthing, I got what I have with my pure blood from the Enemies of my country our House my own Emma is built upon a solid foundation and will last to us when his house and lands may belong to others than his children, I would not have believ'd it from any one but you, but if ever I go abroad again matters shall be settled very differently I am working hard with Gibbs about Bronte but the calls upon me are very heavy, next September I shall be clear I mean Sep^{r}: 1805. I have wrote to both Acton + the Queen about you[1] I do not think she likes M^{r}: Elliot and therefore I wish she had never shown him my letters about you we also know that he has a card of his own to play, D^{r}: Scott who is a good man although poor fellow[2] very often wrong in the head[3] is going with Staines[4] in the Camelion just to take a peep at Naples + Palermo I have introduced him to Acton who is very civil to every body from me, the Admiralty proceedings towards me you will know much sooner than I shall, I hope they will do the thing handsomly [*sic*] and allow of my return in the spring but[5] I do not expect it, I am very uneasy at your ~~+ H^{a}~~ being on the coast for you cannot move if the french make the attempt which I am told they have done and been repulsed, pray God it may be true, I shall rejoice to hear you ~~+ H^{a}~~ are safe at Merton + happy shall I be the day I join you Gannam Justom[6] Gaetano is very grateful for your remembrance of him M^{r}: Chev^{r}:[7] is an Excellent servant, William says he has wrote twice I suppose he thinks that enough.[8] This is wrote within 3 miles of the fleet in Toulon who are looking very tempting, kind regards to M^{rs}: Cadogan Charlotte +^{c}: + comp^{ts}: to all our joint friends for they are no friends of mine who are not friends to Emma. God Bless you, again + again

Cap^{n}: Hardy has not been very well and I fancy Admiral Murray will not be sorry to see England especially since he has been promoted ~~xxx xxx xxx~~ he expects his flag may get up God Bless you my Dearest Emma and be assured I am ever most faithfully yours

[1]Rather: about supporting her to get a pension.

[2]Inserted.

[3]For the causes of this ailment (most probably as a consequence of the stroke of lightning that had hit him) and further references, see Doc. No. 287 and fn.

[4]Thomas Staines (1776–1830).

[5]The following passage from 'I do not expect it' until 'Gannam Justom' is added upside down along the whole width of the two 'inner' pages of the letter.

[6]1814-letters, ii, p. 71, have here '*Gannam Justem*'; whatever either is supposed to mean.

[7]Chevalier.

[8]The following passages are written upside down (judging from the direction of writing in the inside) on the 'outside' of the letter. The passage from 'This is wrote' until '+ again' is below the address. The passage from 'Cap^{n}: Hardy' until 'faithfully yours' is above the address.

341. *To Lady Hamilton*

[BL: Egerton 1614 ff. 106–107, no. 55] Victory
Sep^{r}: 9th: 1804

Since I wrote you my Dearest Emma on Aug^{t}: 30th: not the least change has taken place nor have I received a letter from any place, I have lost my opponent Monsr: La Touche I grieve to think that he died a natural death it was more than I bargain'd for however I hope not to follow his example for many years to come but to live happily many many years with you ~~and my dear H^{a}:~~[1] You will know long before me what are Lord Melville's intentions towards me, who comes and how I am likely to get home, If Cap^{n}: Keats will allow me a passage with my numerous suite I wish to go home in the Superb, but if the Admiralty send out a senior Admiral I must be subject to his will + pleasure, all that I hope is that the Ad^{ty}: will not keep me in quarantine at farthest beyond the return of the Post, for we shall be well crowded 7 or 8 to sleep in one cabbin but I cannot help it, it was the same and very uncomfortable coming out in the Amphion, but then I shall look, my dear Emma for happier moments for I shall not stay three minutes at Portsmouth but fly to dear Merton where all in this world which is dearest to me resides and therefore I would have you remain at Merton being assured I shall lose no time in coming to your dear dear Embrace, God Bless you my Dear Emma I have only a moment to scrawl this line but be assured I am ever most faithfully yours, — The Box you mention'd sending May 18th: has never arrived[2] nor my arms from Mr. Nayler[3] I wish M^{r}: Sprinks[4] may please you in building but he is [a] drunken fellow, I dare say you have made the subterraneus [*sic*] passage so as to stop the kitchen door and windows or you will find the smell of the kitchen I fear very bad, but I think you have provided against that[5]

If not we must provide against that next Spring and whatever becomes of me I can made [*sic*] better arraingements than I did before and not

[1]Here some words are pretty thoroughly crossed out in two dark black groups of about equal size. Somebody has added in the original manuscript above the deletions in pencil 'and my dear H^{a}:'. With cold light, 'and my' can be made out, as can 'H^{a}:'; the word 'dear' appears to be the most convincing addition.

[2]First mentioned in letters of 12. and 13 Aug 1804 (Docs Nos 333 and 334); Nelson reports in his letter of 31 Mar 1805 that it 'is just arrived' (Doc. No. 361).

[3]George Nayler, of the College of Arms.

[4]Pettigrew, ii, p. 423, has here 'Spinks'.

[5]The following passage is added upside down on the top of pages 2 and 3 and is not in Pettigrew, ii, p. 423.

have you for a moment subject to any purse proud man. I am very much hurt, but patience, once more God bless you.

342. *To Lady Hamilton*

[Pettigrew, ii, pp. 423–4] Victory,
September 22nd, 1804.

Your two letters of August 7th and 13th I have received. I am not sure whether I gave the Spanish dresses to Captain Layman, or sent them to the Admiralty; the pieces of Armoisins[1] and Naples shawls I gave him open, or there might be difficulty in getting them on shore. I have been expecting a ship from Naples and Palermo these several days, perhaps the Queen or Acton from Palermo might say something about you, but I can no longer defer sending off my dispatches to catch the Triumph at Gibraltar. Report says, she and the King are likely at last to have a serious rupture, Circello, who is Acton's man, will not give into her wants and wishes. However, I never trouble myself with these matters, they may settle their own affairs, they are *old* enough. Acton will get back to Castel à Mare, and by degrees try to get into office again, he will never go to England if he can help it. I am sure it is not his inclination. Your disposition is too generous to insult a fallen man, however much we may detest the principles which guide his conduct, and I am sure nine-tenths of those who now abuse the Earl and Troubridge were, and would be again, their most abject flatterers were they again in office – for me, I feel myself above them in every way, and they are below my abuse of them; now no longer in power, I care nothing about them, and now they can do no harm to any one I shall not abuse them. Sir William Bolton is going to Gibraltar to refit the Childers. I see no prospect of making him Post. When I come home I will speak to some of the Admiralty about Tom Bowen, but I must stick to Sir William Bolton, for if I ask many favours I may get none. Charles is rated on board the Niger, and I hope he will do well. I have talked much to him and he promises fair. When you receive this letter I shall most probably be upon my passage, in what ship, &c. &c. must be left to the Admiratly or the Admiral who they may send out. I have plenty of candidates for taking me to England. Gore[2] of the Medusa writes in desperation, but I am not my own master. Superb

[1] Armosins [*sic*] is thick, plain silk.
[2] John Gore, with whom Nelson had cooperated in the Channel in 1801.

I think will be the ship. God bless you. Kiss dear Horatia for me, and be assured I am,

Yours, &c.
Nelson and Bronté.

Don't fix anything about Linton's farm till my arrival, perhaps some of it may be sold.

I am anxious to hear from Gibbs and to settle Bronté, then that will be off my mind. It ought to have brought me £3000. a year, instead of a little more than £2000, when all is paid however. However, I have been a great fool in that business, but never mind. God bless us. Amen.

343. *To Lady Hamilton*

[NMM: CRK/19/52] Victory
Sep[r]: 29th: 1804

This day my dearest Emma which gave me birth I consider as more fortunate than common days as by my coming into this world it has brought me so intimately acquainted with you who my soul holds most dear I well know that you will keep it and have my dear H[a]: to drink my health, 46 years of toil and trouble, how few more the common lot of mankind leads us to expect, and therefore it is almost time to think of spending the few last years in Peace and quietness, by this time I should think either my successor is named or permission is granted me to come home, and if so you will not long receive this letter before I make my appearance, which will make us, I am sure, both truly happy, we have had nothing for this fortnight but Gales of Easterly Winds + heavy rains not a vessel of any kind or sort join'd the fleet,

I was in hopes D[r]: Scott would have return'd from Naples and that I could have told you something comfortable for you from that quarter, and it is now 7 weeks since we heard from Malta, therefore I know nothing of what is passing in the world, I would not have you my Dear Emma allow the work of Brick and Mortar to go on in the winter months, it can all be finished next summer when I hope we shall have peace or such a universal war as will upset that vagabond Buonaparte, I have been tolerable well 'till this last bad weather which has given me pains in my breast, but never mind all will be well when I get to Merton,

Admiral Campbell[1] who is on board desires to be remembered to you he does not like much to stay here after my departure, indeed we all draw so well together in the fleet that I flatter myself the sorrow for my departure[2] will be pretty general, Adl: Murray will be glad to get home, Hardy is as good as ever and Mr: Secretary Scott is an excellent man, God Bless you my Dearest Emma and Be assured I am Ever your most faithful + affectionate N. & B. Kiss Dear Ha: I hope she is at Merton fixt

344. *To Lady Hamilton*

[Morrison, ii, pp. 240–41 (No. 782)] *Victory*,
October 2 nd, 1804

It was only yesterday, my dearest Emma, that I received your letter of July 1st, it having travelled in a Spanish smuggling boat to the coast of Italy and returned again to Spain, the boat not having met any of our ships. I am anxious to put you right about my proxy, and that Lord Moira's having it could have had no influence against Mr. Addington, not having done anything for me or my friends; you will see that it was entrusted to support Mr. Addington. Perhaps Davison has been the innocent cause of any one having my proxy, for I never liked giving it. Lord M[oira], in his letter to Davison, says, – 'being intrusted by him with the charge of repelling any attack which envy might even aim at his character, I will give myself the pride of being ostensibly confided in by him, and in Political questions I shall hold myself bound to give his vote as his relation to the Ministry requires, though it may be in contradiction to my own.

On January 13th, 1804, I signed the Proxy and sent it to Davison with the following extract: 'I have intrusted him with what I did not believe I would have intrusted any man, and I hope he will be a firm supporter of Mr. Addington's Administration'.[3] This did not get home till March, therefore no vote was given in Mr. Addington's administration,[4] but you see if any had, it would have been to support Mr. Addington, therefore it could have had no influence upon Mr. Addington if his inclination had

[1]George Campbell.

[2]The following passage is written upside down along the whole length of the top of the sheet.

[3]The proxy was for Earl Moira; the quotation from the letter to Davison is correct (see Nicolas, v, p. 371), but the dating of the proxy not; Nelson had already written to Davison on 12 Dec 1803: 'I have signed the Proxy for Lord Moira' (Nicolas, v, p. 305).

[4]Which ended on 15 May 1804.

led him to do anything; but the fact is, that if my pension was entailed so would Lord St. Vincent's, and at a time he was to be turned out for misconduct, that I take to be the reason. I think I should not have given my vote against Pitt. I am no party man as a tool, if I am to be a part of Administration it alters the case. If Pitt is attentive to me he shall have my vote. I have told you all this that you might see my conduct had nothing to do with *Addington's* conduct.

I have kept myself in this letter entirely to the subject of yours. You see Lord Moira bound himself to support Addington. God bless you.

345. *To Lady Hamilton*

[BL: Egerton 1614 ff. 108–109, no. 56] Victory
Oct^{r}: 5th: 1804

My Dearest Emma,

Hallowell is just arriv'd with your dear dear letters and although I have not in fact one moment of time still I send a line to thank you for them, I have only hastily run over your dear dear letters I never could have thought that you did not give enough to Poor M^{rs}: Bolton I must have meant that you should hold your generous hand[1] for if you have a fault it is that you give away much more than you can afford but respecting her + Tom +^{c}: +^{c}: I will regulate those things to the full extent of what I ought to afford upon due consideration and that shall be regularly paid. I can only touch hastily upon several subjects, I have letters from M^{r}: Elliot and the Queen The King is also in desperation at the thoughts of my going home, The King offered me houses either at Palermo or Naples but what would living in a Palace be without my own Emma, If I am at Sea faithfully serving my Country both Emma + her Nelson knows it is right whatever may be their sufferings at being separated, a few months in England will make us both in every respect much happier + more comfortable than at present, a messenger is now near England with a letter for Castelcicala to present to the King begging that I may be desired to return in the spring, but I do not expect that Pitt will accord with their wishes, although I receive from every part of Administration the most flattering marks of confidence, Acton is also very uncomfortable at the thoughts of my going away he was very kind to D^{r}: Scott. I much fear without great management Naples will be lost, I fear the Emperor of

[1]The misunderstanding appears to have been caused in the letter of 13 Jan 1804 (Doc. No. 299).

Germany[1] is too closely allied to Buonaparte to mind His relations at Naples The Q. is very angry. I have much to tell you when we meet upon all those subjects Your Brother Ball desires to be remembered to his Sister Emma[2] You will not have time to answer this Letters are on the avarage [*sic*] 5 weeks getting via Lisbon to Roses, Gibbs is doing I believe all he[3] can for me at Bronte M^{rs}: G^{r}:[4] will be allowed 100£ a year I see I must do it and then it can never be said but that I have done most nobly by her, Gibbs wants to get her to England and I can see by his letter that he means something. God Bless + preserve you for your only your own,[5]

I must just write a line by Post to Davison to thank him for his letters, he says every thing shall [be] done according to my desires therefore I hope my Dearest Emma that you will have no more trouble about paying for the improvements, Sir W^{m}: Bolton is gone to heave down at Gibralter he is a very good young man I wish I could make him Post and into a good frigate. Kind love + regards to M^{rs}: Cadogan to M^{rs}: Bolton Charlotte +^{c}: +^{c}: God Bless you I shall write by Gibralter in a few days.

346. *To Lady Hamilton*

[NMM: CRK/19/53]

Victory
Oct^{r}: 7th: 2 PM.[6]

I wrote you my dearest Emma this morning by way of Lisbon but a boat which is going to Torbay having brought out a cargoe [*sic*] of potatoes will I think get home before the Lisbon packet I shall only say Guzelle Gannam Justem[7] and that I love you beyond all the world this may be read by French Dutch, Spanish or Englishmen, for it comes from the heart of my Emma your faithful + affectionate

Nelson + Bronte

I think the gentry will soon come out. I cant say more by such a conveyance.

[1]Francis II, nephew of the Queen of Naples.
[2]The terms ‘brother’ and ‘sister’ refer to them both having received the Maltese Order of St John.
[3]The letter is continued upside down on top of pages 3 and 2 (writing across the folding line).
[4]Graefer.
[5]The letter is continued on the outside, upside down, first below (until ‘down at’), then above the address.
[6]The ‘PM’ is strangely connected by a pseudo-deletion.
[7]See Doc. No. 340 (‘happy shall I be the day I join you Gannam Justom’).

347. *To Lady Hamilton*

[*a)* Pettigrew, ii, p. 427;
b) Morrison, ii, p. 241 (No. 783)]

[*a)*] Victory,
October 10th, 1804.

[*b)*] This, my own dearest Emma, will, I dare say, be the last letter you will receive before you see your own Nelson. Whatever arrangements are made about me by the Minsters, it is all settled long before this time. You will know from the Admiralty about my quarantine, but I dare say it will not be longer than return of post. I would wish you, my Emma, to remain at Merton. You are sure I shall lose no time, and it is possible, if I have leave, to strike my flag at that same moment that I get pratique.[1] I shall not land at Portsmouth. As I wrote you before, I think the Superb will carry me, but if a senior Admiral comes out, I am subject to his will and pleasure. If all our house is not finished it can be done next summer, and we shall get through the winter very comfortable I have no doubt. Your last letters were to August 27th. You write so naturally that I fancy myself almost, not *quite*, in your dear company, but that will soon be, and I hope you have fixed Horatia at Merton. We have had much bad weather, and it has disagreed very much with me. Davison will pay all the bills, therefore you will not be more troubled on that matter. I have much to say to you but that I shall reserve to our happy, happy meeting. May God bless you, my dearest Emma, prays ever your faithful. You will to the Duke of Q., &c., &c., say everything that is civil. Love to Mrs. Cadogan, Charlotte,

[*a)*] N. & B.

348. *To Lady Hamilton*

[NMM: CRK/19/54]

Victory Oct^{r}: 13th: 1804

My Dearest Emma the dreadful effects of the yellow fever at Gib^{r}: and many parts of Spain will naturally give you much uneasiness 'till you hear that thank God we are entirely free from it and in the most perfect health not one man being ill in the fleet, the cold weather will I hope cure the disorder, whilst writing this letter a cutter is arrived from England with strong indications of a Spanish War I hope from my heart that it will not prove one, but however thet

[1]Pratique is the licence given to a ship to enter port on assurance from the captain to convince the authorities that his ship is free from contagious disease.

is my die is cast and long before this time I expect another Admiral is far on his way to supersede me, Lord Keith I think a very likely man I should have [*sic*] for your sake and for many of our friends have liked an odd hundred thousand Pounds but never mind, if they give me the choice of staying a few months longer it will be very handsome and for the sake of others we would give up my dear Emma very much of our own felicity if they do not we shall be happy with each other and with Dear H^a: the cutter returns with my answers directly therefore my own Emma you must only fancy all my thoughts and feelings towards you, they are every thing which a fond heart can fancy I have not a moment I am writing + signing orders[1] whilst I am writing to my own Emma my life my soul God in heaven bless you your letter is Sep^r: 16th: your last is Aug^t: 27th: I have not made myself understood about M^rs: Boltons money You give away <u>too</u> much[2] kiss our dear H^a: a thousand times for your own faithful Nelson, I send 200 £ keep it for your own pocket money, You must tell Davison + Haslewood that I cannot answer their letters, Linton[3] cannot be fixt but you will know whether I come home or stay from M^r: Marsden, God Bless you Tell my Brother that I have made M^r: Yonge a Lieutenant into the Seahorse frigate Cap^n: Boyle,[4] once more God Bless my dearest Emma.

Write your name on the back of the bill if you send any person for the money.

I have scrawled 3 Lines to Davison that he should not think I neglected him in his confinement[5]

I have received the enclosed from Allen can we assist the Poor foolish man, with a <u>character</u>[6]

349. *To Lady Hamilton*

[Houghton: MS Lowell 10] Victory
Oct^r: 31st: 1804

My Dearest Emma,

Various circumstances makes [*sic*] me rather believe that it will not be possible to land this letter in Spain and if it is landed I hardly think it will

[1] For (some of) the orders, see Nicolas, vi, p. 238 (to Captain Gore), pp. 241–3 (to Captain Richard Strachan).

[2] Compare Doc. No. 345.

[3] See Doc. No. 342, postscript.

[4] Courtnay Boyle (d. 1844).

[5] This is a reference to Davison's imprisonment in the Marshalsea prison. This note is added in a vertical direction of writing on the outside.

[6] This note is also added in a vertical direction of writing on the outside, but upside down in relation to the previous note.

ever reach Lisbon however as I never miss an occasion of writing I take the chance of saying a very few words, I have prepared every thing for my successor be [he] who he will and a very few hours will suffice me to give him up the cudgels The fleet is perfection not one man ill of any complaint a great thing to say in these dreadful times of sickness I have got Mr: Estes son onboard he wants to get to England but through Spain [it] is impossible as no one is allowed to travel from one Town to another,[1] I purpose sending him via Gibr if we hear more favourable accounts of the fever and from thence he intends to get to Lisbon as [*sic*] so [go] home by the Packet but if my superiors comply with my request I may probably be in England sooner than this letter, The cutter I hope my own Emma arrived safe and I have by her endeavour'd to make some amends for the cruelty of Mr: Greville what can he think of himself, however I shall be happy in sharing my fate with Yours believe my dearest Emma all I would say to You and what I think but I must keep it to myself I am expecting every hour the answer from the Admiralty. The french fleet all well the 29th: Sir Wm: B. is at Malta therefore I have not sent his letter, I have much to tell you on[2] many subjects and what I can tell the Great People (You understand me) will if I return again be most useful to them if not too great to hear what I know God in heaven Bless You + send us a meeting at Dear Merton a happy one I have no doubt but it will be my cough is so so love to Ha: +c: +c: +c:

350. *To Lady Hamilton*

[William Clements: Hubert S. Smith,
Volume 1 'Naval Affairs'] Victory Novr: 1804

I yesterday my dearest beloved Emma had the happiness of receiving your dear kind + affectionate letters of Sepr: 16th: 20th: 27th: + Octr: 1st: I cannot but think that I shall see You before You read this letter it goes by way of Lisbon where I am sending Mr: Este who is very anxious to get to England I have been You will believe as attentive to him as I could, I am glad that You have had so pleasant a trip into Norfolk that You have made them all happy I have no doubt but You have made Yourself Poor, I do not believe that Pitt will give you a Pension any more than Addington who I supported to the last moment of his Ministry there is no gratitude in any of them however if they do not do it I will give it You out of Bronte, You

[1] Probably as a precautionary measure against the spread of yellow fever (see Doc. No. 348).
[2] The text continues upside down at the top of and across pages 3 and 2.

will see what effect Your Queens letter has through Castelcicala a very pretty channel. She has made Roger Dumas, Comdr: In Chief and some other Frenchman something else against both the Kings + Actons consent but I fear she is ruling not so well as we could wish, I did not hear from her by the last vessel from Naples perhaps she is angry[1] at my ill health and going home for a few months to save my life, the china that we heard so much about was never ordered, Mr: Elliot I believe would not be satisfied any where he has by this time he writes me 12 children and is Poor, Geo. Elliot is grown so proud that he scarcely deigns to own them for his cousins and would scarcely speak to a very fine lad which Mr: Elliot has sent to sea and is now on board the Amazon, Capt: Hardy says Geo. Elliot will turn out an ungrateful wretch although he may be a good officer. I have very attentive letters from General Acton but he has no more the Power the Queen has got clear of him and never whilst she rules will [he] be suffer'd to even enter the kingdom, I send you his private letter his Public one goes to Lord Camden[2] Gibbs writes me of the difficultys of settling all my affairs at Bronte he is anxious to remove Mrs: Graefer I shall allow the 100 £ a Year and have done with her, If she intends to go to England I have wrote to Capt: Lamb[3] Agent of Transport [*sic*] to find her a passage which he has promised me to do I shall get nothing from Bronte but accounts till next years crop, and when I let it the Rents will be raised one third at least and I not benefitted till 8 years are expired[4]

You may tell Davison and truly that I have so much fever + head ache that if I had the Kings Ransome [*sic*] I could not write to him but remember me kindly to him and compliments to Haselwood,[5] love to Mrs: Cadogan Charlotte +c +c

351. *To Lady Hamilton*

[Pettigrew, ii, p. 434] Victory,
Nov. 6th, 1804.

Although I have wrote you by the Admiralty, yet I will not allow Mr. Este to leave me without carrying a line from me. I think his father's and his

[1]The 'n' is inserted.
[2]John Pratt, 1st Marquess Camden (1759–1840) was at that time Secretary of State for War and the Colonies.
[3]Philip Lamb.
[4]The letter is continued after this passage upside down across the third and second pages of the letter.
[5]William Haslewood.

own inclination, will induce him to call upon you and deliver this letter. He will be able to tell you how I am, not very stout, although perhaps not very ill. The Kent must have been arrived several days when you wrote October 1st. I am momentarily expecting a vessel from the Admiralty with either another Admiral, or permission or refusal for my return to England.

As Mr. Este is first to go by Lisbon, instead of sharing my fate, I have sent the Termagant to land him there, but I tell him that he had better stay, for that I shall be in England before him, which that god may grant, is the fervent prayer of

Yours,
Nelson and Bronté.

I have this day appointed Mr. Westphaling's friend, Mr. Roberts, to the Anson, it will most probably be my last act of attention during my present command.

352. *To Lady Hamilton*

[NMM, MAM/33, photocopy][1] Victory
Nov^{r}: 15th: 1804 2 AM

My last letters having been sent back from Roses not suffered to be landed assures me that we are at War with Spain but I have not a Word from our Minister at Madrid upon the Subject God knows my dearest Emma what the Admiralty mean to do with me but if I stay much longer I should not much like to arrive in the very depth of Winter I hardly think my shattered constitution would stand such a shock, I am now for the first time in my life likely to pick up some Money which shall make all these we hold dear comfortable, if I had it many of my near Relations should have benefitted by it I am as You may believe sending ships in all directions and this line is wrote at 2 in the Morning, I hope this will reach you it will assure you my Dearest Emma of the constant affection of Your Faithful Devoted

Nelson + Bronte

Think what I would say did I even believe that this letter would reach you, remember me to all our dear friends

[1] I owe information of this source to Jane Knight.

353. *To Lady Hamilton*

[NMM: CRK/19/55]

Victory
Nov[r]: 23rd: 1804

As all our communication with Spain is at an end I can now only expect to hear from my own dear Emma by the very slow mode of Admiralty vessels and it is now more than two months since the John Bull sail'd, I much fear something has been taken for they never would I am sure have kept me so long in the dark, however by management + a portion of good luck I got the account from Madrid in a much shorter space of time than I could have hoped for and I have set the whole Mediterranean to work and I think the fleet cannot fail of being successful and if I had, had the spare[1] Troops at Malta at my disposal Minorca would at this moment have had English colors flying this letter my dearest beloved Emma goes although in M[r]: Marsdens letter such a roundabout way that I cannot say all that my heart wishes, imagine every thing which is kind and affectionate and you will come near the mark, where is my successor, I am not a little surprized at his not arriving, a Spanish War I thought would have hastened him, Ministers could not have thought that I wanted to fly the service my whole life has proved the contrary and if they refuse me now I shall most certainly leave this country in March or April for a few months rest I must have very soon, if I am in my grave what are the mines of Peru[2] to me but to say the truth I have no idea of killing myself I may with care live yet to do good service to the State, my cough is very bad and my side where I was struck on the 14th: Feb[ry]:[3] is very much swelled at times a lump as large as my fist brought on occasionally by violent coughing but I hope and believe my lungs are yet safe, Sir William Bolton is Just arriving from Malta I am preparing to send him [on] a cruize where he will have the best chance I can give him of making 10,000 £[4] He is a very attentive good young man I have not heard from Naples this age I have in fact no small craft to send for news, if I am soon to go home I shall be with you before this letter may God bless you, Thompson desires to be most kindly remembered to his dear wife + children[5] he is most sincerly [*sic*] attatched to them + wishes to save

[1]Inserted.
[2]Regarded as a treasure trove because of its silver mines at Potosí (formerly 'Alto Perú', Upper Peru, nowadays Bolivia).
[3]At the battle off Cape St Vincent in 1797.
[4]Of prize money.
[5]Not 'child'.

what he can for their benefit, as our means of communicating are cut off I have only to beg that you will not believe the idle rumours of battles +^{c}: +^{c}: +^{c}: May heavens bless you prays fervently my Dear Emma Ever your most faithful + affectionate

Nelson + Bronte.

354. *To Lady Hamilton*

[BL: Egerton 1614 ff. 110–111, no. 57] Victory
Dec^{r}: 4th: 1804

If any one could have told me my own dearest Emma that Admiral Campbell[1] would have saild for England before me I should not have believed him, but his state of health is come to that crisis that probably his life would be lost if he was kept here even 48 hours longer therefore he proceeds this day in the Ambuscade and poor fellow I hope he will arrive safe, I have for several months thought that his mind was debilita[te]d but we tried to laugh him out of it I send you his letter when I announced to him in consequence of his application that a frigate should carry him to England immediately All my things are on board the Superb and if my successor would arrive I could be off in two hours, We have reports that Sir John Orde is the man which has thrown a gloom over all the fleet, but I hope unnecessarily, for six years upon the shelf may have taught him[2] a little moderation towards officers,[3] I have made up my mind to overwhelm him with respect and attention and to even make an offer as Ad^{l}: Campbell has gone home to serve 'till the Admiralty can send out another flag officer, but I have wrote to Lord Melville that I should make such an offer and that I entreated him to send out a flag officer as soon as possible but I dare say Sir John Orde is too great a man to want my poor services and that he will reject them, be that as it may you will I am sure my Dear Emma agree with me that I shall show my superiority to him by such an offer and the world will see what a sacrifice I am ready to make for the service of my King + country, for what greater sacrifice could I make than serving for a moment under Sir John Orde and giving up for that moment the society of all I hold dear in this world, many here

[1]George Campbell.

[2]Inserted.

[3]Sir John Orde (1751–1824), described by Roger Knight as 'a universally unpopular officer' (p. 660), had opposed Nelson's appointment to the Mediterranean over himself in 1798 (which meant for him in 1804: 'six years upon the shelf'), since when Nelson had tried to be conciliatory.

think that He is sent out off Cadiz to take a fortune out of my mouth, that would be very curious, the late Admiralty directed Ad^{l}: Cornwallis to send Campbell to cruize at the mouth of the Streights[1] and he took all my sweets and now this Admiralty sends and takes all my golden Harvest,[2] it is very odd, surely I never served faithfully, I have only dreamt I have done my duty to the advantage of my country, but I am above them, <u>I feel it</u>, although not one farthing richer than when I left England, it is this day 75 days since my letters were dated in London from the Admiralty, I can only my dear Emma bring you a most faithful and affectionate heart which is all your own and may God Bless you my own Emma prays Ever for Ever your most attatchd faithful + affectionate

Nelson + Bronte

Kiss dear H. for me and give my kindest regards to M^{rs}: Cadogan Charlotte and all all [*sic*] our friends.

355. *Fifth codicil to Nelson's will*[3]

[TNA: Prob. 1/22/1]

To be added to my Will and Codocils.

N + B.

I hereby confirm my last will + testament bearing date on or about May 13th: 1803, with the codocils and confirm anew my Legacy to Lady Emma Hamilton[4] and to my adopted Daughter Horatia Nelson Thompson and I farther Give to my Dear Friend Emma Hamilton widow of the R^{t}: Honb^{bl}: Sir W^{m}: Hamilton K. Bth: the Sum of Two-Thousand Pounds Sterling, and to my Secretary John Scott Esqr: the Sum of one hundred Pounds to buy a Ring or some token of my remembrance and I request that He will with Capt: Hardy take care of my papers + Effects (for my Executors) and I give to my friend The Rev^{d}: Alex^{r}: Scott the sum of Two hundred Pounds Sterling, Dated on Board the Victory in the Gulph of Palma Sardinia December nineteenth one thousand Eight hundred and four.

Nelson + Bronte

[1]Straits of Gibraltar.
[2]Of prize money.
[3]See Doc. No. 259.
[4]It should be 'Emma, Lady Hamilton'.

356. *To Lady Hamilton*

[Monmouth: E 159]

Victory
Dec[r]: 19th: 1804

My Dearest Emma,

Since I wrote you by the Ambuscade[1] when I was every moment expecting the arrival of the great Sir John Orde I have receiv'd a letter from him telling me that He was in the chief command of a squadron outside the Streights[2] +[c]: +[c]: +[c]: he has treated my ships a little hars[h]ly but never mind he will get all the money and your Poor Nelson all the hard blows, am I to[3] take this act as a proof of Lord Melvilles regard for me, but I submit patiently, but I feel[4] I have not had a scrap of a Pen from England 90 days this day, it is rather long in these critical times, I send this through M[r]: F.[5] at Naples and as it will be read by the French and many others I do not chuse to say anything more than I care for all the world knowing that I love you more than anything in this world and next my D[r]: H[a]: I keep everything packed up and two hours would finish every thing I can have to do with my successor, who must certainly be near at hand, or is Sir John[6] after he has got Riches to come here and get glory, I have certainly much to arrai[n]ge when I get home and the situation of M[rs]: B[n]:[7] shall have serious consideration but such a place as Tysons would very soon involve M[r]: B in difficultys however I will ask, and I fear [I] shall be refused, my cough is still very very bad and I ought at this moment to have been snug at Merton, but I look forward for that day with much pleasure and please God it will arrive very soon, you may tell[8] Lord Melville that the French fleet was safe the 12th: Dec[r]: but my[9] reporter says that they are certainly embarking Troops, but I hope to meet them and to realize the fond wishes of my country may God Almighty keep you prays

[1]See Doc. No. 354; the *Ambuscade* left the fleet on 4 Dec 1804.

[2]Straits of Gibraltar.

[3]Inserted.

[4]This is the end of the first page; the text continues a fair bit down on the second page, so that there was enough space at the top of the second (and third) page(s) left for Nelson to insert text upside down.

[5]Falconet.

[6]Orde.

[7]Bolton.

[8]The letter is continued upside down on the same side of the sheet across pages 2 and 3.

[9]Inserted.

ever yours + only yours[1] remember me kindly to good Mrs: Cadogan Charlotte Miss Connor and all our friends I wish I could be with you all this Xtmas which I fully expected.

357. *To Lady Hamilton*

[Pettigrew, ii, pp. 445–6]

Victory,
December 30th, 1804.

My dearest Emma,

I received by the Swiftsure your letters to October 29th, on your return from your long expedition into Norfolk, on Christmas-day, the day I had devoted to spend most happily with you and our dear adopted Horatia at dear Merton. I received the Admiralty's permission to go to England for the re-establishment of my health,[2] and I think that a few months may enable me to serve another year, and then, except for an expedition, I shall most likely never serve again. The winter has been quite different to the last. We have not had a cold day, nor near so many gales of wind, but my cough is very troublesome, particularly from two in the morning until I have had my breakfast; but a little of your good nursing will set me up again. The Niger has been sent home, I fear by Sir John Orde, who has not behaved very civil towards any of my squadron, therefore I am afraid Mr. Charles Connor will lose his kind protector in Captain Hillyar, which will be a serious misfortune to him, for he was rated Midshipman, and forced by Captain Hillyar to study, which he was not very fond of. The going home of George Campbell has protracted my departure till another Admiral comes out, which may very well be in January, then unless the French fleet is actually at sea, nothing will keep me two hours. I have not heard from Naples for some time, but I hear the French are oppressing both the Sovereigns and the people very much. I wrote you on the 19th through Mr. Falconet.

I have wrote to Lord Melville as strong as possible, and in fact have sold myself to him, if he complies with my desires for Mr. Bolton, but my dear kind hearted Emma, I do not believe he will give me any thing. I only wish I had the power myself, and so I might if the

[1]After this passage the letter is continued, still upside down, on the outside 'under' the address; The letter has been bound in somewhere and the piece of paper glued to it covers the beginnings of the lines, which are (the letters that disappear under the piece of paper are ~~crossed out~~): '~~rem~~ember . . . ~~Ch~~arlotte . . . ~~fri~~ends . . . ~~a~~ll . . .'.

[2]Doc. No. 362: 'although given the 6th: October came to me on Decr: 25th: Xt:mas Day'.

station had not been taken from me, and given to that great officer who has served so much and so well; but as I have asked favours of Lord Melville, I must not grumble. The end of February, or the first week in March, I shall certainly be in England in the Superb, and I only hope that we shall have a very short quarantine, for I shall certainly not communicate with Gibraltar, I cannot say what I would wish in this letter, for it goes by way of Lisbon in the Admiralty packet, and will be smoked, cut, &c. &c. before it gets to you, and I may very probably be with you before the letter, which will give inexpressible happiness to

Yours,
Nelson and Bronté.
Kiss dear Horatia for me.

358. *To Lady Hamilton*

[William Clements: Hubert S. Smith,
Volume 1 'Naval Affairs']

Victory
Jan^{ry}: 14th: 1805.

Although my Dearest Emma I have not heard that M^{r}: Falconet forwarded my other letter of Dec^{r}: 19th: yet I shell take the chance of another crossing the Continent just to say I am not so unwell as I have been the french are certainly preparing for an expedition I only fear they will defer it till my departure, all our friends at Naples are pressing me to stay + save them and certainly their situation becomes every day more critical The Usurper[1] have [*sic*] made most unjust demands upon them and held out threats but the Queen is firm I must not go on with this subject for Lord Nelson insists that I shall put nothing of politicks in my letter therefore I can only assure my dear Emma of my truest affection and love for you ~~xxx xxx xxx xxx xxx~~ I shall probably be at Home long before this letter therefore shall only say God Bless and preserve You for Your own faithful

J. T.[2]

[1]Napoleon Bonaparte?
[2]Nelson signing as Thomson.

359. *Lady Hamilton's poem 'Emma to Nelson'*

[1814-letters, ii, pp. 127–8][1]

Emma to Nelson

I think, I have not lost my heart;
Since I, with truth, can swear,
At every moment of my life,
I feel my Nelson there!

If, from thine Emma's breast, her heart
Were stolen or flown away;
Where! where! Should she my Nelson's love
Record, each happy day?

If, from thine Emma's breast, her heart
Were stolen or flown away;
Where! where! Should she engrave, my Love!
Each tender word you say?

Where! where! should Emma treasure up
Her Nelson's smiles and sighs?
Where mark, with joy, each secret look
Of love, from Nelson's eyes?

Then, do not rob me of my heart,
Unless you first forsake it;
And, then, so wretched it would be,
Despair alone will take it.

360. *To Lady Hamilton*

[Pettigrew, ii, pp. 460–62]

Victory
February 18th, 1805.

[1]In a letter to Davison from 'Clarges Street [26th Jan 1805]', in which this poem was enclosed, Lady Hamilton wrote: 'I send you some of my bad Verses on my soul's idol' (1814-letters, ii, pp. 125–7, at p. 126).

My dear Emma,

When we passed the Faro,[1] on January 31st, I sent friend Broadbent a letter for you,[2] and begged him to forward it to England. Your good heart will readily believe what an anxious time I have had from that period to this moment, and it is still continuing, for I have, as yet, got no tidings of the French fleet. I fear they got crippled, and returned to Toulon, for they were not used to encounter a Gulf of Lyons gale, which we have been in the practice of for these twenty months past. If they are got back, no man regrets the accident which may have happened to them more than myself, for I looked upon my meeting the French Admiral,[3] as the end of all my toil. No man commands a fleet, more anxious to fulfil the wishes of its Chief, than the one I at present command. For this month, I have neither eat nor slept one moment in comfort. However, both the King of Naples and the Turk are obliged, by my care of their dominions. John Bull, we know, calculates nothing right that does not place the British fleet alongside that of France. By the events are we judged; however, I feel that I have done right in going to Egypt, for at this moment, I as firmly believe, that was their destination, as I believed it before, and they have now a much better chance of holding Egypt, with a few men, than they had before, when they landed 40,000, for now, every inhabitant is for them, and they were then against them, and so are the Mamelukes.[4] I have now traversed 1000 leagues of sea after them. Our passage from

[1]Of Messina, on the way to Egypt, where Nelson then supposed the French fleet had gone. As no letter to Lady Hamilton of that period is (yet) known, Nelson's account to Major Misset in Cairo might best explain the situation from Nelson's viewpoint: 'The French fleet having saild on Jan^ry^: 18th: with from 8000 – to 10,000 Troops embarked, their destination not known, but general[l]y believed to be either the Morea or Egypt, a very heavy Gale of Wind seperated some of their ships, one of 80 guns put into Adjaccio in Corsica and three were seen steering for S^t^: Fiorenzo in the same Island, the remainder of the fleet I have not heard of since they were off the South end of Sardinia on the 21^d^:, on the 18th: they had not gone to Naples, on the 31rd: they had not been in Sicily when I passed the Faro of Messina, the Weather has been too bad for me to communicate with the Morea although I was on the 2nd: off Coron + sent a frigate to the pacha of that place, I have therefore but little doubt but that their destination is to take possession of Alexandria, when the French consul writes that all Egypt would declare for the french against the Turks, therefore even should they not be arrived but forced to return into Port, from the very bad weather they have had, yet I would strongly recommend to you to urge the Vizir or Pacha of Egypt whatever he is called to be upon his Guard and in particular to strengthen Alexandria by every means in his power, for Egypt He may rely is one of Buonapartes favorite Objects.' (BL: Egerton 1614 ff. 112–113, no. 58; given, partly incorrectly, in Pettigrew, ii, pp. 458–9).

[2]If this does not refer to the letter of 14 Jan 1805 (Doc. No. 358), it is lost.

[3]Pierre-Charles de Villeneuve (1763–1806).

[4]A member of a former military caste, originally composed of slaves from Turkey, that held the Egyptian throne from c. 1250 until 1517 and remained powerful until 1811.

Messina, round by the Morea[1] to Alexandria, was seven days. I am, at this moment, forty-six leagues from Malta, where I shall communicate to-morrow, but not shorten a rag of canvas. French fleet, French fleet, is all I want to have answered me. I shall never rest till I find them, and they shall neither, if I can get at them. You will believe that this anxiety has not done my general health much good, but had I been absent and the French fleet put to sea, it would have gone hard to kill me, and anxious as I am sure we are to meet, I am sure you agree with me. But I do not despair of yet getting hold of these fellows, and they shall reward me for all my trouble. Your last letter was November 2nd, since when I have not heard a scrap from England. How is Horatia? Neither she or you are ever absent from my thoughts, and all my glory will serve to give you both real happiness. God send it may be so, and soon.

February 20th. Yesterday I was off Malta, in a gale of wind, at south-east, so that a boat could only get to one of the fleet, which brought me intelligence of the return of the French fleet, in a most crippled state, to Toulon, except one ship of the line, which is on shore at Ajaccio, and one frigate dismasted and gone to Genoa. This news was grievous enough for me, but, to-day, I received the further mortifying news, of the capture of a convoy, which sailed from Malta, January 4th. This has hurt me more than the other, but I cannot help it; no blame, I feel, attaches itself to me, whatever may be said, my conduct will bear a scrutiny. I have not heard from Naples how they take my going to Egypt; perhaps the Queen thinks it only necessary for me to look to their safety, and that I have never neglected. I do not think that she and Mr. Elliot exactly hit it off. The court of Naples ought to be most grateful for my constant and unwearied attention to them. I am now off Maritimo,[2] in dreadful bad weather, beating to get off Toulon. Either the enemy will be near putting to sea again, or the summer will, in a few weeks, be so far advanced, that they will not venture to move, when I shall embrace the permission of the Admiralty, and return to England for a few months, but it shall never be said of me, as it has been of another Commander-in-chief, that I gave up the command, when the enemy's fleet was actually at sea. No, I would die 10,000 deaths before such a stigma should be cast upon my character. You may believe my anxiety, not for myself, for I have nothing to reproach myself with, but I cannot bear that the French fleet should have been out and got back again.

Yours,
Nelson and Bronté.

[1]Southern Greece, what is now called the Peloponnese.
[2]Marettimo.

361. *To Lady Hamilton*

[1814-letters, ii, pp. 87–95 (No. LVIII)]

Victory,
March 9th, 1805.

I do assure you, my dearest Emma, that nothing can be more miserable, or unhappy, than your poor Nelson. From the 19th of February, have we been beating from Malta to off Palma, where I am now anchored, the wind and sea being so very contrary and bad. But I cannot help myself, and no one in the fleet can feel what I do: and to mend my fate, yesterday Captain Layman arrived – to my great surprise – not in his brig,[1] but in a Spanish cartel,[2] he having been wrecked off Cadiz, and lost all the dispatches and letters. You will conceive my disappointment! It is now from November 2d, that I have had a line from England. Captain Layman says, he is sure the letters are sunk, never to rise again; but as they were not thrown overboard until the vessel struck the rock, I have much fear that they may have fallen into the hands of the Dons. My reports from off Toulon state the French as still in port: but I shall ever be uneasy at not having fallen in with them.

I know, my dear Emma, that it is in vain to repine; but my feelings are alive to meeting those fellows after near two years' hard service. What a time! I could not have thought it possible that I should have been so long absent; unwell and uncomfortable in many respects. However, when I calculate upon the French fleet not coming to sea for this summer, I shall certainly go for dear England, and a thousand (times) dearer Merton. May Heavens bless you, my own Emma! I cannot think where Sir William Bolton is got to; he ought to have joined me, before this time. I send you a trifle, for a birth-day's gift. I would to God, I could give you more; but, I have it not! I get no prize-money worth naming; but, if I have the good fortune to meet the French fleet, I hope they will make me amends for all my anxiety; which has been, and is, indescribable. How is my dear Horatia? I hope you have her under your guardian wing, at Merton. May God bless her. Captain Layman is now upon his trial. I hope he will come clear, with honour. I fear it was too great confidence

[1]The *Raven*; the court martial on board the *Royal Sovereign* found: 'The Court doth therefore adjudge the said Captain William Layman to be severely reprimanded and put at the bottom of the list of Commanders, and the said Mr: John Edwards is rendered ineligible to promotion for two Years after completing the usual time of servitude for a Lieutenant and the said Captain William Layman and Mr: John Edwards are hereby so sentenced accordingly.' (BL Add. 34,929, f. 41).

[2]Cartel ships were ships employed on humanitarian voyages, in particular, to carry prisoners for exchange between places agreed upon in the terms of the exchange.

in his own judgement that got him in the scrape; but it was impossible that any person living could have exerted himself more, when in a most trying and difficult situation.

March 10th.

Poor Captain Layman has been censured by the Court, but I have my own opinion; I sincerely pity him, and have wrote to Lord Melville and Sir Evan Nepean, to try what can be done. Altogether, I am much unhinged.

To-morrow, if the wind lasts, I shall be off Toulon. Sir William Bolton is safe, I heard of him this morning. I hear that a ship is coming out for him; but, as this is only rumour, I cannot keep him from this opportunity of being made Post, and I dare say, he will cause by his delay, such a tumult, that Louis's son,[1] who I have appointed to the Childers, will lose his promotion, and then Sir Billy will be wished at the devil! But I have done with this subject; the whole history has hurt me. Hardy has talked enough to him to rouse his lethargic disposition.

I have been much hurt at the loss of poor Mr. Girdlestone![2] He was a good man; but there will be an end of us all. What has Charles Connor been about? His is a curious letter! If he does not drink, he will do very well; Captain Hilliar[3] has been very good to him. Colonel Suckling, I find, has sent his son to the Mediterranean; taking him from the Narcissus, where I had been at so much pains to place him. I know not where to find a frigate to place him. He never will be so well and properly situated again. I am more plagued with other people's business, or rather nonsense, than with my own concerns. With some difficulty, I have got Suckling placed in the Ambuscade, with Captain Durban, who came on board at the moment I was writing.

March 31st.

The history of Suckling will never be done. I have this moment got from him your letter, and one from his father. I shall say nothing to him; I don't blame the child, but those who took [him] out of the most desirable situation in the navy. He never will get into such another advantageous ship: but, his father is a fool; and so, my dear Emma, that *ends*.

The box which you sent me in May 1804, is just arrived in the Diligent store-ship.[4]

[1]John Louis (1785–1863), son of Sir Thomas Louis (1758–1807), who had served as captain of the *Minotaur* under Nelson at the battle of the Nile.

[2]Nelson's niece, Eliza Bolton, had married the Rev. Henry Girdlestone.

[3]James Hillyar.

[4]First mentioned in Docs Nos 333, 334, 341 (where he states that the box was sent on 18 May 1804).

I have sent the arms to Palermo, to Gibbs. The clothes are very acceptable; I will give you a kiss, for sending them.

God bless you! Amen.

April 1st.

I am not surprised that we should both think the same about the kitchen; and, if I can afford it, I should like it to be done: but, by the fatal example of poor Mr. Hamilton, and many others, we must take care not to get into debt; for, then, we can neither help any of our relations, and [must] be for ever in misery! But, of this, we [will] talk more, when we walk upon the poop at Merton.

Do you ever see Admiral and Mrs. Lutwidge? You will not forget me when you do.

To Mrs. Cadogan, say every thing that is kind; and to all our other friends: and, be assured, I am, for ever and ever, your's and only your's,

NELSON & BRONTE.

As I know that all the Mediterranean letters are cut and smoaked, and perhaps read, I do not send you a little letter in this; but your utmost stretch of fancy cannot imagine *more* than I feel towards my own dear Emma.

God bless you! *Amen*.

362. *To Lady Hamilton*

[RNM: 223/73] Victory
March 13th: 1805

off Toulon but not in sight

last night my dearest Emma I receiv'd your letters of Sep^{r}: 12th: by way of Naples Nov^{r}: 27th: Dec^{r}: 18th: 27th: 29th: + Jan^{ry}: 8th: sent by Amphion all those by Layman are lost[1] I know your dear love and affection for me is as reciprocal as mine therefore when I see you are hurt at my non arrival I only wish that you would for one moment call your good sense before you + see if it was possible You know I never say anything which I do not mean and every body[2] knows that all my things are on board of the Superb and there they remain, I expected Sir John Orde

[1]Layman had lost his ship, the *Raven*, by shipwreck (see letter of 9 Mar 1805, Doc. No. 361).

[2]Inserted.

was come out to relieve me for I never could have supposed that any Admiralty would have sent any admiral to take from me every prospect of prize money,[1] but my soul is beyond that consideration compared to getting at the french fleet, but to the point, and to have done, my leave of absence although given the 6th: October came to me on Dec[r]: 25th: X[t]:mas Day[2] before that period I could not go, and from that moment I was well assured that the French fleet would put to sea they did so, and only yesterday I return'd off here from the pursuit of them to Egypt, I now find them ready for Sea and the Troops embarked and I am in momentary hopes of their putting to Sea call these circumstances before you and Judge[3] me, your dear dear letters make me miserable very because often[4] for it supposes things which are impossible, you calculated because you knew I had leave of absence not calculating that I had it not till X[t]:mas[5] my anxiety since to fall in with the Enemy has been great indeed and to satisfy you beyond contradiction of my intentions I send you a copy of my letter to the Board of Admiralty and I am sure you will approve, my beloved Emma you know that I live only for you + my Dear H[a]: therefore you may be sure that I shall be as soon as even you could think it right never write me about your going abroad to change the climate +[c]: +[c]: then you give me entirely up, and you may rely that I would never go to Merton, I am vext that[6] Davison should not do all that is right He writes me that he pays every bill the moment it is presented with respect to agency he ought to know that I have not the power of appointing an agent and that if he was agent for this fleet at either Malta or Gibralter he must absolutely decide upon the spot the only thing which I was offered the agency for the Dutch ship Orion was sent to him and he had the Nile + Copenhagen If impossibilities are expected I cannot help it, He ought to know better,

[1]See also Doc. No. 354.

[2]Inserted.

[3]The omission of this underlining by Colin White may not have been completely coincidental, because the passage is disadvantageous to Lady Hamilton and CW claims that underlinings in Nelson's letters were added later by her.

[4]These words are arranged a bit confusingly: 'very stands above the word 'because', which is written in faint ink and difficult to read so that it has been transcribed together with the word 'often' by Colin White (*The New Letters*, 2005, p. 48 [hereafter: *The New Letters*]) to: 'the day after'.

[5]The words till X[t]:mas' are inserted.

[6]The 't' at the end of 'that' is written from the fourth unto the front page; this may explain, how Colin White could misread the letters to mean 'Mr'.

(2)

never mind we shall do very well when I may be able to get all my scraps together, and although not able to keep a carraige, believe me my own Dearest Emma in my pursuit of the Enemy between the 19th: and 21st: of Jan^{ry}: when if the weather had continued moderate we should have fought our battle I did not forget you as you would have found, for you are ever uppermost in my thoughts day or night calm or Gale of wind you are never absent from my thoughts, therefore I entreat by all the love You bear me that You will not either fret yourself or write fretful to your own Nelson who adores you I shall come and stay more than a month with you and I should long ago have been with you had my leave arrived or the french fleet put to sea I have done upon that subject, you will see that both the King + Queen of Naples are angry with me but I cannot help it when I am dead I am of no use to them or any one Else I grieve that Horatia is not at Merton under your watchful care I should give M^{rs}: Gibson a pension of 20£ a year for her life if you do not think it too much. the crying would be over in a day or two and it will be worse the longer it is put off[1] I wish you could manage and have her[2] home, Sir $Will^{m}$: Bolton is got out of the way I have made him into the Amphitrite and he goes directly to England I shall recommend him to Lord Melville for immediate employment he is unlucky not having taken a single vessel, you will remember me most kindly to M^{rs}: Cadogan I am truly sensible of her worth and attention to our interest at Merton you cannot imagine how I long to see it but I fear the kitchen will smell if so I shell build one separate from the House and make the present one a servants Hall I have it all in my head if I have but the money I am glad you have seen Cap^{n}: Hillyar he would be able to tell you about Charles I hope he will behave well and set himself on in the World.[3]

Victory off Toulon March 13th: 1805

[1]For quite a while Nelson had been pursuing the idea of paying Mrs Gibson a pension and taking Horatia out of her care (see letter of 2 April 1804, Doc. No. 310); and he was to pursue the matter further (see letters of 18 May 1805, Docs Nos 372–373). Colin White suggests that 'crying' refers to Nelson's wish that the baby should be inoculated against smallpox (*The New Letters*, p. 49 n.); I disagree for two main reasons: first, Nelson had already commented on the effects of the inoculation in Doc. No. 336; second, the 'crying' in this context in my view rather refers to Mrs Gibson's possible protest at losing the care of Horatia, which provided her with a source of income.

[2]Their daughter Horatia.

[3]The following copy of a letter to Marsden, referred to earlier in this letter, is in Nelson's handwriting.

Sir,[1]

Their Lordships are fully aware of my reasons for not attending to my own health since I received their permission to return to England for its reestablishment. I do assure you that no consideration for self could come into my mind when the Enemys fleet was sure of putting to Sea + they are now perfectly ready in appearance to put to sea again, Therefore although I have suffered very much from anxiety and a very stormy winter yet I shall either stay to fight them which I expect every hour, or until I believe they will not come to sea for the summer, when I shall embrace their Lordships permission and return to England for a few months for the reestablishment of a very shattered constitution. I am Sir +^{c}:

M^{r}: Marsden Esqr:

363. *To Lady Hamilton*

[NMM: TRA/13] Victory
March 16th: 1805.

The Ship is just parting and I take the last moment to renew my assurances to My Dearest beloved Emma of my eternal love affection and adoration, you are ever with me in my Soul, your resemblance is never absent from my mind, and my own dearest Emma I hope very soon[2] that I shall embrace the substantial part of you instead of the Ideal, that will I am sure give us both real pleasure and exquisite happiness, longing as I do to be with you yet I am sure under the circumstances in which I am placed, you would be the first to say my Nelson try + get at those french fellows and come home with glory to your own Emma, or if they will not come out then come home for a short time and arrange your affairs which have long been neglected, dont I say my own love what you[3] would say, only continue to love me as affectionately as I do you and we must then be the happiest couple in the World may God bless you Ever prays yours and only your faithful

Nelson & Bronte
Gaetano is very well and William has sent a letter to his Father.

[1]This letter is given in Nicolas, v, p. 357, with some differences in spelling, punctuation and capitalisation.
[2]Inserted.
[3]Inserted.

364. *To Lady Hamilton*

[Monmouth: E 437]

Victory
March 30th: 1805.

Your letters my own dear beloved Emma by the Ambuscade to Febry: 15th: came to me on the 26th: and now Louis is arrived I shall the moment I think that the french fleet will not come to sea for the summer put myself into the Superb from which my things never have [been] taken from the time I expected the Great and Rich Sir John Orde, I fix in my own mind to start May 1st: for if they are not at sea in April I think they will lay fast unless a very superior fleet should come into the Mediterranean when I am readier to start from England than being here at least [Lady Hamilton][1] for actual service but keep my intended movements to yourself for folks like to chatter, You are sure my Emma that I am as anxious to see you as you can be to see me for I love and revere you beyond all this world because I feel you deserve it of me therefore I shall say[2] no more upon that subject but shall wait to give you much more efficacious proofs of my love than can be convey'd in a letter, I admire dear Ha: writing I think her hand will soon be like her dear mothers and if she is but as clever I shall be content you may rely that when I come home I shall do what I can for Mrs: Bolton but before I can fix a sum I must see what I have at all events I shall be able to keep Tom[3] at College without any expence to his Father that I will certainly do and I must œconemise in something at home, my letter to Lord Melville was strong abt: Mr: Bolton but I have had no answer in short I never had any interest

I am at this moment not a little vext with Sir Wm: Bolton he is Lazy or he might have been worth 30,000 £ but he would not look after it, I never had such a chance or I should have been a very rich man, I am more sorry for his family than himself, I have appointed him Post into the Amphitrite and her and the Renown are prevented sailing for England from Gibraltar by waiting for him and when I am likely to see him I cant tell I am sorely vext he is a very good young man but he never will do any good for himself he has no activity, I move the whole fleet with Ten times the rapidity than he does his Brig, He might have been very Rich and independent this has vext me and all his friends here for every one[4] likes him as a good man, You will agree with me this is but a negative character.

[1]Here, at the bottom of the page, 'Lady Hamilton' is inserted in Nelson's handwriting.
[2]Inserted.
[3]Tom Bolton.
[4]Inserted.

365. *To Lady Hamilton*

[Monmouth: E 445] Victory
April 4th: 1805.

My Emma and God forbid you should belong to any one else that goose Sir William Bolton has lost his frigate Amphitrite[1] and perhaps a month or two's Rank as Post but I have waited three weeks for his joining me and the service will not[2] admit of my waiting any longer, luckily for him Lord Melville has wrote me that He will send out a Post ship for him and therefore I hope he will suffer no harm but it vexes me, the time draws near my Emma my love my everything that's dear ~~xxxxx xxxxxx xxxxx~~ and that we shall be happier perhaps if that is possible than ever, and unless the french fleet should be at sea or a certainty of its putting to sea I shall move to the Superb on the day I have before told you, I need not say more except that I shall fly to Merton dear dear Merton, I shall take care not to speak any thing which may subject me to quarantine, therefore I hope a return of post or at least two will liberate me, (I must not say that) for my liberation makes me all all yours[3] I dare not send a little ~~send a little~~ letter for what with smoking and ~~firing~~ cutting[4] all would be read but let them read this that I love you beyond any woman in this world, and next our dear Ha: how I long to settle what I intend upon her and not leave her to the mercy of any one or even to any foolish thing I may do in my old age, adieu for a very short time and may the Heavens bless you and give us a happy meeting + very very soon, prays your faithful

Nelson + Bronte

366. *To Lady Hamilton*

[BL: Egerton 1614 f. 114, no. 59] Victory 9 PM
April 5th: 1805.

My Dearest Emma,

You will easily conceive my anxiety and indeed misery at not yet having fallen in with these French rascals but I sincerely hope[5] an end may

[1]Pettigrew, ii, p. 467, explains: 'Captain Corbet [d. 1810], of the *Bittern*, was appointed by Lord Nelson Captain of the *Amphitrite*, in the room of Sir W. Bolton, and Captain Louis was transferred to the *Bittern*.'

[2]Inserted.

[3]The word 'yours' is underlined twice.

[4]The word 'cutting' is above the crossed-out 'firing'.

[5]Inserted.

soon be put to my misery, I cannot say enough how much my own Dear Emma I love and revere you and you shall ever glory in your Nelson whether living or dead and your dear approbation will be sweeter to me than all the Honors which Monarchs can bestow, again + again may Heaven Bless you and my Dear H[a]: I could not exist long in this dreadful suspence but I am doing what man can do to find them out God send I may soon meet them The ship parts adieu adieu adieu. Ever Ever to the last Moment only your faithful Nelson + Bronte

367. *To Lady Hamilton*

[BL: Egerton 1614 ff. 115–116, no. 60] Victory
April 19th: 1805.

You will I am sure my own dearest Emma feel for my cruel disappointment in not meeting with the French fleet,[1] but I could not divide myself and guard Sardinia, Naples, Sicily, The Morea + Egypt at the same time Had I gone West and they East 24 hours start of me would have lost any of those places and England never could have regained them, to the Westward they could only get out of the Streights[2] and abandon the Mediterranean in which with their Toulon fleet they found they could not get a move ahead of me, I may be abused by some blockheads but I do assure you that upon a revision of my own conduct, that I approve and that is a great thing for if a man does not approve of his own conduct it is certain nobody Else can, Sir William Bolton is now with me waiting impatiently for the Post ship which Lord Melville promised to send him but I am not sure[3] that he may have an opportunity of writing

I have receiv'd your letters by the Decade they are all grateful to my feelings except one and I am a little vext with you upon that subject I allude to what you have heard that Gore should have said, I do not believe that Gore should have said any thing about her,[4] He never saw her nor is it likely that I should amuse him with such discourse who so well knew my attachment and devotion to you, But you ought not to believe any thing injurious to me, but when I tell you that I joind the fleet July 8th: Gore parted from the fleet the 9th: on the 19th: he receiv'd his final orders to go to Gibralter therefore next July it is two years since

[1]On 19 April Nelson learnt that the French fleet had left Toulon, heading westward (Knight, p. 486).

[2]Straits of Gibraltar.

[3]Inserted.

[4]Lady Nelson.

I have seen Gore and then certainly in company with all the Captains of the fleet therefore the thing is impossible and that must convince you, but such suspicions hurt my feelings, I think it very probable that a very few days will clear me of the Mediterranean, and draw me nearer to dear Merton, my Dearest Emma and H^{a}: of this my own Emma may rely that her Nelson will be with Her as soon as Even Emma could think it possible for him to be circumstanced as I am with the French fleet, may God Bless you my Emma prays fervently

Your faithful
Nelson + Bronte

368. *To Lady Hamilton*

[Monmouth: E 169]

Victory Tetuan Bay
May 4th: 1805.

Your Poor dear Nelson is my dearest beloved Emma very very unwell, after a two years hard fag it has been mortifying the not being able to get at the Enemy, as yet I can get no information about them, at Lisbon this day [a] week they knew nothing about them, but it is now generally believed that they are gone to the West Indies, my movements must be guided by the best judgement I am able to form, John Bull may be angry but he never had an officer who has served Him more faithfully, but Providence I rely will yet crown my never failing exertions with success and that it has only been a hard trial of my fortitude in bearing up against untoward events, you my own Emma are my first and last thoughts and to the last moment of my breath they will be occupied in leaving you independant of the world, and all I beg in the world is[1] that you will be[2] a kind an affectionate Father to my dear ~~xxxxxxx~~[3] daughter Horatia,[4] but my Emma your Nelson is not the nearer being lost to you for taking care of you in case of events which are only known when they are to happen to an all wise Providence, and I hope for many years of comfort with you, only think of all you wish me to say and you may be assured

[1]Inserted.
[2]Inserted.
[3]Here a piece of writing longer than Nelson's word 'daughter' is crossed out with so much energy that part of the paper is torn; Sichel, p. 517, suggests that the word obliterated was 'own', but that would have been much too short.
[4]Both the words – 'daughter' and 'Horatia' – are underlined three times each.

it exceeds if possible your wishes, may God protect you and my dear Horatia[1] prays Ever your most faithful and affectionate

Nelson + Bronté
All letters sent by the Niger + Avenger are gone up the Mediterranean.

369. *To Lady Hamilton*

[BL, Egerton 1614 ff. *116–**116, no. *60]

Victory May 9th: off Cape St: Vincent.

My Dearest beloved Emma I think myself a little better but I can neither drink Porter nor eat cheese and that is enough to satisfy me that I am far from well but I take no Physic, Bark in all ways disagrees with me, but I submit myself to the care of a good Providence and if it is his pleasure I shell soon be restored to my own faithful Emma I have wrote Nepean that they must if I go to the West Indies send out an Admiral for I am not able to remain there not that I fear the country it would agree with me as well as any other half the people kill themselves from fear of the climate, I hope to God I shall get hold of the French fleet. I got through the Gut on the night of the 6th: and am now anxiously waiting the return of the Amazon from Lisbon when my final route will be determined upon, I approve very much the plan of the Kitchen and I hope that we shall live many years to enjoy it, my Emma you are every thing to me and I love you if possible more than ever, I send you a Bill for 300£ 200 of which is for you[r]self and the other 100£ make in little presents for me to those about you I have sent Mrs: Bolton her 100£ so nothing is necessary to be given to her, You see my Emma Lord Melville is out and given away a Commissionership of both the Navy + Victualling Office without considering me, they none of them care for me I may be Poor but I am honest I could say much on that subject but I hope we shall soon talk upon that and many other subjects much more interesting to our mutual happiness, I have sent[2] two Codocils[3] in which you are deeply interested to Mr: Haslewood to be placed with my Will and other Codocils for if I kept them onboard ship they might be lost and then you and my Horatia not get what I intend which would embitter my last moments may heavens bless you,

[1]Underlined twice.
[2]Inserted.
[3]Probably Docs Nos 303 and 355.

Noon[1] Cap^{n}: Sutton has just joined nothing is known[2] of the french fleet and my destination is the West Indies and I only wait to see the Troops under Admiral Knight[3] round the Cape I have wrote to Nepean that I must be relieved The Lively Cap^{n}: Hamond[4] I find has passed the fleet for Gibralter, once more God Bless you, Ever yours faithfully

Nelson + Bronte

370. *To Lady Hamilton*

[Pettigrew, ii, p. 473][5]

My dearest Emma,

In case any thing should happen to the Wasp who is going to England with my dispatches and your letters, I send a duplicate of the draft upon Marsh and Creed, and I beg you to send Mrs. Bolton's to her. I have wrote her a line by the Wasp. We are hard at work victualling the fleet to five months, and hope to start to-morrow. May God be propitious to my wishes, and send me a victor – then, and not till then, can I be happy. Kiss my dear Horatia for me.

Yours,
Nelson and Bronté.

371. *To Lady Hamilton*

[Pettigrew, ii, pp. 474–5]

Victory,
May 13th, 1805.

70 Leagues W.S.W. from Cape St. Vincent.

My dearest Emma,

No letter from any person for England could have left the Victory from the day we passed the Faro, January 31st to March 16th, when the Renown went to Gibraltar. Mr. Marsden, when you recollect his situation, cannot tell you any thing, and if he did, as has been the case at present, he must pretend to know exactly where I was, or it would soon get over London and to France. He is very much hurt that you are

[1]Inserted.
[2]The letter 'n' at the end of the word 'known' is inserted.
[3]John Knight (1748–1831).
[4]Graham Eden Hamond.
[5]This letter is reproduced by Pettigrew before Doc. No. 371 without giving a date; it has therefore been inserted here.

offended with him, for not telling you if I am alive or dead, and when he makes a story on purpose, as he thinks, to please you, by telling you I am well, &c. &c. &c., then you are angry. You should have known that it was impossible that I could write *alone* to him; but I will have done with this subject which, under my present cruel situation, almost cut my feeble thread of life.

The Marquis Circello and Abbé Campbell came on board for a minute in a gale of wind, and with them your letters. I do assure you, that both my health and the arrangement of my affairs, independent of my inclination, demand my serious consideration. I know I am most deeply in debt to Davison, and I want his account that I may close it, for it must not run on in the way it has done, but I cannot get it, nor do I know how I stand with their banking house, I get no account; but things will be on a new footing when I get to dear Merton. I suppose if I do not find the French fleet that I shall be tried. They may do as they please, they will find none who has served them more faithfully, and this going to the West Indies ought to be a proof [of] it, for it must be everything but a party of pleasure to me, but I am sure you will approve of my conduct, however we may feel the consequences. I write this in case of meeting any vessel bound to England, when I shall close it.'

May 20th. Nothing yet have we seen, we are running nine miles *per hour*, 700 leagues from Barbadoes. Sutton, of the Amphion, is with us. I am, as you will believe, very, very uneasy and anxious, but I hope it will all end well. Kiss dear Horatia for me, I never forget for a moment either you or her.

Nelson and Bronté.

372. *To Lady Hamilton*

[Jean Kislak: 2004.006.00.0004][1]

Victory at sea
May 16th: 1805,

My Dearest Lady Hamilton

As it is my desire to take my adopted daughter Horatia Nelson Thompson from under the care of Mrs: Gibson and to place her under your guardianship in order that she may be properly educated and brought up I have therefore most earnestly to entreat that you will undertake this

[1]Christie's catalogue of the 2003-sale (lot 155) states: 'The present letter is presumably the enclosure to the private letter to his 'Dearest Beloved Emma' dated 18 May, where he describes it as 'that sort of letter which may be shown any where or to any body' (Doc. No. 373).

charge, and as it is my intention to allow M[rs]: Gibson as a free will offering from myself (she having no claim upon her having been regularly paid for her care of the child) The Sum of Twenty pounds a Year for the term of her natural life, and I mean it should commence when the child is delivered to You, but should M[rs]: Gibson endeavour upon any pretence to keep my adopted daughter any longer in her care then I do not hold myself bound to give her one farthing and I shall most probably take other measures,[1] I shall write to M[r]: Haslewood upon Your telling him that You have received the child to settle the annuity upon M[rs]: Gibson, and If You think Miss Connor disposed to be the Governess of Horatia I will make her any allowance for her trouble which You may think proper, I again and again my Dearest Friend request Your care of my adopted daughter, whom I pray God to bless, I am Ever for Ever my Dear Lady Hamilton Your most faithful + affectionate

Nelson + Bronte

373. *To Lady Hamilton*

[*c)* Christie's, 3 Dec 2003, lot 156;
d) C. White, p. 50, no. 59] [*c)*] Victory
May 18th: 1805

150 leagues WSW from Madiera [*sic*]

My Dearest beloved Emma, I send you the enclosed that no difficulty may arise about My Dear Horatia in case any accident should happen to me for I know too well the necessity of taking care of those we love whilst we have the power, and these arraingements do not hasten our death I believe quite the contrary as it leaves nothing to corrode the mind in a sick bed, I only hope to get at the french fleet when if it pleases God I shall immediately return to my own dear Emma at Merton [*d)*] 'You will know how to direct Mr Haslewood in making out the paper for the annuity and that Mrs G.[2] must not presume to chatter[3] for if she does the annuity ought to be forfeited, but you will know how to talk to her. You will see I have wrote that sort of letter which may be shown any where

[1]The writing continues a bit lower in the same line, so that it appears that Nelson had a break in writing.
[2]Mrs Gibson.
[3]About who Horatia's parents are.

or to any body.[1] May God in heaven bless you My Emma and send us a happy meeting is the fervent prayer of Your Ever faithful

Nelson & Bronte

374. *To Lady Hamilton*

[Monmouth: E 167] Victory off Carlisle Bay
Barbadoes June 4th: 1805.

My own dearest Beloved Emma Your own Nelsons pride and delight, I find myself within six[2] days of the Enemy, and I have every reason to hope that the 6th: of June will immortalize your own Nelson your fond Nelson, May God send me victory and us a happy and speedy meeting, Ad^{l}: Cochrane[3] is sending ~~hope~~ home[4] a vessel this day, therefore only pray for my success and my Laurels I shall with pleasure lay at your feet and a Sweet Kiss will be an ample reward for all your faithful Nelsons hard fag, for Ever and Ever I am your faithful ever faithful and affectionate

Nelson + Bronte

the Enemys fleet and army are supposed to have attacked Tobago and Trinidada and are now about landing

375. *To Lady Hamilton*

[BL: Egerton 1614 ff. 117–118, no. 61] Victory off S^{t}: Lucia
June 10th: 1805

Your own Dear Nelson my Emma is very sad the French fleet have again escaped me it appears hard to have had the cup at my lip and to have it dashed from me when I wrote you a Line from Barbadoes[5] I would not

[1]The letter to 'William Haslewood Esqr:', dated 'Victory May 16th: 1805.' is preserved in NMM: TRA/14 [Trafalgar House collection of Nelson MSS.; kept also on NMM microfilm SMF/137, where it says: 'Acquired 1947']: 'It is my desire that M^{rs}: Gibson is given an annuity of twenty Pounds a Year when the [*sic*] she gives up my adopted daughter Horatia Nelson Thompson to the Guardianship of my Dear friend Lady Emma Hamilton and promises not to have any thing more to do with the child either directly or indirectly and I have my estate cha[r]geable with this annuity. Nelson + Bronte'.

[2]Somebody has added in a pencilled note here: '(two)'.

[3]Thomas Chochrane (1775–1860), from 1831 10th Earl of Dundonald.

[4]The word 'home' is written above the crossed-out '~~hope~~'.

[5]Doc. No. 374.

have given one farthing to have assured a battle [*sic*], The information from S^{t}: Lucia as you will see by the newspaper was doubted by none, how I grieve at the arrival of that news nothing could have prevented my getting at them on the 6th:, long ago it would have been all over and your Nelson have added I doubt not another sprig of Laurel to his Brow or his memory[1] but it has pleased God to order it otherwise I saild at 8 oclock in the morning of the 5th: with L^{t}: Genl: Sir Willm: Myers[2] and 2000 Troops onboard, on the 6th: we were at Tobago where they had heard of the Enemy being at sea and they supposed them to have arrived at Trinidada on the day before, I now was sure and every thing was fully prepared to decide the contest 12 to 18, but lo on the 7th: when the fleet got into the Gu[l]ph of Paira[3] the Enemy were not there, but we receiv'd an express that they were to sail from Martinico on the 5th for Grenada + Trinidada They did sail in the night of the 5th: but not for Grenada but I fancy to try and effect their escape, on the 8th: at day light I sailed from Trinidada, and on the 9th: at noon I was at S^{t}: Georges Grenada where I receivd the mortifying news that on the 6th: the Enemy 18 Sail of the Line ~~7~~ 6[4] frigates and 3 Brigs + shooners [*sic*][5] were under Dominica on the 7th: they were under Guadalupe I am carrying every rag but my hopes are very faint although I must not despair, if they should attempt Antigua I shall be up with them and if they Run I may by good fortune overtake them before they get to Europe, however mortified I may individually feel at not fighting them yet my happy arrival has saved all our West India Islands and commerce My services have benefited the country a[l]though it brings neither Honor or Riches to me[6] the latter is given by two Admiraltys to others how well deserved to have been taken from me time will shew, You will talk of this letter with prudence for the Public must not know at least from you of my movements but I know my Emma is to be trusted with any secret I shall fill this up as we get on and write you another Line before the Vessel parts from the Fleet, June 11th: we are under Montseratt from whence the Enemy were seen beating to windward on Saturday God knows their intention but I still think it is to get out of my way it has almost broke my heart I shall hear from Antigua

[1]The letters 'ry', which did not fit at the end of the line, are written above the letters 'mo' and inserted by an arrow from below the line.

[2]William Myers (1750–1805).

[3]The Gulf of Paria is a vast natural harbour between the Venezuelan mainland to the west and Trinidad to the east, with entrances from the north and south.

[4]The number '6' is written above the number '7' that is crossed out with one stroke near the top, so that the deletion is barely noticeable.

[5]The words '+ shooners' are above the letters 'gs were'.

[6]Inserted.

to-day, may heavens bless you my Dearest beloved Emma and believe me Ever for Ever Your own faithful

Nelson + Bronte

376. *To Lady Hamilton*

[Pettigrew, ii, p. 479]

Victory, 7 p.m.,
June 12th, 1805.

My own Emma,

I have just anchored in St. John's road[1] to land the troops, and the moment they are on shore I am after Gravina, and I really hope to catch him before he gets to Cadiz.

Yours,
Nelson and Bronté.

377. *To Lady Hamilton*

[Monmouth: E 416]

Victory
June 16th: 1805. 130 Lgs: from

Antigua

As I am sending a vessel to Lisbon and a letter to the Admiralty to tell them I am so far on my return I would not you are sure omit writing you a Line although it will probably be a long while in reaching my Dearest Emma, I yet hope that I shall send a frigate with good news for why may I not at last be so fortunate as to get up with the Enemys fleet, ah my Emma June 6th: would have been a great day to me had I not been led astray by false information, I cannot help myself, what a loss, what a relief it would have been for the last two years of cares and troubles, whenever I do get information it is not worth sixpence and I have ever found if I was left and acted as my poor noddle told me was right I should seldom err[2] my genius carried me direct to the spot, and all would have been as well as heart could wish, when comes across me Genl: Woretons[3] information, I shall give up the command to Sir Richd: Bickerton if they are arrived before me and so I have wrote the

[1]Antigua.
[2]End of first page.
[3]Major-General Robert Brereton (1747–1816), governor of St Lucia 1803–7.

Admiralty and proceed to England I may be abused and neglected but my Dearest Emma I have served the country most faithfully, June 18th: as my letters are closed to the Admiralty, I can tell you what no one knows, that the French fleet are at this moment not 80 Leagues from me, may God Almighty send us up with them, my Emma shall not blush for the conduct of Her Faithful Nelson + Bronte.

Kiss my Angel Horatia, farewell farewell, I love 'till Death, and afterwards will be your Guardian, May God bless you my own dearest beloved Emma If I live I shall soon be with you.

378. *To Lady Hamilton*

[BL: Egerton 1614 ff. 119–120, no. 62] Victory Gibralter
July 20th: 1805.

My Dearest beloved Emma I am sure that you will feel my most severe affliction in not having met the Enemys fleet, my misery is extreme but my heart + head tell me I have done right whatever may be the Judgement of my country I bow to it with submission, had I followed the decision of my own noddle I should have been right but I was forced from circumstances to follow the information of others ag^{t}: my own better Judgement, I tell you my Emma my feelings, but I know your dear affectionate sensible heart will have felt all my misery, The moment the fleet is water'd and victualled I shall get outside the Streights[1] and then when I know that the Enemy is arrived in any port in Europe I shall proceed to England as I have this day wrote the Admiralty for the reestablishment of my health, I need not say what inexpressible pleasure it will give your Nelson to meet and embrace his dear dear Emma and to find her all that his fond and attatchd heart could wish or desire, The Generals and Commissioner having been onboard to make me a visit I have been forced against my inclination to set my feet upon the Rock[2] to return their visits It took me three hours hard work but thank God I am got into my cabbin again and my next step on shore will I hope be Portsmouth and then to dear dear Merton may God Bless you my Emma and Be assured I am Ever for Ever your faithful a[nd][3] affectionate

Nelson + Bronte.

[1]Straits of Gibraltar.
[2]Of Gibraltar.
[3]The greatest part of the word 'and' is hidden under the glue; Nelson did not leave any space unused for a seal or piece of glue.

I find by letters from Naples that they are in a desperate state and longing for my return to protect them I have only a moment, this goes by a merchant Brig. I shall write in a few days by Prevoyante, M[r]: M[c]: Coy[1] who has executed his commission in shaking hands with me as he said you desired him when you shook hands with him, all my letters are I find gone to England.[2]

379. *To Lady Hamilton*

[*a)* Pettigrew, ii, pp. 482–3;
c) Christie's, 3 Dec 2003, lot 157]

[*c)*] Victory
July 24th: off Ceuta

I wrote you on the 20th: My Emma by a merchant Brig under cover to M[r]: Marsden and I think she will get home safe, all my toils will probably end in abuse but I feel I do not deserve any censure we have been to Tetuan to water the fleet and to get[3] some refreshment for our poor fellows who [have] much of the Scurvy, I sailed this morning and I hope in the night to pass thro' the Straights,[4] the moment I find the enemy are safe in Port and out of my reach that moment I shall sett off for England, but I am dreadfully uneasy I have reason to hate the name of Gen[l]: Brereton as long as I live and perhaps our country for ever but it is vain to repine + fret myself ill I know this too well but I cannot help it The name and circumstances absolutely haunt me[5]

[*a)*] *July 25th.* This morning in the Gut, Captain Pettit of the Termagant, brought an account that the French fleet had been seen standing to the northward. I am just going off Cadiz to give some orders to Admiral Collingwood, and to dispatch the Pickle schooner to the Admiralty, with an account that I am steering for Ireland or England, as I may hear my services may be most wanted.

Yours,
Nelson and Bronté.

[1]Robert McCoy (d. 1848), lieutenant 1803–6). The letter is continued upside down across then top of pages 3 and 2, in very long lines across the folding line.

[2]BL, Add. Ms.34968 (Nelson's sea journals/operational notebooks for the period of 6 Mar until 18 Aug 1805), f. 57, states: 'Friday July 19th: at day bore up for Gibralter Bay at 8 the fleet anchored no information of the Enemys fleet / Saturday July 20th: employd compleating the fleet with provisions + stores went on shore for the first time since June 16th: 1803 and from having my foot out of the Victory Two Years wanting Ten days'.

[3]Inserted.

[4]Straits of Gibraltar.

[5]End of page and end of facsimile.

380. *To Lady Hamilton*

[NMM: SUT/2]

Victory Spithead
Aug[t]: 18th: 1805.

I am my beloved and dearest Emma this moment anchored,[1] and as the Post will not go out untill eight oclock and you not get the letter till 11 or 12 oclock tomorrow I have ordered a Post office express to tell you of my arrival I hope we shall be out of Quarantine tomorrow, when I shall fly to Dear dear Merton, You must my Emma believe all I would say + fancy what I think, but I suppose this letter will be cut open smoked + perhaps read, I have not heard from my own Emma since last April by Abbe Campbell but I trust my Emma is all which her Nelson wishes her to be, I have brought home no honors for my Country, only a most faithful servant, nor any Riches, that the Administrations took care to give to others, But I have brought home a most faithful and honorable and beloving heart to my Emma and my Dear dear Horatia, May Heaven Bless you, the boat is waiting and I must finish, This day two years + three months I left you. God send us as happy a meeting as our parting was sorrowful, Ever for Ever yours

Nelson + Bronte
Kindest regards to M[rs]: Cadogan Charlotte and all our friends with you

381. *To Lady Hamilton*

[Jean Kislak: 2003.111.00.0001]

Victory Motherbank
Aug[t]: 19th: 1805

I am now my Dearest Emma in Quarantine for the first time of my Life and I never could have been more mortified by it, but whatever we may feel and greater feeling, I believe cannot be, we must submit, none can come to us nor we go to any one, I hope to be out of Quarantine tomorrow forenoon for we have not a sick man You may believe I shall not stay ten minutes in Portsmouth only to Bow to the Commander In Chief + the Commissioner whilst the post chaise is preparing, the Admiralty leave is arrived, but nothing can be done without an Order in Council,

[1]BL, Add. Ms.34968 (Nelson's sea journals/operational notebooks for the period of 6 Mar until 18 Aug 1805), f. 66, states: 'Sunday Aug[t]: 18th: […? Imt?] 2 Years + 3 Months from my arrival at Portsmouth at day light weighed working up to Spithead at 9 anchored at Spithead.'

and I cannot be at Merton before 9 oclock and if not by that time we have not Pratique[1] therefore do not expect your faithful loving Nelson after that hour

I have this moment got yours of last night from Merton I shall my Emma rejoice to have you in my arms then I need not envy a King I am all all Yours, I shall rejoice to see dear Horatia, Charlotte + Ann + Eliza,[2] and I would not have any Emmas relation go without my seeing her,

M[r]: Marsden has just sent me your letter of Aug[t]: 10th: I must write a line to the Doctor[3] as he is in Norfolk, I shall only say my Heaven sends [*sic*] us a speedy meeting a happy one I am sure it will be

Ever for Ever my Emma Your own faithful.

Nelson + Bronte
Kind regards to M[rs]: Cadogan.

[1]Pratique is the licence given to a ship to enter port on assurance from the captain to the authorities that his ship is free from any contagious disease.

[2]Ann and Eliza were daughters of Nelson's sister Susannah Bolton.

[3]Nelson's brother William; the 'line' Nelson wrote on 19 Aug 1805 was the following, superscribed 'Victory in Quarantine': 'My Dear Brother, / By a letter from Lady Hamilton I find you are in Norfolk and by Horace's letter I see he belongs to Cambridge You will have heard of our arrival but I know you would like better to have it under my hand I am so so but what is very odd the better for going to the West Indies and even with the anxiety. We must not talk of Sir Rob[t]: Calders battle I might not have [done] so much with my small force If I had fell in with them you would probably have been a Lord before I wish'd, for I know they meant to make a dead set at the Victory / Hardy is I am sorry to say very unwell Give my kind love to M[rs]: Nelson + Horace, best regards to the Archdeacon [Yonge] RM Rolfe and our other friends and Be assured I am Ever your most affectionate brother / Nelson + Bronte' (taken from a facsimile in G. Lathom Browne, *Nelson: The Public and Private Life of Horatio, Viscount Nelson*, London: T. Fisher Unwin, 1891, p. 284; reproduced omitting the beginning and with additions, some of which are given here in square brackets, by James Stanier Clarke and John M'Arthur, *The Life of Admiral Lord Nelson, K.B. from His Lordship's Manuscripts*, in 2 vols (London, 1809), ii, p. 419, from where it was copied by Nicolas, vii, p. 13).

CHAPTER V

THE END, SEPTEMBER–OCTOBER 1805

Between arriving at Merton on 20 August and leaving it on 13 September 1805 there were 25 days. Although Nelson referred back to this period a month later, on 12 October: 'I do really feel that the 25 days I was at Merton was the very happiest of my life' [398], one must not be misled into thinking that the time ashore was spent in secluded togetherness. Nelson spent much of his time conversing with ministers, at the Admiralty and with politicians; so much so, that he 'often stayed at Gordon's Hotel in Albemarle Street to save the fifty minutes by post-chaise to Merton'.[1] When Nelson and Lady Hamilton were together at Merton, they were never alone. Members of Nelson's family as well as old friends visited and Lady Hamilton complained to Mrs Ludwidge: 'He has all his Brothers & Sisters at Merton & I go there to see them but for fear of having all the Cats on my back I am over cautious so as to be completely miserable.'[2] At the same time, however, it appears that Lady Hamilton enjoyed the buzz of activity around Nelson, into which she was drawn to a certain extent and to which she had contributed, 'sending to every part of the country to bid Nelson's family join her at Merton'.[3] Lord Minto, one of the visitors at Merton, observed: Nelson's 'conversation is a cordial in these low times . . . Lady Hamilton has improved and added to the house and the place extremely well without his knowing she was about it. He found it all ready done. She is a clever being after all: the passion is as hot as ever.'[4]

During his last days in England, Nelson could hardly move without being feted. Lord Minto wrote to his wife on 26 August:

> I met Nelson to-day in a mob in Piccadilly and got hold of his arm, so that I was mobbed too. It is really quite affecting to see the wonder and admiration, and love and respect, of the whole world; and the genuine expression of all these sentiments at once, from gentle and simple, the moment he is seen. It is beyond anything represented in a play or a poem of fame.[5]

[1]Roger Knight, *The Pursuit of Victory. The Life and Achievement of Horatio Nelson* (London, 2005) [hereafter: Knight], pp. 496–7.

[2]Quoted in Knight, p. 498.

[3]Flora Fraser, *Beloved Emma. The Life of Emma Lady Hamilton* (London, 1986) [hereafter: Fraser], p. 317.

[4]The Countess of Minto (ed.), *Life and Letters of Sir Gilbert Elliot, First Earl of Minto from 1751 to 1806, when his public life in Europe was closed by his appointment to the vice-royalty of India, edited by his great-niece . . .*, 3 vols (London, 1874) [hereafter: Minto], iii, p. 363.

[5]Minto, iii, p. 363.

Bathing in this attention, Lady Hamilton tried to make Nelson speak about it in the presence of the Duke of Devonshire and Lady Elizabeth Foster, who according to Lady Bessborough thought that Nelson:

> so far from appearing vain and full of himself, as one had always heard, he was perfectly unassuming and natural. Talking of Popular Applause and his having been Mobb'd, L[ad]y Hamilton wanted to give an account of it but he stopped her. 'Why,' said she, 'you like to be applauded – you cannot deny it.' 'I own it,' he answered, 'popular applause is very acceptable and grateful to me, but no Man ought to be too much elated by it, it is too precarious to be depended upon, and it may be my turn to feel the tide set as strong against me as ever it did for me.'[1]

Questions of celebration and adulation soon receded into the background of Nelson's and Lady Hamilton's minds as they learned on 2 September of the French fleet's entering Cadiz harbour.

On 4 September Lady Hamilton informed Nelson's sister, Susannah Bolton: 'There seems no doubt of his going immediately to take Calder's fleet.'[2] It was not only 'Calder's fleet' that Nelson was meant to take over, but also the squadron under the command of Collingwood, his old friend of West Indian days (1780s), and he would have another admiral under his command, rear-admiral the Earl of Northesk, whom he had not met before.[3] Nelson and Lady Hamilton now took sacrament together and exchanged rings, in a quasi-wedding ceremony, while at the same time protesting the purity of their relationship.[4] Nelson added another codicil to his will, leaving 'all the Hay belonging to me at Merton' to Lady Hamilton [382]. He also made sure Lady Hamilton would receive £ 100 a month 'till further notice',[5] but later noted at sea: 'Coals, I see, I forgot' [387]. His private matters had to stand behind all the professional affairs still to be sorted. Nelson's obligations ashore kept him busy and with little privacy. Lord Minto wrote to his wife from 'Pall Mall: Friday, September 13, 1805':

[1]Knight, p. 498; for a modest assessment of what he might be able to achieve; see also Nelson's letter to his brother, written on his arrival in England and quoted in a fn. to Doc. No. 379 (last footnote in previous chapter).

[2]Fraser, p. 319.

[3]Knight, p. 499, 502 with fn.

[4]Fraser, p. 320.

[5]Knight, p. 499.

> I went yesterday to Merton in a great hurry, as he, Lord Nelson, said he was to be at home all day, and he dines at half-past three. But I found he had been sent for to Carlton House [residence of the Prince of Wales], and he and Lady Hamilton did not return till half-past five. I stayed till ten at night and took a final leave of him. He is to have forty sail of the line, and a proportional number of frigates, sloops, and small vessels. This is the largest command that any admiral has had for a long time. He goes to Portsmouth to-night . . . Lady Hamilton was in tears all yesterday; could not eat, and hardly drink, and near swooning, and all at table. It is a strange picture. She tells me nothing can be more pure and ardent than this flame. . . .[1]

How exactly Nelson and Lady Hamilton spent their last hours together, remains unknown, but that it was painful to both is obvious. Nelson expressed in his diary the emotional significance of his farewell from Lady Hamilton and his daughter Horatia: 'Friday night at half past Ten drove from dear dear Merton where I left all which I hold dear in this World to go to save my King + Country'; the text merges into a prayer, deals with the possibility of his death and finishes with three times 'amen' [383].

In these emotionally charged days, Nelson had the advantage of distraction, as there still remained much to arrange. After his journey through the night on empty roads to Portsmouth, he sent off a short note to Lady Hamilton [384], before he started a full day of business.[2] Although he was '[ov]erwhelmed by business', he managed to write one more short letter to Lady Hamilton when still ashore, convincingly reassuring her that she was 'never for one moment absent from my thoughts' [385]. As soon as he was on board *Victory*, another letter followed [386]. After having sailed, five more letters followed in close succession [387–390, of which 390 was written on two successive days], documenting his impatience at getting to his fleet: 'Off Cunmore, Sept. 16th, 1805. 11 A.M.' – 'Victory off Portland Sep^{r}: 16th: 1805 at noon, Wind West – foul' – 'Victory off Plyth– Sep^{r}: 17th: 9 oclock in the Morning blowing fresh at WSW dead foul wind.' Nelson's patience was to be sorly tested, as it too Victory three days to get in foul wind from 'off Plyth' to '30 Leg^{s}: S.W. from Scilly' [390 and 391].[3] After four more days Nelson was 'off Lisbon' and sent Lady Hamilton his most recent reading of the

[1]Minto, iii, p. 370.
[2]Knight, p. 500.
[3]See also Knight, p. 501.

French novelist Le Sage [392]. An optimistic account of his proceedings followed a day later [393].

After joining his fleet off Cadiz on his birthday (29 September), Nelson invited his captains in two groups, one on 29 September itself and one on 30 September. He still had to get to know some of them so that much had to be arranged and communicated. Nelson ordered the fleet to be moved out of sight of Cadiz and to have the ships painted in the same way in order to be able to distinguish them in the heat of battle from those of the enemy's fleet.[1] Although Nelson 'was hardly ever better than' on 30 September, he suffered the following 'morning one of my dreadful spasms' [394]. The pain probably helped to focus his mind and thus produce one of the most memorable passages in his letters to Lady Hamilton: his account of the effect of laying out his plan to his admirals and captains:

> when I came to explain to them the Nelson touch it was like an electric shock, some shed tears all approved, it was new, it was singular, it was simple and from Admirals downwards it was repeated it must succeed[2] if ever they will allow us to get at them, You are my Lord surround by friends who you inspire with confidence, some my dear Emma may be Judas's but the majority are certainly much pleased with my commanding them [394]

Nelson's assessment of how he was esteemed in his fleet appears to have been rather modest. From letters of captains in his fleet that have come down to us it is possible to assess that he inspired them with confidence and even joy. One of the captains that had not known Nelson before, George Duff, wrote to his wife: 'I dined with his Lordship yesterday , and had a very merry dinner; he is certainly the pleasantest Admiral I ever served under'; and ten days later: 'He is so good and pleasant a man, that we all wish to do what he likes, without any kind of orders.'[3]

On a technical level, Nelson had to make sure that his fighting force was as numerous as possible, but also well supplied. The need for victualling was the first reason to reduce the numbers of the ships available for fighting the impeding battle, as Nelson had to send Captain Louis

[1]Knight, pp. 502 and 504–5.

[2]Nelson had used similar words in Doc. No. 31, when he described how he convinced others of a plan of attack: 'I have been fighting, with the Marquis [de Niza], Troubridge, Louis, and Hood, my new plan of attack. They all agree it must succeed.'

[3]Knight, p. 505, where the subject of Nelson's personal magnetism is argued for in more detail.

with a little squadron to North Africa. The second factor diminishing his force was Admiral Calder giving Nelson a 'very distressing scene', insisting on being allowed a court martial to clear his name; to which Nelson yielded by allowing him to return to England in his ship and accompanied by two captains who could testify for him [395 and 398].[1] Considering Nelson's assessment that 'our battle must soon be fought' and that 'it is only numbers which can annihilate' [396], 'the arrival of three Ships from England' was a relief [399].

Busy as Nelson was preparing his fleet for battle, his letters to Lady Hamilton are full of declarations of affection in different ways, from straightforward ['I love you dearly tenderly and affectionately', 395] to passionately ['I love and adore you to the very excess of the passion', 389], and these emotions were expressed continuously through to the approaching battle [see 387, 390, 393, 394, 396 and 398]. On 19 October Nelson sat down to write a letter each, to Lady Hamilton and their daughter Horatia [400 and 401]. Both are short and focus on his love for them at the fateful moment on entering into battle. A day later, Nelson added some lines to his letter to Lady Hamilton, informing her about the movements of the enemy, finishing this last letter to her, without signing: 'May God Almighty give us success over these fellows and enable us to get a peace' [401].

On the morning of the actual battle, on 21 October 1805, Nelson sat down and, writing in his diary, added a seventh codicil to his will [402], which he copied onto small sheets.[2] The entry into his diary, kept in a small vellum-bound volume, begins with the much-quoted prayer, which forms the final stage of several similar lines written down in the previous weeks [see for example, 383 and 401]:

> Monday Oct^{r}: 21st: 1805 at day Light saw the Enemys Combined fleet from East to ESE bore away made the signal for order of sailing and to prepare for Battle the Enemy with their heads to the Southward, at 7 the Enemy wearing in succession, May the Great God whom I worship Grant to my Country and for the benefit of Europe in General a great and Glorious Victory, and may no misconduct in any one tarnish it, and may humanity after Victory be the predominant feature in the British fleet, For myself individually I commit my Life to Him who

[1]Knight, p. 505.

[2]The copy is held at the National Maritime Museum. As the (first) version in the diary was later registered with the other codicils (and is kept with them at TNA), I have used this one in this collection.

made me, and may his blessing light upon my endeavours for serving my Country faithfully, to Him I resign myself and the Just cause which is entrusted to me to

Defend,
Amen, Amen, Amen

These fraught words were followed by Nelson's appeal to honour Lady Hamilton's 'Eminent Services' by giving her 'an ample provision to maintain her Rank in Life'. As Nelson himself had not been able to do so, he left her 'a Legacy to my King and Country' [402].

Nelson's last wish was not fulfilled. Lady Hamilton was returned her own letter to him of 8 October 1805 [399; more of her letters have not come down to us] and his last letters to her, on which she noted in despair [401]:

oh miserable wretched Emma.
oh glorious + happy Nelson

382. *Sixth codicil to Nelson's will*[1]

[TNA: Prob. 1/22/1]

I give my Dearest friend Lady Hamilton all the Hay belonging to me at Merton and in Wimbledon Parish September Eleventh 1805

Nelson + Bronte

383. *Nelson's journal*

[NMM: JOD/14:1–2]

friday[2] night at half past Ten drove from dear dear Merton where I left all which I hold dear in this World to go to save my King + Country may The great God whom I adore enable me to fullfill the expectations of my Country and if it is His good pleasure that I should return my Thanks will never cease being offered up to the Throne of His Mercy If it is His good providence to cut short my days upon Earth I bow with the greatest Submission relying that He will protect those so dear to me that I may leave behind, His will be done amen amen amen.

384. *To Lady Hamilton*

[Monmouth: E 180][3]

My Dearest and most beloved of Women Nelsons Emma I arrived here this mom^{t}: and M^{r}: Lancaster takes it, His coach is at the door and only waits for my line Victory is at S^{t}: Helens and if possible shall be at sea this day, God Protect you and my Dear Horatia prays Ever your most faithful

Nelson + Bronte

6 oclock George Inn,[4] Sep^{r}: 14th: 1805

[1]See Doc. No. 259.

[2]13 Sept 1805.

[3]The envelope to go with this letter is kept at the NMM: NWD/12; with the note: 'This is the envelope of the last letter which Lord Nelson wrote on shore – and was written from the "George Inn" Portsmouth Dated 6 o'clock September 14th 1805 –'.

[4]Portsmouth.

385. *To Lady Hamilton*

[Pierpont Morgan: MA321] Portsmouth Sept: 14[1]

My Dearest Emma

Rose is arrived in high [roused?] humour and Mr: Pitt is to be [w]ith[2] him to morrow he promises he will do all possible with him to situate Mr: Bolton, I am going to take Mr: R.[3] + Mr: Canning[4] onboard the Victory at St: Helens and they will eat my scrambling dinner if I do not get under Sail, I have been [ov]erwhelmed[5] with business from the moment of my arrival,[6] but You are never for one moment absent from my thoughts May the Heavens bless You My own Emma and Believe me Ever Your most faithful Affectionate and devoted

Nelson + Bronte

Mr: Rose is much pleased with my letter to Lord Moira[7]

386. *To Lady Hamilton*

[CRC] Victory Sept: 15th: 1805.

My Dearest Emma Most probably some boat will come off to the ship before the tide suits us to weigh, being obliged to anchor it being calm, Messrs: Rose and Canning dined here yesterday they seem'd[8] pleased and I did not dislike letting out a little knowledge before Canning who seems a very clever deep headed man I hope and indeed think that Bolton will get something but I entreat that Perry will not say anything respecting my not having had any favor or honor conferr'd upon me It can do no good and may do harm Rose was astonished at my not being Rich and he said he would tell the[9] ~~my~~ whole[10]

[1]There is a bit of paper remaining of the top right-hand corner with a bit of writing on it ('18'?), so that it appears that the date was continued until the right-hand corner of the letter.

[2]Here part of the paper is lost.

[3]Rose; see also Doc. No. 386.

[4]George Canning (1770–1827), at that time Treasurer of the Navy, later to become Foreign Secretary and Prime Minister.

[5]The part of the paper on which the first two letters (at the beginning of the line) are written is lost.

[6]See Knight, p. 500.

[7]Not published.

[8]After the word 'seem'd' there is a blot or a crossed out '~~a~~'.

[9]The words 'he would tell the' are inserted.

[10]The letter is not continued on the back of the page.

387. *To Lady Hamilton*

[Morrison, ii, p. 212 (No. 716)][1]

. . . to Mr. Pitt, therefore in appearances at least for Mr. Bolton,[2] if not for bettering my income, I seem to stand well. I send you, my Emma, the copy of the paper which Marsh & Creed has, and a copy had better be left with Mrs. Cadogan, then Miss Reynolds can refer to it, and if you can think of anything else for them to pay to save you trouble I will order it. Coals, I see, I forgot, but as the bill is paid up it will not be necessary to pay it before Xtmas, when I hope to be at home. My cabin smells of paint, but I do not think I have suffered from it. I did not sleep very much, although I was dreadfully tired, and all I hope for now is a fair wind. Believe me, my dear Emma, although the call of honour seperates us, yet my heart is so entirely yours and with you, that I cannot be faint hearted, carrying none with me. Kiss our dear god-child and remember me to all our dear friends with you, and for ever and ever I am your faithful and affectionate [&c]

P. S. – Hardy says the king was very inquisitive about our West India trip, and spoke very kindly of me. Col Desboro' sent for him to his brother's to come to the lodge from his brother's; all the courtiers spoke to him, and civilly, except Ld. Hawkesbury,[3] who never said a word to him. You see what a jumble I have made in my hurry with two sheets of paper.

388. *To Lady Hamilton*

[Pettigrew, ii, p. 498]

My beloved Emma,

I cannot even read your letter. We have fair wind, and God will, I hope, soon grant us a happy meeting. The wind is quite fair and fresh. We go

[1]This letter's beginning is missing. Morrison dated it 'June 1803', but I assume it was written after Nelson left England in Sept 1805, because the letter mentions the 'Coals' Nelson 'forgot' (he had been arranging a lot for Merton just before he left; see: Knight, p. 499), 'Xtmas' (which was much closer and a much more likely time of return in Sept. 1805 than in June 1803), 'a fair wind' (they had none on leaving the Solent; see: Knight, p. 501) and 'our West India trip' (achieved in the summer of 1805).

[2]See also Doc. No. 385.

[3]Robert Banks Jenkinson, Lord Hawkesbury (1770–1828), later 2nd Earl of Liverpool; at this time Home Secretary.

too swift for the boat. May Heaven bless you and Horatia with all those who hold us dear to them. For a short time, farewell,

Ever Yours,

Nelson and Bronté.
Off Cunmore, Sept. 16th, 1805. 11 A.M.

389. *To Lady Hamilton*

[Monmouth: E 429] Victory off Portland Sep^{r}: 16th: 1805
at noon, Wind West – foul.

I have read my dearest Emma your truly kind and affectionate letters of Saturday[1] and I can only assure you that every tear is a proof to me of your most warm attatchment which were it possible would make me more yours than I am at present but that is impossible for I love and adore you to the very excess of the passion, but with Gods Blessing we shall soon meet again kiss dear dear Horatia a thousand times for me, I write this letter and I fear I shall too soon have an opportunity of sending it for we are standing near Weymouth the place of all others I should wish to avoid,[2] but if it continues mod^{te}: I hope to escape without anchoring, but should I be forced I shall act as a man and your Nelson neither courting nor ashamed to hold up my head before the greatest Monarch in the World. I have thank God nothing to be ashamed of,

I have wrote a line to the Duke[3] he will show it you, and I shall do it occasionally I prepare this to be ready in case opportunity offers, and I am working very hard with M^{r}: Scott if you see Sir Willm: Scott say how very sorry I am not to have seen him but it was impossible may God bless you my own Emma and believe me Ever most faithfully yours

Nelson + Bronte

[1] 14 Sept 1805.

[2] Nelson apparently wished to avoid having to meet George III, who was spending time at Weymouth; see also Knight, p. 501.

[3] No letter of Nelson's to the Duke of Queensberry is included in Nicolas.

390. *To Lady Hamilton*

[NMM: CRK/19/56]

Victory off Plyth– Sep^{r}: 17th: 9 oclock
in the Morning blowing fresh
at WSW dead foul wind.

I sent my own dearest Emma a letter for you last night in a Torbay boat + gave the man a Guinea to put it in the post office we have had a nasty blowing night and it looks very dirty

I am now signalizing the ships at Plymouth to join me but I rather doubt their ability to get to sea however I have got clear of Portland and have Cawsand bay + Torbay under the Lee,

I entreat my dear Emma that you will cheer up and we will look forward to many many happy years and be surrounded by our childrens child^{n}: God Almighty can when he pleases remove the impediment,[1] my heart + soul is with you ~~+ Horatia~~, I got this line ready in case a boat should get alongside for Ever Ever I am yours most devotedly

Nelson + Bronte

M^{r}: Rose said he would write to M^{r}: Bolton if I was saild but I have forgot to give him the direction,[2] but I will send [it] today. I think I shall succeed very soon if not at this moment

Wednesday Sep^{r}: 18th: off the Lizard I had no opportunity of sending your letter yesterd^{y} nor do I see any prospect at present The Ajax and Thunderer are joining but it is nearly calm with a swell from the westward Perseverance has got us thus far and the same will I dare say get us on, Thomas seems to do very well and content, tell M^{r}: Lancaster that I have no doubt but that his son will do very well God Bless you my own Emma

I am giving my letters to Blackwood[3] to put on board the first vessel he meets going to England or Ireland, once more heavens bless you, Ever for Ever

Your Nelson + Bronte

[1]Nelson's wife, Frances.
[2]Address.
[3]Henry Blackwood (1781–1830) was at that time captain of the frigate *Euryalus*.

391. *To Lady Hamilton*

[Monmouth: E 436] Victory Sep^{r}: 20th: 1805. 30 Leg^{s}: S.W. from Scilly

My Dearest Emma,

A frigate is coming down which we take to be the Decade from the fleet off Cadiz if the battle has been fought I shall be sadly vext but I cannot help myself We have had very indifferent weather + it is still very dirty perseverance has got us thus far and I trust will accomplish all our wishes I write this Line to put onboard her for if she has news I have to write to the Ad^{ty}: May Heavens bless you kiss Dear Horat^{a} for Ever Yours faithfully

Nelson + Bronte

392. *To Lady Hamilton*

[Christie's, 19 Oct 2005, lot 43: *a)* facsimile, *b)* transcription] [*a)*] Victory off Lisbon Sep^{t}: 24th: 1805

I send You my Dearest Emma the very interesting work of Le Sage,[1] have them halfbound with ~~loose~~ hollow[2] back that they may open easy You will find them the most interesting thing in the world for Your happy pupils to read and refer to, Ever my Dearest Emma most affectionately + faithfully Your

Nelson + Bronte

Lady Hamilton

A View of Algiers and of the Consuls Country house, also of the Islands of Capri

[*b)*] views of Algiers, 'the Consuls country house', and Capri and Strombolo, and 'three packs of cards which to those who know French may be very instructive . . . make them put in money and they will soon tell'

[1]Alain-René Le Sage (1668–1747); French novelist and playwright.
[2]The word 'hollow' is written above the crossed out '~~loose~~'.

393. *To Lady Hamilton*

[Monmouth: E 183] Victory off Lisbon Sep^{r}: 25th: 1805

My Dearest beloved Emma for so you are in the very strongest sense of the words We are now in sight of the Rock of Lisbon and although we have very little wind I hope to get round Cape S^{t}: Vincent tomorrow we had only one days real fair wind but by perseverance we have done much I am anxious to join the fleet for it would add to my grief if any other man was to give them the Nelson touch which we[1] say is warranted never to fail, I have read my Emma with much interest your letters which I got at Merton but I must have many others afloat I do feel by myself what you must have felt at not hearing from me from Jan^{ry}: 29th: to after May 18th: at first I fancied that they had been stopt by the Admiralty as the account of Sir John Ordes joining the Channel fleet got to the Admiralty on the 3 or 4th: of May, but I now trace that my dispatches with Layman went home in the Avenger sloop with a convoy and that they had a very long passage I mention all these circumstances that my dearest Emma should never think that her Nelson neglects or forgets her for one moment, no I can truly say[2] you are always present whereso ere [*sic!*] I go, I have this letter ready in case I should fall in with any thing from Lisbon homewards steering, may God Bless you my best my only beloved and with my warmest affections to Horatia be assured I am for Ever your most faithful + affectionate

Nelson and Bronte

Say every kind thing to M^{rs}: Cadogan + the girls, probably this will find you at Canterbury if so to the D^{r}: + M^{rs}: N. say the needful

394. *To Lady Hamilton*

[BL: Egerton 1614 ff. 121–122, no. 63] Victory Oct^{r}: 1st: 1805

My Dearest Emma,

It is a relief to me to take up the Pen and write you a line for I have had about 4 oclock this morning one of my dreadful spasms which has almost enervated me, it is very odd I was hardly ever better than yesterday

[1]Underlined twice.
[2]Inserted.

Fremantle staid with me 'till 8 oclock[1] and I slept uncommonly well but was awoke with this disorder, My opinion of its effect some one day has never altered, however it is entirely gone off and I am only quite weak but I do assure you my Emma that the uncertainty of human life makes the situation of you ~~my~~[2] dearer to my affectionate heart you —[3] fly up to my mind and my last breath happen when it will, will be offered up in a prayer for a blessing on you, The Good people of England will not believe that rest of body and mind is necessary for me, but perhaps this spasm may not come again these six months. I had been writing seven hours yesterday[4] perhaps that had some hand in bringing it upon me

I got round Cape St: Vincent the 26th: but it was the 28th: before I got off Cadiz and joined Adl: Collingwood but it was so late that I did not communicate 'till next morning, I believe my arrival was most welcome not only to the commander of the Fleet but also to every individual in it, and when I came to explain to them the Nelson touch it was like an electric shock, some shed tears all approved, it was new, it was singular, it was simple and from Admirals downwards it was repeated it must succeed[5] if ever they will allow us to get at them, You are my Lord surround by friends who you inspire with confidence, some my dear Emma may be Judas's but the majority are certainly much pleased with my commanding them The Enemys fleet is 35 or 36 Sail of the Line in Cadiz, the french have given the Dons an old 74 to repair and taken possession of the Santa Anna of 112 guns,[6] Louis is going into to Gibralter + Tetuan to get supplies of which the fleet is much in want and Admiral Knight[7] as I

[1]Knight, p. 505, quotes from letter from Fremantle to the marquis of Buckingham of 30 Sept 1805: 'We dined with Lord Nelson – the juniors and I never passed a pleasanter day. I staid with him until eight at night – he would not let me leave before.'

[2]Between the words 'you' and 'dearer' there is nearly a line of crossings out through which only the word 'my' stands out. It stands out so clearly that one might wonder whether anything is hidden under the rest of the crossings out that are in part not covering much of the line. Only at the very end an 'e' appears to be visible through the brownish ink used for the crossings out. A lighter shade of brownish colouring, spreading around the beginning and the end of the crossings out on the paper may indicate an attempt at 'washing away" some letters. The paper is torn in one part (4 cm before the word 'dearer').

[3]Here is another deletion covering about a quarter of the line. Here again, it appears doubtful whether there is anything written underneath.

[4]Ten letters of 30 Sept 1805 are given in Nicolas (vii, pp. 53–60), two of which are dated 'about 30 September 1805'.

[5]Nelson had used similar words in Doc. No. 31, when he described how he convinced others of a plan of attack: 'I have been fighting, with the Marquis [de Niza], Troubridge, Louis, and Hood, my new plan of attack. They all agree it must succeed.'

[6]Here Nelson was misinformed; the *Santa Ana* was commanded by captain José Ramón de Gardoqui y Jaraveitia (1755–1816) at the Battle of Trafalgar.

[7]John Knight.

am told has almost made us quarrel with the Moors of Barbary[1] however I am sending Mr: Ford and money to put us right again God bless you Amen Amen Amen.

395. *To Lady Hamilton*

[Monmouth: E 438]

. . .[2] and when Louis's squadron goes I shall have 23 Sail of the Line to meet them but we shall do very well I am sensible that Ministry are sending me all the force they can and I hope to use it.

Octr: 2nd: last night I got your dear letters Sepr: 19th: 18th:[3] by Adl: Sutton[4] You must not my Emma complain of my short letters for all that I could write was it a Ream of paper might be comprisd in one short sentence that I love you dearly tenderly and affectionately.

I have had as you will believe a very distressing Scene with Poor Sir Robert Calder he has wrote home to beg an enquiry feeling confident that he can fully justify himself I sincerely hope he may, but I have given him the advice as to my dearest friend, He is in adversity, and if he ever has been my Enemy[5] he now feels the pang of it, and finds me one of his best friends.

Our friend Sir Evan[6] is a great courtier whilst we are in prosperity or that your face and voice may please him he will be our admirer in different ways[7] me to feed his ambition, You to please his Passion, but I can and so can you see into such friends, Why dont he serve Poor Brent, Louis Hollowell[8] Hoste are all enquiring about you and desire their kind regards, I am pressed beyond measure for time for I cannot keep the vessel as Vice Adl: Collingwoods and Sir Robt: Calders dispatches were stopt by me off Cape St: Vincent on the 26th: May God Bless You my Dearly beloved Emma Kiss Horatia for me a thousand times I shall write her very soon in 8 or 10 days another Vessel will be sent remember me

[1]Nelson wrote to the Dey of Algiers on 5 Oct 1805 in order to keep good relations (Nicolas, vii, pp. 78–9).

[2]Beginning missing.

[3]*Sic*, in this order.

[4]'by Adl: Sutton' is inserted.

[5]Envying Nelson for having received the Order of the Bath after the Battle of St Vincent at which Calder commanded John Jervis' flagship the *Ville de Paris*; Nelson himself did not always entertain the best of opinions of Calder (see Doc. No. 91).

[6]Nepean.

[7]Inserted.

[8]Benjamin Hallowell.

kindly to M[rs]: Cadogan Miss Connor Reynolds Charlotte, and say every kind [thing] for me to the doctor + M[rs]: Nelson if this finds you at Canterbury and again + for Ever Believe me Your most faithful in every sence of the word Nelson and Bronte,

If you see Lad[y]: Elizth: Forster [*sic!*][1] say that I have delivered to Clifford[2] all his things letters +[c]: and he is to dine with me to day, I have just got your letter of Aug[t]: 6th: recommending a M[r]: O Reilly of the Canopus I fear I can do nothing unless the Combined fleet puts to Sea.

Make my Compliments to M[r]: Perry and our Merton friends I congratulate you on the fall of the Wall and the opening prospect I hope the Kitchen is going o<u>n</u> God Bless you amen amen amen. With all the furore[3]

396. *To Lady Hamilton*

[BL: Egerton 1614 ff. 123–124, no. 64]

Victory 16 Lg[s]:
West from Cadiz
Oct[r]: 6th: 1805.

My Dearest beloved Emma I wrote you on the 2nd: by the Nimble[4] and if she acts up to her name she will have a good passage She will tell you of my arrival in the fleet but as an opportunity now offers of sending a letter by way of Lisbon I will not omit writing to my dearest Emma although most probably other letters will get home before this, and perhaps those of the very greatest importance, the Enemy are I have not the smallest doubt determined to put to sea and our battle must soon be fought, although they will be so very superior in numbers to my present force Yet I must do my best and have no fears but that I shall spoil their voyage, but my wish is to do much more and therefore hope that the Admiralty have been active in sending me ships, for it is only numbers which can annihilate, a decisive stroke on their fleet would make half a Peace, and my Emma if I can do that I shall as soon as possible ask to come home and get my rest at least for the winter and if no other inducement was

[1]Misspelling of 'Foster'; Elizabeth Foster (1758–1824), daughter of the Earl-Bishop of Bristol, had visited Lady Hamilton at Naples in April 1793 together with the Duchess of Devonshire and Lady Spencer (Fraser, p. 184) she met Nelson during his stay ashore, see p. 510.

[2]Lady Elizabeth Foster's illegitimate son by her later (from 1809) husband William Cavendish, 5th Duke of Devonshire (and 7th Baron Clifford; 1748–1811), Augustus Clifford (1788–1877), who had entered the navy in 1800.

[3]*Sic*, not 'fervour'.

[4]This refers to Doc. No. 395, which was continued on 2 Oct 1805.

wanting for my exertion this would be sufficient for what greater reward could the country bestow than to let me come to you ~~+ Horatia~~ and dear dear Merton, and to come to you a Victor, would be a Victory twice gained and the rewards would I know from experience be beyond what any person except yourself could give may God Bless you my Dearest Emma and Be assured I am Ever yours most faithfully + affectionately

Nelson + Bronte

Kiss Dear H[a]: and remember me most kindly to all.[1]

Oct[r]. 7th: since writing yesterday I am more and more assured that the combined fleets will put to sea, happy will they be who are present and disappointed will those be who are absent May God protect us and Heavens bless. I kiss you a thousand times. Defiance is just joined it now blows fresh Easterly and a nasty sea Bless you, Amen, Amen Amen,

Tell M[r]: Bolton to be easy I hope soon something will turn up for him it is useless to complain the best thing is to say nothing of any expectations.

397. *From Lady Hamilton to Nelson*

[CRC] Canterbury October 8th 1805

My Dearest Life,

We are just come from Church for I am so fond of the Church service + the Cannons are so Civil we have every Day a fine anthem for me yesterday Mr Mrs + Miss Harpen Mrs Bridges Marquis of Douglas + Several Thornton + Mr Baker[2] the member dined with us the Dr[3] gave a good Dinner + Mariana dressed the Macroni + [Cary?] so all went off Our Julia is very ill yet by not [being] brought to bed as she is only seven months [pregnant] I do not mean to keep Julia after she gets well I am obliged to send for Mariana down + my mother Can ill spare her – she gives me such an amiable account of our Dearest Horatia she now reeds very clear + is learning her notes + French + Italian + my mother doats on her the other day she said at Table Mrs [Condeying?] I wonder Julia did not [Ran?] out of the Church where she wants to be married for I should

[1]The letter is continued on the next and last page.
[2]William Baker (1743–1824), MP for Hertfordshire.
[3]Nelson's brother William.

seeing my squinting husband come in for my god how ugly he is + how he looks Cross Eyed why as my Lady says he looks 2 ways for Sunday

now Julias husband is the ugliest man you ever saw but how that little thing cou'd observe him but she is Clever is she not Nelson – we go Tomorrow for 2 days to Ramsgate to see our old friends poor Lady Dunmore[1] who is there[2] is in gret afliction for the loss of her son Captain John [Murry?] – to day we dine alone to Eat up the scraps + drink tea with old Mrs Percy Charlotte hates Canterbury it is so dull so it is My dear girl writes every day in Miss Conners letter + I am so pleased with her my heart is broke being from her lot I have not had her so long at Merton That my Heart will not bear to be with out her you will be ever fonder of her when you Return she says I love my dear dear god papa but Mrs Gibson told me he killd all the people + I was afraid Dearest Angel she is oh Nelson how I love her but how do I idolize you my dearest Husband of the Heart you are all in this world to your Emma – may God send you victory + Home soon to your Emma, Horatia, + Paradise Merton for when you are there it will be paradise My[3] own Nelson may god prosper you + preserve you for the sake of your affectionate Emma

I hope Sir Edward Berry has joined you by this time but I now long to have letters from you every bodys full of Sir R Carlder coming Home Captain Staines Called yesterday he is gone to Town as he wishes much to join you Lord Douglas begd me to ask you if you ever met with Turkish Tobaca + if you did he wishes you wou'd send him some write often tell me how you are how the sea agrees with you weather it is a bad port is blocade in short the smallest Trifle that concerns you is so very enteresting to your own[4] faithfull Emma[5]

My compliments to the two Scotts[6] + Mr Ford poor Mary Reccommends her Brother to you Mary has nursed me in many an illness night + day[7] + you will love her for that

Tyson is going to buy a County seat + park for Mrs Tyson near Woolwich my Compliments to Admiral Louis God bless you my own own Nelson

[1]Probably Lady Charlotte Dunmore (d. 1819), daughter of Alexander Stewart, 6th Earl of Gallowy, mother to Lady Augusta Murray.

[2]The words 'who is there' are inserted.

[3]Underlined twice.

[4]Underlined thrice.

[5]The letter is continued in the same direction on the outside of the piece of paper (half a sheet), above and below the address.

[6]Alexander and John Scott.

[7]The words 'night' and 'day' are underlined twice.

398. *To Lady Hamilton*

[Pierpont Morgan: MA321] Victory Oct^{r}: 11th: 1805

My Dearest Emma,

M^{r}: Denis request of L^{t}: Hargraves introduction shall be attended to but it must be considered that very few opportunities offer of ever getting onboard the Commander In Chiefs ship in the Winter Months and our battle I hope will be over long before the summer days.

Oct^{r}: 12th: the wind has blown so fresh these two days that the Enemy if so disposed have not had the power of putting to Sea which I am firmly of opinion they intend God send it for our sakes as well as that of our Country well over, our friend Sutton is going home for his health, Hoste has Amphion and Sir W^{m}: Bolton Eurydice which I hope the Admiralty will approve this is the last chance of Sir Billys making a fortune if he is active and persevering he may do it and be easy for life, Ah my Beloved Emma how I envy Sutton going home his going to Merton and seeing You and Horatia, I do really feel that the 25 days I was at Merton was the very happiest of my life would to God they were to be passed over again but that time will I trust soon come and many many more days added to them, I have been as You may believe made very uneasy or rather uncomfortable by the situation of Sir Robt: Calder he was to have gone home in another Ship and a real jumble however I have given way to his misery and directed the Prince of Wales to carry him to Spithead[1] for whatever the result of the enquiry may be I think he has a right to be treated with Respect, therefore my Dear Emma do not form any opinion ab^{t}: him 'till the trial is over, Oct^{r}: 13th: I am working like a horse in a mill but never the nearer finishing my task which I find difficulty enough in getting in keeping clear from confusion but I never allow it to accumulate, Agamemnon is in sight and I hope to have letters from You who I hold dearer than any other person in this World and I shall hope to hear that all our family goes on well at that dear dear Cottage, believe all I would say upon this occasion but letters being in quarantine may be read not that I care who knows that I love you most tenderly and affectionately, I send You Abbe Campbells letter + copy of those from the King + Queen You see they would never wish me out of the Mediterranean Kiss Dear Horatia a thousand times for Your faithful Nelson + Bronte.

[1]The 'Prince of Wales' refers to a ship; for more information about Nelson allowing Calder to return home, see Knight, p. 503, and Doc. No. 395.

399. *To Lady Hamilton*

[Monmouth: E 195]

Tenthousand thanks my dearest Emma for your truly affectionate letters by Sir Edwd: Berry and for the picture which I am sure I shall admire although it is not yet on board, You will hear how near Agamemnon was being taken by the Rochford Squadron who may perhaps travel my way but I hardly expect it, Sir Thos:[1] Calder is on the Wing and the arrival of three Ships from England[2] fills up my whole time till night therefore I can only say my Love may God Bless you and send us a happy meeting and Be assured I am Ever for Ever Yours most faithfully

Nelson + Bronte

I dont think Davison a good hand to keep such a secret as you told him, I fear I cannot even write him a Line.

400. *To Horatia Nelson Thomson*

[NMM: WAL/46] Victory Oct^{r}: 19th: 1805.

My Dearest Angel,

I was made happy by the pleasure of receiving your letter of Sep^{r}: 19th: and I rejoice to hear that you are so very good a Girl and love my Dear Lady Hamilton who most dearly loves[3] you give her a Kiss from me, The Combined fleets of the Enemy are now reported to be coming out of Cadiz and therefore I answer your letter my dearest Horatia to mark to you that you are ever uppermost in my thoughts, I shall be sure of your prayers for my safety, conquest and speedy return to Dear Merton and our Dearest Good Lady Hamilton, Be a good Girl mind what Miss Connor says to you, Receive my Dearest Horatia the affectionate Parental Blessing of your father

Nelson + Bronte.

[1]Here Nelson appears to have got confused about Calder's Christian name, which was Robert. He wrote it correctly in Docs Nos 395 and 398.

[2]Between 7 and 13 Oct Nelson's fleet was joined by three 64-gun ships, which increased his force from 23 (see Doc. No. 395) to 26 ships (Knight, p. 509).

[3]The letters 'lo' are partly cut away at the bottom, where there is a hole in the paper.

401. *To Lady Hamilton*

[BL: Egerton 1614 ff. 125–126, no. 65][1] Victory Oct^{r}: 19th: 1805
Noon Cadiz ESE 16 Leagues.

My Dearest beloved Emma the dear friend of my bosom the Signal has been made that the Enemys combined fleet are coming out of Port, We have very little Wind so that I have no hopes of seeing them before tomorrow May the God of Battles crown my Endeavours with success at all events I will take care that my name shall ever be most dear to you and Horatia both of whom I love as much as my own life, and as my last writing before the battle will be to you so I hope in God that I shall live to finish my letter after the Battle, may Heaven bless you prays your Nelson + Bronte. Oct^{r}: 20th: in the morning. we were close to the mouth of the Streights[2] but the Wind had not come far enough to the Westward to allow the combined fleets to weather the shoals off Traflagar [*sic*]. but they were counted as far as forty sail of ships of War which I suppose to be 34 of the Line[3] and six frigates, a group of them was seen off the lighthouse of Cadiz this morn^{g}: but it blows so very fresh + thick weather that I rather believe they will go into the Harbour before night, May God Almighty give us success over these fellows and enable us to get a peace[4]

This letter was found open on His[5] Desk + brought to Lady Hamilton by Cap^{n} Hardy

oh miserable wretched Emma.
oh glorious + happy Nelson

[1]On a separate sheet (f. 127), used as an envelope it says: 'The inclosed Letters were / found after the Action and / sealed up in the presence / of the Reverend M^{r}: Scott / T.M.Hardy'.

[2]Straits of Gibraltar.

[3]The combined Franco-Spanish fleet consisted of 33 ships at the Battle of Trafalgar (see: Knight, p. 514).

[4]The following lines are in Lady Hamilton's handwriting.

[5]Underlined three times.

402. *Seventh and last codicil to Nelson's will*

[TNA: PROB 1/22/2]

Monday Oct^{r}: 21st: 1805 at day Light saw the Enemys Combined fleet from East to ESE bore away made the signal for order of sailing and to prepare for Battle the Enemy with their heads to the Southward, at 7 the Enemy wearing in succession, May the Great God whom I worship Grant to my Country and for the benefit of Europe in General a great and Glorious Victory, and may no misconduct in any one tarnish it, and may[1] humanity after Victory be the predominant feature in the British fleet, For myself individually I commit my Life to Him who made me, and may his blessing light upon my endeavours for serving my Country faithfully, to Him I resign myself and the Just cause which is entrusted to me to

Defend,

Amen, Amen, Amen[2]

October the twenty first one thousand Eight hundred and five then is [*sic!*] sight of the Combined fleets of France and Spain distant about Ten miles

Whereas the Eminent Services of Emma Hamilton Widow of the Right Honourable Sir William Hamilton have been of the very greatest Service to Our King & Country, to my knowledge without her receiving any reward from either our King or Country, first that she obtained the King of Spain[s][3] letter in 1796 to His brother the King of Naples acquainting him of his intention to Declare War against England from which letter the Ministry sent out orders to then Sir John Jervis to Strike a Stroke if opportunity offered against either the arsenals of Spain or her fleets, that neither of these was done is not the fault of Lady Hamilton the opportunity might have been offered, secondly the British fleet under my Command could never have return'd the second time to Egypt had not Lady Hamiltons influence with the Queen of Naples caused Letters

[1]The 'm' at the beginning of 'may' stands at the beginning of a line and, perhaps for that reason, appears like a capital 'M'.

[2]After this Nelson left the rest of the page (about a third of it) empty and continued on the next page (numbered 29 in the manuscript at TNA).

[3]Charles IV (1748–1819; reigned 1788–1808); The word stands at the end of the line, so that Nelson felt forced to draw the last line of the 'n' a bit downwards. He may have therefore not had enough space for the 's'.

to be wrote to the Governor of Syracuse that he was to encourage the fleet being supplied with every thing should they put into any Port in Sicily, We put into Syracuse and received every supply went to Egypt + destroyed the French fleet, Could I have rewarded these Services I would not now call upon my Country but as that has not been in my power I leave Emma Lady Hamilton therefore a Legacy to my King and Country that they will give her an ample provision to maintain her Rank in Life. I also leave to the beneficence of my Country my adopted daughter Horatia Nelson Thompson and I desire She will[1] Use in future the name of Nelson only,[2] these are the only favors I ask of my King and Country at this moment when I am going to fight their Battle[3] May God. Bless My King + Country and all those who I hold dear My Relations it is needless to mention they will of course be amply provided for

Nelson and Bronté.

Witness[4]
Henry Blackwood
T. M. Hardy.

[1]Here a new page begins.

[2]Pettigrew, ii, p. 519, explains in a fn.: 'The grant under the King's sign manual, by which Horatia took the name of Nelson only, bears date Sept. 30, 1806.'

[3]Here a new line begins.

[4]The word 'Witness' is written in the same handwriting as Captain Blackwood's signature.

APPENDICES

APPENDIX 1

SELECTED LIST OF PREVIOUS PUBLICATIONS

Printed Primary Sources

[Anon.] (ed.), *The Letters of Lord Nelson to Lady Hamilton with a Supplement of Interesting Letters by Distinguished Characters*, 2 vols, (London: Thomas Lovewell & Co., 1814).

[Anon., A. and M. Gatty], *Recollections of the Life of the Rev. A. J. Scott, D.D. Lord Nelson's Chaplain* (London: Saunders and Otley, 1842).

[Morrison, Alfred], *The Collection of Autograph Letters and Historical Documents formed by Alfred Morrison (Second Series, 1882–1893)–The Hamilton & Nelson Papers*, 2 vols ([n. pl.]: printed for private circulation, 1893).

Naish, George (ed.), *Nelson's Letters to His Wife and other Documents. 1785–1831* (London: Navy Records Society, 1958).

Nicolas, Nicholas Harris (ed.), *The Dispatches and Letters of Vice Admiral Lord Viscount Nelson*, 7 vols (London: Chatham Publishing, 1997; first edited 1844–46).

Parsons, G. S., Nelsonian Reminiscences. Leaves from Memory's Log (London: Saunders and Otley, 1843).

Pettigrew, Thomas Joseph, *Memoirs of the Life of Vice-Admiral Lord Viscount Nelson, K.B. Duke of Bronté etc. etc. etc.*, 2 vols (London: T. and W. Boone, 1849).

White, Colin (ed.), *Nelson. The New Letters* (Woodbridge, Suffolk: The Boydell Press in association with The National Maritime Museum and The Royal Naval Museum, 2005).

Secondary Sources

Bindoff, S. T., E. F. Malcolm Smith and C. K. Webster (eds.), *British Diplomatic Representatives 1789–1852, edited for the Royal Historical Society*, Camden Third Series, Vol. L (London: Camden Society, 1934).

Clarke, James Stanier, and John M'Arthur, *The Life of Admiral Lord Nelson, K.B. from His Lordship's Manuscripts*, in 2 vols (London: T. Cadell and W. Davies, 1809).

Fraser, Flora, *Beloved Emma. The Life of Emma Lady Hamilton* (London: Weidenfeld and Nicolson, 1986).

Harrison, James, *The Life of the Right Honourable Horatio Lord Viscount Nelson . . .*, 2 vols ([London]: C. Chapple, 1806).

Knight, Roger, *The Pursuit of Victory. The Life and Achievement of Horatio Nelson* (London: Allen Lane, 2005).

Lincoln, Margarette, *Naval Wives & Mistresses* (London: National Maritime Museum, 2007).

Rodger, N. A. M., *The Command of the Ocean* (London: Allen Lane, 2004)

Russell, Jack, *Nelson and the Hamiltons* (first published by Anthony Blond, 1969; Harmondsworth, Middlesex: Penguin Books, 1972).

Sichel, Walter, *Emma Lady Hamilton. From New and Original Sources and Documents. Together with an Appendix of Notes and New Letters*, 3rd edn, revised (Edinburgh: Archibald Constable, 1907).

Vincent, Edgar, *Nelson. Love & Fame* (New Haven and London: Yale University Press, 2003).

Williams, Kate, *England's Mistress. The Infamous Life of Emma Hamilton* (London: Hutchison, 2006).

APPENDIX 2

CHRONOLOGY OF NELSON'S LETTERS TO LADY HAMILTON

1798

Month	Day	Time	Doc. No.	Written by	Written to
June	13		1	Nelson	Lady Hamilton
	17		2		
		6 pm	3		
			4	Lady Hamilton	Nelson
	30		5		
July	22		6	Nelson	Lady Hamilton
			7		Sir William and Lady Hamilton
August	11		8		Lady Hamilton
	13		9		
September	8		10	Lady Hamilton	Nelson
October	3		11	Nelson	Lady Hamilton
	16		12		
	20		13	Lady Hamilton	Nelson
	24		14	Nelson	Lady Hamilton
	26		15	Lady Hamilton	Nelson
	27		16	Nelson	Lady Hamilton
			17	Lady Hamilton	Nelson
			18		[verses]
November	2		19		Nelson
	22		20	Nelson	Lady Hamilton
	24	Evening	21	Lady Hamilton	Nelson
	25	Evening	22		
			23		
			24	Nelson	Lady Hamilton
December	25?		25		

1799

Month	Day	Time	Doc. No.	Written by	Written to
January	25		26	Nelson	Lady Hamilton
February	9		27	Nelson and Lady Hamilton	Ball

Month	Day	Time	Doc. No.	Written by	Written to
March	4		28	Nelson	[draft for speech]
May	19	8 o'clock	29		Lady Hamilton
	20		30		
	21		31		
			32		
	22		33		
	24	8 o'clock			
	25		34		[codicil]
	26		35		Lady Hamilton
June	1		36	Nelson, Sir William and Lady Hamilton	Ball
	12	Evening	37	Lady Hamilton	Nelson
	16	7 o'clock	38	Nelson	Lady Hamilton
	18		39	Nelson and Ball	
	19		40	Nelson	
	20	Noon	41		
		3 o'clock			
		4 o'clock			
	29				

1800

Month	Day	Time	Doc. No.	Written by	Written to
January	29		42	Nelson	Lady Hamilton
	30				
February	2	Noon			
	3		43		
	13		44		
	18		45		
		evening			
	20		46		
	25		47		
March	4		48		

Month	Day	Time	Doc. No.	Written by	Written to
November			49	Nelson	Lady Hamilton
			50		
November or December			51		
December	29	6 o'clock, morning	52		

1801

Month	Day	Time	Doc. No.	Written by	Written to
January	13		53	Nelson	Lady Nelson
	14	8 o'clock	54		Lady Hamilton
	16	5 o'clock	55		Lady Nelson
	17	5 o'clock	56		Lady Hamilton
	20		57		Lady Nelson
	21		58		Lady Nelson
			59		Lady Hamilton
	24		60		
			61		
	25		62		
	26		63		
	27		64		
	28		65		
	29		66		
			67		
February	1		68	Nelson	
	2		69		
	3		70		Mrs Thomson
			71		Lady Nelson
	4		72		Lady Hamilton
			73		
	5	noon			
			74		Mrs Thomson
	6		75		
			76		Lady Hamilton
		noon			
	7				
	8		77		
			78		

Month	Day	Time	Doc. No.	Written by	Written to
	9		79	Nelson	Lady Hamilton
	?		80		
	?		81		
	11		82		
		3 o'clock	83		
	12	1 o'clock	84		
			85		
	13		86		
	14		87		
	15				
	15		88		
	16	morning			
			89		
	?		90		
	16	night	91		
	17		92		
	?		93		
	17		94		
		night	95		
	18	Morning			
		Night	96		
	19		97		
		Thursday			
			98		
	?		99		
	?		100		
	19		101		
	20	9 o'clock			
		Night 9 o'clock	102		
		11 o'clock			
			103		Mrs Thomson
	20	10 o'clock at night	104		Lady Hamilton
	21	morning			
		8 o'clock	103		Mrs. Thomson
	22	8 o'clock	105		Lady Hamilton
		8 o'clock			
		noon			

Month	Day	Time	Doc. No.	Written by	Written to
	23		106	Nelson	Mrs Thomson
	24		107		Lady Nelson
	27		108		Lady Hamilton
	?		109	Lady Hamilton	[verses]
March	1	8 o'clock morning	110	Nelson	Lady Hamilton
		noon	111		
		9 o'clock	112		
	2	morning			
			113		
	3	Morning	114		
		11 o'clock			
		2 o'clock			
		½ past 2 o'clock			
	4		115		
		4 o'clock	116		
			117		Lady Nelson
	5		118		[will]
	6		119		Lady Hamilton
		Half-past 8 o'clock			
		Noon			
		3 o'clock			
	6		120		[codicil]
		10 o'clock at night	121		Lady Hamilton
	7				
		9 o'clock	122		
			123		
	9		124		
		Morning	125		
	10		126		
	11		127		
			128		
	?		129		Mrs Thomson
	?		130		

Month	Day	Time	Doc. No.	Written by	Written to
	13		131	Nelson	Lady Hamilton
	14				
	16				
			132		[codicil]
	17		133		Lady Hamilton
	19		134		
	20	8 o'clock	135		
	21		136		
		1 o'clock	137		
	23		138		
	26		139		
	28				
	30	½ past 5 o'clock			
		9 o'clock at night	140		
April	2	8 o'cock at night	141	Nelson	Lady Hamilton
	5		142		
			143		
	6	7 in the morning			
	9		144		
		9 o'clock at night			
		9 o'clock at night	145		
	11		146		
	13		147		
	14		148		
	15		149		
	17		150		
	20		151		
	23		152		
	25		153		
	27		154		
	28		155		

Month	Day	Time	Doc. No.	Written by	Written to
May	2		156	Nelson	Lady Hamilton
	5	2 o'clock	157		
	?		158		
	5		159		
	8	2 o'clock	160		
			161		
			162		
			163		
	11		164		
	12		165		
	13				
	15		166		
			167		
	16		166		
	17		168		
	24		169		
	26		170		
	27		171		
June	1		172	Nelson	Lady Hamilton
		8 am	173		
	5		174		
	8		175		
	10		176		
	11				
	12		177		
		[no time]			
		11 o'clock at night			
	13		178		
	14				
		9 o'clock in the evening			
	15				
	30	½ past 1 o'clock	179		

Month	Day	Time	Doc. No.	Written by	Written to
July	27		180	Nelson	Lady Hamilton
	28		181		
	29		182		
	30		183		
	31		184		
August	1		185	Nelson	Lady Hamilton
	2				
	3		186		
	4		187		
		7 o'clock	188		
			189		
	5		190		
	6		191		
	7		192		
			193		
	9		194		
	10		195		
	11		196		
	12		197		
	13		198		
			199		
	14		200		
	15		201		
	16		202		
	17		203		
	18		204		
	19		205		
			206		
	20		207		
			208		
	21		209		
	22		210		
	23	6 o'clock in the morning	211		
	24		212		

Month	Day	Time	Doc. No.	Written by	Written to
September	?		213	Nelson	Mrs Thomson
	20		214		Lady Hamilton
	21	½ past 7 o'clock	215		
		Noon			
		¼ past 10 o'clock	216		
	23		217		
			218		
			219		
	24		220		
		2 o'clock	221		
	25		222		
	26	8 o'clock	223		
	?		224		
	28		225		
		Half past 1 o'clock			
	29		226		
		Noon			
	39		227		
October	1		228	Nelson	Lady Hamilton
	2		229		
	3		230		
	4	9 o'clock	231		
			232		
	5		233		
			234		
	?	2 o'clock	235		
	6		236		
			237		
	8		238		
		10 o'clock			
		Half past 7 o'clock	239		
	9		240		
	10		241		
			242		

Month	Day	Time	Doc. No.	Written by	Written to
	11		243	Nelson	Lady Hamilton
		11 o'clock			
	12	10 o'clock	244		
	13		245		
		11 o'clock			
	14		246		
		noon			
	15		247		
			248		
	16		249		
			250		
	16	2 pm	251		
	17		252		
	18		253		
	19		254		
	20		255		
			256		
	21		257		
	29		258		

1803

Month	Day	Time	Doc. No.	Written by	Written to
May	10		259	Nelson	[will]
	13		260		[first codicil]
	16	¼ before 6 o'clock	261		Lady Hamilton
	18		262		
	19		263		
	20		264		
		noon	265		
	21		266		
	22	8 o'clock in the morning	267		
	23				
	25		268		
	26				
	30				
June	2			Nelson	Lady Hamilton
	3				

Month	Day	Time	Doc. No.	Written by	Written to
		2 o'clock		Nelson	Lady Hamilton
	4				
	10		269		
	11				
	20		270		
	25		271		
July	?		272		
	8				
	8				
	12		273		
	18				
	21				
August	1		274		
	10		275		
	21		276		
	?		277		
	?		278		
	?		279	Lady Hamilton	Nelson
	24		280	Nelson	Lady Hamilton
			281		
	?		282		
	before 26		283		
	?		284		Mrs Thomson
September	6		285		[second codicil]
	8		286		Lady Hamilton
	10		287		
	18		288		
	19		289		
	26		290		
October	5		291		
	6		292		
	18		293		
	21		294		Horatia
	22		293		Lady Hamilton
	23		295		
November?	?		296		
December	7		297		
	13				
	25				
	26		298		

1804

Month	Day	Time	Doc. No.	Written by	Written to
January	13		299	Nelson	Lady Hamilton
	20		300		
			301		Horatia
February	10		302		Lady Hamilton
	19		303		[third codicil]
	25		304		Lady Hamilton
			305		
March	14		306		
	?		307		
	19				
	?		308		
	?		309		
April	2		310	Nelson	
	7		311		[fourth codicil]
	7		312		Lady Hamilton
	9				
	9		310		
	10		313		
	13		314		Horatia
	14		310		Lady Hamilton
	19		315		
	21		316		
	23		317		
	28		318		
May	3		319		
			320		
	5		321		
	22		322		
	27		323		
	30				
			324		
June	6		325		
	10		326		
	17		327		
	18				
	27		328		

Month	Day	Time	Doc. No.	Written by	Written to
July	1		329	Nelson	Lady Hamilton
			330		
	9		331		
	11				
	12				
	14		332		
August	12		333		
	13		334		
			335		
			336		
	20		337		
	22		338		
	27		339		
	30	Evening [and]	340		
	31				
September	9		341		
	22		342		
	29		343		
October	2		344	Nelson	Lady Hamilton
	5		345		
	7	2 pm	346		
	10		347		
	13		348		
	31		349		
November	?		350		
	6		351		
	15		352		
	23		353		
December	4		354		
	19		355		[fifth codicil]
			356		Lady Hamilton
	39		357		

1805

Month	Day	Time	Doc. No.	Written by	Written to
January	14		358	Nelson	Lady Hamilton
			359	Lady Hamilton	[poem]
February	18		360	Nelson	Lady Hamilton
	20				
March	9		361		
	10				
	13		362		
	16		363		
	30		364		
	31		361		
April	1				
	4		365		
	5	9 pm	366		
	19		367		
May	4		368		
	9		369		
	?		370		
	13		371		
	18?		372		
	18		373		
	20		371		
June	4		374		
	10		375		
	11				
	12	7 pm	376		
	16		377		
	18				
	20		378		

Month	**Day**	**Time**	**Doc. No.**	**Written by**	**Written to**
July	24		379	Nelson	Lady Hamilton
	25				
August	18		380		
	19		381		
September	11		382		[sixth codicil]
	13		383		[journal]
	14	6 o'clock	384		Lady Hamilton
			385		
	15		386		
	?		387		
	16		388		
			389		
	17	9 o'clock	390		
	18				
	20		391		
	24		392		
	25		393		
October	1		394		
	?		395		
	2				
	6		396		
	7				
	8		397	Lady Hamilton	Nelson
	11		398	Nelson	Lady Hamilton
	12				
			399		
	19		400		Horatia
			401		Lady Hamilton
	20				
	21		402		[codicil]

APPENDIX 3

ITEMS MENTIONED IN THE LETTERS, NELSON'S WILLS AND CODICILS TO HIS WILLS

Presents

History of the aigrette, the sword from the King of Naples and the swords from the captains at the Battle of the Nile after Nelson's Death:

<table>
<tr><th>Aigrette/chelengk</th><th colspan="2">Sword from the King of Naples</th><th>Sword from captains at the Battle of the Nile</th></tr>
<tr><td colspan="4">After Nelson's death these items were first handed over to Lady Hamilton, who then handed them over to Nelson's brother William.[1]</td></tr>
<tr><td colspan="4">Went as heirlooms associated with the dukedom of Bronte to Nelson's brother William, 1st Earl Nelson, and from him in 1835 to his daughter Charlotte, who had married Samuel Hood, 2nd Baron Bridport</td></tr>
<tr><td rowspan="2"></td><td colspan="2">separated into:</td><td rowspan="2"></td></tr>
<tr><td>a sword in which the diamonds were replaced with paste</td><td>. . . and a necklace</td></tr>
<tr><td colspan="4">Sold in Bridport sale in 1895</td></tr>
<tr><td>Bought by Frazer & Haws, court jewellers, on behalf of Mrs Constance Eyre Matcham; bought for the nation</td><td>Bought by Lady Llangatock and given by her to Monmouth to be kept at the Nelson Museum</td><td>Bought by Mr Haws</td><td>Bought by Mr Mullens and presented to Greenwich Hospital</td></tr>
<tr><td>Stolen from the National Maritime Museum in 1951</td><td>Stolen from the Nelson Museum at Monmouth in 1953</td><td>Owned by the Earl of Mexborough in 1952</td><td>Stolen from Greenwich Hospital in 1900</td></tr>
</table>

[1]Pettigrew, i, p. 428, refers in a fn. to a receipt found among Lady Hamilton's papers.

Other presents and honours that Nelson received after the battle of the Nile and that he mentioned in his letters to Lady Hamilton are:

Collar of the Bath, medals and Order of St Ferdinand: These honours underwent a similar fate to that of the aigrette.

Pelisse (Lady Hamilton writes 'pelicia' and Nelson writes 'pelesse'): A pelisse was a short fur lined or fur timed jacket that was usually worn hanging loose over the left shoulder of hussar light cavalry soldiers, ostensibly to prevent sword cuts (Wikipedia). Nelson had received his from the Grand Signor after the battle of the Nile.[1]

Boxes: Nelson received two of these precious presents; he himself remembered on 25 May 1799 that he had received them from the Tsar of Russia and 'the Mother of the Grand Signor' (Doc. No. 34). The *Naval Chronicle*, vol. iii, April 1800,[2] however, listed among the 'presents to Lord Nelson for his Services in the Mediterranean between October the First 1798 and October the First 1799' two gold boxes, one from the Emperor of Russia (value estimated at £ 2,500), the other from the King of Sardinia (value estimated at £ 1,200).

Sources

Pettigrew, Thomas Joseph, *Memoirs of the Life of Vice-Admiral Lord Viscount Nelson, K.B. Duke of Bronté etc. etc. etc.*, 2 vols (London: T. and W. Boone, 1849).

Prentice, Rina, *The Authentic Nelson* (London: National Maritime Museum, 2005), pp. 23, 34, 63 and 76.

Munday, John, 'The Nelson Relics', in *The Nelson Companion*, ed. Colin White (Annapolis, MD: Alan Sutton Publishing, 1995), pp. 59–79, 62 and 67.

Paintings of Lady Hamilton

Elisabeth Vigée le Brun's *Lady Hamilton as a Bacchante* (or *Ariadne*): This painting, which Nelson bought from Christies in 1800 for £300 is not to be confused with the painting by the same painter of *Lady Hamilton as a Bacchante* which is now kept at the Walker Art Gallery in Liverpool. On the Gallery's website the painting that

[1]See fn in Pettigrew, i, p. 443.
[2]Quoted by Munday, p. 62.

Nelson bought is referred to as *Emma as Ariadne* and it is described as the earliest painting of the sitter by Madame Vigée le Brun, dating from 1790. This painting, which is now in a private collection, has props such as a leopard skin and a wine goblet, making the sitter resemble a Bacchante and thus explaining the misleading title.

Sir William Hamilton commissioned Henry Bone to paint a copy of this picture in enamel on copper and bequeathed it to Nelson. This copy is now in the Wallace Collection in London. Pettigrew reports of it being 'in the possession of Lord Northwick', who informed him 'that Sir William often complained of the extravagant price he had paid to the French lady for her portrait, and also of Emma's scruples on having afterwards prevailed upon her to clothe her fine form under a tiger's skin, which not only spoilt the picture, but was the dearest skin he had ever heard of, as it cost him £100!'

Johan Heinrich Schmidt, painted companion pieces of Nelson and Lady Hamilton in pastel. The paintings were done in Dresden in 1800 and are now at the National Maritime Museum, London. There used to be a paper fixed to the frame of the painting of Lady Hamilton on which Lady Hamilton had written: 'This Portrait of Emma Hamilton was in all the Battles with the virtuous, gallant and heroic Nelson. He called it his Guardian Angel and thought he could not be victorious if he did not see it in the midst of Battle. He used to say under his Banner. I grieve (or lament) the fatal 21st of October, when he gloriously fell and ordered Captain Hardy to bring it to me.'[1]

Sources

Lynda McLeod, 'James Christie and his auction house', *Art Libraries Journal* 2008, 33/1, pp. 29–34

Pettigrew, Thomas Joseph, *Memoirs of the Life of Vice-Admiral Lord Viscount Nelson, K.B. Duke of Bronté etc. etc. etc.*, 2 vols (London: T. and W. Boone, 1849), i, p. 440.

Walker, Richard, The Nelson Portraits ([Portsmouth]: Royal Naval Museum, 1998), pp. 112–17.

http://www.liverpoolmuseums.org.uk

http://wallacelive.wallacecollection.org

[1]Walker, p. 114, quoting the transcription from Sir Geoffrey Callender, on the Schmidt portraits, in *The Illustrated London News*, 20 March 1943, p. 314.

APPENDIX 4

POETRY REFERRED TO IN NELSON'S LETTERS

'Cheer up Fair Emma', was written to the tune of 'Heart of Oak' and 'addressed to Lady Hamilton on her Birthday, April 26th 1800, on board the Foudroyant, in a gale of wind, by Miss Ellis Cornelia Knight'. The text runs:

Come cheer up, fair Emma, forget all thy grief,
For they shipmates are brave, and a hero's their Chief;
Look around on these trophies, the pride of the main,
They were snatched by their valour from Gallia and Spain.
Heart of Oak are our ships, heart of oak are our men;
We always are ready, steady, boys, steady!
We'll fight and we'll conquer again and again.

Behold yonder fragment, 'tis sacred to fame:
'Mid the waves of old Nile it was sav'd from the flame:
The flame that destroy'd all the glories of France,
When Providence vanquish'd the friends of blind Chance.
Heart of Oak . . .

Those arms the St Joseph once claim'd as her own,
Ere NELSON and Britons her pride had o'erthrown:
That plume there evinces that still they excel:
It was torn from the cap of the fam'd William Tell.
Heart of Oak . . .

Then, cheer up, fair Emma! remember thou'rt free,
And ploughing Britannia's old Empire – the Sea:
How many in Albion each sorrow would check,
Could they kiss but one plank of this conquering deck.
Heart of Oak . . .'.

'See, the Conquering Hero Comes' is a chorus from George Frederic Handel's oratorio *Judas Maccabaeus*, originally meant as a compliment to the Duke of Cumberland's victory at Culloden in 1746.

The original words by Thomas Morell are:	Lady Hamilton's variations (in italics, see Doc. No. 18) are:
Youths	
See, the conqu'ring hero comes!	See, the conqu'ring hero comes!
Sound the trumpets, beat the drums.	Sound the trumpets, beat the drums.

Sports prepare, the laurel bring,	Sports prepare, the laurel bring,
Songs of triumph to him sing.	Songs of triumph to him sing.

Virgins

See the godlike youth advance!	See *our gallant Nelson comes*!
Breathe the flutes, and lead the dance;	[second line of first verse repeated]
Myrtle wreaths, and roses twine,	[third line of first verse repeated]
To deck the hero's brow divine.	Songs of Triumph *Emma sings.*
	[third and fourth lines of second verse]

Israelites

See, the conquering hero comes!
Sound the trumpets, beat the drums.
Sports prepare, the laurel bring,
Songs of triumph to him sing.
See, the conqu'ring hero comes!
Sound the trumpets, beat the drums.

APPENDIX 5

MINUTE OF A CONVERSATION WITH THE PRINCE ROYAL OF DENMARK ON 3 APRIL 1801: TRANSCRIPT OF A MANUSCRIPT WITH A CORRECTION IN NELSON'S HANDWRITING

The manuscript, apparently written by a secretary, is in the Hubert S. Smith Collection (Volume I: 'Lord Nelson and the Battle of Copenhagen), 1801, in the William Clements Library at the University of Michigan, Ann Arbor; it has previously been printed in Thomas Joseph Pettigrew, *Memoirs of the Life of Vice-Admiral Lord Viscount Nelson, K.B. Duke of Bronté etc. etc. etc.*, 2 vols (London: T. and W. Boone, 1849), ii, pp. 23–6.

His Royal Highness began the conversation by saying how happy he was to see me and thanked me for my humanity to the wounded Danes, I then said that it was to me and would be the greatest affliction to every man in England from the King to the Lowest person to think that Denmark had fired on the British flag and became leagued with her Enemies, His Royal Highness stopped me by saying that Admiral Parker had declared War against Denmark, this I denied and requested His Royal Highness to send for the papers and he would find the direct contrary, and that it was the farthest from the thoughts of the British Admiral, I then asked if His Royal Highness would permit me to speak my mind freely on the present situation of Denmark, to which he having acquiesced, I stated to him the sensation which was caused in England by such an unnatural alliance with, at the present moment, the furious enemy of England. His answer was that when he made the Alliance it was for the protection of their trade and that Denmark would never be the Enemy of England, and that the Emperor of Russia was not the Enemy of England when this treaty was formed, that he never would join Russia against England and his declaration to that Effect was the cause of the Emperors (I think he said) sending away His Minister that Denmark was a trading Nation and had only to look to the protection of its lawful commerce, His Royal Highness then enlarged on the Impossibility of Danish Ships under convoy, having on board[1] any contraband trade; but to be subjected to be stopped even a Danish fleet by a pitiful privateer and that she should search all the ships and take out of the fleet ay vessels she might please was what Denmark could not permit, to this my answer was simply what occasion for convoy to fair trade? To which he answered did you find any thing in the convoy of the Freya and that no Commander could tell what contraband goods might be in the convoy, +c +c and as to Merchants they would always sell what was most saleable + as to swearing to property I could get any thing sworn to which I pleased, I then said suppose that England which she never

[1]Here the first page ends; the word 'board' is repeated at the beginning of the second page.

will was to consent to this freedom and nonsence of Navigation, I will tell your Royal Highness what the result would be – ruination to Denmark, for the present commerce of Denmark with the warring powers was half the neutral carrying trade, and any Merchant in Copenhagen would tell you the same. If all this freedom was allowed, Denmark would not have more than the sixth part, for the State of Papenburgh[1] was as good as the State of Denmark in that case; and it would soon be said we will not be stopped in the Sound our flag is our protection and Denmark would lose a great Source of her present revenues and that the Baltic would soon change its name to the Russian Sea. He said this was a delicate subject, to which I replied that His Royal Highness had permitted me to speak out. He then said pray answer me a question for what is the British fleet come into the Baltic My Answer, to crush a most formidable and unprovoked Coalition ag[t]: Great Britain, He then went on to say that His Uncle[2] had been deceived that it was a misunderstanding and that nothing should ever make him take a part against Great Britain for that it could not be his interest to see us crushed nor he trusted ours to see him, to which I acquiesced, I then said there could not be a doubt of the hostility of Denmark for if her fleet had been joined with Russia + Sweden they would assuredly have gone into the North Sea menaced the Court of England, and probably have joined the French if they had been ~~xxx~~ over.[3] His Royal Highness said His ships never shou'd' join any power against England, but it required not much argument to satisfy him, he could not help it by his treaty,[4] In speaking of the pretended Union of the Northern powers I could not help saying that His Royal Highness must be sensible that it was nonsence to talk of a Neutral protection of trade with a power who had none and that He must be sensible that the Emperor of Russia would never have thought of offering to protect the Trade of Denmark if he had not had hostility against Great Britain. He said repeatedly I have offered to say and do offer my Mediation between Great Britain + Russia My answer was a Mediator must be at peace with both parties You must settle Your

[1]On the river Ems, situated west of Bremen and close to the Netherlands, Papenburg had been part of the Duchy of Arenberg, which had been lost with the Peace of Lunéville, on 9 February 1801, as it was (mostly) situated west of the river Rhine, where it was ceded to France; territorial compensation within Germany was not forthcoming (for this purpose territories of the Catholic Church were secularised in 1803); the blind duke ceded his title to his son in 1803 It appears that, between the Peace of Lunéville in 1801 and 1803, Papenburg was somehow regarded as a perfect example of a powerless country.

[2]George III of Great Britain.

[3]Here Nelson deleted a word and wrote 'over' above it

[4]The words 'by his treaty' are inserted in Nelson's handwriting

matter with Great Britain, at present you are leagued with our Enemies and are consider'd naturally as a part of the Effective force to fight us. Talking much on this subject His Royal Highness said what must I do to make myself equal Answer, sign an Alliance with Great Britain, and join your fleet to ours. His Royal Highness their[1] [said] Russia will go to War with Us and my desire as[2] a Commercial Nation is to be at peace with all the world, I told him he renew the offer of Great Britain either to join Us or disarm, + pray Lord Nelson wht do you call disarming, My Answer was, that I was not authorized to give an opinion on the Subject but I considered it as not leaving on foot any force beyond the custom any establishment, 2nd + do you consider the guardships in the Sound as beyond that common establishment. Answer, I do not, 2~: We have always had 5 sail of the Line in the Cattegat and Coast of Norway, Answer I am not authorized to define what is exactly disarming but I do not think much of a force will be allowed. H. R. H., when all Europe is in such a dreadful shade of confusion it is absolutely necessary that States should be on their guard, Answer Your Royal highness, renews the offer of England to Keep, 20 sail of the Line in the Baltic. He then said I am sure my intentions are very much misunderstood. To which I replied that Sir Hyde Parker, had authorized me to say that upon certain conditions H. R. H might have an opportunity of explaining his sentiments at the Court of London. I am not authorized to say on what conditions exactly. 2n:, but what do you think. Answer. First a free entry of the British Fleet into Copenhagen and the free use of every thing we may wish from it, before I could get on he replied quick that you shall have with pleasure, the next is whilst this explanations is going on a total Suspension of Your treaties with Russia, these I believe are the foundation on which Sir Hyde Parker only can build other articles for his justification[3] in Suspending his orders which are plain and positive, His royal Highness desired me to repeat which I had said which having done he thanked me for my open conversation and I having made an Apology if I had said any thing which he might think too strong, His Royal Highness very handsomely bid the same and we parted. He saying that he hoped We would cease from hostilities to Morrow as on such an important occasion. He must call a Council.

[1]Sic.

[2]Here the second page ends; the word 'as' is repeated at the beginning of the third page.

[3]Here the third page ends; the word 'justification' is repeated at the beginning of the fourth page.

APPENDIX 6

THE TAKING OF THE *SWIFT* CUTTER: AN ATTEMPT TO TRACE THE DOCUMENTS CAPTURED BY *L'ESPÉRANCE* IN 1804

In documents 315, 321, 322 and 323 Nelson vents his anger at the loss of the *Swift* cutter. The fate of the ship and the documents it carried can be reconstructed from French documents at the archives of the Foreign Office in Paris and Nantes as well as the National Archives in Paris.

On '21 Germinal an 12',[1] that is on 9 April, the French consul at Barcelona, Pancôme Louis Adélaïde Viot, reported to 'His Excellence' the 'Citizen Minister', Talleyrand, about how and by whom the British *Swift* cutter had been taken:

> on Saturday, the 17th of this month [= 5 April 1804] the French privateer xebec,[2] *l'Esperance*, Captain Escoffier of Nice,[3] entered this port,[4] carrying with her an extremely important prize as her object, the dispatch cutter *Swift*, Captain Leake, coming from Plymouth and Gibraltar with a considerable number of dispatches from the English Admiralty for Nelson and for several officers of his squadron; others are destined for the English troops at Malta; there are probably more than 150 separate letters addressed to officers in the English fleet in the Mediterranean that can give [an idea] about the English presence and perhaps about the horrible conspiration that was so happily discovered.[5] All was s[aved] at the moment the English commander disappeared to t[hrow] the dispatches overboard; he was hit by two balls and fell dead over his papers.
>
> This cutter had sailed from Plymouth on 11 M[arch][6] last. It was met on the 15th of this month [3 April 1804] at 10 nautical miles

[1]21 Germinal of year 12 of the French Republic; the French revolutionary calendar started with the proclamation of the French Republic on 22 September 1792; its years consisted of twelve months of 30 days each and an additional five (or six) days at the end of the year.

[2]The xebec (there are several spellings across the Mediterranean), from Turkish şebeke, was a three-masted Mediterranean sailing ship, usually rigged with lateen sails, with a narrow floor to achieve high speed, which made it the favoured vessel for corsairs. It was characterised by a long overhanging bowsprit, a wide beam and aft-set mizzen mast

[3]Viot himself gives the captain's name as 'Sciuffino' in a letter to the Minister of the Navy (CADN, Centre des Archives Diplomatiques de Nantes: Barcelone A 43 *, page 91, letter of 22 floreal an 12 = 10 May 1804). Nice had been part of Savoy since the 14th century, so that there was a strong influence of the Italian (rather: Ligurian) language and it appears probable that 'Escoffier' was a French version of the captain's real name.

[4]Barcelona.

[5]This most probably refers to the execution of the Duke d'Enghien on 21 March 1804 for supposedly aiding Britain and plotting against France.

[6]Viot probably used the name of the month of the old calender here, as the only month in the French Revolutionary calendar that starts with an M is Messidor that usually begins on 19 June (though in a leap year on 18 June) and it appears highly unlikely that it had taken the *Swift* cutter about ten months rather than 23 days.

[off the coast?] by the French privateer who had sailed the sa[me] day in the morning from [?] and heading to the Roads of Catalonia, between Palomar and St-Antony.[1]

We have [lost?] a sailor in this [action?].

I got the dispatches delivered immediately after the arrival of the privateer in port; they were treated with vinegar; I got them dried, [?] and wrapped into a case, which weighed about 30 to 35 pounds marc,[2] sent all to Perpignan to be handed over to the Prefect of the Department of the Eastern Pyrenees. I requested that the case would be passed on by the fastest and safest [means] to the address of the Minister of the Navy and Colonies – according to article 68 of the regulations on the [?] in force since 2 Prairial of year 11 [= 21 May 1803]. For this purpose I sent my nephew, C[ol] Dornac, candidate for attaché to this office, dispatching him as an extraordinary courier, accompanied by my valet, a brave soldier, who served well in the light infantry of the Republic.

> They left Barcelona on Sunday 18th [= 6 April 1804] at one o'clock after midnight; they should have arrived at Perpignan yesterday[3] early enough for the dispatches to [be] posted with the courier who was due to leave on the 20th in the evening from Perpignan to Paris, so that it is probable that you receive the parcel one delivery before the present letter . . .[4]

[1]The original has here 'palamor et St-[?]', which I assume to refer to El Palomar (an inland town, south of Valencia, which was regarded part of Catalonia) and Sant Antoni (port on Ibiza).

[2]The original has here 'livre de poids de marc'. Before the metric system was introduced in France on 12 February 1812, the weights provided two types of pounds, the 'livre de poids' (subdivided into 12 ounces) and the 'livre de poids de marc' (subdivided into 2 marcs of 8 ounces each, which made it 16 ounces in total); the 'livre de poids de marc' weighed 489.5 g, which makes the weight of the described case about 15 kg.

[3]20 Germinal an 12 = 8 April 1804.

[4]CAD (Centre des Archives Diplomatiques, La Courneuve); Correspondance consulaire et commerciale / Barcelone, vol 21 (1802–1806); microfilm P 9380, pp. 194-5: '... que samedi 17 de ce mois [= 5 April 1804] le chebeck Corsaire français, l'Espérance, Capitaine Escoffier de Nice, est entré dans ce port, Conduisant une prise extrémement importante par son objet, c'est le Cutter Aviso Anglais le Swif[t] Capitaine Leake, venant de Plymouth et de Gibraltar, avec une quantité considérable de depêches de l'amirauté Anglaise pour Nelson et pour divers officiers de son Excadre; d'autres sont destinées pour les Troupes Anglaises qui sont à Malthe, il y a en entre plus de 150 lettres particulieres qui sont adressées aux officiers des Armées Navales Anglaises dans la Mediter[ranée] et qui peuvent donner des [?] sur ce que se presen[ce] Angleterre, et peut-être sur l'horrible Conspiration qu[e] vient d'être si heureusement decouverte, le tout a été s[ecuré] au moment où le commandant Anglais se disparaît à j[èter] des Depêches à la Mer, il á été frappe de deux balles est tombé mort sur ses papiers. / Ce Cutter etait parti de Plymouth le 11 M[?]

The detailed account of what he had done was probably motivated by a certain concern about being reproached for having decided on the wrong way of action to take. Apparently Viot had had an argument with one of his subordinates, 'C^en^ Molin', who wanted to carry the precious parcel in person. In order to avert possible rebuke in this respect, he mentions at the end of his letter Molin's 'zeal' to be commissioned with the transporting of the parcel. Viot, however, comments that this zealous man had been for three months so 'gravely' incapacitated that he was still convalescent and unable to stand the 'fatigue of running the post for a day and two nights without rest'.[1] Citizen Molin was not content having his zeal mentioned in the consul's letter. Instead, the same day that Viot wrote his report to his superiors, he gave his own view of Viot's proceedings to the Minister of Foreign Affairs, Talleyrand, stressing in a rather confused way that he had agreed neither with the means of transport nor with the choice of addressee of the parcel:

> The correspondence of the British cabinet with Lord Nelson was sent in successive stages instead of directly, in view of the importance of the object, to the Minister of the Navy. I beseech your Excellence to believe that I am too anxious to pay tribute to your area of responsibility not to have told Citizen Viot that I thought that the parcel should have been sent to your department; but he insisted to address it according to his views

dernier, il a été rencontré le 15 de ce mois à 10 milles [de] mer par le corsaire français qui etait sorti le mê[me] jour au matin de part-[?] et pris sur la [rade?] de Catalogne entre Palamor et St-[?] / Nous avons p[?] un matelot dans ce [?] / Je me sais fait remettre les depêches aussi[tôt] que le Corsaire est entré dans le port; elles ont été passées aus Vinaigre, Je les ai faites secher, et les [ai?] ensuite [clapées?] et renfermées, dans une valise qui en [?] pleine et pése de 30 à 35 livres pieds de Marc envoye le tout à Perpignan pour être remis a[u] Préfet du département des Pyrennés orientales [?] j'ai prié de faire passer la valise par la [?] la plus prompte et la plus sure à l'adresse du Ministre de la Marine et des Colonies – Conforment à l'Article 68 du règlement sur les armem[?] en course du 2 prairial an 11. J'ai fait partir à cet effet le C^ne^ Dornac, mon neveu, Élève attaché à ce Commissariat, que j'ai depêché en courrier Extraordinaire – accompagné de mon Domestique, brave Militaire, qui abien servi dans les troupes légères de la République. / Ils sont sortés de Barcelone Dimanche 18 à une heure après minuit; ils ont du arriver à Perpignan hier assez tôt pour que les depêches [?] Expediées par le Courrier qui a du partir le 20 au soir de Perpignan pour Paris, [ensuite?] qu'il est probable que la reception de cet envoi précedera d'un ordinaire celle de la présente.'

[1]CAD (Centre des Archives Diplomatiques, La Courneuve); Correspondance consulaire et commerciale / Barcelone, vol 21 (1802–1806); microfilm P 9380, p. 195: 'Le zèle ... mais il-y-a trois mois qu'il est après gravement incomodé, il est à [p?] Convalecent et n'auroit pas pu suporter la fatigue courir la poste pendant un jour et deux nuits sa[ns] arrêter.'

> Allow me, Citizen Minister, to have the honour to inform you, in order that if something [= the parcel] does not come from me, it may not be interpreted as clumsiness, and that I may have the happiness to retain your estimation and your favour.
>
> The object was, I think, important enough that [unlike] Consul Viot I would have made it my duty to take departure and surveillance en route out of mercenaries' hands until I leave [the parcel] in your hands; but it is known that [after a] long illness my strength is not sufficient to have allowed me to take the post from Barcelona to Perpignan, to then go by stagecoach through the night and [up to] Paris, ...[1]

It appears that, keen as everybody was to be connected with the precious parcel, they all wanted to pass it on rather than keep it. Even the Minster of the Navy and the Colonies, Denis Decrès, felt obliged to report to the First Consul, Napoleon Bonaparte, how much he had tried to get it – merely to pass it on to him. He wrote on '30 G^al^. An 12 de la République française [= 18 April 1804]' to 'Citizen Consul':

> I have the honour to send you some documents relating to a parcel that was announced as very important and that had been sent by post from Perpignan to my address. This parcel has been since midday until 9 o'clock in the evening the object of my solicitude. During the afternoon I three times vainly sent [somebody] to the post and they were always rejected with the same response that nothing had arrived. At 9 o'clock I sent my secretary general to Captain La Valette[2] so that he would order a special inquiry. It was only after his

[1]CAD (Centre des Archives Diplomatiques, La Courneuve); Correspondance consulaire et commerciale / Barcelone, vol 21 (1802-1806); microfilm P 9380, 196-197: 'La Correspondance de cabinet britannique avec Lord Nelson a été envoyée de cascade en cascade au lieu de[?] directement, vû l'importance de l'objet, au Ministre de la Marine. Je supplie votre Excellence de croire que je suis trop jaloux de rendre hommage à vos attributions pour que je n'ayer par dit au Citoyen Viot que se croyais que le paquet était de votre département: mais il a persisté à l'adresser selon sa manière de voir. / Permettre-moi, Citoyen Ministre, d'avoir d'honneur de vous en prévenir, a fin que cequi ne vient pas de moi ne me soit pas impreté à gaucherie, et que j'aye le bonheur de me conserver votre estime et votre bienveillance. / L'objet était, je crois, assez important pour qu'au [contraire?] du C^ul^ Viot, je me soit fait au devoir d'eu oter le départ et la surveillance en route à des mains mercenaires, jusqu'à ce que je laisse mis dans les vôtres; mais il est notoire que, [?] longue maladie mes forces ne m'auraient pas encore permis de courir nécessairement la poste du Barcelone à Perpignan, de courir ensuite en chaise de poste la nuit et le [four? fusque? á] Paris, ...'

[2]Antoine Marie Chamans, comte de Lavalette (1769–1830), trusted friend of Napoleon Bonaparte, had become 'Directeur Général des Postes' on 19 March 1804, a position that he maintained until the end of Napoleon's reign.

return that I finally got to know that Captain La Valette had passed the parcel on to you.[1]

A day after Napoleon Bonaparte received the dispatches destined for the British Mediterranean fleet, Nelson learnt of the loss. On 19 April 1804 he wrote to Lady Hamilton not only about the loss of information for his fleet, but also about his worry that the enemy would gain information that they might publish (Doc. No. 313). Such a publication might cause damage to his private reputation as well as to the public interest. Both these worries do not appear to have been justified.

Back in Barcelona Consul Viot, after having discharged the precious parcel of documents from the *Swift*, looked after the prize. On '8 floréal an douze [= 26 April 1804]' he reported his expenses to the Minister of the Navy and on '22 floreal an 12 [= 10 May 1804]' he sent another letter, enclosing a list of (further?) documents that he had found on board the *Swift*.[2] He enumerated letters addressed to the fleet off Toulon, the *Swift*'s muster book, a safe conduct signed by Decrès for a packet boat operating between Dover and Calais, several letters from the Admiralty and even four letters signed by Nelson; to this Viot added an 'inventory of cordage and artillery pieces found in the vessel', but did not mention any private letters or pictures.[3]

Meanwhile, on 5 May 1804, Nelson learned from Alexander Scott, whom he had sent to Barcelona that the French consul was boasting about the pictures of Lady Hamilton that he got from the *Swift* (Doc. No. 319). Beyond the consul's bragging no attempts at publication or mere spreading of the information gained from the taking of the *Swift* cutter appear to have been made. As shown above, neither the consul nor his superiors at the Foreign Office nor the Minister of the Navy even looked at the contents of the dispatches sent to Paris. It is unclear what was done

[1]Archives Nationales [de France]; AF IV 1191 [correspondance du Ministère de la Marine avec the Premier Consul; AF stands for 'Secrétairerie d'état impériale (an VIII-1815)'], p. 212: 'J'ai l'honneur de vous adresser les Pieces relatives à un Paquet annoncé comme très important qui avait été mis à la poste à mon adresse, a Perpignan. Ce paquet a été depuis midi jusqu'à 9 heures du soir l'objet de ma sollicitude. J'ai envoyé vainement trois fois à la poste dans la soirée, et sur la réponse toujour réjétée qu'il n'était point arrivé, J'ai envoyé a 9 heures mon Sécrétaire Général au C^ne^ La Valette pour qu'il en prescrivit une recherche extraordinaire. Ce n'a été qu'à son retour que J'ai [seu ?] enfin que le C^ne^. La Valette vous avoit adressé ce paquet.'

[2]CADN (Centre des Archives Diplomatiques de Nantes): Barcelone A 43 * [French consul's letter book to other ministeries], pp. 90, 91.

[3]CADN (Centre des Archives Diplomatiques de Nantes): Barcelone A 43 * [French consul's letter book to other ministeries], p. 91 'les pièces sont accompaniés de l'inventaire des agrès, apparaux et artillerie existant / trouvé dans le bâtiment'.

with them at the First Consul's Office. I could not trace them and was told at the National Archives in Paris that the Empress (Marie Louise) and Talleyrand destroyed a great number of Napoleonic documents after his fall from power. The collection at the Archives of the Foreign Office in Paris, too, is anything but impressive. For the years 1803 to 1805 the material about 'England' consists of a meagre assembly of documents, such as lists of ships, letters from merchants, prisoners and diplomats.[1] Significantly the collection holds a printed 'List of Papers, Presented by His Majesty's Command, to Both Houses of Parliament, 24th January 1805',[2] thus showing that French knowledge of British undertakings was available in the public domain anyway. At the same time this item indicates why the French did not have any need to publish captured papers: they simply did not have to defend their policies in any political institution, such as a parliament.

[1]CAD (La Courneuve); Correspondance politique / sous-séries Angleterre, vol 602 (24 7bre 1803 – 31 X^{bre} 1805); microfilm P 11777.

[2]CAD (La Courneuve); Correspondance politique / sous-séries Angleterre, vol 602 (24 7bre 1803 – 31 X^{bre} 1805); microfilm P 11777, pp. 283–325.

APPENDIX 7

DOCUMENTATION OF FLOW OF LETTERS IN CHAPTER IV (1803–1805)

No. of document	Date of document	Sent via (information about source in brackets, if other document)	Information about receiving letter(s)
259	10.05.1803		
260	13.05.1803		
261	–	'the duke's servant' [262]	
262	18.05.1803		
263	19.05.1803		
264	20.05.1803		'Your dear kind letters are just come'
265	–		
266	21.05.1803		
267	22.05.1803 23.05.1803		
268	25.05.1803 26.05.1803 30.05.1803 02.06.1803 2 o'clock 04.06.1803		
269	10.06.1803 11.06.1803	'How this letter will get home I know not. It will be read by every post office from Naples to London . . . this letter I send to Gibbs to send by the post'	
270	20.06.1803		
271	25.06.1803		
272	– 08.07.1803		
273	12.07.1803 18.07.1803 21.07.1803		
274	01.08.1803		'You letter of May 31st: which came under cover to Mr: Noble of Naples enclosing Davison's correspondence with Plyh: arrived by the Phœbe two days ago'

No. of document	Date of document	Sent via (information about source in brackets, if other document)	Information about receiving letter(s)
275	10.08.1803		
276	21.08.1803		
277	–		
278	–		
279	From LH	–	–
280	24.08.1803		
281	24.08.1803		
282	–		
283	26.08.1803		'By the Canopus ad[l]: Campbell I have received all your truly kind and affectionate letters from May 20th: to July 3rd: [with the exception of one dated May 31st: sent to Naples)'
284	26.08.1803		
285	2nd codicil	–	–
286	08.09.1803		
287	10.09.1803 16.09.1803		
288	18.09.1803		
289	–	'As this ship goes by Malta, I do not write a line by her unless she should pick them up at Gib[r]'	
290	26.09.1803		
291	05.10.1803		'By a letter from Davison of the 15th: Aug[t]: sent by Lisbon which reached me on the 1st: of this month I was made truly happy by hearing

No. of document	Date of document	Sent via (information about source in brackets, if other document)	Information about receiving letter(s)
			that my Dearest Emma was at Southend and well, and last night I had the happiness of receiving your own dear letters of June 26th: from Hilborough and of Augt: 3rd: from Southend'
292	06.10.1803	'I hope that Captain Murray will be the bearer of a letter from me to you'	
293	18.10.1803 22.10.1803		'Your truly kind and affectionate letters from July 17th: to Augt: 24th: all arrived safe in the Childers the 6th: of this month . . . I have receiv'd your letter with Lord Williams + Mr: Kemble's about Mr: Palmer'
294	21.10.1803		
295	23.10.1803	'the Ship is on the Wing + this is the last moment to say'	
296	–		
297	07.12.1803 13.12.1803 25.12.1803	'Friend Gayner an honest Quaker who lives at Roses in Spain has taken charge of a letter for you he will enclose it to his correspondant at Bristol'	

No. of document	Date of document	Sent via (information about source in brackets, if other document)	Information about receiving letter(s)
298	26.12.1803	'The Phoebe joined me here, and carries my letters to Gibraltar'; 'the Phœbe saild for Gibralter with the English letters on Dec^{r}: 27th:' [322]	
299	13.01.1804		'I rec^{d}: on the 9th: your letters of Sep^{r}: 29th: Oct^{r}: 2, 7, 10, 12, 17th: 21 Nov^{r}: 8th: 5th: to the 24th:'
300	20.01.1804		
301	20.01.1804		
302	10.02.1804		'all your letters to Dec^{r}: 27th: I found just arrived'
303	3rd codicil		
304	25.02.1804	[on the outsiden of the manuscript are a stamp 'CATALUÑA' and the handwritten notes 'Via Lisboa y London' and 'Inglaterra']. . . 'February 25th by Barcelona' [328] [referring to 305?]	
305	25.02.1804	'February 25th by Barcelona' [328] [referring to 304?]	
–	02.03.1804	'March 2nd' [328]; 'by Barcelona; in March, three' [331]	
306	14.03.1804	'the British Fair cutter I hope is arrived safe She has three packets from me to England'; '15th, by Rosas' [328]; 'by Barcelona; in March, three' [331]	'Young Faddy my dearest Emma brought me two days ago your dear and most kind letter of Nov^{r}: 26th:'

No. of document	Date of document	Sent via (information about source in brackets, if other document)	Information about receiving letter(s)
307	– 19.03.1804	'March 19th: the gale seems abating and I shall get off the vessel for Gibralter'; 'I wrote you yesterday going safe thro' Spain' [308]; '19th, by Gibraltar' [328]; 'by Barcelona; in March, three' [331]	
308	–	'I take my chance of a letter . . . I shall write in a few days by Gib^{r}: but I would not miss the trial of friend Quaker Gayner' [308]	'I rec^{d} last night your two letters of Jan^{ry} 15th and 28th'
309	–	'I shall write in a few days by Gib^{r}:' [308]	
310	02.04.1804 09.04.1804 14.04.1804		'Cap^{n}: Capel brought me your letters sent by the Thisbe from Gibralter . . . found none but Dec^{r}: + early in January . . . at last I found one without a date'
311	4th codicil		
312	07.04.1804	'I send this by Captain Layman'; '14th by Captain Layman' [326]; 'by Barcelona; . . . in April six' [331]	
313	10.04.1804	'I have wrote fully and intend to send them by the Argo who I expect to join every minute'; 'April 10th, by Rosas' [328]; 'by Barcelona; . . . in April six' [331]	'I have received all your truly kind and affectionate letters to Jan^{ry}: 25th: by the Thisbe and last night your letter of Jan^{y}: 13th: by Naples'

No. of document	Date of document	Sent via (information about source in brackets, if other document)	Information about receiving letter(s)
314	13.04.1804 To Horatia		
315	19.04.1804	'I shall continue to write thro' Spain . . . Captain Hollowell is so good as to take home for me wine as by the enclosed list, and if I can some honey'; '19th, . . . by the *Argo*' [328]; 'by Barcelona; . . . in April six' [331]	'your letter of feb[ry]: 12th: thro' M[r]: Falconet I have received I know they are all read therefore never sign your name'
316	21.04.1804	'21st, . . . by the *Argo*' [328]; 'by Barcelona; . . . in April six' [331]	
317	23.04.1804	'I have sent last night a box of Marischino Veratable of Zara . . . Hollowell parted last night but being in sight I am sending a frigate with a letter to the Admiralty'; 'Captain Layman, Captian Hallowell, and I believe another packet of letters for you, are now at Gibraltar.' [318]; '23rd, by the *Argo*' [328]; 'by Barcelona; . . . in April six' [331]	
318	28.04.1804	'28th, by Rosas' [328]; 'by Barcelona; . . . in April six' [331]	
319	03.05.1804		
320	03.05.1804	'I am sending a letter to Madrid I cannot let the opportunity slip of saying we are alive this day'; 'May 3rd, by Barcelona' [328]; 'by Barcelona; . . . in May, five; in June to the 19th, three; June 27th, July 1st' [331]	
321	05.05.1804	'5th, by Rosas' [328]; 'by Barcelona; . . . in May, five' [331]	

No. of document	Date of document	Sent via (information about source in brackets, if other document)	Information about receiving letter(s)
322	22.05.1804	'I shall write by Gib^{r}: in a few days this goes thro' Spain by the care of friend Gayner'; 'I wrote you on the 22nd: through Roses in Spain' [323]; 'I wrote you on the 22nd: thro' friend Gayner, the Quaker at Roses' [324]; '12th, by Rosas' [324] [error in date by Nelson or Morrison?]; 'by Barcelona; . . . in May, five' [331]	'Your two letters via Lisbon arrived the same day with those in the Leviathan'; 'from you I had letters April 5th: and the papers to April 9th: receiv'd May 10th with a convoy' [325]
323	27.05.1804 30.05.1804	'I shall write in a few days by Barcelona this goes by Gibralter'; '30th, 31st, by Gibraltar' [328]; 'by Barcelona; . . . in May, five' [331]	
324	30.05.1804	'May 30th: . . . I write you this day by Barcelona' [323]; 'I am writing this day by way of Gibralter + Barcelona to take both chances'; 'I have sent you a case of macaroni by the Agincourt'; '30th, 31st, by Gibraltar' [328] [Nelson appears to have forgotten that one of the two letters was sent 'by Barcelona']; 'by Barcelona; . . . in May, five' [331]	
325	06.06.1804	'this goes thro' friend Gayner'; 'I wrote to you on the 6th: via Roses' [326]; 'June 6th, by Rosas' [328]; 'by Barcelona; . . . in June to the 19th, three' [331]	

No. of document	**Date of document**	**Sent via (information about source in brackets, if other document)**	**Information about receiving letter(s)**
326	10.06.1804	'this goes by Barcelona'; 'I wrote you last on the 10th *viâ* Barcelona' [327]; '10th, by Barcelona' [328]; 'by Barcelona; . . . in June to the 19th, three' [331]	
327	17.06.1804 18.06.1804	'19th, by Rosas' [328]; 'by Barcelona; . . . in June to the 19th, three' [331]	
328	27.06.1804	'I have wrote you . . . a letter by Roses of June 27th: not yet gone' [329]; 'June 27th' [331]; 'I wrote you . . . on the 8th: a letter dated June 27th:' [332]	'Last night, my dearest Emma, I received your three letters of April 13th and 22nd, and May 13th, by way of Naples. It is the only scrap of a pen we have had from England since April 5th, by Leviathan'
329	01.07.1804	'I wrote you yesterday by Gibraltar' [330] [referring to this letter?]	'Your letters of Ap^{l}: 13th: 22nd: + May 13th: through M^{r}: Falconet came safe a few days ago'
330	01.07.1804	'I have a moment, and but a moment, to write you a line through Spain. . . . All my public dispatches go for Gibraltar this day.'; 'July 1st' [331]; 'I wrote you . . . July 4th: by way of Barcelona' [332]	
331	09.07.1804 11.07.1804 12.07.1804	'I send this through Mr. Falconet'; 'I wrote you . . . 9th: and 12th: by way of Naples' [332]	'Last night, my dearest Emma, I received your most kind letter of May 24th'

No. of document	Date of document	Sent via (information about source in brackets, if other document)	Information about receiving letter(s)
332	14.07.1804		
333	12.08.1804	'as the Childers is going to Roses . . . I take my chance of the Post'	'the Ambuscade arrived this day fortnight . . . By her I receiv'd your letters of May 14th: 22nd: + 30th: via Lisbon, and of April 9th:, 18, 15th: May 10th: 18th: 29th: June 1st: 5th:'
334	13.08.1804	'by the Kent I shall write fully' [333]; 'the Kent left us 3 days ago and as the wind has been perfectly fair since her departure I think she will have a very quick passage and arrive long before this letter, but' [337]	'The Ambuscade brought me your letters to June 5th, *viz.* April 9th, 15th, 18th, May 14, 22, 30, *viâ* Lisbon. May 10, 18, 29, June 1, 4, 6, by sea'
335	13.08.1804		
336	13.08.1804		
337	20.08.1804	'as a ship is going to Roses I will not omit the opportunity of writing thro' Spain'	
338	22.08.1804		'The ship was gone for Rosas, when the Spencer yesterday, nineteen days from Plymouth, joined us, by whom I had the happiness of receiving your letters of *viâ* Lisbon, June 28th, and one without a date through Mr. Marsden, July 4th, 7th, 10th, and 19th'

No. of document	Date of document	Sent via (information about source in brackets, if other document)	Information about receiving letter(s)
339	27.08.1804	'this goes by Triumph'; 'yesterday I wrote to you thro' Spain' [340]	'Your dear kind letter by friend Gayner of June 22nd: + July 10th: are just receiv'd and those by Spencer to July 19th:'
340	31.08.1804	'this goes by Naples'	
341	09.09.1804		
342	22.09.1804	'I can no longer defer sending off my dispatches to catch the Triumph at Gibraltar'	'Your two letters of August 7th and 13th I have received'
343	29.09.1804		
344	02.10.1804		'It was only yesterday, my dearest Emma, that I received your letter of July 1st, it having travelled in a Spanish smuggling boat to the coast of Italy and returned again to Spain, the boat not having met any of our ships'
345	05.10.1804	'I wrote you my dearest Emma this morning by way of Lisbon' [346]	'Hallowell is just arriv'd with your dear dear letters'
346	07.10.1804		
347	10.10.1804		'Your last letters were to August 27th'
348	13.10.1804		'your letter is Sep^{r}: 16th: your last is Aug^{t}: 27th:'

No. of document	Date of document	Sent via (information about source in brackets, if other document)	Information about receiving letter(s)
349	31.10.1804		
350	??.11.1804	'this letter . . . goes by way of Lisbon'	'I yesterday my dearest beloved Emma had the happiness of receiving your dear kind + affectionate letters of Sep^{r}: 16th: 20th: 27th: + Oct^{r}: 1st:'
351	06.11.1804	'I will not allow Mr. Este to leave me without carrying a line from me'	
352	15.11.1804	'My last letters having been sent back from Roses not suffered to be landed'	
353	23.11.1804	'As all our communication with Spain is at an end I can now only expect to hear from my own dear Emma by the very slow mode of Admiralty vessels . . . this letter . . . goes although in M^{r}: Marsdens letter such a roundabout way . . .'	
354	04.12.1804	'I wrote you by the Ambuscade' [356]	
355	5th codicil		
356	19.12.1804	'I send this through M^{r}: F. at Naples'; 'I wrote you on the 19th through Mr. Falconet' [357]; 'Although . . . I have not heard that M^{r}: Falconet forwarded my other letter of Dec^{r}: 19th:' [358]	
357	30.12.1804	'this letter . . . it goes by way of Lisbon in the Admiralty packet, and will be smoked, cut, &c. &c. before it gets to you'	'I received by the Swiftsure your letters to October 29th'

No. of document	Date of document	Sent via (information about source in brackets, if other document)	Information about receiving letter(s)
358	14.01.1805	'I shell take the chance of another [letter] crossing the Continent'	
359	Poem by Lady Hamilton		
–	On or before 31.01.1805	'on January 31st, I sent friend Broadbent a letter for you' [360]	
360	18.02.1805 20.02.1805		'Your last letter was November 2nd'
361	09.03.1805 10.03.1805 31.03.1805 01.04.1805		'It is now from November 2d, that I have had a line from England . . . The box which you sent me in May 1804, is just arrived in the Diligent store-ship'
362	13.03.1805		'last night my dearest Emma I receiv'd your letters of Sep^{r}: 12th: by way of Naples Nov^{r}: 27th: Dec^{r}: 18th: 27th: 29th: + Jan^{ry}: 8th: sent by Amphion all those by Layman are lost
363	16.03.1805	'The Ship is just parting and I take the last moment to . . .'; 'March 16th, when the Renown went to Gibraltar' [371]	

No. of document	Date of document	Sent via (information about source in brackets, if other document)	Information about receiving letter(s)
364	30.03.1805		'Your letters my own dear beloved Emma by the Ambuscade to Feb^{ry}: 15th: came to me on the 26th:'
365	04.04.1805		
366	05.04.1805		
367	19.04.1805		
368	04.05.1805	'All letters sent by the Niger + Avenger are gone up the Mediterranean'	
369	09.05.1805	'In case any thing should happen to the Wasp who is going to England with my dispatches and your letters, I send a duplicate' [370]	
370	??.05.1805		
371	13.05.1805 20.05.1805	'I write this in case of meeting any vessel bound to England, when I shall close it'	'The Marquis Circello and Abb' Campbell came on board for a minute in a gale of wind, and with them your letters'
372	16.05.1805		
373	18.05.1805		
374	04.06.1805		
375	10.06.1805 11.06.1805	'I shall fill this up as we get on and write you another Line before the Vessel parts from the Fleet'	
376	12.06.1805		
377	16.06.1805	'As I am sending a vessel to Lisbon and a letter to the Admiralty to tell them I am so far on my return I would not you are sure omit writing you a Line'	

No. of document	Date of document	Sent via (information about source in brackets, if other document)	Information about receiving letter(s)
378	20.07.1805	'I have only a moment, this goes by a merchant Brig.'; 'I wrote you on the 20th: My Emma by a merchant Brig under cover to Mr: Marsden' [379]	
379	24.07.1805	'I shall write in a few days by Prevoyante, Mr: Mc: Coy' [378]	
380	18.08.1805	'as the Post will not go out untill eight oclock and you not get the letter till 11 or 12 oclock tomorrow I have ordered a Post office express to tell you of my arrival'	'I have not heard from my own Emma since last April by Abbe Campbell'
381	19.08.1805		'I have this moment got yours of last night from Merton . . . Mr. Marsden has just sent me your letter of August 10th'

SOURCES AND DOCUMENTS

Archives

British Library
Christie's Corporate Art Collection
Clive Richards Collection
Houghton Library
William L. Clements Library, University of Michigan
Huntington Library
Jean Kislak Collection
Nelson Museum Monmouth
National Maritime Museum
Pierpoint Morgan Library
Royal Naval Museum
The National Archives, Kew, Richmond, Surrey
US Naval Academy Museum

Published Works

Morrison, A. (ed.), *The Collection of Autograph Letters and Historical Documents formed by Alfred Morrison (Second Series, 1882–1893) – The Hamilton and Nelson Papers*, 2 vols (London, 1893).

Naish, George (ed.), *Nelson's Letters to His Wife and other Documents. 1785–1831* (London, 1958).

Nicolas, Nicholas Harris (ed.), *The Dispatches and Letters of Vice Admiral Lord Viscount Nelson*, 7 vols (London, 1997; first edition: 1844–46).

Pettigrew, T. J., *Memoirs of the Life of Vice-Admiral Lord Viscount Nelson, K.B., Duke of Bronté etc. etc. etc.*, 2 vols (London, 1849).

Russell, Jack, *Nelson and the Hamiltons* (first published 1969; Harmondsworth, Middlesex, 1972).

White, Colin (ed.), *Nelson. The New Letters* (Woodbridge, Suffolk, 2005).

Numerical List of Documents

Chapter I: The Beginning of an Enduring Relationship: June 1798–December 1800

1	To Lady Hamilton	13 June 1798	Jean Kislak: 1993.002.00.0001
2	Lady Hamilton to Nelson	17 June 1798	BL: Add. MS 34,989 f. 3
3	To Lady Hamilton		BL: Egerton 1614 ff. 1–2, no. 1
4	Lady Hamilton to Nelson	17 June 1798	BL: Add. MS 34,989 ff. 1–2
5	Lady Hamilton to Nelson	30 June 1798	NMM: CRK 20/55
6	To Lady Hamilton	22 July 1798	Huntington: HM 34077
7	To Sir William and Lady Hamilton	22 July 1798	Harrison, i, p. 256
8	To Lady Hamilton	11 Aug 1798	CRC/18
9	To Lady Hamilton	13 Aug 1798	RNM: 48/64
10	Lady Hamilton to Nelson	8 Sept 1798	BL: Add. MS 34,989 ff. 4–7
11	To Lady Hamilton	3 Oct 1798	BL: Add. MS 34,989 ff. 12–13
12	To Lady Hamilton	16 Oct 1798	BL: Egerton 1614 ff. 3–4, no. 2
13	Lady Hamilton to Nelson	20 Oct 1798	BL: Add. MS 34,989 ff. 14–15
14	To Lady Hamilton	24 Oct 1798	NMM: CRK/19/1
15	Lady Hamilton to Nelson	26 Oct 1798	BL: Add. MS 34,989 ff. 16–17
16	To Lady Hamilton	27 Oct 1798	RNM: 49/64
17	Lady Hamilton	27 Oct 1798	BL: Add. MS 34,989 ff. 18–24
18	Verses to 'Heart of Oak' by Lady Hamilton		BL: Add. MS 34,989 f. 25
19	Lady Hamilton to Nelson	2 Nov 1798	BL: Add. MS 34,989 ff. 26–27
20	To Lady Hamilton	22 Nov 1798	Monmouth: E 425
21	Lady Hamilton to Nelson	24 Nov 1798	BL: Add. MS 34,989 ff. 28–29

22	Lady Hamilton to Nelson		BL: Add. MS 34,989 ff. 30–31
23	Lady Hamilton to Nelson		BL: Add. MS 34,989 ff. 32–33
24	To Lady Hamilton		Monmouth: E 424
25	To Lady Hamilton		NMM: MON/1/111
26	To Lady Hamilton		CRC/19
27	To Ball with a postscript by Lady Hamilton		Morrison, I, pp. 37–8 (No. 374)
28	Draft for speech in Palermo	4 Mar 1799	Christie's, 3 Dec 2003, lot 224
29	To Lady Hamilton	19 May 1799	NMM: CRK/19/3
30	To Lady Hamilton	20 May 1799	NMM: CRK/19/4
31	To Lady Hamilton	21 May 1799	Nicolas, vii, p. clxxxii
32	To Lady Hamilton	[21 May 1799]	NMM: CRK/19/2
33	To Lady Hamilton	22 May 1799	Nicolas, vii, p. clxxxiii
34	Codicil to Nelson's will	25 May 1799	CRC
35	To Lady Hamilton	26 May 1799	Monmouth: E 444
36	Nelson, Lady Hamilton and Sir William to Ball	1 June 1799	Christie's, 3 Dec 2003; Nicolas, iii, p. 371
37	Lady Hamilton to Nelson	12 June 1799	NMM: CRK/20/56
38	To Lady Hamilton	16 June 1799	NMM: CRK/19/7
39	To Lady Hamilton with postscript	18 June 1799	BL: Egerton 1614 ff. 5–6, no. 3
40	To Lady Hamilton	19 June 1799	Monmouth: E71
41	To Lady Hamilton	20 June 1799	NMM: AGC/N/3
42	To Lady Hamilton	29 Jan 1800	CRC/24
43	To Lady Hamilton	3 Feb 1800	NMM: CRK/19/5
44	To Lady Hamilton	13 Feb 1800	Jean Kislak: 1988.013.00.0003
45	To Lady Hamilton	18 Feb 1800	Morrison, ii, p. 86 (No. 456)
46	To Lady Hamilton	20 Feb 1800	NMM: CRK/19/6
47	To Lady Hamilton	25 Feb 1800	CRC/25
48	To Lady Hamilton	4 Mar 1800	BL: Egerton 1614 ff. 7–8, no. 5
49	To Lady Hamilton	Nov 1800	BL: Egerton 1614 ff. 9–10, no. 6

50	To Lady Hamilton		Russell, p. 212
51	To Lady Hamilton		Nov or Dec 1800 Bonhams, 14 Nov 2012
52	To Lady Hamilton		Pettigrew, i, p. 392; Christie's, 21 June 1989, lot 234

Chapter II: The Baltic Campaign: January–June 1801

53	To Lady Nelson	13 Jan 1801	Huntington: HM 34039
54	To Lady Hamilton	14 Jan 1801	NMM: AGC/18/26
55	To Lady Nelson	16 Jan 1801	Huntington: HM 34040
56	To Lady Hamilton	17 Jan 1801	Pettigrew, i, p. 410
57	To Lady Nelson	20 Jan 1801	Huntington: HM 34041
58	To Lady Nelson	21 Jan 1801	Huntington: HM 34042
59	To Lady Hamilton	21 Jan 1801	BL: Egerton 1614 ff. 14–15, no. 8
60	To Lady Hamilton	24 Jan 1801	Pettigrew, i, p. 414
61	To Lady Hamilton	[24 Jan 1801]	Pettigrew, ii, p. 645
62	To Lady Hamilton	25 Jan 1801	Jean Kislak: 1993.151.00.0004
63	To Lady Hamilton	26 Jan 1801	Pettigrew, i, pp. 416–17 & ii, p. 645; Morrison, ii, p. 109 (No. 503); Christie's, 3 Dec 2009, lot 134
64	To Lady Hamilton	27 Jan 1801	Pettigrew, i, p. 417
65	To Lady Hamilton	28 Jan 1801	Monmouth: E 91
66	To Lady Hamilton	29 Jan 1801	BL: Egerton 1614 ff. 63–64, no. 9
67	To Lady Hamilton	[29 Jan 1801]	Pettigrew, i, p. 646
68	To Lady Hamilton	1 Feb 1801	Jean Kislak: 1989.037.00.0001
69	To Lady Hamilton	2 Feb 1801	Huntington: HM 34078

70	To Lady Hamilton (alias Mrs Thomson)	[3 Feb 1801]	Jean Kislak: 2004.006.00.0003
71	To Lady Nelson	3 Feb 1801	Huntington: HM 34043
72	To Lady Hamilton	4 Feb 1801	Pettigrew, i, pp. 421–2 and ii, p. 467; Morrison, ii, p. 111 (No. 507)
73	To Lady Hamilton		BL: Egerton 1614 ff. 18–19, no. 10
74	To Lady Hamilton (alias Mrs Thomson)	[5 Feb 1801]	Jean Kislak: 1989.037.00.0002
75	To Lady Hamilton (alias Mrs Thomson)	[6 Feb 1801]	Pettigrew, ii, pp. 650; Morrison, ii, p. 113 (No. 510)
76	To Lady Hamilton	6 Feb 1801	Houghton: MS Lowell 10
77	To Lady Hamilton	8 Feb 1801	CRC/28
78	To Lady Hamilton	[8 Feb 1801]	Morrison, ii, p. 113 (No. 511)
79	To Lady Hamilton	9 Feb 1801	Pettigrew, i, p. 423
80	To Lady Hamilton		NMM: WAL/1
81	To Lady Hamilton		NMM: WAL/2
82	To Lady Hamilton	11 Feb 1801	NMM: SUT/2
83	To Lady Hamilton	11 Feb 1801	Pettigrew, i, p. 424; Morrison, ii, p. 113 (No. 514)
84	To Lady Hamilton	12 Feb 1801	Christie's sale 1568, Nov 2014, lot 23
85	To Lady Hamilton	12 Feb 1801	Pettigrew, i, p. 424.
86	To Lady Hamilton	13 Feb 1801	Pettigrew, i, p. 425; Morrison, ii, p. 114 (No. 513); Christie's, 3 Dec 2003, lot 139
87	To Lady Hamilton	14 Feb 1801	Pettigrew, i, p. 42; Sichel, p. 520
88	To Lady Hamilton	15 Feb 1801	Pettigrew, i, pp. 425–426.

89	To Lady Hamilton	16 Feb 1801	NMM: CRK/19/8
90	To Lady Hamilton (alias Mrs Thomson)		NMM: CRK/19/10
91	To Lady Hamilton	16 Feb 1801	Jean Kislak: 1990.035.00.0001
92	To Lady Hamilton	17 Feb 1801	Morrison, ii, pp. 116–17 (No. 518)
93	To Lady Hamilton (alias Mrs Thomson)		Huntington: HM 34082
94	To Lady Hamilton	17 Feb 1801	BL: Egerton 1614 ff. 20–21, no. 11
95	To Lady Hamilton	17 Feb 1801	BL: Egerton 1614 ff. 22–23, no. 12
96	To Lady Hamilton	18 Feb 1801	Jean Kislak: 1993.151.00.005
97	To Lady Hamilton	19 Feb 1801	Huntington: HM 34079
98	To Lady Hamilton	19 Feb 1801	Morrison, ii, p. 119 (No. 524)
99	To Lady Hamilton (alias Mrs Thomson)		Morrison, ii, p. 119 (No. 523)
100	To Lady Hamilton		Huntington: HM 34083
101	To Lady Hamilton	19 Feb 1801	Huntington: HM 34080
102	To Lady Hamilton	20 Feb 1801	NMM: CRK/19/9
103	To Lady Hamilton (alias Mrs Thomson)	20 Feb 1801	Huntington: HM 34081
104	To Lady Hamilton	20 Feb 1801	Huntington: HM 34044
105	To Lady Hamilton	22 Feb 1801	Pettigrew, i, pp. 430–31; Morrison, ii, pp. 120–21 (No. 527)
106	To Lady Hamilton (alias Mrs Thompson)	[23 Feb 1801]	William L. Clements Library: Hubert S. Smith, vol. 1 'Naval Affairs'

107	To Lady Hamilton	24 Feb 1801	Huntington: HM 34045
108	To Lady Hamilton	27 Feb 1801	Pettigrew, i, pp. 431–2; Morrison, ii, pp. 121–2 (No. 529)
109	Verses from Lady Hamilton to Nelson		Morrison, ii, p. 143 (No. 572)
110	To Lady Hamilton	1 Mar 1801	Morrison, ii, p. 122 (No. 530); Christie's, 19 Oct 2005, lot 19; Christie's, 20 June 1990, lot 224
111	To Lady Hamilton	1 Mar 1801	Morrison, ii, pp. 122–3 (No. 531)
112	To Lady Hamilton	1 Mar 1801	Houghton: MS Lowell 10
113	To Lady Hamilton	2 Mar 1801	Houghton: pf MS Eng 196.5 (22)
114	To Lady Hamilton	3 Mar 1801	Pierpont Morgan: MA321
115	To Lady Hamilton	4 Mar 1801	Huntington: HM 34084
116	To Lady Hamilton		Huntington: HM 34085
117	To Lady Nelson	4 Mar 1801	NMM: AGC 17/10 BL: Add MS 28333,f f. 3–4
118	Duplicate of Nelson's will of 5 Mar 1801	16 March 1801	CRC
119	To Lady Hamilton	6 Mar 1801	Pettigrew, i, p. 436; Morrison, ii, p. 125 (No. 537)
120	First codicil to Nelson's last	6 Mar 1801	CRC will of 5 Mar 1801

121	To Lady Hamilton	6 Mar 1801	Pettigrew, i, p. 437; Morrison, ii, pp. 126–7 (No. 539)
122	To Lady Hamilton	7 Mar 1801	CRC
123	To Lady Hamilton	[8 Mar 1801]	Pettigrew, i, p. 439
124	To Lady Hamilton	9 Mar 1801	Morrison, ii, p. 127 (No. 541)
125	To Lady Hamilton	9 Mar 1801	Morrison, ii, p. 127 (No. 541)
126	To Lady Hamilton	10 Mar 1801	Pettigrew, i, p. 439; Morrison, ii, pp. 127–8 (No. 542)
127	To Lady Hamilton	11 Mar 1801	BL: Egerton 1614 ff. 24–25, no. 13
128	To Lady Hamilton	11 Mar 1801	Christie's Corporate Art: PH 431
129	To Lady Hamilton (alias Mrs Thomson)		Morrison, ii, pp. 129–30 (No. 545)
130	To Lady Hamilton (alias Mrs Thomson)		Morrison, ii, p. 130 (No. 546)
131	To Lady Hamilton	13 Mar 1801	BL: Egerton 1614 f. 26, no. 14
132	Duplicate of second codicil to Nelson's last will of 5 Mar 1801	16 Mar 1801	CRC
133	To Lady Hamilton	17 Mar 1801	NMM: MON/1/18
134	To Lady Hamilton	19 Mar 1801	Christie's Corporate Art: PH 431
135	To Lady Hamilton	20 Mar 1801	Pettigrew, i, p. 447.
136	To Lady Hamilton	21 Mar 1801	BL: Egerton 1614 ff. 28–29, no. 15
137	To Lady Hamilton	21 Mar 1801	Morrison, ii, p. 131 (No. 549)
138	To Lady Hamilton	23 Mar 1801	Pettigrew, i, p. 448.
139	To Lady Hamilton	26 Mar 1801	BL: Egerton 1614 f. 32, no. 17

140	To Lady Hamilton	30 Mar 1801	Pettigrew, i, p. 452; Morrison, ii, p. 132 (No. 551)
141	To Lady Hamilton	2 April 1801	BL: Egerton 1614 ff. 34–35, no. 18; CRC/33
142	To Lady Hamilton	5 April 1801	BL: Egerton 1614 ff. 36–37, no. 19
143	To Lady Hamilton	5 April 1801	Huntington: HM 34086
144	To Lady Hamilton	9 April 1801	BL: Egerton 1614 ff. 38–39, no. 20
145	To Lady Hamilton (alias Mrs Thomson)	9 April 1801	William L. Clements Library: Hubert S. Smith, vol. 1 'Naval Affairs'
146	To Lady Hamilton	11 April 1801	BL: Egerton 1614 ff. 40–41, no. 21
147	To Lady Hamilton	13 April 1801	BL: Egerton 1614 ff. 42–43, no. 22
148	To Lady Hamilton	14 April 1801	Pettigrew, ii, pp. 31–2
149	To Lady Hamilton	15 April 1801	BL: Egerton 1614 ff. 44–45, no. 23
150	To Lady Hamilton	17 April 1801	Huntington: HM 34087
151	To Lady Hamilton	20 April 1801	Huntington: HM 34088
152	To Lady Hamilton	23 April 1801	Huntington: HM 34089
153	To Lady Hamilton	25 April 1801	BL: Egerton 1614 ff. 46–47, no. 24
154	To Lady Hamilton	27 April 1801	Huntington: HM 23635
155	To Lady Hamilton	28 April 1801	US Naval Academy Museum
156	To Lady Hamilton	2 May 1801	Pettigrew, ii, p. 50; Morrison, ii, pp. 143–4 (No. 573)

157	To Lady Hamilton	[5 May 1801]	Pettigrew, ii, p. 50; Morrison, ii, pp.144 (No. 575)
158	To Lady Hamilton		BL: Egerton 1614 ff. 48–49, No. 25 and ff. 51–52, No. 27
159	To Lady Hamilton	5 May 1801	BL: Egerton 1614 ff. 53–54, No. 28
160	To Lady Hamilton	8 May 1801	BL: Egerton 1614 ff. 55–56, No. 29
161	To Lady Hamilton	8 May 1801	Huntington: HM 34090
162	To Lady Hamilton	8 May 1801	Pettigrew, ii, pp. 54–55
163	To Lady Hamilton	8 May 1801	Pettigrew, ii, p. 56
164	To Lady Hamilton	11 May 1801	BL: Egerton 1614 ff. 57–58, no. 30
165	To Lady Hamilton	12 May 1801	BL: Egerton 1614 ff. 59–60, no. 31
166	To Lady Hamilton	15 May 1801	BL: Egerton 1614 ff. 61–62, no. 32
167	To Lady Hamilton	15 May 1801	Pettigrew, ii, p. 68
168	To Lady Hamilton	17 May 1801	Pettigrew, ii, p. 68
169	To Lady Hamilton	24 May 1801	BL: Add.34, 274, f. 61
170	To Lady Hamilton		Pettigrew, ii, p. 80; Morrison, ii, pp. 149–150 (No. 589)
171	To Lady Hamilton	27 May 1801	Monmouth: vol.320 E321
172	To Lady Hamilton	1 June 1801	Pettigrew, ii, p. 83
173	To Lady Hamilton	1 June 1801	Sotheby's (consulted 19 May 2010)
174	To Lady Hamilton	5 June 1801	Pettigrew, ii, pp. 84–5
175	To Lady Hamilton	8 June 1801	BL: Egerton 1614 ff. 63–64, no. 33
176	To Lady Hamilton	10 June 1801	BL: Egerton 1614, ff. 65–66, no. 34
177	To Lady Hamilton	12 June 1801	Pettigrew, ii, p. 98

178	To Lady Hamilton	14 June 1801	NMM: WAL/47
179	To Lady Hamilton	30 June 1801	NMM: PST/83

Chapter III: The Channel Campaign: July–October 1801

180	To Lady Hamilton	27 July 1801	NMM: MON/1/19
181	To Lady Hamilton	28 July 1801	Pettigrew, ii, pp. 131–2
182	To Lady Hamilton	29 July 1801	Monmouth: E 95
183	To Lady Hamilton	30 July 1801	BL: Egerton 1614 ff. 67–68, no. 35
184	To Lady Hamilton	31 July 1801	NMM: CRK/19/11
185	To Lady Hamilton	1 Aug 1801	Pettigrew, ii, pp. 137–8; Sotheby's, 13 Dec 1990
186	To Lady Hamilton	3 Aug 1801	NMM: RUSI/203
187	To Lady Hamilton	4 Aug 1801	BL: Egerton 1614 ff. 69–70, no. 36
188	To Lady Hamilton	4 Aug 1801	Pettigrew, ii, p. 139
189	To Lady Hamilton	4 Aug 1801	Houghton: pf MS Eng 196.5 (22a)
190	To Lady Hamilton	5 Aug 1801	BL: Egerton 1614 ff. 71–72, no. 37
191	To Lady Hamilton	6 Aug 1801	Pierpont Morgan: MA 321
192	To Lady Hamilton	7 Aug 1801	Huntington: HM 34091
193	To Lady Hamilton	7 Aug 1801	Pettigrew, ii, p. 415
194	To Lady Hamilton	7 Aug 1801	Pettigrew, ii, p. 147
195	To Lady Hamilton	10 Aug 1801	Huntington: HM 34092
196	To Lady Hamilton	11 Aug 1801	NMM: CRK/19/12
197	To Lady Hamilton	12 Aug 1801	BL: Egerton 1614 ff. 73–74, no. 38
198	To Lady Hamilton	13 Aug 1801	Pettigrew, ii, pp. 150–51

199	To Lady Hamilton	13 Aug 1801	Pettigrew, ii, pp. 151–2
200	To Lady Hamilton	14 Aug 1801	Pettigrew, ii, pp. 153–4; Morrison, ii, p. 161 (No. 614)
201	To Lady Hamilton	15 Aug 1801	Pettigrew, ii, pp. 154–5; Christie's 21 June 1989, lot 248
202	To Lady Hamilton	16 Aug 1801	BL: Egerton 1614 ff. 78–79, no. 40
203	To Lady Hamilton	17 Aug 1801	Pettigrew, ii, pp. 157–8
204	To Lady Hamilton	18 Aug 1801	NMM: CRK/19/13
205	To Lady Hamilton	19 Aug 1801	Pettigrew, ii, pp. 161–2
206	To Lady Hamilton	19 Aug 1801	Christie's, 3 Dec 1986, lot 315
207	To Lady Hamilton	20 Aug 1801	Pettigrew, ii, pp. 162–3
208	To Lady Hamilton	20 Aug 1801	Pettigrew, ii, p. 166
209	To Lady Hamilton	21 Aug 1801	NMM: CRK/19/14
210	To Lady Hamilton	22 Aug 1801	Houghton: MS Hyde 77,7.11.
211	To Lady Hamilton	23 Aug 1801	Pettigrew, ii, p. 171
212	To Lady Hamilton	24 Aug 1801	Pettigrew, ii, pp. 171–2
213	To Lady Hamilton (alias Mrs Thomson)		Morrison, ii, p. 165 (No. 621); Christie's 21 June 1989, lot 252 and 3 Dec 2003, lot 145
214	To Lady Hamilton	20 Sept 1801	Pettigrew, ii, pp. 181–2

215	To Lady Hamilton	21 Sept 1801	Pettigrew, ii, pp. 183–4; Morrison, ii, pp. 165–6 (No. 622)
216	To Lady Hamilton	21 Sept 1801	NMM: CRK/19/5
217	To Lady Hamilton	23 Sept 1801	Pettigrew, ii, pp. 184–5
218	To Lady Hamilton	23 Sept 1801	Monmouth: E 107
219	To Lady Hamilton	23 Sept 1801	Pettigrew, ii, p. 187.
220	To Lady Hamilton	24 Sept 1801	Pettigrew, ii, pp. 187–8
221	To Lady Hamilton	24 Sept 1801	NMM: AGC/17/11
222	To Lady Hamilton	25 Sept 1801	Pettigrew, ii, p. 189
223	To Lady Hamilton	26 Sept 1801	NMM: CRK/19/6
224	To Lady Hamilton	27 Sept 1801	Pettigrew, ii, pp. 190–1
225	To Lady Hamilton	28 Sept 1801	Pettigrew, ii, pp. 192–3; Morrison, ii, p. 168 (No. 625)
226	To Lady Hamilton	29 Sept 1801	CRC
227	To Lady Hamilton	30 Sept 1801	Pettigrew, ii, p. 195
228	To Lady Hamilton	1 Oct 1801	Pettigrew, ii, p. 199
229	To Lady Hamilton	2 Oct 1801	Houghton: MS Lowell 10
230	To Lady Hamilton	3 Oct 1801	Pettigrew, ii, pp. 202–3; Christie's, 9 Dec 1998, lot 40
231	To Lady Hamilton	4 Oct 1801	Pettigrew, ii, p. 203
232	To Lady Hamilton	4 Oct 1801	BL: Egerton 1614 ff. 80–81, no. 41
233	To Lady Hamilton	5 Oct 1801	Pettigrew, ii, p. 205
234	To Lady Hamilton	5 Oct 1801	Huntington: HM 34093

235	To Lady Hamilton		Jean Kislak: 1987.004.00.0001
236	To Lady Hamilton	6 Oct 1801	BL: Egerton 1614 ff. 82–83, no. 42
237	To Lady Hamilton	6 Oct 1801	Pettigrew, ii, pp. 207–8; Morrison, ii, pp. 172–3 (No. 631)
238	To Lady Hamilton	8 Oct 1801	NMM: CRK/19/7
239	To Lady Hamilton	8 Oct 1801	Pettigrew, ii, pp. 212–13
240	To Lady Hamilton	9 Oct 1801	BL: Egerton 1614 ff. 84–85, no. 43
241	To Lady Hamilton	10 Oct 1801	NMM: MAM/7
242	To Lady Hamilton		Pettigrew, ii, p. 211
243	To Lady Hamilton	11 Oct 1801	NMM: PBE2591
244	To Lady Hamilton	12 Oct 1801	NMM: CRK/19/18
245	To Lady Hamilton	13 Oct 1801	Monmouth: E 112
246	To Lady Hamilton	14 Oct 1801	Editor's collection
247	To Lady Hamilton	15 Oct 1801	NMM: CRK/19/19
248	To Lady Hamilton	15 Oct 1801	Huntington: HM 34094
249	To Lady Hamilton	16 Oct 1801	NMM: CRK/19/20
250	To Lady Hamilton	16 Oct 1801	NMM: CRK/19/20
251	To Lady Hamilton		NMM: CRK/19/20
252	To Lady Hamilton	17 Oct 1801	1814–letters, ii, pp. 84–7, no. XXI
253	To Lady Hamilton	18 Oct 1801	BL: Egerton 1614, ff. 86–87, no. 44
254	To Lady Hamilton	19 Oct 1801	NMM: CRK/19/23
255	To Lady Hamilton	20 Oct 1801	NMM: CRK/19/24
256	To Lady Hamilton	20 Oct 1801	NMM: CRK/19/25
257	To Lady Hamilton	21 Oct 1801	NMM: CRK/19/26
258	To Lady Hamilton	29 Oct 1801	NMM: CRK/19/27

Chapter IV: Settled: May 1803–August 1805

259	Nelson's last will and Testament (extract)		TNA: Prob 1/22
260	First codicil to Nelson's last will and testament		TNA: Prob 1/22
261	To Lady Hamilton		Morrison, ii, p. 210 (No. 712)
262	To Lady Hamilton	18 May 1803	Houghton: pf MS Eng 196.5 (33)
263	To Lady Hamilton	19 May 1803	NMM: MAM/26
264	To Lady Hamilton	20 May 1803	Pettigrew, ii, p. 300
265	To Lady Hamilton	20 May 1803	Morrison, ii, pp. 210–11 (No. 713)
266	To Lady Hamilton	21 May 1803	Pettigrew, ii, p. 300
267	To Lady Hamilton	22 May 1803	NMM: CRK/19/28
268	To Lady Hamilton	25 May 1803	CRC/46
269	To Lady Hamilton	10 June 1803	Pettigrew, ii, pp. 304–5; Morrison, ii, p. 213 (No. 718)
270	To Lady Hamilton	20 June 1803	Pettigrew, ii, p. 310
271	To Lady Hamilton	25 June 1803	Huntington: HM 34095
272	To Lady Hamilton	8 July 1803	NMM: CRK/19/29
273	To Lady Hamilton	12 July 1803	BL: Egerton 1614 ff. 94–95, no. 49
274	To Lady Hamilton	1 Aug 1803	NMM: CRK/19/30
275	To Lady Hamilton	10 Aug 1803	NMM: CRK/19/31; Pettigrew, ii, p. 326
276	To Lady Hamilton	21 Aug 1803	Pettigrew, ii, p. 331
277	To Lady Hamilton		Pettigrew, ii, p. 332
278	To Lady Hamilton		Pettigrew, ii, p. 332
279	Lady Hamilton to Nelson		Houghton: MS Lowell Autograph

280	To Lady Hamilton	24 Aug 1803	Houghton: MS Lowell Autograph
281	To Lady Hamilton	24 Aug 1803	NMM: CRK/19/32
282	To Lady Hamilton		Pettigrew, ii, pp. 336–7
283	To Lady Hamilton	26 Aug 1803	NMM: CRK/19/33
284	To Lady Hamilton (alias Mrs Thomson)	26 Aug 1803	NMM: CRK/19/34
285	Second codicil to Nelson's will		TNA: Prob. 1/22/1
286	To Lady Hamilton	8 Sept 1803	BL: Egerton 1614, ff. *97–**97, no. *50
287	To Lady Hamilton	10 Sept 1803	NMM: CRK/19/35
288	To Lady Hamilton	18 Sept 1803	Nicolas, v, p. 206
289	To Lady Hamilton	19 Sept 1803	Morrison, i, p. 218 (No. 730)
290	To Lady Hamilton	26 Sept 1803	CRK/19/36
291	To Lady Hamilton	5 Oct 1803	BL: Egerton 1614 ff. 96–97, no. 5
292	To Lady Hamilton	6 Oct 1803	Pettigrew, ii, p. 346; Morrison, ii, p. 219 (No. 733)
293	To Lady Hamilton	18 Oct 1803	NMM: CRK/19/37
294	To Horatia Nelson Thompson	21 Oct 1803	Pettigrew, ii, p. 352
295	To Lady Hamilton	23 Oct 1803	CRC
296	To Lady Hamilton		Morrison, ii, pp. 219–20 (No. 734)
297	To Lady Hamilton	7 Dec 1803	NMM: MAM/28
298	To Lady Hamilton	26 Dec 1803	Pettigrew, ii, p. 359
299	To Lady Hamilton	13 Jan 1803	NMM: CRK/19/38 and 33
300	To Lady Hamilton	20 Jan 1804	Pettigrew, ii, p. 372; Morrison, ii, pp. 222–3 (No. 742); Christie's 3 Dec 2003, lot 150

301	To Horatia Nelson Thompson	20 Jan 1804	Monmouth: E 161
302	To Lady Hamilton	19 Feb 1804	BL: Egerton 1614 ff. 98–99, no. 51
303	Third codicil to Nelson's will		TNA: Prob. 1/22/1
304	To Lady Hamilton	25 Feb 1804	CRC
305	To Lady Hamilton	25 Feb 1804	Morrison, ii, p. 225 (No. 747)
306	To Lady Hamilton	14 Mar 1804	NMM: CRK/19/39
307	To Lady Hamilton	19 Mar 1804	Huntington: HM 34096
308	To Lady Hamilton		Morrison, ii, p. 225 (No. 749); Christie's 3 Dec 2003, lot 151
309	To Lady Hamilton		Huntington: HM 34065
310	To Lady Hamilton	2 April 1804	NMM: CRK/19/40
311	Fourth codicil to Nelson's will		TNA: Prob. 1/22/1
312	To Lady Hamilton	7 April 1804	Pettigrew, ii, p. 382
313	To Lady Hamilton	10 April 1804	NMM: CRK/19/41
314	To Horatia Nelson Thompson	13 April 1804	1814-letters, II, pp. 107–8
315	To Lady Hamilton	19 April 1804	NMM: CRK/19/42
316	To Lady Hamilton	21 April 1804	Pettigrew, ii, p. 384
317	To Lady Hamilton	23 April 1804	NMM: CRK/19/43
318	To Lady Hamilton	28 April 1804	Pettigrew, ii, pp. 389–90; Morrison, ii, pp. 229–30 (No. 758)
319	To Lady Hamilton	3 May 1804	Morrison, ii, p. 230 (No. 759)
320	To Lady Hamilton	3 May 1804	BL: Egerton 1614 ff. 100–101, no. 59
321	To Lady Hamilton	5 May 1804	NMM: CRK/19/44
322	To Lady Hamilton	22 May 1804	CRC

323	To Lady Hamilton	27 May 1804	NMM: CRK/19/45
324	To Lady Hamilton	30 May 1804	BL: Egerton 1614 ff. 102–103, no. 53
325	To Lady Hamilton	6 June 1804	NMM: CRK/19/46
326	To Lady Hamilton	10 June 1804	NMM: CRK/19/47
327	To Lady Hamilton	17 June 1804	Pettigrew, ii, pp. 397–8;
328	To Lady Hamilton	27 June 1804	Morrison, ii, pp. 232–3 (No. 764)
329	To Lady Hamilton	1 July 1804	NMM: CRK/19/48
330	To Lady Hamilton	1 July 1804	Pettigrew, ii, p. 409; Morrison, ii, pp. 233 (No. 765)
331	To Lady Hamilton	9 July 1804	Morrison, ii, pp. 234–5 (No. 768)
332	To Lady Hamilton	14 July 1804	BL: Egerton 1614 ff. 104–105, no. 541
333	To Lady Hamilton	12 Aug 1804	NMM: CRK/19/49
334	To Lady Hamilton	13 Aug 1804	Morrison, ii, pp. 238–9 (No. 777)
335	To Lady Hamilton		Morrison, ii, p. 239 (No. 778)
336	To Lady Hamilton	13 Aug 1804	Morrison, ii, p. 239 (No. 779)
337	To Lady Hamilton	20 Aug 1804	NMM: CRK/19/50
338	To Lady Hamilton	22 Aug 1804	Pettigrew, ii, pp. 419–20
339	To Lady Hamilton	27 Aug 1804	Houghton: pf MS Eng 196.5 (39)
340	To Lady Hamilton	31 Aug 1804	NMM: CRK/19/51
341	To Lady Hamilton	9 Sept 1804	BL: Egerton 1614 ff. 106–107, no. 55
342	To Lady Hamilton	22 Sept 1804	Pettigrew, ii, pp. 423–4
343	To Lady Hamilton	29 Sept 1804	NMM: CRK/19/52

344	To Lady Hamilton	2 Oct 1804	Morrison, ii, pp. 240–41 (no. 782)
345	To Lady Hamilton	5 Oct 1804	BL: Egerton 1614 ff. 108–109, no. 56
346	To Lady Hamilton	7 Oct 1804	NMM: CRK/19/53
347	To Lady Hamilton	10 Oct 1804	Pettigrew, ii, p. 427; Morrison, ii, p. 241 (No. 783)
348	To Lady Hamilton	13 Oct 1804	NMM: CRK/19/54
349	To Lady Hamilton	31 Oct 1804	Houghton: MS Lowell 10
350	To Lady Hamilton	Nov 1804	William L. Clements Library: Hubert S. Smith, vol. 1 'Naval Affairs'
351	To Lady Hamilton	6 Nov 1804	Pettigrew, ii, p. 434
352	To Lady Hamilton	15 Nov 1804	NMM: MAM/33
353	To Lady Hamilton	23 Nov 1804	NMM: CRK/19/55
354	To Lady Hamilton	4 Dec 1804	BL: Egerton 1614 ff. 110–111, no. 57
355	Fifth codicil to Nelson's will	19 Dec 1804	TNA: Prob. 1/22/1
356	To Lady Hamilton	19 Dec 1804	Monmouth: E 159
357	To Lady Hamilton	30 Dec 1804	Pettigrew, ii, pp. 445–6
358	To Lady Hamilton	14 Jan 1805	William L. Clements Library: Hubert S. Smith, vol. 1 'Naval Affairs'
359	Lady Hamilton's poem 'Emma to Nelson'		1814–letters, ii, pp. 127–8
360	To Lady Hamilton	18 Feb 1805	Pettigrew, ii, pp. 460–62
361	To Lady Hamilton	9 Mar 1805	1814–letters, ii, pp. 87–95, no. LVIII
362	To Lady Hamilton	13 Mar 1805	RNM: 223/73

363	To Lady Hamilton	16 Mar 1805	NMM: TRA/13
364	To Lady Hamilton	30 Mar 1805	Monmouth: E 437
365	To Lady Hamilton	4 April 1805	Monmouth: E 445
366	To Lady Hamilton	5 April 1805	BL: Egerton 1614 f. 114, no. 59
367	To Lady Hamilton	19 April 1805	BL: Egerton 1614 ff. 115–116, no. 60
368	To Lady Hamilton	4 May 1805	Monmouth: E 169
369	To Lady Hamilton	9 May 1805	BL: Egerton 1614 ff. *116–**116, no. *60
370	To Lady Hamilton		Pettigrew, ii, p. 473
371	To Lady Hamilton	13 May 1805	Pettigrew, ii, pp. 474–5
372	To Lady Hamilton	16 May 1805	Jean Kislak: 2004.006.00.0004
373	To Lady Hamilton	18 May 1805	Christie's 3 Dec 2003, lot 156; White, p. 50, no. 59
374	To Lady Hamilton	4 June 1805	Monmouth: E 167
375	To Lady Hamilton	10 June 1805	BL: Egerton 1614 ff. 117–118, no. 61
376	To Lady Hamilton	12 June 1805	Pettigrew, ii, p. 479
377	To Lady Hamilton	16 June 1805	Monmouth: E 416
378	To Lady Hamilton	20 July 1805	BL: Egerton 1614 ff. 119–120, no. 62
379	To Lady Hamilton	24 July 1805	Pettigrew, ii, pp. 482–3; Christie's 3 Dec 2003, lot 157
380	To Lady Hamilton	18 Aug 1805	NMM: SUT/2
381	To Lady Hamilton	19 Aug 1805	Jean Kislak: 2003.111.00.0001

Chapter V: The End: September–October 1805

382	Sixth codicil to Nelson's will	11 Sept 1805	TNA: Prob. 122/1
383	Nelson's journal		NMM: JOD/14:1–2

384	To Lady Hamilton	14 Sept 1805	Monmouth: E 180
385	To Lady Hamilton	14 Sept 1805	Pierpont Morgan: MA321
386	To Lady Hamilton	15 Sept 1805	CRC
387	To Lady Hamilton		Morrison, ii, p. 212 (No. 716)
388	To Lady Hamilton	16 Sept 1805	Pettigrew, ii, p. 498
389	To Lady Hamilton	16 Sept 1805	Monmouth: E 429
390	To Lady Hamilton	17 Sept 1805	NMM: CRK/19/56
391	To Lady Hamilton	20 Sept 1805	Monmouth: E 436
392	To Lady Hamilton	24 Sept 1805	Christie's, 19 Oct 2005, lot 43
393	To Lady Hamilton	25 Sept 1805	Monmouth: E 183
394	To Lady Hamilton	1 Oct 1805	BL: Egerton 1614 ff. 121–122, no. 63
395	To Lady Hamilton	2 Oct 1805	Monmouth: E 438
396	To Lady Hamilton	6 Oct 1805	BL: Egerton 1614 ff. 123–124, no. 64
397	From Lady Hamilton to Nelson	8 Oct 1805	CRC
398	To Lady Hamilton	11 Oct 1805	Pierpont Morgan: MA321
399	To Lady Hamilton		Monmouth: E 195
400	To Horatia Nelson Thompson	19 Oct 1805	NMM: WAL/46
401	To Lady Hamilton	19 Oct 1805	BL: Egerton 1614 ff. 125–126, no. 65
402	Seventh and last codicil to Nelson's will	21 Oct 1805	TNA: Prob 1/22/2

INDEX

NAVY RECORDS SOCIETY – LIST OF VOLUMES
(as at 1 July 2019)

Members wishing to order any volumes should do so via the Society's website. All volumes are available on print-on-demand via scanned copies, apart from Volume 34 (for copyright reasons) and the two Occasional Publications (for reasons of size).

1. *State Papers relating to the Defeat of the Spanish Armada, 1588*. Vol. I. Ed. Professor J.K. Laughton.
2. *State Papers relating to the Defeat of the Spanish Armada, 1588*. Vol. II. Ed. Professor J.K. Laughton.
3. *Letters of Lord Hood, 1781–1783*. Ed. D. Hannay.
4. *Index to James's Naval History, 1886*, by C.G. Toogood. Ed. Hon. T.A. Brassey.
5. *Life of Captain Stephen Martin, 1666–1740*. Ed. Sir Clements R. Markham.
6. *Journal of Rear Admiral Bartholomew James, 1752–1828*. Eds. Professor J.K. Laughton & Cdr. J.Y.F. Sullivan.
7. *Hollond's Discourses of the Navy, 1638 and 1659 and Slyngesbie's Discourse on the Navy, 1660*. Ed. J.R. Tanner.
8. *Naval Accounts and Inventories of the Reign of Henry VII, 1485–1488 and 1495–1497*. Ed. M. Oppenheim.
9. *The Journal of Sir George Rooke, 1700–1702*. Ed. O. Browning.
10. *Letters and Papers relating to the War with France, 1512–1513*. Ed. A. Spont.
11. *Papers relating to the Navy during The Spanish War, 1585–1587*. Ed. J.S. Corbett.
12. *Letters and Papers of Admiral of the Fleet Sir Thomas Byam Martin, 1733–1854*, Vol. II (see Vol. 24). Ed. Admiral Sir Richard Vesey Hamilton.
13. *Letters and Papers relating to the First Dutch War, 1652–1654*, Vol. I. Ed. S.R. Gardiner.
14. *Dispatches and Letters relating to the Blockade of Brest, 1803–1805*, Vol. I. Ed. J. Leyland.

15. *History of the Russian Fleet during the reign of Peter the Great, by a Contemporary Englishman, 1724.* Ed. Vice-Admiral Sir Cyprian A.G. Bridge.
16. *Logs of the Great Sea Fights, 1794–1805*, Vol. I. Ed. Rear Admiral Sir T. Sturges Jackson.
17. *Letters and Papers relating to the First Dutch War, 1652–1654*, Vol. II. Ed. S.R. Gardiner.
18. *Logs of the Great Sea Fights, 1794–1805*, Vol. II. Ed. Rear Admiral Sir T. Sturges Jackson.
19. *Letters and Papers of Admiral of the Fleet Sir Thomas Byam Martin, 1773–1854,* Vol. III (see Vol. 24). Ed. Admiral Sir R. Vesey Hamilton.
20. *The Naval Miscellany*, Vol. I. Ed. Professor J.K. Laughton.
21. *Dispatches and Letters relating to the Blockade of Brest, 1803–1805.* Vol. II. Ed. J. Leyland.
22. *The Naval Tracts of Sir William Monson*, Vol. I. Ed. M. Oppenheim.
23. *The Naval Tracts of Sir William Monson*, Vol. II. Ed. M. Oppenheim.
24. *Letters and Papers of Admiral of the Fleet Sir Thomas Byam Martin, 1773–1854*, Vol. I. Ed. Admiral Sir R. Vesey Hamilton.
25. *Nelson and the Neapolitan Jacobins*. Ed. H.G. Gutteridge.
26. *A Descriptive Catalogue of the Naval Mss. in the Pepysian Library*, Vol. I. Ed. J.R. Tanner.
27. *A Descriptive Catalogue of the Naval Mss. in the Pepysian Library*, Vol. II. Ed. J.R. Tanner.
28. *The Correspondence of Admiral John Markham, 1801–1807.* Ed. Sir Clements R. Markham.
29. *Fighting Instructions, 1530–1816*. Ed. J.S. Corbett.
30. *Letters and Papers relating to the First Dutch War, 1652–1654*, Vol. III. Eds. S.R. Gardiner and C.T. Atkinson.
31. *The Recollections of James Anthony Gardner, 1775–1814*. Ed. Admiral Sir R. Vesey Hamilton and Professor J.K. Laughton.
32. *Letters and Papers of Charles, Lord Barham, 1758–1813*, Vol. I. Ed. Professor Sir J.K. Laughton.
33. *Naval Songs and Ballads*. Ed. Professor C.H. Firth.
34. *Views of the Battles of the Third Dutch War*. Ed. J. S. Corbett. **(Out of Print due to copyright)**.
35. *Signals and Instructions, 1776–1794*. Ed. J. S. Corbett.
36. *A Descriptive Catalogue of the Naval Mss. in the Pepysian Library,* Vol. III. Ed. J.R. Tanner.
37. *Letters and Papers relating to the First Dutch War, 1652–1654*, Vol. IV. Ed. C.T. Atkinson.

38. *Letters and Papers of Charles, Lord Barham, 1758–1813*, Vol. II. Ed. Professor Sir J.K. Laughton.
39. *Letters and Papers of Charles, Lord Barham, 1758–1813*, Vol. III. Ed. Professor Sir J.K. Laughton.
40. *The Naval Miscellany*, Vol. II. Ed. Professor Sir J.K. Laughton.
41. *Letters and Papers relating to the First Dutch War, 1652–1654*. Vol. V. Ed. C.T. Atkinson.
42. *Papers relating to the Loss of Minorca, 1756*. Ed. Captain. H.W. Richmond.
43. *The Naval Tracts of Sir William Monson*, Vol. III. Ed. M. Oppenheim.
44. *The Old Scots Navy, 1689–1710*. Ed. J. Grant.
45. *The Naval Tracts of Sir William Monson*, Vol. IV. Ed. M. Oppenheim.
46. *Private Papers of George, 2nd Earl Spencer, 1794–1801*, Vol. I. Ed. J.S Corbett.
47. The Naval Tracts of Sir William Monson, Vol. V. Ed. M. Oppenheim.
48. *Private Papers of George, 2nd Earl Spencer, 1794–1801*, Vol. II. Ed. J.S. Corbett.
49. *Documents relating to the Law and Custom of the Sea*, Vol. I, *1205–1648*. Ed. R.G. Marsden.
50. *Documents relating to the Law and Custom of the Sea*, Vol. II, *1649–1767*. Ed. R.G. Marsden.
51. *The Autobiography of Phineas Pett*. Ed. W.G. Perrin.
52. *The Life of Admiral Sir John Leake,* Vol. I. Ed. G.A.R. Callender.
53. *The Life of Admiral Sir John Leake*, Vol. II. Ed. G.A.R. Callender.
54. *The Life and Works of Sir Henry Mainwaring*, Vol. I. Ed. G.E. Manwaring.
55. *The Letters of Lord St. Vincent, 1801–1804*, Vol. I. Ed. D. Bonner-Smith.
56. *The Life and Works of Sir Henry Mainwaring*, Vol. II. Eds. G.E. Manwaring and W.G. Perrin.
57. *A Descriptive Catalogue of the Naval Mss. in the Pepysian Library*, Vol. IV. Ed. J.R. Tanner.
58. *Private Papers of George, 2nd Earl Spencer, 1794–1801*, Vol. III. Ed. Rear Admiral H.W. Richmond.
59. *Private Papers of George, 2nd Earl Spencer, 1794–1801*, Vol. IV. Ed. Rear Admiral H.W. Richmond.
60. *Samuel Pepys's Naval Minutes*. Ed. Dr. J.R. Tanner.
61. *The Letters of Earl St. Vincent, 1801–1804*, Vol. II. Ed. D. Bonner-Smith.

62. *The Letters and Papers of Admiral Viscount Keith*, Vol. I. Ed. W.G. Perrin.
63. *The Naval Miscellany*, Vol. III. Ed. W.G. Perrin.
64. *The Journal of the 1st Earl of Sandwich, 1659–1665*. Ed. R.C. Anderson.
65. *Boteler's Dialogues*. Ed. W.G. Perrin.
66. *Letters and Papers relating to the First Dutch War, 1652–1654*, Vol. VI (& index). Ed. C.T. Atkinson.
67. *The Byng Papers*, Vol. I. Ed. W.C.B. Tunstall.
68. *The Byng Papers*, Vol. II. Ed. W.C.B. Tunstall.
69. *The Private Papers of John, Earl Sandwich, 1771–1782*. Vol. I, *1770–1778*. Eds. G.R. Barnes & J.H. Owen.
70. *The Byng Papers*, Vol. III. Ed. W.C.B. Tunstall.
71. *The Private Papers of John, Earl Sandwich, 1771–1782*, Vol. II, *1778–1779*. Eds. G.R. Barnes & J.H. Owen.
72. *Piracy in the Levant, 1827–1828*. Ed. Lt. Cdr. C.G. Pitcairn Jones R.N.
73. *The Tangier Papers of Samuel Pepys*. Ed. E. Chappell.
74. *The Tomlinson Papers*. Ed. J.G. Bullocke.
75. *The Private Papers of John, Earl Sandwich, 1771–1782*, Vol. III, 1779–1780. Eds. G.R.T. Barnes & Cdr. J.H. Owen.
76. *The Letters of Robert Blake*. Ed. Rev. J.R. Powell.
77. *Letters and Papers of Admiral the Hon. Samuel Barrington*, Vol. I. Ed. D. Bonner-Smith.
78. *Private Papers of John, Earl Sandwich*, Vol. IV. Eds. G.R.T. Barnes & Cdr. J.H. Owen.
79. *The Journals of Sir Thomas Allin, 1660–1678*, Vol. I, *1660–1666*. Ed. R.C. Anderson.
80. *The Journals of Sir Thomas Allin, 1660–1678*, Vol. II, *1667–1678*. Ed. R.C. Anderson
81. *Letters and Papers of Admiral the Hon. Samuel Barrington*, Vol. II. Ed. D. Bonner-Smith.
82. *Captain Boteler's Recollections, 1808–1830*. Ed. D. Bonner-Smith.
83. *The Russian War, 1854: Baltic and Black Sea*. Eds. D. Bonner-Smith & Capt. A.C. Dewar R.N.
84. *The Russian War, 1855: Baltic*. Ed. D. Bonner-Smith.
85. *The Russian War, 1855: Black Sea*. Ed. Capt. A.C. Dewar.
86. *Journals and Narratives of the Third Dutch War*. Ed. R.C. Anderson.
87. *The Naval Brigades of the Indian Mutiny, 1857–1858*. Ed. Cdr. W.B. Rowbotham.

88. *Patee Byng's Journal, 1718–1720*. Ed. J.L. Cranmer-Byng.
89. *The Sergison Papers, 1688–1702*. Ed. Cdr. R.D. Merriman.
90. *The Keith Papers*, Vol. II. Ed. C. Lloyd.
91. *Five Naval Journals, 1789–1817*. Ed. Rear Admiral H.G. Thursfield.
92. *The Naval Miscellany*, Vol. IV. Ed. C. Lloyd.
93. *Sir William Dillon's Narrative of Professional Adventures, 1790–1839*, Vol. I, *1790–1802*. Ed. Professor M. Lewis.
94. *The Walker Expedition to Quebec, 1711*. Ed. Professor G.S. Graham.
95. *The Second China War, 1856–1860*. Eds. D. Bonner-Smith & E.W.R. Lumby.
96. *The Keith Papers*, Vol. III. Ed. C.C. Lloyd.
97. *Sir William Dillon's Narrative of Professional Adventures, 1790–1839*, Vol. II, *1802–1839*. Ed. Professor M. Lewis.
98. *The Private Correspondence of Admiral Lord Collingwood*. Ed. Professor E. Hughes.
99. *The Vernon Papers, 1739–1745*. Ed. B.McL. Ranft.
100. *Nelson's Letters to his Wife and Other Documents, 1785–1831*. Ed. G.P.B. Naish.
101. *A Memoir of James Trevenen, 1760–1790*. Ed. Professor C.C. Lloyd.
102. *The Papers of Admiral Sir John Fisher*, Vol. I. Ed. Lt. Cdr. P.K. Kemp R.N.
103. *Queen Anne's Navy*. Ed. Cdr. R.D. Merriman R.I.N.
104. *The Navy and South America, 1807–1823*. Eds. Professor G.S. Graham & Professor R.A. Humphreys.
105. *Documents relating to the Civil War*. Eds. Rev. J.R. Powell & E.K. Timings.
106. *The Papers of Admiral Sir John Fisher*, Vol. II. Ed. Lt. Cdr. P.K. Kemp R.N.
107. *The Health of Seamen*. Ed. Professor C.C. Lloyd.
108. *The Jellicoe Papers*, Vol. I, *1893–1916*. Ed. A Temple Patterson.
109. *Documents relating to Anson's Voyage Round the World, 1740–1744*. Ed. Dr. G. Williams.
110. *The Saumarez Papers: The Baltic 1808–1812*. Ed. A.N. Ryan.
111. *The Jellicoe Papers*, Vol. II, *1916–1935*. Ed. A Temple Patterson.
112. *The Rupert and Monk Letterbook, 1666*. Eds. Rev. J.R. Powell & E.K. Timings.
113. *Documents relating to the Royal Naval Air Service*, Vol. I, *1908–1918*. Ed. Capt. S.W. Roskill.
114. *The Siege and Capture of Havana, 1762*. Ed. Professor D. Syrett.

115. *Policy and Operations in the Mediterranean, 1912–1914*. Ed. E.W.R. Lumby.
116. *The Jacobean Commissions of Enquiry, 1608 and 1618*. Ed. A.P. McGowan.
117. *The Keyes Papers*, Vol. I, *1914–1918*. Ed. Professor P.G. Halpern.
118. *The Royal Navy and North America: The Warren Papers, 1736–1752*. Ed. Dr. J. Gwyn.
119. *The Manning of the Royal Navy: Selected Public Pamphlets, 1693–1873*. Ed. Professor J.S. Bromley.
120. *Naval Administration, 1715–1750*. Ed. Professor D.A. Baugh.
121. *The Keyes Papers*, Vol. II, *1919–1938*. Ed. Professor P.G. Halpern.
122. *The Keyes Papers*, Vol. III, *1939–1945*. Ed. Professor P.G. Halpern.
123. *The Navy of the Lancastrian Kings: Accounts and Inventories of William Soper, Keeper of the King's Ships, 1422–1427*. Ed. Dr. S. Rose.
124. *The Pollen Papers: The Privately Circulated Printed Works of Arthur Hungerford Pollen, 1901–1916*. Ed. Dr. J.T. Sumida.
125. *The Naval Miscellany*, Vol. V. Ed. Dr N.A.M. Rodger.
126. *The Royal Navy in the Mediterranean, 1915–1918*. Ed. Professor P.G. Halpern.
127. *The Expedition of Sir John Norris and Sir Francis Drake to Spain and Portugal, 1589*. Ed. Professor R.B. Wernhan.
128. *The Beatty Papers*, Vol. I. *1902–1918*. Ed. Professor B.McL. Ranft.
129. *The Hawke Papers, A Selection: 1743–1771*. Ed. Dr. R.F. Mackay.
130. *Anglo-American Naval Relations, 1917–1919*. Ed. M. Simpson.
131. *British Naval Documents 1204–1960*. Eds. Professor J.B. Hattendorf, Dr. R.J.B. Knight, A.W.H. Pearsall, Dr. N.A.M. Rodger & Professor G. Till.
132. *The Beatty Papers*, Vol. II, *1916–1927*. Ed. Professor B.McL. Ranft.
133. *Samuel Pepys and the Second Dutch War*. Ed. R. Latham.
134. *The Somerville Papers*. Ed. M. Simpson with assistance from J. Somerville.
135. *The Royal Navy in the River Plate, 1806–1807*. Ed. J.D. Grainger.
136. *The Collective Naval Defence of the Empire, 1900–1940*. Ed. Professor N. Tracy.
137. *The Defeat of the Enemy Attack on Shipping, 1939–1945*. Ed. Dr. E.J. Grove.

138. *Shipboard Life and Organisation, 1731–1815*. Ed. B. Lavery.
139. *The Battle of the Atlantic and Signals Intelligence: U-boat Situations and Trends, 1941–1945*. Ed. Professor D. Syrett.
140. *The Cunningham Papers*, Vol. I: *The Mediterranean Fleet, 1939–1942*. Ed. M. Simpson.
141. *The Channel Fleet and the Blockade of Brest, 1793–1801*. Ed. Dr. R. Morriss.
142. *The Submarine Service, 1900–1918*. Ed. N.A. Lambert.
143. *Letters and Papers of Professor Sir John Knox Laughton, 1830–1915*. Ed. Professor A.D. Lambert.
144. *The Battle of the Atlantic and Signals Intelligence: U-boat Tracking Papers, 1941–1947*. Ed. Professor D. Syrett.
145. *The Maritime Blockade of Germany in the Great War: The Northern Patrol, 1914–1918*. Ed. J.D. Grainger.
146. *The Naval Miscellany*, Vol. VI. Ed. Dr. M. Duffy.
147. *The Milne Papers. Papers of Admiral of the Fleet Sir Alexander Milne 1806–1896*, Vol. I, *1820–1859*. Ed. Professor J. Beeler.
148. *The Rodney Papers*, Vol. I, *1742–1763*. Ed. Professor D. Syrett.
149. *Sea Power and the Control of Trade: Belligerent Rights from the Russian War to the Beira Patrol, 1854–1970*. Ed. N. Tracy.
150. *The Cunningham Papers*, Vol. II: *The Triumph of Allied Sea Power, 1942–1946*. Ed. M. Simpson.
151. *The Rodney Papers*, Vol. II, *1763–1780*. Ed. Professor D. Syrett.
152. *Naval Intelligence from Berlin: The Reports of the British Naval Attachés in Berlin, 1906–1914*, Ed. Dr. M.S. Seligmann.
153. *The Naval Miscellany*, Vol. VII. Ed. Dr. S. Rose.
154. *Chatham Dockyard, 1815–1865. The Industrial Transformation*. Ed. P. MacDougal.
155. *Naval Courts Martial, 1793–1815*. Ed. Dr. J. Byrn.
156. *Anglo-American Naval Relations, 1919–1939*. Ed. M. Simpson.
157. *The Navy of Edward VI and Mary*. Eds. Professor D.M Loades and Dr. C.S. Knighton.
158. *The Royal Navy and the Mediterranean, 1919–1929*. Ed. Professor P. Halpern.
159. *The Fleet Air Arm in the Second World War*, Vol. I, *1939–1941*. Ed. Dr. B. Jones.
160. *Elizabethan Naval Administration*. Eds. Professor D. M. Loades and Dr. C.S. Knighton.
161. *The Naval Route to the Abyss: The Anglo-German Naval Race, 1895–1914*. Eds. Dr M.S. Seligmann, Dr F. Nägler and Professor M. Epkenhans.

162. *The Milne Papers. Papers of Admiral of the Fleet Sir Alexander Milne 1806–1896*, Vol. II, *1860–1862*. Ed. Professor J. Beeler.
163. *The Mediterranean Fleet, 1930–1939*. Ed. Professor P. Halpern.
164. *The Naval Miscellany*, Vol. VIII. Ed. B. Vale.
165. *The Fleet Air Arm in the Second World War*, Vol. II, *1942–1943*. Ed. Dr B. Jones.
166. *The Durham Papers*. Ed. Dr H.L. Rubinstein.

OCCASIONAL PUBLICATIONS.

O.P. 1 *The Commissioned Sea Officers of the Royal Navy, 1660–1815*. Eds. Professor D. Syrett & Professor R.L. DiNardo.

O.P. 2 *The Anthony Roll of Henry VIII's Navy*. Eds. Dr. C.S. Knighton & Professor D.M. Loades.